Single Subject Research Methodology
in Behavioral Sciences

This book is written for student researchers, practitioners, and university faculty who are interested in answering applied research questions and objectively evaluating educational and clinical practices. The basic tenet of single subject research methodology is that the individual is of primary importance and that each individual study participant serves as his or her own control. It is because of this focus on the individual that clinicians and educators have been using single subject research designs for over 40 years to answer applied research questions. Although the methodology has its roots in behavioral psychology and applied behavioral analysis, it has been used by applied researchers across a variety of disciplines such as special education, speech and communication sciences, language and literacy, therapeutic recreation, occupational therapy, and social work. Key features include the following. . .

- Applied Focus—More than any other text, this book focuses on the nuts and bolts of how to use single subject research in constructing one's research project or in evaluating one's professional practice.
- Numerous and Varied Examples—The book abounds in examples from special education and other disciplines and populations within the applied research literature.
- Reader Friendly—The text is written in a reader friendly style, features sample data sheets and graphic displays, and includes detailed guidelines for conducting visual analysis of graphic data.
- Expertise—The author's long and distinguished career in teaching single subject research is augmented in this book by contributions from other experts in the field.

David L. Gast (Ph.D. University of Kansas) is Professor of Special Education in the Department of Communication Sciences and Special Education at the University of Georgia. Co-author with Dr. James Tawney of *Single-Subject Research in Special Education*, he has also authored or co-authored 10 chapters and over 100 journal articles. Dr. Gast serves as a consulting editor for *Focus on Autism and Other Developmental Disabilities, Education and Training in Developmental Disabilities*, and *Exceptionality*.

Single Subject Research Methodology in Behavioral Sciences

David L. Gast, Ph.D.

Department of Communication Sciences and Special Education,
University of Georgia

Routledge
Taylor & Francis Group

NEW YORK AND LONDON

First published 2010
by Routledge
711 Third Avenue, New York, NY 10017

Simultaneously published in the UK
by Routledge
2 Park Square, Milton Park, Abingdon, Oxon OX14 4RN

Routledge is an imprint of the Taylor & Francis Group, an informa business

© 2010 Taylor & Francis

Typeset in Minion by
Swales & Willis Ltd, Exeter, Devon

Library of Congress Cataloging-in-Publication Data
Gast, David L.
  Single subject research methodology in behavioral sciences /
  David L. Gast.
    p. cm.
  Includes bibliographical references and index.
  1. Single subject research. 2. Psychology—Research. 3. Educational
  psychology—Research. I. Title.
  BF76.6.S56G37 2009
  300.72—dc22
  2009003726

ISBN10: 0–8058–6276–5 (hbk)
ISBN10: 0–8058–6277–3 (pbk)
ISBN10: 0–203–87793–4 (ebk)

ISBN13: 978–0–8058–6276–8 (hbk)
ISBN13: 978–0–8058–6277–5 (pbk)
ISBN13: 978–0–203–87793–7 (ebk)

Contents

Preface

Throughout my career as a professor of special education, first at the University of Kentucky (1975–1989) and later at the University of Georgia (1990–present), my interest has been to encourage students to be active participants in research, both as a "scientist-practitioner" and as a collaborator with applied researchers. I suppose this was instilled in me when I was a doctoral student at the University of Kansas (1971–1975) in what was then the Department of Human Development and Family Life (HDFL). During that time I was fortunate to be inspired by some of the best behavioral researchers in the field of applied behavior analysis, including Drs. Joseph Spradlin, my mentor, Sebastian Striefel, James Sherman, Donald Baer, Montrose Wolf, and others. The faculty at the K.U. encouraged and supported the active involvement in research by its master's and doctoral students, as well as teachers and therapists working at one of the many research sites supported by federal grants. It was through the mentorship model adopted by HDFL faculty that I learned that some of the best applied research questions are generated by practitioners, and if practitioners are taught research skills, specifically single subject research methodology, they can be active applied researchers and contributors to the applied research literature. It is to this end that this book has been written.

My goal in writing this book was to present a thorough, technically sound, user friendly, and comprehensive discussion of single subject research methodology. The contributing authors and I assume that those who read the book will have had an introduction to applied behavior analysis and that readers will be familiar with basic behavioral terminology, principles, and procedures. The primary audiences, for whom the book was written, are graduate students, scientist-practitioners, and faculty from a variety of disciplines including special and general education; school, child, and clinical psychology; speech, occupational, recreation, and physical therapy; and social work (i.e., anyone from the social and behavioral sciences, and education, who has an interest in researching the effectiveness and efficiency of instructional and treatment programs). In light of the intended audiences, the applied research examples abstracted, tabled, and cited throughout the book sample a wide range of studies published in a variety of refereed professional journals that represent a number of disciplines, thereby showing the versatility of single subject research methodology. These studies were chosen because of their being applied, behavioral, conceptually systematic, technological, analytical, and effective. Most, but not all, studies referred to in chapters describe behavioral investigations that have been conducted with children and adults with special needs, specifically individuals with intellectual disabilities, autism spectrum disorders, and behavioral disorders. Although some faculty teaching a course in single subject research design may choose to supplement the book with recently published full-text examples from the research literature, an attempt was made to include a sufficient number and range of examples so that supplemental readings would not be necessary. That decision is left to the instructor.

The organization of the book, including the sequence in which chapters are presented, is based on my 30-plus years teaching a course on single subject research methodology to graduate students in special education and psychology. Instructors, however, may choose to assign chapters in a different order since earlier chapters are rarely necessary to understanding content presented in later chapters. The exception to this is Chapters 5 ("General Factors in Measurement and Evaluation"), 6 ("Replication"), 7 ("Dependent Measures and Measurement Procedures"), and 9 ("Visual Analysis of Graphic Data"), that are important to the critique of experimental designs and the applied research study examples abstracted in the design chapters. The book begins with a general discussion of Applied Research in Education and Behavioral Sciences (Chapter 1) in which the various research approaches used in the behavioral sciences and education are introduced. Characteristics, strengths and limitations, and established guidelines are presented for each approach. In Chapter 2 ("Scientific Research in Educational and Clinical Settings") a case is made for educators and clinicians to be actively involved in applied research as principal investigators or as collaborators with applied researchers as means for improving their practice. An attempt is made to show how behavioral science research and education are not as dissimilar as one might think if practitioners agree to evaluate their practice within the context of a single subject research design. Through such participation educators and clinicians can add to our understanding on how to better serve our students and clients. Chapter 3 ("Ethical Principles and Practices") addresses the expected professional behaviors of investigators who conduct research in applied settings. It also outlines a common protocol for receiving permission from university Institutional Review Boards (IRB), prior to conducting research with human subjects, and what safeguards must be in place to protect study participants. Several technical writings tasks are important to the design, approval, and dissemination of research. Chapter 4 ("Writing Tasks: Literature Reviews, Research Proposals, and Final Reports") describes how to complete these writings assignments.

A hallmark of single subject research is objective measurement, formative evaluation, and control of common threats to internal validity that could compromise experimental findings. These topics are discussed in Chapter 5 ("General Factors in Measurement and Evaluation"), while Chapter 6 ("Replication") discusses the importance of repeating experimental effects within and across participants in order to have confidence in research findings. The importance of systematic replication in behavioral science research is also addressed in Chapter 6. Throughout the book emphasis is placed on the direct, repeated, and reliable measurement of behavior. These topics and procedures related to each are operationalized in Chapter 7 ("Dependent Measures and Measurement Procedures"). Chapter 8 ("Visual Representation of Data") and Chapter 9 ("Visual Analysis of Graphic Data") both emphasize the importance of graphic displays as a means for communicating and analyzing single subject research findings. Chapter 8 describes guidelines for the construction of graphic displays, as well as tables, while Chapter 9 describes experimental variables that should be attended to when conducting a visual analysis of data plotted on a line graph. How to conduct both within condition and between adjacent conditions visual analyses are presented and exemplified.

In the remaining chapters of the book the various single subject research designs are critically discussed. Each chapter has a common format in that: (a) each design is described; (b) how threats to internal and external validity are evaluated and controlled are discussed; (c) considerations and guidelines for using a design are presented; (d) advantages and limitations are overviewed; (e) applied research examples are abstracted; (f) sample studies are outlined in table format; and (g) key points are summarized. In Chapter 10 ("Withdrawal and Reversal

Designs") baseline logic, quantitative descriptive designs ("A" and "B" designs), simple A-B correlational design, and various repeated time-series designs (A-B-A, A-B-A-B, B-A-B, and A-B-A'-B) capable of demonstrating a functional relation are presented and exemplified. Multiple baseline and multiple probe designs, and their three variations (across behaviors, conditions, and participants) are discussed in Chapter 11 ("Multiple Baseline and Multiple Probe Designs"). Specific attention is given to differentiating multiple baseline and multiple probe designs, as well as describing the two types of multiple probe designs (probe days and probe conditions). In Chapter 12 ("Comparative Intervention Designs") the types of comparative research questions asked by behavioral researchers are presented, as are the single subject research comparative designs used to answer those questions (multitreatment designs, Alternating Treatments Design, Adapted Alternating Treatments Design, Parallel Treatments Design). The more common single subject research designs are sometimes not practical for some research questions, or they may not adequately evaluate and control some threats to internal validity. In these cases some behavioral researchers have used variations of the multiple baseline design (e.g., changing criterion design, "delayed" or nonconcurrent multiple baseline design) that have practical advantages but which have research limitations. Other researchers have combined single subject research designs to strengthen evaluation of experimental control (e.g., multiple baseline across participants combined with multiple probe across behaviors; alternating treatment design combined with multiple baseline across participants) by increasing the number of replication attempts. These designs and topics are discussed and exemplified in Chapter 13 ("Variations of Multiple Baseline Designs and Combination Designs"). Chapter 14 ("Statistics and Single Subject Research Methodology"), the final chapter of the book, addresses the role and place of statistical analysis with single subject research design data. Proposed procedures are presented, as are precautions in their use. A case is made for conducting meta-analyses of single subject research investigations, although still controversial, as a quantitative means for identifying and supporting evidenced-based practice.

Whether you chose to assume the role of scientist-practitioner, collaborator on research projects initiated by others, or merely a consumer of single subject research, the information covered in this book will help you understand the logic behind single subject research design, the importance of repeated, direct, and reliable measurement, the requirements for evaluating and controlling alternative explanations for research findings, the visual analysis of graphic data, and the importance of replication. The guidelines presented throughout the text are just that, guidelines, intended to assist you in the design, analysis, implementation, and dissemination of single subject research. As an applied researcher, use the guidelines to assist you in gaining an understanding of your research site and its practical constraints before beginning your study, and plan accordingly. Through your understanding of single subject research methodology and your research efforts, and those of other behavioral researchers, we will accumulate evidence that supports promising and best practices.

DLG

Acknowledgments

This project would not have been undertaken had it not been for the generosity of my friend and former colleague at the University of Kentucky, Dr. James W. Tawney, who signed over the copyright of a book we co-authored, *Single Subject Research in Special Education*, published in 1984. The purpose of that book, much like the purpose of this book, was to encourage special education students, teachers, therapists, and other professionals working with individuals with special needs, and who adopted a behavior analytic approach, to become active applied researchers. Through Jim's mentorship early in my career and his invitation to co-author the above single subject research design book, I developed better analytical skills that made me a better researcher and university instructor. I want to thank Dr. Mark Wolery, a dear friend and respected colleague for over 30 years, who has been involved with this project from the very beginning. His encouragement to sign the contract, willingness to participate by sharing his time and expertise in writing two chapters, and availability to critique and provide feedback throughout the writing and editing of the book has been greatly appreciated. Because of my being "technology challenged" I can't imagine what the manuscript would have looked like had it not been for Ms. Amy Spriggs and Ms. Diana Hammond, two dedicated and accomplished doctoral students who I have had the privilege of advising and working with for the past few years. I sincerely appreciate the willingness of each author and co-author who provided contributions throughout the book. I also want to thank the graduate students with whom I have worked at the University of Kentucky (1975–1989) and University of Georgia (1990–present). Had it not been for their insightful research questions, persistence, and patience, I am confident my research career would have been less interesting and productive. Thank you for challenging my analytical abilities. And finally, I want to thank my wife, Kathy Boyle-Gast, and daughter, Hunter Gast, for their encouragement and tolerance through the project. Their support has always been appreciated on this and other projects.

1

Applied Research in Education and Behavioral Sciences

David L. Gast

At no time in education and behavioral sciences has accountability been more important. Since the passage of the Individuals with Disabilities Education Act (IDEA) and No Child Left Behind Act (NCLB), "evidence-based practice" has been the guiding principle for determining whether a treatment or instructional program should be implemented or maintained. Though the phrase "evidence-based practice" is relatively new, the idea that research should guide practice is not, particularly for those of us trained in applied behavior analysis. Baer, Wolf, and Risley (1968), in their seminal article that defined applied behavior analysis, emphasized the importance of quantitative research-based decisions for guiding practice whether you were a psychologist, educator, speech/language pathologist, occupational therapist, recreation therapist, etc. Their emphasis on a low-inference decision model, based on repeated measurement of behavior within the context of a single subject experimental design, set a standard for practitioners determining intervention effectiveness more than 40 years ago. At the time of their article, published in the inaugural issue of the *Journal of Applied Behavior Analysis*, there was no shortage of critics who questioned the viability and desirability of an empirical scientific approach for studying and understanding human behavior, a response in part due to the controversial position articulated by B. F. Skinner in his classic book, *Science and Human Behavior* (1953). Having passed the test of time, as evidenced by the numerous single subject research design studies that have influenced practice across many disciplines, it has been shown that a behavioral approach can and does provide a scientific framework for understanding and modifying behavior in positive ways. Few would question that Baer et al. established evidence-based practice as a core value for applied behavior analysts, a value that has yielded best and promising practices across numerous disciplines within the behavioral sciences.

Evidence-Based Practice and the Scientific Method

What constitutes a "practice"? Horner et al. (2005) defined *practice* as "a curriculum, behavioral intervention, systems change, or educational approach designed to be used by families, educators, or students with the express expectation that implementation will result in measurable educational, social, behavioral, or physical benefit" (p. 175). This definition applies to specific interventions and broader approaches used by professionals who provide educational and clinical services. It should not go unnoticed that the definition includes mention of a "measurable" benefit to those who are the focus of the practice.

What constitutes *evidence* that supports implementation of a particular practice? Must evidence be quantitative? Is clinical or professional judgment a consideration? Do data need to be collected within the context of a randomized experimental group design or randomized clinical trial? To what extent can research outcomes based on quasi-experimental group, single subject, or qualitative research designs be used to support implementation of a curriculum, behavioral intervention, systems change, or educational approach? Answers to these questions are important since different research methods and designs yield different types of data and different professionals and researchers have different opinions as to which type of research methodology yields the most reliable and valid results that will generalize across individuals, conditions, and time. *The research question should determine the research method and design (group, single subject, or qualitative) chosen.* In behavioral sciences, "trustworthiness" or credibility of research findings is based on the rigor of the scientific method employed and the extent to which the research design controls for alternative explanations. *The scientific method requires investigator objectivity, reliability of measurement, and independent replication of findings.* As a scientist you will be expected to see things as they are not as you wish them to be; this will necessitate defining the target behavior (or event) clearly and concisely so that two independent observers consistently agree on scoring what they observe. Finally, you will need to be patient to see if your research findings stand up to the scrutiny of other researchers when they attempt to replicate your results. This latter criterion is critical, as *replication is at the heart of the scientific method*, without which you cannot have confidence in study findings.

Behavioral scientists have numerous scientific research designs from which to choose in their quest for answers to research hypotheses and questions. There is general agreement among researchers that different research questions or objectives require different research approaches, i.e., no one research method or design is appropriate for answering all research questions. However, for behavioral scientists, certain research methods and designs are deemed superior to others when generalizing findings to individuals or groups. This judgment is based on the degree to which data-collection procedures, data analyses, and data reporting are viewed as objective, reliable, and valid, and the extent to which it is believed that the study could be replicated and yield similar findings. Studies that are based on investigator perceptions and descriptions, that fail to objectively define and evaluate the reliability of investigator observations, and that lack detailed descriptions of conditions under which data are collected, thus making replication difficult if not impossible, are judged as lacking scientific rigor and "trustworthiness" of findings. Judging the rigor of the scientific method of a study that supports a particular practice is at the heart of determining whether a practice is, in fact, evidence-based.

To that end, in determining the rigor of the science supporting a particular policy, procedure, or practice, most professional organizations have recommendations and guidelines on their websites for evaluating research study adequacy (e.g., American Psychological Association, www.apa.org; American Speech-Language-Hearing Association, www.asha.org; Association of Behavior Analysis International, www.abainternational.org; Council for Exceptional Children, www.cec.org). Odom et al. (2005) point out that interest in and guidelines for the evaluation of research supporting clinical and educational practices has been addressed by medical, social science and educational professional organizations for many years. As a result of No Child Left Behind (NCLB) legislation, families are increasingly holding professionals accountable for their choice of practices used with their children. Parents and others expect to see positive changes in behavior, an expectation that is both reasonable and consistent with ethical standards of educational and clinical service professional organizations. Take, for example, an excerpt from a Policy Statement on "The Right to an Effective Behavioral Treatment," passed by the Association of Behavior Analysis International (ABAI) membership in 1989, that reads:

> An individual is entitled to effective and scientifically validated treatment; in turn, the behavior analyst has an obligation to *use only those procedures demonstrated by research to be effective.* Decisions on the use of potentially restrictive treatment are based on consideration of its absolute and relative level of restrictiveness, the amount of time required to produce a clinically significant outcome, and the consequences that would result from delayed intervention.

> (ABAI, 1989; italics added)

Applied behavior analysts have historically held themselves accountable for designing and employing curricula, interventions, systems for change, and educational/therapeutic approaches that bring about positive behavior change. As will be discussed throughout this book, single subject research methodology will permit you as a *"scientist-practitioner,"* a label coined by Barlow, Hayes, and Nelson (1984) to describe interventionists who make data-based decisions an integral part of their practice, to repeatedly evaluate your practices, allowing you to maintain them when data support their effectiveness; modify them when progress is slow or plateaus; or abandon them when necessary and implement another promising practice with an emerging evidence base. These research decisions can be made while retaining the experimental integrity of a study if you are familiar with measurement and design guidelines presented in later chapters. For now, I recommend that you visit your professional organization's website and review the most recent recommendations for supporting evidence-based practice.

General Guidelines for Evaluating Supportive Evidence

The National Research Council (NRC), at the request of the U.S. Department of Education's Office of Special Education Programs (OSEP), was assigned the task of developing a set of guidelines for evaluating the scientific rigor and trustworthiness of research related to autism spectrum disorders (ASD). A committee of respected researchers in the areas of early childhood education and ASD was asked "to integrate the scientific, theoretical, and policy literature and create a framework for evaluating the scientific evidence concerning the effects and features of educational interventions for young children with autism" (Committee on the Educational Interventions for Children with Autism, 2001, p. 13). The Committee recognized that there are numerous sources for generating evidence, with some approaches yielding greater scientific evidence than others. They also recognized that different research questions require different research methodologies, and in spite of current popularity of some approaches (e.g., clinical descriptions), greater scientific credence was assigned to findings based on quantitative research approaches. Guidelines adopted by the committee and recommended for use when evaluating scientific rigor of research supporting a curriculum, procedure, or policy are presented in Table 1.1. Three primary areas are addressed: Internal Validity, External Validity/Selection Bias, and Generalization. *Internal validity* refers to the degree to which the research design controls for extraneous or confounding variables, variables that could support an alternative explanation for the findings. *External validity/selection bias* refers to the number of study participants and how participants are selected, with greater external validity assigned to studies with a larger number of participants who are randomly assigned to experimental conditions. *Generalization* refers to the extent to which an experimental effect is observed beyond the treatment setting, under natural conditions, and maintained over time. Under each of these three areas there are four categories or descriptions that may or may not represent a study, or series of studies you are evaluating. These categories are presented in a hierarchy from most (first listed) to least (last listed) degree of trustworthiness of research findings. To determine the level of confidence you should have in the evidence supporting a practice, identify the statement under each area that best represents the research reviewed. As a general guideline, if you were to assign a score to each statement (e.g., 1–4), the lower the score the greater the likelihood that the findings are reliable, valid, and will generalize to similar individuals. Unfortunately, deciding the merits of research supporting a practice is not that simple or "cut and dried." Clinical and educational research can be compromised by limited access to a population, ethical concerns regarding random assignment or withholding of a treatment, or the expense of independent replication. As discussed in Chapter 3, professional judgment must be used when evaluating and conducting applied research. When there are few participants in a study, as is typically the case in single subject research design studies, successful independent replications increase confidence. In fact, it has been suggested that such "systematic replications" (Sidman, 1960) have greater trustworthiness when generalizing findings to other individuals who exhibit similar behaviors emitted at a similar frequency or magnitude (Wolery & Ezell, 1993). You should be aware that although the commonly held "gold standard" for research trustworthiness is assigned to research findings generated by randomized experimental group designs, seldom are these studies independently replicated. This is in part due to cost. The point I am making here is that the NRC guidelines for evaluating research are a good starting point, but informed judgment must also be used in determining the credibility of evidence supporting a practice. It is important to understand threats to internal validity (discussed in Chapter 5) and how a research design evaluates and controls for these threats. You must also be familiar with how external validity is established with each research approach and whether findings from a study or series of studies are likely to generalize to individuals with whom you are working and/or studying. As Skinner (1953) noted,

> In general a science is helpful in dealing with the individual only insofar as its laws refer to individuals. A science of behavior which concerns only the behavior of groups is not likely to be of help in our understanding of the particular case.

> (p. 19)

Although the NRC guidelines give the highest degree of trustworthiness to randomized experimental group designs and randomized clinical trials, you must ask whether these studies or trials adequately controlled for threats to internal validity and whether the findings have been independently replicated. Only through independent replication can investigator bias and research skill in controlling threats to validity be truly assessed.

Dissemination of Evidence-Based Practices in Education

It is important that practices supported by research be disseminated to practitioners. To that end, the Education Science Reform Act of 2002 was established within the U.S. Department of Education's Institute of Education Sciences (IES; www.ed.gov/about/offices/list/ies); its mission, to "provide rigorous evidence on which to ground education practice and policy" by government-funded research projects. IES's oversight responsibilities was a direct response to concerns regarding the quality of educational research and the requirement put forth in NCLB that teachers use scientifically proven practices (Odom et al., 2005). To disseminate its findings, IES established the What Works Clearinghouse:

> to provide educators, policymakers, researchers, and the public with a central and trusted source of scientific evidence of what works in education. The WWC aims to promote informed education decision making through a set of easily accessible databases and user friendly reports that provide education consumers with high quality reviews of the

---

Table 1.1 National Research Council's Committee on the Educational Interventions for Children with Austism (2001) Guidelines Used to Evaluate Studies

BOX 1–1 Guidelines Used to Evaluate Studies
Every research report considered by the committee was assigned to one category (I–IV) for each area (A, B, and C).

A. Internal Validity: Control for nonspecific factors, such as maturation, expectancy, experimenter artifacts
  I. Prospective study comparing the intervention to an alternative intervention or placebo in which evaluators of outcome are blind to treatment status
  II. Multiple baseline, ABAB design, or reversal/withdrawal with measurement of outcome blind to treatment conditions or pre-post design with independent evaluation
  III. Pre-post or historical designs or multiple baseline, ABAB, reversal/withdrawal not blind to treatment conditions
  IV. Other

B. External Validity/Selection Biases
  I. Random assignment of well-defined cohorts and adequate sample size for comparisons
  II. Nonrandom assignment, but well-defined cohorts with inclusion/exclusion criteria and documentation of attrition/failures; additionally adequate sample size for group designs or replication across three or more subjects in a single-subject design
  III. Well-defined population of three or more subjects in single-subject designs or sample of adequate size in group designs
  IV. Other

C. Generalization
  I. Documented changes in at least one natural setting outside of treatment setting (includes social validity measures)
  II. Generalization to one other setting or maintenance beyond experimental intervention in natural setting in which intervention took place
  III. Intervention occurred in natural setting or use of outcome measures with documented relationship to functional outcome
  IV. Not addressed or other

Source: Reprinted with permission from the National Academies Press, Copyright 2001, National Academy of Sciences.

effectiveness of replicable educational interventions (programs, products, practices, and policies) that intend to improve student outcomes.

(WWC; http://ies.ed.gov/ncee/wwc)

Prior to 2006 the WWC only "certified" and disseminated practices that were shown to be effective by a randomized experimental group design or random clinical trial. However, in September 2006, in one of its technical working papers, "Study Design Classification" (WWC 2006a), it revised its guidelines to include three additional research designs: "quasi-experiment with equating on pretest, regression discontinuity design, or single-case design with multiple changes of condition." This policy revision showed an understanding by IES and WWC that applied research studies, particularly studies conducted with low-incidence populations and conducted in clinical and classroom settings, require research designs other than those that randomly assign participants to experimental conditions. Standards for evaluating experimental and quasi-experimental group design studies have been put forward (WWC 2006b); however, specific standards for evaluating single subject research design studies have not, as of July 9, 2008. To be kept abreast of current standards, particularly the development of those for single subject research design studies, periodically check the WWC website and its technical reports for updates on evidence standards for reviewing studies.

Research Approaches in the Behavioral Sciences

As the book title connotes, the focus of this text is on single subject research methodology, also referred to as single case research design, and its use by applied researchers in behavioral sciences. In spite of this single research-approach focus, it is important for you to be able to compare and contrast research approaches on the basis of their research logic, strategies for controlling threats to internal validity, and generalization of findings to individual cases. Through your analysis and understanding of research approaches you will be better able to choose the appropriate research design for answering your research question(s). As previously noted, no one research approach or design is appropriate for answering all research questions. Thus it is your responsibility, both as a consumer of and contributor to research, to be familiar with the various research approaches used in behavioral sciences. In the sections that follow common research approaches and designs are briefly overviewed. More detailed design descriptions and analyses are found elsewhere in such general research methodology texts as deMarrais and Lapan (2004), Fraenkel and Wallen (2006), Portney and Watkins (2000), and Schlosser (2003).

Experimental, Quasi-Experimental, and Correlational Designs

Experimental design studies are defined by an investigator's manipulation of an independent variable (e.g., intervention, treatment, or practice; i.e., system of least prompts, self-monitoring, repeated practice) to verify what effect it has on a dependent variable (e.g., frequency, duration of target behavior; i.e., number of steps completed correctly, percentage of time on-task, number of words read correctly per minute). The act of intentionally manipulating some variable (e.g., stimulus presentation pace, response consequence contingency, materials) to see if there is a measurable change in a behavior (or event) differentiates experimental research from other research approaches. Experimental design studies (a) describe the target behavior(s), (b) predict what impact the independent variable will have on the dependent variable(s), and (c) test to see if the prediction is correct. In so doing, the research design must control for alternative explanations for the observed behavior change(s). What differentiates an experimental design study from a *quasi-experimental design* study, at least within the context of the group research design approach, is how research participants are assigned to study conditions. In experimental group design studies participants are randomly assigned to a study condition (e.g., experimental group or control group; intervention A or intervention B), while quasi-experimental group design studies do not use random assignment of participants but other strategies to control for differences in study-group composition, e.g., counterbalancing techniques, participant matching (Fraenkel & Wallen, 2006). Regardless of whether a study uses an experimental or quasi-experimental design, if the prediction "proves" true, it is said there is a *functional relation* (i.e., cause–effect relation) between independent and dependent variables. The demonstration of a functional relation adds evidence in support of the independent variable being a promising and possibly "best practice" if findings are independently replicated. Greater support is attributed to results of an experimental group design study, compared to a quasi-experimental group design study, because of the random assignment of participants.

Correlational design studies, like experimental and quasi-experimental design studies, describe and predict the relation between independent and dependent variables, however, *in correlational studies there is no attempt by the investigator to verify the prediction*. Such studies represent a quantitative-descriptive research approach in which the relation between variables is established by using a correlation coefficient (Fraenkel & Wallen, 2006). When independent and dependent variables co-vary there is said to be a correlational relation between variables. Practices supported by correlational evidence are deemed less trustworthy or convincing than those supported by experimental and quasi-experimental evidence since correlational design studies do not rule out alternative explanations because there is no attempt to replicate the experimental effect of the independent variable on the dependent variable.

Group Research Approach

Gersten, Fuchs, Compton, Coyne, Greenwood, and Innocenti (2005) provide an excellent discussion of indicators for evaluating scientific rigor of group experimental and quasi-experimental research reports and proposals. Much of what is presented in this section is a summary of key points they present in determining the level of support assigned to group studies investigating the efficacy of a practice. They point out that there was not complete agreement among authors on all issues discussed. Nevertheless their presentation provides a framework from which to judge the level of support for an evidence-based practice with group designs. Table 1.2 summarizes the "Essential and Desirable Quality Indicators for Group Experimental and Quasi-Experimental Research Articles and Reports."

Characteristics of Group Design

The basic logic underlying all group research studies is that a large number of individuals are divided and assigned to one of two or more study conditions. Study conditions could be a control condition, in which participants *are not* exposed to the independent variable, and treatment condition, in which participants *are* exposed to the independent variable. When comparing two different treatments, participants would be equally divided between the two treatments. In some group studies more than two conditions may be compared, in which case an equal number of participants would be assigned to each of the conditions (e.g., 30 assigned to control, 30 assigned to treatment A, 30 assigned to treatment B). A critical variable to consider when evaluating a group study is how participants are assigned to study conditions. The optimal method is random assignment of participants (experimental study), but this is not always possible and may depend on the research objective or population being studied. When random assignment of participants is not feasible, it is recommended that

Table 1.2 Essential and Desirable Quality Indicators for Group Experimental and Quasi-Experimental Research Articles and Reports

Essential Quality Indicators

Quality Indicators for Describing Participants
1. Was sufficient information provided to determine/confirm whether the participants demonstrated the disability(ies) or difficulties presented?
2. Were appropriate procedures used to increase the likelihood that relevant characteristics of participants in the sample were comparable across conditions?
3. Was sufficient information given characterizing the interventionists or teachers provided? Did it indicate whether they were comparable across conditions?

Quality Indicators for Implementation of the Intervention and Description of Comparison Conditions
1. Was the intervention clearly described and specified?
2. Was the fidelity of implementation described and assessed?
3. Was the nature of services provided in comparison conditions described?

Quality Indicators for Outcome Measures
1. Were multiple measures used to provide an appropriate balance between measures closely aligned with the intervention and measures of generalized performance?
2. Were outcomes for capturing the interventions effect measured at the appropriate times?

Quality Indicators for Data Analysis
1. Were the data analysis techniques appropriately linked to key research questions and hypotheses? Were they appropriately linked to the limit of analysis in the study?
2. Did the research report include not only inferential statistics but also effect size calculations?

Desirable Quality Indicators
1. Was data available on attrition rates among intervention samples? Was severe overall attrition documented? If so, is attrition comparable across samples? Is overall attrition less than 30%?
2. Did the study provide not only internal consistency reliability but also test-retest reliability and interrater reliability (when appropriate) for outcome measures? Were data collectors and/or scorers blind to study conditions and equally (un)familiar to examinees across study conditions?
3. Were outcomes for capturing the intervention's effect measured beyond an immediate posttest?
4. Was evidence of the criterion-related validity and construct validity of the measures provided?
5. Did the research team assess not only surface features of fidelity implementation (e.g., number of minutes allocated to the intervention or teacher/interventionist following procedures specified), but also examine quality of implementation?
6. Was any documentation of the nature of instruction or series provided in comparison conditions?
7. Did the research report include actual audio or videotape excerpts that capture the nature of the intervention?
8. Were results presented in a clear, coherent fashion?

Note:
* A study would be acceptable if it included only measures of generalized performance. It would not be acceptable if it only included measures that are tightly aligned.

Source: Gersten et al. (2005). Copyright by Society for the Experimental Analysis of Behavior, Inc. Reproduced by permission.

interventionists be randomly assigned to conditions. Gersten et al. (2005) point out that random assignment of participants does not guarantee study group equivalence, an important consideration when analyzing group research findings. *It is the fundamental logic of group design, experimental and quasi-experimental, that groups of participants assigned to each study condition are equivalent on "key" characteristics or status variables (e.g., chronological age, gender, ethnicity, test scores) at the start of a group study* (Rosenberg et al., 1992). By starting with equivalent groups across conditions, it is possible to attribute later differences between groups to the independent variable rather than group composition. Because group equivalence is critical, some investigators have chosen to match participants on key characteristics prior to the start of their study and then randomly assign one matched member to each study condition. Implied in this process is the importance of the researcher providing a detailed description of group members, thereby convincing study evaluators that groups were equivalent at the start of the study.

Other participant and interventionist variables should also be addressed when evaluating or reporting results from group studies, including participant attrition and interventionist characteristics. Specifically, it is important to note the number of participants who have withdrawn from a study and the condition to which they were assigned. If attrition is comparable across conditions there is not a problem, however, if one condition has a substantially higher attrition rate than another condition, problems arise when analyzing the data, since groups will no longer be comparable in number. In such cases it is always important to document and report the reasons for participant withdrawal, noting whether it was in some way due to the condition to which they were assigned. For studies in which one or more interventionists are participating, it is important to describe each interventionist in detail so that there are no critical differences between them (e.g., education, certification, experience), as some differences could influence the consistency and fidelity with which the independent variable is implemented. To avoid this potential problem, researchers randomly assign or counterbalance interventionists across conditions. When neither option is possible for logistical reasons (e.g., clinical group or teacher classroom assignment), *procedural fidelity* data become increasingly important in the analysis of findings, i.e., the degree to which condition procedures were followed as specified in the research proposal.

Controlling Threats to Internal Validity

All quantitative research studies, group and single subject design studies, attempt to evaluate and control for alternative explanations for their results (see Chapter 5 for information on threats to internal validity). To accomplish this, researchers select a research design and measurement system that give reviewers confidence that study findings were, in fact, due to differences in study conditions. This effort begins with a clear and concise description of each study condition. General condition labels or descriptions (e.g., Self-Management, Direct Instruction, Desensitization Strategy) are insufficient, and more detailed "point-by-point" or technological descriptions are required. All condition descriptions (control and treatment) should be described in sufficient detail to allow an independent investigator to replicate procedures or to conduct a meta-analysis or synthesis of research on a topic (see Chapter 14 for information on meta-analyses).

The measurement system should also be described in detail, allowing reviewers to judge the validity and reliability of measures. Multiple measures "closely aligned to the intervention and measures of generalized performance" (p. 158) are encouraged, as is "test-retest reliability," and use of tests that have established validity. Internal consistency reliability (i.e., coefficient alpha) should be calculated and reported (Gersten et al., p. 158–159). While pre/posttest measures are deemed adequate, inclusion of multiple measures over the duration of a study is preferred since more complex statistical analysis procedures are available (e.g., Hierarchical Linear Modeling). Another variable that should be addressed is the degree to which data collectors and interventionists are familiar to participants and "blind" to study hypotheses. Experimenter bias can be avoided if data collectors are equally familiar (or unfamiliar) to participants, however, experimenter or interventionist bias requires frequent reliability checks on independent and dependent variables to ensure procedural fidelity and scoring consistency.

The group research approach is the most common research methodology used in the behavioral sciences. Group research designs are well-suited for large-scale efficacy studies or clinical trials in which a researcher's interest is in describing whether a practice or policy with a specific population, on average, will be effective. With such research questions a group design methodology is recommended. Numerous group designs and statistical analysis procedures are available for your consideration if you choose to study group behavior. As will be discussed in a later section of this chapter, a question you must ask is, "To what extent do results generated by a group design study generalize to a specific individual?" To paraphrase Barlow et al. (1984), generalization of group research findings to individuals requires a "leap of faith," the extent of which depends on the similarity of the individual to study participants for whom the intervention was effective. You must never lose sight when attempting to generalize a practice supported by group research to an individual that some participants performed better, while others performed worse than the average participant. Do not be surprised if results are not replicated if your student or client differs substantially from the average group study participant.

Qualitative Research Approaches

The term qualitative research is an "umbrella" term that refers to a number of *descriptive research* approaches "that investigate the quality of relationships, activities, situations, or materials" (Fraenkel & Wallen, 2006, p. 430). Brantlinger, Jimenez, Klingner, Pugach, and Richardson (2005) define qualitative research as "a systematic approach to understanding qualities, or the essential nature, of a phenomenon within a particular context" (p. 195). A quantitative analysis of outcome measures is typically not of interest to qualitative researchers. The qualitative paradigm is discussed here in spite of its descriptive rather than experimental analysis of behavior due to what appears to be increased interest among some researchers who believe it is "ideal for phenomena that are patently complex and about which little is known with certainty" (Lancy, 1993, p. 9). Table 1.3 identifies and briefly describes 16 different qualitative research approaches that Brantlinger et al. place under the qualitative research paradigm. Of the 16 approaches, three have particular prominence among educational and clinical researchers who conduct qualitative research studies: case study, ethnography, and phenomenology. The *case study* approach entails an in-depth and detailed description of one or more cases (individuals, events, activities, or processes), while *ethnography* refers to the study of culture, defined as "the customary beliefs, social forms, and material traits of a racial, religious, or social group" (*Merriam-Webster Online Dictionary*, 2008), in which the investigator unobtrusively observes people in their natural setting without an attempt to influence their behavior or the event. Sometimes confused with ethnography, *phenomenology* is the study of people's reactions and perceptions of a particular event or situation. For a more in-depth discussion of these and other qualitative research approaches, see Glasser and Strauss (1967), Lincoln and Guba (1985), or Lancy (1993).

Common Characteristics

Qualitative research approaches share a number of common characteristics, not least of which is a desire to provide a detailed, in-depth description of the case or phenomena under study. Data are collected using several methods, including direct observation in which the investigator's role is that of a "participant-observer" in the natural environment, with neither an interest nor attempt to influence the person or event being observed. As a participant-observer the researcher takes field notes, sometimes referred to as "reflective notes," that are intended to capture the "essence" or "themes" of the observations. Other data-collection techniques include audio and video recordings that are summarized and presented in written narratives. Interviews and questionnaires are important data-collection instruments used in qualitative research. In terms of these two data-collection tools and their use in

Table 1.3 Types and Descriptions of Qualitative Research

Case study—exploration of a bounded system (group, individual, setting, event, phenomenon, process); can include autobiography and biography.

Collective case study—a study that takes place in multiple sites or includes personalized stories of several similar (or distinctive) individuals.

Enthnography—description/interpretation of a cultural or social group or system; typically includes observations, interviews, and document analysis.

Action research—researcher brings ideas for practice to fieldwork to have an impact on the setting/participants while collecting data.

Collaborative action research—researcher and practitioner share ideas about how to change practice and work together to modify a situation as well as collect information for a study.

Grounded theory—research done to generate or discover a general theory or abstract analytical hunch based on study of phenomena in a particular situation(s).

Phenomenology—studies the meanings people make of their lived experiences.

Symbolic interactionism—studies interpretive processes used by persons dealing with material and social situations.

Narrative research—collection of personal narratives; based on recognition that people are storytellers who lead storied lives.

Life (oral) history—extensive interviews with individuals to collect first person narratives about their lives or events in which they participated.

Quasi-life-history research—encouraging participants to recall and reflect on earlier as well as current meaningful occurrences in their lives.

Interpretive research—used synonymously with "qualitative work" and/or to refer to research framed within certain (critical, feminist, disability study, critical race) theories.

Content analysis—close inspection of text(s) to understand themes or perspectives (also refers to the analysis stage of qualitative studies).

Conversational analysis—studying interactional situations, structure of talk, and communicative exchanges; includes recording facial expressions, gestures, speed or hesitancy of speech, and tone of voice.

Discourse analysis—deconstructs common sense textual meanings; identifies meanings that undergird normative ways of conceptualizing and discussing phenomena.

Ideological critique—discourse analysis that assumes political meanings (power disparities) or ideologies are embedded in, and infused through, all discourses, institutions, and social practices.

Source: Brantlinger et al. (2005). Copyright by Society for the Experimental Analysis of Behavior, Inc. Reproduced by permission.

phenomenology, Fraenkel and Wallen (2006) describe the role of the researcher as one who "extracts what he or she considers to be relevant statements from each subject's description of the phenomenon and then clusters these statements into themes. He or she then integrates these themes into a narrative description of the phenomenon" (p. 437). Unlike the group study approach in which hypotheses are formulated prior to conducting a study to test a theory, known as a *deductive analysis* approach (i.e., general to specific), researchers who use a qualitative study approach collect data and describe themes or trends in the data without offering a theory, an approach known as *inductive analysis* (i.e., specific to general). In this regard, qualitative and single subject research studies are similar. A critical difference between qualitative and quantitative research approaches is, as Brantlinger et al. (2005) states, "Qualitative research is not done for the purposes of generalization but rather to produce *evidence* based on the exploration of specific contexts and particular individuals" (p. 203). If this is in fact how qualitative researchers view their approach, we as consumers of research must ask the question, "How can qualitative research findings support evidence-based practice if they can not be generalized beyond the case studied?"

Data Analysis, Reliability, and Validity Issues
The issue of credibility and trustworthiness of research findings is central to practitioners using promising, if not best practices in their service to students and clients and their families. Guidelines for evaluating the credibility of qualitative research studies have been developed by Brantlinger et al. (2005) and are presented in Table 1.4. These measures are how qualitative

Table 1.4 Credibility Measures for Qualitative Research

Triangulation—search for convergence of, or consistency among, evidence from multiple and varied daily sources (observations/interviews; one participant & another; interviews/documents).

- *Data triangulation*—use of varied data sources in a study.
- *Investigator triangulation*—use of several researchers, evaluators, peer debriefers.
- *Theory triangulation*—use of multiple perspectives to interpret a single set of data.
- *Methodological triangulation*—use of multiple methods to study a single problem.

Disconfirming evidence—after establishing preliminary themes/categories, the researcher looks for evidence inconsistent with these themes (outliers); also known as negative or discrepant case analysis.

Researcher reflexivity—researchers attempt to understand and self-disclose their assumptions, beliefs, values, and biases (i.e., being forthright about position/perspective).

Member checks—having participants review and confirm the accuracy (or inaccuracy) of interview transcriptions or observational field notes.

- *First level*—taking transcriptions to participants prior to analyses and interpretations of results.
- *Second level*—taking analyses and interpretations of data to participants (prior to publication) for validation of (or support for) researchers' conclusions.

Collaborative work—involving multiple researchers in designing a study or concurring about conclusions to ensure that analyses and interpretations are not idiosyncratic and/or biased; could involve interrater reliability checks on the observations made or the coding of data. (The notion that persons working together will get reliable results is dependent on the "truth claim" assumption that one can get accurate descriptions of situational realities.)

External auditors—using outsiders (to the research) to examine if, and confirm that, a researcher's inferences are logical and grounded in findings.

Peer debriefing—having a colleague or someone familiar with phenomena being studied review and provide critical feedback on descriptions, analyses, and interpretations or a study's results.

Audit trail—keeping track of interviews conducted and/or specific times and dates spent observing as well as who was observed on each occasion; used to document and substantiate that sufficient time was spent in the field to claim dependable and confirmable results.

Prolonged field engagement—repeated, substantive observations; multiple, in-depth interviews; inspection of a range of relevant documents; thick description validates the study's soundness.

Thick, detailed description—reporting sufficient quotes and field note descriptions to provide evidence for researchers' interpretations and conclusions.

Particularizability—documenting cases with thick description so that readers can determine the degree of transferability to their own situations.

---

researchers address the validity and reliability of information in their research reports, but the authors caution against "using credibility measures as a checklist in a rigid and unreflective way," and, although they "encourage" researchers to use credibility measures, "they believe that authors who succinctly clarify the methods used and the rationale for them can convey that their reports are reliable and worthy of attention without alluding to credibility measures" (pp. 200–201). As you may have deduced from the quotes cited (e.g., "extracts what he or she considers relevant"), the primary criticism of qualitative research approaches is their lack of objectivity. A common characteristic of qualitative studies is the position of the researcher as an "insider" who has close personal contact with participants and who is both the data collector and data analyst. Brantlinger et al. acknowledge that they (qualitative researchers) are "the instrument" in their research and that "To do qualitative work well (be *valid* instruments), we must have experience related to our research focus, be well read, knowledgeable, analytical, reflective, and introspective" (p. 197). If true, the position of the qualitative researcher raises concerns because of the subjectivity of the data collected and reported, which in turn influences the validity and reliability of findings since observational safeguards (e.g., independent observations) are rare. This lack of reliability of measurement alone is a major threat to the internal validity of findings, a confounding known as instrumentation (see Chapter 5 and Chapter 7 for detailed information on threats to internal validity and reliability of measurement). The use of field notes, narrative descriptions, and the freedom of investigators to "consider what is relevant" all signal a method that is prone to subjectivity and findings that would be difficult, if not impossible, to replicate. Replication, as previously noted, is at the heart of the scientific method. If replication of a study's findings has not been attempted or not been achieved those findings cannot be considered trustworthy or valid. So, what does qualitative research offer to the science of human behavior? In spite of concerns over subjectivity and lack of replication, qualitative studies can and do provide detailed descriptions of behavior under natural conditions that could subsequently lead to asking research questions, or testing research hypotheses, that employ more objective, quantitative research approaches.

Single Subject Research Approach

Single subject research methodology has a long tradition in the behavioral sciences. Sidman (1960) first described this research approach in his seminal book, *Tactics of Scientific Research: Evaluating Experimental Data in Psychology*, which exemplified its application within the context of basic experimental psychology research. In 1968, Baer, Wolf, and Risley elaborated on single subject research methodology and how it could be used in applied research to evaluate intervention effectiveness with individuals. Since that time numerous articles, chapters, and books have been written describing single subject research methodology and its use in a number of disciplines, including psychology (Bailey & Burch, 2002; Barlow & Hersen, 1984; Johnston & Pennypacker, 1993; Kazdin, 1998; Kratochwill & Levin, 1992; Skinner, 2004), special education (Gast, 2005; Kennedy, 2005; Richards, Taylor, Ramasamy, & Richards, 1999; Tawney & Gast, 1984), "helping professions" (Bloom & Fischer, 1982), literacy education (Neuman & McCormick, 1995), communication sciences (McReynolds & Kearns, 1983; Schlosser, 2003), and therapeutic recreation (Dattilo, Gast, Loy, & Malley, 2000). As Horner et al. (2005) pointed out, over 45 professional journals publish single subject research design studies. A common misconception about single subject research methodology is that it is appropriate only if you subscribe to a behavioral psychology model, which is incorrect. Although it is based in operant conditioning, applied behavior analysis, and social learning theory, interventions based in other theoretical models may be evaluated within the context of a single subject research design. In this section the basic parameters of single subject research methodology are overviewed as a means of comparison with previously described research approaches. Quality indicators for evaluating single subject research studies have been developed by Horner et al. and are presented in Table 1.5. The topics introduced in this section, including criteria for evaluating supportive evidence of a practice, are discussed in detail in the chapters that follow.

Characteristics of Single Subject Research Design

In spite of its name, single subject (or single case) research design, it is important to understand that this research approach is *not* a case study approach in which there is only one participant whose behavior is described, in detail, in written narrative, based on primary data collected using qualitative research techniques (e.g., field notes, interviews). Single subject research design is a quantitative experimental research approach in which study participants

Table 1.5 Quality Indicators Within Single-Subject Research

Description of Participants and Setting
- Participants are described with sufficient detail to allow others to select individual with similar characteristics (e.g., age, gender, disability, diagnosis).
- The process for selecting participants is described with replicable precision.
- Critical features of the physical setting are described with sufficient precision to allow replication.

Dependent Variable
- Dependent variables are described with operational precision.
- Each dependent variable is measured with a procedure that generates a quantifiable index.
- Measurement of the dependent variable is valid and described with replicable precision.
- Dependent variables are measured repeatedly over time.
- Data are collected on the reliability or interobserver agreement associated with each dependent variable, and IOA levels meet minimal standards (e.g., IOA = 80%; Kappa = 60%).

Independent Variable
- Independent variable is described with replicable precision.
- Independent variable is systematically manipulated and under the control of the experimenter.
- Overt measurement of the fidelity of implementation for the independent variable is highly desirable.

Baseline
- The majority of single-subject research studies will include a baseline phase that provides repeated measurement of a dependent variable and establishes a pattern of responding that can be used to predict the pattern of future performance, if introduction or manipulation of the independent variable did not occur.
- Baseline conditions are described with replicable precision.

Experimental Control/Internal Validity
- The design provides at least three demonstrations of experimental effect at three different points in time.
- The design controls for common threats to internal validity (e.g., permits elimination of rival hypotheses).
- The results document a pattern that demonstrates experimental control.

External Validity
- Experimental effects are replicated across participants, settings, or materials to establish external validity.

Social Validity
- The dependent variable is socially important.
- The magnitude of change in the dependent variable resulting from the intervention is socially important.
- Implementation of the independent variable is practical and cost effective.
- Social validity is enhanced by implementation of the independent variable over extended time periods, by typical intervention agents, in typical physical and social contexts.

Source: Horner et al. (2005). Copyright by Society for the Experimental Analysis of Behavior, Inc. Reproduced by permission.

serve as their own control, a principle known as "*baseline logic*" (Sidman, 1960). In single subject design studies each participant is exposed to both a "control" condition, known as baseline, and an intervention condition. The target behavior is repeatedly measured within the context of one of several research designs that evaluate and control for threats to internal validity. Depending on the research design used, baseline (A) and intervention (B) conditions are slowly alternated across time (e.g., A-B-A-B or withdrawal design), or the intervention condition is introduced in a time-lagged fashion across several behaviors (conditions or participants). Return to a previously introduced condition or introduction of a new condition to a new behavior (condition or participant) occurs only after data stability is evident. Data for individual participants are presented on a line graph for each participant and decisions to maintain or change the current condition are made in accordance with visual-analysis guidelines (see Chapter 9 for information on visual-analysis guidelines). Baseline logic is very different from group design logic in which similar or matched participants are assigned to one of two or more study conditions (control or intervention) based on pretest data and, unlike single subject studies, not all participants are exposed to the intervention. At some specified time in the future, not necessarily when participants have reached some pre-established performance criteria, posttest data are collected and analyzed using statistical methods comparing the average performance of participants assigned to one condition to the average performance of participants assigned to other conditions. Where group research data are analyzed using statistical procedures, single subject research data are analyzed primarily using visual-analysis guidelines in which graphed data levels, trends, and stability are reported for each study participant. Descriptive statistics (mean, median, mode, range) are also used to summarize results. Single subject research designs and visual analysis of graphic data for individual participants make them ideal for applied researchers and practitioners who are interested in answering research questions and/or evaluating interventions designed to change the behavior of individuals.

Controlling Threats to Internal Validity
Regardless of the research approach, alternative explanations must be ruled out for there to be confidence that the independent variable was responsible for a study's findings. The extent to which researchers evaluate and control for threats to internal validity will determine the level of confidence we can have in their results. In single subject research studies a participant's behavior is repeatedly measured under at least two experimental conditions, baseline and intervention, using direct observational recording procedures. To ensure data-collection objectivity, independent observers periodically check the accuracy of measures using the same definitions and recording procedures used by the primary observer. These data are typically reported as percentage of interobserver agreement. It is also important that experimental condition procedures (baseline and intervention) be consistently followed. To ensure procedural fidelity, an independent observer collects data on "key" procedural variables (e.g., securing student attention, waiting 5 s for participant's response, delivering correct consequences) and reports the percentage of time *each* variable is correctly followed. To evaluate and control for outside or "extra-experimental" influences and the passage of time that may be responsible for observed changes in behavior, single subject design researchers systematically (a) alternate baseline and intervention conditions (withdrawal, reversal design, multitreatment design, alternating treatments design) or (b) stagger the introduction of the intervention across three or more behaviors, conditions or participants (multiple baseline design, multiple probe design) that are functionally independent but amenable to the same intervention. Other strategies are used to evaluate and control for the influence of participants' awareness of being observed, repeated exposure to test conditions, their withdrawal from a study, variability in their performance, and performance carryover effects when moving from one condition to another. In determining the supportive evidence for a practice a single subject design study must address and report the extent to which threats to internal validity were controlled. Subsequently, independent researchers will need to replicate results of earlier studies in order to extend the generality of findings. Through replication "the scientific method is self-correcting" (Harry, 2006, p. 44).

Research Approaches and Generalization to the Individual

In education and clinical practice, educators, psychologists, speech/language pathologists, occupational, recreation, and physical therapists are expected to evaluate the adequacy of their efforts by measuring changes in each student's or client's behavior over the duration of their programs. While many, if not most, of these professionals are interested in individual performance, other practitioners, as well as administrators and some researchers, will evaluate the adequacy of their system-change efforts (e.g., curriculum revisions, school-wide discipline policy) by focusing on the performance of the group. Many of these professionals, however, will identify those individuals who respond poorly to the system change and modify the program in some way with the intention of bringing about positive change in all group members. There are few occasions, if ever, when it would be acceptable for an educator or clinician to ignore the needs of an individual who has failed to benefit from the first instructional program or treatment attempted. Professional ethics across disciplines dictates an active and concerted effort by practitioners and applied researchers to identify an intervention that will succeed in benefiting each student, client, or research participant, regardless of the number of attempts it may take to find such an intervention. This position is fundamental to applied behavior analysis research as described by Baer et al. (1968). So, what do research reports (i.e., published journal articles) using these three research approaches have to say to practitioners wanting to positively change behavior of their students or clients?

Group Research Approach

Group design studies, regardless of whether they are experimental, quasi-experimental, or correlational, are interested in the average performance of group members, with some individuals assigned to the control group that does not receive the intervention, while other individuals are assigned to ineffective or inferior intervention groups. Even for those individuals assigned to the group in which an intervention was determined to be effective, based on achieving a statistical significance level of $p < 0.05$, the intervention was ineffective for some individuals in the group. That is, group research findings overestimate their generality since not all individuals respond in the same way to the independent variable. In a similar vein some group study participants perform better than the average participant, thus underestimating the impact of the independent variable. If, however, your interest were to evaluate a curriculum or policy change and its effect on group performance, a group research approach would be better suited for answering your research questions or testing your hypotheses.

Concerns with the group research approach, relative to study participants and generalization of findings to other individuals, include ethical issues when study participants do not benefit from their participation. Irrespective of the time lost, introducing an effective intervention after the study has concluded can address this concern, a practice that conscientious group researchers are following. Less easily addressed by the group research approach for the scientist-practitioner is the practical problem of identifying a sufficiently large sample to make any statistical test of findings meaningful. For those of us interested in studying "low-incidence" populations it is nearly impossible to find a large enough population in a single site, thus precluding use of a group research design. As previously discussed, even when a large sample is available, inter-subject variability and a failure to analyze and report individual characteristics decreases the generality of findings unless the individual is similar to individuals who responded positively to the intervention.

Qualitative Research Approaches

Qualitative research approaches attempt to provide an in-depth descriptive report of a single individual, event, or activity without proclaiming that their findings generalize beyond the case studied (Brantlinger et al., 2005). In addition to providing an insightful account of the target case, qualitative research reports can be of value to researchers and practitioners by serving as a source for generating research questions and hypotheses that can be addressed with more objective quantitative research approaches. Practitioner findings from qualitative studies provide minimal, if any, support for a practice since there is no attempt to isolate causes of an observed behavior change, and level of subjectivity in observations, data analyses, and reporting.

Single Subject Design Approach

Single subject research methodology is a "low-inference model" that is based on inductive reasoning and is ideal for the scientist-practitioner. The individual is of paramount importance as evidenced by the in-depth and detailed descriptions of individual participants and their performance in published research reports. Since individual data are presented it is possible, as a consumer of research, to analyze independently the effect an intervention has on each participant. If there is inter-subject variability, it is possible to analyze individual characteristics that may account for performance differences. For those participants for whom the initial intervention was not effective, applied researchers will continue to search for an effective intervention while still demonstrating experimental control. The dynamic nature of the research methodology allows the researcher to respond to individual differences, and in so doing identify intervention modifications or alternatives that may prove effective for other individuals for whom the original intervention failed. Because of its emphasis on providing a detailed description of study participants and procedures, objectivity in measurement, evaluation and control of alternative explanations for findings, individual visual presentation and analysis of data, and systematic replication of findings, single subject research studies provide an important evidence base for supporting a practice.

Summary

There are a number of research approaches available to the scientist-practitioner who chooses to add evidence in support of a particular practice he or she is currently using or is considering using. As a contributor to research evidence, it is important to choose the appropriate research methodology that best answers the research question. Group research methodology is appropriate and best suited for testing hypotheses when your interest is in the average performance of a group of individuals, but it will have limited generality to individuals who differ from those for whom the intervention was effective. Unfortunately for practitioners who are consumers and evaluators of group design research, sufficient details are seldom provided on individual participants that would allow them to make an informed decision as to the likelihood of their student or client responding positively to the intervention studied. Qualitative research approaches (e.g., case study, ethnography, phenomenology) may be appropriate if your interest is in an in-depth qualitative (as opposed to quantitative) descriptive report of an individual, activity, or event. Studies using this research approach make no attempt to intervene, control for common threats to internal validity, or generalize findings beyond the case studied. The single subject research approach focuses on individual performance and permits practitioners and researchers to independently evaluate the merits of a study or a series of studies since all primary data are presented on all participants in graphic displays and tables. In accordance with scientific method principles, sufficient detail is typically presented in single subject research reports to permit replication by independent researchers. It is through such replication efforts that the generality of findings of a single study is established and evidence generated in support of an intervention. In the chapters that follow we have attempted to provide sufficient detail on the parameters of single subject research methodology to allow you to objectively evaluate and conduct single subject research studies. Through your efforts and the efforts of other applied researchers it is possible to advance our understanding of human behavior and add evidence in support of effective practices. To this end, scientist-practitioners must disseminate their research findings in professional journals, at professional conferences, and during clinic or school inservices.

References

Association of Behavior Analysis International. (1989). *The right to an effective behavioral treatment.* Retrieved June 30, 2008 from www.abainternational.org/ABA/statements/treatment/asp.

Baer, D. M., Wolf, M. M., & Risley, T. R. (1968). Some current dimensions of applied behavior analysis. *Journal of Applied Behavior Analysis, 1,* 91–97.

Bailey, J. S., & Burch, M. R. (2002). *Research methods in applied behavior analysis.* Thousand Oaks, CA: Sage Publications.

Barlow, D. H., Hayes, S. C., & Nelson, R. O. (1984). *The scientist practitioner: Research accountability in clinical and educational settings.* New York: Pergamon Press.

Barlow, D. H., & Hersen, M. (1984). *Single case experimental designs: Strategies for studying behavior change* (2nd ed.). New York: Pergamon Press.

Bloom, M., & Fischer, J. (1982). *Evaluating practice: Guidelines for the accountable professional.* Englewood Cliffs, NJ: Prentice-Hall, Inc.

Brantlinger, E., Jimenez, R., Klingner, J., Pugach, M., & Richardson, V. (2005). Qualitative studies in special education. *Exceptional Children, 71,* 195–207.

Committee on the Educational Interventions for Children with Autism. (2001). (The NRC, 2001 book).

Dattilo, J., Gast, D. L., Loy, D. P., & Malley, S. (2000). Use of single-subject research designs in therapeutic recreation. *Therapeutic Recreation Journal, 34,* 253–270.

deMarrais, K., & Lapan, S. D. (Eds.). (2004). *Foundations for research: Methods of inquiry in education and the social sciences.* Mahwah, NJ: Lawrence Erlbaum Associates.

Fraenkel, J. R., & Wallen, N. E. (2006). *How to design and evaluate research in education* (6th ed.). New York: McGraw-Hill.

Gast, D. L. (2005). Single-subject research design. In M. Hersen, G. Sugai, & R. Horner (Eds.), *Encyclopedia of behavior modification and cognitive behavior therapy* (pp. 1520–1526). Thousand Oaks, CA: Sage Publications, Inc.

Gersten, R., Fuchs, L. S., Compton, D., Coyne, M., Greenwood, C., & Innocenti, M. (2005). Quality indicators for group experimental and quasi-experimental research in special education. *Exceptional Children, 71,* 149–164.

Glasser, B. G., & Strauss, A. L. (1967). *The discovery of grounded theory: Strategies for qualitative research.* Chicago, IL: Aldine.

Harry, G. J. (2006). Requirements for good scientific inquiry. *Autism Advocate, 45,* 44–47.

Horner, R. H., Carr, E. G., Halle, J., McGee, G., Odom, S., & Wolery, M. (2005). The use of single-subject research to identify evidence-based practice in special education. *Exceptional Children, 71,* 165–179.

Johnston, J. M., & Pennypacker, H. S. (1993). *Strategies and tactics for human behavioral research* (2nd ed.). Hillsdale, NJ: Erlbaum.

Kazdin, A. E. (1998). *Methodological issues and strategies in clinical research.* Washington, DC: American Psychological Association.

Kennedy, C. H. (2005). *Single-case designs for educational research.* Boston, MA: Pearson/Allyn & Bacon.

Kratochwill, T. R., & Levin, J. R. (1992). *Single-case research design and analysis: New direction for psychology and education.* Hillsdale, NJ: Lawrence Erlbaum.

Lancy, D. F. (1993). *Qualitative research in education.* New York: Longman.

Lincoln, Y. S., & Guba, E. G. (1985). *Naturalistic inquiry.* Newbury Park, CA: Sage Publications, Inc.

McReynolds, L. V., & Kearns, K. P. (1983). *Single-subject experimental designs in communicative disorders.* Baltimore, MD: University Park Press.

Neuman, S. B., & McCormick, S. (Eds.). (1995). *Single subject experimental research: Applications for literacy.* Newark, DE: International Reading Association.

Odom, S. L., Brantlinger, E., Gersten, R., Horner, R. H., Thompson, B., & Harms, K. R. (2005). Research in special education: Scientific methods and evidence-based practices. *Exceptional Children, 71,* 137–148.

Portney, L., & Watkins, M. P. (2000). *Foundations of clinical research: Applications to practice.* Upper Saddle River, NJ: Prentice Hall.

Richards, S. B., Taylor, R. L., Ramasamy, R., & Richards, R. (1999). *Single subject research: Applications in educational and clinical settings.* San Diego, CA: Singular Publishing Group, Inc.

Rosenberg, M. S., Bott, D., Majsterek, D., Chiang, B., Gartland, D., Wesson, C., et al.(1992). Minimum standards for the description of participants in learning disabilities research. *Learning Disability Quarterly, 15,* 65–70.

Schlosser, R. W. (2003). *The efficacy of augmentative and alternative communication.* Boston, MA: Academic Press.

Sidman, M. (1960). *Tactics of scientific research: Evaluating experimental data in psychology.* New York: Basic Books.

Skinner, B. F. (1953). *Science and human behavior.* New York: Macmillan.

Skinner, C. H. (2004). Single-subject designs for school psychologists. *Journal of Applied School Psychology, 20,* 2.

Tawney, J. W., & Gast, D., L. (1984). *Single subject research in special education.* Columbus, OH: Charles E. Merrill.

What Works Clearinghouse. (2006a). *Study design classification.* Retrieved July 9, 2008 from http://ies.ed.gov/ncee/wwc/pdf/studydesignclass.pdf.

What Works Clearinghouse. (2006b). *Study standards.* Retrieved July 9, 2008 from http://ies.ed.gov/ncee/wwc/pdf/study_standards_final.pdf.

Wolery, M., & Ezell, H. (1993). Subject descriptions and single subject research. *Journal of Learning Disabilities, 26,* 642–647.

2

Scientific Research in Educational and Clinical Settings

David L. Gast and James W. Tawney (from his earlier contributions to this chapter)

In recent years there has been a call by government for educators and clinicians to adopt evidence-based practices. This call is reflected in research, personnel preparation, and service grant programs directed by such agencies as the U.S. Department of Education, Office of Special Education Programs (OSEP, www.ed.gov/about/offices/list/osers/osep/index.html), and National Institute of Mental Health (NIMH, www.nimh.nih.gov). These grant competition sponsors require that grant applicants guarantee the incorporation of evidence-based practices into the delivery of services and preparation of personnel funded under their sponsored programs. It is interesting to many of us behavior analysts that this emphasis on evidence-based practice is viewed as new . . . something that has only recently been emphasized in the fields of psychology and education. For those of us who were educated in the tradition of applied behavior analysis in the 1960s and 1970s, the importance of "research-based" practice and "data-based" instruction were at the core of our training. Tawney and Gast (1984) described what they termed "The Behavioral Revolution" that traced the contributions of behavioral psychologists to the field of education by such pioneers as B. F. Skinner, Sidney Bijou, Donald Baer, Monte Wolf, Todd Risley, Ogden Lindsey, Nathan Azrin, Jay Birnbrauer, Norris Haring, Hugh McKenzie, Richard Whelan, and Thomas Lovitt. These behavioral psychologists, and many others, called for an objective, scientific approach to educational and clinical practices, an approach based on inductive reasoning, rather than deductive reasoning, and one that adopted a "low-inference model" that focused on observable, quantifiable behavior. The point here is that there is nothing new about the call for evidence-based practice ... it has been an integral part of the behavioral tradition from the beginning, as articulated in the works by Skinner (1953, 1968), Bijou and Baer (1961), Bijou (1966), and Baer, Wolf, and Risley (1968).

Whether you view education and many of the therapies as "art" or "science" will likely depend on your history. When we observe clinicians delivering therapy or educators teaching, and we ask, "What are you doing and why are you doing it that way?", rarely will we get a response that links the observed practice to research. We would not be completely surprised if respondents explain its connection to some theory, but if pressed it is unlikely that they would cite specific research reports that support their intervention strategy. As students, clients, parents, and advocates of "best" and "promising" practices it is our responsibility to ask difficult questions of teachers and clinicians as it relates to the instruction and services they deliver. As clinicians and educators we should be prepared to answer these questions.

In this chapter we define the goals of science and the goals of educational and clinical practice. Given that our history is in the field of special education, our discussion focuses primarily on the integration of science and practice by teachers, though the points we make are equally applicable to speech/language, behavior, physical, occupational, and recreation therapists. It is our position that teachers and clinicians have some of the best research questions, questions that, if answered, could improve how teachers teach and therapists deliver therapy. For that reason we call on teachers and therapists to develop a repertoire of applied research skills and to initiate single subject research design studies as a part of their practice.

The Goal of Science

The *Merriam-Webster Online Dictionary* (2008) defines science as "the state of knowing: knowledge as distinguished from ignorance or misunderstanding"; "knowledge or a system of knowledge covering general truths or the operation of general laws especially as obtained and tested through scientific method." Simply put, the goal of science is to *advance knowledge*. In the popular view, within a discipline the accumulation of knowledge often proceeds in a somewhat haphazard fashion. From the efforts of many come the grand discoveries of the few, the findings that move society forward. As the process unfolds, the major body of research yields findings that may go unnoticed for years. Some findings are of immediate interest and generate new research programs that may be abandoned when more fruitful approaches appear on the horizon. Thus, while the individual scientist follows a defined set of procedures applied systematically to an area of inquiry and moves from one logical question to another, science itself advances in a less orderly fashion. Sidman (1960) illustrates the point from the perspective of the scientist:

> It sometimes seems that a brilliantly creative experimenter does not possess the qualities of patience and plodding thoroughness that most of us feel are vital for scientific progress. While it would, of course, be desirable for all investigators to be simultaneously

brilliant and plodding, such a combination is, in fact, rare. Most of us are elaborators of other workers' discoveries; a few of us are creators; only a handful are both. We are all necessary, for even the most creative scientist builds upon an established foundation. A scorn for the everyday scientific laborer will blind the student to the immensely valuable and necessary contributions that can come only from hard and often uninspired "pick and shovel" work. On the other hand, if the student is taught, as many are, that pick and shovel labor *is Science*, then he will inevitably fail to appreciate the results of important, but unelaborated, discoveries.

(p. 24)

To student-researchers and scientist-practitioners their contribution to the advancement of science may seem small. A replication of a published study, the application of a standard procedure in a new environment or with a new population—these efforts may seem minor in the grand scheme of science. However, if they adhere to the fundamental principles of the scientific method by (a) operationally defining and reliably measuring behavior, (b) consistently implementing procedures, (c) controlling extraneous variables, and (d) repeating treatment effects, their contribution will likely positively impact "best" and "promising" practices. Such research efforts are a necessary part of the elaboration of our general understanding of behavior and the growth of applied behavior analysis.

The Goal of Education and Clinical Practice

The goal of education and clinical practice is to *change behavior in a positive direction.* One need not be a behaviorist to adopt this definition, although many educators and therapists would disagree with the definition, and with that assumption. A brief example will illustrate this point.

Many years ago, when proponents of "behaviorism" and "humanism" were tilting at each other over the "proper approach" to education, the second author was asked to consult with a group of regular and special educators in a small college. The invitation was tendered because of the author's work in the area of "competency based teacher education." The task was to develop a philosophy statement, a set of general goals, and a set of specific competencies to be demonstrated by graduates of this teacher-education program. After the amenities, and the coffee, the group set about its first task—developing a philosophy statement. There was little discussion, not uncommon at the beginning stage of a group project. Finally the consultant raised the question, "What is the fundamental goal of education?" Then, to end the silence that followed, he asked, rhetorically, "Isn't the goal of education to change behavior?" No silence this time! A distinguished committee member jumped to his feet, threw down his working materials, shot a withering glance at the consultant, shouted "Oh, my God no! You're one of those behaviorists!" He wheeled and left the room, never to return. At the very least, those actions broke the ice, and the committee proceeded. Being or not being a "behaviorist," of course, had nothing to do with the task at hand—though few, other than the consultant, would have agreed at that point. The lesson to be learned was that long-time educators, however they defined their work, did not define it as changing behavior. However, there is a general social expectation that the educational process will produce a change in children's behavior. Students are expected to "know more" at the end of the school year. Further, teachers are expected to be responsible for that change. The legal contract between a teacher and the employing district is the observable manifestation of a social contract that offers a livelihood in return for the enhancement of the next generation. Whether one chooses to describe the contract in euphemisms or concrete terms, the expectation is the same. For the classroom teacher, and therapists working in schools or community-based clinics, the goals of education and clinical practice are clear: to produce a positive change in behavior and, at the same time, to establish some personal responsibility for the change.

Integrating Science into Educational and Clinical Practice

Is it possible to incorporate scientific methodology into the daily routine of the school classroom? . . . clinic program? . . . therapy room? It is, but it's not an easy task. We have stated the benefits of this strategy in general terms: to advance science, to document child performance change, and to establish teachers' and therapists' responsibility for the change. Before moving on to the research task itself, we would like to restate and elaborate on the importance of these goals.

Advancement of Science

Through the work of Skinner and Bijou a system of behavior analysis has been developed that includes a philosophy of behavior development, a general theory, a methodology for translating theory into practice, and a specific research methodology. This system was new in the scope of human evolution and the advancement of science. It has gained acceptance and verification through the successful application of concepts and principles. One general "test" of the system has been the demonstration of effectiveness in a variety of settings, in basic and applied applications. Baer et al. (1968) suggested some benefits that occur from an analysis of individual behavior:

> A society willing to consider a technology of its own behavior apparently is likely to support that application when it deals with *socially important behaviors*, such as intellectual disabilities, crime, mental illness, or education. Such applications have appeared for many years. Their current number and the interest that they create apparently suffice to generate a journal for their display. That display may well lead to the widespread examination of these applications, their refinement, and eventually their replacement by better applications. Better applications, it is hoped, will lead to a better state of society, to whatever extent the behavior of its members can contribute to the goodness of a society. Since the evaluation of what is a "good" society is in itself a behavior of its members, this hope turns on itself in a philosophically interesting manner. However, it is at least a fair presumption that behavioral applications, when effective, can sometimes lead to a social approval and adoption.
>
> (p. 91)

Applied behavior analysis has been adopted and made an integral part of special and general education, speech/language therapy, clinical psychology, recreation therapy, and many other disciplines. Applied research, be it conducted in a classroom, clinic office, or community environment, derived from a system of behavior analysis and focused on specific problems of learning and reinforcement, supports the elaboration of a system of behavior analysis. In this way the student-researcher, teacher-researcher, and therapist-researcher may contribute to the advancement of science.

Not all teachers and therapists may choose to be applied researchers, but they certainly can contribute to the advancement of science, and their discipline, by collaborating with those who do. Eiserman and Behl (1992) addressed this point in their article describing how special educators could influence current best practice by opening their classrooms to researchers for the purpose of systematic research efforts. They pointed out the potential benefits of such collaborations, not least of which teachers becoming interested in conducting their own research and bridging the gap between research and practice (p. 12). Their position is not new, but one that behavior analysts have advocated for years (Barlow, Hayes, & Nelson, 1984; Borg, 1981; Odom, 1988; Tawney & Gast, 1984). Encouragement of practitioner involvement in applied research efforts, as defined by Baer et al. (1968, 1987), acknowledges their potential contribution by addressing "real" problems, which need to be addressed under "real" conditions, with available resources. It cannot be overstated that practitioners are often confronted with issues or problems overlooked by researchers. Thus, if practitioners collaborate with researchers, or acquire the skills to conduct their own research, they can generate answers to questions that will improve educational and clinical practice. Through such collaborations and research initiatives both science and practice will advance to the benefit of those served by teachers and therapists.

Advancement of Educational and Clinical Practice

Public education can make a difference. The applied researcher who demonstrates positive changes in children's behavior, in academic performance as well as in social behavior, produces evidence of a benefit of the instructional process. When looking at special education, you do not have to look far to learn that many of the materials and teaching approaches used have a limited research base. In response to this, the What Works Clearinghouse (http://ies.ed.gov/ncee/wwc) was established to disseminate educational practices that have been scientifically evaluated and shown to be effective. Much of the applied research, in special education, psychology, speech pathology, occupational therapy, etc., has been conducted in controlled environments (lab schools, research institutes, private clinics, medical centers) by highly educated research professionals who have access to resources beyond those typically available in public schools and clinics. Research generated in such centers is important to advancing our understanding of human behavior and how to positively affect change, however, the extent to which effective interventions generalize to settings outside these "resource rich" and controlled environments needs to be shown. Thus, there are many research possibilities that the teacher/therapist-researcher can conduct in their public school classroom or community-based clinic that will add to our understanding on how to better serve those under their care.

Baer et al. (1987) addressed the need for applied researchers to determine the context with which interventions succeed and fail. When research is conducted under highly controlled conditions, as often found in lab schools and university clinics, replication of conditions by those working in "typical" community settings may be difficult, if not impossible. That is, interventions found to be effective in resource "rich" controlled settings may not be able to be carried out at the same level of fidelity, thus affecting the outcome of the intervention. It is important for applied researchers to identify the versatility and latitude of a particular intervention and still be effective prior to advocating its use. In fact, through "failures to replicate" we seek out answers to "why?", and with perseverance, identify modifications to the original intervention that result in the desired behavior change. Such discoveries are important to the advancement of practice in that our goal is for changes in behavior to generalize and maintain in natural environments. Through collaboration with applied researchers, the contribution made by teachers and therapists will increase the probability that instructional strategies and interventions under study will improve practice as delivered by other teachers and therapists working in community schools and clinics.

Empirical Verification of Behavior Change

Successful teachers and therapists must demonstrate they can bring about positive behavior change in their students or clients. You should expect that increasingly informed parents will ask for data on child performance change, and then will ask for some verification that your efforts were responsible for that change. Computer and instructional technologies have developed sufficiently to enable you to meet these requests for data. As discussed in Chapter 7, computer-based data management systems are now available to most teachers and clinicians that assist in collecting, organizing, graphing, and analyzing data. Currently those teachers and therapists who employ "best" and "promising" practices, who develop direct data-collection systems, and who use single subject research designs to evaluate their interventions will be able to answer questions parents ask. The task may require extra effort, but the data should provide sufficient reinforcement to maintain these teaching and research behaviors.

Challenges of Applied Research in Community Environments

Researchers encounter common problems when conducting research in public school class-rooms and clinic environments. In Chapter 3 some of the logistical problems that confront applied researchers, such as recruiting and maintaining support and participation, are discussed. Here, we focus on the day-to-day problems of conducting research in the community settings (schools, clinics, recreation programs, etc.). Some of these logistical problems translate into research design problems, which are discussed in subsequent chapters.

Obtaining Resources for Classroom Research

The classroom is, or can be, rich in resources for the teacher-researcher. The classroom is where the kids are. Instructional materials are the stimuli for experiments. Students emit a wide array of behaviors. Some are of ecological concern, particularly when children emit them with such intensity or frequency that they interfere with personal development and/or the order of the classroom environment. Reinforcement procedures and schedules have long been a part of instructional technology that the materials for reinforcement systems are no longer considered foreign or difficult to obtain. If you wanted to establish a token economy in your class it is unlikely that you would be confronted with objections. Such was not the case 25 years ago, but research on token economy systems, in their many forms, has demonstrated their effectiveness (Cooper, Heron, & Heward, 2007).

Unless a study requires special equipment, e.g., SMARTBOARD, the resources required for applied research projects in classroom and clinical settings are generally low-cost. Today most teachers and therapists have access to personal computers, DVD players and recorders, digital cameras, digital watches, and a host of software programs that permit them to develop study materials, record and store data, and graphically display participant performance. Students from local colleges and universities can be recruited as volunteer data collectors or reliability observers, or they may earn credit for their service. Paraprofessionals may also assist with your research project by serving as an instructor, collecting data, or supervising students not participating in the investigation. Depending on the school's philosophy, daily class schedule, and student's age range, it may be possible to obtain support from older students. Parent volunteers, administrative staff, other teachers and therapists may also lend support to your research project. The resources listed above are illustrative, not exhaustive. They are intended to serve as suggestions to generate other likely alternatives. To the teacher or therapist who wishes to proceed with a study, but questions whether there are sufficient resources, we say, "Look around you, most of what you need is at hand."

The Pragmatics of Applied Research

Here we consider what happens when "nothing proceeds as planned." Figure 2.1 and the following examples illustrate how reality impinges on the ideal outcome of a study—reliable data that clearly demonstrate a powerful effect. There are solutions for some of the problems, but in other instances there is no alternative but to start over. Figure 2.1 represents two experimental conditions, baseline (A) and intervention (B), which are meant to represent the first two conditions of any type of single subject research design. Graph 1 represents the ideal; subsequent graphs show reality.

1. *Ideal case.* A clear effect is demonstrated by an immediate and abrupt change in level upon introduction of intervention. The effect is maintained over time.

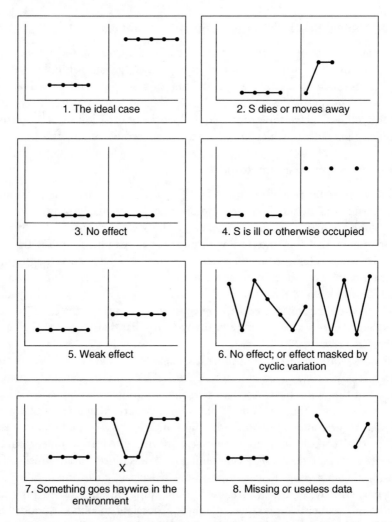

Figure 2.1 Graphic representations of two experimental conditions, baseline (A) and intervention (B), which are meant to represent the first two conditions of any type of single subject research design.

2. *Participant dies or moves away.* The ideal, of course, is that once initiated the study is brought to completion. Here, after only three days in intervention, the study had been interrupted due to the loss of the participant, a threat to validity known as attrition.

3. *No effect.* Graph 3 shows no effect of the intervention; the participant's behavior is not brought under stimulus control. Whatever has happened, the experimenter has started in the wrong place and is very far off base. When might such a problem occur? Suppose that the intervention represented the academic performance of a child with a moderate intellectual disability and that the student had been poorly assessed. An instructional program requiring performance far beyond the student's skill level might produce such a result.

4. *Participant is ill or otherwise occupied.* This is a variation on Graph 2. Here the child participates, but only sporadically. The intervention appears to be effective but due to intermittent exposure to the intervention its implementation may have to be shifted to the home environment (or wherever the child is when not in attendance). If a pool of potential participants is available, it is important to review attendance records before selecting participants.

5. *Weak effect.* There appears to be a differential effect as identified by an immediate change in level, but the effect is weak. Weak effects should not be discounted, but they may lack educational or clinical significance, i.e., criterion performance level was not achieved. This situation requires an intensive analysis of procedures to determine possible ways that the intervention can be enhanced to bring about the desired level change.

6. *No effect; or effect masked by cyclic variation.* Here it is impossible to tell if there is an effect, i.e., the data in both conditions are functionally equivalent and appear to show a cyclical pattern across days regardless of the condition in effect. Any effect is masked by failure to extend the baseline condition until a stable pattern is established. The extreme range of responses during the intervention condition indicates that behavior is not under stimulus control. The recommended response to such data patterns is to study the variability and attempt to establish a stable level and trend in performance before introducing an intervention.

7. *Something goes haywire in the environment.* Here, after two days in intervention, something that happens that is outside the researcher's control. While X may be explained (if it is identified), it will require an extension of the study to provide a more substantial demonstration of experimental control. In a school setting, X may be a substitute teacher, school celebration, family matter, or classroom visitor . . . the possibilities are many. When research is conducted in community schools and clinics, and study participants live at home, the number of outside variables that may affect behavior is considerable. When a brief, temporary change occurs in a data series as shown in Graph 7, and data return to earlier levels, the researcher may not identify the cause of the temporary change in performance. Because of the number of uncontrolled variables outside the research site, it is imperative that applied researchers control for possible alternative explanations to their intervention being responsible for the behavior change observed. Their choice of single subject research design and ability to identify and control for outside influences will determine the degree of confidence we can have in their intervention.

8. *Missing or useless data.* Theoretically, in small-scale research projects that are the focus of this text, data should not disappear. The sad fact is that they do. Sometimes data sheets may be lost or misplaced during the course of a busy day. Sometimes human

error in recording or a computer malfunction renders the data useless. Or, suppose that a researcher is following a written procedure and inadvertently makes an error, one that persists until the next periodic observation by a third-party reliability check. Such procedural *infidelity* necessitates dropping the participant from the study, or, at minimum, starting over with him with a new target behavior or set of stimuli, and describing the procedural error and action taken in the research report. Some "loss of data" problems can be alleviated by maintaining strict control over the data sheets (e.g., securing data sheets and graphs in a locked drawer or cabinet). If data are collected or stored on computer, back-up measures and security precautions should be taken. Preplanning can prevent some of these problems.

Teachers and Therapists as Applied Researchers

Similarities Between Research and Practice

Knowing that teaching (or therapy) and research are considered by some to be antithetical, we would like to draw some parallels between the behaviors we consider to be fundamental to both science and educational/clinical practice.

A teacher or therapist must:

1. Analyze an individual's performance to identify the initial instructional performance level; a form of hypothesis testing.
2. Specify instructional/therapy objectives that contain antecedents, behaviors, and defined criterion performance levels.
3. Operationally define instructional/therapy procedures so that another informed adult is able to implement procedures with fidelity.
4. Conduct concept and/or task analyses as a means of sequencing instructional/intervention programs for individual learners.
5. Implement procedures consistently.
6. Collect repeated measures on each individual's performance.
7. Analyze data and make program decisions based on the data.
8. Maintain data records.
9. Share an individual's performance regularly with significant others.
10. Follow professional/ethical guidelines.

An applied researcher must:

1. Identify a behavior challenge, i.e., behavior excess or deficit.
2. Generate a research question in the form: "If I do this, what might happen?"
3. State specific research-program objectives.
4. Define the elements of the research procedure: stimuli, arrangement, materials and equipment, target response topography, consequent events.
5. Write specific, replicable research procedures and implement with fidelity.
6. Collect direct, repeated, and reliable measures of performance.
7. Analyze graphically displayed data and make research decisions based on data.
8. Maintain data records.
9. Share research progress with research team members and significant others.
10. Conduct research in an ethical manner.

The similarities in these sets of behaviors are apparent. They can be synthesized by noting that both the teacher/therapist and applied researcher must (a) be able to identify and analyze problems, (b) generate creative solutions, (c) implement an intervention in a systematic manner, (d) document the effect of the intervention, and (e) act on the data in an ethical and responsible way. Barlow et al. (1984) referred to those teachers and therapists who engage in applied research as "scientist-practitioners," a reference we believe aptly describes those who conduct applied research as part of their daily service-delivery activities.

Some Differences Between Research and Practice

Public school classrooms and community-based programs and clinics seldom have the same level of resources as found at university-sponsored lab schools and clinics. As previously mentioned, in spite of some inconveniences, community-based programs provide adequate resources for conducting applied research. The fact that teacher/therapist-researchers who work in community settings often must utilize existing resources can add to the generality of their research findings. In recent years there has been concern that some "applied" research being disseminated may not be so "applied" after all, in that it requires special resources that are out of reach of most teachers and therapists working in typical community service and educational settings. In fact, in response to this concern, the Association of Behavior Analysis International (ABAI) launched a new practitioner-focused applied research journal in 2008, *Behavior Analysis in Practice* (BAP).

The point we want to make here is that the typical classroom is obviously not a Skinner box, nor does it approximate a sterile experimental space consisting of a table, a chair for the teacher/therapist and one for the student, and a stimulus-management device. Or does it? It is certainly not the norm, or where the majority of instruction occurs, but some teaching does occur in distraction-free, partitioned-off areas (if not separate rooms), in which a teacher/therapist and student are seated across the table from one another (Discrete Trial Training; Lovaas, 2003) or in front of a computer screen in public school classrooms and clinics. When instruction occurs under such controlled conditions it is important to evaluate the functional use of what was learned and to assess whether skills learned maintain and generalize to more natural environments. In special education, speech/language therapy, and child psychology, however, the trend is for most instruction to occur within the context of natural activities and routines implemented across the day. If this is the context in which you plan to conduct your research, it is important for you to know that you may need to create more rigorous conditions for data collection and environmental control. This may not be an easy task, but the more familiar you are with measurement and design alternatives the easier it will be. What follows are suggestions on how to proceed and questions you should ask if you are: (a) planning to conduct your own research project in your own classroom or clinic setting as both the primary researcher and service provider; (b) a collaborating teacher or therapist opening your work environment to someone else who will serve as the primary researcher; or (c) a visiting researcher who needs to be sensitive to the demands placed on the collaborating teacher or therapist. These questions are framed from the teacher/therapist perspective, i.e., the person who has primary responsibility for ensuring that teaching or therapy is not disrupted by the research process (Eiserman & Behl, 1992).

1. Does the research question address an educational or therapy objective? Will participants benefit from their participation?
2. Is there a research base that leads you to believe that your participation is likely to improve practice?
3. Are the research objectives and procedures consistent with current agency policies?

4. Do you have an interest in the answer to the research question?
5. How will participation affect your daily schedule and the schedule of participants? Will the current daily schedule have to be altered?
6. How does the intervention under study affect continuation of interventions currently in use? Are you willing to modify or abandon current interventions and replace them with the new intervention for a period of time?
7. Will participation disrupt other activities or events typically attended by participants?
8. How much of your time, and that of each student, will be required each day? How many days, weeks, or months are you willing to commit to this project? Is this commitment reasonable and justifiable?
9. How will participants, in your judgment and experience, respond to their participation?
10. Will significant others (parents, guardians, agency administrators, etc.) support the research objective and participation?
11. Are the necessary resources available (e.g., data collectors, reliability observers, computers, software programs, cameras, assistive or adaptive equipment) for conducting the research? If a piece of equipment breaks down is there back-up equipment available?
12. Do you have any ethical concerns?

Answers to these questions, which only sample the range of questions you must ask, are important prior to committing yourself and others to a research project. In that single subject research design studies typically occur over several weeks, if not months, you must understand the practical implications of your commitment from the outset. We encourage you to enter any research project with a thorough understanding of its research base, potential contributions, logistical challenges, procedural requirements, and ethical implications. All studies are not equal in their research requirements (data-collection procedures, intervention procedures, research designs, etc.), and the more you understand measurement and design alternatives, the more likely you are to design a study that will be practical for your setting while advancing both science and practice.

Summary

In this chapter we have defined the goals of science, education, and clinical practice. Our contention is that practitioners identify instructional and behavioral challenges, often overlooked by researchers not working in their settings, that, if addressed in a systematic research approach, will add to our knowledge and positively change behavior. We hold that teachers and therapists can and do contribute to the advancement of science and practice by acquiring applied research skills and conducting their own studies, and through their collaboration with applied researchers at universities, research institutes, and medical clinics. As a teacher/ therapist, your participation in applied research is encouraged as a means for ensuring that the practical constraints of working in community-based public school classrooms, clinics, or programs are addressed. Without the participation of practitioners the research questions asked may be esoteric, basic, and have little to do with improving practice. By addressing the logistical constraints inherent in most community-based programs, knowledge generated through applied research efforts can truly be "applied," benefiting all parties who participate in the research effort. Collaboration is encouraged as a practical means for advancing our understanding the parameters of "best" and "promising" practices.

References

Association of Behavior Analysis International. (ABAI, www.abainternational.org).

Baer, D. M., Wolf, M. M., & Risley, T. R. (1968). Some current dimensions of applied behavior analysis. *Journal of Applied Behavior Analysis, 1,* 91–97.

Baer, D. M., Wolf, M. M., Risley, T. R. (1987). Some still-current dimensions of applied behavior analysis. *Journal of Applied Behavior Analysis, 1,* 91–97.

Barlow, D. H., Hayes, S. C., & Nelson, R. O. (1984). *The Scientist practitioner: Research accountability in clinical and educational settings.* New York: Pergamon Press.

Bijou, S. W. (1966). A functional analysis of retarded development. In N. R. Ellis (Ed.), *International review of research in mental retardation* (vol. 1, 1–20). New York: Academic Press.

Bijou, S. W., & Baer, D. M. (1961). *Child development 1: A systematic and empirical theory.* New York: Appleton-Century-Crofts.

Borg, W. R. (1981). *Applying educational research: A practical guide for teachers.* New York; Longman.

Cooper, J. O., Heron, T. E., & Heward, W. L. (2007). *Applied behavior analysis* (2nd ed.). Upper Saddle River, NJ: Prentice-Hall, Inc.

Eiserman, W. D., & Behl, D. (1992). Research participation: Benefits and considerations for the special educator. *Teaching Exceptional Children, 24,* 12–15.

Lovaas, O. I. (2003). *Teaching individuals with developmental delays.* Austin, TX: Pro-Ed.

Merriam-Webster's Online Dictionary. (2008). Retrieved April 16, 2008, from www.merriam-webster.com/dictionary.

National Institute of Mental Health (NIMH, www.nimh.nih.gov).

Odom, S. L. (1988). Research in early childhood special education: Methodologies and paradigm. In S. L. Odom & M. B. Karnes (Eds.), *Early intervention for infants and children with handicaps* (pp. 1–22). Baltimore, MD: Paul H. Brookes.

Sidman, M. (1960). *Tactics of scientific research: Evaluating experimental data in psychology.* New York: Basic Books.

Skinner, B. F. (1953). *Science and human behavior.* New York: Macmillan.

Skinner, B. F. (1968). *The technology of teaching.* New York: Appleton-Century-Crofts.

Tawney, J. W., & Gast, D. L. (1984). *Single subject research in special education.* Columbus, OH: Charles E. Merrill.

U.S. Department of Education, Office of Special Education Programs. (OSEP, www.ed.gov/about/offices/list/osers/osep/index.html).

What Works Clearinghouse. (http://ies.ed.gov/ncee/wwc).

3

Ethical Principles and Practices

Linda Mechling and David L. Gast*

You may be in for a shock upon learning that the research project, independently conceived and carefully designed, must undergo formal scrutiny before it is carried out. Later, in the midst of the institutional review process, it may come as an even greater shock to hear members of a human subjects review committee raise serious questions about potential harmful effects as they consider what you perceive to be a most benign intervention program. Or, review team members may question whether the benefits of the proposed study outweigh the risks, as *they* perceive them. It may seem that some interventions are primarily educational or

*We wish to thank Dr. James W. Tawney for his earlier contributions to this chapter.

therapeutic and thus need not be presented for human subjects review. Depending on the interpretation of the university, research institute, or agency, that may be the case. Yet, any intervention that presumes to alter the social or academic behavior of research participants and that presumes to have scientific merit, i.e., to contribute to a knowledge base, raises fundamental ethical and specific procedural questions. Under present federal regulations (The Public Health Service Act as amended by the National Institutes of Health Revitalization Act of 1993, P.L. 103–143), sponsoring institutions must "assure" that the rights of research participants are protected. These assurances are made only after the proposed study has been brought under public scrutiny through examination by a human subjects review committee and the investigator has undergone completion of a training program for conducting research with human subjects.

This chapter presents the ethical issues that must be considered in applied research, describes the steps that you must go through to obtain institutional approval to conduct thesis, dissertation, or independent research, and then describes the ethical guidelines behavior analysts and "scientist-practitioners" must follow when using single subject research methodology to answer research questions related to the effectiveness of their instructional and treatment programs.

Common Ethical Concerns

As the 21st century progresses, it is apparent that humankind will benefit from, or bear the consequences of (depending on one's point of view), an unprecedented explosion in the growth of science and technology. Technology has made possible: exchange of ideas and knowledge in "real time"; increasingly miniaturized and sophisticated computer systems; wireless communication; and Internet access systems. The advancement of science has made possible a host of life-sustaining agents and medical advancements to increase the survival rate of at-risk infants and the human life expectancy of adults. It is also apparent that the moral, philosophical, and ethical issues will be debated, unresolved, long after the practices are firmly in place.

The goal of science is the advancement of knowledge. All forms of scientific inquiry are presumed to be important, whether they seem to offer benefits that are immediate and practical or long-range and esoteric. Thus, the scientist pursues knowledge, along whatever path that may take her; at least that is the common view. The physicist or biochemist may work unimpeded and in relative anonymity. Not so the scientist who studies—and attempts to modify—human behavior.

Psychologists, therapists, and educators engage in their professions within a framework of general standards of conduct. The Council for Exceptional Children (CEC) has developed a Code of Ethics containing eight fundamental ethical premises for guiding teachers of students with exceptionalities (Council for Exceptional Children, 2003), while psychologists have developed ethical principles for conducting research (American Psychological Association, 2002). These serve as models for social science research and, in large part, address issues of concern to human subjects review committees. In the broadest terms they suggest researchers acknowledge and evaluate potential risk, conduct research so that risk is minimized, inform study participants of their rights, and if risk is inevitable, take all steps necessary to reverse the psychological duress imposed. These principles, succinctly delineated by the American Psychological Association's *Ethical Principles in the Conduct of Research with Human Participants* (1992), as follows:

a. In planning a study, the investigator has the responsibility to make a careful evaluation of its ethical acceptability. To the extent that the weighing of scientific and human values suggests a compromise of any principle, the investigator incurs correspondingly serious obligation to seek ethical advice and to observe stringent safeguards to protect the rights of human participants.

b. Considering whether a participant in a planned study will be a "subject at minimal risk," according to recognized standards, of primary ethical concern to the investigator.

c. The investigator always retains the responsibility for ensuring ethical practice in research. The investigator is also responsible for the ethical treatment of research participants by collaborators, assistants, students, and employees, all of whom, however, incur similar obligations.

d. Except in minimal-risk research, the investigator establishes a clear and fair agreement with research participants, prior to their participation, that clarifies the obligations and responsibilities of each. The investigator has the obligation to honor all promises and commitments included in that agreement. The investigator informs the participants of all aspects of the research that might reasonably be expected to influence willingness to participate and explains all other aspects of the research about which the participants inquire. Failure to make full disclosure prior to obtaining informed consent requires additional safeguards to protect the welfare and dignity of research participants. Research with children or with participants who have impairments that would limit understanding and/or communication requires special safeguarding procedures.

e. Methodological requirements of a study may make the use of concealment or deception necessary. Before conducting such a study, the investigator has a special responsibility to (1) determine whether the use of such techniques is justified by the study's prospective scientific, educational, or applied value; (2) determine whether alternative procedures are available that do not use concealment or deception; and (3) ensure that the participants are provided with sufficient explanation as soon as possible.

f. The investigator respects the individual's freedom to decline to participate in or to withdraw from the research at any time. The obligation to protect this freedom requires careful thought and consideration when the investigator is in a position of authority or influence over the participant. Such positions of authority include, but are not limited to, situations in which the research participant is a student, client, or employee of the investigator.

g. The investigator protects the participant from physical and mental discomfort, harm, and danger that may arise from research procedures. If risks of such consequences exist, the investigator informs the participant of that fact. Research procedures likely to cause serious or lasting harm to a participant are not used unless the failure to use these procedures might expose the participant to risk of greater harm or unless the research has great potential benefit and fully informed and voluntary consent is obtained from each participant. The participant should be informed of procedures for contacting the investigator within a reasonable time period following participation should stress, potential harm, or related questions or concerns arise.

h. After the data are collected, the investigator provides the participant with information about the nature of the study and attempts to remove any misconceptions that may have arisen. Where scientific or humane values justify delaying or withholding this information, the investigator incurs a special responsibility to monitor the research and to ensure that there are no damaging consequences for the participant.

i. Where research procedures result in undesirable consequences for the individual participant, the investigator has the responsibility to detect and remove or correct these consequences, including long-term effects.

j. Information obtained about a research participant during the course of an investigation is confidential unless otherwise agreed upon in advance. When the possibility exists that others may obtain access to such information, this possibility, together with the plans for protecting confidentiality, is explained to the participant as part of the procedure for obtaining informed consent.

These principles were derived after extensive dialogue among groups of psychologists. They are stated in the broadest possible terms since they must apply to basic research in laboratory settings as well as applied research in natural environments. Similarly, they apply to procedures that involve the presentation of noxious or aversive stimuli as well as those that are based on positive consequences. Because they must cover such a broad range of applications, more specific guidance is provided for the individual researcher in a listing of specific problems or issues related to each principle; the implications of possible actions are discussed. In this way, you hopefully are guided to make appropriate and ethical decisions. You should realize that this is a judgmental process and that hard and fast rules do not exist to determine "ethical" research behavior.

Core Ethical Values

In their book, *Ethics for Behavior Analysts*, Bailey and Burch (2005) detail guidelines adopted by the Behavior Analyst Certification Board (BACB) of the Association of Behavior Analysis International (ABAI; www.abainternational.org) regarding the professional conduct of behavior analysts. These guidelines, which are explained and richly exemplified, are based on a set of moral principles that are widely accepted in our culture. In his discussion on "core ethical values," Bailey refers to Koocher and Keith-Spiegel's (1998) description of nine principles of behavior for psychologists, which are so fundamental that they apply to teachers, therapists, and other helping professionals in the execution of their professional duties and/or applied research agenda. Specifically, these core ethical principles, paraphrased from Bailey and Burch (pp. 12–24), are:

1. "Do No Harm" by practicing only within your realm of knowledge and expertise.
2. Respect the autonomy of others by promoting self-sufficiency.
3. Benefit others by identifying treatment or educational goals that are valued by them.
4. Be fair, or put simply, "treat others like you would like to be treated."
5. Be truthful with clients, students, family members, and colleagues.
6. Treat others with dignity and respect; help those without a voice to have a voice.
7. Treat others with care and compassion in the design of treatment and educational programs and research.
8. Pursue excellence by using current best practices that are evidence-based.
9. Accept responsibility for your behavior, regardless of the outcome of your actions.

It is beyond the scope of this chapter to delineate each of the BACB guidelines discussed by Bailey and Burch, but Guideline 7 (7.0–7.13), "The Behavior Analyst and Research," is important to student- or practitioner-researchers who are proposing single subject research design investigations for the first time. Therefore, these Guidelines are presented verbatim, without commentary and examples provided in the text. A complete list of "Behavior Analyst Certification Board® Guidelines for Responsible Conduct of Behavior Analysts" is available on the BACB website (www.bacb.com).

7.0 THE BEHAVIOR ANALYST AND RESEARCH.

Behavior analysts design, conduct, and report research in accordance with recognized standards of scientific competence and ethical research. Behavior analysts conduct research with human and non-human research participants according to the proposal approved by the local human research committee, and Institutional Review Board.

(a) Behavior analysts plan their research so as to minimize the possibility that results will be misleading.

(b) Behavior analysts conduct research competently and with due concern for the dignity and welfare of the participants. Researchers and assistants are permitted to perform only those tasks for which they are appropriately trained and prepared.

(c) Behavior analysts are responsible for the ethical conduct of research conducted by them or by others under their supervision or control.

(d) Behavior analysts conducting applied research conjointly with provision of clinical or human services obtain required external reviews of proposed clinical research and observe requirements for both intervention and research involvement by client-participants.

(e) In planning research, behavior analysts consider its ethical acceptability under these Guidelines. If an ethical issue is unclear, behavior analysts seek to resolve the issue through consultation with institutional review boards, animal care and use committees, peer consultations, or other proper mechanisms.

7.01 Scholarship and Research.

(a) The behavior analyst engaged in study and research is guided by the conventions of the science of behavior including the emphasis on the analysis of individual behavior and strives to model appropriate applications in professional life.

(b) Behavior analysts take reasonable steps to avoid harming their clients, research participants, students, and others with whom they work, and to minimize harm where it is foreseeable and unavoidable. Harm is defined here as negative effects or side effects of behavior analysis that outweigh positive effects in the particular instance, and that are behavioral or physical and directly observable.

(c) Because behavior analysts' scientific and professional judgments and actions affect the lives of others, they are alert to and guard against personal, financial, social, organizational, or political factors that might lead to misuse of their influence.

(d) Behavior analysts do not participate in activities in which it appears likely that their skills or data will be misused by others, unless corrective mechanisms, i.e., peer or external professional or independent review, are available.

(e) Behavior analysts do not exaggerate claims for effectiveness of particular procedures or of behavior analysis in general.

(f) If behavior analysts learn of misuse or misrepresentation of their individual work products, they take reasonable and feasible steps to correct or minimize the misuse or misrepresentation.

7.02 Using Confidential Information for Didactic or Instructive Purposes.

(a) Behavior analysts do not disclose in their writings, lectures, or other public media, confidential, personally identifiable information concerning their individual or organizational clients, students, research participants, or other recipients of their services that they obtained during the course of their work, unless the person or organization has consented in writing or unless there is other ethical or legal authorization for doing so.

(b) Ordinarily, in such scientific and professional presentations, behavior analysts disguise confidential information concerning such persons or organizations so that they are not individually identifiable to others and so that discussions do not cause harm to participants who might identify themselves.

7.03 Conforming with Laws and Regulations.

Behavior analysts plan and conduct research in a manner consistent with federal and state law and regulations, as well as professional standards governing the conduct of research, and particularly those standards governing research with human participants and animal subjects.

7.04 Informed Consent.

(a) Using language that is reasonably understandable to participants, behavior analysts inform participants of the nature of the research; they inform participants that they are free to participate or to decline to participate or to withdraw from the research; they explain the foreseeable consequences of declining or withdrawing; they inform participants of significant factors that may be expected to influence their willingness to participate (such as risks, discomfort, adverse effects, or limitations on confidentiality, except as provided in Standard 7.05 below); and they explain other aspects about which the prospective participants inquire.

(b) For persons who are legally incapable of giving informed consent, behavior analysts nevertheless (1) provide an appropriate explanation, (2) discontinue research if the person gives clear signs of unwillingness to continue participation, and (3) obtain appropriate permission from a legally authorized person, if such substitute consent is permitted by law.

7.05 Deception in Research.

(a) Behavior analysts do not conduct a study involving deception unless they have determined that the use of deceptive techniques is justified by the study's prospective scientific, educational, or applied value and that equally effective alternative procedures that do not use deception are not feasible.

(b) Behavior analysts never deceive research participants about significant aspects that would affect their willingness to participate, such as physical risks, discomfort, or unpleasant emotional experiences.

(c) Any other deception that is an integral feature of the design and conduct of an experiment must be explained to participants as early as is feasible, preferably at the conclusion of their participation, but no later than at the conclusion of the research.

7.06 Informing of Future Use.

Behavior analysts inform research participants of their anticipated sharing or further use of personally identifiable research data and of the possibility of unanticipated future uses.

7.07 Minimizing Interference.
In conducting research, behavior analysts interfere with the participants or environment from which data are collected only in a manner that is warranted by an appropriate research design and that is consistent with behavior analysts' roles as scientific investigators.

7.08 Commitments to Research Participants.
Behavior analysts take reasonable measures to honor all commitments they have made to research participants.

7.09 Ensuring Participant Anonymity.
In presenting research, the behavior analyst ensures participant anonymity unless specifically waived by the participant or surrogate.

7.10 Informing of Withdrawal.
The behavior analyst informs the participant that withdrawal from the research may occur at any time without penalty except as stipulated in advance, as in fees contingent upon completing a project.

7.11 Debriefing.
The behavior analyst informs the participant that debriefing will occur on conclusion of the participant's involvement in the research.

7.12 Answering Research Questions.
The behavior analyst answers all questions of the participant about the research that are consistent with being able to conduct the research.

7.13 Written Consent.
The behavior analyst must obtain the written consent of the participant or surrogate before beginning the research.
  (Association of Behavior Analysis International, *Behavior Analyst Certification Board*®
Guidelines for Responsible Conduct of Behavior Analysts, 2004. Reprinted with permission)

Conducting Research in Applied Settings

The process outlined here begins after a student has selected a research topic and obtained approval from an academic advisor or thesis research sponsor to proceed with the project and prior to obtaining permission to conduct research by satisfying a human subjects Institutional Review Board (IRB). In some cases the investigator may also have to present a proposal and obtain approval from the research site's board of directors. At the very least a letter of support from a school or agency administrator is required by most review boards as part of the human subjects protocol form to document permission to use a targeted site. You must follow a specified procedure to obtain permission to enter schools, clinics, or other service environments. When the study is in progress, good relations must be maintained with parents, school/ clinic personnel, and community agencies. After the study is completed, parents, teachers, therapists, and other personnel will expect a debriefing. Copies of the final report may be requested by the school or agency as a condition for permission to conduct the research. At every stage, the behavior of the researcher *is* critical to successful completion of the project. Further, personal interactions between the researcher and others may determine, in large part, whether other researchers are subsequently permitted to work in the system. We assume that basic courtesy is a firmly established part of the researcher's repertoire and thus we will refrain from sermonizing on how to behave in schools, clinics, and community agencies. Some inherent problems, however, deserve mention.

Recruiting Support and Participation

Each institution has a set procedure to follow to request permission to work in schools and clinics. In some cases, in a university, a request may be transmitted to a coordinator of field experiences in their college (College of Education, College of Liberal Arts and Sciences, College of Public Health) and then transmitted to a specific individual in the proposed school district or agency. In smaller school systems or agencies, that person may forward the request to the school board or board of directors for approval; then, if approved, to the principal or on-site administrator. In a clinical setting permission may be required from the clinic director or even the department chair which houses the clinic. Undoubtedly, the process varies from place to place but in each system there is a clearly defined channel. However, these channels hardly represent reality and therein lies the problem. In an active College of Education, for example, there are many channels of communication. Many teachers are program gradu-ates, maintain close working relations with former professors, and offer an open invitation to work in their classrooms. On some occasions, teachers will request help directly from the university for students who represent eminently researchable behavioral challenges. In other situations, when faculty have close working relationships with principals and faculty, it will seem logical to informally discuss a project which then becomes tacit approval to carry out the research. In other situations, you may be encouraged to proceed along formal and informal channels at the same time. Little advice can be offered that applies across settings and situations except that (a) a request to conduct research should be submitted through formal channels as soon as human subjects approval is granted; (b) when invited into the schools informally, specifically ask the person issuing the invitation who should be apprised of the visit; and (c) when discussing a potential study during informal contacts (e.g., when you are in the school on community business), stress the fact that the project is only a possibility, describe what stage of development the study has reached, state when it is likely to be formally submit-ted, and clearly indicate that teacher/principal/manager reaction, rather than approval, is being sought.

Emphasis on real-life, community-based experiences requires that research no longer be conducted within the confines of clinics and classrooms. Projects may require collaboration with community agencies and companies, public or private. Students should be aware that permission to conduct research in community settings, such as a local grocery-store chain, may take weeks and even months to obtain. Local managers will often be required to obtain approval from district-level managers and in some instances from corporate headquarters. The level of approval will depend on the type of research involved and the format proposed (i.e., video taping, involvement of the company's employees, interaction with the business's customers).

Common Courtesies

Student-researchers who have taught or conducted therapy in school or clinic settings should be sensitive to the disruption which a research project may cause, however, they may be less familiar with the concerns that will be presented by community employers and managers. For example, questions may be raised concerning: (a) time of day proposed to be on-site for conducting research (peak business hours and maximum demands on employees); (b) days of the week the proposed research will be conducted (peak shopping day for senior citizens); and (c) liability risk to the company. If the research project holds promise of making life more comfortable for the school faculty member, clinician, or business manager, for example, an educational intervention provides tutorial instruction for a child and thus frees the teacher for other work, or includes job training for future company employees, any reasonable disruption is likely to be tolerated. If the benefit is most direct for the researcher and holds only potential benefits for the achievement of science, disruption is less likely to be tolerated. Researchers should consider how to contribute time, technical assistance, or other needed resources to research sites.

Divulging information during the study may create a dilemma. Teachers, clinicians, parents, and participants may want to know how things are going. Full, open, and honest disclosure of information is fundamental to ethical practice and the protection of participants' rights. However, specific feedback given frequently may constitute another independent variable in some studies. Suppose that a novel intervention is employed to shape a desired social behavior, that parents request and receive daily progress (Ralph said "please" and "thank you" three more times than yesterday), and that the parents naturally increase the opportunities and reinforcement at home. The change in behavior may occur for two reasons, thus confounding the study. One solution to the problem is to decide ahead of time what type of honest but neutral response will be given ("things seem to be going as expected"). If the project goes badly and parents request that you terminate the project, remember that one element of informed consent is the participant's or parents' right to withdraw participation at any time without repercussions. Since the response cost of that decision might mean an extra term for the researcher, it is not unreasonable to expect that she will attempt to encourage continued participation. If parents claim an increase in crying or other emotional behaviors at home and attribute that to the intervention, the researcher may have a difficult time convincing them otherwise. If the intervention is being videotaped and it clearly shows that the child smiles often and manifests other signs of pleasure, it is reasonable to show a brief segment of tape and to indicate what percentage of the remainder of the tapes show positive interactions. If an independent observer is recording data and can verify that the intervention is positively received, she may be requested to share information with parents. Or, the classroom teacher may be able to see positive change that can be shared. The researcher, in this situation, may walk a fine line between encouragement and coercion and, further, must judge whether sharing information to salvage the research project will introduce a potential source of confounding. The situation requires objective analysis and a good sense of ethics.

Recognition and Reinforcement of Participation

Researchers should realize that they have an obligation to others who may follow them. One way to meet this obligation and leave the research site on a positive note is to spontaneously provide information about the outcome of the study and to recognize those who participated. Having plotted data daily, graphs will be available for discussion as soon as the research project is finished. The written narrative from the human subjects review protocol or the written thesis proposal provides a frame of reference to discuss what was done, and the graphs provide a referent for the outcome. Immediate feedback to parents, teachers, and others is likely to be positively reinforcing. When the researcher has made commitments to provide written reports, it would seem advisable to provide them before they are due. Hand delivered, with an additional word of thanks for the research opportunity, they should leave a favorable impression and increase the probability that the next researcher will be well received.

You should further consider recognition to participating teachers and clinicians, or public recognition to the community agency or business. Within a published manuscript some authors will recognize the school or business with an "acknowledgement statement" as a footnote to the article. Businesses may also be recognized with a local newspaper or corporate news article following the completion of the study. Some businesses may also request, or you may suggest, that a presentation be made on a local or corporate level concerning the company's contribution and the purpose of the research. Participating teachers, clinicians, and agencies can also be nominated for various awards and certificates (i.e., "Making a Difference") within the community or through state and national agencies (Autism Society of America).

Finally, some researchers choose to recognize participation by including monetary support for participating professionals. This may be accomplished through an "honorarium" line in the budget of a research grant or by providing a "small" gift at the completion of the study (i.e., a gift card from a local grocery for participation in a study to teach purchasing skills; end-of-the-year pizza party for the class; or contribution to a school fundraising effort).

Securing Institutional and Agency Approval

The process outlined here begins after a student has selected a research topic and obtained approval from an academic advisor or thesis-research sponsor to proceed with the project. The process of institutional review varies from school to school. Two typical procedures are outlined; one requires researchers to defend a written proposal before an Institutional Review Board (IRB) (full review), the other does not (expedited review). The process starts with a very mundane act: locating the proper forms. The forms will be accompanied, in most cases, by guidelines for preparation of the narrative portion of the protocol. These deserve intensive study by the student. Representative forms from the University of Georgia are shown in Figures 3.1 and 3.2. Also deserving your attention is the submission-approval process presented in Figure 3.3. Preparation of a clearly written proposal, submitted early, should increase the probability that approval is obtained in sufficient time to conduct the research. A second requisite of early attention is completion of "training for human subject researchers" which is required prior to the IRB reviewing the research application and fulfills the National Institute of Health's human subjects training requirement (www.citiprogram.org). This mandatory training is provided online and available through university research foundations, sponsored programs, or Offices of the Vice President for Research, as well as agencies like the National Cancer Institute. Free, web-based tutorials provide information about the rights and welfare of human participants in research, and are based on the all-important Belmont Report (1979) that details basic ethical principles on the conduct of research with human subjects.

Increasing the Probability of Approval

The best recommendation to increase the probability of approval on the first submission of the application is to write clearly and succinctly elaborating on those points that are likely to be viewed critically, easily misunderstood, or sensitive. In other words, the skill required for preparing an article submission to the *Journal of Applied Behavior Analysis* or *Journal of Autism and Developmental Disorders* will serve to prepare a research application for human subjects review. The application should also use technical jargon-free language which can be understood by a review board which may comprise an array of disciplines. The suggestions that follow are elaborations, in part, on the items contained in the guidelines in Figure 3.2. Investi-

CHECK	ELEMENTS
	1. Statement that activities are related to research
	2. Title of research
	3. Name(s), department, institution, phone number of researcher(s)
	4. Name(s), department, institution, phone number of faculty advisor (if applicable)
	5. Statement that participation is voluntary
	6. Freedom to withdrawal without penalty
	7. Purpose of research
	8. Description of procedures in lay terms
	9. Appropriate alternative procedures or courses of treatment that may be advantageous (if applicable)
	10. Expected duration of subject's participation
	11. Description of any reasonably foreseeable risks and/or discomforts
	12. Contact in case of distress or discomfort related to research participation (if applicable)
	13. Statement regarding expected benefits to subject or others that may be reasonably expected
	14. Financial or other compensation/incentive (if applicable). This may include any compensation, incentive, or reimbursement (money, subject pool credits). Indicate how any payment will be prorated, in case the subject withdraws from the study prior to completing his/her participation in it
	15. Explanation regarding the extent of confidentiality The participation and responses will be made public. (OR) The results of this participation will be anonymous. (OR) The results of this participation will be confidential, and will not be released in any individually identifiable form, unless otherwise required by law
	16. Procedures for maintaining confidentiality or anonymity
	17. Disposition of tapes/photos (if applicable)
	18. An explanation of the circumstance that could lead to the subjects' participation being terminated by the researcher without regard to the subjects consent (if applicable)
	19. Deception Statement (if applicable) "In order to make this study a valid one, some information about my (or my child's) participation will be withheld until after the study."
	20. Offer to answer any questions or to accept any comments & a phone number for that contact
	21. Subject's signature and date line
	22. Researcher's signature Line
	23. Final agreement and consent form copy statement

Figure 3.1 UGA IRB review checklist.

Check One
Human Subjects Office
New Application: ☐
Resubmission*: ☐ **Revision** ☐
(All changes must be highlighted)

University of Georgia
612 Boyd GSRC
Athens, GA 30602-7411
(706) 542-3199

*NOTE: A new application is required every five years.

IRB APPLICATION

MAIL 2 COPIES OF APPLICATION TO ABOVE ADDRESS

(Check One) **Dr.** ☐ **Mr.** ☐ **Ms.** ☐   *(Check One)* **Dr.** ☐ **Mr.** ☐ **Ms.** ☐

(Check One) **Faculty** ☐ **Undergraduate** ☐ **Graduate** ☐   *(Check One)* **Faculty** ☐ **Undergraduate** ☐ **Graduate** ☐

Principal Investigator   **UGA ID – last 10 digits only**   **Co-Investigator**   **UGA ID – last 10 digits**

Department, Building and + Four   **Department, Building and + Four**
(Include department even if living off campus or out of town)

Mailing Address (if you prefer not to receive mail in dept.)   **Mailing Address (if you prefer not to receive mail in dept.)**

Phone Number (s)   E-Mail (REQUIRED)   **Phone Number (s)   E-Mail**

Signature of Principal Investigator   **Signature of Co-Investigator (use additional cover sheets for more than one Co-Investigator)

UGA Faculty
Advisor: _____
          Name   **Department, Bldg+ Four**   **E-Mail (REQUIRED)**   **Phone No.**

Signature: _____   **UGA ID – last
                              Date: _____   **10 digits only** _____
**Your signature indicates that you have read the human subjects guidelines and accept responsibility for the research described in this application.

If funded: _____
          ***Sponsored Programs Proposal#   **Name of Funding Agency**
***By listing a proposal number, you agree that this application matches the grant application and that you have disclosed all financial conflicts of interest (see Q6a)

TITLE OF
RESEARCH:

NOTE: SUBMIT 4-6 WEEKS PRIOR TO YOUR START DATE
APPROVAL IS GRANTED ONLY FOR 1 YEAR AT A TIME

CHECK ALL THAT APPLY:

Investigational New Drug ☐   **Exceptions to/waivers of Federal regulations** ☐
If yes to the above, provide details:

Data Sets ☐ **Existing Bodily Fluids/Tissues** ☐ **RP Pool** ☐ **Deception** ☐
Illegal Activities ☐ **Minors** ☐ **Moderate Exercise** ☐ **Audio/ Video taping** ☐
MRI/EEG/ECG/NIRS/Ultrasound/ Blood Draw ☐ **X-RAY/DEXA** ☐ **Pregnant Women/Prisoners** ☐
HUMAN SUBJECTS RESEARCH APPLICATION

Figure 3.2 UGA IRB application form.

INSTRUCTIONS:
1. *Type responses to all 11 questions (all parts) listed below (12 pt. font only).*
2. *Do not answer any question with "see attachments" or "not applicable".*
3. *Submit original plus one copy to the Human Subjects Office.*
4. *We will contact you via email if changes are required. Allow 4-6 weeks.*

IMPORTANT: Before completing this application, please determine if the project is a research project. Check the federal definition of research at http://www.ovpr.uga.edu/faqs/hso.html#7 or call the Human Subjects office at 542-3199. The IRB only reviews research projects.

1. **PROBLEM ABSTRACT**: *State rationale and research question or hypothesis (why is this study important and what do you expect to learn?).*

2. **RESEARCH DESIGN**: *Identify specific factors or variables, conditions or groups and any control conditions in your study. Indicate the number of research participants assigned to each condition or group, and describe plans for data analysis.*

3. **RESEARCH SUBJECTS**:
    a. *List maximum number of subjects   , targeted age group   (this must be specified in years) and targeted gender   ;*

    b. *Method of selection and recruitment - list inclusion and exclusion criteria. Describe the recruitment procedures (including all follow-ups).*

    c. *The activity described in this application involves another institution (e.g. school, university, hospital, etc.) and/or another country.* Yes☐ No☐
    If yes, provide the following details:
    1) **Name of institution:**
    2) **County and state:**
    3) **Country:**
    4) *Written letter of authorization (on official letterhead only)/* IRB approval:
       Attached: ☐
       Pending: ☐

    d. *Is there any working relationship between the researcher and the subjects?*
    Yes☐ No☐, *If yes, explain.*

    e. *Describe any incentives (payment, gifts, extra credit).*
    Extra credit cannot be offered unless there are equal non-research options available.

4. **PROCEDURES**: *State in chronological order what a subject is expected to do and what the researcher will do during the interaction. Indicate time commitment for each research activity. And detail any follow-up.*

    Duration of participation in the study: Months
    No. of testing/training sessions: Length of each session:
    Start Date:

Figure 3.2 (Continued)

Only if your procedures include work with blood, bodily fluids or tissues, complete below:
Submit a MUA from Biosafety: Attached☐ Pending☐
If you are exempted from obtaining a MUA by Biosafety, explain why?

Total amount of blood draw for study: ml   Blood draw for each session: ml

5.   **MATERIALS**: *Itemize all questionnaires/instruments/equipment and attach copies with the corresponding numbers written on them.*

Check all other materials that apply and are attached:
Interview protocol☐   Debriefing Statement☐   Recruitment flyers or advertisements☐
Consent/Assent forms☐
If no consent documents are attached, justify omission under Q. 8

6.   **RISK**: *Detail risks to a subject as a result of data collection and as a direct result of the research and your plans to minimize them and the availability and limits of treatment for sustained physical or emotional injuries.*
        NOTE: **REPORT INCIDENTS CAUSING DISCOMFORT, STRESS OR HARM TO THE IRB IMMEDIATELY!**
        a. **CURRENT RISK**: *Describe any psychological, social, legal, economic or physical discomfort, stress or harm that might occur as a result of participation in research. How will these be held to the absolute minimum?*

        Is there a financial conflict of interest (see UGA COI policy)? Yes☐ No☐
        If yes, does this pose any risk to the subjects?

        b. **FUTURE RISK**: *How are research participants to be protected from potentially harmful future use of the data collected in this project? Describe your plans to maintain confidentiality, including removing identifiers, and state who will have access to the data and in what role. Justify retention of identifying information on any data or forms.*
                DO NOT ANSWER THIS QUESTION WITH "NOT APPLICABLE"!
        Anonymous☐   Confidential☐   Public☐   *Check one only and explain below.*

        Audio-taping☐   Video-taping☐
        If taping, how will tapes be securely stored, who will have access to the tapes, will they be publicly disseminated and when will they be erased or destroyed? Justify retention.

7.   **BENEFIT**: *State the benefits to individuals and humankind. Potential benefits of the research should outweigh risks associated with research participation.*
        a. *Identify benefits of the research for participants, e.g. educational benefits:*

        b. *Identify any potential benefits of this research for humankind in general, e.g. advance our knowledge of some phenomenon or help solve a practical problem.*

Figure 3.2 (Continued)

8. **CONSENT PROCESS:**
   a. *Detail how legally effective informed consent will be obtained from all research participants and, when applicable, from parent(s) or guardian(s).*

   Will subjects sign a consent form? Yes☐ No☐
   If No, request for waiver of signed consent – Yes☐
   Justify the request, including an assurance that risk to the participant will be minimal. Also submit the consent script or cover letter that will be used in lieu of a form.

   b. **Deception Yes☐ No☐**
   If yes, describe the deception, why it is necessary, and how you will debrief them. The consent form should include the following statement: "In order to make this study a valid one, some information about my participation will be withheld until completion of the study."

9. **VULNERABLE PARTICIPANTS: Yes☐ No☐**
   Minors☐ Prisoners☐ Pregnant women/fetuses☐ Elderly☐
   Immigrants/non-English speakers☐ Mentally/Physically incapacitated☐ Others☐ *List below.*
   Outline procedures to obtain their consent/assent to participate. Describe the procedures to be used to minimize risk to these vulnerable subjects.

   ILLEGAL ACTIVITIES: Yes☐ No☐
   If yes, explain how subjects will be protected.

   <u>*NOTE: Some ILLEGAL ACTIVITIES must be reported, e.g. child abuse.*</u>

   <u>*STUDENTS*</u>

   This application is being submitted for :
   Undergraduate Honors Thesis☐
   Masters Applied Project, Thesis or Exit Exam Research☐
   Doctoral Dissertation Research☐

   Has the student's thesis/dissertation committee approved this research? Yes☐ No☐
   The IRB recommends submission for IRB review only after the appropriate committees have conducted the necessary scientific review and approved the research proposal.

Figure 3.2 UGA IRB application form.

gators new to the field of research may also find it helpful to consult other investigators who have recently had successful submissions.

Special Populations

Student-researchers will note that special populations receive specific attention in the checklist portion of the application and may require full review by the IRB, depending on the nature of the intervention and vulnerability of proposed participants. Since this chapter was prepared with researchers working with individuals with disabilities in mind, it is apparent that this is an item of concern for student-researchers who are expected to draw on their knowledge of the learning-behavioral characteristics of participants with whom they wish to work and to describe the population (a) in general terms, (b) in traditional categorical terms, and (c) with respect to the specific target behaviors that they intend to investigate.

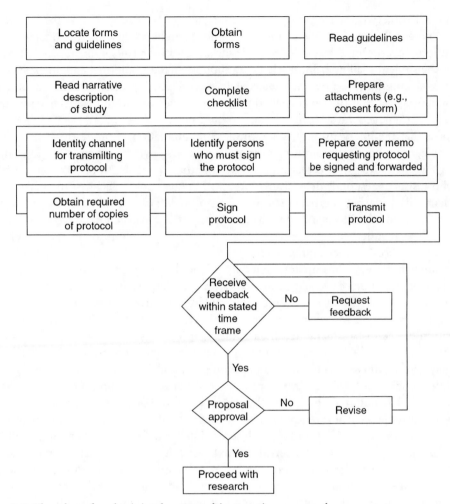

Figure 3.3 Flowchart for obtaining human subjects review approval.

Guidelines also require a rationale for selecting this special population and a description of safeguards for their protection. An adequate rationale might indicate how or why the target behavior interferes with functioning and why the intervention, if successful, will make life better for participants. It might also include a concise reference to an existing literature that verifies that the target behavior is commonly present (or absent) in the population and requires intervention.

Potential Risk

Student-researchers will be required to indicate the level of potential risk to participants and whether the level constitutes "minimal" or "more than minimal" risk. Minimal risk is considered to be the same risk that a person would encounter in daily life or while performing routine physical or psychological examinations (United States Department of Health and Human Services: Code of Ethics, 2005). At first glance, it might seem that the issue of potential risk is easily dismissed in a classroom-based academic intervention or in a social behavior change project employing positive consequences. However, risk may be interpreted broadly. Suppose that the researcher engages a student in an intervention during a time when the student would otherwise be receiving academic instruction; then suppose that the intervention does not succeed. The student's behavior is unchanged and he has lost instructional time. If the intervention proceeds for an extended period without positive results, is the researcher responsible for the student's falling behind schedule? Suppose that a traditional and an experimental instructional program are presented alternately to students who perform better under the traditional program. Has the experimental program interfered with more effective instruction and thus disadvantaged the students?

Suppose that the intervention involves physical manipulation of the research participants, for example, using physical prompting of motor responses (switch activation by pointing and touching) with children with cerebral palsy. What is the potential risk of physical injury to a child who resists or responds defensively? How will the researcher decide if the participant is being "harmed" and what alternate plan will be employed to ensure that the element of risk is removed? What are the risks involved with community-based instruction where research participants will be required to cross streets, ride public transportation, or learn to seek adult assistance when "lost" in the community?

We assume that student-researchers generally will not be permitted to conduct research that involves the presentation of aversive or noxious stimuli and, thus, that is not a topic of concern here. However, suppose that an intervention involves positive consequences for a correct response and extinction for an incorrect response. What level of risk is present due to this intervention or the distress exhibited by a student? In response to these issues, the student-researcher might consider that the length of an intervention may constitute only a fraction of a school day and that there may be ways to make up potentially lost instruction time. Further, it is possible to describe how one "feels" physical resistance during prompting, or to list the obvious signs of "emotional" responses that signal distress. For example, suppose in a small project conducted as a course requirement, a professor and a graduate student attempted to shape *drinking from a glass* by a student with severe intellectual disabilities and minor physical limitations. Having observed and determined that the child could complete all movements in the response chain, they developed a program to shape a consistent and durable response using physical guidance, extinction (looking away), and withholding a preferred drink until a correct approximation response was emitted. In the midst of the program, the child began to whine, cry, and then tantrum when the drink was withheld. At this point, the classroom teacher intervened to terminate the intervention since it was obviously so distressful to the student (in the teacher's opinion). Suppose that this intervention had been a student research project and had been challenged by a human subjects review committee member; the protocol might have been developed in this way:

1. The target is drinking from a glass, without assistance, at every meal.
2. The benefits—the child will acquire a new skill and adults will be freed from the necessity of helping the child with the task.
3. The teaching sequence will be:
    a. set glass in front of student;
    b. bring the student's hand and arm to proper position;
    c. physically prompt drinking by placing hand over the child's and initiating the grasp, lift, tilt, drink response chain;
    d. gradually withdraw physical assistance (operationally defined);
    e. praise at each step;
    f. when resistance occurs:
        i. remove glass from the child's hand,

ii. turn away for 5 s,

iii. if tantrum behaviors occur, continue with intervention for three sessions or until tantrum behaviors are not emitted,

iv. if the previous step is unsuccessful after three sessions, go to plan B (which must be further defined).

This brief outline of a strategy contains two important elements. It acknowledges that an emotional response may occur and sets a limit on the length of time that the behavior will occur before the intervention is modified. This strategy sets the stage for the researcher to account for tantrum behaviors as a typical response in an extinction procedure and then allows for the development of an alternate strategy.

The questions raised here are intended to sensitize the student-researcher to different perspectives on the issue of risk, to raise issues that cannot be answered definitely, and to suggest in one instance a strategy to account for the possibility of duress. Student-researchers may find it helpful to share their protocols with fellow students to identify potential sources of risk and challenge the rationale for engaging in the project.

Defining the Methods and Procedures

The human subjects review application requires an abbreviated version of the written thesis research proposal. While requirements for the scope of the research proposal will vary from university to university, from an advisor's verbal approval of a general description of the study to written approval of a fully developed proposal designed for submission for extramural funding, at some point a complete manuscript must be prepared. We recommend that the human subjects review prospectus be drawn from a fully developed proposal to ensure you begin the task of technical writing early in the research process.

A careful look at Figure 3.2 shows that the human subjects review process focuses on specific elements of the procedures. The protocol requires a complete but abstracted description of the procedures. Then, special attention is directed to two questions, "What will happen to the subjects?" and "What will happen to the data?"

Researchers with a background in education, psychology, and the various therapies (speech, occupational, physical) should be skilled in task analysis and should be adept at writing an explicit description of the steps or sequence of events in the research procedure. You will find it helpful to "walk through" the procedure as you write it and "talk through" the procedures with colleagues. Much of the research conducted using single subject research methodology involves discrete trials, making it easy to describe antecedent stimuli, the topography of the participant's response, and the events that follow the response (reinforcement, correction, etc.). A review committee is less likely to take special interest in antecedent events that are common or easily defined than in esoteric or potentially noxious stimuli. If academic behavior-change research projects use common materials, e.g., a well-known basal reading series, it should be sufficient to identify the materials by publisher, content area, and daily "units" of instruction. If academic stimuli are experimental and designed specifically for the study, you may be questioned to determine why they are expected to produce positive results. If assistive technology is used, the dimensions or features of the device should be presented. If visual stimuli are presented and the discriminability of one stimulus is increased by adding then fading a feature of the stimulus, the fading steps can be described. If a procedure involves a series of statements and actions by the researcher, these should be written exactly as they will occur. If the procedure involves physical prompting, the nature and degree of effort should be described, for example, the researcher will say, "Ralph, throw me the ball," and if no spontaneous response occurs, she will gently grasp him at the wrist and lift the hand/arm so that it rests on the ball. Physical assistance will be terminated if the child pulls away, cries, or shows other signs of distress. If consequences involve preferred edibles or liquids, the review committee is likely to request justification and assurances by the researcher that nutritional and allergy factors will be considered. That challenge should be satisfied by describing what is now common practice: assessing a child's preferences; consulting with teachers, parents, professionals, and significant others; identifying a menu of reinforcers, using a schedule of reinforcement, and so on. If not a natural consequence of the target response, you will need to explain how you plan to transfer stimulus control to more natural consequences directly related to the response.

General Considerations

The concern for "What happens to the data?" is based on three factors: (a) Is the information sensitive?; (b) Can individual participants be identified?; (c) To insure confidentiality, is there a plan to control access to the data and then to destroy it when it is no longer needed?

Data Storage
Most of the data student-researchers collect will not be classified as sensitive information. In our view, intelligence-test scores constitute the only sensitive data collected on school-age children. Children's records may contain sensitive information on the child and family, but these data are not typically reported in single subject research investigations and are unlikely to be of concern to the student-researcher. A case can be made, however, that achievement-test scores on individual students are sensitive, though we would argue against that position. In any case, the student-researcher should expect to yield on that point and treat those scores as the review committee requests. These data are clearly not sensitive:

- Units of academic content, e.g., number of math problems completed per session;
- Percentage of correct verbal responses to teacher's questions;
- Number of words read correctly per minute;
- Frequency, intensity, or duration of generally acknowledged inappropriate or interfering social behaviors, e.g., hitting, kicking, talking out, self-injurious behavior;
- Percentage of intervals on-task behavior during study time.

Anonymity
Protecting the anonymity of participants is obviously a problem in single subject research studies—one that is easily solved. You should (a) describe how participants will be coded, for example, by fictitious names or initials; (b) verify that the researcher will be the sole holder of the code (or the researcher and academic advisor); and (c) state where the code will be stored, for example, in a locked file in the advisor's office. When a study is prepared for publication, you may use a fictitious name and so label it, fictitious initials, or the real initials of the participant. The location where the study was conducted may be described in ambiguous terms, for example, a resource room in an elementary school in a medium-sized city in the Northeast. Participants should be informed about how all data, including photographs and audio and video recordings, will be used and stored. You should also be cognizant of the vulnerability of information exchanged electronically through the Internet. Expert advice may be necessary to learn how to protect data and confidential information and participants should be informed of the risks to privacy and limits of confidentiality of information exchanged electronically (Smith, 2003b).

A special problem arises when a study is conducted in a small school or community, when a participant is unique, for example, the only child with cerebral palsy in the school. Under such circumstances, the review committee may question the disposition of the final report (master's or doctoral thesis) and the number of individuals who have access to it. Unless the thesis is prepared for publication, few people will actually read it—one to five faculty members and, at some universities, a graduate school representative. Academic review committee members will be well aware of the disposition of the research and who will have access to it. If a study is prepared for publication, the committee may question whether anonymity can be sufficiently guaranteed, arguing that any person reading the article would recognize the participant. Professional journals, however, are specialized and have a relatively limited circulation. Thus, the probability is low that someone from the local community would have access to the information. Presumably one who did have access would treat the information in a professional manner, but that is outside the scope of concern for the researcher.

Confidentiality

Confidentiality is an extremely complex issue that requires considerable attention by applied researchers. Accepted confidentiality procedures have been delineated in the Belmont Report (1979), APA (1992, section 5), BACB (2004, section 7.02), and incorporated into IDEA. At the end of the research project, the student-researcher should have a file of raw data sheets, coded for anonymity, and, in a separate place, the key to the code. Whether this information should be destroyed is a matter of judgment. If the study is publishable, good scientific practice dictates that the raw data should be kept intact so that other researchers have access to it if they challenge the findings or otherwise wish to examine the data. The American Psychological Association (2001) position, as stated in the *Publication Manual of the American Psychological Association*, is that raw data be retained for a minimum of 5 years after publication of the research. Researchers take great care in protecting the confidentiality of study participants; however, in rare cases the legal system may require divulging information.

Informed Consent and Assent

Figures 3.4 and 3.5 present samples of an informed consent and assent form, respectively, that are intended as guides for construction of such forms. The critical elements of informed consent are:

1. Written *consent* must be obtained from the participant or the participant's parent or legal guardian; or *assent* and permission must be obtained if working with minors who are capable of understanding the nature of their participation and rights, including individuals with intellectual disabilities.
2. The procedures must be described fully, including purpose and expected duration.
3. Potential risks, as well as benefits, should be discussed.
4. Consent can be revoked at any time, and the participant is free to withdraw from participation. Some Institutional Review Boards now require that the consent form include a statement which identifies behaviors that will be recognized as indicating the participant with a disability no longer wishes to participate (i.e., turns his head away from the investigator).
5. The consent form and the description of the study must be communicated in simple language, clear to uneducated individuals.
6. Information as to who to contact if questions or concerns arise during the study should be shared with parents or guardians.

SAMPLE PARENTAL PERMISSION FORM

I agree to allow my child, _____, to take part in a research study titled, "Computers and Math", which is being conducted by Mr. Mark Investigator, from the Elementary Education Department at the University of Georgia (542-XXX) under the direction of (UGA faculty advisor, department and phone number). I do not have to allow my child to be in this study if I do not want to. My child can refuse to participate or stop taking part at any time without giving any reason, and without penalty. I can ask to have the information related to my child returned to me, removed from the research records, or destroyed.

The reason for the study is to find out if using computers helps young children learn math.

Children who take part may improve their math skills. The researcher also hopes to learn something that may help other children learn math better in the future.

If I allow my child to take part, my child will be asked to do some math problems and play some math games on a computer while the researcher watches. The researcher will ask my child to do these activities once a week for 20 minutes for six weeks. This activity will take place during free study time and will not interfere with math lessons. If I do not want my child to take part then she/he will be allowed to study as usual.

The research is not expected to cause any harm or discomfort. My child can quit at any time. My child's grade will not be affected if my child decides to stop taking part.

Any information collected about my child will be held confidential unless otherwise required by law. My child's identity will be coded, and all data will be kept in a secured location.

The researcher will answer any questions about the research, now or during the course of the project, and can be reached by telephone at: ###-###-####. I may also contact the professor supervising the research, Dr. Faculty Advisor, Elementary Education Department, at 542-XYXY.

I understand the study procedures described above. My questions have been answered to my satisfaction, and I agree to allow my child to take part in this study. I have been given a copy of this form to keep.

_____	_____	_____
Name of Researcher	Signature	Date
Telephone: _____		
Email: _____		

_____	_____	_____
Name of Parent or Guardian	Signature	Date

Please sign both copies, keep one and return one to the researcher.

Additional questions or problems regarding your child's rights as a research participant should be addressed to The Chairperson, Institutional Review Board, University of Georgia, 612 Boyd Graduate Studies Research Center, Athens, Georgia 30602-7411; Telephone (706) 542-3199; E-Mail Address IRB@uga.edu

Figure 3.4 UGA Parental Permission Form (informed consent format).

In most circumstances, applied researchers will successfully obtain consent from parents or guardians of participants if they see the advantages to their child, family, or significant others. Student-researchers should bear in mind that parents represent the full range of human variation. Researchers may be closely questioned by intelligent, informed, and articulate parents who may have many more questions than the human subjects review committee. In many instances, parents will sign a consent form without questioning because they are willing to participate in any activity that has promise to help their child. In other circumstances, the researcher will approach parents who are poorly educated and of limited ability. In these cases, in particular, ethical practice requires that parents fully understand the intervention,

DATE

Minor Assent Form

Dear Participant,

You are invited to participate in my research project titled, "(Project Title)." Through this project I am learning about how boys and girls learn to read and write in a second language.

If you decide to be part of this, you will allow me to work with you on your reading and writing. You will talk to me about your reading and writing. You will allow me to watch you and take notes while you are reading, writing or playing. Your participation in this project will not affect your grades in school. I will not use your name on any papers that I write about this project. However, because of your participation you may improve your ability to read and write in English. I hope to learn something about reading and writing that will help other children in the future.

If you want to stop participating in this project, you are free to do so at any time. You can also choose not to answer questions that you don't want to answer.

If you have any questions or concerns you can always ask me or call my teacher, Dr. _____ at the following number: _____.

Sincerely,

(Your Full Name)
Department and University Affiliation
Contact Information

_____

I understand the project described above. My questions have been answered and I agree to participate in this project. I have received a copy of this form.

_____
Signature of the Participant/Date

Please sign both copies, keep one and return one to the researcher.

Additional questions or problems regarding your rights as a research participant should be addressed to The Chairperson, Institutional Review Board, University of Georgia, 612 Boyd Graduate Studies Research Center, Athens, Georgia 30602-7411; Telephone (706) 542-3199; E-Mail Address IRB@uga.edu

Figure 3.5 UGA Minor Assent Form sample.

its risks, and its benefits. For participants between the ages of 8 and 17, who are capable of giving informed consent, including individuals with intellectual disabilities, you may be required to seek the individual's "assent," as well as the appropriate permission from a parent or guardian. Assent may be waived if a person cannot be consulted either because of the severity of his or her disability, or if the intervention being studied is likely to be beneficial to the child and can only be investigated within a research context. As with the consent form, the assent form must present information in a language that can be understood by the participant.

Sharing of Information
Parents, as well as other persons involved in the research project, are likely to be interested in the outcome of the study. Human subjects review committees require that such information be provided. In order to conduct a study, at a minimum, you may be expected to share information with participants' teachers and therapists, and sometimes the school principal or clinic administrator. Other professionals, for example, speech, occupational, and physical therapists, may benefit from knowing the results of the study as well. You should learn what is typical, or expected, in the school system, clinic, or community business where the study is to be conducted, and should list those who will be informed of study outcomes. You should decide in advance how detailed an explanation will be given to those who have limited direct involvement with the participant. Parents, teachers, and therapists may request a step-by-step review of the study, focusing on daily sessions where performance was well above or below other data points. Others will be satisfied with a general description of the procedure and the extent to which it was successful. A simple explanation of the sequence of intervention, for example, three social communication skills taught and empirically verified within the context of a multiple baseline design across behaviors, focuses on the fact (we will assume) that no change occurred until intervention was introduced. That this occurred three times suggests that the intervention was responsible for the change. This should be easily understood by most people. Finally, parents may wish to know how much information will be shared with others. An explanation should be prepared in advance in the likelihood that the review committee, too, shows a special interest in that information.

Expertise of the Researcher

Human subjects review committees require assurance that the student-researcher knows what she is doing and that she is going to be supervised by a knowledgeable faculty member. Student-researchers who have teaching or clinical experience should list and describe the length and type of the experience. Certification, licensures, and endorsements should be shared. For teachers, the committee may wish to be assured that the researcher has worked with children, has worked in and/or understands the protocol of working in schools, and has experience with the procedure under study. The description of the procedure, included in a previous section, should assure committee members that they pose no, or limited risk.

Publication Ethics and Reporting of Results

You will face additional challenges regarding the preparation and submission of a written manuscript for publication consideration (also refer to Chapter 4) after the completion of the formal research procedures.

Publication Credit: Authorship

The *Ethical Principles of Psychologists and Code of Conduct* (American Psychological Association, 2002) recommends under Standard 8.12c that faculty advisers clearly discuss publication credit with students from the onset of their research relationship and that discussion continue throughout the research process. Some institutions may have formal procedures for establishing credit and obtaining an authorship agreement among students and faculty. Others may rely on a verbal agreement or "understanding" between contributors to the research. Standards 8.12b and 8.12c specifically address provision of credit for students who substantially contribute to the conceptualization, design, and implementation of the research and who analyze or interpret results of the study (Smith, 2003a). For doctoral students this implies first authorship, while master's students may be listed as the primary author on "work substantially based on their thesis" (Smith, 2003b). It is important that early agreements contain information on the tasks to be completed, the level of credit that should be given (order of authorship), and that students, new to research and publishing, be made aware of the guidelines set forth by the American Psychological Association (2002) and the Behavior Analysis Certification Board (2004, sections 7.15–7.16) on publication credit.

Reporting of Results

Student-researchers will likely be familiar with ethical procedures for preparing manuscripts and professional documents which avoid the issue of plagiarism or the use of other's ideas and work without proper credit being given to the author or originator of the work. They may be unaware, however, that these procedures apply to their work as student-researchers, even if the work is completed under the direction of faculty advisors. They may be even less familiar with provision of intellectual credit for non-published material including information shared at meetings, conferences, and through informal conversations with advisors, other students, and professionals. You should be given appropriate acknowledgement for your original ideas, and your work, whether published or unpublished, should not be used by others for personal gain (Sales & Folkman, 2000). You should also be aware that your unpublished work is "copyrighted from the moment it is fixed in tangible form—for example, typed on a page" and that this copyright protection is in effect until the author transfers the copyright on a manuscript accepted for publication (*Publication Manual of the American Psychological Association*, 2001, p. 355). Finally, you will be required to present a statement with a manuscript submitted for publication consideration that the manuscript is not being simultaneously submitted to any other journal.

Ethical Practice

A teacher or clinician is likely to use single subject research designs under two conditions—as part of graduate training or as part of evidence-based practice. In the first instance, you will follow the processes described in the first part of this chapter. In the second instance, you have a somewhat different set of responsibilities. When single subject research methodology is used as an integral part of the instructional or therapeutic process, you will seldom need to seek approval from the school or clinic administration. However, to the extent that such applied research represents an innovation, you are advised to make public the strategies (data collection, experimental design, baseline and intervention procedures, etc.) that will be employed. When single subject research investigations address *social behavior change*, ethical considerations for the use of positive behavior supports must be employed.

The major element of ethical practice that applies to empirically verified intervention, i.e., is the *principle of full and open disclosure of information.* Critical elements of IDEA require that individual students' programs be planned in conjunction with parents and in collaboration with other specialists and school administrators, i.e., Individual Education Program (IEP) committee. The scientist-practitioner's major tasks are to set up data systems, explain the logic for the specific research design, and describe how the design permits certain conclusions, i.e., evaluates threats to internal validity. Since these events go beyond typical practice, little disagreement should be encountered.

Summary

In this chapter we have provided a context for conducting applied research within a set of ethical principles. We have stated our assumptions about the prerequisite behaviors necessary to conduct academic and social behavior-change programs within the framework of single subject research methodology. Specific procedures have been listed, designed to help you obtain approval to conduct research in a manner that protects the rights of participants. We close by stating again that there are no clear answers to the problems we have raised, and finally, that these guidelines are useful only to those applying mature judgment to the problems they confront.

References

American Psychological Association. (1992). Ethical principles of psychologists and code of conduct. *American Psychologist, 47,* 1597–1611.

American Psychological Association. (2001). *Publication manual of the American Psychological Association* (5th ed.). Washington, DC: Author.

American Psychological Association. (2002). *Ethical principles of psychologists and code of conduct.* Washington, DC: Author. Retrieved August 13, 2007, from www.apa.org/science/research/regcodes.html.

Bailey, J. S., & Burch, M. R. (2005). *Ethics for behavior analysts.* Mahwah, NJ: Lawrence Erlbaum Associates.

Behavior Analysis Certification Board. (2004). *Behavior analysis certification board guidelines for responsible conduct for behavior analysts.* Retrieved August 27, 2007, from www.bacb.com/cues/frame_about.html.

CITI. (n.d.). *Course in the protection of human research subjects.* Retrieved August 27, 2007, from www.citiprogram.org.

Council for Exceptional Children. (2003). *What every special educator should know: Ethics, standards, and guidelines for special educators* (5th ed.). Arlington, VA: Author.

Koocher, G. P., & Keith-Spiegel, P. (1998). *Ethics in psychology: Professional standards and cases* (2nd ed.). New York: Oxford University Press.

National Cancer Institute: U.S. National Institute of Health. (n.d.). *Human participants protection education for research teams.* Retrieved August, 13, 2006, from www.cancer.gov/clinicaltrials/learning/humanparticipant-protections.

National Commission for the Protection of Human Subjects of Biomedical and Behavioral Research. (1978). *The Belmont Report: Ethical principles and guidelines for the protection of human subjects of research.* (DHEW Publication No. OS 78–0012). Washington, DC: Government Printing Office. Retrieved August 27, 2007, from http://ohsr.od.nih.gov/guidelines/belmont.html.

Sales, D. B., & Folkman, S. (Eds.). (2000). *Ethics in research with human participants.* Washington, DC: American Psychological Association.

Smith, D. (2003a). Five principles for research ethics. *Monitor, 34,* 56. Retrieved August 13, 2007 from www.apa.org/monitor.jan03/newcode.html.

Smith, D. (2003b). What you need to know about the new code. *Monitor, 34,* 62. Retrieved August 13, 2007, from www.apa.org/monitor.jan03/newcode.html.

United States Department of Health and Human Services (2005.). *Code of federal regulations: Title 45 public welfare; Part 46 Protection of human subjects.* Retrieved August 13, 2007, from www.hhs.gov/ohrp/human-subjects/guidance/45cfr46.htm.

4

Writing Tasks: Literature Reviews, Research Proposals, and Final Reports

Mark Wolery and Kathleen Lynne Lane

Reviewing the Literature
  Process for Conducting Literature Review
Selecting and Stating Research Questions
  Finding Research Topics and Research Questions
  Asking Research Questions Rather than Testing Hypotheses
  Stating Research Questions
  Summary
Writing a Research Proposal
  Abstract
  Introduction
  Method
  Data-Analysis Procedures
Writing a Final Report
  Introduction
  Method
  Results
  Discussion
Dissemination of Research
  Deciding Authorship
  Poster Presentations
  Conference Seminar Presentations
  Web-Based Publishing
  Refereed (Peer-Reviewed) Journals
Summary

Written language is a major way scientists establish a record of their work and communicate with one another and with practitioners. As in other writing forms, technical scientific writing has its own organization, style, and standards. Across disciplines those styles and standards vary, but value is placed on organization, factual reporting requiring minimal inference, precise and concise detail, and brevity. Learning to write technically is similar to many other skills; it requires attempting the skill, purposeful attention to the act, feedback from others, and an ongoing commitment to improve. Scientific writing is so important that Baer, Wolf, and Risley (1968), in their seminal article on applied behavior analysis, included it as a major dimension (i.e., technological). Their guideline for judging the quality of technological writing is: "The best [test] for evaluating a procedure description as technological is probably to ask whether a typically trained reader could replicate that procedure well enough to produce the same results, given only a reading of the description" (p. 95). Technological descriptions are especially critical in applied research, because the procedures are used in non-standard settings (not in laboratories).

Fortunately, a number of helpful resources exist such as the *Publication Manual of the American Psychological Association* (5th edition). This manual provides guidance on preparing written documents and is used by most journals in psychology, education, and other fields. Additional information can be found at www.apastyle.org. However, as noted in the preface to the fifth edition, the *Publication Manual* is not a solution to every stylistic question; rather, it provides standards in an area which is constantly changing.

The purposes of this chapter are to describe some of the standards for preparing technical documents and to present suggestions for helping readers acquire and use a scientific writing style. The chapter presents information on reviewing the literature, stating research questions, writing research proposals for evaluation by others, and describing completed studies. The chapter concludes with information on disseminating information from studies.

Reviewing the Literature

Research is conducted for many reasons such as satisfying your curiosity about how nature works, solving problems presented by individuals to whom you provide services, fulfilling the requirements of a degree or grant, challenging or supporting a policy or practice, convincing others about the effectiveness of a technique, and many others. Regardless of the reason for doing research, it starts with learning what has already been studied, which means reviewing the literature!

Reviewing the literature is an extremely beneficial use of time. A careful review allows you to discover what is known about a topic; what implications exist for practice or policy; what factors qualify or limit the findings; and what questions are answered, partially answered, or unasked. Reviewing the literature also allows you to develop an argument for doing specific studies. In essence it is an opportunity to satisfy your curiosity. For example, studies may support using a procedure in a particular way to produce desired results, but if no one has studied a variation of the procedure that may make it easier to apply, then it is logical to focus on that variation in future studies. Reviewing the literature also allows you to benefit from the successes and problems encountered by other researchers. How other researchers measured the behaviors of interest, controlled or failed to control for certain threats to internal validity, or applied an independent variable may give important clues about how to plan your study. Thus, a literature review has three main functions: (a) articulating what is known and not known about a topic; (b) building a foundation and rationale for a study or series of studies; and (c) improving plans for future studies by identifying successful procedures, measures, and designs used by other investigators and detecting issues and problems they encountered.

Process for Conducting Literature Review

Several steps are involved when reviewing the literature. These include (a) selecting a topic; (b) narrowing that topic; (c) finding the relevant sources; (d) reading and coding relevant reports; (e) sorting the sources with sound information from those with less trustworthy information; and (f) organizing the findings and writing the review. Two common products of literature reviews are: introductions for study reports (i.e., proposals and articles), and stand-alone products such as review articles or chapters in books, theses, or dissertations. The processes for both types of products are similar, but they are different in how the literature is described and in how current published reviews on the topic are used. Introductions to study reports contain less detailed information about the reviewed studies than do stand-alone reviews. When writing an article introduction, recent reviews are very useful; however, when writing a stand-alone literature review, the presence of a recently published review of the topic means you may need to switch topics. The following paragraphs place emphasis on conducting stand-alone literature reviews, but will provide information for writing introduction sections to studies.

Selecting the Topic of the Review

Selecting and subsequently narrowing a topic for the literature review can be a challenging task. A primary reason for selecting a topic should be you are interested in it! Searching for, summarizing, evaluating, and describing the literature can be tedious and time consuming; it is painful if one is not interested in the topic. If you have many interests, then you must select a topic from among several viable candidates. It is useful to determine whether recent published reviews of the topics exist. A topic for which there is no recently published review should be selected. On the other hand, if you are not sure what is interesting, you can establish an interest by reading about the field you are studying, including the journals and text books. Find several issues of relevant journals, and read the abstracts of all the studies published in those issues. Identify the ones that pique your interest and read those articles. Another complementary suggestion is to talk with professionals who are practicing in your field. Identify what issues they face and what dilemmas they encounter. Finally, no substitute exists for being involved in the profession you are studying. This can be done through volunteer work, field experiences, and so forth.

Narrowing the Topic

Often interesting topics are really quite broad. Examples might be how to teach reading; how to make schools more effective; how to help families of children with Down syndrome; inclusion of children with disabilities in general education classes; the causes of and treatments for aggression; how to deal with the problem behaviors of adolescents; and the effects of neurotransmitters on daily functioning. These are interesting and important topics, but they could, and often have, filled entire books and then only in a cursory manner. Sometimes by reading the literature on the broader topic, a more refined or narrower topic will emerge. Of course there is no pure definition of what is too broad or too narrow. Generally, however, a manageable review has 10 to 30 sources. Some reviews may include many more sources; for example, Doyle, Wolery, Ault, and Gast (1988) reviewed 90 articles on a single procedure, the system of least prompts. However, reviews are more manageable when fewer than 30 sources are involved. Having fewer than 10 sources usually is not sufficient for a review.

A useful technique for narrowing a broad topic is to generate a list of questions about it. For example, if one was interested in the inclusion of children with disabilities in regular education classrooms, a number of questions could be asked: What are the legal and social reasons for inclusive practices? What do general education teachers find helpful in implementing inclusive practices? What strategies are successful in training general education teachers for inclusion? What teaching practices are effective in inclusive classes? How prevalent is the use of inclusion? What types of children with disabilities tend to be included? What barriers exist to inclusive practices? What effects does inclusion have on children with disabilities? What effects does inclusion have on children without disabilities? What are the roles of special educators in inclusion? Once a list of questions is generated, one or two of them are selected as being of special interest, and these can be the focus of the review.

Another useful strategy for narrowing a broad topic is to conceptualize it by various study components. Common elements would be the independent variable (e.g., intervention, practice, treatment), how the independent variable is implemented, the participants, the context, and the behaviors involved. Focusing on the independent variable often is highly useful. Examples of reviews using this strategy are reviews of milieu teaching (Kaiser, Yoder, & Keetz, 1992), instructive feedback (Werts, Wolery, Holcombe, & Gast, 1995), simultaneous prompting (Morse & Schuster, 2004), alternative treatments (Green et al., 2006). In each of these, the review focused on a specific identifiable independent variable. This can be narrowed even further by limiting the review of the independent variable to other variables (e.g., population, measure, setting). For example, Baranek (2002) reviewed an independent variable (i.e., sensory and motor interventions) but focused only on a given population, children with autism. Lane (2004) focused on academic and tutoring interventions for students with emotional and behavioral disorders. Another variation is to combine the independent variable with a given context or setting. For example, Hitchcock, Dowrick, and Prater (2003) reviewed the literature on video self-modeling but restricted the topic to studies conducted in schools. Still another variation is to restrict the review to how the independent variable was applied; for example, Wolery, Reichow, Barton, and Busick (in press) reviewed a teaching procedure called time delay, but only included articles focusing on embedding the procedure in ongoing activities of the learners' day. Similarly, Schuster et al. (1998) reviewed the literature on constant time delay, but restricted the review to a specific type of behaviors, chained behaviors.

In other instances, a broad topic can be narrowed by focusing on specific behaviors or skills. For example, McConnell (2002) reviewed interventions for promoting social interactions in children with autism. Ledford and Gast (2006) reviewed the literature on feeding problems in children with autism. Similarly, one can focus on measures used in research; for example, Wolery and Garfinkle (2002) focused on measures used in intervention research with children who had autism. Another option is to focus on specific measurement or assessment practices. For example, Munson and Odom (1996) focused on the use of ratings scales for measuring parent–infant interactions. Lane, Umbreit, and Beebe-Frankenberger (1999) conducted a review of the research on functional assessment for students with emotional and behavioral disorders. Logan and Gast (2001) were interested in identifying reinforcers for students with significant disabilities, and they narrowed their review to preference assessments. Finally, the focus of reviews can be narrowed by focusing on methodological issues or by restricting the review to specific research methods. Lane, Robertson, and Graham-Bailey (2006) focused on methodological considerations related to school-wide interventions in secondary schools. Odom and Strain (2002) reviewed the literature for a specific set of recommended practices, but restricted themselves to the research using single subject research designs.

In three special cases, a method for narrowing a broad topic is to limit the review to recently published research. These special cases are (a) the past publication of a comprehensive review of a topic: (b) the publication of a major conceptual paper or seminal article on the topic: and

(c) the literature published after a specific event that should impact the research field in a given way. In the first case, if a review on the topic was published 10 years earlier, then limiting that review to research published since the first review is appropriate. When this is done, you should account for the publication lag. For example, a review published in 1998 was probably completed and submitted to the journal in 1996 or 1997; thus, papers published in 1996 and 1997 may not be included in the original review, and those dates should be searched in a new review of the topic. In the second case, a major conceptual paper may have impacted subsequent research. For example, Stokes and Baer's (1977) review of procedures for promoting generalization was a major milestone in the applied behavior analysis literature. Reviewing the research on generalization since publication of that paper would be relevant. Finally, in the third case, examples of events that may impact the research field would be federal laws, such as No Child Left Behind or the Individuals with Disabilities Education Improvement Act of 2004.

In isolated situations, authors have restricted their review to a specific journal. For example, Gresham, Gansle, and Noell (1993) conducted a review of studies reporting treatment-integrity measures. Because they were interested in children, they restricted their review to studies involving children. They also restricted the review to the *Journal of Applied Behavior Analysis*. The restriction to this journal was done because they reasoned a methodological advance such as measuring treatment integrity would be most obvious in the journal which was the flagship journal for applied behavior analysts.

In summary, four methods are suggested above for narrowing a broad topic. First, a list of questions can be generated about the broader topic, and one or two of those questions can be selected for review. Second, a broad topic can be thought of as a series of study components. The review can be restricted to one component (e.g., independent variable) or to one component limited by another (e.g., an independent variable in a specific setting). Third, in some cases you can narrow a review by date, but this is generally not recommended unless there is a specific reason for doing so. Finally, in select cases, the review can be narrowed by focusing on a specific journal. In some cases, you may not realize the topic you are attempting to review is too broad. When this happens, you will start searching for the literature and find many more relevant articles than you can possibly review. Reading these, or their abstracts, may provide information for narrowing the search; also, you may need to apply the above strategies.

Find the Relevant Sources

Finding the relevant literature requires persistence and use of systematic search strategies. The goal of literature reviews often is to describe what is known about a topic; as such, you are obliged to find all the relevant sources. Before starting a search, however, identify what you are trying to find. This is determined, in part, by narrowing your topic (discussed above); nonetheless, it is wise to identify inclusion and exclusion criteria. These criteria are used to sort relevant from irrelevant sources. Inclusion criteria are the specific factors or characteristics a study or article must have to be included in your review; and exclusion criteria are the specific factors or characteristics of a study or article that exclude it from being reviewed. These criteria vary greatly across reviews and often are related to how the topic was defined and narrowed. Common inclusion and exclusion criteria focus on the type, source, and language of publication; sometimes they include the date of publication and population characteristics.

The "data" for most literature reviews are research articles rather than chapters, discussion articles, and other reviews of the topic. A common inclusion criterion is to include only research articles, and often only research of a given type (e.g., experimental rather than descriptive or causal-comparative). This does not mean that chapters or discussion and review articles on the topic are irrelevant; they are relevant. They may provide useful information on the topic, but they are not the primary sources for understanding what is known from research.

Another common inclusion/exclusion criterion is the source of publication: books, professional journals, dissertations, conference presentations, and so forth. Many reviewers include only journal articles, because such documents have undergone peer review, meaning some impartial judges have read and evaluated the study and concluded it was worthy of publication. Also, journal articles are often accessible in university libraries or through inter-library loan. Dissertations, conference presentations, final reports and similar documents may be peer reviewed, but the level of evaluation may less rigorous. These sources tend to be less accessible and sometimes they are eventually published as journal articles. However, using unpublished sources may be a way to minimize publication biases if only published literature is used.

A third strategy, which actually is rather ethnocentric, is to include only sources published in the English language and exclude sources published in other languages. This practice is often done for expedience, because the time, difficulty, and cost of translating the source into English can be excessive. Nonetheless, limiting the review to English-language publications may limit the knowledge about the topic.

The date of publication often is used as an inclusion criterion; reviewers only search for reports published in the last 10 or 15 years. While the logic for this seems defensible (the recent research will be more informative than older research), setting an artificial date limit (e.g., 10 years) can unduly restrict the information included in the review. A better alternative is to find previous reviews of the topic, and then include papers (as described above) published a couple years before the review article was published.

Finally, many individuals include characteristics of their population of interest as an inclusion/exclusion criterion. These may be the age of the population (e.g., preschoolers, adolescents), their diagnoses, or other characteristics (e.g., incarcerated, homeless). While this is useful, some practices of interest are used across these demographic characteristics. For example, some practices (e.g., providing choices) have been studied with preschool-, elementary-school, middle-school-, and high-school-aged participants (e.g., Kern et al., 1998; Shogren, Fagella-Luby, Bae, & Wehmeyer, 2004). If a search was limited by age, then the reviewer would get a partial picture of what is known about this intervention. Similarly, many practices used with a given diagnostic group may have been studied with participants with other diagnoses as well. There is a balance here, between finding all research reports relevant to the topic vs. the specific focus of the review. A compromise is often to delve into all the literature on a topic, and then decide whether the limitation by population characteristics changes the findings.

Once the inclusion and exclusion criteria are identified, the reviewer should write a description of each criterion. This information will become part of the method section (described below) of the literature review. It is also useful to retain the references of some reports (particularly well-known and widely cited reports) that are excluded. These may need to be cited in the review with a justification of why they were excluded.

Five systematic search strategies are suggested: electronic searches, ancestral searches, hand searches, author searches, and expert nomination. For a comprehensive yet practical discussion of how to conduct literature searches, see Lucas and Cutspec (2005). Perhaps the most widely known search strategy is the use of electronic search engines. This does not mean typing a term into general search engines; rather it means taking advantage of specific databases of scientific publications available in most university libraries or online through a library connection. Common examples of such search sources are PsycINFO, Medline, and ERIC. Others exist and others will appear in the future, but these are established and widely recognized in behavioral sciences. Other disciplines, such as sociology, will have their own databases; thus, select the databases most relevant to your topic. Lucas and Cutspec (2005) and McHugo and Drake (2003) identify other databases.

An important issue in using electronic searches is the terms entered for the search. Most databases have instructions or suggestions for selecting and entering terms to identify the largest number of relevant sources. They often allow for combining terms to make the focus of the search more precise. Reading and following the instructions for the various databases is highly recommended. Lucas and Cutspec (2005) provide an extensive discussion of issues related to terms used in electronic searches. Most of these databases have an option for displaying an abstract of the study, which is useful in making an initial decision about whether a report potentially meets the inclusion criteria. It is often wise to use multiple electronic databases, because some studies might be found using one but not another.

Keep a record of (a) what search terms were used; (b) how many sources were found on each search; and (c) how many of the found sources met the inclusion criteria. This information is often reported in the literature review. After each search, make a list of the reports which appear to meet the inclusion criteria. This list should contain the complete reference and should be written as an APA-style reference list.

After conducting electronic searches and finding the full body of the selected reports, a second search strategy should be implemented. This strategy, called an ancestral or bibliographic search, involves examining the reference list of each report as well as the reference lists of reviews of your topic. This strategy often results in finding additional reports meeting the inclusion criteria. These reports may have been published in journals not included in the electronic database or may be relevant but for one reason or another did not appear during the electronic search. This is also a useful way to identify non-research reports (e.g., reviews or chapters) which can help in describing the topic.

Another useful search strategy is to conduct a "hand" search of selected journals. Usually, research reports on given topics are published in a few journals. These journals can be selected based on their reputation or on the frequency with which they appear in the list of reports generated from other search strategies. When doing a hand search, it is useful to read the abstracts of each article published in the journal as compared to going by article titles in the table of contents. Hand searches are time consuming but often yield relevant reports.

From the reference list of reports meeting the inclusion criteria or appearing to meet the inclusion criteria, scan the list for authors who have multiple entries. If there are authors who have published multiple times on a topic, which is common, then it is wise to do an electronic search of those authors' names. Many of the electronic databases allow for searching by author name. This strategy may well identify additional relevant reports.

After completing the above search strategies and finding all reports that appear to meet the inclusion criteria, read the reports and make a final determination of whether they will be included in the review. Once a list of reports is established, it is useful to identify authors who appear to be actively conducting research in the topic. Two strategies are useful; you can search at their academic institution and see if their curriculum vitae is posted. If it is up to date, you can scan through the list of publications to identify ones relevant to your area. You also can contact them through email or regular mail. Send a message saying you are conducting a literature review on the topic and include the reference list of identified sources. In the message, ask whether they are aware of any other reports, whether they have any relevant reports accepted but not yet published (i.e., in-press papers), and if they would send you a copy of in-press papers. This strategy is a useful check on whether you have successfully found all relevant reports. Not everyone will respond, but many will. Keep track of to whom such messages are sent as well as their replies. Such information will be included in the method section of the literature review.

In most cases, using the above search strategies will result in finding all relevant sources. Often after completing two or three of these strategies, no new reports will appear. When this occurs, it often indicates that the relevant sources have been found. If, however, each search strategy produces multiple relevant reports, review Lucas and Cutspec's (2005) suggestions.

Reading and Coding the Relevant Reports

After finding the relevant reports, they must be read and information gleaned from them. A coding sheet (or electronic database) should be constructed to enter the information from the reports. Often a set of rules and definitions is written to guide the coding of reports. Although coding sheets will vary by topic, some general information is needed: the reference and study purpose or research questions. In addition, information is needed about participants (e.g., age, gender, diagnosis, race), the setting, materials, response definitions, measurement procedures, independent variable, and findings. Often, information is recorded about the methodological rigor of the study, including the design, number of replications, and presence of specific threats to internal validity. The function of the coding sheet is to summarize information from each study which in turn will allow more efficient and accurate description of the studies. When deciding what components to code, one option is to review and code the quality features of single subject experimental designs posed by Horner et al. (2005).

Sorting Reports by the Rigor of the Study Procedures

Some published studies are of higher quality in terms of controlling for threats to internal validity (see Chapter 5), having an adequate number of intra- and inter-subject replications in the study (see Chapter 6), using superior measures (see Chapter 7), and employing defensible experimental designs (see Chapters 9–12). The question becomes, should the same confidence be put in the findings of a poorly conducted study or a well-conducted study? The answer obviously is, "No." Three strategies exist for dealing with this conclusion. First, the rigor of study methods can be rated (e.g., Shernoff, Kratochwill, & Stoiber, 2002), and then those ratings can be used to give differential weight to the findings of the more highly rated papers. Second, studies can be sorted into two groups: those with weak rigor and those with acceptable rigor. The findings from those in the weak-rigor group would be compared to the findings of those in the high-rigor group. If the findings are the same, then both groups of studies would be retained. Third, studies can be sorted into two groups: those with weak rigor and those with acceptable rigor. Those with weak rigor would be discarded or excluded from the review, and the findings of the review would be based on the studies with accepted or high methodological rigor. This tactic is called the best-evidence synthesis (Slavin, 1987a, 1987b). This third approach is the most practical way to identify what is known about a topic with confidence, especially when the literature is relatively large.

Organizing the Findings and Writing the Review

Literature reviews and articles often have parallel sections: an abstract, introduction, method, results, and discussion. The *abstract* is often a single paragraph. The *introduction* also usually is relatively short (2–3 pages), identifying the topic, describing the rationale for reviewing the literature on the topic, and ending with a purpose statement. Although sometimes not included, the purpose statement can contain a series of questions about the literature. Generating such a list is useful for organizing the results section. For example, when reviewing the research on embedding time delay, the purpose statement and guiding questions were:

> The purpose of this manuscript is to review the progressive and constant time delay research when trials are embedded into ongoing activities of the day. The questions guiding the review were (a) what was the stated purpose of the studies, (b) who taught what to whom in which contexts, (c) what procedural aspects characterize the embedding research, (d) has embedded instruction with time delay procedures resulted in learning, (e) how rigorous are the methods used in this research, (f) what conclusions can be drawn from this research, and (g) what questions remain unanswered in this research?
>
> (Wolery et al., in press)

These questions are similar to research questions for a data-based experimental study (see below). Specifically, they indicate what the reviewer wants to learn from the studies.

The second section of the literature review is the *method*, and it too is relatively brief. This section includes a description of the search strategies used to find the literature and what the results of each strategy were. If electronic searches were conducted, then the terms entered into the search engine should be listed. The method section also should specify the inclusion and exclusion criteria for selecting individual study reports. Finally, this section includes a description of the coding manual and coding procedures used to analyze the study reports. Ideally, two or more individuals would review a subset of the study reports using the same coding definitions to calculate inter-coder agreement (see Chapter 7). The proportion of study reports coded by two or more persons, the method for calculating interobserver agreement, and the results of those calculations should be described in the method section. Sometimes two or more individuals use the same search procedures to see if they identify the same articles for review; if this is done, the agreement in finding articles also should be reported here. Random selection of included and excluded studies can be used to calculate inter-rater agreement of the inclusion and exclusion criteria.

The third section of the paper is the *results* section. This is the most idiosyncratic section of a literature review; it varies greatly by the content being studied as well as the purpose of the review. This section almost always is the longest section; thus, a good outline and organizational strategy is necessary to assist in the writing. A logical organization, of course, also is helpful to the reader. Some reviews describe each study separately and sequentially—one study after another. This organizational structure should be avoided, because it does not allow for easy synthesis of the findings across studies for the writer or reader.

To assist in the synthesis, a useful method is to put the coded information from each study in a table. Such tables are often constructed with each study occupying a row and the variables of each study occupying the columns. The tables are often long (many columns), but allow quick examination of various variables across studies. For example, this would allow you to scan the table and get a picture of who the participants were, what locations were studied, what measures were used, variations on the use of the independent variables, and many other important elements of the studies. Such tables make major differences across studies obvious; for example, you can readily scan the table and identify the studies in which a generalization measure was included, or the studies in which persons indigenous to the participants' service systems implemented the independent variables, which designs were used, and so forth. Such tables in their totality rarely are included in the final written document. Rather they are used to get an overview and identify elements for description and discussion. Sometimes parts of such tables (e.g., a table of the participants' characteristics and settings; a table of results) may be included in the final review.

In some reviews, a natural division of the reviewed studies may appear. For example, a review may focus on studies used to measure or assess a phenomenon (e.g., some type of play, some type of communicative skill, attention maintained problem behaviors) and studies evaluating procedures to change the behavior. These two types of studies (assessment and intervention) would suggest a logical division of the results section. Some studies may have information for both sections of the review, but this is fine as long as you make this clear.

Generating a list of questions, as described above for the introduction section of the literature review, is a useful organizational strategy. It assists in focusing the writing on one issue at a time—the "answer" to each question may become a major subsection of the results. Often some of the questions focus on the methods used in the research, such as who participated in the studies; where the studies occurred; how were the behaviors measured; what procedures, independent variables, and designs were used, and so forth. Other questions may focus on which research practices (e.g., interobserver-agreement assessment, procedural-fidelity assessment, elements of the design) were in place to detect and then control for threats to internal validity. Of course, you should not be bound only by the questions generated before actually reading and coding the reports; sometimes important issues/questions will emerge as the review progresses. These may constitute additional subsections in the results of the document.

In addition, some of the questions focus on the results of the studies. When studies have multiple outcomes measures, the results section may include separate subsections for each measure. For example, one subsection may be devoted to the initial behavior change (acquisition or control), and another subsection may focus on the generalization or the maintenance of those changes. Some authors have suggested the effects of interventions should be quantified and summed across studies. For example, Scruggs and Mastropieri (1987, 1998) suggested using the percentage of non-overlapping data from baseline to intervention. While examining data overlap can be useful when attempting to decide whether a change in data occurred from one condition to the next (e.g., from a baseline condition to the intervention condition) (see Chapter 8), major limitations exist in using this method for judging whether one study had larger effects than another or for quantifying the size of the change across conditions (Salzberg, Strain, & Baer, 1987; White, 1987; Wolery, Busick, Reichow, & Barton, in press). Several other methods have been proposed (Allison & Gorman, 1993; Dunst, Hamby, & Trivette, 2004; Olive & Smith, 2005); however, each of these holds significant weaknesses. It is beyond the scope of this chapter to critique these methods. Nonetheless critical literature reviews which do not use such statistics have been helpful and made significant contributions to describe what is known about a topic, what should be studied, and what practice implications exist. Thus, a defensible option is to do a critical review (non-quantitative) of the topic. This mitigates the possibility of ignoring subtle but critical procedural differences across studies which may occur when a quantitative summary technique is used.

The *discussion* section, sometimes called *implications* or *conclusions*, is the final section of the literature review. This section should restate the purpose of the review and it should summarize the major findings from the review. Often, a helpful way to discuss the individual findings is to report the limitations or qualifications of each finding. It is more useful to know when, with whom, and under what conditions a finding (e.g., functional relation) appears to exist than to simply state a functional relation exists. It also is important to note when, with whom, and under what conditions a given functional relation does not appear to exist. From the reporting of the findings, implications can be drawn for future research and for practice.

Finally, the literature review should contain an articulation of the limitations of the review. The limitations often go back to the inclusion and exclusion criteria. For example, if only reports published in peer-reviewed journals were included, then it is useful to qualify this restriction to that fact. Also, other restrictions placed on the reviewed studies (e.g., conducted in a given location such as home, school, or clinic) by the exclusion criteria also should be noted. Another part of the discussion section is to identify issues needing more research. This can be in the context of discussing each of the major findings or can be a separate section of the discussion. Similarly, drawing implications for practice is often a subsection of the discussion section.

Using the Literature Review
When a comprehensive, critical review of the literature has been conducted, it should be used. As noted above, the function of literature reviews are (a) to describe what is known about a topic; (b) to build a rationale for a study or series of studies; and (c) to identify research procedures to strengthen a study. For the latter two functions (building a rationale, and identifying procedures), the review may be primarily useful to the person who conducted the review. However, when the first function (describing what is known) is met, then the review may be useful to other individuals. It can be used as a chapter in a book, thesis, or dissertation, but it also may be suitable for submission for review and possible publication in a professional journal. Many journals accept review articles from time to time, and the author of any review should look at the submission guidelines published in the journal or on its website. Reviews having implications for practice as well as research are more welcome in some journals than others.

Selecting and Stating Research Questions

This section focuses on issues related to starting new studies; specifically, how you can find topics to study and then translate those topics into research questions. The purpose, elements, and forms of research questions are discussed. Finally, various types of research questions are described.

Finding Research Topics and Research Questions

Using the Literature
As noted, research is often reviewed to build a rationale for a study and to identify a new study or series of studies to do. From a review of the literature, specific study ideas or researchable questions may arise. Those study ideas and research questions may come from the limitations of the existing research. For example, if a procedure for reducing challenging behaviors has been studied only at one level of intensity (e.g., only for parts of the school day), then a gap exists in our knowledge about how the procedure would work if it was used at other intensity levels (e.g., all day). Conducting studies on those other intensity levels would help reduce the limitations in the existing research.

Sometimes research questions come from a single study rather than a review of several studies. The discussion sections of studies often note avenues for future research, which are timely and important areas of future research. The method sections of completed research also identify the conditions under which procedures have been studied. Systematic replication of completed studies (see Chapter 6) is an ideal way to find new studies. In systematic replications, the investigator attempts to use participants, settings, procedures, measures, and designs similar to those used in the original study. The research questions for the replication focuses on a variation of one aspect of the study while attempting to keep other elements the same as the original study. For example, Filla, Wolery, and Anthony (1999) studied the effects of an environmental arrangement and adult prompts to increase the frequency of preschoolers' conversations with classmates during play. Cuneo (2007) replicated the study by using similar procedures but measured the content and frequency of what children said to one another.

An advantage of systematic replications is that other investigators have solved many of the procedural aspects of the experiment. Thus, when embarking on your first study or your first study in a new area, relying on the success of others increases your likelihood of success. Another advantage, however, is that complete knowledge about a topic rarely comes from a single study; rather it comes from a series of studies (systematic replications) on that issue or topic. Clearly, evidence-based practice recommendations are from a series of similar studies focused on how an independent variable is related to important dependent measures rather than from a single study (Dunst, Trivette, & Cutspec, 2002; Horner et al., 2005). In many ways, generality (see Chapters 5 and 6) about a functional relation from a study is inherently tied to replication (Birnbrauer, 1981). Before attempting a systematic replication of a given study, however, you should review the related literature to ensure the planned variation has not already been studied adequately and appears defensible.

Other Sources
Not all research questions come from the literature; in fact, "too 'slavish' a reliance on archival literatures as a source of experimental questions carries its risks" (Johnston & Pennypacker, 1993, p. 40). Those risks include not looking afresh at phenomena and potential relations in nature, not considering alternative explanations for behavior, and minimizing the chances of discovering interesting relations.

Several alternatives exist to relying solely on the literature, and one is observing individuals similar to your potential participants in their usual environments. There is no substitute for knowing one's organism and its behavior in context; and there is no better way to acquire such knowledge than spending attentive time watching and interacting with them in their usual settings. If your potential participants are children with disabilities, then spending time watching them at home, in their classrooms, on the playground, and in their communities is critical for planning studies of their behavior. Careful observation often generates questions about potential relations between environmental events and structures and behavior. Those questions often can be converted into good research questions.

Other alternatives for research questions arise from day-to-day practice, and the problems and issues encountered. For example, when constant time delay was initially studied with chained behaviors, the studies involved delivering the instruction in a 1:1 instructional arrangement (one teacher, one child). A teacher, Ann Griffen, who participated in earlier studies, suggested that the 1:1 arrangement was not practical in classrooms. Based on her suggestion, a study was conducted evaluating an arrangement where one child was taught while two others observed. Fortunately, the two observing children learned by observation what was being taught directly to one child (Griffen, Wolery, & Schuster, 1992). Thus, a practical problem was solved, and a more efficient instructional arrangement was found effective. In some cases, a procedure appears to be working well, and a study is initiated to evaluate its effectiveness. Jolivette, Wehby, Canale, and Massey (2001) conducted a classroom study where the teacher was providing students with choices about the order with which three required assignments were completed. This appeared to be resulting in high levels of task engagement and low levels of disruptive behavior. Systematic data collection and use of choice vs. no-choice condition across children confirmed that the choice of the order in which assignments were completed was indeed related to higher levels of task engagement and lower disruptive behavior.

Some research questions come from principles derived from research. For example, the Premack principle states that if high-probability behaviors (frequently occurring behaviors) follow low-probability behaviors (behaviors that do not occur often), then the frequency of the low-probability behaviors will increase (Premack, 1959). Many children with disabilities frequently emit stereotypic behaviors that are repetitive behaviors (rocking, hand flapping, flipping things in front of the eyes) which appear to have few social consequences. These stereotypic behaviors often are high-probability behaviors. Thus, for children for whom other reinforcers are not readily available or deliverable, investigators asked: If stereotypic behaviors are high-probability behaviors, will their contingent use result in increases in correct responding (Wolery, Kirk, & Gast, 1985) and decreases for challenging behaviors when used in a differential reinforcement of other behaviors contingency (Charlop, Kurtz, & Casey, 1990; Charlop-Christy & Haymes, 1996)? In these cases, as predicted, the stereotypic behaviors (high-probability behaviors) functioned as positive reinforcers for low-probability behaviors (Charlop et al., 1990; Wolery et al., 1985).

Other Factors in Selecting Research Questions
The literature, practice issues or problems, and principles of behavior may serve as sources of research questions. Two additional factors should be considered; these are the investigators' interest in the question, and the feasibility or practicality of conducting the proposed study. Being interested in the research questions and study are not prerequisites for conducting studies with rigor, but it is much better when investigators are interested in what they are studying.

Unlike interest, assessing the feasibility of doing a study is a critical step in deciding whether to attempt to answer specific research questions. Little is as disheartening as planning and starting a well-conceptualized and important study only to realize it is not feasible. Evaluating feasibility varies by study, but some common issues can be proposed. You should consider whether an adequate number of appropriate participants are available. Specifying narrow and precise participant-selection criteria is recommended because it is likely to lead to consistent findings, but this can reduce the number of individuals who will be eligible to participate. Also, you must ensure you have access to sites where potential participants are educated, treated, or reside. This may involve getting approval from multiple institutional review boards or groups. Other critical feasibility issues focus on data collection. Most single subject experimental studies require repeated direct observation over many days, weeks, and months; having adequate observer time which can match the schedule of the study are critical issues. Also, interobserver-agreement assessment should occur often (e.g., minimum of 33% of the sessions for each participant and condition), thus, additional observer time is needed for this data collection. When data are collected using video cameras, personal assistance devices, or hand-held computers, additional expense and resources are required. Of course, when data are not collected from live observations, then time is needed for coding the data. Because decisions are made as the study progresses (e.g., are the data stable, when should the conditions be changed), data must be summarized and graphed on a daily or regular basis, and evaluating whether adequate time exists for coding and analysis must be considered. You must also consider whether the implementers of the experimental conditions can carry out the procedures with sufficient precision and integrity, what training they need, how much time it would take, and whether demands exist which preclude their implementation of your procedures. You also must judge whether adequate time exists to complete the study before inalterable deadlines such as the close of school or student graduation occur. Using the past literature is one way to judge this issue, but certain events outside the investigator's control are likely to occur, such as participant illness, scheduled holidays and breaks, snow days, and so forth. Thus, it is wise to start studies when you have 1.5 or 2 times the amount of time you think you will need.

Asking Research Questions Rather than Testing Hypotheses

A hypothesis is a statement about the likely relations existing in nature to be confirmed by the outcome of a study. While many investigators in education and psychology structure their studies to test hypotheses, an alternative is to ask experimental or research questions about those potential relations (Kennedy, 2005). By tradition, single-case experimental investigators ask experimental questions rather than state and test hypotheses. This is done, in part, because research is viewed as a way to build an explanation of why behavior occurs as it does in nature rather than evaluating a theory. Another reason for asking neutral questions about nature is it may introduce fewer biases into the research enterprise than stating the likely outcome (a hypothesis) before the study is initiated (Johnston & Pennypacker, 1993). However, in nearly all studies, researchers begin with some prediction or bias about the outcome. The task for the investigator is not to be blinded by the prediction but to be open to all potential outcomes; thus, asking neutral research questions is simply a way to help guard against those inherent biases.

Stating Research Questions

The function of research questions is to focus the investigator on the purpose or goal of the study. The research question provides broad boundaries for making decisions about which measures, procedures, participants, and designs are relevant. For example, if the research question focuses on whether a given environmental manipulation (teaching procedure) will result in particular participants learning a specific skill (behavior), then the measures selected must address that skill directly. Similarly, it would eliminate participants who did not meet the inclusion criteria. Finally, certain research designs would be more appropriate for evaluating teaching procedures than other research designs. Thus, the research question focuses the investigator on key elements of the study plan.

Stating the research question in the written proposal for a study or in a report of a study after it is completed functions to orient readers' attention to the purpose and nature of the study. The introduction of such reports should build the rationale for the study, and the last paragraph should state the purpose of the study and include the research questions. This allows readers to know what the investigator wants to learn, and thus, allows readers to evaluate independently whether the study method actually will allow a defensible answer to the questions.

Research questions have three elements: participants, independent variable, and dependent measures (Kennedy, 2005). All research questions should have these three elements, but the order in which the elements are included in the question can vary. For example, the same research question could take the following forms: (a) Does "X" independent variable influence "Y" dependent variable for "Z" participants? (b) For "Z" participants, does "X" independent variable influence "Y" dependent variable? Or (c) Is "Y" dependent variable of "Z" participants influenced by using "X" independent variable? The three elements are present in each question, but the sentence structure is different.

Research questions ideally are stated in neutral language rather than predictive language. For example, "does a procedure influence a behavior?" or "what relations exist between a procedure and a behavior?" rather than "does a procedure increase/decrease a behavior?"

However, in practice, directional questions often are asked. This style is probably defensible when the existing literature confirms a direction; however, in initial studies on a topic, a neutral question may be more defensible.

Studies may have more than one research question. When multiple questions are used, their number should be limited (e.g., to three or four) to ensure the study is manageable. Often multiple dependent measures are involved, and in such cases, a separate question can be asked for each dependent measure. To assist the reader, it is wise to use a parallel sentence structure for each question. For example, a teacher of fifth-grade students may be interested in the effects of assigned seating or students choosing where they sit on their problem behavior, accuracy of their assigned work, and on-task behavior. Rather than grouping these different measures into one question, parallel questions could be asked for each behavior of interest:

- What are the relations between teacher assignment of seating and students' choice of seating on the frequency of disruptive classroom behaviors for fifth-grade students?
- What are the relations between teacher assignment of seating and students' choice of seating on the percentage correct on assignments for fifth-grade students?
- What are the relations between teacher assignment of seating and students' choice of seating on the percentage of intervals on on-task behavior for fifth-grade students?

By asking these three questions, the investigator and reader can focus on whether the method section will allow each to be answered. The questions provide a focus for planning the study, but do not prescribe how each element of the study will occur. For example, the above questions do not specify the duration of the observations, the definitions of the behaviors, which recording systems will be used, how students will be told which condition is in effect, what content will be taught, what students' tasks will be, how the teacher will make the seating assignments, or how seats will be arranged in the classroom.

In practice, we think about the teaching procedures, interventions, and treatments (independent variables) we use to help individuals learn and function better in their lives. These procedures and interventions are what we as educators, psychologists, and therapists can do to help them change. Our questions about those independent variables are: Does this procedure work? Does more or less of this procedure work better? Does it work better with some or all of its parts? Does it work better than some other procedure? Implicit in each of these questions are the behaviors we want to change. Four types of research questions are useful (Kennedy, 2005), and they parallel the questions we have about procedures and treatments. Examples of these four types of questions (demonstration, parametric, component, and comparative) are shown in Table 4.1.

A common type of question is a *demonstration question* (Does it work?). Demonstration questions follow the form: "What relations exist between an independent variable and a behavior for a given set of participants?" Demonstration questions are straightforward; they ask whether and how use of an independent variable changes our participants' behaviors. Some demonstration questions are stated in a directional way: Does use of a teaching procedure increase children's percentage of correct responses on mathematics worksheets? Or, Does the use of a given reinforcement schedule for other behaviors reduce the rate of aggressive behavior on the playground? These are important questions because they ask whether particular environmental arrangements or events are related to patterns in participants' behaviors.

Another type is a *parametric question* (Does more or less of this procedure work better?). Parametric questions focus on the amount of the independent variable and the effects of those various amounts on behavior. They follow the form of: "What relations exist between one level of the independent variable and another level of the independent variable on a given behavior

Table 4.1 Sample Research Questions

Question type
Form
Example

Demonstration questions
    What relations exist between an independent variable and a behavior for given participants?
        What relations exist between point-of-view video modeling and percentage of intervals of pretend play behaviors of preschoolers with autism?
        Does contingent observation during free-play time influence the number of aggressive acts by preschoolers with disabilities in inclusive classrooms?

Parametric questions
    What relations exist between one level of the independent variable and another level of that independent variable on a given behavior for given participants?
        What relations exist between 3 or 8 trials per behaviors with the constant time delay procedure on the number of trials to criterion by preschoolers with language delays?
        What relations exist between daily and weekly feedback on the number of social initiations during recess attempted by elementary-age students with internalizing behavior problems?

Component analysis questions
    What relations exist when a component of the independent variable is added or subtracted on a behavior for given participants?
        Does contingent observation with reinforcement for appropriate behavior or contingent observation only result in a more rapid decrease in aggressive acts by young children with behavior disorders?
        Does self-monitoring with reinforcement for work completion or self-monitoring in isolation result in higher rates of work completion for middle school students with learning disabilities?

Comparative questions
    Does one independent variable or another have a differential influence on a behavior for a given participants?
        Is the system of least prompts or video modeling more effective in teaching numeral naming to young children with intellectual impairments?
        Are teacher-led or peer-based strategies more effective in teaching self-determination skills to high school students with behavioral disorders?

for specific participants?" Examples might be: Does 30- or 50-minute speech-therapy sessions each week result in fewer articulation errors by 8-year-old children with articulation disorders? Or, Does self-monitoring and self-reinforcement every 10 minutes or every 20 minutes for working on assignments result in faster reduction of disruptive behavior? These are important questions because they help us understand how much of a procedure or treatment must be used to get the desired effects for given participants.

The third type of research question is a *component-analysis question* (Does it work better with some or all of its parts?). Component-analysis questions are an acknowledgment that many of our procedures and interventions have many different parts (components); in short, many of these are treatment packages. A study can demonstrate (using a demonstration question) that a given package is related to consistent shifts in participants' behaviors. The question then becomes, are all of the components of the package necessary? These questions follow the form of: "What relations exist when a teaching procedure is used with or without a given component on a specific behavior of given participants?" An alternative is to study whether a given package becomes more or less effective when another component is added. For example, we might ask, Does participation in a check-in-check-out procedure implemented in conjunction with a school-wide primary prevention positive behavior support plan influence work completion of middle school students initially identified as being non-responsive to the primary positive behavior support plan? These types of questions are important, because they allow us to take apart treatment packages as well as build treatment packages.

The final type of research question is *comparative questions* (Does one procedure work better than another procedure?). Although there are many pitfalls in such research questions (Johnston, 1988), there are many times when these questions are highly useful (see Chapter 12). The questions take the form of: "Does one teaching procedure or another teaching procedure result in more rapid learning of a specific behavior for given participants?" When two or more procedures or interventions are compared, each usually has been shown to be effective. These types of questions are useful for making recommendations about which practices should be used, and about which of a couple procedures is more efficient under given situations.

Summary

Research questions function to help investigators articulate the focus of a study and to set broad boundaries for making decisions when planning a study. Research questions have three primary elements (participants, independent variable, and dependent variable), and the syntax used in writing them is flexible. Ideally, questions are stated in a neutral sense, but in practice they often are not. Four common types of research questions are: demonstration questions, parametric questions, component-analysis questions, and comparative questions.

Writing a Research Proposal

Research proposals are written to communicate to others your plans about conducting a study. Research proposals are often submitted to students' research committees to evaluate whether the studies are worthy of being a master's degree thesis or a doctoral dissertation, and to determine what changes are needed in the plans to increase the chances of successful completion of quality studies. Grant proposals submitted to funding agencies also often contain research proposals. Emphasis is placed below on writing research proposals for thesis and dissertation studies. Research proposals have four sections: an abstract, introduction, method, and data analysis.

Abstract

The abstract is a challenging writing task, because a lot of information is summarized into a few sentences. Different journals have varying length requirements, but it ranges from 120 to 250 words; check in the journal to which you wish to submit your paper. It is wise to read the abstracts of several other studies to see how they are structured. The information needed is (a) a sentence about the general topic or purpose of the study; (b) an overview of the method, particularly the participants, measured behaviors, setting, and type of design; (c) a sentence or two about the results of how behavior changed; and (d) a statement about the implications for future research or of how the findings fit with previous research.

Introduction

The writer has three tasks in the introduction. The first is to introduce the topic to the readers; this is usually done in the first paragraph, which starts with a general statement. The second task is to provide a summary of existing literature while building a rationale for the study. This task comprises the major portion of the introduction. Several models for organizing the literature summary and stating the rationale are presented in Table 4.2. Other models can be

Table 4.2 Various Models for Writing the Introduction to a Research Proposal

---

Model 1—Accumulating evidence approach
  A. General statement about the topic/issue
  B. Series of referenced statements about the current knowledge of the topic
  C. Statement about gap in knowledge—leading to the rationale for the proposed study
  D. Purpose statement and research questions

Model 2—Contrasting options approach
  A. General statement about the topic/issue
  B. Description of one alternative or option
  C. Description of the other alternative or option
  D. Contrasts of the two alternatives or options
  E. Rationale for current study
  F. Purpose statement and research questions

Model 3—Historical perspectives approach
  A. General statement about the topic/issue
  B. Description of the emergence a body of evidence about the topic
  C. Identification of the next steps in extending the body of evidence
  D. Rationale or justification for studying the particular step
  E. Purpose statement and research questions

Model 4—Deficit in knowledge about a practice approach
  A. General statement about the practice
  B. Description of the practice with discussion of supporting research
  C. Identification of consistent weakness in the studies supporting the practice and statement about why this weakness is problematic
  D. Purpose statement and research questions

Model 5—Discrepant knowledge approach
  A. General statement about the topic/issue
  B. Description of one body of knowledge about the topic/issue
  C. Description of the second (discrepant) body of knowledge about the topic/issue
  D. Potential resolution of the discrepant body of knowledge—leading to the rationale for the study
  E. Purpose statement and research questions

Model 6—Expanded application approach

  A. General statement about the topic/issue
  B. Description of previous applications of the approach with the effects
  C. Rationale for expanding the application (e.g., to a new population, new context, new skill, new implementers)
  D. Purpose statement and research questions

---

used, but these are common. Finally, the last paragraph of the introduction states the purpose and lists the research questions. The length of the introduction will vary greatly across universities and committees; generally, 4–8 pages are sufficient.

Method

The method section is the main body of research proposals; it is a detailed plan of the study being proposed. Because the study has not yet been conducted, it should be written in the future tense. This section should have the same sections as commonly found in articles describing research studies in professional journals: participants, setting, materials, response definitions and measurement procedures, experimental design—with a description of each experimental condition. Other common sections include interobserver-agreement assessment, procedural-fidelity assessment procedures, and social-validity procedures. These sections are described below. Some studies, particularly comparative studies, will have a general procedures section. Although the participants, setting, and materials sections usually appear in that order at the beginning of the method section; the order of other sections may vary across studies. The method section should include detailed operational description of the procedures. As Baer et al. (1968) indicated; this description should be sufficiently detailed and precise that a trained individual could read the proposal and then implement the study as you intended without additional guidance. In general, a research proposal should be more detailed than a method section in a published article.

Participants

Almost always when proposals are written, your participants are not known. You will know, however, how many you need. It is wise to start with more participants than the minimum required by your design. This section may include adult as well as student participants. Generally, three types of information are needed about participants (Wolery & Ezell, 1993). First, it should include the demographic characteristics such as gender, age, diagnoses, race, ethnicity, and socioeconomic status. This should also include the types and intensity of services they are receiving. If you do not know who the participants are, your proposal should state whether each of these will be used as inclusion criteria, and in some cases give ranges (e.g., ages) or options (e.g., children with behavior disorders or learning disabilities). These characteristics are not the basis for making generalizations from single subject studies (Birnbrauer, 1981), but they should be reported for archival purposes.

Second, you should identify the measures (e.g., tests) used to describe your participants' academic and functional performance. These measures may not be used to make decisions about including or excluding participants, but will be used to present a description of who participated. The full name and APA citation should be included when using published tests or scales. For young children and individuals with significant disabilities, specific tests and scales may be less relevant than detailed descriptions of each participant from repeated observations and from interviews with their parents and teachers.

Third, you need to identify the inclusion and exclusion criteria and how those criteria will be measured. While age, diagnosis, and occasionally other demographic categories will be used, the more important criteria are functionally based. Specifically, these include how participants behave under the baseline conditions of the study, what events are related to the behaviors of interest, and whether participants have specific behaviors needed to respond successfully to the independent variable or to acquire the behaviors in the dependent variable (Birnbrauer, 1981; Lane, Little, Redding-Rhodes, Phillips, & Welsh, 2007; Wolery & Ezell, 1993). If reinforcers are used in the independent variable, then you should describe how reinforcers will be identified. Similarly, if you use a functional behavioral assessment to select participants whose challenging behaviors are maintained by specific factors, then you should state this in this section. The procedures used in the assessment should be described later in the method; but the criteria should be stated here.

Setting

The setting section should describe the location of all experimental procedures and conditions that are implemented, including where primary, side-effect, and generalization measures are collected; where assessment procedures were conducted; and where the independent variable was implemented. The description of these locations should include their physical dimensions—reported in metric units—and how those spaces are arranged. The description should identify in the larger space where the experimental activities will occur (e.g., on the floor, at a table). An important aspect of the arrangement describes the relative location of the implementer to the participants (e.g., seated across a table from one another). If quality measures (e.g., rating scales) of those settings are available, then these should be reported. For example, the *Assessment of Practices in Early Elementary Classrooms* (Hemmeter, Maxwell, Ault, & Schuster, 2001) is a measure of the quality of kindergarten through third-grade classrooms. If an investigator used such a measure and reported the results, then readers would have a summary of the quality of the classrooms in which a study occurred. Likewise, if a study was conducted in a school that was listed as failing by the state, then information is provided about the context in which the study occurred.

Materials
This section should include a description of the materials, supplies, and equipment used. This includes the materials participants use during experimental sessions and observations. When published curricula are used, the citation should be included. Any equipment used to collect the data (e.g., video camera) should be reported by name, make, and model. When trade-marked materials are used, include the trademark symbol (™). This section may include the criteria and rules used for selecting materials.

Response Definitions and Measurement Procedures
This section is a complete description of the dependent variable. Each behavior being measured in the study should be defined in this section. The definitions should not be generic descriptions of the construct, but should be the definitions that will be used during the observations or the coding of video records. Also, any rules to be used in recording the data should be reported. The type of recording system to be used during the observations should be identified and described operationally. For example, if a partial-interval recording system is used, then the duration of the interval should be identified and whether a continuous or discontinuous system will be used should be reported (see Chapter 7). In many studies, multiple dependent measures are used; if this is true in your study, then each one should be described. This section also should identify how long each observation will be; how often observations will occur; and if more than one observation occurs within a day, when and how much time will occur between observations. It is acceptable and desirable to use definitions and measurement procedures used in other similar research. When appropriate, citations of the published literature should be included. When data-collection forms are used, these should be included in an appendix of the proposal.

In this section and sometimes in a section labeled interobserver agreement, plans for training observers and documenting how they are trained should be described. Finally, this section should describe the interobserver-agreement assessment procedures. You should indicate how often interobserver agreement will be assessed, what formula will be used to calculate the agreement estimates, and what levels of agreement will be considered acceptable.

Experimental Design
This section usually includes a paragraph describing the experimental design you will use. Often a citation to the design is included. However, it is important to describe the manner in which the design will be implemented in your study. Some student committees will require a description of how the proposed design addresses threats to internal validity (see Chapter 5). Under the experimental design section, each experimental condition should be described as a subsection. This would include the baseline condition and treatment conditions. Sometimes, especially in comparative studies, a general procedures section is included that describes procedures to be used across all conditions.

The description of the baseline condition, called probe condition in some designs, should include a description of the procedures used and the parameters (quantification) of those procedures (Lane, Wolery, Reichow, & Rogers, 2006). In Table 4.3, a number of dimensions of baseline procedures are listed. These dimensions might not be included in each study, but most are relevant for most studies. Some of these dimensions may be addressed in other sections of the method. The intervention conditions should include a description of the independent variable. As with other procedures, the procedures used to implement the independent variable must be described, as should the parameters of those procedures. Ideally, the only difference between the baseline and intervention conditions is the independent variable or the level at which the independent variable is used. However, if other factors are different across the conditions, these should be specified. The goals of this section are to describe in detail who will do what to whom (Wolery & Dunlap, 2001). When a condition is repeated, include a description of how its second and subsequent use is similar to or identical to the first time the condition is used.

Table 4.3 Description of Factors to Be Described in Baseline Conditions

Question
  Dimensions

Who did what to whom?
Individuals other than participants
- How many were present
- Role in study
- Preparation relative to those roles
- Relationship to the participant before the study
- Participant's familiarity with those individuals
- Any unique factors relative to their involvement

Procedures
- Behaviors of the person(s) conducting the experimental procedures/sessions
- Contingencies in effect for the studied behaviors
- The consistency with which the contingencies were delivered
- Activities, tasks, materials, or curriculum used
- Familiarity or history of the participant with the routines and procedures

Participants
- Familiarity with the baseline procedures
- Familiarity with the persons conducting the study
- Participant's peers also experienced the procedures of the baseline condition or whether it was applied only to the participant

Where were those actions taken?
- Size of the setting
- The arrangement of the equipment and materials of the settings
- Participant's location compared to the person(s) implementing the study
- The setting(s) in which ancillary measures were taken
- Qualitative ratings of the setting
- The participant's familiarity with the setting

When did those actions occur?
- Frequency and consistency with which observations occurred
- When within the day did observations occur
- Duration of each observation

Source: Lane, Wolery, Reichow, and Rogers, 2006. Table 1. With kind permission from Springer Science+Business Media.

Procedural Fidelity

This section should describe how the implementation of the procedures will be measured (Billingsley, White, & Munson, 1980). The goal is to have data from direct observation of how accurately and frequently each important procedure in the study is implemented. This measurement should include the procedures used in the baseline (probe) condition as well as the independent variable. Although some investigators only measure whether their independent variable is implemented accurately, we recommend measuring implementation in both the baseline and intervention procedures. This section also should report how often these data will be collected and how they will be calculated.

Social Validity

Wolf (1978) described the importance of assessing the social validity of studies. This section should describe how the social validity of the study will be assessed. This should include what aspects of social validity (goals, procedures, and effects) will be assessed, when the assessment will occur, and procedures used in that assessment. Finally, the consumers who will judge the social validity of the study should be identified. We recommend assessing social validity before implementing an intervention to inform significant others about the intervention process and after intervention to compare and evaluate consumers' perspectives regarding goals, procedures, and outcomes (Lane & Beebe-Frankenberger, 2004).

Data-Analysis Procedures

In research proposals, the data-analysis plan should be presented. This section should have two subsections: formative evaluation, and summative evaluation. The formative evaluation section should describe (a) how often interobserver agreement will be assessed; (b) what levels will be considered acceptable; (c) what actions will be taken if the agreement estimates are unacceptable; (d) how often procedural-fidelity assessments will occur; (e) what levels of procedural fidelity will be considered acceptable; (f) what actions will be taken if the procedural-fidelity data are too low; (g) how the data on the primary dependent variables will be graphed; and (h) how the graphed data will be analyzed to make decisions about changing experimental conditions. The summative evaluation section should describe (a) how the interobserver agreement data will be summarized and presented in your final report; (b) how the procedural-fidelity data will be summarized and presented in your final report; (c) how the dependent-measure data will be summarized and presented; and (d) what rules you will use to make a judgment that a functional relation exists. Sample graphic displays and tables are recommended.

Writing a Final Report

The final report of a study can take several forms, such as a master's thesis, doctoral dissertation, and a manuscript for submission to a journal for review and possible publication. These reports usually include five sections (abstract, introduction, method, results, and discussion), although some thesis and dissertation reports have university-unique sections.

Introduction

The introduction of a final report is similar to the introduction for research proposals. However, while you are conducting your study, you should be reading the literature to identify new articles bearing on your study. When new articles appear, these should be integrated into your introduction.

Method

The method section of a final report should include an exact, precise, detailed operational description of what you did in your study. The sections are identical to those for the research proposal, but it should be written in the past as compared to future tense. Nonetheless, writing the method of a final report is more than simply changing the tense of the research proposal. It involves ensuring you provide an accurate, thorough description of what occurred and present enough information to allow another to replicate your study.

Participants, Setting, and Materials

Some sections are quite different from the proposal. For example, the section describing the participants is a description of who actually participated. This would include the same content (demographic information, abilities, and inclusion criteria), but it is a report of those who were involved. Often, including this information in a table will conserve space and make accessing the information easier for readers. The setting and material sections should also be changed to describe the actual locations and materials.

Response Definitions and Data Collection

Sometimes in the process of conducting a study, the proposed definitions of the behaviors will change slightly as observers are trained and data collection is initiated. Thus, ensure the definitions in the final report represent the definitions used in the actual data collection. This is true of the measurement procedures as well. The description of the percentage of sessions (by condition and participant) that interobserver-agreement data were collected, the formula used to calculate the percentage of agreement, and the results can be reported in the method or at the beginning of the results section.

Experimental Design

As in other sections, this section should be revised to describe what actually occurred. Procedural changes from the proposal to the actual study should be reported.

Procedural Fidelity

This section includes a listing of the specific variables measured and the procedures for measuring them.

Social Validity

This should be a description of the methods used to assess the social validity. The results of the assessment should be presented at the end of the results section.

Results

This section begins by describing the results of the interobserver and procedural-fidelity assessments. Some authors describe the results of the interobserver-agreement data in the method section, and others put it in the results section. For the procedural-fidelity data, the following should be reported: (a) the percentage of sessions/observations on which procedural fidelity was assessed by condition and participant; (b) the formula used to calculate implementation accuracy; and (c) the results of the assessment (e.g., percentages and ranges) by variable, condition, and participant. Sometimes this information is most easily and clearly presented in a table. Those data indicate whether further analysis of the data are warranted; if the study procedures were not implemented with fidelity to the planned procedures, then the resulting data are suspect (i.e., threats to internal validity are present). In most cases, however, implementation errors would be detected and corrected as the study is conducted; thus, data analysis can proceed.

The purpose of the results section is to describe how the data paths changed, or did not change, with the experimental manipulations. This section is *not* the place to describe the meaning of the findings, to speculate about what influenced the behavior, to suggest other research, or to draw implications for practice. This is the place to describe the patterns in the data. Two major ways exist for organizing the results: by dependent measure, and by participant. The former is preferred particularly when the data are consistent across participants. If the participants required multiple modifications to the procedures before change reliably occurred, then organizing the results by participant may be used.

The results section almost always contains figures depicting participants' data across experimental conditions. The narrative should include a general description of the data, and comments about data stability, systematic changes in the data (e.g., changes in stability, level, trend), the extent to which changes co-occurred with the experimental conditions, and potentially the ranges of performance within and across conditions. Although some authors report means and ranges for each condition, this should be avoided unless the data are neither accelerating nor decelerating within and across conditions and only changes in level are evident. The description should be about the patterns existing within the data and the shifts in those patterns that occurred or did not occur when the experimental conditions changed. Thus, describing the baseline data (e.g., high, low, accelerating, decelerating, variable, stable) and describing how the data changed when the intervention was introduced are critical elements. This style of describing the patterns in the data across time as conditions changed is the type of description appropriate for single-case experimental designs. Unusual events (e.g., extended absences, changes in implementer) should be described and may be represented on figures also.

Discussion

The purpose of this section is to describe the relevance of the study's data; it can be a relatively brief section (e.g., 3–5 pages). The cardinal rule is: "Say no more than the data permit" (Tawney & Gast, 1984, p. 364). The first paragraph should restate the purpose of the study and note the major findings from it. After this paragraph, you should accomplish three things in the discussion section: (a) describe your findings by tying them to the existing research—much of which you will have cited in the introduction section; (b) identify areas for future research; and (c) note the limitations and qualifications of the study. In most cases, you may also want to draw implications for practice.

There are a couple ways to organize the discussion section. First, if several findings exist, then each finding can be discussed sequentially. The similarities and differences with previous research should be addressed and referenced. It is important to connect your findings to the literature, citing how findings from your study converge with or diverge from existing studies. During this discussion, you may point to future research, particularly modifications of your procedures. You also can describe how each finding is limited or qualified by the manner in which you conducted your study. The second way to organize this section is to have separate sections discussing these elements (findings and relevance to literature, future research, limitations, and implications for practice). You may be hesitant to note the limitations of your study; however, this is part of being skeptical about one's own work and it is a legitimate scientific behavior. Scientific knowledge is necessarily conditional—functional relations exist in the contexts of studies in which they are identified. All studies are limited in many ways; thus, acknowledging those limits is not a sign of weakness but evidence you are being objective in dealing with the realities of your study. Further, addressing your limitations and providing recommendations for future studies can help shape future investigations.

Dissemination of Research

Once you have completed your study or literature review, the next step is to disseminate what you have learned. The word disseminate literally means "to plant, propagate" (from the Latin word, *seminare*) "in every direction" (from the Latin word, *disseminatus*; *The American heritage dictionary of the English language*, 2000). Not every study or review should be disseminated, but if new information is learned about a functional relation, then dissemination seems appropriate.

Accurate dissemination of your work is important for two reasons. Specifically, sharing your findings with the research and teaching communities will potentially inform future studies and shape educational practices. As illustrated above, reading previous investigations will help researchers (a) conduct more rigorous studies addressing limitations recognized in earlier works, and (b) extend the knowledge base by addressing unanswered questions. For example, constant time delay had been shown to be effective in teaching preschoolers many skills in multiple studies (e.g., Alig-Cybriwsky, Wolery, & Gast, 1990; Doyle, Wolery, Gast, Ault, & Wiley, 1990). However, in each study, the procedure's use was monitored carefully and occurred at high degrees of accuracy. The question became, would teachers actually implement it that way? As a result, two levels of procedural accuracy (i.e., high and low) were compared experimentally (Holcombe, Wolery, & Snyder, 1994). The data showed correct implementation was indeed important for nearly all children.

Similarly, forward-thinking practitioners have the ability to glean information on "what works" (or does not work), which can then be used to improve practices. For example, a teacher working in an inclusive classroom who is struggling to support students with emotional and behavioral disorders could benefit from reading about function-based interventions conducted with similar students being educated in a similar setting (Lane, Weisenbach, Little, Phillips, & Wehby, 2006). Thus, research findings should be shared to benefit others and help influence research and practice. Now the question becomes, how do I disseminate what has been learned?

Many methods exist for distributing your information, some are informal (e.g., conversations with your colleagues or students; information-sharing sessions with practitioners and parents) and others are more formal. Some formal venues include poster presentations, conference seminar presentations, web-based publications, and refereed journal articles. This section describes each of these. However, first, an important issue of all dissemination activities is discussed: deciding on authorship and order of authorship.

Deciding Authorship

The issue of authorship is important because it carries implications for scientific contribution and productivity, which potentially influence hiring, promotion, and tenure decisions. Moreover, authorship and the order of authorship can be conceptualized as expressions of intellectual property rights—individuals who contribute substantially have a right, because of ownership, to be included as authors. Authorship can be a point of contention between contributors if clear guidelines are not established to determine who should be an author and the order in which the names are listed. This section describes: (a) inappropriate practices, (b) assumptions, and (c) general guidelines.

Inappropriate Practices

Two practices violate ethical guidelines with respect to publication credit: under-inclusion (fraud) and over-inclusion. Under-inclusion or fraud refers to omitting individuals as authors who have contributed substantially to the research or product. In brief, this can be thought of as not giving sufficient credit when due. Over-inclusion refers to including individuals as authors who did not make a substantial contribution to the research or product. In brief, this can be thought of as giving undue credit.

Assumptions

Individuals should be included as an author if they have made a substantial contribution to the study or product. These contributions can be defined as *intellectual*—providing conceptualizations and making decisions related to the design, implementation, and/or analysis of the research, activity, or product; *material*—providing funding, space, and/or resources to the research or activity; *operational*—conducting the research or activity under the guidance and supervision of another person; and *descriptive*—writing the actual product or parts of the product. In Table 4.4, we suggest operational definitions of contributions that may and may not meet threshold for a substantial contribution. Combinations of the behaviors specified

Table 4.4 Behaviors Constituting Substantial and Not Substantial Contributions

Substantial contribution	(1) Participating in the conceptualization, design, implementation, analysis, and description of a study or activity entitles a person to be an author on the products of that work. However, membership on a research team where the research or activity is discussed regularly but with no other involvement does not entitle a person to serve as an author.
	(2) Conceptualizing, developing an outline, or designing a product, activity, or study is sufficient contribution.
	(3) Conducting a substantial amount of the experimental sessions is sufficient contribution.
	(4) Supervising the day-to-day implementation of experimental sessions is sufficient contribution.
	(5) Securing funding and participating in decisions about the conceptualization, design, implementation, analysis, or description of the research, activity, or product is sufficient contribution. However, only securing funding is not a sufficient contribution.
	(6) Collecting, coding, entering, summarizing, *or* conducting statistical analyses of the data *and* participating in the decisions about the design and analysis are sufficient contribution.
	(7) Writing a major portion of a product based on the research or activities conducted by others is sufficient contribution.
Not a substantial contribution	(1) Collecting data, coding data, entering data, summarizing data, maintaining a data base, conducting literature searches under the guidance of another, *or* conducting statistical analyses under the direction of another *without* participating in the decisions related to the design, implementation, or analysis of the research or activity do not constitute sufficient contribution.
	(2) Reading pre-submission/publication drafts of products and providing feedback do not constitute sufficient contributions.
	(3) Providing access to subjects does not constitute sufficient contribution.
	(4) Serving as a subject or as a rater of some aspect of a product (e.g., social validity, validation of a questionnaire) does not constitute sufficient contribution.
	(5) Providing periodic consultation to a person or group on a study or on a product does not constitute sufficient contribution.
	(6) Providing funding for a study but not being involved in the study does not constitute sufficient contribution.
	(7) Providing individuals with opportunities to develop a product (e.g., introducing an author to a publisher) does not constitute sufficient contribution.

under the category of "not a substantial contribution" from a single individual may constitute a meaningful contribution.

Once the decision to include an individual as an author is made, the next step is to determine the order of authorship. In other words, who is first, second, or third author? The order of authorship should be guided by the amount of contribution to the research, activity, or product. The person who contributes the most should be placed in the first-author position, and those with the least (but still substantial) contribution should be placed in the last-author position. The statements in Table 4.5 are provided as suggestions in making this decision. Regardless of position, it is essential for all authors to consent to being an author. Everyone has the right to decline authorship for whatever reason, despite their contribution to the research, activity, or product. For those individuals who do not contribute substantially to the research or activity, but who provide support for it, should be acknowledged in an author footnote.

General Guidelines

This section has some general guidelines for determining issues of authorship. First, decisions about authorship (inclusion and order) should be made based on the contributions of each individual with a goal of including only individuals who offer a substantial contribution. Second, if an error (over- or under-inclusion) is made, we encourage over-inclusion rather than under-inclusion, with fraud being the more serious violation of the two. Third, decisions regarding inclusion and order should be made *early* in the development of a product or a study rather than after it is completed. However, changes to the initial decision can be made if the planned contributions change over the course of the study. Fourth, disputes about authorship should be discussed first with the senior author and/or principal investigator and then with all persons concerned. Fifth, maintain a list of all individuals who contribute to the research, activity, or product. The list should include those who will be authors and those who will be acknowledged. Sixth, allow each author to read the product before it is submitted or disseminated and ask each person to sign a statement indicating that they recognize they are included as an author on the product and they affirm the accuracy and integrity of the product. Finally, when a product (e.g., book, chapter, manual) is developed for publication or distribution and may result in financial gain, then the amount of the financial rewards should be negotiated

Table 4.5 Guidelines for Determining the Order of Authorship

1. Intellectual contribution takes precedence over material, operational, or descriptive contributions.

2. Material contribution takes precedence over operational or descriptive contributions.

3. Operational contribution takes precedence over descriptive contributions.

4. Combinations of these contributions may take precedence over other single contributions (e.g., operational and descriptive contributions could take precedence over material contributions).

5. When a study is a student thesis or dissertation, then the student is always the first author, but others should be included based on their contribution (intellectual, material, operational, and/or descriptive).

6. When a report is based on a student thesis or dissertation, the student maintains rights such as deciding whether, when, and where the manuscript is submitted and who is included as a co-author and order of authorship. However, when the student's study was part of an investigator's funded project, then the investigator and student share in the rights to make these decisions and a responsibility to disseminate the findings.

7. When multiple products are completed by a set of authors and the contributions to those products are essentially equal, then the order of authorship should be counterbalanced across products.

among the authors when the product is initially conceived. This amount should be reviewed when the product is completed to ensure it reflects actual contributions. A written agreement among authors is recommended.

Once the issues of authorship (inclusion and order) are addressed, it is time to move forward with dissemination activities. We will offer brief input on the following dissemination activities: (a) poster presentations, (b) conference seminar presentations, (c) web-based publications, and (d) refereed journal articles.

Poster Presentations

Poster presentations at conferences provide an opportunity to disseminate studies in a format that is potentially less nerve-wracking than a formal presentation. When presenting a poster, you prepare a visual display of the study and stand near it. The visual display has the same sections as a written study report: title, abstract, introduction, method, results, and discussion. The poster should not have dense prose; rather, less text, more bullets, large font size, and more graphics are recommended. Individuals walk by, look at the poster, read the information, and can ask questions. Be prepared to give a 2–3-minute overview of the study. It also is wise to prepare a 1–2-page description of the study with graphs to give to people who are interested. This format allows for brief conversations as well as extended conversations with highly interested people.

Conference Seminar Presentation

A conference seminar presentation will include the same study components presented in a manuscript. Often you will need to prepare a visual presentation (e.g., PowerPoint™) to guide your oral discussion. Below are some suggestions for preparing and delivering presentations:

Preparation Activities
Prior to submitting a presentation, be certain the study will be sufficiently complete to have meaningful data to discuss. Also, be sure you will have sufficient time to analyze the data. When making the presentation, the slides must be readable (e.g., font size of 20 or more) from the back of the room. Usually, a brief background to the study is followed by the research questions, overview of methods, and the results. If possible, practice with an audience of your peers to get feedback and gain confidence in responding to questions. Another reason to practice ahead of time is to ensure that you abide by the timeframe allotted. Often conference seminars will have three or four studies presented by different authors in an hour. If you are given 15 minutes, do not exceed that limit, because you will use the time allotted to others.

Delivering Presentations
When it is time to present, dress professionally, find your presentation room well before the start of your presentation, restrict your presentation to the time limit, and answer questions respectfully and thoughtfully. In terms of dress, some conferences are more casual than others. If possible, consult those who have attended the conference before to determine the level of formality. Conferences often occur in large hotels with a variety of different rooms for presentations. Unless you find your room beforehand, you might miss your time slot. As mentioned above, pace the presentation to allow sufficient time to cover the intended content and still answer questions. People attend conferences to seek information and time needs to be devoted to answering their questions. Some individuals will pose questions that appear challenging or thought provoking, whereas others will pose questions or comments that may appear inane.

Respond respectfully in all instances; it is acceptable to say, "I don't know" to questions for which you do not know the answer. Present your work completely, with candor, and with integrity.

Web-Based Publishing

The Internet is widely accessible to many individuals and this makes it a tempting means of disseminating information. As is widely known, nearly anyone can put nearly anything on the Web. We do not recommend simply putting your study reports on the Web on your own homepage or some other non-scientific outlet. Some journals (e.g., *Journal of Early and Intensive Behavioral Intervention*) are only published on the web; they do not have a corresponding paper version of the journal. Some of these are legitimate outlets for scientific products. The defensible ones are similar to hard-copy journals in the following ways: they have an editor, they have an editorial board composed of reputable scientists, their review process is described, and they use a peer-review process (described below). Such journals are likely to become progressively more common. While it is acceptable to publish in such web-based journals, we recommend avoiding those that do not have an editorial board and do not use the peer-reviewed process.

Refereed (Peer-Reviewed) Journals

Conducting research and learning something relevant is a major accomplishment and the findings should be shared. One of the most prestigious and rigorous methods of sharing study results is publication in refereed journals. This section describes how to (a) select a journal for submission; (b) write the article and prepare for submission; (c) submit the manuscript; and (d) participate in the review process.

Select a Journal for Submission
Journals vary greatly in terms of the types of papers published, readership, type of research methods accepted, and perceived quality and rigor. Many journals exist; therefore, you should examine a variety of journals and use the following suggestions in selecting a journal. First, identify the types of readers who are most appropriate for your manuscript and identify journals most apt to have such a readership. For example, if you are interested in sharing your behavioral research with other scholars with interest in rigorous applied behavior analytic studies, you might consider publishing in the *Journal of Applied Behavior Analysis*. However, if you are more interested in reaching both researchers and practitioners, you might consider publishing in *Journal of Behavioral Education* or *Journal of Positive Behavior Supports*. Second, of those with an appropriate readership, identify the journals publishing papers similar to your study in terms of independent and dependent variables and similar in terms of research methods. Finally, of those with an appropriate readership and matching methods, identify the one with the highest perceived quality. Look at the reference list in your study; consider publishing in the journals where many of the authors you cited published.

Write the Article and Prepare for Submission
Once a journal is selected, examine a recent issue of the journal (or the journal's website) to obtain some key information such as (a) the desired length of manuscripts—most journals present some upper limit; (b) any unique formatting or presentation guidelines; (c) number of copies to submit; and (d) how manuscripts are submitted (electronically, hard copy, etc.). Often there is a section titled "guidelines for authors" or "information for authors." This section often is on the inside cover of the journal. Some journals (e.g., *Topics in Early Childhood*

Special Education, Topics in Language Disorders) have topical issues—meaning they are seeking papers on a specific topic and have specific due dates for such manuscripts.

Because most theses and dissertations exceed article length, students often need to do a major revision in which the length of their initial document is decreased and reorganized to adhere to APA and journal guidelines. Generally, consider the following: (a) the introduction is between four and six pages in length; (b) the method section is completed with sufficient details about participants' characteristics, participant-selection criteria, overall procedures, intervention procedures, measures (including treatment integrity and social validity), and experimental design; (c) the results section must be quite succinct with narrative and only the key figures and tables; and (d) the discussion section should be relatively short (3–5 pages), focusing on how the study confirms or extends previous investigations, limitations, future directions, and educational implications. Horner et al. (2005) and Wolery and Dunlap (2001) present recommendations and guidelines for conducting and reporting research using single-case experimental designs.

In preparing a paper for submission, attend carefully to the APA style manual. All authors should read the paper before it is submitted, give feedback, and give explicit approval for their name to be included on the paper. It is good practice to have someone unassociated with a manuscript read it prior to submission. The intention is to obtain feedback on the logic, readability, presentation, and mechanics. The goal is to submit a clean manuscript free of presentation errors (spelling, formatting, grammatical, punctuation).

Submitting the Manuscript

Submitting the paper includes two major steps: having the correct number of copies and writing the cover letter. Most journals require four or five copies of the manuscript, if hard copy. This information is usually published in the journal under the instructions to authors.

The cover letter is a request for a review of the paper. Sometimes editors want specific information addressed in the cover letter (contact information, information on approval from the institutional review board [IRB], etc.). The letter is usually addressed to the editor (see the author guidelines). The letter usually starts by saying, "Attached are (X) copies of a manuscript titled, [give title]. Please consider it for possible review and publication in [Journal Title]." If the manuscript has multiple authors, it is often wise to state that all authors agreed to submit it to the journal. If it contains original data, state that IRB approval was received before the study was initiated. State that you will not submit the paper to another journal during the time it is under review by the journal to which you are submitting. It is an ethical violation to submit the same manuscript to more than one journal at a time, and it is a legal violation (copyright infringement) to publish the same article in more than one journal or other source. Generally, you may present a paper at a conference (as a poster or formal publication) and also submit it to a journal for publication. Give the contact information (address, email, phone number) of the corresponding author. Finally, thank them for their consideration of the paper.

Most editors notify the author via email, post card, or letter when a paper is received. If you do not receive notification of a paper in 2 or 3 weeks, it is wise to contact the editor to be sure it was received.

Participate in the Review Process

When editors receive a manuscript for review (which is often done electronically), they send it to three to five reviewers. Sometimes they send it to an associate editor who in turn sends it to the reviewers. The reviewers are typically given a date by which they are to submit their reviews and specific guidelines for conducting the review. After the editor has received the reviews a decision is made, which often includes one of the following: accept, accept contingent upon revisions, reject but invite resubmission, or reject. These are defined in Table 4.6. The editor makes the decision, communicates that in a letter to the author, and often describes the needed changes. The reviewers' comments also are sent to the author. Some journals use a "blind" review process; specifically, the reviewers are not told who authored the paper. The authors rarely know who the reviewers are, unless the reviewer makes this explicit (e.g., signs their review). Other journals (e.g., *Journal of Applied Behavior Analysis*) have used an open review process in which the reviewers know who the authors are.

After receiving the review, read the decision letter carefully. Sometimes (particularly when the review is less than favorable) it is helpful to set the review aside and read it after the initial reaction passes. You do not need to respond to the editor when a manuscript is rejected or when it is a rejection with an invitation to resubmit (unless asked to do so). It is almost always futile to argue with an editor.

When the decision is to accept with revisions, attend carefully to the reviews and to the editor's letter about the nature of the needed revisions. Make the revisions as quickly as possible, and send them back to the editors. Most editors want a letter describing what and how the changes were made, and they want a justification for any requested revisions which were not done. Depending upon the editor and journal, there may be multiple rounds of revisions. Also, just because your paper was accepted contingent upon the revisions, it is not really accepted until the editor is satisfied with the revisions.

Once a paper is finally accepted, the editor generally sends a message or writes telling you the paper has been accepted. If the process has dealt with hard copies to that point, the editor will usually request an electronic copy. Although this is a major hurdle, the process is not complete. Nearly all journals have a copyeditor who reads and copyedits your paper. After the

Table 4.6 Description of Editorial Decisions

Decision	Description
Accept	Very rarely is a paper accepted without revisions—once or twice in a life time of publishing, unless of course it is an invited commentary on something and even then revisions are likely.
Accept contingent upon revisions	This decision means the editor is willing to publish the paper if the authors are able to make the requested revisions in a satisfactory way. The editor often, but not always, is explicit about what revisions are needed. Even when the editor's letter details the needed revisions, it is useful to examine the reviewers' comments about the paper. When this is the decision, you should make the revisions quickly and submit the required number of copies. Often the editor's letter includes a specific date by which the revisions need to be done. Do not send it to another journal.
Reject but invite resubmission (revise/resubmit)	This decision means the editor is not ready to accept it and not ready to reject it. Usually, fairly major revisions are requested, and sometimes this involves reanalysis of the data, inclusion of additional data, inclusion of new information, or reframing the paper in a major way. Sometimes editors are explicit about what needs to be changed, and at other times they may just refer you to the reviewer's comments. If you get such a decision, carefully determine whether you can respond adequately to the concerns. If a revision is submitted, the manuscript is almost always sent back out for review, often to a couple of the original reviewers and one or two new reviewers. With a reject but resubmit decision, you are free to send it to another journal or revise and resubmit it to the original journal (but not both!). Often, but not always giving the original journal another try is worth the effort.
Reject	This means the editor will not publish the paper. When this occurs, you are free to submit it to another journal, although you should attend to the reviewer's comments in making the decision to submit the paper to another journal

copyediting is complete, you will likely receive your manuscript in one of two forms. First, it may be your manuscript with copyediting marking on it (hard or electronic). Second, they may send your paper formatted for publication (i.e., page proofs). They will ask you to read it again to make sure they have not changed your meaning and to catch any typographical errors. Often, the copyeditor also will include "author queries." This will be a list of questions asking you for a response. They rarely allow major changes in the paper at this stage. They often give a 24- or 48-hour turn-around deadline. It is an important step; read your paper carefully, make sure the tables and figures are correct, and make sure the references to the figures/tables are what you intended. This will be your last opportunity to edit your manuscript. Check the paper, respond to their queries, and return it as soon as you can.

Often with the copyediting or page proofs, two additional things will be included: (a) a copyright transfer agreement, and (b) a reprint order form. The copyright transfer agreement is a legal document transferring the copyright from the authors to the publisher. Journals will not publish a paper if the copyright transfer is not signed. Sometimes the corresponding author can sign this form, but most publishers require all authors to sign the form.

Finally, the reprint request form is essentially an order form asking you how many reprints of your article you want to purchase. The price varies by the number of pages, but is often excessive. Some journals have gone to having a pdf file available for purchase—usually at a more reasonable rate. The reprint request form usually must be returned even if you are not ordering reprints. At this point, you wait. Some months later the manuscript will appear in the journal as published form! Now, celebrate!

Summary

In this chapter, we provided an overview of some key standards for preparing documents adhering to scientific writing: the specific guidelines for reviewing the literature, writing different types of research questions, writing research proposals, and describing completed investigations. We also made some recommendations for disseminating what you have learned.

References

Alig-Cybriwsky, C. A., Wolery, M., & Gast, D. L. (1990). Use of a constant time delay procedure in teaching preschoolers in a group format. *Journal of Early Intervention, 14*, 99–116.

Allison, B. D., & Gorman, B. S. (1993). Calculating effect sizes for meta-analysis: The case of the single case. *Behavior, Research, and Therapy, 31*, 621–641.

The American heritage dictionary of the English language (4th ed.). (2000). Boston, MA: Houghton Mifflin.

American Psychological Association (2001). *Publication manual of the American Psychological Association* (5th ed.). Washington, DC: American Psychological Foundation.

Baer, D. M., Wolf, M. M., & Risley, T. R. (1968). Some current dimension of applied behavior analysis. *Journal of Applied Behavior Analysis, 1*, 91–97.

Baranek, G. T. (2002). Efficacy of sensory and motor interventions for children with autism. *Journal of Autism and Developmental Disorders, 32*, 397–422.

Billingsley, F. F., White, O. R., & Munson, R. (1980). Procedural reliability: An example and rationale. *Behavioral Assessment, 2*, 129–140.

Birnbrauer, J. S. (1981). External validity and experimental investigation of individual behavior. *Analysis and Intervention in Developmental Disabilities, 1*, 117–132.

Charlop, M. H., Kurtz, P. F., & Casey, F. G. (1990). Using aberrant behaviors as reinforcers for autistic children. *Journal of Applied Behavior Analysis, 23*, 163–181.

Charlop-Christy, M. H., & Haymes, L. K. (1996). Using obsessions as reinforcers with and without mild reductive procedures to decrease inappropriate behaviors of children with autism. *Journal of Autism and Developmental Disorders, 26*, 527–546.

Cuneo, A. (2007). *Enhancing preschoolers' conversation during themed play using in-school play dates.* Unpublished master's degree thesis. Vanderbilt University (Nashville Tennessee).

Doyle, P. M., Wolery, M., Ault, M. J., & Gast, D. L. (1988). System of least prompts: A review of procedural parameters. *Journal of the Association for Persons with Severe Handicaps, 13,* 28–40.

Doyle, P. M., Wolery, M., Gast, D. L., Ault, M. J., & Wiley, K. (1990). Comparison of constant time delay and the system of least prompts in teaching preschoolers with developmental delays. *Research in Developmental Disabilities, 11,* 1–22.

Dunst, C. J., Hamby, D. W., & Trivette, C. M. (2004). Guidelines for calculating effect sizes for practice-based research syntheses. *Centerscope, 2*(2), 1–10.

Dunst, C. J., Trivette, C. M., & Cutspec, P. A. (2002). Toward an operational definition of evidence-based practices. *Centerscope, 1*(1), 1–10.

Filla, A., Wolery, M., & Anthony, L. (1999). Promoting children's conversations during play with adult prompts. *Journal of Early Intervention, 22,* 93–108.

Gresham, F. M., Gansle, K. A., & Noell, G. H. (1993). Treatment integrity in applied behavior analysis with children. *Journal of Applied Behavior Analysis, 26,* 257–263.

Griffen, A. K., Wolery, M., & Schuster, J. W. (1992). Triadic instruction of chained food preparation responses: Acquisition and observational learning. *Journal of Applied Behavior Analysis, 25,* 193–204.

Hemmeter, M. L., Maxwell, K. L., Ault, M. J., & Schuster, J. W. (2001). *Assessment of practices in early elementary classrooms.* New York: Teachers College Press.

Hitchcock, C. H., Dowrick, P. W., & Prater, M. A. (2003). Video self-modeling intervention in school-based settings: a review. *Remedial and Special Education, 24,* 36–46.

Holcombe, A., Wolery, M., & Snyder, E. (1994). Effects of two levels of procedural fidelity with constant time delay on children's learning. *Journal of Behavioral Education, 4,* 49–73.

Horner, R. H., Carr, E. G., Halle, J., McGee, G., Odom, S. L., & Wolery, M. (2005). The use of single-subject research to identify evidence-based practices in special education. *Exceptional Children, 71,* 165–179.

Johnston, J. M. (1988). Strategic and tactical limits of comparison studies. *The Behavior Analyst, 11,* 1–9.

Johnston, J. M., & Pennypacker, H. S. (1993). *Strategies and tactics of behavioral research* (2nd ed.). Hillsdale, NJ: Lawrence Erlbaum Associates.

Jolivette, K., Wehby, J. H., Canale, J., & Massey, N. G. (2001). Effects of choice-making opportunities on the behavior of students with emotional and behavioral disorders. *Behavioral Disorders, 26,* 131–145.

Kaiser, A. P., Yoder, P. J., & Leetz, A. (1992). Evaluating milieu teaching. In S. F. Warren and J. Reichle (Eds.), *Causes and effects in communication and language intervention* (pp. 9–47). Baltimore, MD: Brookes.

Kennedy, C. H. (2005). *Single-case designs for educational research.* Boston, MA: Allyn & Bacon.

Kern, L., Vorndran, C. M., Hilt, A., Ringdahl, J. E., Adelman, B. E., & Dunlap, G. (1998). Choice as an intervention to improve behavior: A review of the literature. *Journal of Behavioral Education, 8,* 151–170.

Lane, K. L. (2004). Academic instruction and tutoring interventions for students with emotional/behavioral disorders: 1990 to present. In R. B. Rutherford, M. M. Quinn, & S. R. Mathur (Eds.), *Handbook of research in emotional and behavioral disorders* (pp. 462–486). New York: Guilford Press.

Lane, K. L., & Beebe-Frankenberger, M. E. (2004). *School-based interventions: The tools you need to succeed.* Boston, MA: Allyn & Bacon.

Lane, K. L., Little, M. A., Redding-Rhodes, J. R., Phillips, A., & Welsh, M. T. (2007). Outcomes of a teacher-led reading intervention for elementary students at-risk for behavioral disorders. *Exceptional Children, 74,* 47–70.

Lane, K. L., Robertson, E. J., & Graham-Bailey, M. A. L. (2006). An examination of school-wide interventions with primary level efforts conducted in secondary schools: Methodological considerations. In T. E. Scruggs & M. A. Mastropieri (Eds.), *Applications of research methodology: Advances in learning and behavioral disabilities* (vol. 19, pp. 157–199). Oxford: Elsevier.

Lane, K. L., Umbreit, J., & Beebe-Frankenberger, M. (1999). A review of functional assessment research with students with or at-risk for emotional and behavioral disorders. *Journal of Positive Behavioral Interventions, 1,* 101–111.

Lane, K. L., Weisenbach, J. L., Little, M. A., Phillips, A., & Wehby, J. (2006). Illustrations of function-based interventions implemented by general education teachers: Building capacity at the school site. *Education and Treatment of Children, 29,* 549–671.

Lane, K. L., Wolery, M., Reichow, B., & Rogers, L. (2006). Describing baseline conditions: Suggestions for study reports. *Journal of Behavioral Education, 16,* 224–234.

Ledford, J. R., & Gast, D. L. (2006). Feeding problems in children with autism spectrum disorders: A review. *Focus on Autism and Other Developmental Disabilities, 21,* 153–166.

Logan, K. R., & Gast, D. L. (2001). Conducting preference assessments and reinforcer testing for individuals with profound multiple disabilities: Issues and procedures. *Exceptionality, 9,* 123–134.

Lucas, S. M., & Cutspec, P. A. (2005). The role and process of literature searching in the preparation of a research synthesis. *Centerscope, 3*(3), 1–26.

McConnell, S. R. (2002). Interventions to facilitate social interaction for young children with autism: Review of available research and recommendations for education intervention and future research. *Journal of Autism and Developmental Disorders, 32,* 351–372.

McHugo, G. J., & Drake, R. E. (2003). Finding and evaluating the evidence: A critical step in evidence-based medicine. *Psychiatric Clinics of North America, 26,* 821–831.

Morse, T. E., & Schuster, J. W. (2004). Simultaneous prompting: A review of the literature. *Education and Training in Developmental Disabilities, 39,* 153–168.

Munson, L. J., & Odom, S. L. (1996). Review of rating scales that measure parent-infant interaction. *Topics in Early Childhood Special Education, 16,* 1–25.

Odom, S. L., & Strain, P. S. (2002). Evidence-based practice in early intervention/early childhood special education: Single subject design research. *Journal of Early Intervention, 25,* 151–160.

Olive, M. L., & Smith, B. W. (2005). Effect size calculations and single subject design. *Educational Psychology, 25,* 313–324.

Premack, D. (1959). Toward empirical behavioral laws: I. Positive reinforce. *Psychological Review, 66,* 219–233.

Salzberg, C. L., Strain, P. S., & Baer, D. M. (1987). Meta-analysis for single-subject research: When does it clarify, when does it obscure? *Remedial and Special Education, 8,* 43–48.

Schuster, J. W., Morse, T. E., Ault, M. J., Doyle, P. M., Crawford, M. R., & Wolery, M. (1998). Constant time delay with chained tasks: A review of the literature. *Education and Treatment of Children, 21,* 74–106.

Scruggs, T. E., & Mastropieri, M. A. (1987). The quantitative synthesis of single-subject research: Methodology and validation. *Remedial and Special Education, 8,* 24–33.

Scruggs, T. E., & Mastropieri, M. A. (1998). Summarizing single-subject research: Issues and applications. *Behavior Modification, 22,* 221–242.

Shernoff, E. S., Kratochwill, T. R., & Stoiber, K. C. (2002). Evidenced-based interventions in school psychology: An illustration of Task Force coding criteria using single-participant research design. *School Psychology Quarterly, 17,* 390–422.

Shogren, K. A., Faggella-Luby, M. N., Bae, S. J., & Wehmeyer, M. L. (2004). The effects of choice-making as an intervention for problem behavior: A meta analysis. *Journal of Positive Behavior Interventions, 6,* 228–237.

Slavin, R. E. (1987a). Ability grouping student achievement in elementary schools: A best-evidence synthesis. *Review of Educational Research, 57,* 293–336.

Slavin, R. E. (1987b). Best-evidence synthesis: An alternative to meta-analysis and traditional reviews. In W. R. Shadish & C. S. Reichardt (Eds.), *Evaluation studies: Review annual* (Vol. 12, pp. 667–673). Thousand Oaks, CA: Sage Publications.

Stokes, T. F., & Baer, D. M. (1977). An implicit technology of generalization. *Journal of Applied Behavior Analysis, 10,* 349–367.

Tawney, J. W., & Gast, D., L. (1984). *Single subject research in special education.* Columbus, OH: Charles E. Merrill.

Werts, M. G., Wolery, M., Holcombe, A., & Gast, D. L. (1995). Instructive feedback: Review of parameters and effects. *Journal of Behavioral Education, 5,* 55–75.

White, O. R. (1987). The quantitative synthesis of single-subject research: Methodology and validation: Comment. *Remedial and Special Education, 8,* 34–39.

Wolery, M., & Dunlap, G. (2001). Reporting on studies using single-subject experimental methods. *Journal of Early Intervention, 24,* 85–89.

Wolery, M., & Ezell, H. K. (1993). Subject descriptions and single subject research. *Journal of Learning Disabilities, 26,* 642–647.

Wolery, M., & Garfinkle, A. N. (2002). Measures in intervention research with young children who have autism. *Journal of Autism and Developmental Disorders, 32,* 463–478.

Wolery, M., Kirk, K., & Gast, D. L. (1985). Stereotypic behavior as a reinforcer: Effects and side-effects. *Journal of Autism and Developmental Disorders, 15,* 149–161.

Wolery, M., Reichow, B., Barton, E. E., & Busick, M. (in press). Embedding constant and progressive time delay in ongoing activities. *Journal of Early and Intensive Behavioral Interventions.*

Wolf, M. (1978). Social validity: The case for subjective measurement or how applied behavior analysis is finding its heart. *Journal of Applied Behavior Analysis, 11,* 203–214.

5

General Factors in Measurement and Evaluation

David L. Gast

Applied Behavior Analysis

If educators and clinicians are to effectively design, implement, and evaluate intervention programs, they must measure the effects of their intervention on their students' or clients' behavior. Just as applied research requires the systematic and repeated measurement of behavior (Baer, Wolf, & Risley, 1968), so does effective instruction and therapy. The similarities between applied research and data-based interventions are far greater than their dissimilarities. Each of the following characteristics, which were described by Baer et al. in their 1968 seminal article, distinguish applied research from non-applied research, and also differentiate data-based intervention from non-data-based intervention.

1. *Applied*: The participant or society benefits from the research involvement.
2. *Behavioral*: The intervention focuses on and measures observable events.
3. *Analytical*: The effect the intervention has on behavior is "believable," i.e., a cause–effect relation is demonstrated; internal validity.
4. *Technological*: The procedures are described in sufficient detail to permit replication.
5. *Conceptually systematic*: The format and terminology used to describe the intervention is consistent with professional guidelines and literature.

   6. *Effective*: The effects of the intervention are large enough to be of practical value to the participant or society, i.e., social validity.

   7. *Generality*: Behavioral change is maintained over time and carries over to the natural environment, i.e., ecological validity.

This chapter describes general issues in measurement and evaluation, with emphasis on (a) direct and systematic measurement of behavior through the use of direct observational recording procedures; (b) reliability; and (c) validity. The discussion focuses on how you as a scientist-practitioner, through repeated measurement of student or client behavior within the context of a single subject research design, can accurately monitor child performance and evaluate program effectiveness and, in so doing, contribute to the applied research literature. The compatibility between data-based instruction/therapy and applied research is addressed from a teacher/therapist perspective. Also, the importance of the reliability and validity of measurement are discussed, as are common threats to internal validity as they relate to single subject research methodology.

Characteristics of Measurement and Evaluation

Measurement

In recent years teachers and therapists have increasingly emphasized the development of systems for monitoring student and client progress toward instructional and therapy objectives. This interest in accountability has necessitated practitioners becoming proficient in objectively measuring behavior.

   Measurement may be defined as the systematic and objective quantification of objects, events, or behaviors according to a set of rules. Basic steps or rules to be followed in the measurement process include (a) identifying what is to be measured; (b) defining the behavior or event in observable terms; and (c) selecting an appropriate data-recording procedure for observing, quantifying, and summarizing behavior.

Identifying What Is to Be Measured

As an applied researcher what you decide to measure will depend directly on the research question and the objective of your intervention. Several sources are available to help you determine what to measure. In addition to using personal observations, you can consult with significant others (parents, other teachers and therapists, psychologists, etc.), as well as examine previous assessments. For school-aged study participants, a recent Individual Education Plan (IEP) will incorporate instructional priorities from each of the above sources, facilitating the process.

Defining What Is to Be Measured

In accordance with the behavioral approach to teaching and clinical practice, you should define target behaviors in observable and measurable terms. Rather than define a child's behavior in such global terms as "disruptive," "bored," or "passive" without further behavioral elaboration, describe the behavior(s) to be observed in specific terms. For example, if a teacher frequently has observed a student leaving his desk without permission, talking with classmates during class presentations, and dropping pencils and books, you would have a much clearer idea as to what the teacher considers disruptive behavior. In addition to describing and record-

ing the topography and frequency of a target behavior it is often important to record the
duration, magnitude, inter-response time or some other characteristic of the behavior. It is also
advised to provide examples and non-examples of target behaviors to increase interobserver
agreement. With greater behavioral specificity and clarity you can more effectively document
observations and communicate them to colleagues, the child, and the child's parents.

Selecting a Data-Recording Procedure

After having identified the behavior to be measured and defining it in observable terms, you
must decide upon a method for quantifying the behavior. There are a variety of recording
procedures available to behavior analysts, each with its own advantages and disadvantages. You
must decide what it is about the behavior that deserves attention (i.e., frequency, duration,
latency, intensity, magnitude, or accuracy) and then select a recording procedure that is practical, sensitive to behavior change, and reliable. Several direct observational recording systems
are available, including event recording, duration recording (total and per occurrence), interval
recording (partial and whole), and time-sample recording (fixed, variable, and PLACHECK).
Specifics regarding these direct observational recording procedures are discussed in Chapter 7.
Variables that require consideration before selecting a data-recording procedure include (a) the
target behavior; (b) the objective of the academic or behavioral intervention program; (c)
practical constraints of the setting(s) in which the behavior is to be measured; and (d) sensitiv-
ity to document behavior change across time and conditions of the study. No single recording
system is appropriate for all behaviors, all educational or therapeutic objectives, or for use in
all settings.

Evaluation

Before discussing the parameters of measurement it is important to make a distinction between
measurement and evaluation. Measurement was defined in the previous section. *Evaluation* is
the analysis or comparison of data, collected during the measurement process, upon which
instructional and therapeutic decisions can be based. When the basic rules of measurement
have been adhered to and when an accurate analysis of the data has been conducted, program
evaluation generates information that facilitates an understanding of the relation between
child performance and the independent variable (e.g., instructional arrangement, task
sequence, pace, materials, instructional method, etc.). Through such understanding, we can
better individualize the intervention by objectively deciding whether to maintain, modify, or
abandon the current intervention strategy.

In applied research there are two basic requirements for evaluating the relation between a
study participant's behavior and the independent variable. First, accurate, reliable, and frequent measures of behavior are needed. Second, the measurement system must be paired with
a single subject research design. This chapter highlights the parameters of measurement, while
later chapters detail the various single subject experimental designs appropriate for evaluating
behavior. Only when both requirements are met can a *functional relation* (i.e., cause–effect
relation) between the independent and dependent variables be isolated. Without such pairing,
measurement at best yields only a *correlational relation*.

Summative Evaluation

A frequently used educational evaluation strategy for measuring student performance is the
pretest/posttest paradigm. Representative of this evaluation procedure is the annual assessment
of student progress toward short-term instructional objectives as specified in the IEP. The

literature pertaining to the IEP repeatedly cites the need to objectively evaluate pupil progress toward reaching the goals stated in the IEP. For many educators and therapists who work in educational settings, an annual evaluation of student progress is viewed as grossly inadequate for making instructional and therapeutic decisions. Such summative evaluations do not permit ongoing modifications or corrections of ineffective instructional or therapy programs, and thus considerable teacher, therapist, and student time may be wasted. Summative methods for evaluating pupil performance should be viewed only as the peripheral ends of a continuum for monitoring and evaluating individual progress and program effectiveness. The data generated by such annual evaluations are more likely to be of interest to school and clinic administrators in determining educational placements, rather than "frontline" teachers and therapists responsible for daily instructional and intervention programs.

The pretest/posttest evaluation paradigm represents a commonly used summative evaluation strategy. *Summative evaluation*, a static process, is the documentation of progress or change in performance by measuring and comparing an individual's performance at two points in time. In an educational context, it evaluates teaching and learning *post hoc*, i.e., after teaching and learning have occurred. Both the teach-test and test-teach-test paradigms, in which data are *not* collected during the teaching process, are representative of the summative evaluation strategy.

The summative evaluation of child behavior can be controversial, depending on the conditions under which the assessment is conducted. For example, when a child is tested at an educational-assessment clinic or in the office of an educational diagnostician or school psychologist, several variables come into play that may adversely affect how a child performs during the test situation. Consider for a moment the following conditions under which educational testing may take place:

- The child is separated from familiar persons, removed from familiar surroundings, and taken to a strange room.
- "Ideal" testing rooms, equipped with two-way mirrors, microphones, video cameras, barren walls, overhead fluorescent lighting, hard chairs and a table, bring images of police interrogation rooms.
- An evaluator (most likely never seen by the child before) takes the child through a series of activities ranging from requesting responses to questions like: "Do bananas fly?" to buttoning, lacing, and zipping the appendages of a polka-dot octopus.

Without belaboring the point, under the best of conditions (i.e., familiar examiner, familiar setting, or after a period of adaptation to a new person and environment) the data gathered from such assessments may only approximate those representing the child's actual capabilities. You cannot ignore the potential adverse influence of these novel variables on child performance. Summative information obtained under these conditions should be approached with caution. An alternative approach for acquiring summative information is to observe and evaluate child performance on functional tasks (e.g., buttoning his shirt, asking to tell her address) in the child's natural environment (classroom and/or home) using familiar materials, over an extended period of time (2–4 weeks). This latter evaluation approach is likely to generate information that more accurately reflects a child's educational and behavioral strengths and weaknesses.

It should be noted that the pretest/posttest paradigm is sometimes used in applied research to supplement a formative evaluation paradigm as a means for evaluating generalization of performance across settings, materials, or tasks. In such cases, behaviors related to the primary research question (e.g., acquisition of three greeting responses) may be evaluated within the context of a formative evaluation paradigm (i.e., multiple baseline across behaviors), while secondary research questions (e.g., greeting familiar adults not used in training when approached in non-training settings) may be evaluated within the context of a pretest/posttest design. This use of a summative evaluation paradigm is both appropriate and recommended ✓ when your interest is in evaluating the breadth or side effects of your intervention strategy.

Formative Evaluation
In order to go beyond perfunctory "paper compliance" by conducting annual static summative assessments of student progress, it is necessary to measure and evaluate the appropriateness of intervention programs on a more frequent and regular basis. Formative evaluation is an alternative to, or a strategy to be used in conjunction with, summative evaluation. *Formative* ✓ *evaluation*, a dynamic or *ongoing process*, emphasizes the frequent and repeated measurement of performance on functional and age-appropriate tasks, assessed under natural conditions, over time. Unlike summative data, formative data can be used to guide instructional and treatment programs by providing you with a frequent measure (i.e., gathered at least weekly) of behavior toward a target therapeutic or instructional objective. Such information allows you to modify your intervention in a systematic manner when deterioration of performance is first evident. In addition, formative data can confirm achievement, thereby reassuring you that your intervention is appropriate and effective.

Of course many variables must be considered before determining whether child progress is real or contrived. Assuming that instructional or behavioral objectives are appropriate, appropriate dependent measures have been selected, and data collected are reliable, frequent, and repeated measures of child performance can be both informative and reinforcing to you. However, the simple recording of behavior at frequent and regular intervals does not in itself merit the label of formative evaluation. Only if these data are analyzed and used to determine ✓ whether to maintain, modify, or abandon the current intervention is the evaluation strategy considered formative.

Formative Evaluation: Objections and Considerations
The idea of keeping precise and reliable data often is seen as prohibitive by many educators and therapists who are required to assume responsibility for a number of children with a wide range of individual differences. Too often when requested to collect child-performance data, a teacher's response is, "I don't have time to collect data; I have to teach." Such an argument reveals a misconception that teaching (or therapy) and data collection are incompatible behaviors. This need not be the case. When appropriate preparations are made, formative evaluation can save you time by confirming the effectiveness, or signaling the ineffectiveness, of an intervention strategy.

Formative program evaluation has one purpose: to assist in deciding whether to maintain, modify, or abandon the current program (Bijou, 1977). It serves no purpose to collect data on ✓ the effectiveness of a program unless the data are used to help in the decision-making process. In fact, you should avoid the "trap of recording any and all behavior, simply for the sake of data collection" (Scott & Goetz, 1980, p. 66). A critical question to ask before collecting perform- ✓ ance data is, "To what practical end can the data be used?" Several researchers have provided guidelines to help practitioners and researchers make data-based decisions as to when to maintain, modify, or change program conditions (Haring & Liberty, 1990; Liberty & Haring, 1990; Liberty, Haring, White, & Billingsley, 1988). Practicality is a key factor when deciding what type of data to collect, how frequently the data should be collected, and what method for collecting the data should be used. If you have a thorough understanding of measurement options (dependent measures, recording systems, continuous and intermittent data-collection procedures) and know how to visually analyze graphed data, the systematic and frequent measurement of behavior need not be a time-consuming and aversive process that conflicts with your teaching or therapy program.

The objection that direct measurement procedures are too rigid and time-consuming, and thus detract from teaching or the delivery of therapy, are common complaints heard by university faculty and educational consultants. There may be some justification for this objection if the data collected are summative and if the data are not used to modify the intervention. Summative evaluations tend to be time-consuming and rigid and, therefore, it is understandable why some practitioners object to collecting such data. In contrast, formative evaluation can assist in the implementation of your intervention. The direct and systematic observation of behavior can facilitate your: (a) understanding of each child's strengths and weaknesses; (b) general observational skills; (c) awareness of emerging or recurring behaviors; (d) interactions with team members (e.g., parents, administrators, therapists, educators, psychologists) by providing more accurate information; and (e) objective monitoring of program effectiveness, permitting program modification, if necessary, before valuable teacher and student instructional time is wasted (Scott & Goetz, 1980).

The initial implementation of systematic measurement procedures may prove time-consuming and cumbersome; however, the benefits derived from the time spent in the initial phases of the data-collection process will justify the effort. The amount of time necessary to implement a data-collection system will depend directly on your familiarity with direct measurement procedures and your organization of the classroom or therapy setting. The more familiar you are with direct observational recording procedures and the more organized the environment (e.g., activity schedules, staff responsibilities), the less time it will take and the less cumbersome it will be to implement an effective and efficient data-based program.

Data collection must be individualized (i.e., the type of data collected and the recording procedure employed will depend upon the type of information sought). Parsimony coupled with practicality should be the rule in teaching and therapy, and in applied research. Collecting data that will not be used and the use of recording systems that lack simplicity and economy should be avoided. The measurement system should be as simple as possible and still provide the necessary information upon which program and research decisions can be based. As Bancroft and Bellamy (1976) pointed out, objections to systematic direct measurement "result from an inability to structure classroom activities for efficient measurement or an unwillingness to use the resulting data to modify a 'tried and true' technique" (p. 28).

It would be naive to presume that all teachers and therapists in all educational or clinical settings, regardless of the number of students or clients served, or the staffing patterns, should and could collect trial-by-trial data on all programs for all students and clients. This simply is not practical. Although daily measures are considered ideal, they may prove to be impractical because of time constraints. *Weekly measures typically are considered the minimum acceptable frequency for formatively evaluating progress.* Failure to evaluate progress weekly increases the risk of continuing an ineffective program which wastes time, and which may produce inappropriate interfering behaviors.

Continuous measurement (i.e., daily, session-by-session or trial-by-trial data) can provide you with constant feedback upon which to base decisions. Although continuous measurement yields a wealth of information upon which you can base your intervention decisions, such rigor may at times prove too cumbersome and too time-consuming to be practical. An alternative to continuous measurement is non-continuous or intermittent measurement. For example, rather than evaluating a student's performance every instructional session, progress is measured every other session. Although data are not collected daily, they are collected frequently, allowing you to modify the program, if necessary, without wasting instructional time. As with continuous measurement, non-continuous measurement requires that the data be collected systematically and reliably, using one of the many direct observational recording procedures discussed in Chapter 7. The implementation of a *non-continuous measurement* strategy will provide you with information relative to child progress. If data are variable and difficult to analyze, a continuous measurement strategy can be adopted. The particular recording system employed will depend upon the type of information sought. Weekly measures, using a non-continuous measurement strategy, will generally suffice to provide you with feedback regarding child progress, unless of course the intervention program is part of a single subject applied research project, in which case more frequent data typically will be required.

Formative Evaluation Guidelines
Formative evaluation requires that you become competent in the selection, implementation, and evaluation of data-recording procedures and single subject research designs. By familiarizing yourself with the strengths and weaknesses of each recording procedure and research design, you will be in a better position to select a data-collection procedure and research design that is sensitive, reliable, effective, efficient, and answers your research questions. General guidelines in the measurement and formative evaluation of behavior during an applied research include:

1. Define target behavior(s) in observable terms.
2. Collect data repeatedly and frequently on behaviors central to your research question(s).
3. Measure that aspect (frequency, accuracy, duration, etc.) of your participants' behavior that directly relate to your research question(s) and intervention objective, i.e., do not restrict data collection to simple responses and ignore more interesting and important aspects of your participants' behavior.
4. Familiarize yourself thoroughly with data-collection and research-design alternatives.
5. Select a measurement procedure that is practical and that can be consistently and reliably used within the constraints of your setting.
6. Structure your setting so that data collection does not interfere with teaching or therapy.
7. Graphically display data and visually analyze the data regularly.
8. Base decisions to maintain, modify, or abandon the current intervention on your analysis of the graphed data.
9. Collect interobserver agreement and procedural-reliability data frequently to ensure that measurement and experiment condition procedures are followed.
10. Maintain a "research log" in which you record interesting and unusual happenings during the course of the study that may be included in the discussion section of your research report.

The direct and frequent measurement of behavior, when paired with a single subject research design, can yield information that can facilitate the design of an effective intervention and a positive change in participants' behavior. It can assist you in the early identification of learning and behavior problems, provide information on program effectiveness, signal the need for program modification, increase the rate with which a child attains program objectives, and facilitate communication among significant others. Systematic data collection is the "foundation of pragmatic instruction and an antidote to dogmatic and theoretical teaching" (Bancroft & Bellamy, 1976, p. 29).

Reliability and Validity

There are two fundamental issues that must be confronted in research: reliability and validity of measurement. These terms have different meanings in science, evaluation, and general usage. These key terms are considered here. Specific applications are considered throughout the following chapters on measurement and research design.

Reliability

In the vernacular, when you ask, "Is she reliable," you mean, "Can we count on her?" In the field of test construction and evaluation, "to be reliable" means that a test will yield the same results if administered more than one time. These two referents are reflected in *Merriam-Webster's Online Dictionary* (2008) definitions: "suitable or fit to be relied on"; "giving the same result on successive trials." Within the context of single subject research methodology, there are three referents for the term reliability, all of which relate to consistency, i.e., "free from variation or contradiction" (Merriam-Webster): reliability of effect; reliability of measurement; procedural reliability.

Reliability of effect concerns your confidence that the outcome of an intervention is "real"; that is, that if the experiment is repeated, the outcome will be the same. Or, if you or others repeat the same experiment many times, would the outcomes be similar across the series of experiments? To determine if results are reliable, experiments are repeated or replicated. A full discussion of replication is presented in Chapter 6.

Reliability of measurement addresses what you observe or record during the course of a study. There are two facets of reliability of measurement that must be considered. First, you must ask the question: "Are the data accurate?" *Accuracy of measurement*, as described by Cooper, Heron, and Heward (2007, p. 103), refers to the degree to which the "observed value" of a behavior or event being measured corresponds to the "true value" of the behavior or event as it occurs under natural conditions. As described here, the term accuracy is very similar to the term validity, in that both accuracy and validity refer to the degree to which the data collected are a "true" and representative sample of the behavior or event as it occurs the real world. You must answer the question: "Does the definition and the dimension of the behavior being measured (rate, latency, duration, etc.) correspond with how others define the behavior or event?" If "yes," then your data will be viewed as an accurate and valid measure of the target behavior or event. A second aspect of reliability of measurement pertains to the consistency with which data are collected, i.e., interobserver agreement. If the data collected are permanent products (e.g., students' answers to worksheet problems), it is important that they are scored accurately and consistently. To verify that they are accurate is a simple matter of checking the scores against an answer key or asking another person to double-check your scoring. However, many studies are concerned with the observable behavior of children as they interact with a parent, teacher, therapist, and/or other children. The target behavior occurs in a stream of events that are lost to history, unless they are permanently recorded. Sometimes they can be captured through video and/or audio recordings, which can be checked again and again, just as a math worksheet or written essay. Many behavioral researchers, however, rely on on-site human observers to document the occurrence or nonoccurrence of behavior in real time. Usually, a second observer, independent from the first observer, is recruited to determine whether observations are recorded accurately and consistently. In this context, the question is:

"To what extent do two independent observers using the same behavioral definition(s) and the same direct observational recording procedure agree that the target behavior(s) occurred or didn't occur?" The answer to this question is critical because if it is not possible to determine the accuracy, frequency, or duration of a target behavior with some degree of precision, then you will have little basis for claiming that your intervention was successful. In this discussion of reliability, it is important to note that interobserver agreement reliability, like accuracy and validity, "is a relative concept; it is a matter of degree" (Cooper et al., 2007, p. 104). Some degree of disagreement is to be expected, particularly when research is conducted in natural settings (classrooms, homes, community businesses); however, the greater the disagreement, the less confidence you and others will have in the findings. As presented in Chapter 7, simple procedures have been developed to calculate interobserver agreement with the various direct observational recording procedures used in behavioral research.

Procedural reliability, also referred to as procedural or treatment fidelity, is critical to believ- ✓ ing whether the independent variable under investigation is responsible for observed changes in behavior (Vollmer, Sloman, & Pipkin, 2008; Fiske, 2008). Billingsley, White, and Munson (1980) introduced the importance of measuring procedural fidelity at a time when interventions were becoming more complex (instructional and intervention packages), were being conducted in community settings (public schools, mental health centers, recreation programs), and were being implemented by service providers (teachers, therapists) rather than trained researchers or researchers in training. Procedural fidelity refers to the degree to which the procedures of an experimental condition (baseline, intervention, maintenance, generalization), as described in the methods section of a research proposal, are implemented. Since Billingsley et al., several behavior analysts have discussed the importance of measuring procedural reliability (Cooper et al., 1987; Gresham, Gansle, & Noell, 1993; Wolery, 1994), however, the focus of their discussions have been on "treatment integrity" to the exclusion of discussing the importance of collecting procedural-reliability data across all experimental conditions. In order to determine whether an intervention has an effect on behavior, you need to (a) identify and compare the *procedural differences between experimental conditions,* and (b) measure the degree to which procedures in each condition are followed. If, for example, you are interested in evaluating the effectiveness of a visual activity schedule on the independent transitioning behavior of children who have a history of verbal-prompt dependency (Bryan & Gast, 2000; Spriggs, Gast, & Ayres, 2007), it would be important that adults in the classroom not provide verbal prompts in both baseline and intervention conditions. To ensure independent transitioning is being measured, you would want to collect data on the frequency with which adults verbally prompt children to change activities across both conditions. Only if procedural-reliability data are collected across conditions will you be able to identify the procedural differences between conditions, and thus determine what variables may be responsible for observed behavior changes.

Collecting reliability data on the dependent variable entails (a) two trained independent observers, (b) observing and recording the behavior(s) of study participants using the same behavioral definition(s) and the same direct observational recording procedure, who (c) afterwards compare their records using one of the interobserver agreement formulas (discussed in Chapter 7), and (d) report a percentage agreement of observers. Procedural reliability, by contrast, entails (a) a trained independent observer who is thoroughly familiar with condition procedures, (b) observing and recording the behavior of the interventionist (therapist, teacher, parent, peer tutor) implementing the condition as described in the methods section of the research proposal, (c) comparing the record of the interventionist's behavior on each planned procedural variable to the plan itself, and (d) reporting the percentage agreement on each procedural variable that the interventionist's behavior matched the planned procedures. *The formula for calculating procedural reliability is: number of observed behaviors divided by number of planned behaviors multiplied by 100.* This formula yields a percentage that reflects the degree to which the interventionist followed prescribed procedures. This formula should be used to calculate procedural fidelity on *each* procedural variable of the condition (e.g., presentation of the planned stimulus, presentation of the attentional cue, waiting 5 s for the learner to emit an attentional response, presenting the task direction only after an attentional response by the learner, waiting 3 s before delivery of the controlling prompt, waiting 5 s for the learner to emit a response, delivering the appropriate consequence based on the learner's response). Table 5.1 presents a portion of a procedural-reliability data-collection sheet that depicts the procedural variables using a constant time delay (CTD) transfer of stimulus-control procedure to teach object naming in a discrete trial format (Wolery, Ault, & Doyle, 1992). By collecting procedural-reliability data on each procedural variable of a condition it is possible to identify errors in implementation that can be corrected, assuming reliability data are collected frequently, i.e., at least once per condition or 20% of the sessions or days of a condition, whichever is more. It should be noted on the procedural-reliability data sheet in Table 5.1 that reliability on the interventionist's behavior (independent variable) and reliability on the learner's behaviors (dependent variables; attentional response and target response) are recorded on each trial, on the same data sheet, and presumably during the same session, thus making the collection of reliability data more time efficient.

Validity

The Merriam-Webster (2008) *Online Dictionary* offers several definitions of validity, including position or proposal that is "well-grounded or justifiable: being at once relevant and meaningful," "logically correct," and "appropriate to the end in view." It "implies being supported by objective truth or generally accepted authority." As previously noted, the terms validity and accuracy are closely related. In research, if we profess that a behavior count is valid or accurate, we must convince our audience that the "observed value" corresponds to the "true value." This requires that the behavioral definition, the dimension of the behavior being measured, and the conditions under which data are collected represent reality, i.e., the true occurrence as it appears in nature. If our observation periods are too short, conducted at times of the day or in activities when the behaviors are unlikely to occur, we will not get a true measure of the behavior or the conditions under which it is emitted. To obtain a valid or true measure requires that we observe our target behaviors at appropriate times of the day, within appropriate activities when the behaviors are likely to occur, and for an appropriate length of time. When these conditions are met, and when data are collected reliably, the observed effects of the independent variable on the dependent variable will increase the generality of the findings beyond the original research conditions. Thus, as an applied researcher and behavior change agent, you should take great care in how you define and measure your target behavior(s), as well as the conditions under which you collect data.

Internal and External Validity

Two validity issues that are of paramount importance to all research are internal and external validity. Both terms are the focus of Chapter 6, in which direct and systematic replication are discussed. When we ask, "Does this study demonstrate internal validity?", we are really asking, "Is the independent variable and only the independent variable responsible for the observed changes in behavior?" The question is critical because in the universe of events that occur during the course of a study, some are likely to influence the outcome of a study. Controlling

Table 5.1 Procedural Reliability Data Sheet (CTD, expressive labeling)

Student: _____ Instructor: _____
Date: __/__/__ Session: _____ Start Time: _____ Stop Time: _____
Behavior: Restaurants Total Session Time: _____ Delay Interval: 4 seconds
Condition/Phase: _____ Reliability/Observer: _____
Directions: While observing teacher, please record whether teacher emitted behavior during instructional procedure for each trial.
Key: (+) = occurrence; (–) = nonoccurrence

Trial	Stimulus	T presents stimulus	T gives attending cue	T ensures subject attends	T gives instructional cue	T waits 4 s	Student Responding			T consequates correctly	T waits intertrial interval
							Correct	Incorrect	No Response		
1											
2											
3											
4											
5											
6											
7											
8											
9											
10											
11											
12											
13											
14											
15											
16											
17											
18											
Reliability Percentage											

Comments:

for possible sources of confounding or alternative explanations from these events is a major consideration in the selection of a research design. The primary purpose of the single subject research design you select is to control for and evaluate the influence that variables, other than the independent variable, have on the observed effect, i.e., decrease the likelihood of alternative explanations for the observed changes in behavior. The term *internal validity* is synonymous with the phrase "reliability of effect." If the observed effect of an intervention can be repeated while controlling for potentially confounding variables (i.e., threats to internal validity), then the intervention is said to have internal validity. It is our responsibility as researchers to control for threats to internal validity, thus enhancing the believability of our findings.

Two questions are basic to the consideration of *external validity*. The first is specific to the effectiveness and the generality of an independent variable: "Given that an intervention produced a measurable effect with this study participant, will it have a similar effect with other individuals, in other settings, when implemented by other investigators, and when implemented with minor variations in the basic procedure?" The second question strikes at the heart of the field of applied behavior analysis (ABA) and single subject research methodology. "Is it possible to make statements about the generality of an intervention when single subject research designs are employed in a study?" Those who ask this question are often proponents of "large N" contrast group designs and who are disinclined to accept "yes" as an answer. Chapter 6 addresses these questions in depth in the discussion of direct and systematic replication.

Other Types of Validity

There are many types of validity discussed in the behavioral (Johnston & Pennypacker, 1993), social (Babbie, 1995), educational (deMarrais & Lapan, 2004), and clinical (Portney & Watkins, 2000) research literatures. In addition to internal and external validity, you should be aware of four other types of validity that have direct bearing on the design and critique of single subject research investigations.

Social validity. The concern for social validity has been paramount since the inception of ABA. Baer et al. (1968) set the stage for this concern when they specified that the domain of ABA was "behaviors that are socially important, rather than convenient for study" (p. 92). Wolf (1978) reaffirmed this concern in his essay on the use of subjective measures in applied behavioral research. His article argued that subjective feedback data have a place in ABA. Wolf recommended that ABA researchers address *three levels of social validation: goals, procedures, and effects.* Whether a therapy goal or educational objective, treatment program or instructional strategy, or educational gains or therapy outcomes have social significance should be left up to "significant others," i.e., those who have a direct interest in the study participant including, but not limited to, study participants themselves, parents, guardians, teachers, therapists, employers, etc. Single subject research design investigations should include one or more strategies for obtaining "consumer satisfaction data," either through opinion surveys, questionnaires, or interviews. These social-validity data tend to be of secondary importance to applied behavioral researchers, unless of course the social, educational, or clinical perceptions of significant others are the primary focus of the investigation. Generally speaking, social-validity results are presented in discussion sections of reports, rather than result sections, since data reflect opinions, perceptions, and feelings. The exception is if a Likert rating scale is used to collect social-validity data (Reimers & Wacker, 1988) and numerical scores (mean, median, range) can be calculated, in which case reporting social-validity findings in a results section would be appropriate. Social validity should not take the place of direct measures of behavior, but used to supplement primary data by providing insights into how clients, students, and others view aspects of your study.

② *Ecological validity.* Ecological validity, within the context of single subject research methodology, refers to the extent to which a study has "relevance" and the intervention can be reliably implemented in the "real world" (Kratochwill, 1978). Many published applied behavioral research studies have been conducted in "resource rich" university or private clinics, lab schools, and medical centers. These centers are "rich" in terms of the abundance of highly educated staff who are providing and/or receiving research support by having access to the latest material and equipment, low therapist–client or teacher–student ratios, availability of reliability observers and other technical-support staff, and a host of other resources not typically found in community public schools and clinics. You must also assess whether study participants in these settings are representative of those served in your setting because of their control over admissions (e.g., family program affordability, specific entry criteria) and study participation contingencies (e.g., number of hours of direct family member involvement, attendance at training sessions). The question you must ask is,

> Do I have the necessary resources (skills, staff, time, materials, etc.) and do I control similar contingencies (family member implementation at home, attendance at meetings, etc.), to implement the intervention that was shown to be effective in a research report I read?

If "yes," and the results show that the intervention can be implemented with fidelity with a similar effect, you can conclude that the intervention has ecological validity. Simply stated, ecological validity refers to translating "research to practice." ⟵

③ *Content validity.* In the field of test construction and evaluation, validity is a critical concern. Here, there is one basic question, "Is the test appropriate to use in a given situation?" In the area of achievement testing, the proper variation of the question is, "Does the test measure what was taught?" The answer is judgmental even though that judgment may be supported by a statistical analysis. Poor scores (low student achievement) may occur when a radically new curriculum is introduced but student performance is evaluated on a traditional measure. The same result can occur when a traditional curriculum is substantially altered but the program is evaluated with traditional measures.

In single subject research design, content validity refers to the degree to which baseline or probe conditions and measures truly measure what is the focus of the treatment or instructional program. For example, if a probe condition is designed using a "single-opportunity" probe procedure, one in which a student's error on the first step of a response-chain skill results in scoring all subsequent steps as errors, these probe measures would have low content validity. It is possible that the student is simply unable to perform the first step of the task analysis, but can perform some or even all subsequent steps. In this example, a "multiple-opportunity" probe procedure, one in which performance on all steps are assessed (Cooper et al., 2007; Schuster, Gast, Wolery, & Guiltinan, 1988), would yield a "truer" measure of a student's ability, and thus greater content validity.

④ *Criterion-related validity.* Sometimes referred to as "predictive validity" (Babbie, 1995) and "concurrent validity" (Barlow & Hersen, 1984), criterion validity addresses the degree to which two alternative assessments measure the same behavior or content of knowledge. In single subject research the question is, "Do alternative baseline or probe test forms, or different observation periods (e.g., morning and afternoon) administered across days, yield similar behavioral measures?" A test of criterion validity is the substitutability of assessments or observations and the degree to which they yield consistent measures regardless of test form or observational period.

Threats to Internal Validity

Two concepts are important to understanding the pragmatics of experimental control. First, it is impossible to control every possible threat to internal validity. Second, a possible threat may not be an actual threat. Each possible threat should be addressed in the design of your study and the analysis of other researchers' studies. The extent to which threats to validity are evaluated and controlled will determine the level of confidence you should have in the findings. You should not be disheartened to learn that just as there is no free lunch, there is no perfect experiment. Instead, there are carefully designed experiments, experiments that are executed as carefully as they were planned and that provide "adequate and proper data" (Campbell & Stanley, 1963, p. 2) for analysis. Your task is to describe what happened during the course of the experiment and to be able to account for planned and unplanned outcomes, i.e., those that may have influenced the findings.

History

History refers to events that occur *during* an experiment, and after the introduction of the independent variable, that may influence the outcome. Generally speaking, the longer the study the greater the threat due to history. Potential sources of history threats, when a study is conducted in community settings, are the actions of others (parents, siblings, peers, child-care providers) or of study participants themselves (independent online research, observational learning, serendipitous exposure through the media). For behaviors that demand immediate attention in the eyes of significant others, there may be an attempt to intervene prior to the scheduled intervention time. Also, participants may learn target content through television or learn target social behaviors through observing the consequences delivered to others. Single subject research designs address history threats by withdrawing and reintroducing the independent variable (A-B-A-B design and its variations) or by staggering the introduction of the independent variable across behaviors, conditions, or participants (multiple baseline and multiple probe designs and their variations). When a study participant's behavior is inconsistent with previous performance it is important to investigate what might have caused this discrepancy, for example, seizure the night before, fight on the school bus, medication change, sibling instructed.

Maturation

Maturation refers to changes in behavior due to the passage of time. In a "short" duration study (4–6 weeks) maturation is not likely to influence the analysis of the effectiveness of an independent variable that focuses on improving language or motor skills of a child who has a history of slow development. If, however, the study is carried out over several months (4–6 months) with the same young child, there is a greater likelihood that maturation may play a role in observed behavioral changes. As with history confounding, potential maturation threats to internal validity are addressed through the withdrawal or the staggering of the introduction of the independent variable. There are those who refer to "session fatigue" as a maturation threat to validity. Session fatigue refers to a participant's performance decreasing over the course of a session, e.g., 80% accuracy over the first 20 trials and 20% accuracy over the last 20 trials of a 40-trial session. We may debate whether session fatigue is a maturation threat but we would certainly agree it is a threat to the validity of the findings. To avoid session fatigue it is important to be sensitive to a participant's age and attention span, scheduling shorter sessions with fewer trials for younger children and individuals who have a shorter attention span. It may also be helpful in restoring attention to task and responding to take a short break (3–5 minutes) midway through a lengthy session.

Testing

Testing is a threat in any study that requires participants to respond to the same test repeatedly during a baseline or probe condition. As will be discussed in Chapter 11, repeated testing may have a *facilitative effect* (improvement in performance over successive baseline or probe testing or observations sessions) or an *inhibitive effect* (deterioration in performance over successive baseline or probe testing or observations sessions) depending on how the "test" condition is designed. A test condition that repeatedly presents the same academic task, prompts correct responses through a correction procedure, or delivers reinforcement contingent upon a correct response may result in a facilitative effect. Test sessions of long duration, requiring "substantial" participant effort, with minimal or no reinforcement for attention and active participation may result in an inhibitive effect. It is important to design your baseline and probe conditions so that they yield participants' best efforts so that you neither overestimate nor underestimate the impact of the independent variable on the behavior.

Facilitative effects of testing can be avoided by randomizing stimulus presentation order across sessions; not reinforcing correct responses, particularly on receptive tasks; not correcting incorrect responses; and not prompting (intentionally or unintentionally) correct responses. Procedural-reliability checks will help with detecting these procedural errors that could influence participant performance. Inhibitive effects of testing can be avoided by conducting sessions of an appropriate length, i.e., avoid session fatigue; interspersing known stimuli with unknown stimuli and reinforcing correct responses to known stimuli; and reinforce correct responses on expressive, comprehension, and response-chain tasks. These strategies may be helpful in avoiding the testing threats.

Instrumentation

Instrumentation threats refer to concerns with the measurement system, i.e., behavioral definitions, recording procedures, frequency of reliability observations, formula used to calculate interobserver agreement (IOA), independence of observers, observer bias, observer drift, etc. In single subject research the percentage agreement between two independent observers is the most common strategy for determining whether there is a threat to internal validity due to instrumentation. Generally speaking, percentage agreement at or above 90% is viewed as acceptable in applied research, while percentage agreement below 80% is considered unacceptable or at least a matter of concern. Unfortunately, determining what percentage IOA is acceptable, or unacceptable, is not as easy as it may seem since some behaviors are easier to record (permanent products, behaviors of long duration, gross motor responses) than others (high-rate behaviors, behaviors of short duration, vocal responses). In addition, the conditions under which data are collected will influence what percentage agreement you find acceptable. Assuming behavioral definitions are clearly written and observers are properly trained, you would expect measurement errors to be lower when data are collected from permanent products (audio or video recordings, written assignments, assemblies, computer printouts), compared to live observations in "real time." Issues related to reliability of measurement are discussed in Chapter 7. Suffice it to say here you must attend to the details of your measurement system to avoid instrumentation threats to internal validity.

Procedural Infidelity

Earlier in this chapter the importance of procedural reliability was discussed. If the procedures of an experimental condition (baseline, probe, intervention, maintenance, generalization) are *not* consistently implemented across behavior episodes, time, interventionists, etc., as described in the methods section of the research proposal or report, this constitutes a major threat to the internal validity of the findings. It is recommended that a percentage agreement be calculated and reported for *each* interventionist (parent, teacher, clinician) behavior in order to measure the degree to which *each* component of the prescribed condition procedures has been followed. Frequent checks of procedural reliability are recommended across the course of the study, i.e., at least once per condition or 20% of all observation periods, whichever is more.

Attrition

√ Participant attrition refers to the "loss of participants" during the course of a study, which can limit the generality of the findings. As will be discussed in Chapter 6, external validity is primarily enhanced in single subject research design when an investigation is systematically replicated, i.e., similar outcomes are reported when a study is repeated by different investigators, with different participants, at different research sites, targeting different behaviors. A *minimum* of three participants is typically recommended for inclusion in any one single subject research design investigation. However, since it is unlikely that you will have much control over participants who choose to withdraw from your study, or who are required to withdraw due to the family moving, incarceration, hospital admission, or school expulsion, it is recommended that you start with four or more participants when available and if practical. With four participants, the loss of one participant will have less of an impact on your analysis of independent variable generality.

Multiple-treatment Interference

√ Multiple-treatment (or intervention) interference can occur when a study participant's behavior is influenced by "treatments" or interventions, other than the independent variable alone, during the course of a study. An interactive effect may be identified due to *sequential confounding* (the order in which experimental conditions are introduced to participants may influence their behavior) or a *carryover effect* (the effect a procedure used in one experimental condition influences behavior in an adjacent condition). To avoid sequential confounding, the order in which experimental conditions are introduced to participants is counterbalanced (e.g., Participant 1, A-B-A-C-A-B-A-C; Participant 2, A-C-A-B-A-C-A-B). Carryover effects, however, are less easily controlled. It is imperative, however, that, if they exist, they be identified. In Chapter 12 strategies for identifying and controlling threats to validity due to multiple-treatment interference are discussed.

Data Instability

√ Instability refers to the amount of variability there is in the data (dependent variable) over time. As Kratochwill (1978, p. 15) noted,

> Experiments involving repeated measurement of a single subject or group over time typically evidence some degree of variability. If this "instability" is large, investigators could attribute an effect to the intervention when, in fact, the effectiveness was no larger than the natural variation in the data series.

Your attention to the amount of variability in a data series is important in deciding if, or when, it is appropriate to move to the next experimental condition. As will be discussed in Chapter 9, during a visual analysis of graphic data, both level and trend stability must be considered before changing conditions if there is to be a clear demonstration of experimental control. The premature introduction of the independent variable into a data series may preclude such a demonstration. As a consumer of research, you should determine if there is high percentage overlap between data points of two adjacent conditions, (e.g., if 30% or more of the data points of Condition B fall within the range of the data-point values of Condition A) and, if there is, you should be skeptical of any statements a researcher might make regarding the effectiveness of the independent variable. In your own research, when data variability is observed, it is best to (a) maintain the condition until the data stabilize, or (b) attempt to isolate the source of the variability. Threats to internal validity due to data instability are preventable if you are patient and analytical in your research decisions, rather than following some predetermined schedule that dictates when to move to the next experimental condition, e.g., every 7 days the experimental conditions will change.

Cyclical variability

Cyclical variability is a specific type of data instability that refers to a repeated and predictable pattern in the data series over time. When experimental conditions are of equal length (e.g., 5 days in each condition of an A_1-B_1-A_2-B_2 withdrawal design) it is possible that your observations coincide with some unidentified natural source that may account for the variability. For example, if your experimental condition schedule coincides with a parent's work schedule (away from home for 5 days, at home for 5 days) you may incorrectly conclude that the independent variable is responsible for changes in behavior when in fact it may be due to the presence or absence of the parent at home. To avoid confounding due to cyclical variability it is recommended that you vary condition lengths across time.

Adaptation

Adaptation refers to a period of time at the start of an investigation in which participants' recorded behavior may differ from their natural behavior due to the novel conditions under which data are collected. It is recommended that study participants be exposed to unfamiliar adults, settings, formats, data-collection procedures (e.g., video recording), etc. prior to the start of a study, through what is sometimes referred to as *history training*, to increase the likelihood that data collected on the first day of a baseline condition is representative of participants' "true" behavior. A "*reactive effect*" to being observed has been reported and discussed in the applied-research literature for quite some time (Kazdin, 1979), leading to recommendations to be as unobtrusive as possible during data collection (Cooper et al., 2007; Kazdin, 2001).

Hawthorne Effect

The Hawthorne Effect, which refers to participants' observed behavior not being representative of their natural behavior as a result of their knowledge that they are participants in an experiment (Kratochwill, 1978; Portney & Watkins, 2000), is a specific type of adaptation threat to validity related to participants knowing they are part of an ongoing investigation. Self-management studies, in which participants record their own behavior, are particularly susceptible to a Hawthorne Effect. As Cooper et al. (2007) state, "When the person observing and recording the target behavior is the subject of the behavior change program, maximum obtrusiveness exists, and reactivity is very likely" (p. 591). Like adaptation, familiarizing participants with experimental conditions, specifically data-recording conditions, prior to the start of a study may decrease the likelihood of a Hawthorne Effect.

These potential threats to validity require your undivided attention during both the design and evaluation of single subject research. It is imperative that you and those researchers whose studies you read, evaluate and control as many threats to internal validity as possible. Although there is no perfect experiment, it is your responsibility to reduce, to as close to zero as possible, the number of alternative explanations for your findings and conclusions. Be objective in your analysis and conservative in drawing conclusions so as not to overstate the effectiveness of the intervention under investigation. Be particularly sensitive to study conditions that may influence the ecological validity of the findings.

Summary

This chapter has focused on general factors or issues in measurement and evaluation as it relates to single subject research methodology. I have emphasized the distinction between collecting objective information (measurement) and making decisions based on those data (evaluation). I have attempted to show some critical differences between formative or ongoing evaluation and summative evaluation. Possible benefits of, as well as objections to, formative evaluation have been identified. General guidelines for repeated measurement and formative evaluation of behavior in educational and clinical settings have been listed. The terms reliability and validity, paralleling general usage of the terms with their specific use in the context of single subject research design have been presented. The various types of validity (internal, external, social, ecological, content, criterion-related) and how they relate to single subject research methodology were introduced. Common threats to internal validity (history, maturation, testing, instrumentation, procedural infidelity, multiple-treatment inter-ference, data instability, cyclical variability, adaptation, Hawthorne Effect) were described and exemplified. This general discussion of measurement and evaluation has presented concepts that are used repeatedly throughout the remainder of the text. The issues addressed in this chapter apply to classroom teaching, clinic therapy, and applied research. They set the stage for the design and evaluation of single subject research design studies and evidence-based practice.

References

Babbie, E. (1995). *The practice of social research* (7th ed.). Belmont, CA: Wadsworth Publishing Company.

Baer, D. M., Wolf, M. M., & Risley, T. R. (1968). Some current dimensions of applied behavior analysis. *Journal of Applied Behavior Analysis, 1*, 91–97.

Bancroft, J., & Bellamy, G. T. (1976). An apology for systematic observation. *Mental Retardation, 14*, 27–29.

Barlow, D. H., & Hersen, M. (1984). *Single case experimental designs: Strategies for studying behavior change* (2nd ed.). New York: Pergamon Press.

Bijou, S. W. (1977). Practical implications of an interactional model of child development. *Exceptional Children, 44*, 6–14.

Billingsley, F. F., White, O. R., & Munson, A. R. (1980). Procedural reliability: A rationale and an example. *Behavioral Assessment, 2*, 229–241.

Bryan, L. C., & Gast, D. L. (2000). Teaching on-task and on-schedule behaviors to high functioning children with autism via picture schedules. *The Journal of Autism and Developmental Disabilities, 30*, 553–567.

Campbell, D. T., & Stanley, J. C. (1963). *Experimental and quasi-experimental designs for research*. Chicago, IL: Rand McNally.

Cooper, J. O. (1981). *Measuring behavior*. (2nd ed.). Columbus, OH: Charles E. Merrill.

Cooper, J. O., Heron, T. E., & Heward, W. L. (2007). *Applied behavior analysis* (2nd ed.). Upper Saddle River, NJ: Prentice-Hall, Inc.

deMarrais, K., & Lapan, S. D. (Eds.). (2004). *Foundations for research: Methods of inquiry in education and the social sciences*. Mahwah, NJ: Lawrence Erlbaum Associates.

Fiske, K. (2008). Treatment integrity of school-based behavior analytic interventions: A review of the research. *Behavior Analysis in Practice, 1*(2), 19–25.

Gresham, F. M., Gansle, K. A., & Noell, G. H. (1993). Treatment integrity in applied behavior analysis with children. *Journal of Applied Behavior Analysis, 26*, 257–263.

Haring, N. G., & Liberty, K. A. (1990). Matching strategies with performance in facilitating generalization. *Focus on Exceptional Children, 22*(8), 1–16.

Johnston, J. M., & Pennypacker, H. S. (1993). *Strategies and tactics for human behavioral research* (2nd ed.). Hillsdale, NJ: Erlbaum.

Kazdin, A. E. (1979). Unobtrusive measurement in behavioral assessment. *Journal of Applied Behavior Analysis, 12,* 713–724.

Kazdin, A. E. (2001). *Behavior modification in applied settings* (6th ed.). Belmont, CA: Wadsworth.

Kratochwill, T. R. (Ed.). (1978). *Single subject research—Strategies for evaluating change.* New York: Academic Press.

Liberty, K. A., & Haring, N. G. (1990). Introduction to decision rules systems. *Remedial and Special Education, 11,* 32–41.

Liberty, K. A., Haring, N. G., White, O. R., & Billingsley, F. F. (1988). A technology for the future: Decision rules for generalization. *Education and Training in Mental Retardation, 23,* 315–326.

Merriam-Webster's Online Dictionary. (2008). Retrieved March 18, 2008, from www.merriam-webster.com.

Portney, L. G., & Watkins, M. P. (2000). *Foundations of clinical research: Applications to practice.* Upper Saddle River, NJ: Prentice-Hall, Inc.

Reimers, T., & Wacker, D. (1988). Parents' rating of the acceptability of behavior treatment recommendations made in an outpatient clinic: A preliminary analysis of the influence of treatment effectiveness. *Behavioral Disorders, 14,* 7–15.

Schuster, J. W., Gast, D. L., Wolery, M., & Guiltinan (1988). The effectiveness of a constant time delay procedure to teach chained responses to adolescents with mental retardation. *Journal of Applied Behavior Analysis, 21,* 169–178.

Scott, L., & Goetz, E. (1980). Issues in the collection of in-class data by teachers. *Education and Treatment of Children, 3,* 65–71.

Spriggs, A. D., Gast, D. L, & Ayres, K. M. (2007). Using picture activity schedule books to increase on-schedule and on-task behaviors. *Education and Training in Developmental Disabilities, 42,* 209–223.

Vollmer, T., Sloman, K., & Pipkin, C. (2008). Practical implications of data reliability and treatment integrity monitoring. *Behavior Analysis in Practice, 1*(2), 4–11.

Wolery, M. (1994). Procedural fidelity: A reminder of its functions. *Journal of Behavioral Education, 4,* 381–386.

Wolery, M., Ault, M., & Doyle, P. (1992). *Teaching students with moderate to severe disabilities.* New York: Longman

Wolf, M. M. (1978). Social validity: The case for subjective measurement or how applied behavior analysis is finding its heart. *Journal of Applied Behavior Analysis, 11*(2), 203–214.

6
Replication

David L. Gast

Replication is defined by the Merriam-Webster *Online Dictionary* (2008) as the "action or process of reproducing or duplicating"; and "the performance of an experiment more than once." In both applied and basic research, replication can be described as an investigator's ability to repeat the effect an independent variable has on the dependent variable(s). Sidman (1960), in *Tactics of Scientific Research*, provided the definitive word regarding replication, in which he discussed two types of replication: direct replication and systematic replication. Although much of his discussion was written in the context of basic experimental psychology laboratory studies, the impact his insightful discussion of replication has had on applied behavioral research has been far reaching. It is not likely that you will find a text devoted to single subject research methodology, or applied behavior analysis, that does not reference Sidman (1960) and his contributions to behavioral science. His differentiation of direct replication (intra-subject and inter-subject), and its importance for evaluating the reliability of findings, and systematic replication, and its importance for evaluating the generality of findings, has provided behavior analysts with a framework for evaluating research. It is important to recognize that replication is at the heart of all science, and only through successful replication attempts can we gain confidence that experimental findings have both internal and external validity. Our confidence in research findings is directly related to the consistency within and across research attempts. This chapter addresses the parameters of replication that you will want to attend to in the design, implementation, and evaluation of your research efforts and those of others.

Why Replicate?

"The soundest empirical test of the reliability of data is provided by replicating" (Sidman, 1960, p. 70). Any study that you propose to conduct should be placed into the context of other studies that have addressed the same or similar presenting problem or instructional challenge, and manipulated the same or similar independent variable. Through a comprehensive literature review you will gain insight into what interventions have been effective, what modifications have had to be made to make the original independent variable effective, and what gaps there are in the research conducted to date. There are few research studies that are truly novel or unique, most are extensions or modifications of previous research "with a twist." That is, most research investigations attempt to expand our knowledge beyond what we currently know. This is accomplished by identifying gaps in the research literature and investigating whether a previously studied intervention will be as effective with other populations, or with other presenting behavioral problems or instructional challenges, or can be modified to be more effective and/or efficient.

Most studies are conducted to answer simple questions. Suppose that you conduct one study, using an A-B-A-B withdrawal design, with one participant and suppose further that the data show a clear effect, i.e., the behavior levels in B are different than the levels in A (direct intra-subject replication). Your reaction will be an enthusiastic and joyful "I did it and it worked!" to which the scientific community will (or should) reply "Yes, but . . .?" You have demonstrated the reliability of effect for Condition B, relative to Condition A, but with only one participant. The next question, then, is "If I repeat the experiment with similar but different participants, holding all other variables constant used with the original participant, will I get the same effect?" In other words, "Are my results reliable across other similar participants?" This question addresses both the reliability of effect and, to the extent to which participants (and conditions) differ, generality of effect (direct inter-subject replication). Suppose that you were successful in your replication attempt with three similar participants and you were able to keep all "pertinent" condition variables the same. Will these data quiet the scientific community? Possibly . . . but not for long. A single study, conducted with three or four similar participants, in which the independent variable consistently has a positive effect on behavior will gain the attention of the research community, and may be published in a refereed journal, assuming all threats to internal validity were controlled, procedures clearly described, data accurately analyzed, and reported according to APA (2001) publication guidelines. The questions others in the research community will ask, having read your research report, are: "Will I get the same results that you got with different participants, at a different research site?" (i.e., different participants, different investigator, different environmental conditions); "How broadly will the results generalize beyond the original experiment?" (systematic replication). The greater the number of differences from the original study, the greater the risk of not replicating the effect, but if successful, the greater the generality of the findings.

If the results of an intervention are spurious and cannot be reproduced reliably across participants in a single investigation, it is unlikely anyone will attempt to use the intervention. However, you should not be discouraged when there is a "failure to replicate," rather it should inspire you to attempt to identify the reasons for the failure. It is unlikely, in today's research journal world, that if your study has mixed results (i.e., one or more participants were unaffected by the intervention) that your study would be published. The exception to this outcome would be if you demonstrated that a modification to the original intervention, or alternative intervention, were effective in bringing about positive behavior change. As an applied researcher, as defined by Baer, Wolf, and Risley (1968), it is your responsibility to see that participants in your study benefit from their participation.

Why replicate? There are three primary reasons or purposes for attempting to replicate the findings of a study or series of studies:

1. Assess the reliability of findings (internal validity).
2. Assess the generality of the findings (external validity).
3. Look for exceptions.

Each of these reasons for replication will be addressed in the discussion of direct and systematic replication. Sidman (1960) succinctly and cogently addressed the importance of replication when he wrote:

> To the neutral observer it will be obvious that science is far from free of human bias, even in its evaluation of factual evidence. Experimental findings, furthermore, are so fragile when considered within the total matrix of natural phenomena from which they are lifted, and conclusions from such data often so tenuous, that one can only feel surprise at the actual achievements of experimental methodology. What must we work with in any experiment? Uncontrolled, and even unknown, variables; the errors of selective perception arising out of theoretical and observational bias; indirect measurements; the theory involved in the measurement techniques themselves; the assumptions involved in making the leap from data to interpretation. In short, we have a margin of error so great that any true advance might be considered an accident were it not for the fact that too many genuine advances have occurred in too short a time for the hypothesis to be entertained seriously.
>
> (p. 70)

It is through replication that we reduce the margin of error and increase confidence that findings that withstand repeated tests are real, not accidental.

Types of Replication

Direct Replication

Sidman (1960) defines direct replication as "the repetition of a given experiment by the same experimenter . . . accomplished either by performing the experiment again with new subjects or by making repeated observations on the same subject under each of several conditions" (p. 73). Two types of direct replications are described: intra-subject (or intra-group) direct replication and inter-subject (or inter-group) direct replication. Both intra-subject and inter-subject direct replications refer to an investigator's attempts to repeat an experimental effect with the same participant (intra-subject), or across participants in the same study (inter-subject). Assuming a study you design is an attempt to evaluate a functional, rather than correlational, relation between independent and dependent variables, and your study includes more than one participant, your investigation will address both intra- and inter-subject replication. In its narrowest and most conservative definition, direct replication is only possible in laboratory studies using infrahuman subjects (rats, pigeons, etc.), however, in applied research with human participants direct replication is more broadly defined.

Direct Intra-Subject Replication

Direct intra-subject replication refers to *repeating the experimental effect with the same partici-* ✓ *pant* more than once in the same study. For example, when an investigator uses an A_1-B_1-A_2-B_2 withdrawal experimental design, if the removal in the independent variable in A_2 results in a return to levels observed in A_1, and the reintroduction of the independent variable in B_2 results in a return to observed levels in B_1, intra-subject replication has been achieved, i.e., the investigator has been able to show that the presence or absence of the independent variable will determine the level of the dependent variable. If an investigator uses a multiple baseline (or multiple probe) design across behaviors, in which the intervention is systematic-ally introduced across three or more similar but independent behaviors, intra-subject replica-tion is achieved if there is a change in the dependent variable only upon introduction of the independent, not before. Figures 6.1 and 6.2 graphically exemplify intra-subject direct replica-tion with an A-B-A-B withdrawal design, and multiple baseline design across behaviors, respectively. Cooper, Heron, and Heward (2007) have described the intra-subject replication process in four stages, as noted on the graphic displays: prediction (A_1); affirmation (B_1); verification (A_2); replication (B_2). During A_1 the data trend is used to *predict* the data trend if there is no change in experimental condition; B_1 data trend *affirms* that the independent variable may have had an effect on the behavior; A_2 data trend *verifies* there is a cause–effect relation between independent and dependent variables at the simplest level; B_2 data trend *replicates*, or repeats the effect that the independent variable has on the dependent variable, thus increasing confidence that there is functional relation between independent and depend-ent variables. Through the intra-subject direct-replication process you gain confidence that you have demonstrated "reliability of effect," i.e., internal validity, with this one participant. Your objective now is to establish this same effect with other participants included in your study.

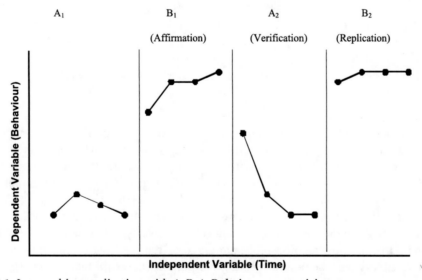

Figure 6.1 Intra-subject replication with A-B-A-B design, one participant.

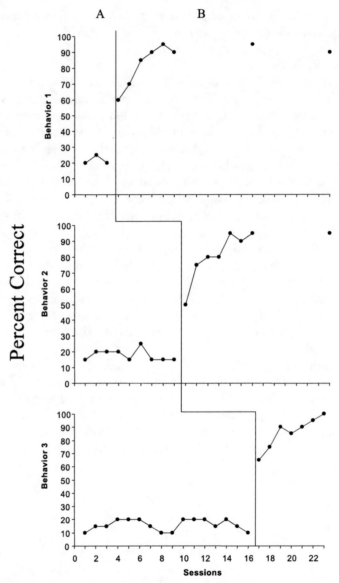

Figure 6.2 Intra-subject replication with multiple baseline design across behaviors.

Direct Inter-Subject Replication

Inter-subject direct replication, as with intra-subject direct replication, refers to one investigator repeating the experimental effect in the same study, however, while intra-subject direct replication refers to repeating the effect with the same participant, inter-subject direct replication refers to *repeating the experimental effect with different participants*. The importance of inter-subject replication was concisely stated by Sidman (1960) when he wrote, "When an experiment is performed with a single organism as the subject, intersubject replication is often demanded on the grounds that the original subject may have been a 'freak'," and he went on to write, "The purpose of intersubject replication is to determine whether uncontrolled and/or unknown variables might be powerful enough to prevent successful replication" (p. 74). It is important to realize that the level of confidence you can have in a study, yours or others', is limited with only one participant. Although "N = 1" studies appear in refereed research journals, such as the *Journal of Applied Behavior Analysis*, findings of these studies must be accepted with caution since the generality of their findings across other individuals and conditions has not been established. A common reason for the publication of single-participant studies is that they frequently address novel interventions or unusual behaviors that journal editors and editorial boards believe warrant dissemination with the hope of stimulating others to attempt a replication. Although a study with only one participant is acceptable under some circumstances, it is recommended that you start your investigation with a minimum of three participants regardless of the single subject research design chosen.

Figure 6.3 presents three graphic displays that illustrate inter-subject replication with an A-B-A-B design, multiple baseline design across behaviors, and multiple baseline design across participants, respectively. In Figure 6.3 the effectiveness of the independent variable is repeated across Participant 1, Participant 2, and Participant 3 in the same study with the same investigator. Figure 6.4 illustrates how inter-subject replication is addressed when using a multiple baseline (or multiple probe) design across behaviors. The effect of the independent variable on the dependent variable is repeated across each of the three participants. As with studies that employ an A-B-A-B design, intra-subject and inter-subject replications are addressed by repeating the effectiveness of the intervention with each participant and across participants. In the case of Figure 6.3's A-B-A-B design, intervention B shows its impact on the dependent variable six times (two demonstrations × three participants), while Figure 6.4 shows nine demonstrations of intervention B effectiveness. Generally speaking, two demonstrations of effectiveness with each participant (intra-subject replication), and three demonstrations across participants (inter-subject replication) is considered sufficient to consider the findings having

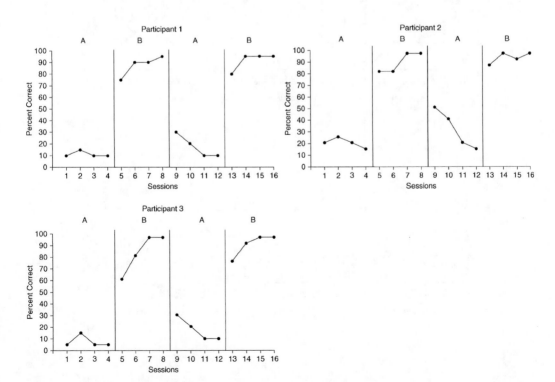

Figure 6.3 Inter-subject replication with A-B-A-B design, three participants.

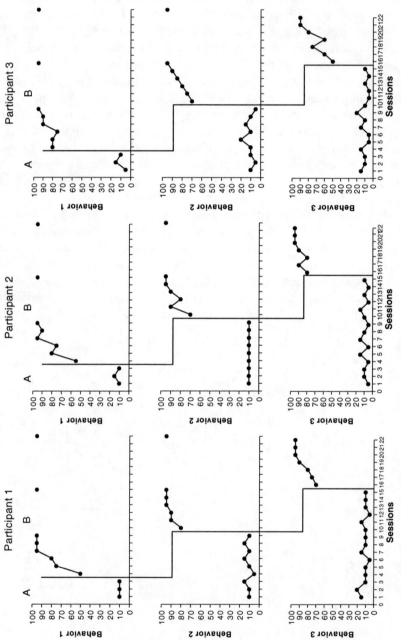

Figure 6.4 Inter-subject replication with multiple baseline design across behaviors and participants.

reliability and, to the extent to which participants differ, generality. As will be discussed, the generality of findings is primarily established through systematic replication.

Figure 6.5 illustrates a multiple baseline design across participants. Unlike the A-B-A-B design and multiple baseline (or multiple probe) design across participants, intra-subject

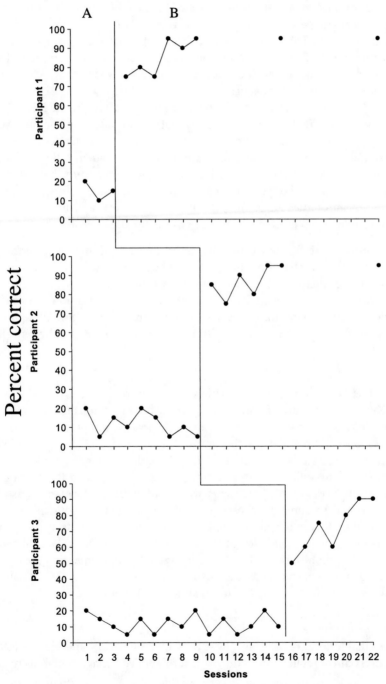

Figure 6.5 Inter-subject replication with multiple baseline design across participants.

replication is not addressed. As will be discussed further in Chapter 11, the demonstration of experimental control (reliability of effect) and the generality of the findings with this design rests with the number of successful inter-subject replications out of the number attempted, and similarity in the data patterns (level and trend) across participants. Many, if not most, behavioral researchers would consider a multiple baseline design across participants a "weaker" evaluation and demonstration of experimental control compared to a multiple baseline design across behaviors or an A-B-A-B design because of the lack of intra-subject replication. From a strictly numerical perspective, Figure 6.5 illustrates that with the same number of study participants as shown in Figure 6.3 and 6.4, three, there are only three demonstrations of independent-variable effectiveness, and for that reason I recommend that more than the minimum number of participants be included in your study when using a multiple baseline (or multiple probe) design across participants.

Sidman (1960) discusses a variation of inter-subject replication that he labels "inter-group" replication. Inter-group replication refers to repeating the effects of an intervention with different groups of individuals by comparing measures of central tendency (mean, median, mode). As with any comparison using measures of central tendency, the findings will both underestimate and overestimate the effectiveness of the intervention by not reporting the individual data of "outliers," i.e., participants who perform considerably worse or considerably better than the mean or median of the group. In this context, and in contrast to an inter-subject replication in which individual data are reported, Sidman writes:

> As a criterion of reliability and generality, intersubject replication is a more powerful tool than intergroup replication. Intergroup replication provides an indicator of reliability insofar as it demonstrates that changes in central tendency for a group can be repeated. With respect to generality, however, intergroup replication does not answer the question of how many individuals the data actually represent. With intersubject replication, on the other hand, each additional experiment increases the representativeness of the findings.
>
> (p. 75)

In light of this limitation associated with inter-group replication, behavior analysts who study the behavior of groups of individuals, and who make research decisions based on group performance rather than each individual's performance, will present, analyze, and report individual data on each member of the group. Stinson, Gast, Wolery, and Collins (1991) exemplified this in their study of observational and incidental learning by four students with moderate intellectual disabilities. They presented one graph in which the mean performance of the group was plotted, and four graphs in which individual performance was plotted. Two tables were also used to summarize each individual's acquisition of incidental and observational information. It is important to remember, if research decisions are being made based on some measure of central tendency of the group, it is the group's data that should "take center stage" and be graphically displayed and analyzed. By supplementing these primary data with each individual's data, you allow readers to independently analyze the data and draw their own conclusions regarding the extent of inter-subject replication.

Direct Replication Guidelines
The guidelines that follow are based on those presented by Barlow and Hersen (1984, p. 346), since they address direct replication in the context of applied behavior analysis research.

1. Investigator(s), setting(s), material(s), instructional arrangement(s), format(s), etc.

should remain constant across replication attempts with the same participant and across participants in the same study.

2. Dependent variable (target behavior and measure) should be similar across participants, but it need not be identical. For example, in a study in which you want to evaluate the effectiveness of a system of least prompts (SLP) procedure to teach chain-task skills to three children with moderate intellectual disabilities, you may identify three different chain-task skills for each of the three students. The SLP procedure must be the same across students and behaviors until the ineffectiveness of the original procedure occurs, at which time you may modify the original procedure. In the case of a study that addresses aberrant behaviors, it is recommended that behaviors be topographically similar, though they need not be identical, and are maintained by the same function (attention seeking, tangible item seeking, escape, automatic reinforcement), as identified through a Functional Behavior Analysis (FBA). The independent variable should be the same across behaviors and participants until failure ensues.

3. Participants should be similar in chronological age, cognitive functioning, sensory abilities, etc. It is generally believed that replication failures are more likely when there are large differences between participants. Birnbrauer (1980) and Wolery and Ezell (1993) address this notion of individual characteristics (status variables) and their importance, or lack of importance, in predicting and evaluating when an intervention is likely to be effective. The topic of participant descriptions and matching study participants on the basis of status variables will be addressed later in this chapter. Suffice it to say here, that in educational and clinical research, the pool of possible study participants will likely be based on your teaching or clinical assignment. That is, you will likely be working with individuals within a certain age range, cognitive level, etc., and it will be these individuals with whom you will conduct your study. As discussed in Chapter 4, it is important that you identify and report the similarities and differences between participants.

4. Independent variable should be the same across participants until progress toward the therapeutic or instructional objective stalls, at which time you may choose to modify the original intervention or replace it with a new intervention. Modification is generally preferred since you may be able to identify a procedural variation that will apply to other individuals in which the original intervention was ineffective.

5. Three direct replications are generally considered the minimum acceptable number of direct replications within the same study. As previously noted, three inter-subject replications are all that is possible when employing a multiple baseline (or multiple probe) design across participants when only three participants are included in the study. When employing other single subject designs, three successful inter-subject (or inter-group) replications are considered the minimum acceptable before moving on to a systematic replication attempt. Variables you should consider in determining whether three replications are an adequate number include: (a) baseline data stability; (b) consistency of effect with related findings; (c) magnitude of effect; and (d) adequacy of controlling threats to internal validity.

Mixed results will require additional replication attempts.

Clinical Replication

Hersen and Barlow (1976) introduced a third type of replication that they called "clinical replication," a form of direct replication, in which direct replication guidelines are followed. Clinical replication, as defined by Hersen and Barlow, refers to the administration of a treatment package containing two or more distinct treatment procedures by the same investigator or group of investigators . . . administered in a specific setting to a series of clients presenting similar combinations of multiple behavioral and emotional problems, which usually cluster together.

(1976, p. 336)

They refer to this as an advanced process, the end of years of research in "technique building." Their context was the clinical setting and their participants, individuals with many types of "emotional" and behavioral problems, thus the use of the term clinical, rather than educational, in their labeling this type of replication. Within this context we can observe their view of the scientific process, as it relates to the field of clinical psychology. It is a three-stage process. First, a researcher working with a series of clients with a similar problem establishes that an intervention produces behavior change. This is direct replication. Next, in clinical replications the researcher (and associates), combining techniques, demonstrates the effectiveness of an intervention package with participants who demonstrate similar clusters of problem behaviors, for example, children with autism. The outcome of this long-term process is an empirically verified intervention program (package): a product, in the broad sense, that may be "tested" by others in systematic replications. The outcome of the whole process would be an effective intervention package that "works" with a range of individuals within the target population. This goal is different from replication as Sidman (1960) described it, in regard to the scientific process. It is not, however, any different from the goal of education, which is to build the most effective and efficient instructional program that incorporates "distinct procedures" (e.g., specific attentional cues/responses, instructional pace, response prompting procedure, positive reinforcement) that have been individually researched and shown to be effective through a series of systematic replication studies. Much of applied research today, whether clinical or educational in nature, is the study of a treatment or educational package. Although it is ideal to change only one variable at a time when moving from one experimental condition to the next (e.g., baseline to intervention), research conducted in community settings (schools, mental health clinics, therapeutic recreation programs) frequently investigate the effectiveness of intervention packages. In such cases, at minimum, it is the responsibility of the applied researcher to identify and report all differences, procedural and otherwise, between experimental conditions. Only through such disclosure will it be possible to identify those variables that may have contributed to observed behavior changes. As discussed in Chapter 12, there are single subject research designs that can be used to evaluate the relative contribution, if any, of intervention package components.

Systematic Replication

Sidman (1960, p. 111) notes that the fundamental dictum of science is that all research "subjects" be treated alike except for the independent variable; however, if adhered to, this rule would strangle "systematic replication as a primary method for establishing reliability and generality." He explains,

> If the psychologist's experience has given him confidence in his techniques, he will choose systematic replication rather than direct replication as his tool for establishing reliability. Instead of simply repeating the experiment, he will use the data he has collected as a basis for performing new experiments and obtaining additional related data.

He continues, "systematic replication demonstrates that the finding . . . can be observed under conditions different from those prevailing in the original experiment," and suggests that the experimenter's judgment (history) will dictate how far he can move from the original experiment. Systematic replication is a gamble, which, if successful, "will buy reliability, generality, and additional information" (p. 112).

What constitutes a systematic replication in applied research? When a researcher carries out a planned series of studies that incorporate systematic changes from one study to the next and identifies them as a replication series, that clearly is systematic replication. If a researcher tries another researcher's procedure and states his intent to replicate, that is another instance. Suppose that a researcher initiates a study based on current findings in an area, such as time-delay transfer of stimulus-control procedure, and develops an intervention that contains several elements of existing procedures. Is this an instance of systematic replication? It is at this point that the definition of systematic replication is in the mind of the beholder. Suppose the researcher combines elements of three time-delay studies as a foundation for a new intervention. Then nothing is the same; we have a different researcher, different study participants, a different environment, and a different intervention. Some researchers may not consider this an instance of systematic replication. It might be called "doing research in an interesting area," and while there may be a link to previous research, there is no single common element. The situation is different if the researcher (a) sets out to replicate; (b) states an intention to replicate; (c) contacts the researcher whose work she wishes to replicate in order to verify correspondence with a published procedure; (d) carries out the study; and then (e) reports results that can be evaluated in relation to the original work. This is a more restricted definition than what Sidman offers. However, in the experimental laboratory serendipity plays a larger part than it does in educational and clinical settings. For while the basic researcher approaches a problem with the question "What will happen if . . .?" the applied researcher, especially in classroom and therapy environments, will approach the problem of behavior change with the question, "How can I make X work?" or, as noted, "How can I do X better?", or, "If X worked for someone else, how can I produce a more powerful effect?"

Systematic replication was defined by Hersen and Barlow (1976, p. 339) as "any attempt to replicate findings from a direct replication series, varying settings, behavior change agents, behavior disorders, or any combination thereof." As pointed out by Tawney and Gast (1984), this definition presents some problems as it relates to their use of the word "series," in that their definition requires that systematic replication follow from a series of direct-replication studies. This qualification, however, places a severe limitation on the definition, i.e., if systematic observation can only follow from a direct-replication study, what is the status of studies designed to replicate another researcher's single study—one that has shown interesting and promising results? This restriction notwithstanding, the phrase "any attempt to replicate" is, at the same time, perhaps too broad. To illustrate, Hersen and Barlow (1976) presented a table of systematic-replication studies in the reinforcement of children's differential attention (pp. 346–349). These 55 studies were conducted by many investigators and were reported from 1959 through 1972. It is doubtful that these studies meet Hersen and Barlow's definition of systematic replication. Whether, collectively, they are systematic replication is a matter of personal opinion. Perhaps Jones' (1978) analysis of Hersen and Barlow (1976) will clarify the point.

Replication is clearly a canon of applied behavioral science, and is discussed frequently, but executed less frequently. Despite the exemplar series of studies described by Hersen and Barlow as illustrative of replications in applied behavior analysis, this reviewer is concerned that replications may be labeled as such, but in fact not be replications. Absolutely pure replication probably happens seldom, if ever. Pure replication would require a point-by-point duplication of a research design, varying nothing except the time the study was conducted. Such replication is considered trivial by most researchers and probably unpublishable as well. When behavioral interventions lead to large and dramatic effects, and there is no question about the experimental control demonstrated in the study, then such pure replication is trivial. But, when researchers change procedures (the inherent flexibility of single-case designs), plan to use the technique with different kinds of subjects in different settings, or anticipate changing any salient aspect of the design, then pure replication, of course, is impossible. Replication then becomes more a matter of repeating the work with systematic modifications. Modified procedures, subject populations, measurement systems, etc., are tested to see if comparable results occur. The value of replication in single-case experimentation occurs when there is a substantial accumulation of parallel or convergent findings from a set of similar, but not identical, procedures, techniques, measurement devices, subject samples, etc. In the end, convergence among results from many such replications determines the generality of findings. This is the big goal to be achieved by the field of applied behavior analysis.

(p. 313)

Suffice it to say, systematic replication, as discussed by applied researchers today, is more broadly defined than the definition offered by Hersen and Barlow (1976), in that (a) a systematic replication attempt may follow a single study, and (b) variations (i.e., systematic modifications) from the original study or studies are included in the definition and, in fact, are encouraged as means for extending the generality of experimental findings. On the topic of systematic replication Tawney and Gast (1984) wrote,

systematic replication, as applied to research conducted in educational settings, is an attempt by a researcher to repeat his own procedure, employing variations in the procedure, with the same or different participants. Or, it is a series of planned experiments, conducted by one researcher that utilizes the same basic procedure, but systematically varies it based on results of the first experiments. Or, it is an attempt by a researcher to reproduce the published findings of others, adhering closely to the original procedure.

(pp. 97–98)

In writing this we considered our definition to reflect the reality that in classroom-based research, as in clinical research, very little is the same from day to day, and from study to study. It focuses on the goal of the researcher to repeat a procedure that has been successful (or at least seems promising). Or, viewed from the perspective of the teacher-researcher, "If intervention X has been used effectively with students like mine, will it work with my students?" By asking such a question you will address the three purposes or goals of systematic replication: (a) demonstrate reliability of effect; (b) extend generality of findings; or (c) identify exceptions. Whatever the outcome of a systematic-replication attempt, our understanding of the phenomenon being studied has been enhanced.

Failure to replicate can lead, and has led, to the discovery of limitations of current interventions and the discovery of new interventions. Regardless of whether a failure to replicate occurs within a direct or systematic replication attempt, the failure should "spur further research rather than lead to a single rejection of the original data" (Sidman, 1960, p. 74). "Science progresses by integrating, and not by throwing out, seemingly discrepant data" (Sidman, 1960, p. 83). In this regard, as an applied researcher, your responsibility is to identify modifications to the original intervention, or identify an alternative intervention, that will be successful and beneficial to the participant. It is not acceptable to simply note that there was a failure to replicate and move on. Baer et al. (1968), in their description of applied behavior analysis, were clear in assigning behavior analysts the responsibility of ensuring that study participants, or society, benefit from research involvement. Thus, after a failure of an intervention to bring about the desired and expected therapeutic behavior change, the appropriate question you should ask is, "What modification can I make to the original intervention, to make it successful?", or, "What other intervention can I employ to bring about the desired therapeutic behavior change?" Failures should stimulate interest in why the failure occurred and what can be done to bring about success. Modification of the original intervention is advised as the first course of action, rather than abandoning the original intervention and replacing it with a new and different intervention. The likelihood of your making the correct decision will be directly dependent on your familiarity with the research literature.

Systematic Replication Guidelines
Different applied researchers may put forward slightly different definitions of systematic replication (e.g., Barlow & Hersen, 1984; Hersen & Barlow, 1976; Jones, 1978; Tawney & Gast, 1984), however, general guidelines on when and how to proceed with a systematic replication attempt are quite similar.

1. Begin a systematic-replication study when reliability of effect has been established through a direct-replication study or series of studies. It does not matter whether the replication attempt follows a single study by one researcher or several studies conducted by several researchers over a number of years. The important factor in deciding when to initiate a systematic replication of an earlier study is the belief that threats to internal validity in the original study were evaluated and controlled, and the findings are accurate (reliable) and true (valid).

2. Identify and report the differences between the systematic-replication attempt and the original study or studies. In the case of a replication attempt following a series of studies it is important to identify the number and types of differences (researcher or research team, participants, variations in the independent variable, dependent measures, experimental design, etc.). Only through reporting these differences will potential reasons for a failure to replicate be identified and subsequently studied, and the extent to which earlier findings generalize. It is important to remember that generalization is not an "all or none" phenomenon, but a matter of degree across different variables. It is your responsibility to identify and report these variables after a successful systematic replication attempt.

3. After a failure to replicate, first modify the original intervention, and if necessary employ a different intervention to bring about the desired therapeutic or educational effect. Much is learned by failures to replicate if we can identify the cause of the failure and identify modifications or alternatives to the original independent variable. Surely one participant's failure to respond as expected is not so unique that other individuals won't respond in a similar fashion? Isn't that what is special about special education and clinical practice . . . interest in identifying procedural adaptations, accommodations, and alternatives to that which is considered the norm?

4. Systematic replication attempts are never over. In addition to strengthening the reliability and generality of findings, "systematic replication is essentially a search for exceptions" (Barlow & Hersen, 1984, p. 364), thus there is no predetermined time to stop, regardless of the number of studies that have successfully demonstrated the reliability and generality of effect. In Sidman's (1960) words, "a negative instance may just be around the corner" (p. 132).

External Validity and Single Subject Research

Generality of Findings: Group vs. Single Subject Research Methodology

A common criticism directed at single subject research methodology has always been that findings cannot generalize beyond the individual . . . there simply are too few participants in studies that employ single subject research designs. By contrast, group research methodology, which randomly assigns a large number of participants to two or more groups, one that serves as a control group and the other(s) experimental comparison group(s), is considered the "gold standard" for establishing external validity. Few would argue that findings generated by large group research generalize better to other large unstudied groups if individuals in the unstudied group are "similar" to participants in the studied group. Wolery and Ezell (1993) point out, "The more similar the two populations, the greater the likelihood of accurate generalizations, and thus the greater the likelihood that findings will be replicated" (p. 644). At first glance these positions regarding research methodology and external validity seem to make sense; however, what if your interest is generalizing findings to a specific individual, rather than a group of individuals? Remember, in large group research the data reported are measures of central tendency, thus there are always individuals within the group who perform better and worse than the average participant. Seldom do these studies provide detailed descriptions of individual participants nor do they often report how individual participants respond to the independent variable. Their focus is on the group, not the individual. Sidman (1960) was clear in his position regarding the importance of reporting individual participant data and the reliability and generality of findings between inter-subject and inter-group replication when he wrote: "Indeed replication of an experiment with two subjects establishes greater generality for data among the individuals of a population than does replication with two groups of subjects whose individual data have been combined" (p. 75). It is also important to understand that seldom are large-N studies repeated, due in part to their cost in time and funds. This means that it is rare that different researchers, or research teams, attempt replications of large group experimental studies, which in and of itself can and does raise concerns, since some investigators may have a vested interest in the outcomes. A final point regarding limitations of large group research is that intra-subject replications are seldom attempted. In a typical group-research investigation, individuals in the experimental group are exposed to the independent variable with no attempt to repeat its effect by either staggering its introduction across behaviors, or withdrawing and then reintroducing it to see if the effect can be repeated. Most behavior analysts would agree that intra-subject replication is a more convincing demonstration of reliability than inter-subject replication, a design characteristic and limitation of many, if not most, large-group research designs, as well as some single subject research designs, most notably multiple baseline design across participants.

Single subject research methodology has a long history in which the primary focus has been on the individual. Even when the focus of a research investigation has been on changing the behavior of a group, individual data of group members have been reported. There is a clear understanding among behavioral researchers that if your interest is in designing and implementing effective interventions for individuals, many of whom differ from the norm, it is imperative that you study the behavior of individuals. As previously discussed, direct intra-subject replication is the primary means by which single subject researchers establish the reliability of their findings and, to the extent that study participants differ, address the generality of their findings through direct inter-subject replication. External validity in single subject research is primarily accomplished through a series of systematic replication studies in which investigators, participants, settings, etc. differ from previous studies and yield the same outcome. The question for you, as you attempt a systematic replication, or are considering using an intervention with a student or client is, "What individual characteristics or variables should I consider in determining the likelihood that the intervention under consideration will be successful?"

There are several variables that you may consider when attempting to determine the similarities and differences between research and "service" populations, the most common being status variables. Status variables are participant descriptors including gender, chronological age, ethnicity, intelligence quotient, academic achievement level, grade level, educational placement, and geographic location; descriptors that were considered "minimal" by the Research Committee of the Council for Learning Disabilities (Rosenberg et al., 1992), when conducting studies with fewer than 10 participants. This type of descriptive information is common and expected in research reports, but is it sufficient for determining whether an intervention will generalize to an individual with similar status-variable descriptors?

Wolery and Ezell (1993) hold that status variables are only "part of the picture" for determining external validity, "that failure to replicate in subsequent research or in clinical and educational settings is undoubtedly related to many other variables than the precise description of subject characteristics" (p. 643). Through a brief review of constant time delay (CTD) research they concluded that in spite of consistent findings across several studies, procedural modifications were necessary even though participants "were nearly identical on status variables" and that the procedure's success was independent of status variables and was likely due to students' "different learning histories" (p. 644). You need only look at published literature reviews and meta-analyses to appreciate the success of single subject research predicting and confirming the reliability and generality of findings to other individuals. But if status variables are not the best predictors of generalization, what variables are?

Behavior analysts support the position that external validity is directly related to baseline condition performance, that predicting the effectiveness of an intervention will be determined by the similarities in response patterns by two individuals under the same or similar environmental conditions. Birnbrauer (1981) summarized the position when he wrote,

> we should look for similarities in baseline conditions, the functional relations that appear to be operative during those pretreatment conditions, and the functional changes that implementation of treatment entailed for previous subjects. These are the keys to generalizing from single-subject studies.
>
> (p. 129)

This is not to say you should discount status variables when writing your research report. As discussed in Chapter 4, detailed participant descriptions are important, including reporting on status variables, but when it comes to predicting generalization success, emphasis should be placed on what Wolery and Ezell (1993, p. 645) termed functional variables, i.e., "the effects of specific environmental-subject interactions." Specifically, you should describe the characteristics of the baseline condition (time of day, response contingencies, number of opportunities to respond, etc.) and the behavior patterns generated by your study participants to predict, with greater confidence, whether your intervention will or will not be effective. Prediction of inter-subject replication success, be it a direct or systematic replication attempt, is more about your attention to baseline condition data, experience with the independent variable, and visual-analysis skills, than it is about matching participants on status variables.

Generalization Continuum

Generalization is not an all-or-nothing proposition. The generality of experimental findings are viewed along a continuum in which the number of variables that change between studies will determine the extent of generalization. Figure 6.6 illustrates the point. At the far left of the horizontal line is direct inter-subject replication. As discussed, few if any condition variables are changed between participants in the same investigation, with the same investigator, conducted during the same time period. Study participants are different, but they tend to be similar in age, cognitive abilities, entry skills, need for behavioral intervention, etc. On status variables they look quite similar. If you will, generalization is "close-in" and, therefore, limited to the degree to which participants differ, which often is not very much. At the far right of the horizontal line is systematic replication with a multitude of differences from previous studies. Systematic replication, at the extreme, has a different investigator, different research site, different types of participants based on status variables, different target behavior or class of behaviors, different dependent measure(s), different single subject experimental design, variation of the independent variable, etc. The differences are many; the similarities are few. Except for the independent variable being "similar" to independent variables studied in previous investigations, it is close to being considered a novel study. At these two extremes the risks of replication are quite different, direct inter-subject replications are much less of a gamble than are systematic replications in which numerous variables are changed from earlier studies. Most replication attempts, however, fall somewhere between these two extremes. The number and types of variables that are changed between separate studies will determine the degree of risk and the extent of generalization. For this reason it is imperative that researchers delineate each and every difference between their study and those that preceded it.

"N of 1" Single Subject Studies and Their Contribution

In some of the most prestigious applied behavior analysis journals, such as the *Journal of Applied Behavior Analysis*, single subject research investigations are published that have been conducted with only one participant. They are truly "N = 1" studies and, thus, in and of themselves contribute little to the external validity of the independent variable under study. Their "stand-alone" contribution is a quantitative evaluation and demonstration of intervention effectiveness, in which threats to internal validity have been adequately evaluated and controlled

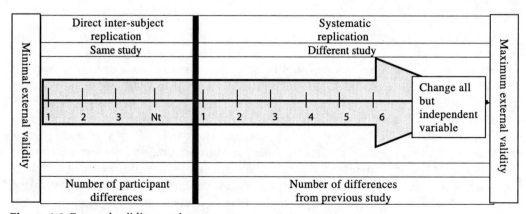

Figure 6.6 External validity continuum.

through direct intra-subject replication, thereby lending support for the intervention that addressed a novel or rare challenging behavior. Through the publication of such research reports, systematic replication is encouraged, which in turn will add to our understanding of the reliability and generality of the intervention. However, as a consumer of research, you should proceed with caution before implementing an intervention reported on only one individual with your client or student. As an applied researcher you are encouraged to attempt to replicate the effect. It is important not to discount the findings of these studies but you need to understand their limitations and need for replication to build confidence in their findings. On this topic, Sidman (1960) wrote:

> Often, especially in a young science, an experiment is performed for the sole purpose of determining if it is possible to obtain a certain phenomenon. In such an experiment, demonstration of the phenomenon in one organism, with reliability established by intrasubject replication is all that is necessary.
>
> (p. 93)

Such studies are the impetus for further research.

General Recommendations for Starting a Systematic Replication

If you wish to initiate a systematic replication attempt, here are few suggestions on how to proceed:

1. Read those studies that relate to your research interest(s) or question(s). Look for recently published literature reviews and meta-analyses on your topic as they may provide you with a comprehensive reference list of empirical investigations that addressed the same or similar research question(s).
2. Develop two tables, one that identifies similar elements, and the other dissimilar elements, across studies you identified.
3. Analyze the data entered in these tables and identify the similarities and differences between studies.
4. Read and list researchers' suggestions for future research on the topic. These are commonly found in the discussion section of research reports.
5. Write your research question(s), if you haven't already, taking into account researchers' suggestions and the practical constraints of your setting (e.g., access to participants, daily schedule, availability to materials and equipment, control of contingencies).
6. Identify and report the specific differences between your proposed study and those which will have preceded it.

Once your study begins you should note whether the effects of the independent variable were replicated with all or only some participants. Regardless of whether your replication attempt was a "success" or "failure," your ability to identify the differences between participants who responded positively to the intervention, and those who did not, is important. In cases of "failure to replicate," your ability to implement a successful variation of, or alternative to the original intervention, will advance our understanding of the reliability, generality, and limitations of the intervention. This contribution is further expanded when you analyze your findings, including the functional and status variables associated with intervention success or failure, with participants in earlier studies.

Summary

Replication is a critical part of the scientific process. Through direct intra-subject replication the reliability of research findings is established. By including multiple participants in the same study an investigator extends the generality of findings to the extent that participants differ on both status variables and functional variables. In single subject research the generality of research findings is primarily established through systematic replication, a series of studies conducted over several years in which the investigator, target population, behavior, dependent measures, etc. differ from earlier studies. Systematic replication is ongoing, never over, as a failure to replicate may be just around the corner. When a "failure to replicate" is evidenced and an exception to previous research findings identified, the limitation of the intervention is revealed. Applied behavioral researchers approach such failures as a challenge and attempt to identify their cause, as well as identify modifications to the original intervention that will bring about the desired behavior change. Through the replication process the science of human behavior is advanced and our ability to design effective and efficient instructional and treatment programs enhanced.

References

American Psychological Association. (2001). *Publication manual of the American Psychological Association* (5th ed.) Washington, DC: Author.

Baer, D. M., Wolf, M. M., & Risley, T. R. (1968). Some current dimensions of applied behavior analysis. *Journal of Applied Behavior Analysis, 1*, 91–97.

Barlow, D. H., & Hersen, M. (1984). *Single case experimental designs: Strategies for studying behavior change* (2nd ed.). New York: Pergamon Press.

Birnbrauer, J. S. (1981). External validity and experimental investigation of individual behavior. *Analysis and Intervention in Developmental Disabilities, 1*, 117–132.

Cooper, J. O., Heron, T. E., & Heward, W. L. (2007). *Applied behavior analysis* (2nd ed.). Upper Saddle River, NJ: Prentice-Hall, Inc.

Hersen, M., & Barlow, D. H. (1976). *Single case experimental designs: Strategies for studying behavior change.* New York: Pergamon Press.

Jones, R. R. (1978). Invited book review of Single-case experimental designs: Strategies for studying behavior change by Michel Hersen and David H. Barlow. *Journal of Applied Behavior Analysis, 11*, 309–313.

Merriam-Webster's Online Dictionary. (2008). Retrieved April 7, 2008, from www.merriam-webster.com.

Rosenberg, M. S., Bott, D., Majsterek, D., Chiang, B., Bartland, D., Wesson, C., Graham, S., et. al. (1992). Minimum standards for the description of participants in learning disabilities research. *Learning Disabilities Quarterly, 15*, 65–70.

Sidman, M. (1960). *Tactics of scientific research—Evaluating experimental data in psychology.* New York: Basic Books.

Stinson, D.M., Gast, D. L., Wolery, M., & Collins, B. (1991). Acquisition of nontargeted information during small group instruction. *Exceptionality, 2*, 65–80.

Tawney, J. W., & Gast, D., L. (1984). *Single subject research in special education.* Columbus, OH: Charles E. Merrill.

Wolery, M., & Ezell, H. (1993). Subject descriptions and single subject research. *Journal of Learning Disabilities, 26*, 642–647.

7

Dependent Measures and Measurement Procedures

Kevin Ayres and David L. Gast

Having considered general issues of concern to the applied researcher, we now progress to specific steps for measuring behavior and conducting applied behavior research. In this chapter we describe (1) how to select a dependent measure; (2) systematic recording procedures; (3) design of data sheets; and (4) procedures for insuring reliable measurement. Having acquired this information you should be ready to conduct single subject design research in classroom and clinical settings.

Parameters of Measurement

The applied researcher must make two decisions before collecting data on a research partici-pant's behavior. First, you must decide (1) what characteristic or dimension of the target behavior should be measured, and (2) what method of recording should be used to measure this aspect of behavior.

The first decision relates to the selection of a dependent variable, or dependent measure. White (1971) defined a *dependent variable* as "a variable which changes as a function of a change in another variable" (p. 186). Dependent measures frequently used by applied researchers include *number* (e.g., number of task-analysis steps completed independently); *frequency* or *rate* (e.g., number of words read correctly per minute); *percent correct* (e.g., percent of addition problems performed correctly per page); *duration* (e.g., number of seconds a child maintains his head control at midline); and *latency* (e.g., number of seconds it takes a student to return to his desk after instructed to do so by the teacher). Other measures also are available but are less frequently reported (e.g., *magnitude, inter-response time, intensity, trials to criterion, errors to criterion*).

The type of dependent measure selected will depend on the target behavior and the intervention objective. For example, an appropriate objective for a student who reads accur-ately but slowly would be to increase the number of words accurately read per minute. For another student, who reads at an acceptable rate but who emits a large number of errors, an appropriate objective would be to increase the percentage of words she reads correctly. In selecting a dependent measure it is important to base the decision on the intended purpose of the instructional or treatment program (e.g., to increase rate, to increase accuracy, or both).

The "other variable" referred to in White's (1971) definition of dependent variable is known as the *independent variable*. The independent variable of an experimental investigation is a variable that is manipulated or observed by the researcher to determine its effect on the dependent variable. It is equivalent to the intervention, treatment, or instructional conditions under which a behavior is repeatedly measured and evaluated.

Selecting a Dependent Measure

The dependent variable selected will relate directly to the research question and the objective of the intervention. Therefore, it is imperative that you decide what it is about the behavior under investigation that you wish to change, i.e., frequency, duration, accuracy, and/or latency. The decision as to whether a behavior is occurring at an acceptable or unacceptable level should not be made arbitrarily; it is a decision that should be based on reliable data. Contrary to what some may believe, educators, clinicians, and applied researchers do not base their decisions to intervene on subjective evaluations and without conferring with "significant others" (parents, other teachers, ancillary personnel). All decisions, particularly those that focus on decreasing the frequency of a behavior, require an objective (empirical) appraisal of the behavior, in addition to parent consultation. To accomplish this, applied researchers focus attention on that aspect of the target behavior of concern, and begin to systematically collect data to verify whether the concern is justified. Only after these initial measures are collected and analyzed is a decision made regarding what course of action to take. This decision is a collective one.

Table 7.1 summarizes the more frequent dependent measures used in applied research. Each of these measures is defined and exemplified in the remainder of this section.

Table 7.1 Summary of Dependent Measures

Dependent Measure	Definition	Considerations
1. Number	Simple count of the number of times a behavior or event occurs	1.1. Requires constant time across observational periods with free-operant behaviors
		1.2. Requires constant number of trials across sessions/days with teacher-paced instruction
2. Percent	Number of occurrences divided by the total number of opportunities for the behavior to occur multiplied by 100	2.1. Equalizes unequal number of opportunities to respond across sessions/days
		2.2. Easily understood
		2.3. Frequently used measure for accuracy
		2.4. Efficient means for summarizing large numbers of responses
		2.5. No reference to the time over which behavior was observed
		2.6. Generally, should be used only when there are 20 or more opportunities to respond
3. Rate	Number of occurrences divided by the number of time units (minutes or hours)	3.1. Converts behavior counts to a constant scale when opportunities to respond or observation time varies across sessions/days
		3.2. Reveals response proficiency as well as accuracy
		3.3. Reported as responses per minute or responses per hour
		3.4. Appropriate for behaviors measured under free-operant conditions
		3.5. Cumbersome to use with behaviors measured under teacher-paced conditions
4. Duration (total)	Amount of time behavior occurs during an observation period	4.1. Expressed as the percentage of time engaged in behavior
		4.2. Does not yield information about frequency or mean duration per occurrence
5. Duration per occurrence	Amount of time engaged in each episode of the behavior	5.1. Yields behavior frequency; mean duration per occurrence and total duration information
6. Latency	Elapsed time from the presentation of the S^D and the initiation of the behavior	6.1. Appropriate measure with compliance problem behaviors (long response latency)
		6.2. May yield information regarding high error rate when there is a short response latency
7. Magnitude	Response strength or force	7.1. Direct measure requires automated-quantitative instrumentation
		7.2. Indirect measure of magnitude possible by measuring effect response has on environment
8. Trials to criterion	Number of trials counted to reach criterion for each behavior	8.1. Yields information on concept formation (learning-to-learn phenomenon)
		8.2. Post hoc summary measure

Number

Number refers to a simple count of the number of times a behavior or event occurs during a constant time period. Number is an appropriate dependent measure only when the observation period during which data are collected is held constant from session to session, or day to day, or when a student has the same number of opportunities to respond on a teacher-paced activity. For example, if each day you read 20 words aloud which students are required to spell correctly within a 10-minute period, the number of words spelled correctly could be used as the dependent variable. In this example both the number of words to be spelled (i.e., opportunities to respond) and the time students have to spell the 20 words are held constant. When number is used to quantify a behavior under free-operant conditions where there is no ceiling or upper limit on the frequency of the behavior, number can be used if the observation period is held constant each day. For example, you could monitor and report the number of talk-outs per day provided the time period during which talk-outs are recorded is the same each day. Number has been used frequently in applied research that has studied free-operant social behaviors. For example, Marckel, Neef, and Ferreri (2006) reported the number of improvisational uses of the Picture Exchange Communication system by children with autism. Other researchers have used number to report on number of successful transitions by toddlers (Cote, Thompson, & McKerchar, 2005).

Throughout the applied-research literature the term *frequency* has been used interchangeably with *number* to refer to the number of times a target behavior occurs (e.g., Williams, Perez-Gonzalez, & Vogt, 2003; Ellis, Ala'i-Rosales, Glenn, Rosales-Ruiz, & Greenspoon, 2006; Singh et al., 2006). This substitution in terms is appropriate only when the observation period is constant across observation periods, for example, days. Generally, when the occurrences of a behavior are tallied it is preferable to use the phrasing "number of occurrences" rather than "frequency of occurrences" to avoid possible confusion with the term *rate*.

Percent

Percent data are perhaps the most frequent dependent measures used by teachers when conducting research. *Percent* refers to the number of times a behavior occurs per total number of opportunities for the behavior to occur, multiplied by 100 (e.g., number "correct" divided by the number of opportunities, multiplied by 100 = percentage of "correct" responses). It is a particularly useful measure when accuracy is of primary concern and when some permanent product is generated, as in the case of many academic instructional programs (e.g., percent of addition problems summed correctly on independent worksheets). Percent data also have been used to summarize the number of responses emitted over a series of constant "time-ruled" observation intervals, as when using an interval recording system:

Number of 10 s intervals during which a response occurred divided by the total number of observation intervals $\times$ 100 = Percentage of intervals the response occurred.

Percent data have several advantages over number and other types of dependent measures (Cooper, 1981; Gentry & Haring, 1976):

1. They convert unequal opportunities to respond across sessions or days to a common scale, thereby "equalizing" the number of opportunities to respond for purposes of data summation and evaluation.
2. They are an efficient means of summarizing large numbers of responses.

3. They are a simple way of summarizing overall performance on a graph or chart.
4. They are more familiar to people than other measures (e.g., rate, latency, magnitude) and, therefore, facilitate communication of performance.

Percent data, however, do have their disadvantages or limitations:

1. They make no reference to the time over which a behavior was observed, thus limiting what can be said about response proficiency.
2. They place upper and lower limits (i.e., 100% and 0%) on reporting data by not referring to the actual number of responses or opportunities to respond.
3. They can mask trends in the data by not revealing when a response occurs during a particular observation period.
4. They should not be used, generally speaking, when the total number of opportunities to respond is less than 20, in which case one change in the numerator will produce a greater than 5% change.

Rate

Rate has been referred to as the basic datum of science (Skinner, 1966). Synonymous with the term *frequency*, rate refers to the number of times a behavior occurs within a timed observation period. Unlike number, rate can serve as the dependent measure when a behavior is observed across variable time periods (e.g., Day 1, 10 min; Day 2, 7 min; Day 3, 12 min). The rate of a behavior is calculated by counting the number of times a behavior occurs and dividing the total number of occurrences by the total number of minutes (or hours) in the observation period.

A distinction has often been made between the terms *rate* and *frequency* based on the manner in which the data are reported. Rate data are commonly reported as the number of responses per minute or hour (White & Haring, 1980) and may be visually displayed on semilogarithmic graph paper as shown in Figure 7.1. Although semilogarithmic graph paper is frequently used to display rate data, equal-interval graph paper can be used (Hoch, McComas, Thompson, & Paone, 2002; Ingersoll & Gergans, 2007). Frequency data are typically reported as the number of responses per total observation period (i.e., data are not converted to responses per minute or hour) and are summarized on the more conventional equal-interval graph paper. It is important that when reporting frequency data in this manner that the observational period be help constant across days.

Rate is an appropriate dependent measure when it is important to know how often a behavior occurs. It is a particularly useful measure when the intervention focuses on academic and social behaviors under free-operant conditions. Though it may be used during experimenter- or teacher-paced activities, it can become a cumbersome process. If used with teacher-paced instruction (i.e., the teacher controls the presentation of materials, cues, prompts, and consequences), the teacher has to start the stopwatch after the task direction has been presented and stop the stopwatch after the student has responded. By starting and stopping the stopwatch on each trial, an accurate measure of student-response frequency can be attained. If this start and stop timing procedure were not employed, the time the teacher took to present task stimuli would be included in the total observation period, thereby affecting the response rate reported and reflecting teacher as well as student proficiency. In such instances the data would reflect changes in either the student's or teacher's rate of responding, or both. Controlled presentations by computer-based instruction, on the other hand, can automatically record a student's response latency and duration, thus allowing a more accurate summary of response rate. Beck, Jia, and

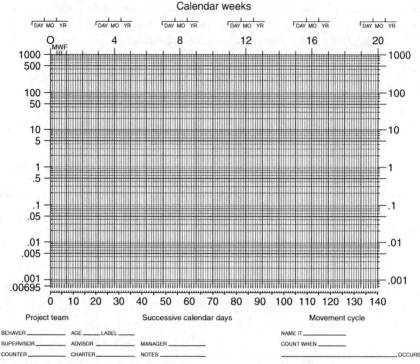

Figure 7.1 Semilogarithmic graph paper.

Mostow (2004), for example, report on the use of a computerized reading tutor that is able to measure inter-word response latencies as students are engaged in a reading-fluency program. These data were then reported with rate data to evaluate changes in student responding.

Another example of when rate may be of interest is when the instructional goal is to increase response fluency. If a student is working toward improving his automaticity with multiplication facts, he might be given a written test and told to accurately complete as many problems as he can in a specified amount of time. Burns (2005) reported number of "digits correct" per minute in an evaluation of incremental rehearsal as a method to increase fluency in single-digit multiplication problems. Another common academic example relates to reading fluency. Begeny, Daly, and Vallely (2006) reported number of words read correctly per minute by students when reading a passage. This allowed the researchers to evaluate how quickly and accurately students read passages of various lengths during two different treatment conditions.

Rate measures have several advantages (Eaton, 1978; Gentry & Haring, 1976; Haring, Liberty, & White, 1980):

1. They are extremely sensitive to behavior changes.
2. They convert behavior counts to a standard or constant scale (e.g., responses per minute), and when plotted on semilogarithmic graphs, they permit behavior comparison across different days and different activities when the amount of time to respond or the number of opportunities to respond varies.
3. They may be evaluated using "data decision" rules.

Rate data have two primary drawbacks. First, when the data are displayed visually on semilogarithmic graph paper, many people have difficulty analyzing the data because of their unfamiliarity with standard celeration charts. This disadvantage can be overcome by plotting rate data on the more conventional and familiar equal-interval line graph. The second disadvantage of frequency measures relates to their use during teacher-paced instruction, which is not recommended. To ensure an accurate measure of student behavior during teacher-controlled instructional activities it is necessary, and cumbersome, to measure only the actual amount of time the student has to respond. You are advised to use number or percent correct as the dependent measure on most teacher-paced activities. Researchers interested in using standard celeration charts should see Graf and Lindsley (2002) for more detailed information on their use.

Duration

The choice of duration as a dependent measure is appropriate when you are interested in knowing how long a behavior occurs once initiated. There are two types of duration measures: total duration and duration per occurrence. *Total duration* refers to the total amount of time a student is engaged in a behavior during the entire observation period. Data are expressed in either the percentage of time or number of minutes engaged in the behavior. Although appropriate in some instances, total duration typically is paired with some other measure (e.g., number or rate).

Unlike total duration, *duration per occurrence* provides data on both the frequency and the duration of a response (e.g., MacDonald et al., 2007). It is the preferred duration measure because it permits you to calculate the frequency of the behavior, the total duration of the behavior, as well as the range, mean, median, and mode duration of each episode of the behavior. This combination of frequency and duration measures yields a measure that is sometimes referred to as *intensity*. Through the use of the duration per occurrence measure both frequency and duration data can be obtained simultaneously. Both measures may prove helpful to you when deciding upon an intervention. For example, if you were concerned about one of your students who "appears" to be engaging in a considerable amount of off-task behavior (e.g., staring at the ceiling) but do not know whether this behavior is characterized by a high frequency and short duration or a low frequency and long duration, by employing a duration per occurrence measure you will be able to identify which of the behavior patterns best characterizes the student's off-task behavior. By having this information available you can then determine whether your intervention should focus on the frequency or duration of the student's off-task behavior. The more information you have on the target behavior, the more likely you are to design and implement an effective intervention. With this in mind, it is recommended that you record duration per occurrence rather than total duration.

Latency

The latency of a response refers to the amount of time it takes a person to begin a response once the task direction or cue has been presented. Latency is an appropriate dependent measure when a student is slow to initiate a response, as in the case of following teacher directions: "Go to your desk" or "Close your book." In addition to signaling a potential compliance problem, a latency measure can provide information regarding a student's understanding of a task's response requirements. A student with a long response latency may require additional instruction or modeling to clarify what response she is to make. In addition to long latencies, you should also be aware of students who have short latencies accompanied by high error rates. You might want to teach a student who manifests this behavior pattern to increase her response latency by requiring that she demonstrate an observing or specific attending response prior to emitting the terminal task response, for example, copying or calling the letters of a word before reading it; matching an object to a sample before naming it; repeating the directions before beginning the task (Wolery, Ault, Gast, Doyle, & Mills, 1990; Wolery, Cybriwsky, Gast, & Boyle-Gast, 1991).

Trials, Sessions, Time, and Errors to Criterion

Trials-to-criterion is a dependent measure that is particularly useful when teaching concepts and operations. It refers to the number of trials (or opportunities to respond) that a student takes to reach a predetermined criterion. Reporting the number of opportunities it takes to reach criterion over successive examples of a concept or operation provides you with valuable information regarding the student's forming a "learning set" (Reese & Lipsitt, 1970). Learning set, sometimes referred to as "learning to learn," is evident when, over successive examples of a concept, fewer trials are required to reach criterion. When a learner responds correctly to a novel example of a concept on the first trial, the learner is said to have learned that concept. Thus, instruction may cease on that concept and begin on another. In the case of motor imitation training, which is intended to teach a child to imitate an adult's model after the verbal direction, "do this," a learning-to-learn phenomenon would be demonstrated if with each new behavior modeled the child requires fewer trials to criterion. When the child can imitate a novel behavior in response to the adult's model, the child is said to have acquired a generalized motor imitation repertoire.

Trials-to-criterion, sessions-to-criterion, and direct instructional time-to-criterion are all appropriate measures to report when you want to gauge the efficiency of instruction. Counting how many trials, sessions, and minutes that are required before a student masters a skill allows you the opportunity to evaluate how quickly an effective intervention works. Further, it provides a measure that can be used to compare the efficiency of different interventions on the same types of dependent measures. Errors-to-criterion is another measure that is often reported when comparing the efficiency of two or more instructional procedures. This measure is important in identifying teaching strategies that may be effective but which generate a large number of errors that may not be tolerated by some learners. These data could be arranged in a table showing the number of sessions to criterion, number of errors to criterion, percentage of errors to criterion, direct instructional time/minutes to criterion (See Tables 8.2 and 8.3). It is important to remember that these measures provide a summative rather than formative evaluation of learner progress. For this reason it is advisable that some other dependent measure, such as percentage correct, be graphed and analyzed daily to guide instruction.

Magnitude

Magnitude, or intensity, infrequently used as dependent measures in applied research, refers to the force or strength of a response. Typically, when magnitude is used as a dependent measure, some automated-quantitative apparatus is required to accurately measure the force of a behavior. Such has been the case in behavior-management research designed to reduce bus or classroom noise levels (e.g., Greene, Bailey, & Barber, 1981; Wilson & Hopkins, 1973). Magnitude is one of many measures used in speech therapy (Shipley & McAfee, 2004). For example, Huber and Chandrasekaran (2006) used measures of magnitude in the form of sound pressure to evaluate the relation between sound production and different movements of the lip and jaw. Sapir, Spielman, Ramig, Story, and Fox (2007) also used a measure of loudness as a dependent measure in their evaluation of a treatment package for improving vowel articulation. In both of these cases, automated recording equipment was essential to collect accurate and reliable data.

In some cases, the magnitude of a response may be determined by evaluating the effect a response has on the environment. For example, muscle strength may be inferred by recording how much weight one can lift, how far one can throw a ball, or how far one can jump. Though an indirect measure of strength, the above measures correlate with more sophisticated automated-quantitative measurement procedures. In addition to these measures of magnitude, the force of a response may be determined as being acceptable or unacceptable according to some criterion included in an operational definition of a behavior. For example, you may define acceptable speech volume on the basis of an observer being able to hear and understand what a child says when positioned no less than 5 feet and no more than 20 feet from the child. As is the case with all dependent measures, the important factor in determining the adequacy of a measure is whether two independent observers can agree on the occurrence and nonoccurrence of a behavior (i.e., interobserver reliability). For clarity it is best to operationalize a response and state exactly what measure (e.g., distance, weight) is being used to infer response magnitude when a more sophisticated automated-quantitative apparatus is not being used. LaVigna and Willis (2005) suggested that magnitude needs greater consideration in applied research because "episodic severity" is a concern to practitioners but is infrequently considered when selecting dependent measures for analysis. In this case, they are referring to events like the severity of a child's tantrum behavior, recommending measures like duration or objective rating scales, to help capture the magnitude of target behavior.

Selecting a Measurement Procedure

To this point we have presented a general overview of the basic characteristics and parameters of measurement. The remainder of this chapter focuses on the process of systematically recording behavior. Three basic methods are used to measure and record behavior: (1) automated-quantitative recording; (2) direct measurement of permanent products; and (3) direct observational recording. Emphasis is given to those direct observational recording systems commonly used by teachers, therapists, and researchers who work in classroom, clinical, and community settings and that facilitate the reliable measurement of behavior.

Automated and Computer-Based Recording

Automated-quantitative recording, sometimes referred to as automatic recording, is the use of an automatic recording device in which an "organism's response activates an electrical or mechanical apparatus which in turn makes a record, automatically recording each response" (Hall, 1974, p. 1). Though primarily associated with controlled laboratory research, automated-quantitative recording has been used in classroom and clinical research. For example, Ayres and Langone (2002) and Ayres, Langone, Boon, and Norman (2006) used software to record student responses to functional math problems. Koscinski and Gast (1993) similarly used software to automatically record and deliver constant time-delay instruction of multiplication facts to students with learning disabilities. Automated-quantitative recording has the advantage of eliminating the error element associated with human observers. There is, however, no guarantee that these sometimes sophisticated apparatuses will always operate properly. Therefore, their accuracy and reliability require monitoring. Koscinski and Gast reported testing the software for "bugs" in the 3 weeks prior to their investigation by having another student, who was not participating in the study, use the program. This allowed a very realistic way to judge the fidelity of the program to the procedural protocol while also letting the researchers check for scoring reliability prior to beginning their investigation.

One common classroom application of automated recording relies on computers to collect data as students engage instructional programs. Students who have basic computer skills can interact directly with their computer as they progress through academic materials. Students with significant physical challenges can interact directly with computers through assistive technology devices (micro-switches). With the growing database supporting the efficacy of computer-based instruction there are more options available to researchers who are studying the impact of technology on student learning and, in many cases, researchers are able to rely on computer-based data collection. Reliance on the computer for data collection will not relieve you of the responsibility for ensuring the integrity of the data-collection procedures (as well as the delivery of instruction). Both of these factors should be considered when collecting reliability data on both the dependent and independent variables.

Beyond direct automated recording facilitated by a computer, other data-collection systems are becoming more widely available that allow the collection of a wide range of dependent measures on hand-held computers "in real time." Dixon (2003) published step-by-step instructions outlining how to create customized direct-observation software for PocketPCs using Microsoft Excel. Those unfamiliar with programming should not be intimidated by the process. Dixon's instructions are task analyzed and include screen captures of critical steps. When you have completed creating the small program in Excel, you are ready to collect real-time direct-observational data.

Most of these systems provide the researcher with customizable data-collection options that facilitate tracking student performance with simple key strokes. This type of data-collection tool is frequently available to run on both laptop as well as hand-held devices (e.g., Palm Pilot, PocketPC). By allowing real-time data collection, these devices can generate graphic displays immediately following data collection, allowing you to save time and make data-based decisions quickly.

Kahng and Iwata (1998, 2000) reviewed several systems that were on the market at the time of their writing, many of which have been updated. Commercially produced products also are available, but to review all current options on the market would quickly date this portion of the chapter; therefore we will describe two of the more common systems. One of these systems, Behavioral Evaluation Strategy and Taxonomy (BEST), has been reviewed by Sidener, Shabani, and Carr (2004). BEST allows users to collect data in "real time" or while watching video of the target behaviors. Sidenar, Shabani, Carr, and Roland (2006) had observers view video footage of students with autism engaged in social interactions. The observers used BEST on a desktop computer to score the behavior. One of the inherent values in using a system like this is that it facilitates the calculation of interobserver-agreement (IOA) data when more than one user scores a session. BEST is available from Educational Consulting Inc. (www.skware.com).

Another data-collection tool that has been cited in several research articles in the past decade is MOOSES (Multiple Option Observation System for Experimental Studies; Tapp, Wehby, & Ellis, 1995). Like BEST, MOOSES allows real-time data collection or post-session data collection by review of video. The software allows frequency and duration recording and calculates IOA in addition to allowing other forms of data analysis. For example, with MOOSES, one is able to analyze the relation between events that occur in sequences during an observation period (e.g., ABC analysis). This would allow, for example, a researcher to analyze free-operant situations where he or she believes that one behavior (teacher demand) influences some other behavior that is also being coded with MOOSES. Free operant situations are those in which a behavior can be emitted at almost any time. A demonstration version of MOOSES can be downloaded from http://jc.vanderbilt.edu/mooses/download.html. MOOSES can be integrated with ProCoderDV which is a software application that digitizes video to allow observers to view events after the fact.

ProCoderDV is software that allows an observer to collect video footage of events and then view them after the fact (Tapp & Walden, 2000). Collecting data from video rather than live observation has many advantages. First, this allows the user to slow down the action so they have an opportunity to see many events that happen too quickly in the natural environment. Footage can be replayed and reviewed by multiple observers (IOA). Software like ProCoderDV used in conjunction with MOOSES offers features that facilitate momentary time sampling and interval recording because the video can be set to pause at the end of set time intervals. There are countless advantages of video-based observation systems but the ease with which one can ensure the collection of accurate data for hard-to-measure behaviors and the ability to score a wide range of behaviors simultaneously or after multiple viewings on numerous participants shown in the video trumps live observation. Researchers have to use caution, though, to guard these live "artifacts" and ensure that they are stored properly (locked office and locked cabinets) with access only available to those on the research team. As with any media that contains important and sensitive information, researchers are urged to make copies of the materials stored and store the copies in a location separate from the originals.

Direct Measurement of Permanent Products

The direct measurement of permanent products refers to the measurement of some product following a response. It is undoubtedly the most common measurement strategy used by teachers. When teachers grade written assignments (e.g., math worksheets, spelling tests, English papers), evaluate the completion of assembly tasks (e.g., puzzles, bicycle brakes, circuitry boards), or review audio or video recordings of student behavior, they are engaged in the measurement of permanent products. This type of behavior recording is then translated into some numerical term, usually number, rate, or percent.

The direct measurement of permanent products has several advantages for the teacher-researcher. First, it is practical with a large number of students in the class, a situation in which it is impractical for a teacher to directly observe each student performing each assignment. Second, it is nonintrusive; that is, it does not detract attention from an ongoing lesson. Third, it yields precise records of student behavior that can be stored for later comparison (e.g., written assignments, audio and video recordings). Fourth, it permits the objective evaluation of IOA by presenting observers with completed assignments in random order. Fifth, it is conducive to "seat work" and other auto-instructional or independent work assignments.

Generally, the measurement of permanent products is recommended for research that focuses on academic or vocational behaviors. In addition, audio and video recordings can prove helpful when conducting research on more basic skills (e.g., oral reading, assembly tasks, self-care skills) and when the focus is on shaping more appropriate social behavior. When a study participant's behavior is being recorded continuously through the use of an audio or video recording system (e.g., oral reading of a passage), the dependent measure (e.g., number of mispronounced words) is counted by using one of the direct observational recording procedures (e.g., event recording, interval recording).

Direct Observational Recording

√ Direct observational recording refers to observing and quantifying behavior as it occurs; it is a fundamental component of applied behavior analysis research. There are several types of direct observational recording procedures; the more common ones are summarized in Table 7.2. The choice of recording procedure is determined by the topography of the target behavior (i.e., the form, or what the behavior looks like) and by which attribute or parameter of the behavior is of interest to you. Some academic targets, such as correct math problems completed per 10-minute session, can be calculated from permanent products, such as the written responses on the math paper. These are not of concern here since scorers' agreement is straightforward (the answer is correct/incorrect, assuming it is legible). Other academic targets, for example, correct vocalization of speech sounds, however, will require a different recording system, as will social behavior targets. Our focus here is on recording procedures that require direct human observation of behavior—not permanent products.

No recording system will measure everything. Each represents a trade-off; it will "catch" the behavior of interest—most of the time—but will also miss much. Your task is to select a procedure that represents the most accurate picture of the target behavior change. One way to record behavior is simply to write down in narrative form everything that occurs, as qualitative researchers do when they take field notes (e.g. Eisner, 1998; Lancy, 1993; Lincoln & Cuba, 1985). Within the context of the classroom or clinical setting, the observer would write, in simple sentences, what the participant does during the observation period, for example, free play. There are problems with this system. Writing and watching are incompatible behaviors. While the observer is writing, some behaviors and events likely will be missed and thus the written record is a partial record. Or, the child may be emitting a behavior at a high rate, and it will be impossible to record each instance. In other words, the flow of the "behavior stream" is too fast for the observer (Wright, 1967). Yet another problem is that two observers are unlikely to write equivalent narratives, and thus it will be difficult to obtain an accurate description of

√ **Table 7.2** Summary of Direct Observational Recording Systems

Procedure	Operation
Event recording	Count or tally each time the target behavior occurs within the observation period.
Duration recording	a. Total duration: Start the stopwatch when behavior begins and stop the stopwatch when behavior ends. Do *not* reset the stopwatch after each occurrence of the behavior. Record the total length of the observation period.
	b. Duration per occurrence: Start the stopwatch when the behavior begins and stop the stopwatch when it ends. Record the elapsed time on a data sheet and reset the stopwatch. Repeat the process for the observation period. Record the total length of the observation period.
Latency recording	Start the stopwatch immediately after the presentation of the S^D (task direction) and stop the stopwatch upon the participant's initiation of the response. Record the elapsed time on a data sheet and reset the stopwatch. Repeat the process for each trial or opportunity to respond.
Interval recording	Divide the observation period into small equal intervals. Record the occurrence or nonocurrence of the target behavior *during* each interval.
Time sample recording	Divide the observation period into equal or unequal intervals. Record the occurrence or nonoccurrence of the target behavior at the *end* of each interval.
PLACHEK recording	Divide the observation into equal or unequal intervals. At the *end* of each interval count the number of participants engaged in the target behavior (or at each available activity).

the observed behavior, i.e., poor IOA. Finally, it is possible for observers' judgments and biases to creep into the report by their choice of words in describing the observed behavior or event. Writing down everything as it happens is cumbersome and does not allow the researcher to summarize and analyze data in an efficient or reliable fashion.

Event Recording

Event recording is the most straightforward method for recording the frequency of a behavior. ✓ It entails tallying, typically by means of placing a mark on a piece of paper or "clicking" a counter, every time the target behavior occurs. This results in a count of the number of times the target behavior occurred within the total observation period. Provided you accurately timed the period of observation, it is possible to calculate and report a participant's rate of responding. For example, when the target behavior is being observed during a free-operant period, you need only record the start and stop times of the observational period, subtract the latter from the former, convert the remainder to minutes, and divide the number of behavior counts into the number of minutes in which the participant was observed. This will yield the standard measure of rate (responses per minute). When the target behavior is being counted during a "teacher-paced" activity, calculating an accurate rate measure becomes more cumbersome as previously discussed.

It is important to note that if a behavior occurs at a low and steady rate it is possible that every response will be recorded; if behavior is emitted at a high rate, for example, nearly continual fist hits to the forehead, some occurrences will be lost. A major problem, described in the next section, is obtaining IOA. Another problem with this, and all occurrence records, is that an instance of behavior tells nothing about the topography of the response. If a child cries, does she wail or just sob quietly? If a student looks away from his assignment, how long does he have to look away to be considered off-task? These problems are addressed when the researcher develops the behavioral definition, but rarely is it possible to provide an exact and exhaustive record.

There are numerous commercially available and practitioner-made devices that will facilitate collecting frequency data and aid in the collection of reliable data. These include wrist golf counters, hand-tally digital counters, wrist-tally boards, masking-tape bracelets, beaded-tally bracelets, digital counters that attach to pencils, and tally note cards that are taped to students' desks. Figure 7.2 shows a sample data-recording form appropriate for collecting frequency data. This data-collection sheet, as well as the above-mentioned event recording devices, also can be used with audio and video recordings of student behavior when number or rate is the dependent measure.

Trial Recording

Trial recording provides one way to break the "behavior stream" into quantifiable elements and consequences. It entails scoring a child's response that occurs within a set response interval ✓ after the presentation of a discriminative stimulus, for example, child requests the preferred toy that is out of reach, by name, within 10 s of making eye contact with the toy. Scoring may be as simple as recording whether the child emitted a correct, incorrect, or no response. An "approximation" may also be scored if her response is topographically similar to the target response. The acceptable response topography will be defined and/or exemplified in the data-collection section of a research proposal or report. A trial ends (a) after the child emits a response; (b) a specified amount of time passes (e.g., 10 s response interval); or (c) a planned consequence has been delivered. This type of recording is common with many types of instructional programs (e.g., Lovaas, 1987) but is less common with social behavior targets

S's Name _____   Date_____

T's Name _____   Behavior _____

Session # _____   Condition _____

Start Time _____ Stop Time_____ = Total Time _____

Directions: Tally number of occurrences

Summary: 1. Total number of occurrences   _____

2. Rate (Rs/minute)   _____

3. Reliability percentage   _____%

Figure 7.2 Sample event recording data-collection form.

studied under free operant conditions. Figure 7.3 provides an example of a data-collection form that might be used to collect data on student responses during a match-to-sample task. Figure 7.4 shows an example of a data sheet that could be used to collect data during a session of trials requiring an expressive language response. Figure 7.5 is an example of a data sheet that might be used to collect data on chained tasks which are often measured in a controlled trial type presentation.

Interval Recording

Whole- and partial-interval recording procedures are frequently used data-collection procedures in applied research, even though they generally require the undivided attention of observers. Interval recording involves defining an observation period and then dividing that period into small equal intervals of time and recording the occurrence or nonoccurrence of the target behavior(s) *during* each interval (e.g., Bryan & Gast, 2000; Hoch et al., 2002; Ingersoll & Gergans, 2007). With interval recording observers are typically cued when to record their observations by audio signals (private audio recording that says "record one," "record two," etc.), vibration signals (VibraLITE vibration watch), or visual signals (subtle hand gesture by an assistant). Schilling and Schwartz (2004) reported on the use of a wireless headset that

Trial	S^D	Choices			Student response	Consequence
1	"spoon"	__fork__	__knife__	__spoon__	+ / –	S^{r+}
2	_____	_____	_____	_____	+ / –	
3	_____	_____	_____	_____	+ / –	
etc.						

Figure 7.3 Sample data sheet performance information section appropriate for match-to-sample or receptive language tasks during teacher-paced instruction.

Trial	S^D	Student Response	Consequence		
			S^{r+}	Correction	S^{r-}
1	__that__	+	✓		
2	__the__	–		✓	
3	_____				
etc.					

Figure 7.4 Sample data sheet performance information section appropriate for expressive language tasks during teacher-paced instruction.

Steps	Trials									
	1	2	3	4	5	6	7	8	9	10
1 _____										
2 _____										
3 _____										
4 _____										
5 _____										

Code: FP = full physical prompt   G = gestural cue

PP = partial physical prompt   V = verbal cue

M = model   I = independent

Figure 7.5 Sample data sheet performance information section appropriate for task-analyzed skills during teacher-paced instruction.

alerted the data collector of times to record. It is important that these signals be private events and not noticeable to research participants. Figure 7.6 exemplifies a typical interval recording data sheet. Both interval recording procedures, and their variations, will prove useful to you if you design studies that focus on social and communication behaviors that occur under free operant conditions.

Whole Interval

Whole-interval recording, as the name implies, documents whether or not the child engaged in the target behavior for the entire observation interval. The whole-interval method is well suited to collecting data on behaviors of long duration that are difficult to measure. For example, counting on-task behavior may not be practical. Measuring duration per occurrence would be the ideal method for evaluating this behavior because it would yield the exact frequency and duration of the behavior, however, whole-interval recording may be more practical and can provide an *estimate of total duration*. It is not an appropriate measure if your interest is an estimate of frequency. Data are generally reported as either percentage of total intervals of occurrence or non occurrence. Peterson, Young, Salzberg, West, and Hill (2006) reported data on student on-task behavior using a whole-interval recording system. Students were observed during a 40-min class period. Observers scored students as "on-task" if their behavior fit the operational definition and they were observed to be on-task for the entire 10-s observation

S's Name _____   Date_____

T's Name _____   Behavior _____

                               Condition _____

Start Time _____ Stop Time_____ = Total Time _____

(Code: ✓ occurrence; - nonoccurrence)

1'				2'				3'				4'				5'			
15"	15"	15"	15"	15"	15"	15"	15"	15"	15"	15"	15"	15"	15"	15"	15"	15"	15"	15"	15"
6'				7'				8'				9'				10'			
15"	15"	15"	15"	15"	15"	15"	15"	15"	15"	15"	15"	15"	15"	15"	15"	15"	15"	15"	15"

Summary: Number of nonoccurrences ___   Percentage of nonoccurrences ___%

Number of occurrences ___   Percentage of occurrences ___%

Figure 7.6 Sample interval recording data-collection form for recording behavior occurrences (√) and nonoccurrences (–) or tallying within intervals.

interval. With a whole-interval system, the amount of time engaged in a target behavior can be *estimated.* For example, if a student was on-task for 100 of the 240 intervals in the observation period, researchers could estimate that the student was on task for approximately 41.7% of the observational intervals (100 intervals divided by 240 intervals multiplied by 100) or 16.7 min (100 intervals multiplied by 10 s divided by 60 s).

Procedurally, with the observation period divided into equal intervals, the observer watches the child and for each time interval records whether the behavior occurred for the entire length of the interval, i.e., yes/no scoring. If the interval is 10 s, the child would be required to be on task the entire 10 s for the interval to be scored as an "occurrence" of on-task. If the student was on task for 3 s, off task for 3 s, and back on task for the remaining 6 s of the interval, the interval would be scored as a "nonoccurrence." This example illustrates the importance of carefully setting the length of the observation interval to avoid underestimating the occurrence of the target behavior. If the interval length is too long, the observer will not be able to capture the occurrence of the target behavior. The shorter the interval length, the more accurate the estimate of total duration. As a general guideline, using a duration-per-occurrence recording procedure, record the duration of the target behavior over several occurrences. Use the median duration, or shorter duration, to set your observational interval length. Typically, interval lengths are in seconds rather than minutes.

Partial Interval

Partial-interval recording is similar to whole-interval recording in that the observer scores the occurrence or nonoccurrence of a behavior during the observation interval. Procedurally they are similar in that you continuously observe the child and, if the child emits the target behavior at any time during the interval you record an "occurrence." Typically no minimum response duration is specified, although it can be in the behavior definition. The difference between whole- and partial-interval recording rests with how an occurrence is defined with each procedure. For a behavior to be scored as an "occurrence" with whole-interval recording, study participants would have to be engaged in the behavior the entire duration of the interval, however, with partial-interval recording they would merely have to engage in the behavior long enough for the behavior to be observed. Once the behavior is observed, that interval would be scored an "occurrence." These data are expressed as the "percentage of intervals" in which the behavior occurred. O'Callaghan, Allen, Powell, and Salama (2006) reported the percentage of intervals in which participants engaged in disruptive behavior in the dentist office. They divided the observation period into 15 s intervals and scored each interval as an occurrence or nonoccurrence of a disruptive behavior. Disruptive behavior was recorded as an occurrence when the participant cried, complained, or moved around "too much" for the dentist to work. This allowed them to estimate the percentage of time that the participant was disruptive.

The advantage with partial-interval recording is that it captures behaviors of high frequency and short duration yielding an *estimate of behavior frequency* and possibly total duration. To yield an estimate of duration you must insure that observational interval size is similar in average duration of a behavior occurrence. This can be determined by using the duration-per-occurrence recording procedure to measure several occurrences of the behavior. As with the whole-interval recording procedure recommendation, use the median behavior duration, or shorter, to set your observation length. You need to be aware that partial-interval recording is an estimate of frequency, and possibly duration, and that as such it may underestimate frequency and duration since more than one occurrence may occur within an observation interval.

Deciding on whether to use whole- or partial-interval recording comes down to two primary questions: (1) What is the dimension (rate, duration, latency, etc.) of interest for the target behavior? and, closely related, (2) What is the research question? If the behavior of interest is low frequency and occurs for long durations (5 s or more) then a whole-interval recording procedure may be preferable. If the behavior is high frequency and short duration

(5 s or less) partial-interval recording would be the logical choice. Remember, both are estimates and may underestimate frequency and/or duration. If frequency is the behavior dimension of interest, and event recording and duration-per-occurrence recording are impractical, partial-interval recording should be considered.

Variations

Variations on these basic interval recording procedures will allow you to fine tune your data-collection system to better meet the needs of your research project. The four variations discussed are common variations of the partial-interval recording procedure.

Due to the possibility of timing problems when two observers are recording behavior, you may want to alternate observation intervals with recording intervals, for example, 10 s observe, 5 s record. In practice, for example, this would allow you to watch the child for the entire 10 s, and then during the following 5 s record what was observed. This technique has the advantage of allowing the observers to look down at their data sheet at a predetermined time, decreasing the likelihood that either observer will miss an occurrence of the behavior. This "observational control" procedure may be helpful when you have concerns that observers may miss an occurrence or when one observer may record an occurrence in one interval and the other observer record in an adjacent interval.

A variation of partial-interval recording that you may choose to use when several behaviors are of interest is a set of codes to record the "occurrence" or "nonoccurrence" of each behavior during each interval. Suppose you are evaluating the effect of an intervention package on the cooperative play of young children with autism. You have identified three different behaviors you want to monitor: cooperative play (CP), alone play (AP), and stereotypy (S). You continuously watch during the observation interval and then after that interval you record each code for each behavior you observed. With this variation you may choose to also use the observational control procedure described in the previous paragraph. Figures 7.7 and 7.8 exemplify two different data-sheet formats for recording multiple behaviors during the same interval. As a general rule, we recommend that no more than three behaviors be targeted for recording at any one time due to reliability concerns. It is also important that the definitions of these behaviors be clearly distinguishable from one another. See Figure 7.6 for an example of a data sheet that could be used to code multiple behaviors in the partial-interval system.

Tally within interval is another variation that is particularly useful when you want to collect frequency data on a specific behavior but do not want to rely on event recording alone. With this variation you record (tally) the number of times the target behavior occurs in each interval. This method of recording is valuable for two reasons. First, you can see the temporal pattern in the behavior (e.g., several occurrences of the target behavior at the beginning of the observational period and fewer at the end). Perhaps the greater benefit is in terms of calculating reliability. With event recording, IOA is calculated by dividing the smaller number of occurrences by the larger number of occurrences and multiplying by 100 (total agreement). This reliability calculation method is the only method available when using event recording alone, and it can increase the perception of IOA, when in fact observers may not be observing the same behavior at the same time. This and other points related to calculating IOA will be discussed in a later section of this chapter. When event recording occurs in combination with a partial-interval recording system you are able to refine this calculation and compute the percentage agreement per interval. That is, each observer's tallies are aligned for each interval to determine if observers actually observed the same occurrence of the behavior. This is useful when behaviors occur at a low rate and are recorded over an extended period of time (e.g., recording instances of elopement attempts across a school day). In this example, the

S's Name _____ Date Condition

_____ _____

O's Name _____ Behavior(s)

_____

Other Students Present _____ _____

_____ _____ _____ _____

Start Time _____ Stop Time _____ = Total Time _____

| Code: | + positive | P peer |
| | – negative | S subject |

Directions: For each interaction, record who initiated the interaction (P or S), whether it was appropriate or inappropriate (+ or –), and the response to the initiation (P+ or P-; S+ or S–). *(Note:* Refer to behavioral definitions for + and – responses.)

1 Minute Intervals			
1	2	3	4
5	6	7	8
9	10	11	12

Summary:	P+ S+ : _____		S + P+ : _____
	P+ S– : _____		S + P– : _____
	P– S+ : _____		S – P+ : _____
	P– S– : _____		S – P– : _____

Comments:

Figure 7.7 Sample interval recording data-collection form using behavioral codes.

observation period may be 6 hours and the observation interval may be 15 min. The behavior may occur 10 times across the day. If observers simply used event recording it may be that they are recording different attempts and different times of the day, though both recorded 10 elopement attempts. By recording each occurrence within a 15-min interval it is possible to determine with greater precision whether observers are recording the same occurrence of the behavior (see Figure 7.8). The shorter the observational interval the greater confidence we have that observers are recording the same event. Peyton, Lindauer, and Richman (2005) used this method of data collection when evaluating the frequency of noncompliant verbal behavior by a child with autism. Observers tallied the number of noncompliant statements made by the child

S's name _____	Date _____
O's name _____	Behavior _____
	Condition _____

time	occur.	nonoccur.	time	occur.	nonoccur.	
1:00			1:30			Summary:
1:05			1:35			Total occurrence _____
1:10			1:40			Percent occurrence % _____%
1:15			1:45			Total nonoccurrence _____
1:20			1:50			Percent nonoccurrence% _____%
1:25			1:55			

Figure 7.8 Second sample of an interval recording data-collection form using behavioral codes.

during each 10-s interval. The value for the researchers was that by using event recording within intervals they could calculate IOA using the point-by-point method, thereby increasing confidence in their measurement system.

A final variation worthy of consideration is scheduling observations randomly across participants when collecting data on more than one participant using partial-interval recording. This strategy also can be used with momentary time-sample recording discussed in the next section. If, for example, you are interested in observing the on-task behavior of four students during an independent work activity, you could try to collect data on each student's on-task behavior each observation interval. This, however, could prove cumbersome and could cue students that data are being collected on their behavior by observing the data recorder looking at one student and then writing on the data sheet. This would adversely influence the validity of the data. An alternative is to randomly alternate observations across students. For example, during a 15-min observation period in which a 15-s partial-interval recording procedure is used, you could observe each student for 15 s during each 1-min time block, randomly rotating across students so that each student is observed once for 15 s each minute. Carr and Punzo (1993) used a system of "spot checks" similar to this when measuring on-task behavior of three students. Within a 10-min evaluation period, each student was observed in a set order at the end of every 5 s. The drawback with this variation is that less data are collected on each participant but it can provide a representative sample of behavior, particularly during longer observation periods when at least 20 observations are recorded for each participant. Using this partial-interval recording variation, Carr and Punzo were able to collect 30 observations on each student during each session.

Time-Sample Recording

√ Time-sample recording, also referred as momentary time sampling, is similar to partial-interval recording in that an observation period (e.g., 30 min) is divided into short (1–2 min) observation intervals, however, rather than observing the child during the interval, the observer is cued to observe the child at the *end* of the observational interval (e.g., Bryan & Gast, 2000; Schilling & Schwartz, 2004). Data are reported as the "percentage of intervals occurred." From the perspective of a teacher or clinician who is conducting an applied research project, time-sample recording has the practical advantage of not requiring continuous observation while trying to deliver instruction or therapy. As with interval recording, time-sample recording yields an *estimate of behavior frequency and duration,* with a tendency to underestimate frequency and overestimate duration, the extent depending on the size of the observation interval. Gunter, Venn, Patrick, Miller, and Kelly (2003) found that intervals of 2 min or less, rather than 4 min and 6 min, generated data that correlated more highly with data collected continuously, thus it is recommended that observation intervals of 1–2 min be scheduled. It is also recommended that time-sample recording be used with behaviors of relatively high frequency and long durations, rather than behaviors of low frequency and short durations. It has been recommended that it be used to "measure continuous activity behavior, such as engagement with a task or activity" (Cooper, Heron, & Heward, 2007, p. 93). When using a time-sample recording procedure it is important to know that you will miss a considerable amount of behavior and, thus, shorter intervals are superior to longer intervals. To exemplify this point, if your observation period is 30 min and you divide this period into 2-min intervals, you would only record if the behavior occurred at the 2, 4, 6, 8, etc. minute marks (e.g., fixed time-sample recording), therefore, you may miss the opportunity to capture behavior that occurred between the 2 min, 1 s and 3 min, 59 s marks. This would result in an underestimate of frequency. In terms of behavior duration, the underlying assumption is that if a person is engaging in the behavior at the observation point (2 min) then he was engaging in the behavior during the preceding interval (and presumably for a substantial portion of it). This can result in overestimate of duration. While there are definite limitations of this system, it provides the applied researcher with the advantage to delivering instruction or therapy while only having to observe the student or client at pre-set intervals.

There are three variations of time-sample recording: fixed interval, variable interval, and Placheck. With *fixed time-sample recording* the observation period is divided into equal observation intervals (2, 4, 6, 8, etc. min), at the end of which the observer is cued to record ("record 2," "record 4," etc.) what was seen or heard. This could entail recording occurrence/nonoccurrence or some behavior code. This variation has been used frequently in research but it does have the disadvantage of possibly signaling to research participants that their behavior is being observed and recorded every 2 min. If they become aware of a predictable observation schedule they could time their behavior accordingly, e.g., on-task for 10 s near the end of every 2-min interval and off-task the other 1 min, 50 s (e.g., Spriggs, Gast, & Ayres, 2007).

Variable time-sample recording addresses this potential problem by scheduling unpredictable observation intervals that vary in length. For example, a 30-min observation period may be divided into an *average* of 2-min intervals, yielding 15 observations. The time between observations may look like this: 1 min, 30 s; 45 s; 2 min, 45 s; 1 min, 15 s; 2 min, 15 s; 3 min, 30 s, with the mean time between observations being 2 min. Such a random and unpredictable observation schedule yields the same number of observations as fixed time-sample recording but with the advantage of not inadvertently signaling to those being observed when they will be observed.

PLACHECK or "planned activity check" works much like time-sample recording but was specifically designed to measure group behavior (Risley, 1971; Doke & Risley, 1972) and treat the measure of the group's behavior as the unit of analysis. For example, the behavior for the entire class for one observation session would be plotted as one data point: the classroom is "the participant." Fixed or variable observational intervals may be scheduled. As with other time-sample recording procedures the observer is cued at the end of an observational interval to record. Unlike the other procedures the observer counts the number of individuals engaged in the target behavior or activity. These data are reported as the percentage of individuals engaged in the target behavior/activity. Placheck is ideal for measuring behaviors of long duration, like on-task or in-seat behavior, when an intervention is being applied to a group. It is also a procedure that can be used to measure activity preferences and other back-up reinforcers, allowing a teacher or therapist to place higher token values on the more highly preferred reinforcer menu items. To accomplish this, the practitioner would count the number of children engaged in or waiting for the opportunity to engage in an activity, divide the number by all children present, and multiply by 100. Data would be reported as the percentage of individuals engaged in the behavior or each of the activities available. The higher the percentage, the greater the demand, and the higher the token value.

As with any dependent variable that will include a composite score for a group (e.g. the number of observed off-task behaviors during an observation period), participant attrition can pose a serious threat to internal validity. Suppose three classrooms each with 15 students. A researcher is using PLACHECK to measure on/off-task behavior in both classes and reporting a composite variable (i.e., no single student accounts for the data point plotted but the behavior of all students, when observed with the PLACHECK system, contribute to the variable total). If one classroom has a student who tends to exert disproportionate influence on the dependent variable (they are the one student who is *always* off-task) and that student moves to another classroom, the researcher's data will reflect this change. After this point, the researcher is essentially measuring the behavior of a different "participant" (classroom of students) and has fundamentally altered the study.

Duration and Latency Recording

Duration recording involves collecting data on how long a behavior occurs. As previously discussed, there are two types of duration measures: total duration and duration per occurrence. *Total duration* is recorded by starting a stopwatch when the behavior is initiated and stopping the stopwatch when the behavior ends. When the next episode of the behavior is initiated, the observer starts the timing device again *without* resetting the time. At the end of the observation period the observer has data on the total number of minutes (or seconds) the behavior occurred during the observation period. Provided you have an accurate measure of the total observation period, it is possible to report the percentage of time the participant engaged in the behavior. However, when total duration is the dependent measure, there are no data on the frequency of the behavior. If frequency data are also desired, you should use the duration-per-occurrence recording procedure.

When recording *duration per occurrence*, the observer starts and stops the stopwatch with each occurrence of the behavior. Each time the behavior occurs, the observer records the duration (length of time) of the response. After recording the time on a separate data form, the observer resets the stopwatch and prepares to record the duration of the next behavior occurrence. A primary advantage of the duration-per-occurrence method is that it yields data on behavior frequency, duration of each behavior occurrence, and total duration. Therefore, this procedure provides several alternative methods for summarizing the data: total number of behavior occurrences; rate of occurrence; mean, median, and range of duration occurrences; total duration per observation period; and percentage of time engaged in the behavior per observation period. Zhang, Gast, Horvat, and Dattilo (2000) measured duration per occurrence when studying the effects of a 4-s constant time-delay procedure on the motor completion durations of four adolescents with severe intellectual disabilities in learning three recreation/leisure skills. Using a multiple probe design across behaviors, they showed that in addition to acquiring the target behaviors, participants also improved their fluency by shortening their response durations. It is recommended that when behavior acquisition and fluency are of interest, duration–per-occurrence recording be used (MacDonald et al., 2007).

S's Name _____   Date _____

T's Name _____   Behavior/Task _____

Session # _____   Condition _____

Start Time _____ Stop Time _____ = Total Time _____

N	N duration/latency per occurrence	N	N duration/latency per occurrence
1		6	
2		7	
3		8	
4		9	
5		10	

Summary: 1. Total number of occurrences   _____

2. Mean duration/latency per occurrence _____

3. Range   _____

Figure 7.9 Sample latency or duration-per-occurrence data-collection form.

When interested in inter-response time or intervals, duration-per-occurrence recording can also be used. The data collector would record the behavior start time (e.g., 1:30:15 p.m.), start the stop watch, and when the behaviors stop, stop the stop watch and record both the duration of that episode of the behavior (5 min, 5 s) as well as the stop time (e.g., 1:35:20 p.m.). When the next behavior begins the observer records the start time (e.g., 2:15:20 p.m.) and repeats the process. By subtracting the end time of the first behavior from the start time of the second behavior the inter-response time is identified (2:15:20 p.m.–1:30:25 p.m. = 40 min, 5 s). Recording the time of day (start and stop times) of each episode provides you with all the information duration per occurrence generates, as well as allows you to identify time between behavior occurrences and any time of day patterns that might be present, e.g., higher frequency of occurrences in afternoons compared to mornings. Figure 7.9 shows a data recording sheet appropriate for collecting and summarizing duration-per-occurrence data.

Duration recording is the appropriate direct observational recording procedure when the target behavior occurs at unacceptable long durations or inappropriate short durations. In both cases the focus of intervention would likely be to positively affect the response duration of the target behavior (e.g., decrease the duration of body rocking; increase the duration of working on an assignment unassisted). As a general rule, when you are concerned with how long a child engages in a behavior, duration-per-occurrence recording should be used.

Latency recording, in contrast to duration recording, focuses on the time elapsed from when a student has an opportunity to respond (e.g., presentation of the task direction, "Begin reading aloud" or natural cue, water in a pan boiling over on the stove) to when the student initiates the response (reads the first word aloud, or initiates to remove the pan from the burner). Latency recording entails starting the stopwatch immediately after the presentation of the task direction (or natural cue) and stopping the stopwatch when the child initiates the response. The observer then records the elapsed time on a data sheet similar to that presented in Figure 7.9. These data can be used to compute *latency per opportunity to respond* as well as mean, median, and range of response latency per opportunity. Latency recording is a particularly useful when collecting data on individuals who have a long response latency or who have a particularly short response latency accompanied by a high error rate. For example, Wehby and Hollahan (2000) measured latency from teacher request to compliance with the request by elementary-aged students with learning disabilities. To facilitate data collection they used the MOOSES data-collection system (described previously). Latency recording may be used with free-operant activities when you are interested in how long it takes a child to acknowledge another child's presence (e.g., eye contact, spoken greeting, etc.), as in a free play situation, or how long it takes a child to put in a second puzzle piece after the first puzzle piece is in place. Both latency and duration recording are important direct observational recording procedures when response proficiency is of primary concern. Automated recording of latency is available in some commercially produced direct instruction software programs, however, this is infrequently the focus of the measurement and more often a byproduct of the software being used to measure fluency (e.g. *Math Blaster*, Knowledge Adventure, Inc. 2005).

Data-Collection Forms

Figures 7.2 through 7.9 present several sample data-collection sheets. You will note that each data sheet presents three types of information: (1) situational, (2) performance, and (3) summary, as recommended by McCormack and Chalmers (1978). Each section and type of information presented is important to the data-collection and analysis process. Though data-sheet formats vary depending on the type of data collected, recording procedure employed, target behavior and task, type of observational period (adult-paced or free-operant), and independent variable, each data sheet should present at minimum the information discussed below. These forms can be easily generated using the "Insert>Table" function available in most word processors. Changing the formatting and borders of cells will allow the researcher to create customized forms to meet their data-collection needs.

Situational Information

Situational information should reflect the following:

1. Research participant's name/initials (or in some cases, participant ID number if other identifiers are not allowed)
2. Date of observation
3. Starting and stopping times of observational period (i.e., time of day)
4. Target behavior(s) or task(s) (intervention objective) on which data are collected
5. Experimental condition and phase (e.g., Probe 1; System Least Prompts CRF; System Least Prompts VR3)
6. Instructor's or data collector's name/initials.

Performance Information

The performance-information section of a data sheet is that portion of the data sheet where participants' responses are recorded during the observation period. It is important that this section be as simple as possible yet provide sufficient information for analyzing participants' response patterns. Several different performance-information sections have been presented in Figures 7.2 through Figure 7.9. When recording data during adult-paced instructional programs, the following information should be provided:

1. Participant response codes (+, −, or 0 = correct, incorrect, and no response, respectively; or I, G, V, M, P = independent, gesture, verbal, model, or physical prompt needed for correct response);
2. Trial number (or response occurrence number);
3. Discriminative stimulus (S^D);
4. Stimulus choices (if receptive task);
5. Participant's response (use response code and, if incorrect, write response emitted or circle stimulus chosen);
6. Consequence delivered (reinforcer, correction, 5 s ignore, etc.).

Summary Information

Summary information should include the following:

1. Total observation period or session time in minutes;
2. Total number of correct and incorrect responses (or total number of occurrences or duration);
3. Percentage or rate of correct responses (percentage of time);
4. Percentage of IOA;
5. Percentage (overall) procedure fidelity;
6. Comments.

The importance of the data-collection sheet, and an investigator's proficient use of it, cannot be overstated. It is the means through which a research participant's behavior is quantified and analyzed and, therefore, it deserves your time and careful attention when developing it. It is advisable to design data sheets so that all reasonable variables that might influence behavior are recorded (e.g., time of day, length of session, consequences delivered, instructor, choice stimuli). Such detail will permit an analysis of errors in the event that variable response patterns emerge. If practical constraints require deletion of some information from the data-collection form, you should take great care in deciding which information to include and which to exclude. Such caution is warranted because the most obvious data are not necessarily those that provide clues to identifying those variables that influence behavior.

In summary, there is no one best way to develop a recording system and data-collection form. Whatever decision is made, something will be gained and something lost. You are advised to read carefully those published studies that closely relate to the topic you wish to study. These studies will describe the most frequently used data-collection systems (definitions, measures, recording procedures, reliability protocol) for your target behaviors. Narrative accounts in the discussion sections of those articles may discuss the limitations of the measurement system and recommend alternatives. For example, one of our master's degree students recently completed a study designed to improve several social behaviors of preschool children with special needs. The recording system, including the behavior definition, was insensitive to the change of one child's behavior from "wailing" to "barely audible crying." On that target behavior, crying, there was no documented effect, although there was a change in the magnitude of the behavior because of the way the behavior was originally defined. Such considerations are important when conducting applied research, particularly when changes in behavior may be on a continuum. You are urged to test your data-recording system prior to beginning your study so that adjustments can be made a priori.

Reliable Measurement

Obtaining reliable measurement is a major task for every researcher. It is a simple matter for the experimental laboratory researcher to describe the physical properties of a Plexiglas press panel and the grams of force required to close a microswitch that is triggered by a peck or paw press or describe the properties of an icon on a computer screen that is accessed by a mouse click. However, that microswitch or mouse is attached to complex electronic circuitry and mechanical/computer recording devices, all preprogrammed to self-destruct at different times, each at a maximally inopportune time—or so it must seem to the experimenter. Thus, while it is easy to describe behavior in this setting, achieving reliable measurement involves a continual fight against mechanical failure. In applied research settings it is possible to develop computerized recording procedures for some behaviors, but often it is not practical to do so. Further, there is a wide range of behaviors that cannot be measured by computer devices alone, i.e., without the input by a human observer. Consequently, applied behavioral research utilizes human observers to record behavioral events.

The use of multiple human observers offers many advantages to the researcher. One observer provides an independent record of data; two or more observers generate additional data. Under certain conditions, it is typical for researchers to report high percentages of agreement between or among observers, and thus increase readers' confidence that the data present a "true picture" of the events that actually occurred. However, using human rather than mechanical or computer recording systems simply trades one set of problems for another. The problems that arise with human observers are easily identified and well reported in the literature.

For example, developing observer training programs may be expensive and time consuming. Observers are intrusive and may require long periods of pre-experiment adaptation in the research setting. Observers' recordings can be biased and may drift away from a standard (i.e., definition) during the course of an experiment. The recording system used will influence an observer's recording; if simple, behavior definitions may be too broad; if complex, and thus difficult to score, the possibility of error increases. Once recorded, reporting IOA data presents another set of problems. Simple calculations will present a false picture in some circumstances. Conversely, available statistical procedures may be little understood by student or novice researchers. Others may object to the statistical procedures on philosophical grounds (Baer, 1977). Here, we discuss the design of human observations and behavior-recording schemes. Our focus is on how to do it, and further, how to increase the probability that reliable results will be obtained. In essence, we have task analyzed the process and then identified typical problems that might be anticipated.

Selection and Training of Human Observers

Selection of observers is usually done pragmatically, i.e., who's around to do the job? Funded researchers may support graduate students who serve as observers or they may train paid undergraduates. Unfunded graduate students, as we suggest later, may form a pool of peer volunteers who assist on each other's research projects. In schools, a teacher-researcher might call upon students, parents, paraprofessionals, or supervisors to conduct reliability checks. Though observer selection is dictated by environmental conditions and though there is no data base indicating that one group or another represents a better choice of individuals for training, there is sufficient research to identify maximally effective training procedures. The following conditions represent the ideal:

1. Observers should remain naive to the purposes of the study.
2. Observers should be trained to a high degree of proficiency *before* the start of the study.
3. Observers should be retrained, or "recalibrated," during the course of an investigation, particularly if it extends over a long period of time.
4. Interobserver communication should be constrained, or clearly defined, to limit possible bias or reinterpretation of behavior definitions.
5. The observation training system should be a close approximation of the situation to be observed.
6. Observers should collect data independent of one another.

These conditions may be difficult to approximate in ongoing classroom and clinical research. Yet, given these standards, you should be able to develop an alternative strategy to compensate for potential weaknesses, for example, if the purpose of a study must remain hidden, then student volunteers would be a better choice than your paraprofessional, all things considered.

The observer training system should be kept as simple as possible. The researcher should:

1. Develop a training protocol using a minimum number of directions stated in simple sentences.
2. Search relevant published studies for commonly used behavior definitions and use or model from them to avoid ambiguity.
3. Define the rules (etiquette) for observing:
   a. How and when to enter the research setting,

  b. Where to sit,
  c. How to interact or avoid specific topics with adults or children in the setting,
  d. How to handle problem situations, for example, ignoring a nonparticipating child who is pulling at your shirt for attention,
  e. What to do with the data, once it has been recorded.
4. Obtain or develop training tapes that are closely related to the setting and circumstances in which the study will be conducted. These tapes might be obtained by:
  a. Contacting other researchers who have conducted similar studies to obtain copies of their tapes.
  b. Seeking out tape libraries in the university, clinic, or school. It is possible that a university preschool might have a library of tapes of certain types of activities or interactions, and, further, that parental permission has been obtained for professional use of the tapes. In schools, the central administration might have copies of "model projects" conducted within the system. Or, individual teachers or colleagues may have similar records.
  c. Obtaining video equipment and develop training tapes on your own. This may require obtaining permission, as discussed in the chapter on ethical procedures.
5. With the tapes, and the recording system that has been selected, observe tapes with others to develop a scoring chart so that trainees' records can be compared to an accurate, defined standard.
6. Implement the training program.
7. Collect data on observers' performance and permit them to collect reliability data only after they have met your high IOA standard, for example, 90% accuracy over three observation periods or videotapes. Also be certain to consider potential difference in agreement with high-frequency vs. low-frequency behaviors. You want the observer to be accurate with both situations because often your intervention is attempting to alter a behavior pattern from one extreme (low rates) to the other (high rates) and you need to be sure that your observer is adequately trained to record behavior at both extremes.

These basic procedures should result in an observer training program that is clear and simple to learn, the complexity of the recording system notwithstanding. When implemented, the outcome should be a group of observers who can accurately record observations in the presence of a defined standard. Whether these observers will agree when they observe in the research setting is yet another matter. That will depend in large part on the extent to which training conditions match actual conditions and on the nature of the recording system. While observer training typically occurs in modified settings, often with video-taped examples, a researcher should "field test" observers in natural environments that are less controlled to make sure that the observer is capable of collecting the required data in a setting with a great many more distractions. This can be done with nonparticipants in the study who may still benefit from the target intervention.

Calculation of IOA

All the efforts described thus far (train observers well; use unambiguous behavior codes; maintain accurate observer recording; develop a recording system that best approximates reality) are intended to produce one outcome. They increase the probability that two observers will observe the same event and agree on what they saw or heard. For if there is little agreement, then there are two views of reality. The greater the discrepancy between them, the less confidence we have in the findings. Without consistently high percentages of agreement between observers, i.e., reliability of measurement, there is no basis for entertaining the validity of an intervention program. This constitutes a threat to internal validity known as instrumentation. The problem is that when you ask the question, "Did both observers see the same thing/events?", the answer is not a simple "yes" or "no." Instead, it is "Sometimes they did, and sometimes they didn't." The next question, then, is to what extent did they agree? That answer is influenced by the way the recording system is constructed and how the data from two observer records are compared. Both topics are addressed here.

Event Recording Systems

Event recording, as noted, simply requires that you record all the target behaviors that occur during the session, lesson, or observation period. At the end of the observation, events are summed. When two observers record during the same observation period, the agreement between their records is obtained by dividing the smaller number by the larger number and multiplying by 100; yielding a *total percent agreement*. This method has frequently been referred to as the *gross method* or *total method* for calculating reliability. If both observers record the same number of events, then their agreement is 100%. The problem is that this method does not permit you to state that both observers saw the same thing at the same time. Table 7.3 illustrates the problem. The top row represents the true case. The next row shows that Observer 1 made an *x* for every talk-out she saw (heard). The bottom row contains an *x* for each event Observer 2 recorded. How could this have happened? Suppose that the study was conducted in an old school building in poor repair. Suppose that, just as the teacher announced, "Class, your 30-minute study period will begin now," a large fly slipped through a torn screen and settled on the nose of Observer 1. Preoccupied with the fly, she missed the first five events that were recorded by Observer 2, who recorded all the events until the 16th, when the fly settled on her nose. Given that 20 talk-outs were emitted, what can be said about these records? First, to calculate percent agreements, remember that each observer provides the researcher only with a record of frequencies. Dividing the smaller number by the larger number, 14 divided by $15 = 0.93 \times 100 = 93\%$ agreement. Not bad—but since we have arranged these records so they can be compared with the true case to show how each observer treated each event, it is clear that the 93% agreement statistic does not tell all there is to know.

Remember that we have created the true case (assume it is a video recording obtained through a permanently installed camera that "caught" all of Grace's talk-outs) for the purpose of illustration. Observer 2 recorded 14/20 or 70% of the events; Observer 1 recorded 15/20 or 75%. These percentages are less impressive than the total agreement percentage, but in the typical study these data can seldom be computed because seldom are videotaping (or audio) records available to document "the true case." As a side note, when practical and with permission it is a good idea to videotape observational periods.

Now, to look at the record again, to what extent did the observers record the same behavior? Both observers scored 9 of the same events out of 20, or 45%. Much less impressive—but remember that, once again, this statistic cannot be computed since each observer's record is

Table 7.3 Grace's "Talk-Outs"

True Case	T	T	T	T	T	T	T	T	T	T	T	T	T	T	T	T	T	T	T	T	20
Observer 1					x		x	x	x	x	x	x	x	x	x	x	x	x	x	x	15
Observer 2	x	x	x	x	x	x	x	x	x	x	x	x	x	x							14

only a series of checks and it is not possible to align them as we have. Because of these limitations, researchers have constructed recording systems that divide observation periods into short intervals and provide some time-sequencing system (e.g., interval or time-sample recording) so that it is possible to document what two observers see or hear "at the same time."

Interval Recording Systems

In a partial-interval recording system, where the first behavior is recorded across continuous time intervals, the data will be influenced by the match between the topography of the behavior and the length of the interval. Long intervals underestimate the frequency of rapidly occurring behaviors. Short intervals overestimate the frequency of long-duration behaviors. In the first instance, the child strikes his forehead rapidly, but is measured on 1-min intervals, so only 1 of 50 may be caught. Conversely, if another child is out of seat once and remains out of his seat for 10 consecutive intervals, unless properly defined, his out-of-seat record will be inflated by a factor of 10. In the first case, when two observers are recording, the assumption is that they are both recording the same behavior, but that may not be the case. In the second case, frequency is inflated because the child left his seat only once and the time out of his seat (duration) was extensive. A basic problem, with both interval and time-sample recording procedures, is keeping observers synchronized on the same interval. If Observer 1 records accurately for each of 50 short intervals, but Observer 2 misses interval 3 and records interval 4 on the line for interval 3 and never corrects the error, then the two observers will be out of sync on 48 out of 50 observations. To avoid this possibility from happening it is recommended that observational intervals be cued by a "private" audio recording that calls out the interval number in which observers are to score (e.g., "record 1," "record 2," etc.).

When it is important to verify that observers saw *exactly* the same thing, time-sample recording is recommended. In contrast to other procedures, this requires that observation points or times be predetermined and that observers score only on these predetermined points in time. Records of these points are compared and calculated in the same ways that interval scores are treated.

If using partial- or whole-interval recording, or momentary time sampling, several calculations can be made and reported that complement one another and provide the most conservative measures of interobserver agreement. The most common method, referred to as the point-by-point (or interval-by-interval) method, which can be used any time the record of two observers can be directly linked to a specific event (like with interval systems, trial-by-trial recording, etc.). It entails examining the records of two observers and counting one for each interval in which they is agree that a behavior occurred or did not occur. The sum of this count, divided by the total of agreements plus disagreements multiplied by 100 yields a percent of agreement measure; one that increases confidence that observers recorded the same behavior at the same time. This estimate may be influenced by the rate of the behavior.

Agreements / (Agreements + Disagreements)	× 100 =	Percent of agreement

If calculating point-by-point agreement it is recommended that you also calculate occurrence agreement and nonoccurrence agreement. An *occurrence percentage agreement* should be computed and reported when observers are recording dichotomous events (occurrence/nonoccurrence) and always when the target behavior is reported to have occurred in *less than 75%* of the intervals (i.e., low to moderate frequency behaviors). To calculate occurrence agreement, use only those intervals in which at least one of the observers recorded an occurrence. For example, in reference to the data record of two observers presented below, only 4 of the 10 intervals are used to calculate occurrence agreement. The percentage-occurrence agreement for these data would be 50%.

Interval	1	2	3	4	5	6	7	8	9	10
Observer 1	+	−	−	+	−	−	−	−	+	−
Observer 2	−	−	−	+	−	+	−	−	+	−

Agreements (2)	× 100 =	2/4 = 50% occurrence agreement
Agreements (2) + Disagreements (2)		

The point-by-point method, which would take into account all 10 intervals, would yield IOA of 80%, an inflation of the level which the two observers actually agreed that they saw the behavior occur.

In contrast to occurrence agreement, *nonoccurrence agreement* should always be computed when the target behavior is reported to have occurred in *more than 75%* of the intervals (i.e., high-frequency behavior). Calculation of nonoccurrence agreement entails using only those intervals in which at least one of the observers recorded a nonoccurrence. For example, in reference to the data below, only 3 of the 10 intervals would be used to calculate nonoccurrence agreement. Nonoccurrence agreement for these data would be 33.3%, while the point-by-point method would yield 80% agreement.

Interval	1	2	3	4	5	6	7	8	9	10
Observer 1	−	+	+	−	+	+	+	+	+	+
Observer 2	+	+	+	−	+	+	+	+	−	+

Agreements (1)	× 100 =	1/3 = 33.3% nonoccurrence agreement
Agreements (1) + Disagreements (2)		

When using an interval or time-sample recording procedure we recommend that you calculate reliability percentages using the point-by-point method, and both occurrence and nonoccurrence agreement methods.

There are objections to these procedures as there are to others. The major problem is that some agreements are assumed to occur by chance alone. Much of the literature consists of statistical formulas to partial out the effect of chance, for example, Hartmann (1977). Others (Baer, 1977) have suggested that the use of complex statistics is antithetical to the applied behavior analysis tradition. One of the underlying premises of research is to clearly and conservatively communicate the results of a study. This not only involves being conceptually systematic and technologically sound (Baer, Wolfe, & Risley, 1968) but also involves making the material accessible to one's audience. The straightforward methods of reliability discussed above accomplish much of this but may fall short in some areas. In cases where they are more refined, perhaps more conservative estimates of reliability are required.

General Guidelines

After identifying how IOA data will be collected there are two other important considerations to make when planning a study. First, the researcher has to determine how frequently to collect IOA data. In an ideal situation, the IOA data would be collected during every observation session. This is not difficult to do when the sessions are videotaped or permanent products are generated but is not terribly practical or efficient. Typical recommendations for IOA data collection range from a minimum of 20% of sessions up to 33% of observation sessions. Using the minimum as a starting point, a researcher should plan to collect IOA for at least 20% of sessions in each condition for each participant in a study. This would mean, if using an A-B-A-B withdrawal design with three participants, the researcher would plan to collect data in at least 20% of the sessions in each A condition and each B condition for each participant. Another logistical and planning consideration that a researcher needs to make is in regard to how the IOA will be collected. Ideally, the primary observer will not be aware of reliability being collected (i.e., it will be covert). This prevents "reactivity" or the response of one under observation from influencing data collection. In this case, even though the reliability observer is watching the participant in the study, they are, by proxy also observing the performance of the primary data collector. Therefore, when practical, reliability should be taken without the knowledge of the primary observer. This is simple to do when data are being collected via video or permanent product because the primary data collector would never know when someone else was collecting data on the same session. Since this is often not possible, however, IOA data collection should be set up in such a way that the observers (primary and reliability observer) cannot see each other's data-recording sheets at a minimum. In a classroom situation, you would want to position the data collectors in such a way that neither could see when and what the other was recording. This is critical because you do not want the primary or reliability observer scoring a behavior as occurring because they saw the other data collector score the behavior.

After the data are collected, the researcher has to interpret the data to determine if the data fall within acceptable limits. A frequently cited minimum for IOA is 80% agreement. For example, one might accept lower IOA for dependent measures related to spoken articulation of certain sounds but expect much higher (i.e., 100%) for written spelling words. A researcher can often search for guidelines relative to their dependent measure of study in the literature to see what other researchers have used. In any case, low IOA must be explained.

When designing a study and a measurement system, it is prudent to field test your instrument and collect IOA data to evaluate your preliminary plans before beginning actual data collection. If you notice low IOA in this testing there are several things to consider. First, you may need to revisit your behavioral definitions. Your observers may be having difficulty determining if certain behaviors fit the definitions. For example, if one were interested in trying to quantify eye contact made by an individual with autism, observers may struggle to determine precisely what constitutes eye contact not because they do not know what it means in a conventional sense but because in measurement you have to clearly delineate, in black and white, what is eye contact and what is not; when eye contact begins and when it ends. Even if the definitions do not need refinement, a common solution for improving IOA before beginning a study (or during a study) is to provide additional training and practice to observers. This can become a particular issue if, over time, you notice IOA data deteriorating. This may indicate that "observer drift" is occurring. This is the result of one or more observers straying from the original definition of the target behavior(s). For example, in-seat behavior may be initially defined as: bottom in seat, feet on floor, back against back of chair, and facing forward. Over time, one of the participants may begin crossing his or her leg under their bottom and essentially sitting on their ankle and foot. One observer may decide to begin scoring this behavior because, functionally, it is similar to the target behavior in their view. This can be addressed with retraining and perhaps revisiting the definition. In other cases, field testing will reveal that the intended measurement system is far too cumbersome for observers to consistently and accurately score behavior. For example, in free-operant social situations, if observers are required to tally the number of verbal exchanges between two participants as well as time the length of the interaction and note how many individuals are engaged in the conversation, critical pieces of data may be omitted. In these cases, either streamlining the data-collection process (if it is being collected in real time) or opting to use videotaped observation sessions may assist with resolving low IOA problems. Regardless, if IOA appear consistently low in field testing or begins to decline, the researcher would be advised to re-evaluate the behavioral definitions, measurement system and retrain observers.

Reporting IOA

IOA data are typically reported in the narrative portion of a research study. Some journals request that IOA be reported in the Methods section of the manuscript where the method for collecting and calculating IOA is placed, while others prefer that reliability be the first thing reported in the Results section of the paper. Regardless, the form generally consists of first reporting the percentage or number of sessions in which IOA data were collected (e.g., IOA were collected in 34% of baseline sessions and 35% of intervention sessions for Ashton). When embedded in the narrative, the data usually follow with a reporting of the range and then median values for IOA (e.g., in baseline, IOA ranged from 80 to 95% with a median of 93%). Alternatively, the actual IOA data can be embedded in a summary table that shows median and range IOA data for each participant in each condition. This might also include information regarding the percentage of sessions in each condition for which IOA were collected. Procedural-fidelity data can then be included in this type of table or likewise embedded in the narrative.

Another way to consider reporting IOA data is to plot the data from the second observer on the graphs with the primary observer's data. This would take the form of additional data points plotted at the same points along the abscissa (i.e., on the session on which two observers scored data) and then at the place on the ordinate corresponding to what the second observer recorded. This helps to contextualize IOA because the reader would then be able to see not only how often IOA data were collected but also see exactly how those data relate to the data collected by the primary observer.

Summary

We have focused on two major topics in this chapter. First, we have defined and described dependent measures common to conducting research in educational, clinical, and community settings. We have described how to select the most appropriate dependent measures and suggested how to design data forms for applied research studies. In the second section of the chapter we have provided you with a rationale for increasing the reliability of the results obtained in an investigation. We have suggested where to look for behavior definitions appropriate to your area of interest. We have presented strategies for training observers. We have discussed problems in maintaining accurate recording and listed the trade-offs among the various recording procedures. We also have presented common formulas for calculating inter-observer reliability. We have thus provided you with a starting point for developing one part of the procedures for a study. The remainder of this text follows the same format, recommending what to do (sometimes) and how to do it. Across the remaining chapters, you will find recommendations for graphically displaying data, analyzing data, and selecting an appropriate design for your research question(s).

References

Ault, M. J., Gast, D. L., & Wolery, M. (1988). Comparison of progressive and constant time-delay procedures in teaching community-sign word reading. *Journal of Mental Retardation, 93,* 44–56.

Ayres, K. M., & Langone, J. (2002). Acquisition and generalization of purchasing skills using a video enhanced computer instructional program. *Journal of Special Education Technology, 17,* 15–28.

Ayres, K. M., Langone, J., Boon, R., & Norman, A. (2006). Computer based instruction for purchasing skills. *Education and Training in Developmental Disabilities, 41,* 253–263.

Baer, D. M. (1977). Reviewer's comment: Just because it's reliable doesn't mean that you can use it. *Journal of Applied Behavior Analysis, 10,* 117–119.

Beck, J. E., Jia, P., & Mostow, J. (2004). Automatically assessing oral reading fluency in a computer tutor that listens. *Technology, Instruction, Cognition, and Learning, 1,* 61–81.

Begeny, J. C., Daly, E. J., & Vallely, R. J. (2006). Improving oral reading fluency through response opportunities: A comparison of phrase drill error correction with repeated readings. *Journal of Behavioral Education, 15,* 229–235.

Bryan, L. C., & Gast, D. L. (2000). Teaching on-task and on-schedule behaviors to high-functioning children with autism via picture activity schedules. *Journal of Autism and Developmental Disorders, 30,* 533–567.

Burns, M. K. (2005). Using incremental rehearsal to increase fluency of single-digit multiplication facts with children identified as learning disabled in mathematics computation. *Education and Treatment of Children, 28,* 237–249.

Carr, S. C., & Punzo, R. P. (1993). The effects of self-monitoring of academic accuracy and productivity on the performance of students with behavioral disorders. *Behavioral Disorders, 18,* 241–250.

Cooper, J. O. (1981). *Measuring behavior* (2nd ed.). Columbus, OH: Charles E. Merrill.

Cooper, J. O., Heron, T. E., & Heward, W. L. (2007). *Applied behavior analysis.* Columbus, OH: Pearson.

Cote, C. A., Thompson, R. H., & McKerchar, P. M. (2005). The effects of antecedent interventions and extinction on toddler compliance with transitions. *Journal of Applied Behavior Analysis, 38,* 235–238.

Dixon, M. R. (2003). Creating a portable data-collection system with Microsoft Embedded Visual Tools for Pocket PC. *Journal of Applied Behavior Analysis, 36,* 271–284.

Doke, L. A., & Risley, T. R. (1972). The organization of day-care environments: Required vs. optional activities. *Journal of Applied Behavior Analysis, 5,* 405–420.

Eaton, M. D. (1978). Data decision and evaluation. In N. G. Haring & C. L. Hansen (Eds.), *The fourth R: Research in the classroom.* Columbus, OH: Charles E. Merrill.

Eisner, E. W. (1998). *The enlightened eye: Qualitative inquiry and the enhancement of educational practice.* Columbus, OH: Merrill.

Ellisa, E. M., Ala' i-Rosales, Glenn, S. S., Rosales-Ruitz, J., & Greenspoon, J. (2006). The effects of graduated exposure, modeling, and contingent social attention on tolerance to skin care products with two children with autism. *Research in Developmental Disabilities, 27,* 585–598.

Gentry, D., & Haring, N. (1976). Essentials of performance measurement. In N. G. Haring & L. Brown (Eds.), *Teaching the severely handicapped Volume 1.* New York: Grune and Stratton.

Graf, S., & Lindsley, O. (2002). *Standard celeration charting 2002.* Youngstown, OH: Graf Implements.

Green, B. F., Bailey, J. S., & Barber, F. (1981). An analysis and reduction of disruptive behavior on school buses. *Journal of Applied Behavior Analysis, 14,* 177–192.

Gunter, P. L., Venn, M. L., Patrick, J., Miller, K. A., & Kelly, L. (2003). Efficacy of using momentary time samples to determine on-task behavior of students with emotional/behavioral disorders. *Education & Treatment of Children, 26,* 400–412.

Hall, R. V. (1974). *Managing behavior—behavior modification: The measurement of behavior.* Lawrence, KS: H & H Enterprises.

Haring, N. G., Liberty, K., & White, O. R. (1980). Rules for data-based strategy decisions in instructional programs: Current research and instructional implications. In W. Sailor, B. Wilcox, & L. Brown (Eds.), *Methods of instruction for severely handicapped students.* Baltimore, MD: Paul H. Brookes Publishers.

Hartmann, D. P. (1977). Considerations in the choice of interobserver reliability estimates. *Journal of Applied Behavior Analysis, 10,* 103–116.

Hoch, H., McComas, J. J., Thompson, A. L., & Paone, D. (2002). Concurrent reinforcement schedules: Behavior change and maintenance without extinction. *Journal of Applied Behavior Analysis, 35,* 155–169.

Huber, J. E., & Chandrasekaran, B. (2006). Effects of increasing sound pressure level on lip and jaw movement parameters and consistency in young adults. *Journal of Speech, Language, and Hearing Research, 49*, 1368–1379.

Ingersoll, B., & Gergansa, S. (2007). The effect of a parent-implemented imitation intervention on spontaneous imitation skills in young children with autism. *Research in Developmental Disabilities, 28*, 163–175.

Kahng, S., & Iwata, B. A. (1998). Computerized systems for collecting real-time observational data. *Journal of Applied Behavior Analysis, 31*, 253–261.

Kahng, S., & Iwata, B. A. (2000). Computer systems for collecting real-time observational data. In T. Thompson, D. Felce, & F. J. Symons (Eds.), *Behavioral observation: Technology and applications in developmental disabilities* (pp. 35–45). Baltimore, MD: Brookes.

Kelly, M. B. (1977). A review of the observational data-collection and reliability procedures reported in the *Journal of Applied Behavior Analysis. Journal of Applied Behavior Analysis, 10*(1), 97–101.

Koscinski, S. T., & Gast, D. L. (1993). Computer-assisted instruction with constant time delay to teach multiplication facts to students with learning disabilities. *Learning Disabilities Research & Practice, 8*, 157–168.

Lancy, D. F. (1993). *Qualitative research in education: An introduction to the major traditions.* White Plains, NY: Longman Publishing Group.

LaVigna, G. W., & Willis, T. J. (2005). An overlooked dependent variable in the application of behavior analysis to challenging behavior. *Journal of Positive Behavior Interventions, 7*, 47–54.

Lincoln, Y. S., & Cuba, E. G. (1985). *Naturalistic inquiry.* Newbury Park, CA: Sage Publications.

Lovaas, O. I. (1987). Behavioral treatment and normal educational and intellectual functioning in young autistic children. *Journal of consulting and Clinical Psychology, 55*, 3–9.

MacDonald, R. Green, G., Mansfield, R., Geckelera, N., Gardeniera, J., Anderson, W., & Sancheza, J. (2007). Sterotypy in young children with autism and typically developing children. *Research in Developmental Disabilities, 28*, 266–277.

Marckel, J. M., Neef, N. A. and Ferreri, S. J. (2006). A preliminary analysis of teaching improvisation with the picture exchange communication system to children with autism. *Journal of Applied Behavioral Analysis, 39*, 109–115.

McCormack, J., & Chalmers, A. (1978). *Early cognitive instruction for the moderately and severely handicapped.* Champaign, IL: Research Press.

O'Callaghan, P. M., Allen, K. D., Powell, S., & Salama, F. (2006). The efficacy of noncontingent escape for decreasing children's disruptive behavior during restorative dental treatment. *Journal of Applied Behavior Analysis, 32*, 161–171.

Peterson, L. D., Young, K. R., Salzberg, C. L., West, R. P., & Hill, M. (2006). Self-management procedures to improve classroom social skills in multiple general education settings. *Education & Treatment of Children, 29*, 1–21.

Peyton, R. T., Lindauer, S. E., & Richman, D. M. (2005). The effects of directive and nondirective prompts on noncompliant vocal behavior exhibited by a child with autism. *Journal of Applied Behavior Analysis, 38*, 251–255.

Reese, H. W., & Lipsitt, L. P. (1970). *Experimental child psychology.* New York: Academic Press.

Risley, T. R. (1971). Spontaneous language in the preschool environment. In J. Stanley (Ed.), *Research on curriculums for preschools.* Baltimore, MD: Johns Hopkins.

Sapir, S., Spielman, J. L., Ramig, L. O., Story, B. H., & Fox, C. (2007). Effects of intensive voice treatment (the Lee Sliverman Voice Treatment [LSVT]) on vowel articulation in dysarthric individuals with idiopathic Parkinson Disease: Acoustic and perceptual findings. *Journal of Speech, Language, and Hearing Research, 50*, 899–912.

Schilling, D. L., & Schwartz, I. S. (2004). Alternative seating for young children with autism spectrum disorder: Effects on classroom behavior. *Journal of Autism and Developmental Disorders, 34*, 423–432.

Shipley, K. G., & McAfee, J. G. (2004). *Assessment in speech-language pathology: A resource manual.* Clifton Park, NY: Delmar Learning.

Sidener, T. M., Shabani, D. B., & Carr, J. E. (2004). A review of the behavioral evaluation strategy taxonomy (BEST) software application. *Behavioral Interventions, 19*, 275–285.

Sidener, T. M., Shabani, D. B., Carr, J. E., & Roland, J. P. (2006). An evaluation of strategies to maintain mands at practical levels. *Research in Developmental Disabilities, 27*, 632–644.

Singh, N. N., Lancioni, G. E., Winton, A. S. W., Curtis, W. J., Wahler, R. G., Sabaawif, M., Singh, J., & McAleavey, J. K. (2006). Mindful staff increase learning and reduce aggression in adults with developmental disabilities. *Research in Developmental Disabilities, 27*, 545–558

Spriggs, A. D., Gast, D. L., & Ayres, K. M. (2007). Using picture activity schedule books to increase on-schedule and on-task behaviors. *Education and Training in Developmental Disabilities, 42*, 209–223.

Tapp, J. T., Wehby, J. H., & Ellis, D. N. (1995). A multiple option observation system for experimental studies: MOOSES. *Behavior Research Methods, Instruments and Computers, 27*, 25–31.

Tapp, J. T., & Walden, T. (2000). Procoder: A system for collecting & analysis of observational data from videotape. In T. Thompson, D. Felce, & F. Symons (Eds.), *Behavioral observation: Innovations in technology and applications in developmental disabilities* (Ch. 5). Baltimore, MD: Paul H. Brookes Publishing Co., Inc.

Wehby, J. H., & Hollahan, M. S. (2000). Effects of high-probability requests on the latency to initiate academic tasks. *Journal of Applied Behavior Analysis, 33*, 259–262.

Williams, G., Perez-Gonzalez, L. A., & Vogt, K. (2003). The role of specific consequences in the maintenance of three types of questions. *Journal of Applied Behavior Analysis, 36*, 285–296.

White, O. R. (1971). *Glossary of behavioral terminology.* Champaign, IL: Research Press.

White, O. R., & Harring, N. G. (1980). *Exceptional teaching* (2nd ed.). Columbus, OH: Charles E. Merrill.

Wilson, C. W., & Hopkins, B. L. (1973). The effects of contingent music on the intensity of noise in junior high home economics classes. *Journal of Applied Behavior Analysis, 6*, 269–275.

Wolery, M., Ault, M. J., Gast, D. L., Doyle, P. M., & Mills, B. M. (1990). Use of choral and individual attentional responses with constant time delay when teaching sight word reading. *Remedial and Special Education, 11*, 47–58.

Wolery, M. Cybriwsky, C. A., Gast, D. L., & Boyle-Gast, K. (1991). Use of constant time delay and attentional responses with adolescents. *Exceptional Children, 7*, 462–474.

Wright, H. F. (1967). *Recording and analyzing child behavior.* New York: Harper & Row.

Zhang, J., Gast, D. L., Horvat, M., & Dattilo, J. (2000). Effect of constant time delay procedure on motor skill completion durations. *Education and Training in Mental Retardation and Developmental Disabilities, 35*, 317–325.

8

Visual Representation of Data

Amy D. Spriggs and David L. Gast

In the preceding chapters we have discussed parameters of applied research and the importance of direct, frequent, and reliable measurement of behavior. We have addressed the point that measurement alone does not permit identification of functional relations between independent and dependent variables. This is accomplished only when a behavior is measured within the context of an appropriately chosen single subject research design. Through such pairing, it is possible to formatively evaluate a particular intervention's effect on behavior and subsequently use that information to develop positive behavior-change programs with students or clients. In pursuit of this information, applied researchers (a) repeatedly measure behavior; (b) provide a technological and conceptually systematic description of conditions under which the behavior is being measured; (c) evaluate behavior change by employing an appropriate single subject research design; (d) identify those variables which affect the behavior by ideally manipulating only one variable at a time; (e) regularly plot the data on a line graph; and (f) conduct visual analyses of the graphically displayed data, maintaining or modifying conditions accordingly. Through this sequence of operations, applied researchers have been able to isolate variables that influence behavior and, in so doing, further our understanding of human behavior and design effective intervention programs.

In this chapter we discuss the importance of regularly and accurately plotting data on a line graph. An explanation of the purpose, types, and basic components of graphic displays is accompanied by multiple examples of graphs found in current applied research. Guidelines for selecting and constructing appropriate graphs and tables are also included. Adhering to the procedures set forth in this chapter for constructing graphs allows you to complete the last step of formative evaluation, visual analyses of graphic data, accurately and reliably. Following procedures outlined for constructing tables allows you to concisely include summative data in your reports.

The Purpose of Graphic Displays

Graphic displays (e.g., line graphs, bar graphs, cumulative graphs) and tables serve two basic purposes. First, they assist in organizing data during the data-collection process, which facilitates formative evaluation. Second, they provide a detailed numerical summary and description of behavior, which allows readers to analyze the relation between independent and dependent variables. The underlying purpose or function of the graph is communication. For the person collecting data the graph is a vehicle for efficiently organizing and summarizing a participant's behavior over time. It allows the researcher to analyze, point by point, the effect a particular event has on a participant's behavior. For behavior analysts "the graph is the primary form of data processing; research decisions, judgments, and conclusions are based almost exclusively on graphed data" (Parsonson & Baer, 1978, p. 133–134). In addition to behavior analysts' reliance on graphically displayed data for communication and analysis, teachers, therapists, and other practitioners find graphing economical in terms of time saved by not having to review daily data forms prior to making program decisions and by not maintaining ineffective intervention programs.

Independent analysis of relations between variables is one of many strengths characteristic of applied behavior analysis and single subject research methodology. By reporting all data, readers can determine for themselves whether a particular intervention has a reliable and "significant" effect on a participant's behavior. The graph, as a compact and detailed data-reporting format, permits independent analysis. Although data could be reported in written narrative day by day or condition by condition, such a format would prove cumbersome. Also, difficulties would arise when attempting to reliably analyze data trends both within and across experimental conditions.

Graphic representation of data provides you with an efficient, compact, and detailed summary of participant performance. It communicates to readers (a) sequence of experimental conditions and phases; (b) time spent in each condition; (c) independent and dependent variables; (d) experimental design; and (e) relations between variables. Therefore, it is not surprising that applied researchers rely heavily on graphic displays.

Types of Graphic Displays

Four basic principles help graphs communicate information to readers: clarity, simplicity, explicitness, and good design (Parsonson & Baer, 1978). A well-constructed graph will (a) use easily discriminable data points and data paths; (b) clearly separate experimental conditions; (c) avoid clutter by keeping the number of behaviors plotted on one graph to a minimum;

(d) provide brief descriptive condition labels and legends; and (e) use appropriate proportions and scales that do not deceive readers. In addition, it is your responsibility to select an appropriate graphic display for presenting data. The type of display will depend upon type of data collected and intended communication. Generally, behavior analysts present all data (e.g., baseline, intervention, probe, and review data) on one or more types of graphs. By presenting all data you enable readers to independently analyze data patterns.

There are three basic types of graphic displays used by applied researchers: line graphs, bar graphs, and cumulative graphs. Although this chapter discusses only the simplest figures within each of the three categories, you should be aware that there are numerous variations within each category.

Before discussing each type of graph, you should be familiar with basic components and symbols used in graphic representations. Figure 8.1 presents major components of a simple line graph; Figure 8.2 presents basic components of a simple bar graph. As shown, there are several common components across the two types of figures. These include:

- Abscissa: horizontal line (*x* axis) that typically identifies the time variable (e.g., sessions, days, dates)

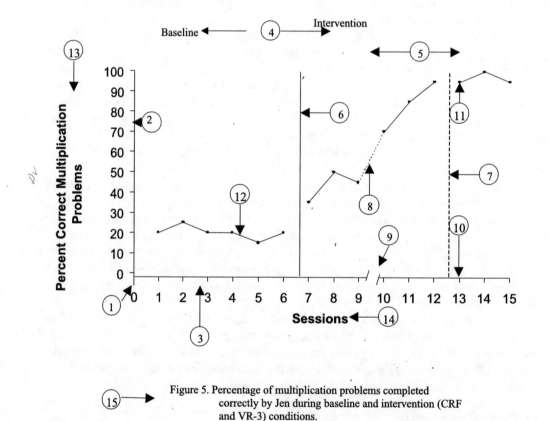

Figure 5. Percentage of multiplication problems completed correctly by Jen during baseline and intervention (CRF and VR-3) conditions.

Figure 8.1 The basic components of a simple line graph: (1) origin, (2) ordinate scale (y), (3) abscissa scale (x), (4) condition identification, (5) condition phase identification, (6) condition change line, (8) data path break, (9) scale break, (10) tic mark, (11) data point, (12) data path, (13) identification of ordinate value (dependent variable), (14) identification of abscissa variable (time), and (15) figure number and legend.

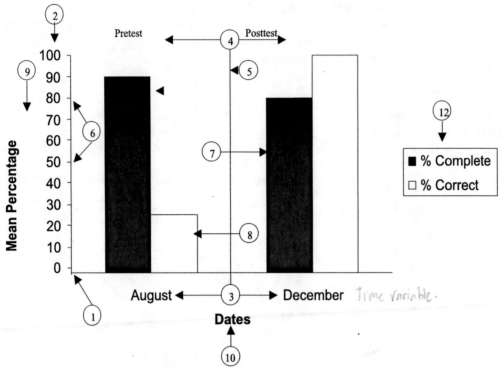

Figure 7. Mean percentage complete and correct addition problems before (pretest) and after (posttest) self-monitoring instruction.

Figure 8.2 The basic components of a simple bar graph: (1) origin, (2) ordinate scale (y), (3) abscissa scale (x), (4) condition identification, (5) condition change line, (6) tick marks, (7) percent complete data bar, (8) percent correct data bar, (9) identification of ordinate variable, (10) identification of abscissa variable, (11) figure number and legend, and (12) figure key.

- Ordinate: vertical line (*y* axis) that typically identifies the dependent variable (e.g., percentage, number, duration, responses/minute)
- Origin: common point of intersection of the abscissa and ordinate
- Tic marks: points along both the abscissa and ordinate where values are shown (e.g., 0%, 10%, 20%; Sessions 1, 2, 3)
- Condition labels: one or two descriptive words or common abbreviations that identify each experimental condition (e.g., Baseline, Social Reinforcement, CTD, DRO–15 min)
- Condition change lines: vertical lines that identify when there has been a change in experimental conditions. If there are phases within a condition, do not connect data points between phases of the condition. It is recommended you use solid condition lines and dashed phase lines; otherwise, it does not matter.
- Key: one or two words describing each type of data point and path or bar plotted on the graph
- Figure number and legend: the figure number is used in the narrative to direct a reader's attention to the appropriate graph, and the legend provides a brief and explicit description of dependent and independent variables.

Though not shown in Figures 8.1 and 8.2, most graph paper is printed with a grid. The grid facilitates accurate plotting of data when plotting by hand. When preparing a graph for publication or formal presentation, however, the grid is typically omitted (see *Using Computer Software to Construct Graphs* presented later in this chapter).

Simple Line Graphs

Line graphs represent the most commonly used graphic display for presenting daily data. Figure 8.3 shows two simple line graphs on which percentage of trials with compliance is measured at varying integrity levels (100%, 50%, and 0%) across two children. In the interest

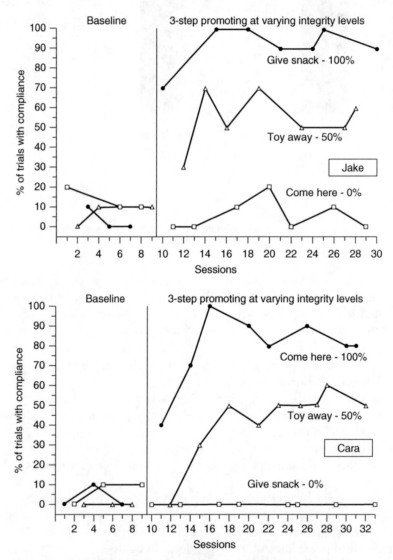

Figure 1. Percentage of trials with compliance across baseline and three-step prompting integrity levels (i.e., 100%, 50%, and 0%).

Figure 8.3 Graph showing two simple line graphs on which the dependent variable (% compliance) is measured at varying integrity levels across two students (source: Wilder et al., 2006. Copyright by Society for the Experimental Analysis of Behavior, Inc. Reproduced by permission).

of simplicity and clarity, seldom are more than three behaviors plotted on a single graph. If additional behaviors are being monitored, as in the case of monitoring the effect of an intervention on non-target behaviors (i.e., response generalization), additional graphs can be used. Figure 8.4 shows one way to present data on several non-target behaviors that are being monitored concurrently.

The line graph has several advantages, the most important of which is that it is familiar to most readers and, thus, easily read and understood. In addition, it is easy to construct and permits the researcher, teacher, or therapist to continuously evaluate the effect an intervention has on dependent variable(s), thus facilitating formative evaluation and the decision to maintain or modify the intervention.

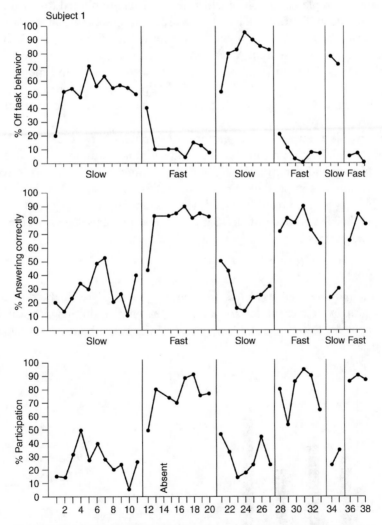

Figure 2. Percent occurrence of off-task, answering correctly, and participation for Subject 1 during the slow- and fast-rate presentation phases. The dotted lines indicate when Subject 1 was absent. The student-teacher taught during the final phases (Sessions 34 through 38).

Figure 8.4 Simple line graph showing three behaviors being monitored concurrently (source: Carnine, 1976. Copyright by Society for the Experimental Analysis of Behavior, Inc. Reproduced by permission).

Simple Bar Graphs

Bar graphs traditionally have been used by applied researchers to display discrete data and comparative information. The great versatility of a bar graph is indicated by its numerous variations. There are two basic types of simple bar graphs: those that present a single bar in an experimental condition and those that present several. As shown in Figure 8.5, the simple single bar graph can be used to summarize a student's performance or behavior across several sessions and days. Figure 8.6 shows how multiple bars can be used to compare effects of three error-correction procedures on trials-to-mastery of word-to-picture pairs for six children with autism. With simple bar graphs, the height of the bar indicates magnitude of data.

An example of a simple bar graph in which several bars are plotted for each experimental condition is presented in Figure 8.7. Figure 8.7 presents a simple bar graph that uses two bars to compare percentages of verbally and physically disruptive behaviors during baseline and intervention conditions for five children. A variation of a simple bar graph is the subdivided bar graph. Figure 8.8 uses the subdivided bar graph format to show mean time spent in various levels of play across four participants. This method of plotting summarizes the magnitude of target behavior with a single bar, which permits a quick and easy comparison of data, in addition to conserving space.

Bar graphs provide a simple and straightforward summary of data that is easily understood and analyzed. Though it is not recommended for displaying continuous data, it is an excellent format for displaying and communicating important comparisons in a final research report. In their construction, it is important to remember to keep the width of each bar identical and thus not perceptually mislead readers. In addition to simplicity and clarity indicative of a well-designed bar graph, it is easy to construct. Bar graphs may prove useful when communicating a child's progress to parents.

Cumulative Graphs

Cumulative graphs have been used less frequently by applied researchers than either line graphs or bar graphs. Few examples are found in the empirical applied research literature. Cumulative graphs do, however, provide an excellent visual summary of participant progress toward goal mastery.

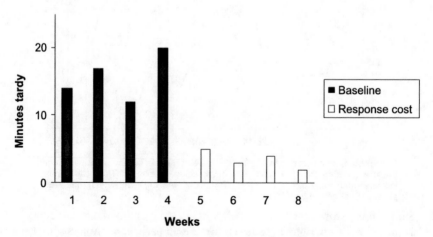

Figure 8.5 Single bar graph showing a student's behavior (minutes tardy) across several weeks.

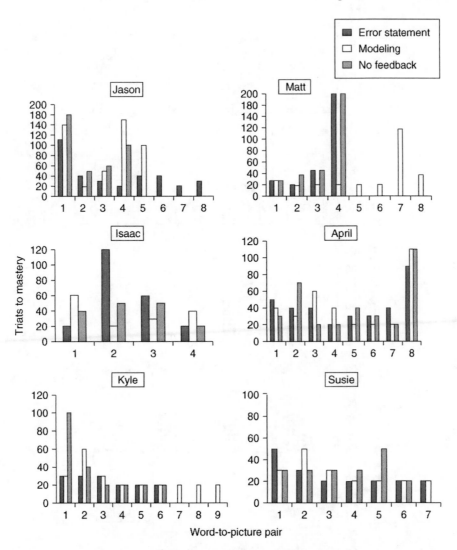

Figure 2. Trials to mastery for each word-to-picture pair. Points with asterisks on the x-axis refer to training that involved random rotation between different word-to-picture pairs; all other points refer to training of an individual word-to-picture pair.

Figure 8.6 Graph showing multiple bars used to compare effects of three different interventions on similar skills (source: Smith et al., 2006. Copyright by Society for the Experimental Analysis of Behavior, Inc. Reproduced by permission).

When cumulative records are plotted . . . the number of responses recorded during each observation period is added (thus the term *cumulative*) to the total number of responses recorded during all previous observation periods. In a cumulative record the y axis value of any data point represents the total number of responses recorded since the beginning of data collection.

(Cooper, Heron, & Heward, 2007, pp. 135–136)

Figure 8.9 shows a cumulative graph on which the effects of continuous error-correction procedures are compared to intermittent error-correction procedures for cumulative number

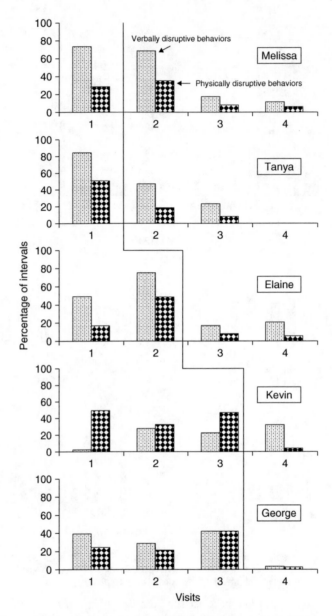

Figure 2.   Percentage of verbally disruptive behavior (light shaded bars) and physically disruptive behavior (dark shaded bars) per visit for each child across baseline and treatment.

Figure 8.7 Bar graph showing two bars used to compare two disruptive behaviors across baseline and intervention conditions for five students (source: O'Callaghan et al., 2006. Copyright by Society for the Experimental Analysis of Behavior, Inc. Reproduced by permission).

of words mastered by six adults with developmental disabilities. Figure 8.10 illustrates a cumulative graph where criteria have been reached. When plotting data on a cumulative graph and a priori criteria are met, the cumulative number returns to zero. The number of correct responses for the second step begins accumulating from zero. This is also the case if the cumulative number reaches the upper limit on the y axis (Cooper et al., 2007). Plotting data in

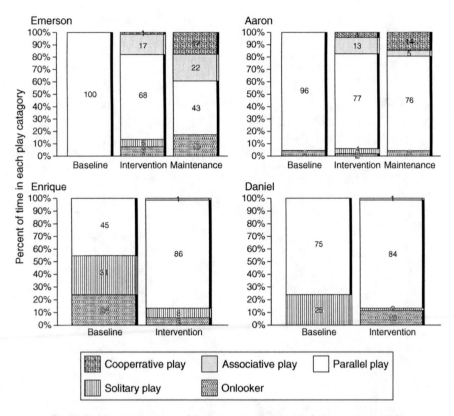

Figure 3. Mean percentage of time spent in each level of play across participants

Figure 8.8 Subdivided bar graph used to show time spent in various levels of play for four students (source: Nelson et al., 2007. Copyright by Society for the Experimental Analysis of Behavior, Inc. Reproduced by permission).

this manner allows readers to see, as shown in Figure 8.10, that after Step 1, the participant met criteria for subsequent steps in much fewer trials. In the case that a participant's cumulative graph is reset to zero due to reaching limits on the *y* axis, the numbers would simply be added together to figure cumulative number, rate, etc. Figure 8.11 illustrates using a cumulative graph within an A-B-A-B withdrawal design. In this example, eye-goggles nearly stopped eye-poking while used. Using a cumulative graph in this manner allows a clear demonstration of intervention effect on the behavior.

According to Cooper et al. (2007), cumulative graphs should be chosen over simple line graphs or bar graphs when: (a) total number is important for reaching a specific goal; (b) giving feedback to participant; (c) opportunities to respond are consistent; and (d) behavior-change patterns would be more accurately reflected by using a cumulative graph.

Semilogarithmic Charts

Semilogarithmic charts are used when absolute changes in behavior (which are what we have discussed to this point) are not the focus of research. Absolute behavior changes are documented by equal-interval data recording, where amounts are "equal" between tic marks on the graph. In contrast, relative behavior changes can be captured when the distance between tic marks are proportionally equal. "For example, a doubling of response rate from 4 to

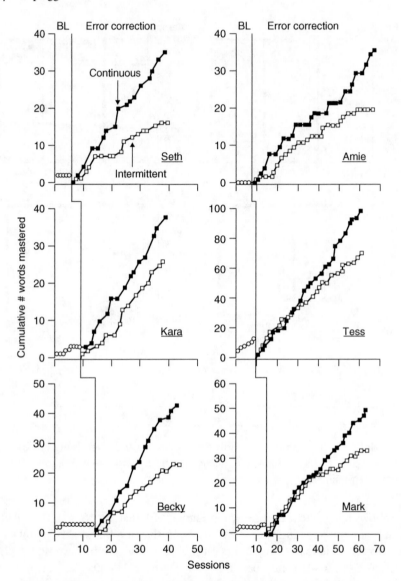

Figure 3. Cumulative number of words mastered during BL, continuous MR, and intermittent MR.

Figure 8.9 Cumulative graph showing the cumulative number of words mastered across sessions (source: Worsdell et al., 2005. Copyright by Society for the Experimental Analysis of Behavior, Inc. Reproduced by permission).

8 per minute would appear on a semi-logarithmic chart as the same amount of change as a doubling of 50 to 100 responses per minute" (Cooper et al., 2007, p. 139) (see Figure 7.1 for an example of semilogarithmic graph paper).

Guidelines for Selecting and Constructing Graphic Displays

Before analyzing graphically displayed data, it is important to evaluate the appropriateness of the format to display your data. The primary function of a graph is to communicate without

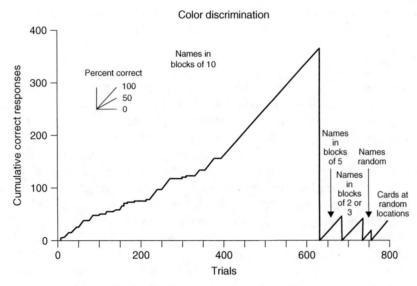

Figure 1. Cumulative record of correct responses. Vertical lines indicate reset of the record after meeting criterion on a step.

Figure 8.10 Cumulative graph showing how to continue recording data after criteria are reached for a step (source: Williams et al., 2005. Copyright by Society for the Experimental Analysis of Behavior, Inc. Reproduced by permission).

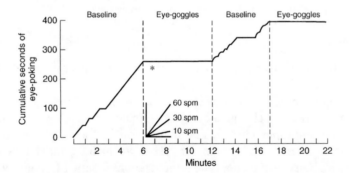

Figure 3. Cumulative seconds of eye poking across baseline and goggles conditions. Spm = seconds per minute. The asterisk indicates the occasion when Geof briefly removed the goggles. The goggles were replaced within 5s by his teacher, who reminded him to continue to wear them.

Figure 8.11 Cumulative graph used within an ABAB withdrawal design (source: Kennedy & Souza, 1995. Copyright by Society for the Experimental Analysis of Behavior, Inc. Reproduced by permission).

assistance from the accompanying text. This requires that you (a) select the appropriate graphic display (line graph, bar graph, or cumulative graph) and (b) present the data as clearly, completely, and concisely as possible. How data are presented and how figures are constructed directly influences a reader's ability to evaluate functional relations between independent and dependent variables. Though there are few hard-and-fast rules that govern figure selection, graph construction, or data presentation, there are recommended guidelines for preparing graphic displays (Parsonson & Baer, 1978; *Publication Manual of the American Psychological Association*, 2001; Sanders, 1978). A brief overview of figure selection, graph construction, and data-presentation guidelines follows. These guidelines should facilitate objective evaluations of graphically displayed data.

Figure Selection

✓Line graphs are used to present serial data. It is inappropriate to use line graphs to present discrete or non-serial data when the actual data path between two data points is unknown. ✓Bar graphs are used to present discrete data. For example, when a comparison of pretest and posttest performance is important, a bar graph is often used.

Combination bar and line graphs are sometimes used when more than three variables appear within a single graph (see Figure 8.12) to simplify "clutter." As previously mentioned, avoiding clutter by keeping the number of behaviors plotted on one graph to a minimum is a key component to a well-constructed graph; with more than three data paths on a single graph, "the benefits of making additional comparisons may be outweighed by the distraction of too much visual 'noise' " (Cooper et al., 2007, p. 132). In Figure 8.12, for example, four concurrently monitored behaviors are graphed using a combination of lines (matching tasks) and bars (naming tasks). Visual clutter was reduced and easy comparisons can be made across relevant variables (e.g., across students, comparing matching tasks, comparing naming tasks).

Combination bar and line graphs are also occasionally used when concurrently monitoring two behaviors where one is intended to replace the other. Figure 8.13 illustrates an example of this; bars represent frequency of incontinent urinations across various conditions (the right ordinate value captures frequency); lines represent percentage of continent urinations across the same conditions (the left ordinate value captures percentage).

Graph Construction

✓The preferred proportion of ordinate (y axis) to abscissa (x axis) is a ratio of 2:3. This is viewed by researchers as limiting the degree of perceptual distortion. If the ordinate scale were longer than this recommended proportion, a steeper slope in the data path would be presented, exaggerating the magnitude of change along the ordinate, while a longer distance between points on the abscissa (in proportion to the ordinate) visually distorts the data by presenting a more shallow data path than if the 2:3 ratio were used, which could mislead the reviewer as to the extent of the variability in the data. The same data are graphed in Figure 8.14 using the correct ratio (Figure 8.14a) and incorrect ratios (Figure 8.14b and c). It is important to use the same ordinate size on all graphs reporting the same measurement units in the same research report (Kennedy, 1989).

Separation of experimental conditions (e.g., A-B) is often indicated by bold solid vertical lines; a phase change within an experimental condition is frequently separated by a thinner, shorter, or dashed vertical line. Different journals request different types of condition lines. In Figure 8.15, Phase 3 of PECS instruction is divided into four phases, distinguished by number of pictures that were discriminated by Gail. Dashed lines are used to separate each phase in PECS instruction; dashed lines using a different pattern are used to distinguish phases within Phase 3. Figure 8.16 shows baseline, intervention, and follow-up conditions separated by solid lines. Phases of intervention for the third teacher–student dyad are divided by dashed lines. In Figure 8.17, both conditions and phases are divided by dashed lines. Phase lines in the second intervention condition are simply shorter than condition-change lines.

A scale break is used when the entire ordinate or abscissa scale is not presented. The ordinate

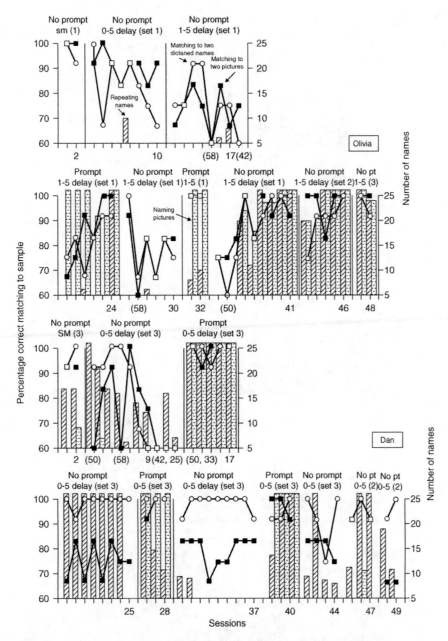

Figure 4. Results for Olivia and Dan across simultaneous, delay, prompt, and no-prompt conditions: Open circles and solid squares reflect percentages of correct matching. Striped bars and shaded bars reflect the number of names spoken on trials with two-picture samples, respectively. Bars with extended tic marks on the abscissa indicate that the number of names exceeded 25.

Figure 8.12 Combination bar and line graph used to concurrently monitor four behaviors (source: Gutowski & Stromer, 2003. Copyright by Society for the Experimental Analysis of Behavior, Inc. Reproduced by permission).

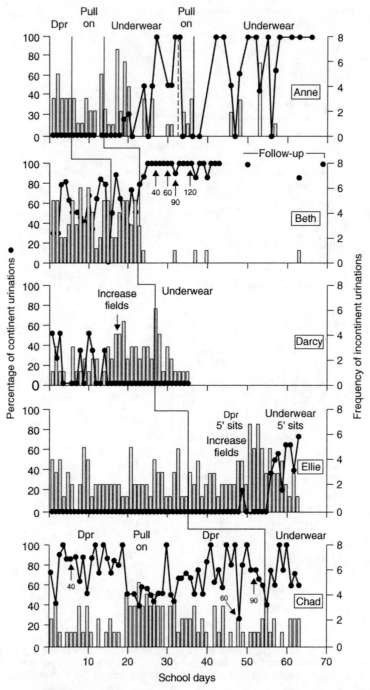

Figure 1. The percentage of continent urinations and frequency of incontinent urinations for all participants during the diaper, pull-on, and underwear conditions. School days without data points reflect days on which the child did not urinate during the experimental conditions. Arrows indicate changes to the toileting schedule or an increase in the amount of fluid offered.

Figure 8.13 Combination bar and line graph used to concurrently monitor two behaviors where left and right ordinates are used to measure behavior (source: Simon & Thompson, 2003. Copyright by Society for the Experimental Analysis of Behavior, Inc. Reproduced by permission).

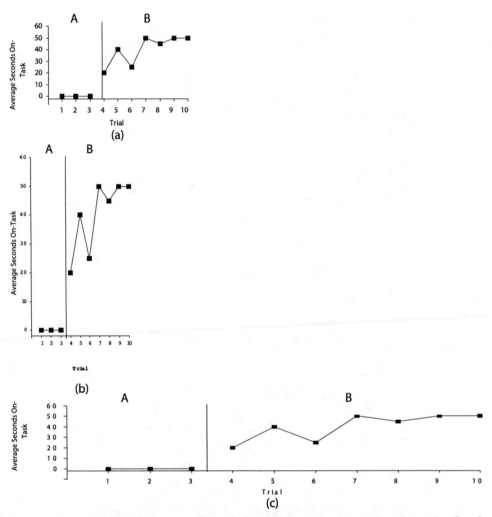

Figure 8.14 Correct (a) and Incorrect (b and c) graph construction proportions: On the above graphs, exact data are displayed using various abscissa/ordinate ratios. Graph (a) illustrates the preferred 2:3 ratio which is thought to minimize the degree of perceptual distortion. Graph (b) uses a ratio of approximately 3:2 which creates a steeper slope, exaggerating the change along the data path. Graph (c) uses a ratio of approximately 2:5. This extra space between tic marks creates a more shallow data path which could mislead readers as to the variability of data or change over time.

scale should show the lower (e.g., 0%) and upper (e.g., 100%) limits of the scale. For example, if mean percent correct is plotted along the ordinate, both 0% and 100% levels should be indicated. If data are consistently below the 50% level, the height of the ordinate may be shortened by placing a scale break above the 50% tic mark, above which the 100% level is marked. Figure 8.18 exemplifies shortening the height of the ordinate by placing a scale break above 20 grams; all but one data point fall below 20 grams. The abscissa scale should be divided into equal interval sessions, days, time, etc. When data are not collected continuously, a scale break should be inserted on the abscissa between the two non-consecutive data points. Figure 8.19 illustrates a scale break on the abscissa after session 30, with the next data point occurring at session 70 for all three sets. Similarly, a scale break occurs between session 82 and 89 for Set 2.

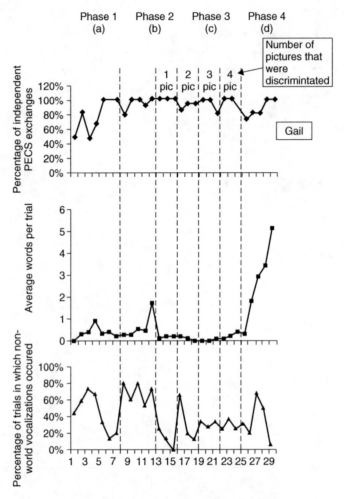

Fig. 1. PECS Proficiency (top panel), words per trial (middle panel),
and non-word utterances (bottom panel) for participant 1, Gail.

Figure 8.15 Graph using phase change lines to distinguish number of stimuli discriminated by the student where both conditions and phases are separated by dashed lines, but of different patterns (source: Ganz & Simpson, 2004. Copyright by Society for the Experimental Analysis of Behavior, Inc. Reproduced by permission).

The zero origin tic mark along the ordinate ideally should be placed slightly above the abscissa when any data point value is zero. When constructing line or bar graphs, it is particularly important not to mistake a zero level for the absence of plotted data. If there are no zero-level data points to be plotted on a line graph, the zero origin tic mark need not be raised above the abscissa.

The dependent measure should be clearly and concisely labeled along the ordinate. Most often, a single dependent measure is labeled along the left ordinate. When more than one dependent measure is graphed, the right ordinate may also be used. Figure 8.20 exemplifies using the left and right ordinate to graph two different measures on the same graphic display; rate is shown on the left ordinate and percent is shown on the right ordinate. Abbreviations and symbols (e.g., %, #) are discouraged in favor of descriptive labels. The frequency with which data are collected (e.g., sessions, days, weeks) should be noted along the abscissa on line graphs.

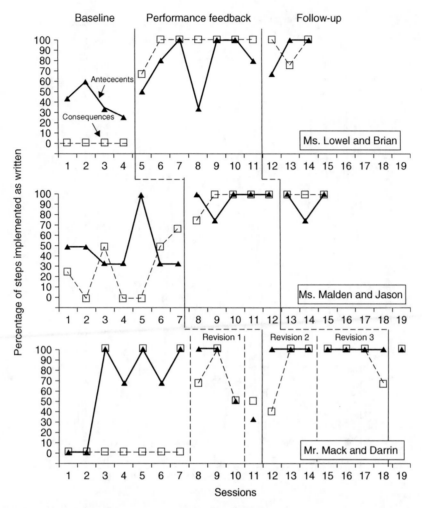

Figure 2. Percentage of antecedent and consequence components implemented as written across teacher–student dyads for Classroom 2.

Figure 8.16 Graph using phase change lines to highlight phases of intervention for the third teacher-student dyad where solid lines separate conditions and dashed lines separate phases (source: Codding et al., 2005. Copyright by Society for the Experimental Analysis of Behavior, Inc. Reproduced by permission).

Figure titles, legends, experimental-condition labels, and condition-phase labels should be concise but explanatory. They should provide sufficient information to allow readers to identify dependent and independent variables as well as experimental design.

Data Presentation

Data points should be marked distinctly using geometric forms (e.g., circles, squares, triangles). You should be able to determine the value of each data point on the ordinate and abscissa scale (e.g., 80% on Day 5).

A data path using a solid line to connect two points implies that there is continuity in the data-collection process. Dashed or omitted data-path lines are used to identify discontinuous data. Dashed lines have, on occasion, been used to connect two points between which no data

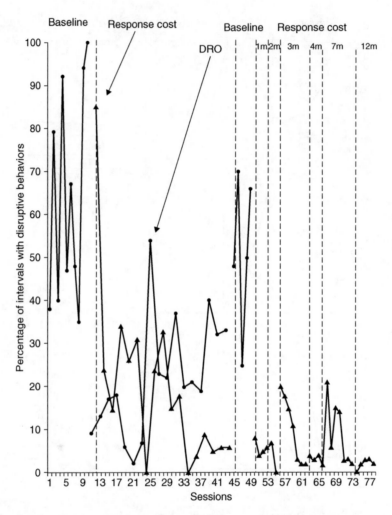

Figure 1. The percentage of intervals with disruptive behavior in baseline and treatment phases. Triangles represent response-cost sessions, and circles represent DRO sessions.

Figure 8.17 Graph using phase change lines that are simply shorter than the condition change lines (source: Conyers et al., 2004. Copyright by Society for the Experimental Analysis of Behavior, Inc. Reproduced by permission).

have been collected (such as connecting data points when the participant has been absent). It is inappropriate to connect data points of two different experimental conditions or condition phases (i.e., data paths should not cross experimental-condition and phase lines).

When plotting data using a line graph, it is recommended that no more than three different data paths be plotted on the same grid. We recommend that additional graphs be used when more than three data paths are necessary to represent the data. When graphing more than one behavior on a single graph, it is sometimes appropriate to use both the left and right ordinate to capture more than one dependent variable. Figure 8.20 exemplifies how both ordinates are used to graph two different measures (rate on left; % on right) on the same grid or graphic display. When graphing similar behaviors on multiple graphs, it is important to maintain ordinate size consistency. Figure 8.21 illustrates how "the intensity and generality of the effects

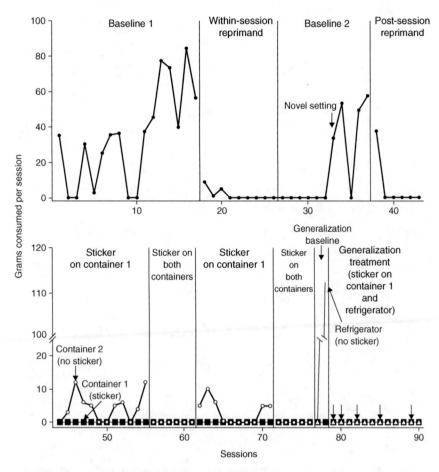

Figure 1. Grams of prohibited food consumed per session during the evaluation of within-session and postsession reprimands (top panel) and grams of prohibited and permitted foods consumed per session during the stimulus control assessment (bottom panel). Arrows indicate sessions in which the refrigerator was checked for missing food in the presence of the participant.

Figure 8.18 Graph showing a scale break on the ordinate (source: Maglieri et al., 2000. Copyright by Society for the Experimental Analysis of Behavior, Inc. Reproduced by permission).

of an experimental intervention may be overestimated, and/or restrictions in the intervention [can occur]" when ordinate sizes are not consistent (Kennedy, 1989, p. 338).

When logistically feasible, behavioral analysts present all data. On occasion, however, when data have been collected over an extended period of time, it may be necessary to condense data in order to present it on a single grid. A procedure for condensing data, commonly referred to as "blocking," is sometimes used to reduce the number of data points plotted on a graph. This procedure entails calculating mean or median performance level of two or more adjacent days' data, thereby reducing the length of the abscissa and the number of data points presented on the graph. When blocking is used, proceed with caution. It is appropriate to block data only if blocking does not mask the variability of the data. The procedure is dangerous in that it is possible for a researcher to distort the actual data trends, and therefore it is rarely used. When data points are blocked, you should (a) note that the data have been blocked; (b) specify how many adjacent data points have been blocked within each condition (the number of data

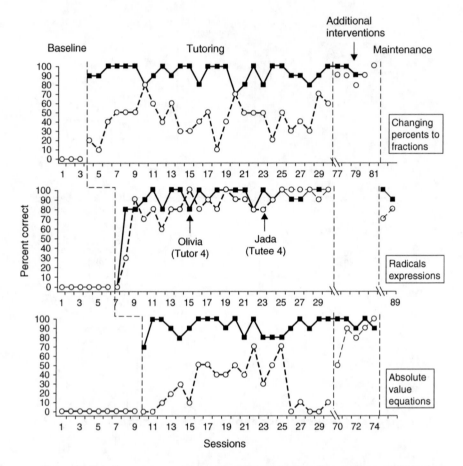

Figure 4. Pair 4's accuracy on the math skills across baseline, tutoring, additional interventions, and maintenance. The five sessions prior to the tutee achieving the mastery criterion are displayed in the additional interventions phase. The filled squares represent the tutor's performance, and the open circles represent the tutee's performance.

Figure 8.19 Graph showing scale breaks on the abscissa (source: Mayfield & Vollmer, 2007. Copyright by Society for the Experimental Analysis of Behavior, Inc. Reproduced by permission)

points blocked across conditions should be the same); (c) provide a rationale for blocking, assuring the reader that blocking was not used to mask data variability, but rather to accentuate data trend and/or reduce figure size due to practical constraints (e.g., not blocking the data would have resulted in an illegible figure when duplicated); and (d) present a minimum of three blocked data points for each condition or phase, thereby allowing the reader to evaluate trend within each condition. As a rule, blocking is done *post hoc*; during the course of research all data are plotted. It is only after the study has been completed, and all data collected, that you can evaluate the appropriateness of the blocking procedure. The general rule regarding blocking is: don't; if you must, proceed with caution and assure your reader that blocked data trends parallel and accurately represent unblocked data.

Trend, median, and mean lines may be drawn to supplement point-by-point data plotted on a line graph; they should not be drawn as an alternative to plotting actual data points and data paths. This should be done sparingly, and as a general rule, we do not recommend their use. Their function is to highlight data trends and averages within and across

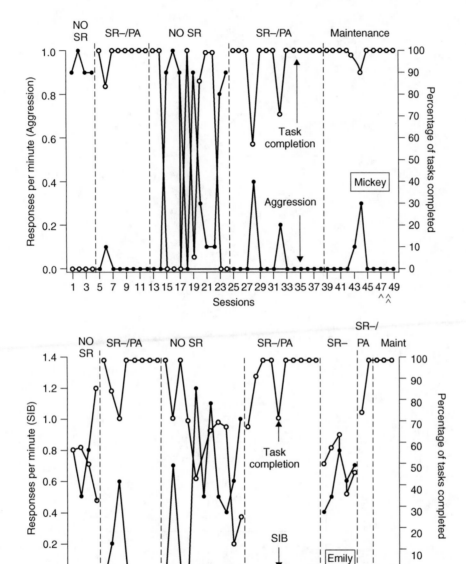

Figure 2. Rate of aggression (left *y* axis) and percentage of tasks completed (right *y* axis) across conditions of the intervention for Mickey (top panel). The single carat indicates probe with novel tasks. The double carat indicates probe with novel instructor. Rate of SIB (left *y* axis) and percentage of tasks completed (right *y* axis) across conditions of the intervention for Emily (bottom panel). The carat indicates probe with novel instructor and novel tasks.

Figure 8.20 Graph showing how left and right ordinates are both used to graph two different measures (rate on left; percent on right) on the same grid or graphic display (source: Hoch et al., 2002. Copyright by Society for the Experimental Analysis of Behavior, Inc. Reproduced by permission).

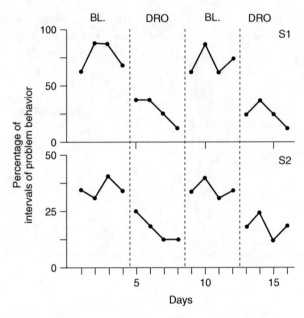

Figure 1. An example of inconsistent vertical axis scales.

(a)

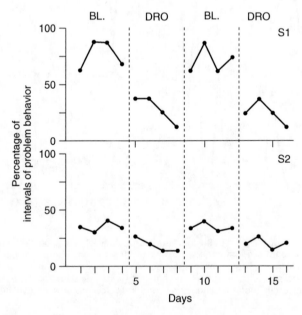

Figure 2. The same data as Figure 1 replotted using consistent
vertical axis scales.

(b)

Figure 8.21a and b Graphs showing the effects of using inconsistent ordinate scales (a) vs. consistent ordinate scales (b) (source: Kennedy, 1989. Copyright by Society for the Experimental Analysis of Behavior, Inc. Reproduced by permission).

conditions. When present on a graph, reviewers should not allow these to distract them from actual day-to-day data. These lines can draw attention away from actual trend and variability in data.

When plotting a statistical average (mean, median, or mode) of a participant's (or several students') responses, you should generally plot, or specify in the text, the numerical range of responses. The range of responses for a group of participants has sometimes been shown on a figure by drawing a vertical line above and below the plotted data point to the upper and lower levels along the ordinate, thereby showing the two levels between which all students' responses fell. When an individual participant's data are averaged within a condition, range is typically reported in the results section of the research report. Range is an important statistic to readers when averages are plotted. It permits readers to evaluate consistency or stability of an individual's behavior within each condition. When a group average is plotted, range indicates degree of variability across participants within a condition.

Using Computer Software to Construct Graphs

Most authors rely on computer software to graph their data. Several reasons contribute to this fact: (a) several journals, including *Journal of Autism and Developmental Disabilities* and *Education and Treatment of Children*, require online submissions; (b) data-plotting software is becoming increasingly available; (c) using computer software allows for accurate data plotting; and (d) if using a spreadsheet to enter data, "data can be stored and analyzed within the spreadsheet, preventing redundant data entry" (Carr & Burkholder, 1998, p. 245). According to Lo and Konrad (2007), "creating professional quality computer generated SS design graphs often presents a challenge even for veteran researchers and practitioners" (p. 156). Efforts to aide teachers, therapists, and other applied researchers have been made by several authors specifically focusing on the Microsoft Office software that is typically "included with or purchased with desktop and laptop computers" (Barton, Reichow, & Wolery, unpublished). Lo and Konrad (2007) and Carr and Burkholder (1998) outline steps for using Microsoft Excel to create a variety of single subject research design graphs while Hillman and Miller (2004) describe using Microsoft Excel for creating multiple baseline graphs. (See Appendix 8.1 and 8.2 for a detailed task analysis using Microsoft Excel to create simple line and bar graphs.) Alternatives to graphing within spreadsheets (e.g., Microsoft Excel) include using Microsoft Word (Grehan & Moran, 2005) and Microsoft PowerPoint (Barton et al., unpublished). With the availability of graphing software, it is important to note that adherence to all aforementioned guidelines for selecting and constructing graphic displays is crucial and "careful examination should be made of the range of scales available and the printer's capability for both accurate data point placement and precise printing of data paths" (Cooper et al., 2007, p. 149).

This overview of general guidelines for selecting a graphic display, constructing graphs, and presenting data is by no means exhaustive. Rather, it has highlighted those guidelines that are important to the objective analysis of graphically displayed data. Certainly, over time, new and improved computer graphing software will become available, simplifying the construction of graphic displays.

Tables

An alternative format for reporting data is the table. Data often reported in tables include: participant demographics, condition variables, efficiency data, reliability data, social validity, generalization, trials-to-criterion, errors-to-criterion, etc. Using a table to report supplemental or summative data can accomplish several things. Given the limited space of journal articles, presenting lengthy information in tabular form can condense it considerably. Table 8.1 shows a table with a considerable amount of information; displayed in a table, the data are organized and more comprehensible to readers. Tables also enable easy comparison of data. The trials-to-criterion and errors-to-criterion found in Table 8.2 are easily compared across sets of stimuli and participants. Occasionally tables are used to demonstrate magnitude of data. Table 8.3 illustrates this by showing the acquisition and maintenance of observational and incidental information (nutritional facts) by high school learners with moderate intellectual disabilities, while being taught to bag groceries. Inserting the solid line draws the readers' attention to the immediate effect intervention had on students' behavior and that the effect was replicated within a multiple probe design across dyads. Data gathered using a Likert scale are frequently summarized in tables. The information in Table 8.4 is a summary of selected social validity questions. Without having to read each question and answer, the table allows readers to determine teacher responses to each intervention component listed. Although tables efficiently highlight and summarize information, seldom are they used to present point-by-point data; rather, tables are primarily used for reporting supplemental or secondary data in single subject research studies. Tables provide an excellent format for summarizing some types of data but they are rarely used as a substitute for graphically displayed data.

Table Construction

The *Publication Manual of the American Psychological Association*, 5th edition, outlines the parameters of table construction. Here, we discuss the elements most pertinent to applied single subject research; these components are outlined in Table 8.5. Tables are double spaced and numbered in numerical order in the order they are mentioned in your text. Table titles are written in italics and should be succinct. Headings within the body are used to concisely organize the information you are sharing. Subheadings may also be used under each heading, when necessary. All headings should aide readers in finding pertinent information. Lines within tables should be limited to separating parts of the table to aide clarity for readers (e.g., around headings but not within the body). Vertical lines are not used. The size of a table will depend on the information being shared; careful consideration should be taken to fit the table within the text. "Turning a journal sideways to read a table is an inconvenience to readers" (APA, 2001, p. 174).

Summary

In this chapter we discussed the basic components and types of graphs and tables used to visually organize data collected in your research. Using the guidelines outlined in this chapter, you will be able to develop graphic displays appropriate for conducting visual analysis (see Chapter 9). While the information presented may appear cumbersome, it is imperative that you collect and organize your data accurately to ensure reliable data analysis. Selecting improper graphic displays or graphing data incorrectly may lead to unwarranted changes in instructional programs, incorrect conclusions of relations between dependent and independent variables, or unclear effects of interventions.

Table 8.1 Table Showing Organization of an Extensive Amount of Information

Student/Set	No. training sessions	No. training trials	No. training errors	% training errors	Training time (min:sec)	Daily probe time (min:sec)	No. of Probe errors	% probe errors
Erol								
1	15	45	0	0	135 min 18 s	45 min 05 s	17	37
2	11	33	0	0	99 min 16 s	33 min 08 s	9	27
3	5	15	0	0	45 min 44 s	15 min 12 s	5	33
Total	31	93	0	0	280 min 18 s	93 min 25 s	31	33
Yunus								
1	16	48	0	0	144 min 01 s	58 min 23 s	13	27
2	8	32	0	0	96 min 55 s	24 min 01 s	8	25
3	5	15	0	0	45 min 22 s	15 min 15 s	4	26
Total	29	95	0	0	286 min 18 s	97 min 39 s	25	26
Yasemin								
1	12	60	0	0	96 min 36 s	48 min 36 s	21	35
2	16	80	0	0	128 min 19 s	64 min 42 s	39	48
3	5	25	0	0	40 min 05 s	20 min 23 s	11	44
Total	33	165	0	0	265 min 00 s	133 min 41 s	71	43
Grand Total	93	353	0	0	831 min 36 s	324 min 45 s	127	35

Source: Birkan (2005). Copyright by Society for the Experimental Analysis of Behavior, Inc. Reproduced by permission.

Table 8.2 Table Showing Trials and Errors to Criterion Across Stimuli Sets for Three Students

Participant & behavior set	Stimuli	# trials (days) to criterion	Errors to criterion (%)
Colin			
Set 1	blue, six	40 (5)	7.5
Set 2	pink, nine	24 (3)	0.0
Set 3	yellow, one	24 (3)	0.0
Set 4	red, three	24 (3)	0.0
Derek			
Set 1	from, with	32 (4)	0.0
Set 2	down, once	32 (4)	0.0
Set 3	little, pretty	24 (3)	0.0
Set 4	left, walk	32 (4)	0.0
Dustin			
Set 1	$3 \times 4, 5 \times 6$	36 (5)	0.0
Set 2	$4 \times 7, 6 \times 10$	64 (8)	12.5
Set 3	$7 \times 3, 8 \times 4$	88 (11)	13.6
Set 4	$6 \times 7, 3 \times 8$	—	—

Source: Wolery et al. (2002). Copyright by Society for the Experimental Analysis of Behavior, Inc. Reproduced by permission.

Table 8.3 Table Showing Acquisition of Observational and Incidental Information. Lines are Inserted to Further Organize Data

Dyads	Learners	Probe Sessions and Dates							
		1 8/30	2 9/13	3 9/26	4 10/11	5 10/23	6 11/1	7 11/8	8 11/15
1	Adam	0	20	20	40	20	20	40	40
	Pete	0	100	100	100	100	100	100	80
2	Robert	0	0	60	60	40	60	20	20
	Barbara	0	0	60	60	60	60	60	20
3	Emma	0	0	0	100	100	100	100	100
	Danny	0	0	0	60	60	60	40	40
4	Dot	0	0	0	0	100	80	100	80
	Jim	0	0	0	0	60	60	20	20
5	Mary	0	0	0	0	0	100	80	100
	Cindi	0	0	0	0	0	80	60	0
6	Michael	0	0	0	0	0	0	40	40
	Cathy	0	0	0	0	0	0	100	80

Mean percentage correct responding at FR10 probe = 73.3% (range: 20%–100%)
Mean percentage correct responding at Probe 8 = 51.6% (range 0%–100%)
[a] Solid lines represent the occurrence of instruction and exposure to incidental information. The first probe after the vertical line for each dyad represents data collected after each dyad had reached the FR10 criterion point in the grocery-bagging program. Intermittent probe sessions were conducted when each dyad reached FR10 criterion. The Probe Session 8 column represents probes conducted for each learner 1 week after Dyad 6 reached FR10 criterion for the grocery-bagging skill.

Source: Wall & Gast (1999). Copyright by Society for the Experimental Analysis of Behavior, Inc. Reproduced by permission.

Table 8.4 Table Organizing Likert-Type Social Validity Data

Intervention components	Teacher responses on selected social validity issues[a]					
	Importance	n	Difficulty	n	Appropriateness	n
Creating communicative opportunities	Very (6–7)	9	Very (6–7)	0	Very (6–7)	9
	Moderately (3–5)	9	Moderately (3–5)	3	Moderately (3–5)	0
	Not (1–2)	0	Not (1–2)	6	Not (1–2)	0
Modeling desired skill	Very (6–7)	9	Very (6–7)	0	Very (6–7)	8
	Moderately (3–5)	0	Moderately (3–5)	1	Moderately (3–5)	1
	Not (1–2)	0	Not (1–2)	8	Not (1–2)	0
Providing specific guidance	Very (6–7)	7	Very (6–7)	0	Very (6–7)	9
	Moderately (3–5)	2	Moderately (3–5)	1	Moderately (3–5)	0
	Not (1–2)	0	Not (1–2)	8	Not (1–2)	0

Notes:

$n = 9$

[a] Teacher responses selected from anchored 7-point Likert scale.

Source: Johnston et al. (2003). Copyright by Society for the Experimental Analysis of Behavior, Inc. Reproduced by permission.

Table 8.5 Basic Component of a Table: (1) Table Number, (2) Title, (3) Headings, (4) Body, and (5) Lines ✓

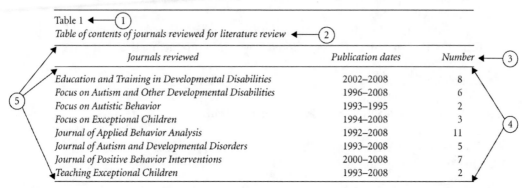

Appendix 8.1

Task Analysis for Creating a Simple Line Graph in Microsoft Excel (versions 97–2003).
*In Excel, there are cells. They correspond to the columns (letters) and rows (numbers).

1. Enter session/trial numbers in column A. Begin in row 2 (cell A2) with #0. You need to start with zero to bring the origin below zero on the ordinate.
2. Label conditions, beginning in column B (cell B1) (for example, column B—baseline, column C—intervention 1, etc.).
3. Enter data in corresponding column/row (for example, trial 1 in baseline would be recorded in cell B3, trial 2 would be recorded in cell B4, etc.).
4. Highlight all information (cell A1 to, for example, C13).
5. Click the "Chart Wizard" icon on the standard toolbar.
6. On the "Standard Types" thumbnail, click "Line."
7. Click "Next" (Excel defaults to the correct line graph).

8. Click "Next" again.
9. Move through the thumbnails by clicking directly on the names (titles, axes, etc.).
   a. Title—Chart Title—this is where you can name your graph (if you have more than one condition, it is recommended to leave this blank); Category (X) Axis—time (i.e., trials, sessions, etc.); Category (Y) Axis—dependent variable (i.e., % correct, # behaviors, etc.)
   b. Axes—no action needed
   c. Gridlines—uncheck "Value (Y) axis—Major gridlines"
   d. Legend—uncheck "Show Legend"
   e. Data Labels—no action needed
   f. Data Table—no action needed
10. Click "Finish."
11. Double click in gray area on graph to open "Format Plot Area" screen.
12. Select Border—None; Area—None; click "OK."
13. Double click on a data series to open "Format Data Series" screen.
14. On Patterns thumbnail—
    a. Line—leave defaults, change color to black by clicking arrow next to color and clicking on the black square
    b. Marker—leave defaults (if geometric shape), change foreground and background to black
    c. Click "OK"
15. Repeat steps 13–14 with each data series (data representing data taken on the same behavior (i.e., percent correct) should have the same geometric shape regardless of condition).
16. Double click on X axis to open "Format Axis" screen.
17. On "Scale" thumbnail:
    a. Unclick "Value (Y) axis crosses between categories
    b. Click "OK"
18. Double click on Y axis to open "Format Axis" screen.
19. On "Scale" thumbnail change the following:
    a. Minimum–5
    b. Maximum100
    c. Major Unit5
    d. Minor Unit1
    e. Category (X) axis crosses at –2
    f. Click "OK"
20. Left click in **chart area** until squares appear in the border around entire graph area.
21. Double click in chart area to open "Format Chart Area" screen.
22. Select Border—None; Area—None; click "OK."
23. With squares still around entire graph area, click "Edit," "Copy" from standard toolbar.
24. Open Microsoft Word.
25. Click "Edit," "Paste" from standard toolbar.
26. Click "View," "Toolbars," "Drawing" from standard toolbar (if needed).
27. Click the "Line" icon from drawing toolbar.
28. Draw a line between conditions.
29. Click the rectangle icon from drawing toolbar.
30. Draw a rectangle around the –5 on the ordinate and the 0 on the abscissa.

31. Double click on rectangle to open "Format Auto Shape" screen
32. On Colors and Lines thumbnail:
    a. Fill: no action
    b. Line: Color: No Line
    c. Arrows: no action
    d. Click "OK"
33. Click on "Text Box" from drawing toolbar.
34. Draw text box over graph.
35. Label each condition in text box.
36. If border appears around text box, double click on text box to open "Format Text Box" screen.
37. Select:
    a. Fill: Color: No Fill
    b. Line: Color: No Line
    c. Arrows: no action
38. To create multiple baseline or multiple probe graphs, simply follow steps 1–25 for each graph (you will need to enter data for each single graph independent of each other).
39. For all graphs but the bottom graph, you will need to add a step to number 17; while in the "Format X axis" tab, click the "Pattern" thumbnail; select "None" under tick mark labels.
40. If you do not move your curser during these steps, the graphs will line up one on top of the other. If they do not all fit one page, place your arrow on one of the corner black squares, click, and drag toward the middle of the graph. Note where you stopped so you can perform the same change to all graphs (they will need to end up with identical dimensions so the phase change lines will line up).
41. When all graphs are lined up, complete steps 26–37.

Appendix 8.2

Task Analysis for Creating a Simple Bar Graph in Microsoft Excel (versions 97–2003).
*In Excel, there are cells. They correspond to the columns (letters) and rows (numbers).

1. Enter abscissa variable (date/time) in column A. Begin in row 2 (cell A2).
2. Label conditions, beginning in column B (cell B1) (for example, column B—pretest, column C—posttest, etc.).
3. Enter data in corresponding column/row (for example, mean % complete pretest would be recorded in cell B2 and mean % complete posttest in cell B3, etc.).
4. Highlight all information (cell A1 to, for example, C3).
5. Click the "Chart Wizard" icon on the standard toolbar.
6. On the "Standard Types" thumbnail, click "Column."
7. Click "Next" (Excel defaults to the correct bar graph).
8. On the "Data Range" thumbnail, select Series in: "Columns."
9. Click "Next."
10. Move through the thumbnails by clicking directly on the names (titles, axes, etc.).
    a. Title—Chart Title—this is where you can name your graph (if you have more than one condition, it is recommended to leave this blank); Category (X) Axis—time (i.e., Date, etc.); Category (Y) Axis—dependent variable (i.e., % correct, # behaviors, etc.)

     b. Axes—no action needed

     c. Gridlines—uncheck "Value (Y) axis—Major gridlines"

     d. Legend—no action needed

     e. Data Labels—no action needed

     f. Data Table—no action needed

11. Click "Finish."

12. Double click in gray area on graph to open "Format Plot Area" screen.

13. Select Border—None; Area—None; click "OK."

14. Double click on a data series (bar) to open "Format Data Series" screen.

15. On Patterns thumbnail—

     a. Border—leave defaults, change color to black by clicking arrow next to color and clicking on the black square

     b. Area—click black square.

     c. Click "OK"

16. Repeat steps 14–15 with each data series (bar), changing the 2nd data series to white. If there are more than two series of data (bars), repeat steps 14–15, but for 14b, click "fill effects"; on "Gradient" thumbnail, click "One Color." On "Pattern" thumbnail, select a pattern. Click "OK," and then "OK" again.

17. Double click on X axis to open "Format Axis" screen.

18. On "Patterns" thumbnail:

     a. Select Major tick mark type: None.

     b. Click "OK"

19. Double click on Y axis to open "Format Axis" screen.

20. On "Scale" thumbnail change the following:

     a. Minimum–10

     b. Maximum100

     c. Major Unit10

     d. Minor Unit1

     e. Category (X) axis crosses at –2

     f. Click "OK"

21. Left click in **chart area** until squares appear in the border around entire graph area.

22. Double click in chart area to open "Format Chart Area" screen.

23. Select Border—None; Area—None; click "OK."

24. With squares still around entire graph area, click "Edit," "Copy" from standard toolbar.

25. Open Microsoft Word.

26. Click "Edit," "Paste" from standard toolbar.

27. Click "View," "Toolbars," "Drawing" from standard toolbar (if needed).

28. Click the "Line" icon from drawing toolbar.

29. Draw a line between conditions.

30. Click the rectangle icon from drawing toolbar.

31. Draw a rectangle around the –10 on the ordinate.

32. Double click on rectangle to open "Format Auto Shape" screen

33. On Colors and Lines thumbnail:

     a. Fill: no action

     b. Line: Color: No Line

     c. Arrows: no action

     d. Click "OK"

34. Click on "Text Box" from drawing toolbar.
35. Draw text box over graph.
36. Label each condition in text box.
37. If border appears around text box, double click on text box to open "Format Text Box" screen.
38. Select:
    a. Fill: Color: No Fill
    b. Line: Color: No Line
    c. Arrows: no action

References

American Psychological Association. (2001). *Publication manual of the American Psychological Association* (5th ed.). Washington, DC: American Psychological Association.

Barton, E. E., Reichow, B., & Wolery, M. *Guidelines for graphing data with Microsoft® PowerPoint™.* Unpublished manuscript, Vanderbilt University, Nashville, TN.

Birkan, B. (2005). Using simultaneous prompting for teaching various discrete tasks to students with mental retardation. *Education and Training in Developmental Disabilities, 40,* 68–79.

Carnine, D. W. (1976). Effects of two teacher presentation rates on off-task behavior, answering correctly, and participation. *Journal of Applied Behavior Analysis, 9,* 199–206.

Carr, J. E., & Burkholder, E. D. (1998). Creating single-subject design graphs with Microsoft Excel™. *Journal of Applied Behavior Analysis, 31,* 245–251.

Codding, R. S., Feinberg, A. B., Dunn, E. K., & Pace, G. M. (2005). Effects of immediate performance feedback on implementation of behavior support plans. *Journal of Applied Behavior Analysis, 38,* 205–219.

Conyers, C., Miltenberger, R., Maki, A., Barenz, R., Jurgens, M., Sailer, A., et al. (2004). A comparison of response cost and differential reinforcement of other behavior to reduce disruptive behavior in a preschool classroom. *Journal of Applied Behavior Analysis, 37,* 411–415.

Cooper, J. O., Heron, T. E., & Heward, W. L. (2007). *Applied behavior analysis* (2nd ed.). Columbus, OH: Pearson.

Ganz, J. B., & Simpson, R. (2004). Effects of communicative requesting and speech development of the picture exchange communication system in children with characteristics of autism. *Journal of Autism and Developmental Disorders, 34,* 395–409.

Grehan, P., & Moran, D. J. (2005). Constructing single-subject reversal design graphs using Microsoft Word™: A comprehensive tutorial. *The Behavior Analyst Today, 6,* 235–256.

Gutowski, S. J., & Stomer, R. (2003). Delayed matching to two-picture samples by individuals with and without disabilities: An analysis of the role of naming. *Journal of Applied Behavior Analysis, 36,* 487–505.

Hillman, H. L., & Miller, L. K. (2004). Designing multiple baseline graphs using Microsoft Excel™. *The Behavior Analyst Today, 5,* 372–424.

Hoch, H., McComas, J. J., Thompson, A. L., & Paone, D. (2002). Concurrent reinforcement schedules: Behavior change and maintenance without extinction. *Journal of Applied Behavior Analysis, 35,* 155–169.

Johnston, S., Nelson, C., Evans, J., & Palazolo, K. (2003). The use of visual supports in teaching young children with autism spectrum disorder to initiate interactions. *Augmentative and Alternative Communication, 19,* 86–103.

Kennedy, C. H. (1989). Selecting consistent vertical axis scales. *Journal of Applied Behavior Analysis, 22,* 338–339.

Kennedy, C. H., & Souza, G. (1995). Functional analysis and treatment of eye poking. *Journal of Applied Behavior Analysis, 28,* 27–37.

Lo, Y., & Konrad, M. (2007). A field-tested task analysis for creating single-subject graphs using Microsoft® Office Excel. *Journal of Behavioral Education, 16,* 155–189.

Maglieri, K. A., DeLeon, I. G., Rodriguez-Catter, V., & Sevin, B. M. (2000). Treatment of covert food stealing in an individual with prader-willi syndrome. *Journal of Applied Behavior Analysis, 33,* 615–618.

Mayfield, K. H., & Vollmer, T. R. (2007). Teaching math skills to at-risk students using home-based peer tutoring. *Journal of Applied Behavior Analysis, 40,* 223–237.

Nelson, C., McDonnell, A. P., Johnston, S. S., Crompton, A., & Nelson, A. R. (2007). Keys to play: A strategy to increase the social interactions of young children with autism and their typically developing peers. *Education and Training in Developmental Disabilities, 42,* 165–181.

O'Callaghan, P. M., Allen, K. D., Powell, S., & Salama, F. (2006). The efficacy of noncontingent escape for decreasing children's disruptive behavior during restorative dental treatment. *Journal of Applied Behavior Analysis, 39*, 161–171.

Parsonson, B. S., & Baer, D. M. (1978). The analysis and presentation of graphic data. In T. Kratochwill (Ed.) *Single subject research: Strategies for evaluating change* (pp. 101–165). New York: Academic Press.

Sanders, R. M. (1978). *How to plot data*. Lawrence, KA: H & H Enterprises.

Simon, J. L., & Thompson, R. H. (2006). The effects of undergarment type on the urinary continence of toddlers. *Journal of Applied Behavior Analysis, 39*, 363–368.

Smith, T., Mruzek, D. W., Wheat, L. A., & Hughes, C. (2006). Error correction in discrimination training for children with autism. *Behavioral Interventions, 21*, 245–263.

Wall, M. E., & Gast, D. L. (1999). Acquisition of incidental information during instruction for a response-chain skill. *Research in Developmental Disabilities, 20*, 31–50.

Wilder, D. A., Atwell, J., Wine, B. (2006). The effects of varying levels of treatment integrity on child compliance during treatment with a three-step prompting procedure. *Journal of Applied Behavior Analysis, 39*, 369–373.

Williams, G., Perez-Gonzalez, L. A., & Queiroz, A. B. (2005). Using a combined blocking procedure to teach color discrimination to a child with autism. *Journal of Applied Behavior Analysis, 38*, 555–558.

Wolery, M., Anthony, L., Caldwell, N. K., Snyder, E. D., & Morgante, J. D. (2002). Embedding and distributing constant time delay in circle time and transitions. *Topics in Early Childhood Special Education, 22*, 14–25.

Worsdell, A. S., Iwata, B. A., Dozier, C. L., Johnson, A. D., Neidert, P. L., & Thomason, J. L. (2005). Analysis of response repetition as an error-correction strategy during sight-word reading. *Journal of Applied Behavior Analysis, 38*, 511–527.

9

Visual Analysis of Graphic Data

David L. Gast and Amy D. Spriggs

Educators and therapists who are engaged in applied research must be in constant contact with their data if they are to ensure that research participants are benefiting from their involvement. Provided participant data are collected repeatedly, graphed regularly, and analyzed frequently within the context of an appropriate single subject research design, it is possible for applied researchers to evaluate the effectiveness of their intervention. Formative evaluation of program effectiveness requires a strategy for analyzing data across time and conditions.

The visual analysis of graphic data, in contrast to statistical analysis of data, represents the most frequently used data-analysis strategy employed with single subject research designs. It has several advantages for educators, therapists, and other direct service personnel. First, the visual-analysis approach can be used to evaluate data of individuals or small groups. Second, it is a dynamic process in that data are collected repeatedly, graphed regularly, and analyzed frequently. Third, data plotted on line graphs permit you to make data-based decisions throughout your research project. Fourth, it focuses on the analysis of individual data patterns, thereby facilitating individualization. Fifth, visual analysis of graphic data permits discovery of interesting findings that may not be directly related to the original research question or program objective. Serendipitous findings (Sidman, 1960; Skinner, 1957) are possible because "primary" data are collected, graphed, and analyzed regularly. Sixth, the graphic presentation of "primary" data permits independent analysis and interpretation of results, thus permitting others to judge for themselves whether an intervention has merit and whether findings are reliable and have social and ecological validity. Seventh, by graphing and analyzing data for all research participants, the effectiveness of an intervention with an individual participant is neither overestimated nor underestimated. For these reasons, visual analysis of graphic data is the strategy preferred by behavioral researchers working in applied settings. It is an approach that has proven to be both practical and reliable; therefore, we recommend its adoption by educators and clinicians involved in applied research when using single subject research designs.

Design Notation

Behavior analysts have adopted an "ABC" notation system to assist them in their analysis of single subject research. Through the use of this system we are able to convey information regarding our analyses without having to rely on lengthy narrative descriptions. Although alternative notation systems have been used by some researchers (Campbell & Stanley, 1966; Glass, Willson, & Gottman, 1975), the "ABC" notations are used more frequently. Table 9.1 summarizes, and briefly explains, the more common symbols used by behavior analysts in their description of single subject research designs.

The capital letter A is used to refer to baseline or probe conditions during which the target behavior is repeatedly measured under pre-intervention conditions. It is typically the first condition of a single subject experiment. Its primary purpose is to generate data in the absence of intervention, against which data collected in subsequent conditions can be compared. Though data collected under a baseline or probe condition may represent the natural frequency of the target behavior, as in free-operant research, they need not. The capital letter B is used to refer to the first experimental condition introduced into a data series. Subsequent experimental conditions, which differ procedurally from the first, will be noted with the letters C, D, etc., in the order of their introduction into the study. A single dash (–) is used to separate adjacent conditions (A-B-C-B-C). When two experimental condition procedures are combined to make a new experimental condition, letters denoting each of the two conditions are paired without use of the dashed line (BC). For example, if A refers to a baseline condition during which tokens are dispensed noncontingently, and B refers to contingent token delivery, and C refers to a response cost procedure, then the combination of the contingent token procedure (B) and the response cost procedure (C) would result in the new experimental condition BC. The sequence of conditions in this example might be presented as an A-B-A-BC-A-BC design in which the researcher is interested in comparing B and BC to A in

Table 9.1 "ABC" Notation System

Notation	Explanation
A	Represents a baseline condition in which the independent variable is not present.
B	Represents the first intervention introduced into the data series.
C	Represents the second intervention introduced into the study that is different from the first intervention.
A–B	A dashed line is used to separate adjacent conditions.
BC	Two letters not separated by a dashed line represent the introduction of two interventions in combination.
B–B′–B″	Primes are used to show a slight variation from the original procedure.
A_1–B_1–A_2–B_2	A numeral placed at the lower right of a letter notation indicates whether this was the first, second, third, etc., time that this condition was introduced into the data series.

this multitreatment experimental design. Referencing the new condition as BC, rather than C alone, assists reviewers in distinguishing between an experimental condition that introduces a novel procedure in isolation, and an experimental condition that reintroduces a procedure that now is paired with another procedure. This simple differentiation in the labeling of experimental conditions facilitates identification of the relation between experimental conditions.

In addition to the above notations, "primes" (e.g., ′, ″, ‴) are added to condition letters (e.g., B, B′, B″) to direct attention to slight variations in experimental procedures. For example, an instructional program designed to teach a student a new skill typically begins with a continuous reinforcement schedule (CRF) for each correct response. Upon reaching a predetermined criterion it is desirable to begin thinning the schedule of reinforcement. Reinforcement schedule thinning may entail reinforcing every second correct response (FR-2), followed by reinforcing on the average of every third correct response (VR-3). This reinforcement schedule thinning (CRF to FR-2 to VR-3) would be referenced as B, B′, and B″.

Another helpful notation practice is to number all similar conditions in sequence. For example, when conducting a visual analysis of graphic data presented within the context of an A-B-A-B design, you should number both A conditions and both B conditions in order (A_1-B_1-A_2-B_2). This assists in differentiating data patterns for similar conditions that were introduced at different points in time over the course of a study.

Visual Analysis of Graphic Data: General Guidelines

In this section we overview general guidelines for inspecting and interpreting line-graphed single subject research data. (The guidelines presented should not be viewed as hard-and-fast rules for interpreting graphic data.) Throughout our discussion we refer to two basic properties of data that need to be analyzed critically when conducting a visual analysis: level and trend. These terms, and operations for computing each, are discussed within the context of data plotted on equal interval rather than ratio (logarithmic) graphs. Therefore, our presentation of guidelines for conducting visual analyses is based on absolute rather than relative changes in data patterns. In their discussion of data-based decision rules for teaching, White and Haring (1980) addressed similar visual-analysis procedures but from a Precision Teaching perspective, which advocates using ratio charts and thus focuses on relative changes in data patterns. Regardless of which type of graph is used to plot data, equal interval or ratio, adherence to the visual-analysis guidelines that follow will result in a reliable evaluation of data.

Though there may be some disagreement among behavior analysts regarding what type of graph paper to use, what criterion to use to determine data stability, or when to refer to change in level as abrupt, there is little disagreement regarding what properties of data demand attention. Specifically, behavior analysts attend to (a) number of data points plotted within a condition; (b) number of variables changed between adjacent conditions; (c) level stability and changes in level within and between conditions; (d) trend direction, trend stability, and changes in trend within and between conditions; and (e) percentage of data points in one condition that fall with the range of data plotted in an adjacent condition. In the remainder of this chapter we address each of these visual-analysis components by defining terminology, describing how to compute each, and pointing out considerations and/or precautions. For the purpose of clarity, visual-analysis guidelines are discussed and graphically presented within the context of an A-B design. These same guidelines, however, are used regardless of conditions being compared (A-B, B-C, B-BC) or the single subject design within which data were collected.

Within-Condition Analysis

Condition Length

✓*Condition length* refers to how long a particular condition or phase is in effect. To determine the length of a condition simply count the number of data points plotted within a condition. ✓A minimum of three separate, and preferably consecutive, observation periods (e.g., sessions, days) are required to determine level stability and data trend. The specific number of observation periods will depend on the variability of the data: *the more variable the data, the longer the condition should be.* Baer, Wolf, and Risley (1968) recommend continuing a condition until "stability is clear." In regard to length of a baseline or probe condition, it is sometimes necessary for applied researchers to take into account both practical and ethical considerations before locking in to the "stability is clear" guideline. Some classes of behavior (self-injury, physical aggression, severe disruption) may require more immediate intervention when the target behavior jeopardizes health and/or safety of participants or those who are in close proximity to them. With such behaviors, a shorter baseline condition may be justified for practical and ethical reasons. When visually analyzing data, or conducting research with these classes of behavior, a shorter baseline condition is understandable and tolerated, though demonstration of experimental control will likely be weakened.

Level

✓The term *level* refers to the magnitude of data as indicated by the ordinate scale value. When inspecting data, there are two basic aspects of level that are important: level stability and level change. *Level stability* is the amount of variability, or range in data-point values, in a data series. ✓When the range of values is small (low variability), data are said to be stable. Generally, if 80% of the data points of a condition fall within a 20% range of the median level of all data-point values of a condition, applied researchers will consider the data stable. To calculate the *median level* of a data series, sequence the data-point values from low to high. If there are an odd number of entries, the median is the middle data-point value; if there is an even number of entries the median is the average of the two middle values. A *median line* is then drawn parallel to the abscissa at that value and a stability envelope is placed over the median line. A *stability envelope* refers to two parallel lines where one line is drawn above and one line drawn below the median line, the distance or range between the two lines indicating how much "bounce" or variability there can be in the data series to be considered "stable." These two lines must remain parallel to the median line. Using the "80%–20%" criteria, if 80% of the data points fall on or within 20% of the median value (represented by the stability envelope), the data would be described as stable. Figure 9.1 summarizes the operations for calculating median level (a), level stability with an odd number of data points (b), and level stability with an even number of data points (c).

The specific percentage (10, 15, 20, 25) used to determine level stability varies depending on such things as the number of opportunities to respond (as with a teacher-paced task) or the ✓frequency of the target behavior (as with a free-operant behavior). As a general rule, *the fewer the number of opportunities to respond, the larger the percentage used to calculate level stability.* If, for example, a student has 20 opportunities to respond during an instructional session, a 10% criterion for calculating stability is not uncommon. If, however, a student has only five opportunities to respond, a stability criterion of 20% would not be unreasonable. When studying a free-operant behavior, the general rule is to use a smaller percentage (10%) to calculate level stability when the data cluster around the uppermost values on the ordinate scale, and use a larger percentage (15–20%) when the data points fall within the middle or

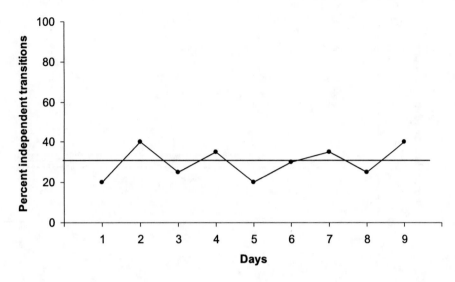

Range of data points (in order, low to high)	Median	Stability envelope
20, 20, 25, 25, 30, 35, 35, 40, 40 ⬆ (when there are an odd number of data points, the middle data point is the median)	30	

Figure 9.1 (a) Calculating median level.

lower range of ordinate values. Thus, before selecting a percentage for calculating level stability, note whether it is a regulated or free-operant behavior and within what range the data fall on the ordinate scale. Difficulty arises in determining a stability criterion when the behavior does not occur in the initial baseline condition (0 occurrence) and the dependent measure is frequency (number or rate) of occurrence. One strategy is to calculate the median level for the first experimental condition (B), since the baseline condition (A) data cannot be used. This stability envelope would be used for this and future conditions. The primary question you must ask yourself is whether the data are sufficiently stable to provide a convincing demonstration of experimental control when experimental conditions are changed. You should remember that the greater the variability in a data series, the greater the risk of not convincing your audience of experimental control.

When conducting a visual analysis on graphed percentage data (e.g., percentage of intervals, percentage correct) a 10–20% stability envelope is common. That is, a data series will be labeled as "stable" if 80% of the data points fall on or within a 20% range. The purpose of a stability envelope is to ensure you are consistent when using the term "stable" to describe the data in your report. *The stability envelope is calculated only once for a behavior and it is placed over the median line of the original condition (A) and all other conditions introduced to that behavior (B, BC, etc.).* If you are collecting data on multiple behaviors, as with a multiple baseline design across behaviors or when concurrently monitoring several behaviors within the context of an A-B-A-B design, you will use the same formula for calculating your stability envelope (e.g., 80% of the data points falling on or within 20% of the median level) but the

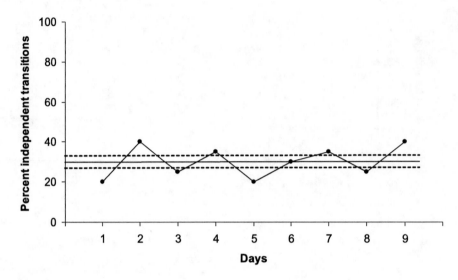

Range of data points (in order, low to high)	Median	Stability envelope
20, 20, 25, 25, 30, 35, 35, 40, 40 ▲ (when there are an odd number of data points, the middle data point is the median)	30	20% of 30 6

Figure 9.1 (b) Calculating level stability–odd numbers of days.

actual range of the envelope may vary depending on the median value of each of the behaviors in their respective baseline or probe condition. If percentage data are graphed, the envelope range should remain the same for all behaviors (e.g., 20%).

It should be noted that some researchers choose to base their visual analyses on the *mean level* rather than the median level of data points of a data series. While *mean* (sum of the data-point values divided by the number of data points) is a more familiar statistic, it has the disadvantage of being influenced by extreme values. For this reason the *median is recommended while conducting visual analyses of graphed data*.

A second aspect of level that is of interest to behavior analysts is the amount of change in level within the same condition. Level change within a condition may be reported in two ways. The *absolute level change within a condition* is computed by (a) identifying the ordinate values of the first and last data points of a condition; (b) subtracting the smallest from the largest; and (c) noting whether the change in level within the condition is in a therapeutic (improving) or contratherapeutic (deteriorating) direction, as indicated by the intervention objective. This provides a gross measure of level change. Calculating a *relative level change within a condition* is more representative. It is computed by (a) calculating the median value of the first half of the data series; (b) calculating the median value of the second half of the data series; (c) ignoring the middle data point if there are an odd number of data points across the condition; (d) subtracting the smallest median value from the largest median value; and (e) noting the difference between median values. Level stability is important, particularly in the second half

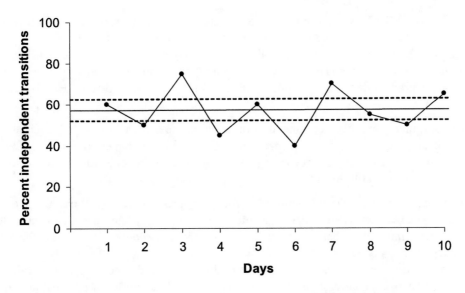

Range of data points (in order, low to high)	Median	Stability envelope
40, 45, 50, 50, 55, 60, 60, 65, 70, 75 (when there are an even number of data points, the average of the two middle data points is the median)	57.5	20% of 57.5 11.5

Figure 9.1 (c) Calculating level stability–even number of days.

of a long data series (seven or more data points), when determining whether it is appropriate to move to the next planned condition in the design sequence. *We recommend that the last 3–5 data points in a data series be analyzed for level stability, trend stability, and contratherapeutic trend direction before deciding whether to move to the next condition.*

Trend
When conducting a visual analysis the *trend* (slope or angle) of a data series is as important, if not more important, as the level of performance. In combination, a careful analysis of level and trend permits a reliable determination of experimental control. *Trend direction,* or slope, refers to the steepness of the data path across time. Typically a trend is referred to as *accelerating* (increasing in ordinate value over time), *decelerating* (decreasing in ordinate value over time), or *zero celerating* (data series is parallel to the abscissa). In addition to referring to the direction of trend, it is important to note whether the direction of a trend is improving or deteriorating.

Two methods are commonly used to estimate trend: freehand method and split-middle method. The *freehand method* entails visually inspecting the data of a condition and drawing a straight line that bisects the data points (Parsonson & Baer, 1978, 1992). Though this method takes very little time, without considerable practice the reliability of drawing a freehand *trend line* (sometimes referred to as a line of progress) that accurately depicts the slope of the data series is apt to be low. The *split-middle method,* as described by White and Haring (1980), provides a more reliable *estimate of trend* and, therefore, is recommended for use with variable data patterns. However, as noted by M. Wolery (personal communication, January 15, 2008), the predictive power of the split-middle line of trend estimation has been established with ratio graphs, rather than equal-interval graphs and, therefore, it is not clear how useful it may be in predicting trend direction with equal-interval graphed data. He went on to say that with

> most computer graphing programs, it is quite simple to switch from equal interval to semi-log graphic displays, so the impediments of the old ratio paper are not as great as they used to be. However, for reviewing someone else's figure, one would have to find the values and re-graph the data.

In spite of this precaution, the split-middle method may prove useful in estimating the overall trend within a condition when using equal-interval graph paper when the data are variable. It is important to remember that this method yields only an *estimate* of trend and the actual trend is depicted by the data on the graph.

The split-middle method, which relies on middle dates and median ordinate values to estimate trend across a condition, is outlined in Figure 9.2. It is important to note that a trend line is calculated using the data series of a single condition (A) and never across adjacent conditions (A-B). As recommended by Cooper, Heron, and Heward (2007), "A trend line can not be drawn by any method through a series of data points spanning a scale break on the vertical axis and generally should not be drawn across a scale break on the horizontal axis" (p. 152). A notable exception, however, is when estimating trend across the pre-intervention or initial probe condition (Probe 1) with a multiple probe design in which data are collected repeatedly but intermittently prior to the introduction of the independent variable (see Chapter 11 for additional information on multiple probe designs).

Having drawn the trend line for a condition you should re-inspect the same data series to see whether there are *multiple data paths within the trend*. Since some conditions of a study may not have a sufficient number of data points to calculate a trend line for each half of a data series, the freehand method is used. If all the data points approximate the direction of the condition trend line, you need go no further to analyze trend within that condition. If, however, two distinct data paths are visible, it is important to identify each (see Figure 9.3, graphs

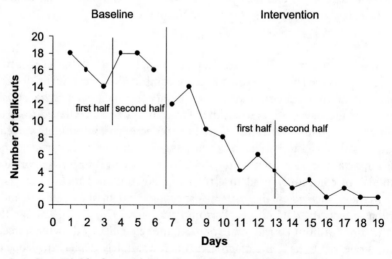

Figure 9.2a Step One: Divide data within each condition in half.

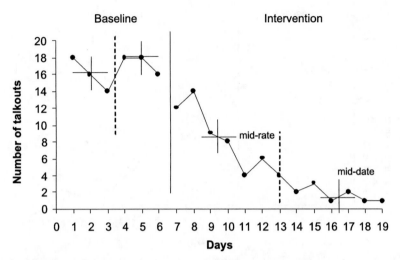

Figure 9.2b Step Two: Find the intersections of the mid-rate and mid-date for each half. The mid-rate is the middle data point counting up or down the data path (if even number of data points, mid-rate is between the two); the mid-date is the is the middle data point when counting left or right on the data path (if even number of data points, mid-date is between the two).

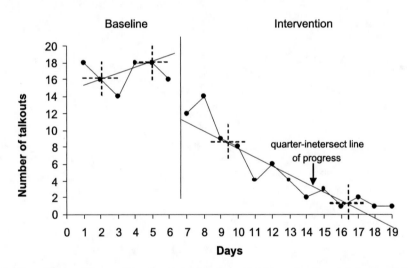

Figure 9.2c Step Three: Draw a line through the data which passes through both of the intersections found in step two (this is the quarter-intersect line).

"c" and "d"). The last data path within the trend should guide your decision whether to introduce a new condition into a data series (provided there are three or more data points that fall in line). It is important to remember that the trend line itself, as generated by the split-middle method, is an estimate of trend and, like the median and mean lines, can divert attention away from the actual, point-by-point data path.

In addition to determining trend direction, it is also important to determine *trend stability*. Similar to evaluating level stability, trend stability is evaluated by determining the number of data points that fall on or within a predetermined range along the condition trend line. Using the same level stability envelope that was calculated using the 80%–20% formula (80% of the data points falling on or within 20% of the median value) and placing it over the trend line,

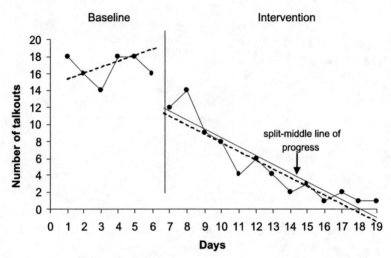

Figure 9.2d Step Four: Move the line(s) drawn in step three up or down so that there is an equal number of data points above and below the line . . . this is your split-middle line of progress. (In this example, the baseline data have 2 data points above and 2 data points below the quarter-intersect line, so the quarter-intersect line is also the split-middle line.)

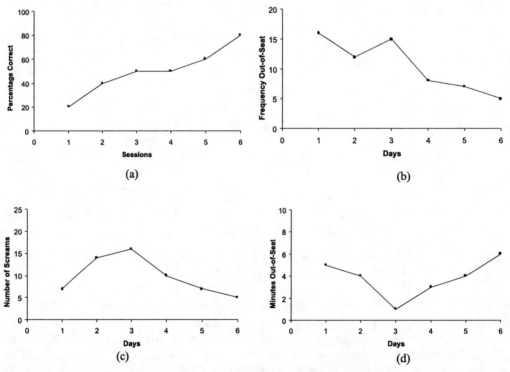

Figure 9.3 Common "within condition" data patterns showing accelerating, decelerating, and combination trends. (a) Improving acceleration trend (unacceptable). (b) Improving deceleration trend (unacceptable). (c) Deteriorating–improving trend (unacceptable). (d) Improving–deteriorating trend (acceptable).

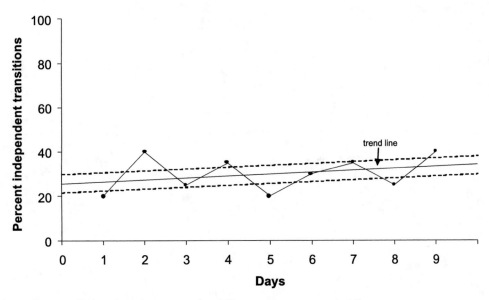

Figure 9.4 Graph showing placement of stability envelope over trend line.

trend stability can be evaluated. If 80% of the data points fall on or within the stability envelope, trend would be considered stable. It is important to remember that both sides of the stability envelope must remain parallel to the trend line, but the envelope may be moved up or down to capture as many data points as possible. Figure 9.4 exemplifies the positioning of the stability envelope over the trend line. In your report, whether it be oral or written, it is important to state your stability criterion. This permits reviewers to independently judge the rigor of your definition of stability.

Common Within-Condition Data Patterns
The visual analysis of data within a condition is concerned primarily with level and trend stability of the data. Figure 9.5, graph "a," depicts a stable data path across five data points. The range of scores is consistently between the 30% and 40% level. With this type of baseline data it would be appropriate to introduce the independent variable in Session 6. Figure 9.5, graph "b," however, presents variable data. The behavior analyst confronted with these data has two options: (1) continue measuring behavior under baseline conditions until the data stabilize, or (2) begin systematically searching for the source(s) responsible for the variability. Figure 9.5, graphs "c" and "d," present data depicting "deteriorating" or contratherapeutic trends, i.e., data paths that are in the direction opposite of improvement. In both cases, despite consistent changes in level across time, the trend direction is stable and, therefore, you could implement intervention in Session 6.

Figure 9.6 presents four examples of data paths in which variability is present. Figure 9.6, graph "a," shows an initial period of variability followed by stabilizing of the data. The initial period of data instability may have resulted from the participant not knowing the task response requirement or her knowing that she was being observed, which in turn diverted her attention from the task. In other words, she had not adapted to the new situation and her responding was affected. Once she adapted to the situation her responding stabilized. This type of data path shows that it is sometimes important to continue a condition to give a research participant sufficient time to adjust to novel environmental variables. A pattern of this type is acceptable

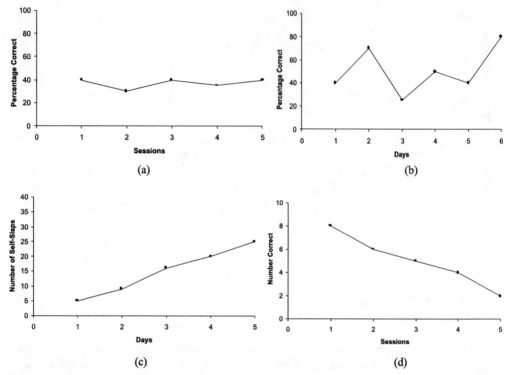

Figure 9.5 Common *"within condition" data patterns.* (a) Stable level and trend (acceptable). (b) Variable level and trend (unacceptable). (c) "Deteriorating" acceleration trend (acceptable). (d) "Deteriorating" deceleration trend (acceptable).

because of the stability in level and trend in the last half of the data series and it would be appropriate to change conditions on day 11.

Figure 9.6, graph "b," shows a data path that was initially stable but that became variable across time. Such trends pose a difficult problem. Variability may be a function of extraneous events (e.g., problems at home, illness), which may be temporary or permanent. Whatever the case, it is recommended that the condition be extended before conducting an experimental analysis.

A data path not uncommon to applied researchers is shown in Figure 9.6, graph "c." These data show high variability with a gradual accelerating trend in the direction of improvement. A change in condition in Session 9 would not provide a convincing demonstration of experimental control even if the data stabilized during the subsequent condition. If for practical or ethical reasons a change in condition is necessary, drawing a trend line using the split-middle procedure for each condition will facilitate the analysis of experimental effect. As a general rule, however, you should *identify and control sources of variability before beginning the next condition.*

A less common data path is presented in Figure 9.6, graph "d." These hypothetical data, collected on Mondays, Wednesdays, and Fridays, show an increase in the number of talk-outs on Fridays. They indicate that there is a regularly recurring event that is responsible for the *cyclical variability* across the condition. Although rare, when confronted with cyclical variability, you must identify and control the source before introducing the next scheduled condition.

The types of data paths shown in Figure 9.3, graphs "a" and "b," require you to continue

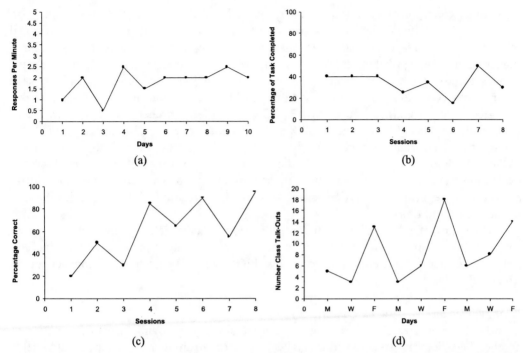

Figure 9.6 Common "within condition" data patterns showing variability. (a) Variable level and trend that stabilizes (acceptable). (b) Stable level and trend that becomes variable (unacceptable). (c) Variable level and improving trend (unacceptable). (d) Cyclical variability (unacceptable).

the condition until the data stabilize. If the improving trend is gradual, you may decide to introduce the next condition, in which case a trend line could be drawn to permit a comparison of trends across adjacent conditions. However, a change in conditions at this time will provide a "less clear" demonstration of experimental control. The preferred tactic is to continue collecting data until the data stabilize. Figure 9.3, graphs "c" and "d," show a "deteriorating–improving" trend and an "improving–deteriorating" trend, respectively. As noted, whether a trend is acceptable depends upon the dependent variable and the intervention. In Figure 9.3, graph "c," the last three data points are in the direction of improvement, and you should withhold introducing the independent variable until the data stabilize or reverse. Figure 9.3, graph "d," shows the duration of out-of-seat behavior decreasing (i.e., improving) on the first 3 days of the condition, signaling a possible adaptation effect, however, the trend began to reverse on day 4 and continued to increase on the following 2 days. Because of this reversal in trend over the last 3 days it would be appropriate to introduce intervention, although an additional 2–3 days in the condition would be desirable.

Between Adjacent Condition Analysis

The between adjacent condition analysis is based on observations and calculations performed during the within-condition analysis. When conducting a between-condition analysis it is important to remember that *only data in adjacent conditions can be directly compared*. The objective of a between-condition analysis is to determine what effect, if any, a change in condition (baseline to intervention, intervention to return to baseline, intervention B to intervention C) has on the dependent variable. In all experimental single subject design studies a particular condition (B) is introduced and reintroduced into one (A-B-A-B) or more than one (multiple baseline design) data series in order to evaluate whether there is a functional relation between independent and dependent variables. With such designs the researcher is interested in knowing what effect B has on A, and whether the effect can be replicated. In some single subject research comparison studies researchers are interested in comparing a specific experimental condition (B) to more than one condition (A, BC), as in an A_1-B_1-BC_1-B_2-BC_2 multitreatment design. In an A_1-B_1-BC_1-B_2-BC_2 design the researcher would be interested in comparing the effect of B to A and BC to B on the dependent variable. In the case of the B to A condition analysis, only correlation conclusions can be drawn since there is no reintroduction of the A condition into the data series. In the case of the BC to B analysis, a functional relation conclusion is possible since there are two opportunities to compare the effect of BC to B (intra-subject direct replication). Nothing can be said about the relation of BC to A since they are not adjacent conditions.

The analysis of data between adjacent conditions entails determining: (a) number of variables that change between adjacent conditions; (b) changes in level (magnitude and stability); (c) changes in trend (direction and stability); and (d) percentage of nonoverlapping data (PND).

Change One Variable Between Conditions

A cardinal rule in research is to change only one variable when moving from one condition to another. Behavior analysts go to considerable lengths to ensure that the independent variable is present in the experimental condition (B) and not present in the adjacent non-experimental or baseline condition (A). When the only difference between two adjacent conditions is the presence of the independent variable, you can evaluate the influence that variable has on the target behavior. To determine how many variables have changed between adjacent conditions, you carefully read the procedures for each condition described in the methods section, noting differences in procedures (e.g., prompting, reinforcement, correction), materials (e.g., two-dimensional, three-dimensional, color-coded), settings (e.g., location, adults), arrangement (e.g., 1:1, group), task format (e.g., expressive, receptive), etc. Sometimes subtle differences between conditions are overlooked that may influence behavior. For example, if during a language-training research project test (baseline or probe) sessions have 40 trials and instructional sessions have 20 trials, the doubling of the number of trials in test sessions will lengthen session time. Depending on whether some child behavior is reinforced (correct responses, response attempts, sitting properly, etc.) in the test condition, and on what schedule, a decrease in response attempts in the second half of a 40-trial test session may be observed. If such a response pattern were to be observed, it would be reasonable to suspect that the difference in the number of trials and session length between conditions adversely influenced the child's performance in test sessions.

It is common for applied researchers working in clinical and educational settings to develop and evaluate the effectiveness of treatment or instructional packages. Such packages typically include a number of procedures, each of which have been studied and shown to be effective in their own right. When the purpose of an investigation is to compare the effectiveness of an intervention package against other experimental or non-experimental conditions, it is important that the differences between conditions adjacent to the intervention package condition be identified. When analyzing data in such studies, you can only discuss the effect the intervention package, as a whole, had on the target behavior; you cannot evaluate the relative contribution of any one of its variables or procedures. In such studies it is important that each time the intervention package is in effect, all components of the package are present. It is recommended that a table be constructed, as shown in Table 9.2, which compares and contrasts variables across experimental and non-experimental conditions.

As both a designer and reviewer of experimental research, it is important to attend to this basic rule: *Change only one variable at a time and, if evaluating the effect of an intervention package, identify and report the number of differences between adjacent conditions, ensuring that each time the intervention package is used, those differences are in effect.* This rule holds true regardless of the condition (A, B, BC) to which you are moving. Adherence to this principle is fundamental for identifying functional relations.

Identify Level Change Between Adjacent Conditions
In discussing level change, you can report absolute and relative level change between conditions. The *absolute level change between two adjacent conditions* is computed by (a) comparing the ordinate values of the last data point of the first condition and the first data-point value of the second condition; (b) subtracting the smallest value from the largest value; and (c) noting whether the change in level is in an improving or deteriorating direction relative to the intervention objective. The absolute level change between conditions will indicate immediate strength or impact an intervention has on the dependent variable. When a "large change in level" occurs immediately after introduction of a new condition, level change is frequently referred to as an "abrupt" change in level, which is indicative of an immediately "powerful" or

Table 9.2 Comparison of Study Conditions

Three Study Conditions

Probo Procedures (Condition A)	Imitating Child's Dance, Play, and Vocalization (IC. Condition B)	Imitating Child with Expansion Intervention (ICE, Condition BC)

• Participant chooses an instrument
• Researcher takes a different instrument
• Researcher starts audio recording
• Researcher starts musical cassette tape
• Music plays for 20 seconds
  • Participant, plays instrument, dances, vocalizes
  • Researcher plays instrument, dances, vocalizes in parallel play without imitation for 20 seconds
• Music stops for 10-second response interval
  • Researcher stops and presents action and word pair models
  • Researcher verbally reinforces correct imitations
  • Researcher verbally describes participant's imitating response
• Music begins again
• Researcher records results on data sheet
	• Participant chooses an instrument
	• Researcher takes an identical instrument
	• Researcher starts audio recording
	• Researcher starts musical cassette tape
	• Music plays for 20 seconds
	  • Participant plays instrument dances, vocalizes
	  • Researcher plays instrument, dances vocalizes in parallel play without imitation for 5 seconds
	  • Researcher imitates participant's actions and sounds for 15 seconds
	• Music stops for 10-second response interval
	  Researcher stops and presents action and word pair models
	  • Reseracher reinforces correct imitations with cheers, puts hugs and/or smiles
	  • Researcher verbally describes participant's imitating response
	• Music begins again
	• Researcher records results on data sheet
		(Criterion for: introducing CE Participants fails to imitate behavior for at least 5 sessions during IC condition)
		  • Probe is implemented
		  • Add expansion with the following procedures
		    • If a participant imitates only the action or word model during the response interval the researcher expands by modeling the behavior not imitated by the child during the trial ("Also do (researcher demonstrates action)" or "Also say (researcher says word)").
		    • If a participant does not imitate during a trial, the researcher presents expansion with "Do (researcher demonstrates action) and "Say (researcher says word)" after that trial ends.
		• Music begins again
		• Researcher records results on data sheet

Source: C. Stephens (2005).

immediately effective intervention. Powerful interventions are desirable with most behaviors but critical with self-injurious and aggressive behaviors.

Relative level change between conditions is also reported. To calculate the *relative level change between two adjacent conditions* (a) identify the median value of the last half of the first condition and the median value of the first half of the second condition; (b) subtract the smallest value from the largest value; and (c) note whether the level change is in the direction of improvement or deterioration. This calculation will indicate whether there was a change in behavior in the initial phase after the introduction of the independent variable, but it will not necessarily reveal that the change was immediate, i.e., the first day of intervention. With some interventions (e.g., self-management programs) and some populations (e.g., young children or individuals with severe disabilities) a delayed effect may be predicted a priori. Although not ideal, in such cases when the delayed effect is anticipated and replicated across data series (participants and/or behaviors) it should have less of an effect on your analysis of findings and drawing conclusions of a functional relation being demonstrated.

Identify Change in Trend Direction

Change in trend direction between two adjacent conditions is probably the most important visual analysis determination you will make. By comparing trend lines across two adjacent conditions (A_1 and B_1) and within similar conditions (A_1 and A_2; B_1 and B_2) it is possible to determine the reliability of effect a change in conditions has on the dependent variable. Changes in trend between adjacent conditions are frequently expressed in terms of "accelerating to decelerating" (see Figure 9.7, graph "f"), "zero celerating to accelerating" (see Figure 9.7, graph "h"), or other similar phrasing. Note whether there was a change, and if there was, whether it was improving or deteriorating based on the intervention objective.

Calculate Percentage of Non-Overlapping Data (PND)

Finally, when comparing the data of two adjacent conditions, you should determine the *percentage of non-overlapping data point values (PND)*. PND is calculated by (a) determining the range of data-point values of the first condition; (b) counting the number of data points plotted in the second condition; (c) counting the number of data points of the second condition that fall *outside* the range of values of the first condition; and (d) dividing the number of data points which fall outside the range of the first condition by the total number of data points of the second condition and multiplying this number by 100 (Scruggs & Mastropieri, 1998). Figure 9.8 shows how to calculate PND. The percentage yielded by this computation reflects the PND between the two conditions. Generally, the higher the PND, the greater the impact the intervention has on the target behavior. An alternative to calculating PND is to calculate percentage of overlapping data points. *Percentage of overlapping data* (POD) is calculated by (a) determining the range of data-point values of the first condition; (b) counting the number of data points plotted in the second condition; (c) counting the number of data points of the second condition which fall *within* the range of values of the first condition; and (d) dividing the number of data points which fall within the range of the first condition by the total number of data points of the second condition and multiplying this number by 100. The percentage yielded by this computation reflects the percentage of overlap between the two conditions. Generally, the lower the percentage of overlap, the greater the impact the intervention has on the target behavior. Either computation, PND or POD, is acceptable though PND is reported more frequently. When using PND (or POD) it is important to be aware of the problems associated with it. Figure 9.9 graphically depicts how reliance on PND alone can compromise your analysis of findings and lead to an incorrect conclusion regarding inter-

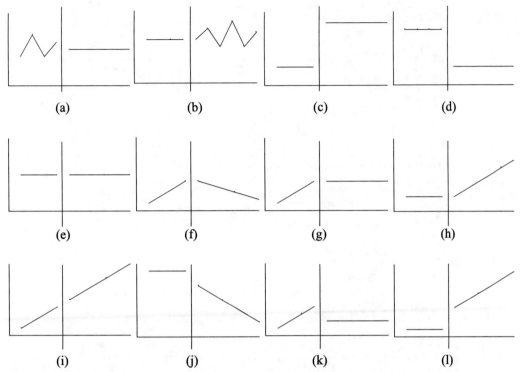

Figure 9.7 Common "between condition" data patterns. Summary of data patterns across two conditions: Graphs (a) and (b), change in variability; Graphs (c) and (d), change in level; Graphs (e) and (i), no change in data; Graphs (f), (g), and (h), change in trend; Graphs (j), (k), and (l), change in level and trend.

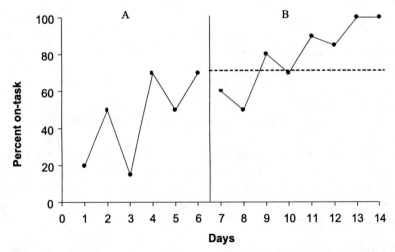

Figure 9.8 Calculating PND. (a) Determine the range of data point values of first condition (15–70); (b) count the number of data points plotted in the second condition (8); (c) count the number of data points of the second condition that fall outside the range of values of the first condition (5); (d) divide the number of data points which fall outside the range of the first condition by the total number of data points of the second condition and multiplying this number by 100 ($5/8 \times 100 = 62.5\%$).

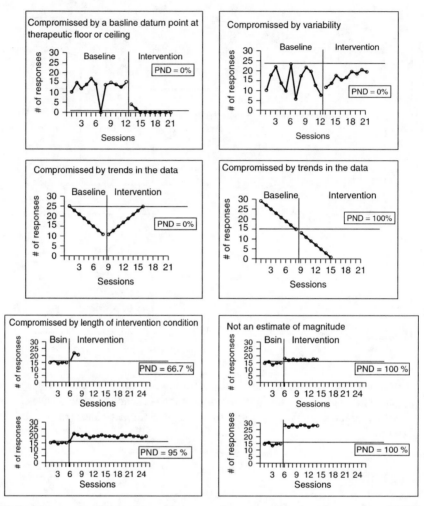

Figure 9.9 Problems associated with percentage of non-overlapping data points (PND) (source: M. Wolery, personal communication, January 15, 2008).

vention effectiveness. Regardless of which you choose to compute, one or the other should be reported along with the other calculations discussed when conducting a detailed visual analysis of graphic data.

We would like to make one last point before leaving the discussion of PND and POD. The methods for calculating PND and POD discussed here are used with all single subject research designs except the alternating treatments design (ATD), also referred to as the multi-element design. The method for calculating PND and POD within an ATD is discussed in Chapter 12, Comparative Intervention Designs.

Common Between-Condition Data Paths

Figure 9.7 presents several common between-condition data patterns. A stable data path should be present in the condition immediately preceding the condition being analyzed. For example, when baseline data are variable (Figure 9.7, graph "a"), it is difficult to inter-pret the experimental effect. The degree of experimental control that can be demonstrated with variable data paths within either condition will depend upon change in level from one condition to the next and percentage of non-overlapping data (PND) in both conditions (Wolery & Harris, 1982). That is, small changes in the dependent-variable values during intervention, which follow a variable data path in baseline condition (Figure 9.7, graph "a"), provide a weaker demonstration of experimental control than small changes in intervention preceded by a stable baseline data path (Figure 9.7, graph "b"). Also, the higher the PND (or the lower POD) between two adjacent conditions the more convincing the demonstration that the intervention was responsible for experimental effect. Data patterns presented in Figure 9.7, graphs "a" and "b" depict variable data paths within a condition and data overlap between conditions. Both cases permit only a statement about change in level and trend stability when the intervention was introduced, not trend direction.

Figure 9.7, graphs "c" and "d" show data patterns frequently encountered by behavior analysts. Figure 9.7, graph "c" represents an increase in level following a stable trend at a lower level in the preceding condition; graph "d" represents an decrease in level following a stable trend at a higher level in the preceding condition. Figure 9.7, graph "c" presents a data pattern in which there is an immediate and abrupt change in the dependent variable upon introduction of the independent variable, a pattern representative of an effective, if not ideal, behavior acceleration program. Figure 9.7, graph "d" represents a data pattern of an immediately effective behavior deceleration program. Both patterns are easily interpreted.

Generally, reviewers are more impressed with an intervention that results in an immediate and abrupt change in response level. Birnbrauer (1981), however, recommended that applied researchers not lose sight of the fact that level of effect during intervention is directly related to the procedures in effect during a baseline condition. A lengthy baseline condition, or a baseline condition in which a thin schedule of reinforcement is operating, has a tendency to depress level of responding. If such baseline conditions are followed by a "rich" intervention package that includes task novelty, stimulus prompts or cues, response prompts, and a dense schedule of reinforcement, there is an increased probability that an immediate and abrupt change in response level will result. Therefore, when conducting a visual analysis of changes in level, as well as in trend, it is important to pay particular attention to (a) the length of the first condition in the comparison and (b) the *procedural contrast* or differences between the two adjacent conditions. When the procedural differences between conditions are small, the change in level need not be large to conclude that the independent variable was effective. When procedural contrast is minimized, it also is easier to isolate the controlling variable.

Figure 9.7, graph "e" shows no change in level of the dependent variable across the two adjacent conditions, i.e., the two conditions are said to be *functionally equivalent*. If these data represent baseline (A) and intervention (B) conditions, respectively, you can treat the two conditions as equivalent and immediately introduce a new intervention (C or BC). The notation of these two adjacent and functionally equivalent conditions is A = B rather than A-B. When two adjacent conditions are functionally equivalent, it is one of the few times that you are *not* required to reintroduce the A condition before introducing a novel condition, e.g., B or BC.

The remaining graphs in Figure 9.7 (f, g, h, I, j, k, and l) exemplify the more common changes in trends between adjacent conditions. Graphs "f," "g," and "h" display changes in trend in the second condition (B) that are not accompanied by an absolute change in level. Figure 9.7, graph "f" shows that the trend was reversed when the intervention was introduced. Figure 9.7, graph "g" shows that the increasing trend in A changed to a zero-celerating trend in B. Figure 9.7, graph "h" shows that a zero-celerating trend in baseline condition changed to an accelerating trend when the independent variable was introduced. In each example, when intervention was introduced, trend direction was influenced. Whether change in trend was improving depends upon the objective of the intervention. If the dependent variable in Figure 9.7, graph "h" were the percentage correct in calculating addition problems, these data would represent an accelerating improving trend during instruction. If, however, the dependent variable were the number of talk-outs during a 30-min independent work activity, these data would represent a deteriorating trend. The acceptability of a trend change cannot be determined without referring to the intervention objective.

Figure 9.7, graph "i" shows no change in trend direction as a function of the independent variable, i.e., the slope of the data path in intervention is the same as in baseline condition. These data are interpreted in the same manner as data presented in Figure 9.7, graph "e," i.e., the independent variable had no effect and therefore the two conditions are functionally equivalent. In this example (graph "i"), if you were to base your analysis solely on mean or median change, range of data values, and/or PND between adjacent conditions, you would incorrectly conclude that the independent variable had a positive effect on the dependent variable.

Figure 9.7, graphs "j," "k," and "l" exemplify changes in trend accompanied by changes in level immediately upon the introduction of the intervention. In all three examples, baseline condition trend is stable; however, introduction of the independent variable resulted in a decelerating trend in graph "j," a zero-celerating trend in graph "k," and an accelerating trend in graph "l."

The 12 data patterns presented in Figure 9.7 represent the more common patterns you will encounter when evaluating single subject research. Figure 9.10 presents three additional patterns, which were discussed by Glass et al. (1975). These patterns represent: (a) a temporary change in level and trend (Figure 9.10, graph "a"); (b) a delayed change in level and trend (Figure 9.10, graph "b"); (c) a decaying change in level and trend (Figure 9.10, graph "c"). For each of these three data patterns an example is presented for an acceleration program (graph on left) and a deceleration program (graph on right).

Temporary and deteriorating change patterns (Figure 9.10, graphs "a" and "c," respectively) indicate that the introduction of the independent variable resulted in an abrupt change in level, but over time the data path returned to near baseline levels. Such data patterns may be a function of weak behavior consequences, reinforcer satiation, or some extraneous event that coincided with the introduction of the independent variable. When confronted with a temporary or deteriorating data pattern, begin an experimental analysis to determine the cause. The delayed change data pattern shown in Figure 9.10, graph "b" could be a function of a weakness in the initial phase of an instructional or therapy program or the child's need for a period of adaptation to discriminate changes between conditions. If condition lengths were short (e.g., 3 days), it would not be possible to detect such transitory changes. In either case, you must decide whether a more abrupt and rapid change in the participant's behavior is desirable. If it is, a systematic analysis of the initial phase of the intervention program should be conducted.

Analysis of Changes Across Similar Conditions

The discussion thus far has focused on the visual analysis of data within conditions and between two adjacent conditions. In order to simplify the presentation of visual-analysis guidelines, data were displayed across two conditions (baseline and intervention). As previously mentioned, the A-B design precludes demonstrating a functional relation between independent and dependent variables. If cause–effect conclusions are to be drawn, the experimental

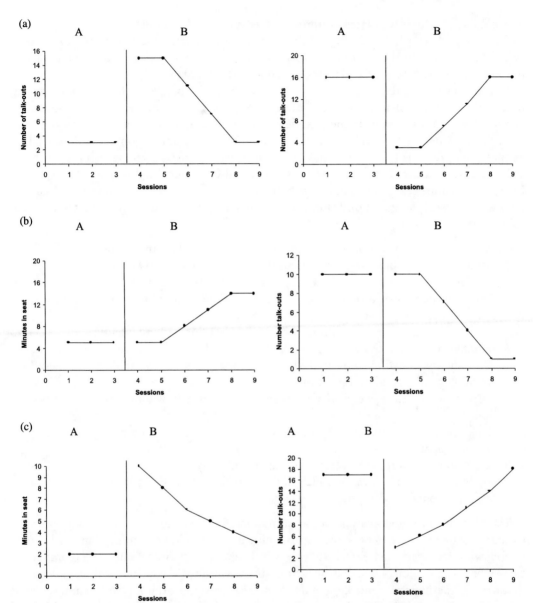

Figure 9.10 Temporary, delayed, and decaying data patterns across conditions. (a) Temporary change in level and trend. (b) Delayed change in level and trend. (c) Decaying change in level and trend.

effect must be replicated either through systematic withdrawal and reintroduction of the independent variable (A-B-A-B design) or through systematic introduction of the independent variable across behaviors, participants, or conditions (multiple baseline or multiple probe designs). This replication of effect is necessary to demonstrate a functional relation between an independent and dependent variables.

The analysis of changes across similar conditions focuses on two questions: (1) Are baseline levels maintained until the independent variable is introduced (multiple baseline or multiple probe design) or retrieved or approximated in subsequent baseline conditions (A-B-A-B design)? And (2) Do level and trend improve immediately after introduction of the independent variable? If guidelines for analyzing within- and between-condition data have been followed, and if the answers to these two questions are "yes," then an experimental analysis of the relation between intervention and target behavior has been accomplished.

Due to practical and ethical constraints, however, it is not always possible for applied researchers to adhere strictly to all recommended guidelines. On these occasions you must decide whether deviations from these guidelines jeopardize a demonstration of experimental control. Some degree of deviation may be acceptable, depending upon the guideline. For example, some degree of data variability may be acceptable; a lower percentage of PND may be acceptable; and, under some circumstances, shortened condition lengths may be acceptable. Under no circumstances, however, can there be deviations from other recommended guidelines without weakening demonstration of experimental control. Guidelines that should be adhered to strictly include:

1. Repeated measurement of the dependent variable across time and conditions;
2. Use of a single subject research design that adequately controls for extraneous and potentially confounding variables (i.e., threats to internal validity);
3. Systematic manipulation of only one variable at a time, or, at minimum, the identification of differences between adjacent conditions;
4. Implementation of each condition with a high level of procedural fidelity;
5. Maintenance of relatively stable baseline levels and trends in a zero-celerating or contratherapeutic direction until the independent variable has been introduced (multiple baseline and multiple probe designs);
6. Retrieval of baseline levels of responding with A-B-A-B withdrawal and reversal designs;
7. Replication of experimental effect across similar experimental conditions, behaviors, and participants;
8. Inspection of multiple characteristics (e.g., level, trend, PND) of graphed data across conditions prior to drawing conclusions as to the effect the independent variable had on dependent variable(s).

The objective of visual analysis of data across similar conditions is extremely important if accurate statements are to be made regarding the internal validity of an experimental effect. By following recommended guidelines you will be able to determine whether experimental control has been demonstrated. When a visual analysis results in your questioning a demonstration of experimental control, you must identify why the experimental demonstration was weakened or jeopardized. Through such *post hoc* analysis you will be able to redesign a study controlling for previously uncontrolled variables. In addition, these analyses provide an excellent source for identifying research questions.

As discussed in Chapter 14, Statistics and Single Subject Research Methodology, there continues to be disagreement among some researchers, particularly those who advocate a statistical analysis of data, as to the reliability of conclusions based on a visual analysis of graphic data. Few would argue that the greater the variability in the data, and reliance on only one or two visual-analysis variables (trend, PND, etc.) is likely to increase disagreements among visual analysts. However, agreement between analysts can be increased if proposed visual-analysis guidelines are followed. It is important to remember that visual analysis of graphic data, a dynamic process, allows scientist-practitioners to adjust their intervention in response to *each* participant's behavior while maintaining the experimental integrity of their study. The data analyzed are the primary or "raw data" of each individual participant, rather than some measure of central tendency of a group, and conclusions are dependent on the degree to which individual analysts agree that the intervention is replicated across participants. For you to be responsive to your research participants' needs while evaluating the effectiveness of the intervention program, visual analysis of graphic data is recommended.

Sample Visual Analysis

In this section we outline a process for conducting a visual analysis addressing those properties of a data series that we have found helpful when analyzing data within and between conditions of a study. Table 9.3 summarizes these data-path properties and the operations for evaluating each. Although not necessary when conducting a visual analysis, you may find Tables 9.4 and 9.5 helpful for organizing and summarizing your calculations, determinations, and analyses. With repeated practice these tables may not be needed. If you choose not to use these summary tables, you are encouraged to develop a visual-analysis summary format that will help you organize and analyze your observations and calculations. It is important to note that the tables are done by data series, i.e., if there are three participants in an A-B-A-B design study these tables would be completed for each participant; if you used a multiple baseline design across behaviors, they would be done for each behavior.

To simplify our discussion of the visual-analysis process, the hypothetical data presented in Figure 9.11 are used. These hypothetical data represent the number of minutes a child, enrolled in a 3-hour after school program, was engaged with peers. Data were collected using a total-duration recording procedure for 2 hours each afternoon during baseline and intervention conditions. For the purposes of our example, the baseline condition (A) represents after-school program staff's engagement with the child when he was alone; during the intervention condition (B) program staff's attention was contingent upon the child being in the

Table 9.3 List of Within and Between Visual Analysis Variables

Within condition	Between conditions
1. Condition sequence	1. Number variables changed; specify

2. Condition length	2. Changes in trend
	  2.1 Direction change
	  2.2 Effect relative to objective
	  2.3 Stability change

3. Level
  3.1 Median
  3.2 Mean
  3.3 Range
  3.4 Stability envelope range
	3. Change in level
	  3.1 Relative change
	  3.2 Absolute change
	  3.3 Median change
	  3.4 Mean change

4. Level change
  4.1 Relative change
  4.2 Absolute change
	4. Data overlap
	  4.1 PND
	  4.2 POD

5. Trend
  5.1 Direction
  5.2 Improving or deteriorating
  5.3 Stability
  5.4 Multiple paths	

Table 9.4 Within Condition Analysis Format

	1	2	3	4
1. Condition sequence:	___	___	___	___
2. Condition length:	___	___	___	___
3. Level:				
3.1 Median	___	___	___	___
3.2 Mean	___	___	___	___
3.3 Range	_ .	_ .	_ .	_ .
3.4–3.6 Stability envelope				
(___/___=___)	___	___	___	___
4. Level change:				
4.1 Relative change	___	___	___	___
4.2 Absolute change	___	___	___	___
5. Trend:				
5.1 Direction	___	___	___	___
5.2 Stability	___	___	___	___
5.3 Multiple paths within trend	___	___	___	___

Table 9.5 Between Conditions Anaylsis Format

Condition comparison	___	___	___	___	2nd condition / 1st condition
1. Number variables changed; specify	1 ___	1 ___	1 ___	1 ___	
	2 ___	2 ___	2 ___	2 ___	
	3 ___	3 ___	3 ___	3 ___	
2. Change in trend					
2.1 Direction change	_I_ .	_I_ .	_I_ .	_I_ .	
2.2 Effect	___	___	___	___	
2.3 Stability change	___	___	___	___	
	to	to	to	to	
	___	___	___	___	
3. Change in level					
3.1 Relative change	___	___	___	___	
	to	to	to	to	
	___	___	___	___	
3.2 Absolute change	___	___	___	___	
	to	to	to	to	
	___	___	___	___	
3.3 Median change	___	___	___	___	
	to	to	to	to	
	___	___	___	___	
3.4 Mean change	___	___	___	___	
	to	to	to	to	
	___	___	___	___	
4. Data overlap					
4.1 PND	___	___	___	___	
4.2 POD	___	___	___	___	

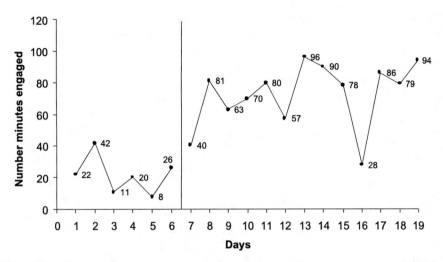

Figure 9.11 Hypothetical data for a contingent attention study to increase number of minutes engaged with peers.

Table 9.6 Summary of "Within Conditions" Visual Analysis of Hypothetical Data Plotted in Figure 9.11

	A$_1$	B$_1$		
1. Condition sequence:	1	2	3	4
2. Condition length:	6	13		
3. Level:				
3.1 Median	21	79		
3.2 Mean	21.5	72.46		
3.3 Range	8–42	28–96	–	–
3.4–3.6 Stability envelope				
(80. / 25. = 5.4)	variable	variable		
4. Level change:				
4.1 Relative change	22–20	66.5–82.5		
4.2 Absolute change	22–26	40–94		
5. Trend:				
5.1 Direction	decelerating	accelerating		
5.2 Stability	variable	variable		
5.3 Multiple paths within trend	no	no		

presence of one or more peers, i.e., independent variable. A functional-behavior assessment (FBA) conducted prior to deciding on an intervention showed that adult attention served as a positive reinforcer. The objective of intervention was to increase number of minutes the child was engaged with peers during the 2-hour observation period, i.e., dependent variable. The completed visual analysis of data graphed in Figure 9.11 is presented in Tables 9.6 and 9.7.

Analysis Within Condition (Refer to Table 9.6)

Step 1: Identify condition sequence. Using the "ABC" letter notation system; assign a letter to each different condition of the study.

Condition Sequence	A$_1$	B$_1$

Table 9.7 Summary of "Between Conditions" Visual Analysis of Hypothetical Data Plotted in Figure 9.11

Condition comparison	B . A				2nd condition 1st condition
1. Number variables changed; specify	– .				
	1 contingency	1 _____	1 _____	1 _____	
	2 _____	2 _____	2 _____	2 _____	
	3 _____	3 _____	3 _____	3 _____	
2. Change in trend					
2.1 Direction change	– $\bigvee$ +	_____	_____	_____	
2.2 Effect	positive	_____	_____	_____	
2.3 Stability change	variable				
	to	to	to	to	
	variable	_____	_____	_____	
3. Change in level					
3.1 Relative change	66.5 .	_____	_____	_____	
	to	to	to	to	
	20 .	_____	_____	_____	
3.2 Absolute change	40 .	_____	_____	_____	
	to	to	to	to	
	26 .	_____	_____	_____	
3.3 Median change	79 .	_____	_____	_____	
	to	to	to	to	
	21 .	_____	_____	_____	
3.4 Mean change	72.5 .	_____	_____	_____	
	to	to	to	to	
	21.5 .	_____	_____	_____	
4. Data overlap					
4.1 PND	84.6%	_____	_____	_____	
4.2 POD	15.4%	_____	_____	_____	

Step 2: Determine condition length. Count the number of data points plotted in Condition A. Count the number of data points plotted in Condition B.

Conditions	A_1	B_1
Condition length	6	13

Step 3: Determine level stability and range.

Find the median level (middle value) of Condition A (and then Condition B) by arranging the data points from lowest to highest and locating the middle data point (odd number of data points in the data series) or average of the two middle data points (even number of data points in the data series).

Condition A								
Day	1	2	3	4	5	6		
Data point value	22	42	11	20	8	26		
Median	21							

Condition A data-point values from low to high: 8, 11, 20, 22, 26, 42.

Median = 21 (average of two middle values, 20 and 22; 20 + 22 = 42/2 = 21).

Condition B													
Day	7	8	9	10	11	12	13	14	15	16	17	18	19
Data point value	40	81	63	70	80	57	96	90	78	28	86	79	94
Median	79												

Condition B data values from low to high: 28, 40, 57, 63, 70, 78, 79, 80, 81, 86, 90, 94, 96.
   Median = 79 (middle data point).

Find the mean for Condition A (and then Condition B) by adding the values of all the data points in a condition and dividing by the number of data points.

Condition A									Total
Day	1	2	3	4	5	6			
Data point value	22	42	11	20	8	26			129
Mean									129/6 = 21.5

Condition B														Total
Day	7	8	9	10	11	12	13	14	15	16	17	18	19	
Data point value	40	81	63	70	80	57	96	90	78	28	86	79	94	942
Mean														942/13 = 72.46

Draw a median line across Condition A at the median-level value (21) and Condition B median-level value (79). See Figure 9.12a.

Using the median level of Condition A and the stability criterion, 80% of the data points falling within 25% of the median, calculate 25% of the median value by multiplying $0.25 \times 21 = 5.25$. The width, or range, of the stability envelope (two lines parallel to and superimposed over the median line) will be 5.25. See Figure 9.12b.

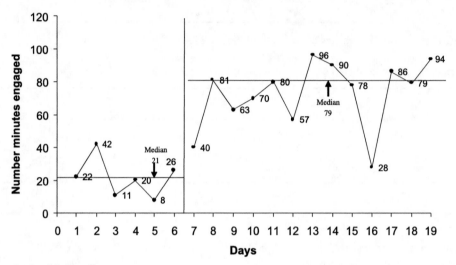

Figure 9.12a Median lines.

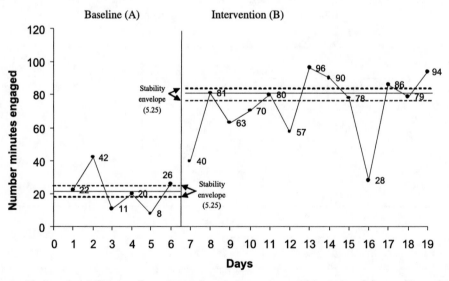

Figure 9.12b Level stability envelope (80% data points on or within 25% of the median of A).

Calculate the percentage of data points that fall on or within the level stability range as shown by the stability envelope. The stability envelope may be moved up or down along the ordinate to "capture" as many data points as possible on or within the stability range but it must remain parallel to the median line.

	Condition A	Condition B
Number of data points in the condition	6	13
Number of data points on or within the envelope	3	4
Percent on or within the envelope	$3/6 \times 100 = 50\%$ variable	$4/13 \times 100 = 30.8\%$ variable

The level of data in both A and B conditions would be described as variable since less than 80% of the data points fall within 25% of the median values of each condition. The assignment of "variable" to these two data paths refers only to level, not trend. Trend stability is calculated separately using the trend line.

Identify the range of values in Condition A (and then Condition B) by recording the lowest data-point value and the highest data-point value.

	Condition A	Condition B
Range	8–42	28–96

Step 4: Determine level change with Condition A and Condition B:

4.1 Identify *relative level change* within each condition by calculating the median value of the first half of the data path in a condition and the median value of the second half of the data path in a condition. If there are an odd number of data points in the condition the middle day's data-point value is not included in the calculation. Subtract the smallest value from the largest value and note whether the change is in the direction of improvement or deterioration.

	Condition A	Condition B
Median 1st half	22	66.5
Median 2nd half	20	82.5
Relative level change	−2 deteriorating	+16 improving

4.2 Identify *absolute level change* within each condition by recording the data-point value of the first day of the condition and the data-point value of the last day of the condition. Subtract the smallest value from the largest value and note whether the change is in the direction of improvement or deterioration.

	Condition A	Condition B
First data point value	22	40
Last data point value	26	94
Absolute level change	−4 deteriorating	+54 improving

The relative and absolute level changes in Condition A indicate little or no change in level within the condition, something one strives for in a condition, particularly in a baseline or probe condition. The relative and absolute level changes in Condition B indicate a positive-level change in the direction of improvement, which is desirable after introduction of an intervention condition. Level change within a condition is only one of several properties of the data path that is considered when analyzing the stability of the data within a condition.

Step 5: Estimate trend direction. Use the freehand or split-middle method to estimate trend direction for Condition A and Condition B. Figure 9.2 task analyzes the split-middle procedure. Figure 9.12c visually depicts the estimate of trend calculated using the split-middle procedure for Condition A in which there are an even number of data points, and Condition B in which there are an odd number of data points. Table 9.6 indicates the direction of the trend for Conditions A (decelerating) and B (accelerating). It also identifies the trend in Condition A as "deteriorating" and trend in Condition B as "improving" based on the objective of the intervention to increase minutes engaged. It is important to note that the actual trend is the graphed data path and that the split-middle, like any statistical procedure, provides only an estimate of reality.

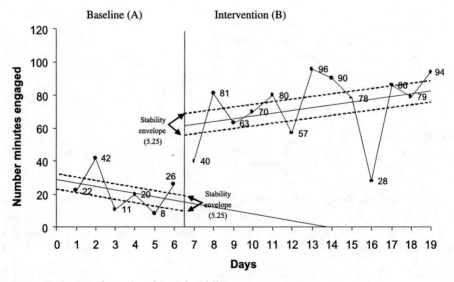

Figure 9.12c Estimate of trend and trend stability.

Step 6: Determine trend stability. Superimpose the stability envelope used to determine level stability over the trend lines for Condition A and Condition B. The stability envelope may be moved up or down to capture as many data points as possible but must always remain parallel to the trend line. Using the same criteria for level stability (80% of data points falling on or within 25% of median value; stability envelope range = 5.25), calculate the percentage of data points that fall on or within the stability envelope placed over each trend line. Figure 9.12c shows the placement of the stability envelope over Condition A and B trend lines. Table 9.6 indicates that trends are variable for both Condition A and Condition B.

	Condition A	Condition B
Number of data points in the condition	6	13
Number of data points on or within the envelope	2	5
Percent on or within the envelope	2/6 × 100 = 33.3% variable	5/13 × 100 = 38.5% variable

Step 7: Determine data paths within trend. Using the freehand method, note whether there are two distinct data paths within a condition (accelerating–decelerating, zero celerating–accelerating, decelerating–zero celerating, etc.). In Condition A only one data path is present (accelerating trend). As noted in Table 9.6 no data paths in Condition A and B were discrepant from the condition trend lines.

Table 9.6 summarizes the completed "within-condition visual analysis" for the graphic data presented in Figure 9.11.

Analysis Between Adjacent Conditions (Refer to Table 9.7)

The objective of this component of the visual-analysis process is to determine what effect contingent adult attention only, when engaged with one or more peers (independent variable), had on number of minutes the child was engaged with peers (dependent variable). This effect can be identified by comparing data of Condition B with data of Condition A. Refer to your "within-condition analysis" calculations and recordings when conducting a "between-adjacent-conditions analysis." Information presented in Table 9.6 was used to complete Table 9.7 in our between-conditions (B to A) analysis example.

Step 1: Determine the number of variables that changed between conditions. To determine the number of variables that change between adjacent conditions, carefully read the procedure sections where condition procedures are described. In our hypothetical example, Condition A represents the staff's attention when the child was alone and B represents their attention contingent upon the child being in the presence of at least one peer. Assuming all other variables were constant across conditions, only one variable was changed. Specify the identified difference(s) between adjacent conditions. Table 9.7 shows that one difference was identified as the contingency.

Step 2: Determine if there was a change in trend direction. Note whether there was a change in trend direction when moving from one condition to the next condition. Also note whether there was a change in trend direction relative to the intervention objective. In our example, there was a "positive" change in trend direction as evidenced by a "decelerating–deteriorating" trend in Condition A that changed to an "accelerating–improving" trend in Condition B.

Step 3: Determine change in trend stability. In Step 6 of the "within-condition analysis," the trend stability of each condition was calculated and noted as being "stable" or "variable." Simply make a note of the change you recorded. In our example, Table 9.6 indicates that the trends in Conditions A and B were both variable. Thus the trend description of the data series graphed in Figure 9.11 is described as: a variable decelerating trend in a contratherapeutic direction where, upon introduction of intervention, there was a change in trend direction to a variable accelerating trend in a therapeutic direction.

Step 4: Determine level change between conditions.

4.1 Relative level change: To determine the relative change in level from Condition A to Condition B, subtract the median value of the second half of A from the median value of the first half of Condition B. Note the direction of change.

	Condition B:A	
Median 1st half B	66.5	
Median 2nd half A	20	
Relative level change	+46.5 improving	

4.2 Absolute level change: To determine absolute change in level from Condition A to Condition B, subtract the last data-point value of A from the first data-point value of B Condition. Note the direction of change.

	Condition B:A	
First data point value B	40	
Last data point value A	26	
Relative level change	+14 improving	

This information is used to determine immediacy and "abruptness" (i.e., large change in magnitude) of the effect of intervention.

4.3 Median level change: Subtract the median value of Condition A from the median value of Condition B. Note the direction of change.

	Condition B:A	
Median value of B	79	
Median value of A	21	
Median level change	+58 improving	

4.4 Mean level change: Subtract the mean value of Condition A from the mean value of Condition B. Note the direction of change.

	Condition B:A	
Mean value of B	72.5	
Mean value of A	21.5	
Mean level change	+51 improving	

Step 5: Determine the percentage of overlap. There are two methods for calculating and reporting the overlap in data-point values between two adjacent conditions.

5.1 Percentage of nonoverlapping data (PND): Count the number of data points in Condition B that fall *outside* the range of A. When the intervention (B) objective has been designed to increase the target behavior, count the number of data points that fall above the highest data point in A. If the intervention (B) objective has been designed to decrease the target behavior, count the number of data points that fall below the lowest data point in A. Divide the number of data points that fall on or outside the range of A by the number of data points in B, and multiply by 100. This will yield the PND. Refer to Figure 9.12d to calculate PND in our example. PND is reported in Table 9.7.

$$\boxed{\text{PND} = 11/13 \times 100 = 84.6\% \text{ (B to A)}}$$

5.2 Percentage of overlapping data (POD): Count the number of data points in Condition B that fall *within* the range of A. When the intervention (B) objective has been designed to increase the target behavior, count the number of data points that fall below the highest data point in A. If the intervention (B) objective has been designed to decrease the target behavior, count the number of data points that fall above the lowest data point in A. Divide the number of data points that fall on or within the range of A by the number of data points in B, and multiply by 100. This will yield the POD. Refer to Figure 9.12d to calculate POD in our example. POD is reported in Table 9.7.

$$\boxed{\text{POD} = 2/13 \times 100 = 15.4\% \text{ (B to A)}}$$

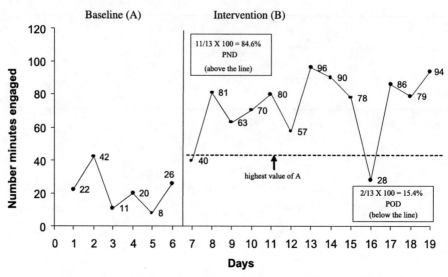

Figure 9.12d Percentage of non-overlapping data (PND) for hypothetical data in Figure 9.11.

Analysis Between Similar Conditions

The purpose of this phase of the analysis is to determine whether similar conditions of an experiment have a similar effect on the dependent variable. In the case of our example in Figure 9.11 that depicts an A-B design, neither Condition A nor Condition B were reintroduced, thus precluding the analysis of a functional relation between independent and dependent variables. You can only conclude that there is a correlation between independent and dependent variables since threats to internal validity (maturation, history, etc.) were not evaluated or controlled. Alternative explanations are possible. It is possible that the passage of time or some variable outside the experimenter's control may have brought about the observed change. A functional relation can only be concluded when (a) there is an successful attempt to replicate the effects of a condition and (b) when similar conditions generate similar levels and trends within (intra-subject replication) and across (inter-subject replication) participants in a study. Generality of findings are further enhanced when similar conditions generate similar effects across different researchers, research programs, and research participants, behaviors, and conditions (systematic replication).

To analyze data between similar conditions (A_1 to A_2; B_1 to B_2; BC_1 to BC_2), you would compare: (a) immediacy of effect (level and trend change) the condition has on the dependent variable when following the same condition (when B_1 follows A_1; when B_2 follows A_2); (b) median and mean levels; (c) range of values; (d) level stability; (e) trend direction; and (f) trend stability. You are directed to Chapter 4 on how to write a technological description of results of your visual analysis of graphic data. The results section of your research report should be restricted to objective statements that summarize your observations and calculations. You should describe how to read complex graphic displays, supplement your narrative with tables that summarize important information related to your research questions (pre/posttest data comparison, generalization results, etc.), and the integrity of your research procedures (interobserver and procedural-reliability data), and avoid use of adverbs and undocumented statements. Save your opinions and impressions for the discussion section of the report.

Summary

This chapter has overviewed general guidelines for conducting visual analyses of graphed data. As previously stated, there are few hard-and-fast rules when it comes to sequence and format for inspecting data. The three phases of the visual-analysis process (within condition, between adjacent conditions, across similar conditions) that have been discussed and the properties of data that we have addressed are familiar to applied behavior analysts. Although the visual-analysis sequence and organizational format may vary, the properties of data (level, trend, data overlap) that require attention do not. In the chapters that follow, visual analyses are presented for each type of single subject research design. As you practice conducting visual analyses on graphic displayed data using the general guidelines outlined in this chapter, you will discover that the process is far less cumbersome than you may now think. Therefore, as you read single subject research investigations and the overviews of studies we present, conduct visual analyses on the graphed data . . . with practice comes proficiency.

References

Baer, D. M., Wolf, M. M., & Risley, T. R. (1968). Some current dimensions of applied behavior analysis. *Journal of Applied Behavior Analysis, 1,* 91–97.

Birnbrauer, J. S. (1981). External validity and experimental investigation of individual behavior. *Analysis and Intervention in Developmental Disabilities, 1,* 117–132.

Campbell, D. T., & Stanley, J. C. (1966). *Experimental and quasi-experimental designs for research.* Chicago, IL: Rand McNally.

Cooper, J. O., Heron, T. E., & Heward, W. L. (2007). *Applied behavior analysis* (2nd ed.). Columbus, OH: Pearson.

Glass, G. V., Willson, V. L., & Gottman, J. M. (1975). *Design and analysis of time-series experiments.* Boulder, CO: Colorado Associated University Press.

Parsonson, B. S., & Baer, D. M. (1978). The analysis and presentation of graphic data. In T. R. Kratochwill (Ed.), *Single subject research: Strategies for evaluating change* (pp. 101–165). New York: Academic Press.

Parsonson, B. S., & Baer, D. M. (1992). The visual analysis of graphic data, and current research into stimuli controlling it. In T. R. Kratochwill & J. R. Levin (Eds.), *Single subject research design and analysis: New directions for psychology and education* (pp. 15–40). New York: Academic Press.

Sidman, M. (1960). *Tactics of scientific research: Evaluating experimental data in psychology.* New York: Basic Books.

Skinner, B. F. (1957). *Verbal Behavior.* New York: Appleton-Century-Crofts.

White, O. R., & Haring, N. G. (1980). *Exceptional teaching* (2nd ed.). Columbus, OH: Charles E. Merrill.

Wolery, M., & Harris, S. R. (1982). Interpreting results of single-subject research designs. *Physical Therapy, 62,* 445–452.

10

Withdrawal and Reversal Designs

David L. Gast and Diana Hammond

> *Variations of the A-B-A-B Design*
> *B-A-B Design*
> *A-B-A′-B Reversal Design*
> *Withdrawal vs. Reversal Design Distinction*
> *Multitreatment Designs*
> **Summary**

Baseline Logic

Single subject research methodology is based on what Sidman (1960) and others have referred to as *baseline logic*. Simply stated, baseline logic refers to the repeated measurement of behavior under at least two adjacent conditions: baseline (A) and intervention (B). If there is a measurable change in behavior after the introduction of intervention, when compared with baseline measures, it is probable, but *not* proven, that the introduction of intervention was responsible for that change (A-B design). To verify this hypothesis you can withdraw (or reverse) the intervention condition by returning to the previous baseline condition (A-B-A design). If the behavior returns to or approximates the level measured during the initial baseline condition there is a greater likelihood that the intervention was responsible for the behavior change, i.e., there was an immediate change in level and trend direction upon the return to the baseline condition. It is imperative that behaviors be "reversible" with A-B-A-B designs and their variations. By reintroducing the intervention condition (A-B-A-B design) a more convincing demonstration of experimental control is possible. The more replications of effect, the greater the confidence we have that the intervention was responsible for the change in behavior.

Baseline logic serves as the foundation for all single subject research paradigms. That is, all single subject research designs are mere extensions or elaborations of the basic A-B paradigm. This chapter describes, analyzes, and exemplifies those single subject designs commonly referred to as "withdrawal" or "reversal" designs. Historically these designs have been referred to as simple and repeated time series designs (Campbell & Stanley, 1966; Glass, Willson, & Gottman, 1975; Birnbrauer, Peterson, & Solnick; 1974). Specifically, discussion focuses on A, B, A-B, A-B-A, A-B-A-B, B-A-B, and A-B-C-B designs. Several variations of the A-B-A-B design are presented and briefly discussed.

A and B Designs

The "A" design and "B" design represent two types of investigations commonly associated with the case-study approach. Unlike the traditional case-study approach, which relies heavily on descriptive narrative of an investigator's observations (Fraenkel & Wallen, 2006; Irwin & Bushnell, 1980; Leary, 1995; Lincoln & Guba, 1985), the "A" and "B" designs require investigators' observations be summarized and reported in numerical terms. With both designs investigators pinpoint one or more characteristics of the behavior or event under investigation and, using some systematic measurement system (behavioral definitions, direct observational recording procedure, repeated measures, interobserver-agreement measures), quantify their observations. It is important to note that neither of these paradigms constitutes an experimental design, i.e., identification of a functional relation between dependent and independent variables is not possible; rather both designs are considered *quantitative-descriptive paradigms*.

The *"A" design* represents a purely descriptive investigation during which an investigator has no plans to intervene or in any way alter the phenomenon under study. Ecological psychologists, anthropologists, and sociologists who are often involved in systematic observation of people in their natural environments use this approach when mapping behavior patterns relative to ecological variables. Because the investigator does not wish to intrude or intervene during repeated observations of the phenomenon of interest, this quantitative-descriptive approach can be viewed as an extended baseline condition; thus the label *"A" design*. Observations are commonly summarized through use of descriptive statistics (mean, median, mode, range) and a sequential analysis of events, i.e., A-B-C analysis.

The "A" design has also been used for *post hoc* analysis of behavior. For example, Dunlap, Clarke, and Reyes (1998) studied the trends in authorship in both the *Journal of Applied Behavior Analysis* (JABA) and the *American Journal on Mental Retardation* (AJMR) from 1975 through 1997. As shown in Figure 10.1, their findings revealed "a trend away from the appearance of new authors with an increase in the publication of works by frequent contributors" (p. 497). They also found this trend more prevalent for JABA than for AJMR.

The *"B" design* is a second type of quantitative-descriptive design. Like the "A" design an investigator who employs the "B" design systematically measures a participant's, or group of participants', behavior under identified stimulus conditions. Unlike the "A" paradigm, measurement in the "B" paradigm occurs during or soon after an intervention has been introduced—not before, i.e., there are no baseline measures. The "B" design does not specify how frequently observations of the target behavior(s) or event(s) must be made, however, the more frequent the measurement the more representative are the data in describing the behavior.

Clinicians and educators often use the "B" design to monitor changes in a client's or student's behavior over time once an intervention has been introduced. For example, a teacher who records weekly spelling test scores after several days of instruction is employing the "B" design. She can determine whether a student has learned target words, but she cannot verify that her instruction was responsible for the student's achievement. Without pre-intervention (i.e., baseline or probe) data on target spelling words, and without adequate measures to control for maturation and historical threats, it is impossible to make an objective empirical evaluation of instructional program effectiveness.

Internal and External Validity

At best, "A" and "B" designs generate quantitative-descriptive information that allows investigators to hypothesize a correlational rather than functional relation between independent and dependent variables. Because investigators using these "designs" do not attempt to control for potential confoundings (e.g., history, maturation, testing), findings cannot be said to be internally or externally valid. Such statements must be derived from an experimental design that replicates a positive effect with the same participant (internal validity, i.e., intra-subject direct replication) as well as across similar participants (external validity, i.e., direct inter-subject and/ or systematic replication).

Considerations

Guidelines
An investigator who chooses to study behavior using either the "A" or "B" design should:

1. Behaviorally define target behavior(s).
2. Select a measurement system that permits an analysis of antecedent and consequent events relative to target behavior(s).

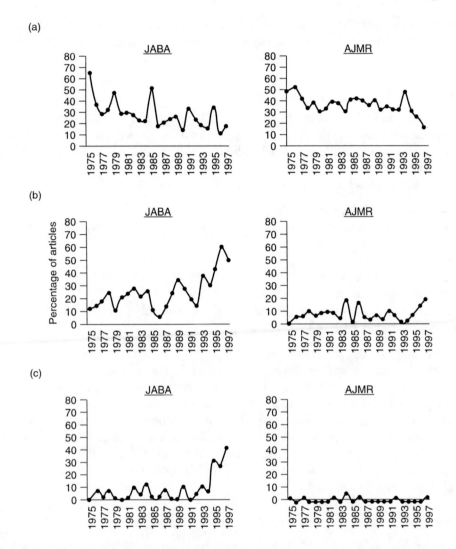

Figure 10.1 Percentage of articles in *JABA* and *AJMR* in which (a) no author had any publications in the journal during the previous 5 years (top graphs); (b) at least one author had a minimum of five publications in the journal during the previous 5 years (middle graphs); and (c) at least one author had a minimum of 10 publications in the journal during the previous 5 years (bottom graphs) (source: Dunlap et al., 1998. Copyright by Society for the Experimental Analysis of Behavior, Inc. Reproduced by permission.)

3. Thoroughly describe conditions under which the target behavior is measured.
4. Schedule frequent observation periods of the target behavior(s).
5. Collect interobserver-agreement reliability data and, with a "B" design, collect procedural-reliability data.
6. Avoid inferring cause–effect conclusions.

"A" and "B" designs will permit you to make only correlational statements regarding the relation between independent and dependent variables. In order to make such statements it is imperative that the dependent variable be operationally defined, the conditions under which the behavior is measured be technologically described, and the observation periods scheduled frequently. Even under the best of conditions you must avoid stating or implying cause–effect conclusions.

Advantages

One might question both the utility and importance of an investigation that employs an "A" or "B" design. Lazarus and Davison (1971), as summarized by Hersen and Barlow (1976), suggested the following advantages associated with case-study approaches. These advantages apply to both "A" and "B" designs.

The case study method can be used to:

1. Foster clinical investigations,
2. Cast doubt on theoretical assumptions,
3. Permit study of rare phenomena,
4. Develop new technical skills,
5. Buttress theoretical views,
6. Result in refinement of techniques, and
7. Provide clinical data to be used as a departure point for subsequent controlled investigations (Hersen & Barlow, 1976, p. 168).

Both "A" and "B" designs can be expanded to provide an experimental analysis of the relation between independent and dependent variables. This can be accomplished by expanding the "B" design to a B-A-B design, provided dependent and independent variables are operationally defined, stimulus conditions are concisely described, target behavior is repeatedly measured, and data are stable before experimental conditions are changed. Under similar circumstances, with the exception of *post hoc* studies of events (e.g., Dunlap et al., 1998; Weisberg & Waldrop, 1971), the "A" design may be expanded to an A-B-A or A-B-A-B design. Whether, in fact, these expansions are possible depends upon a number of factors, including practical and/or ethical constraints.

Limitations

The shortcomings of "A" and "B" designs should be apparent. Neither paradigm permits a functional analysis of behavior. Without repeatedly measuring a target behavior under both baseline *and* intervention conditions it is impossible to isolate those variables responsible for behavior change. At best, "A" and "B" designs permit you to report on the level and trend of the data over time and within a broadly defined condition. As a starting point for a more thorough investigation, these "designs" may suffice for the previously discussed advantages.

Concluding Comments

"A" and "B" designs provide a framework within which you can objectively measure behavior. Though both are an improvement over the traditional narrative-descriptive case-study method, neither permits an experimental analysis of behavior change. There are no occasions in which the "A" or "B" design would be appropriate to evaluate the effectiveness of a therapeutic or instructional program. The "B" design, however, does permit an objective empirical description of individual performance relative to pre-established therapy or instructional objective criteria. Determination of whether achievements are due to your intervention strategy requires use of an experimental design (e.g., A-B-A-B, multiple baseline, multiple probe) that controls for the many potentially confounding variables. There are few occasions when you would choose the "A" or "B" design over more rigorous and informative experimental designs.

A-B Design

The A-B design, sometimes referred to as the "simple time series design" (Birnbrauer et al., 1974), represents the most basic "quasi-experimental" single subject research design. This design requires that the dependent variable be measured repeatedly under controlled baseline (A) and intervention (B) conditions. After repeated observations under a baseline condition, and after the data trend and level have stabilized, the intervention is introduced. During intervention the target behavior continues to be repeatedly measured, noting changes in the dependent variable. Any changes in the target behavior are *presumed* to be a function of the independent variable, i.e., only correlational conclusions are possible.

Internal and External Validity

The A-B design is subject to numerous threats to both internal and external validity (Campbell & Stanley, 1966; Glass et al., 1975; Kratochwill, 1978; Tawney & Gast, 1984). Since there is no direct intra-subject replication (i.e., the effect is not replicated with the same participant) there is no assurance that the independent variable is responsible for observed behavior changes. More specifically, since there is (a) no return to baseline condition and (b) no concurrent monitoring of similar, yet functionally independent behaviors, the natural course of the target behavior in the absence of the intervention (B) cannot be determined. It may very well be that changes in the dependent variable are occurring naturally or in response to some unidentified and uncontrolled variable (i.e., maturational and historical confounding, respectively). In light of these and other threats to internal validity, the A-B design yields correlational conclusions at best, and then only if changes in level and trend direction are observed immediately following introduction of the independent variable.

Considerations

Guidelines
When using the A-B design, you should:

1. Behaviorally define target behavior(s).
2. Select a measurement system that permits an analysis of antecedent and consequent events relative to the target behavior(s).
3. Thoroughly describe baseline and intervention conditions under which the target behavior is measured.
4. Collect continuous baseline data (A) over a minimum of 3 consecutive days or until stable before introducing intervention (B).
5. Collect interobserver agreement (dependent variable) and procedural (independent variable) reliability data in baseline and intervention conditions.
6. Avoid inferring cause–effect conclusions.
7. Replicate experimental effect with similar research participants.

Advantages

The A-B design provides a framework within which behavior can be objectively measured under clearly described and controlled environmental conditions. It improves upon the "B" design by adding repeated measurement of a target behavior under "natural" or baseline conditions prior to introduction of the independent variable. Though the A-B design does not permit a functional analysis of behavior, it may provide a convincing demonstration that behavior change is not a function of the passage of time (i.e., maturation). This may be accomplished when behavior change measured in the intervention condition is immediate and abrupt and follows a long and stable baseline data trend. There are circumstances in educational and clinical settings that may preclude the use of more extensive experimental designs that require the repeated withdrawal (or reversal) of the independent variable (A-B-A-B). When confronted with such practical and/or ethical constraints the A-B design may be the only evaluation paradigm available to teachers and clinicians for monitoring program changes in child or client behavior.

Limitations

Conclusions drawn from studies that employ the A-B design are limited by numerous threats to internal validity (history, maturation) and external validity (Hawthorne effect, novelty and disruption effects, experimenter effects). The most notable limitation of the A-B design is the lack of information on the natural course of the target behavior in the absence of intervention. Without such information it is impossible to rule out the influence of uncontrolled variables (i.e., historical confounding) or the passage of time (i.e., maturational confounding) on the dependent measure.

Suffice it to say that the A-B design provides weak correlational conclusions; for this reason, it has been described as "quasi-experimental." If a full experimental analysis of behavior is desired it is necessary to extend the design to an A-B-A or A-B-A-B design. Only when the A-B design is expanded in these ways is a functional analysis of behavior possible. Seldom will you find an A-B design published in the research literature. When found, it is likely to be with only one of several research participants in the study with the intervention being evaluated for other participants within the context of an A-B-A-B experimental design.

Applied Example: A-B Design

Azrin, N. H., & Wesolowski, M. D. (1974). Theft reversal: An overcorrection procedure for eliminating stealing by retarded persons. *Journal of Applied Behavior Analysis, 7,* 577–581.

Azrin and Wesolowski (1974) evaluated the effectiveness of an overcorrection procedure, compared to a simple correction procedure, as a deterrent to stealing. The participants were 34 ambulatory and nonverbal adults with severe or profound intellectual disabilities (average CA = 41 years; mean IQ = 15; 16 males, 18 females) who resided in a state residential institution. The presenting problem was a high frequency of stealing on the ward, particularly during meal times and during commissary periods between meals. The study was conducted in the hospital commissary.

The dependent variable was the total number of stealing episodes committed by the 34 residents each day. To ensure an accurate detection of each theft the 34 residents were divided into three approximately equal groups; only one group participated in a commissary period at a time. In addition, the two trainers who accompanied residents to the commissary independently collected data on the number of stealing episodes during the 30-minute commissary period. These observers were also responsible for delivering consequences for any instance of stealing they observed in accordance with the intervention that was in effect at the time. Interobserver agreement on the number of stealing episodes recorded was "almost perfect," with only one disagreement recorded during the course of the study.

The two interventions that were compared, relative to their impact on the frequency of stealing episodes, were simple correction (A) and overcorrection (B). In simple correction a staff member required the "thief" to immediately return the stolen food item to the victim. The overcorrection or "theft-reversal procedure" required the offender to return the stolen item to the victim *and* give the victim of the theft an additional identical item obtained from the commissary item display area. Both simple correction and overcorrection procedures included the trainer (a) verbally reprimanding the "thief," (b) verbally instructing the individual to return or obtain the items stolen, and (c) manually assisting the resident in doing so if verbal instructions were not followed.

An A-B design was employed to evaluate the effects of the simple correction (A) and overcorrection (B) procedures on the frequency of the residents' stealing. There was no attempt to compare either procedure with a no-intervention condition for ethical reasons. The simple correction condition was in effect for 5 days, followed by a 20-day condition in which the overcorrection procedure was administered for each instance of stealing.

Figure 10.2 displays the data on the total number of thefts committed by the 34 residents. During the simple correction condition approximately 20 stealing episodes occurred each day. When the overcorrection procedure was introduced, thefts decreased by approximately 50%. After only 4 days of overcorrection procedures, no instances of stealing occurred. This trend and level continued over the remaining 16 days of the overcorrection condition. Measures on the amount of time required by staff to complete each correction procedure revealed that the

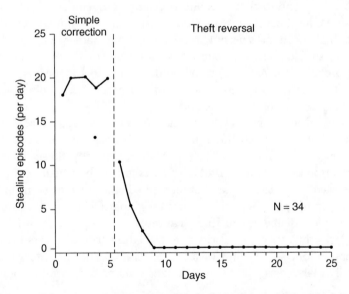

Fig. 1. The number of stealing episodes committed each day by 34 adult retarded residents in an institution. During the five days of simple correction, the thief was required to return the stolen item. During the theft-reversal (overcorrection) procedure (subsequent to the vertical dashed line), the thief was required to give the victim an additional item identical to the one stolen, also returning the stolen item. The stealing episodes consisted of stealing food items from the other retarded residents during commissary periods.

Figure 10.2 Theft reversal: An overcorrection procedure for eliminating stealing by retarded persons (source: Azrin & Wesolowski, 1974. Copyright by Society for the Experimental Analysis of Behavior, Inc. Reproduced by permission).

simple correction procedure required an average of 7 seconds (±2) and the overcorrection procedure 106 seconds (±17).

The data presented in Figure 10.2 show a clear difference in both level and trend of the number of stealing episodes between the simple correction and overcorrection conditions. The relative effectiveness of the overcorrection procedure compared to the simple correction procedure is, however, at best correlational. Because the effect was not replicated with the same group of residents (direct intra-group replication) or with other groups of residents (direct inter-group replication), the findings lack internal and external validity. This is not to say that the overcorrection procedure was not responsible for decreasing the frequency of thefts; rather, there was no experimental demonstration of a cause–effect or functional relation. If investigators had expanded the A-B design to an A-B-A, and if the frequency of thefts increased during the second baseline or simple correction condition (A$_2$), then an experimental analysis of the effects of overcorrection on the frequency of stealing would have been possible. The reintroduction of the overcorrection procedure (B$_2$) would have further strengthened the internal validity of the findings (A-B-A-B). An alternative strategy to enhance the believability of the results would have been to replicate the study with additional groups of residents, preferably within the context of a multiple baseline (or multiple probe) design across participants (see Chapter 11).

Concluding Comments

The A-B design provides a framework for repeated measurement of a target behavior during baseline and intervention conditions. Though the design does not permit a functional analysis of behavior, it can be useful to clinicians and educators in documenting changes in behavior when practical and ethical constraints preclude the repeated introduction and withdrawal of the intervention. If circumstances permit, and if a functional rather than correlational conclusion is desired, you should select an expanded version (A-B-A-B) or variation (multiple baseline or multiple probe) of the A-B design. Without a replication of effect and an evaluation of threats to internal validity, maturation and history in particular, an objective evaluation of effectiveness of the intervention is not possible.

As will be discussed in Chapter 11, a variation of the A-B design that is appearing more frequently in the applied research literature is the "delayed" or "nonconcurrent" multiple baseline design (e.g., Freeman, 2006; Harvey, May, & Kennedy, 2004; Tincani, Crozier, & Alazetta, 2006; Watson & Workman, 1981). This design can best be described as a series of separate and "stacked" A-B designs, each implemented at a different point in time (e.g., one in January, one in April, one in September) that are graphically presented to appear as if they are tiers in a multiple baseline design study. However, the nonconcurrent (delayed) multiple baseline design lacks the experimental rigor in evaluating critical threats to internal validity (history and maturation, specifically) of a "true" multiple baseline design and, therefore, should be critically analyzed as separate A-B designs yielding correlational conclusions at best.

A-B-A Design

The A-B-A design represents the simplest single subject research design for demonstrating cause–effect relations. Like the A-B design, the target behavior is repeatedly measured under baseline (A$_1$) and intervention (B) conditions. After the dependent variable has stabilized during intervention, you reintroduce baseline condition (A$_2$) to the target behavior. The addition of this second baseline condition enhances the strength of the simple A-B design by assessing maturation and history threats to internal validity, thus allowing functional, rather than correlational, conclusions.

Internal and External Validity

The A-B-A design is preferable to the A-B design, at least from a research standpoint, since it permits an experimental analysis of behavior. As with all experimental designs, the key to determining a functional relation between independent and dependent variables is replication of effect. If withdrawal of the intervention results in an immediate change in trend direction, one which approaches a level similar to that in the first baseline, you can conclude with a reasonable level of certainty that the intervention was responsible for the observed change. Although the reintroduction of the baseline condition and the subsequent retrieval or approximation of initial baseline responding levels strengthens the argument that the independent variable was responsible for observed changes in the dependent variable, it does not preclude alternative explanations (e.g., historical confounding). This is particularly true if there are an equal number of days or sessions in each condition of the study making it difficult to identify cyclical variability. The demonstration of experimental control is strengthened with the A-B-A design when a stable data trend in the intervention condition (B_1) is followed by an immediate and abrupt change in level and trend in the second baseline condition (A_2). Conclusions can be strengthened further by extending the design to an A-B-A-B design and/or by replicating the experimental effect with other individuals (inter-subject replication), thereby strengthening internal and external validity.

Considerations

Guidelines
When using the A-B-A design you should:

1. Behaviorally define target behavior(s).
2. Collect continuous baseline data (A_1) over a minimum of 3 consecutive days or until stable.
3. Introduce intervention (B) only after a stable "contratherapeutic" or zero-celerating baseline trend has been established in A_1.
4. Collect continuous data during intervention (B) over a minimum of 3 days.
5. Collect interobserver agreement (dependent variable) and procedural (independent variable) reliability data in baseline and intervention conditions.
6. Withdraw (or reverse) the intervention and return to the original baseline condition (A_2) after acceptable stability in level and trend has been established in the intervention condition (B).
7. Replicate the experimental effect with other participants (direct inter-subject replication).

Advantages

The primary advantage of the A-B-A design, when compared with the A-B design, is that it allows a functional analysis of behavior. This permits you to conclude with greater certainty that the intervention was responsible for changes in the target behavior. Conclusions can be further substantiated and strengthened when the experimental effect is replicated with similar participants within the same study. Though inter-subject replications enhance the external validity of findings, it is the first change in the dependent variable, when the intervention is introduced for the first time (A_1-B_1), that are more likely to be observed in similar non-study participants, and hence the most important demonstration of the impact the intervention has on the dependent variable (Barlow & Hayes, 1979).

Limitations

Although the A-B-A design permits a functional, rather than correlational analysis of behavior, it is susceptible to numerous threats to internal and external validity. First, and foremost, is the possibility, however remote, that introduction and withdrawal of the independent variable coincided with naturally occurring cyclical variations of the target behavior. This threat to internal validity can best be evaluated by decreasing or increasing the number of observation periods in the second baseline condition (A_2) and/or reintroducing the intervention (B_2), i.e., expanding the design to an A-B-A-B design. This second replication of experimental effect greatly enhances the demonstration of experimental control. Second, there is the likelihood that A_1 dependent variable levels will not be fully retrieved in A_2, though they should be approximated. Such sequential confounding is not uncommon to A-B-A, A-B-A-B, and multi-treatment (e.g., A-B-C-B-C, A-B-A-C-A-D) designs. To evaluate sequential confounding with multitreatment designs it is necessary to counterbalance or vary the order in which conditions are introduced to participants (e.g., Participant 1, A-B-C-B-C; Participant 2, A-C-B-C-B). Third, the A-B-A design is not appropriate for evaluating program effectiveness with behaviors that are difficult, if not impossible, to reverse (e.g., academic skills). And fourth, there are practical as well as ethical problems associated with terminating a study in a baseline condition. This criticism is voiced understandably by practitioners who are more concerned with improving a student's or a client's behavioral repertoire, rather than an experimental analysis of behavior. It is important to remember that you would *not* select the A-B-A design, a priori, to evaluate the impact of an intervention on a target behavior. The A-B-A design appears in the literature primarily due to participant attrition during the course of an investigation.

Applied Example: A-B-A Design

Christle, C. A., & Schuster, J. W. (2003). The effects of using response cards on student participation, academic achievement, and on-task behavior during whole-class math instruction. *Journal of Behavioral Education, 12,* 147–165.

Christle and Schuster (2003) evaluated the effectiveness of a "response-card" intervention for increasing the number of student-initiated opportunities to respond, number of student responses, percentage of intervals on-task, and percentage correct on weekly math quizzes during large-group instruction. The study was conducted within the context of an A-B-A withdrawal design in which the "hand-raising" condition represented A and the "response-card" condition represented B. The design was intended to be an A-B-A-B design, however, due to "scheduling conflicts" it was not possible to reintroduce the response-card (B) condition. The study was conducted in a fourth-grade general education classroom serving 9 boys and 11 girls (CA 9–11 years). Data were collected and reported on five of the 20 students, two boys (Brad, Charles) and three girls (Shawna, Emily, Marcella), all of whom were identified by the classroom teacher as having a good attendance record and representing the overall performance range of students in the class.

Event recording was used to measure the number of student-initiated opportunities to respond and number of student responses, while a 5-min momentary time-sampling procedure was used to record on-task behavior. Math quizzes were administered after each experimental condition, and percentage correct scores recorded to measure students' academic performance. Reliability data were collected once per condition for each of the five students by an independent observer. The "simple" or gross method (smaller number divided by the larger number multiplied by 100) was used to calculate interobserver agreement (IOA) on data collected using event recording (number of student-initiated opportunities and number of student responses). The point-by-point method (number of observer agreements divided by the total number of observation intervals multiplied by 100) was used to calculate IOA for on-task and quiz performance data. IOA for student-initiated opportunities to respond ranged from 94% to 100% and 90% to 100% for student responses across all conditions. Reliability for on-task behavior across all students and conditions ranged from 80% to 92%, while IOA for scoring students' quizzes was 100%. Procedural reliability was 98% for the response-card (B) condition and ranged from 91% to 93% for the hand-raising (A) condition.

During baseline condition (A_1 and A_2) the teacher instructed students to raise their hands if they wanted to respond to a question. The teacher would then call on one student whose hand was raised. During the response-card condition (B) the teacher asked the whole class a question, instructed all students to write their answer on their individual response card, and when she said "Cards up," all students were to hold up their response card for her to see. Once she had an opportunity to view all students' cards she announced and showed the correct answer. This response-card procedure was taught to students prior to the start of the study.

Figure 10.3 summarizes number of student-initiated opportunities to respond (closed squares) and number of student responses (open squares). A visual analysis of number of opportunities to respond (students raising their hands) in the hand-raising condition (A_1) shows a stable zero-celerating trend (Brad) or a variable decelerating trend (Shawna, Marcella, Charles, Emily). Students seldom raised their hands to be called on by the teacher. Student responses to teacher questions were also low as indicated by stable, zero-celerating trends near the floor (range = 0–3) for each of the five students. Upon introduction of the response-card condition (B), there was an immediate and abrupt change in the number of teacher questions asked (A_1, mean = 15; B, mean = 22), with a concomitant increase in number of student-initiated opportunities to respond and number of student responses. These changes were, however, temporary as indicated by stable decelerating trends in number of teacher questions asked in B (27, 20, 33, 15, 13), student-initiated opportunities to respond, and number of student responses. It is important to note, however, that in spite of a decrease in teacher questions asked over sessions, each student responded to 100% of the teacher's questions. When the hand-raising condition was reintroduced (A_2), both level and trend changes approximated those of A_1 for all measures, including number of teacher questions. Without reintroduction of the response-card condition (B_2), it is impossible to determine whether decelerating trends in number of teacher questions asked, number of student-initiated opportunities to respond, and number of student responses would be reversed in B_2, replicating levels in the first response-card condition.

Figure 10.4 summarizes percentage of intervals on-task for each student across conditions. During the hand-raising condition (A_1), data were stable (only one data point falling outside the "stability envelope") for Brad, Charles, and Shawna. Upon introduction of response cards (B) there was an immediate and abrupt change in level in a therapeutic direction for each student. Percentage of overlapping data (POD) points between B_2 and A_1 for Brad, Charles, and Shawna was 0%, i.e., PND = 100%. During the first hand-raising condition for Emily and Marcella, percentage of intervals on-task were variable (Emily, mean = 37.5%, range = 0%–100%; Marcella, 70.8%, range = 34%–100%). Percentage of overlapping data points was 100%, i.e., PND = 0%. Upon withdrawal of response cards (B) and a return to the hand-raising condition (A_2), Charles, Shawna, Emily, and Marcella had 0% overlapping data points between conditions, while Brad had 33.3% overlapping data points between the two conditions, i.e., one of three data points of A_2 falling within the range of B.

Quiz scores for each of the five students was higher in the response-card condition, when

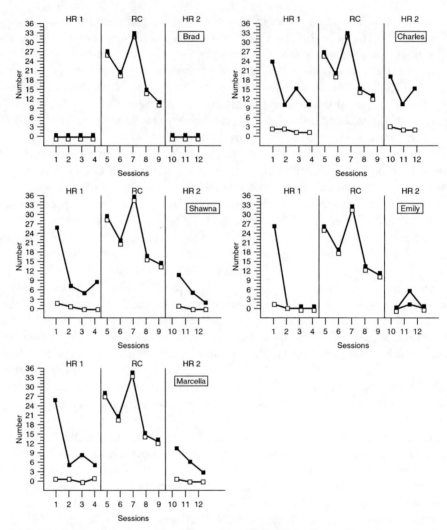

Figure 10.3 Summarizes the number of student-initiated opportunities to respond (closed squares) and the number of student responses (open squares) (source: Christle & Schuster, 2003. Copyright by Society for the Experimental Analysis of Behavior, Inc. Reproduced by permission).

compared to the initial hand-raising condition (A_1), and for four of the five students, when compared to the second hand-raising condition (A_2). Before definitive conclusions can be drawn regarding the effectiveness of response cards on academic performance, it would be necessary to hold a number of potentially confounding variables constant across conditions (content difficulty, time devoted to instruction, teaching methods). For all students, response cards were effective in increasing time on-task, student-initiated response opportunities, and student responses when compared to the hand-raising condition. They also influenced the frequency that the teacher asked questions of the group, although this effect was temporary. In terms of social-validity results, the general education teacher reported that the response-card strategy was "enjoyed" by students, easy to implement, and allowed her to see at a glance how her students were performing. When asked which condition they preferred, all 24 students in the class preferred the response-card condition. The investigators recognized the shortfalls of an A-B-A design and encouraged an attempt to replicate using an A-B-A-B design.

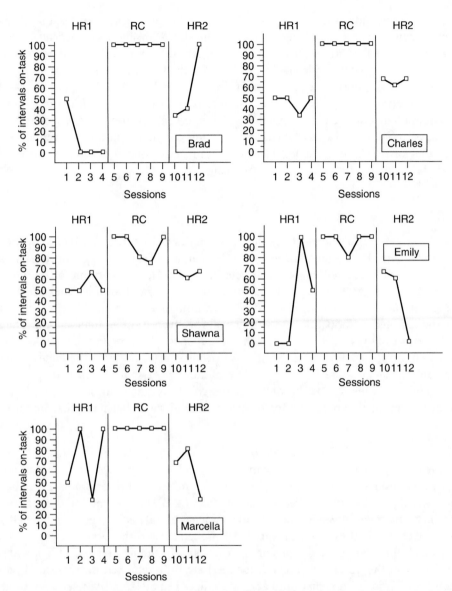

Figure 10.4 Summarizes the percentage of intervals on-task for each student across conditions (source: Christle & Schuster, 2003. Copyright by Society for the Experimental Analysis of Behavior, Inc. Reproduced by permission).

Concluding Comments

The A-B-A design is more useful than the basic A-B design, from an experimental perspective, because it permits a functional analysis of behavior. However, you would not select this design at the outset to evaluate intervention effectiveness due to the practical and ethical considerations of a study participant ending an investigation in a baseline condition. As emphasized by Baer, Wolf, and Risley (1968), participants in applied research studies must benefit from their participation, otherwise it should not be identified as "applied." For practitioners the A-B design is appropriate for documenting behavior change in a client or student but it cannot be concluded that the treatment or instructional program was responsible for the observed change. From a research perspective, if ethically defensible and practical, it would be far more appropriate for you to expand an A-B or A-B-A design to an A-B-A-B design, thereby replicating the impact of the independent variable on the target behavior. In order to build a convincing case to support conclusions generated by an A-B or A-B-A design, several direct inter-subject (or inter-group) replications using A-B, A-B-A, or A-B-A-B designs should be conducted simultaneously to increase confidence in intervention effectiveness. When an A-B or A-B-A analysis is supported by systematic replications, confidence in the intervention's influence on behavior is enhanced. Table 10.1 briefly summarizes studies that report the use of an A-B or an A-B-A design to evaluate behavior change.

A-B-A-B Design

The A-B-A-B design, also referred to as the "reversal design" (Baer et al., 1968), "withdrawal design" (Leitenberg, 1973), "operant design" (Glass et al., 1975), and "equivalent time series design" (Campbell & Stanley, 1966; Birnbrauer et al., 1974), has been one of the most frequently used single subject designs in behavioral research. Regardless of its label, the A-B-A-B design permits a clear and convincing demonstration of experimental control because it requires the repeated introduction and withdrawal (or reversal) of an intervention. The most important feature of the A-B-A-B design is that it *evaluates* a direct replication of effect, i.e., the last two conditions (A_2-B_2) replicate the first two conditions (A_1-B_1) with the same participant and the same behavior (direct intra-subject replication). In spite of reservations by some educators and clinicians to use the A-B-A-B design, it continues to be the simplest, most straightforward evaluation paradigm for evaluating causality with behaviors that are reversible.

Internal and External Validity

The A-B-A-B design demonstrates experimental control when the level and trend of a target behavior improves under intervention condition (B_1 and B_2) and deteriorates under baseline condition (A_1 and A_2). With each replication of effect (A-B), the internal validity of results is strengthened. The internal validity of the independent variable is further strengthened when magnitude of change in the dependent variable is immediate and abrupt (e.g., correct responding improves from 50% in the last session of A_1 to 90% in the first session of B_1), and when levels observed in the first baseline condition (A_1) are fully retrieved in the second baseline condition (A_2). Though immediate and abrupt changes in both trend and level are desirable, a believable demonstration of causality is still possible when a gradual reversal in trend is observed and when the first baseline condition level is approached, though not fully recovered. This failure to fully retrieve initial baseline levels within the same number of observation periods of previous conditions is not uncommon to researchers who use the A-B-A-B design. This phenomenon, primarily attributed to historical factors, necessitates changing conditions only after a stable contratherapeutic trend has been established. If changes in conditions are based solely on an "equal condition length" guideline, which we do not recommend, you could seriously jeopardize an otherwise believable demonstration of experimental control.

As with all empirical investigations, the external validity of results is achieved only when cause–effect relations are replicated with other similar participants under the same or similar experimental conditions. Consequently most researchers will try to include three or more participants in their investigation. By doing so they can immediately expand upon the

Table 10.1 A-B and A-B-A Design Study Summaries

Reference	Participants	Setting/arrangement	Independent variable	Dependent variable
Chafoules, S. M., Riley-Tillman, T. C., Sassu, K. A. LaFrance, M. J., & Patwa, S. S. (2007). Daily behavior report cards: An investigation of the consistency of on-task data across raters and methods. *Journal of Positive Behavior Interventions, 9,* 30–37.	Number: 3 Sex: male Age range: 8 yr 5 mo–9 yr 1 mo Disability/diagnosis: Learning disabilities	Setting: general education classroom (2nd and 3rd grades) Arrangement: individual	Daily behavior report cards	Percent on-task behavior
Egel, A. L. (1981). Reinforcer variation: Implications for motivating developmentally disabled children. *Journal of Applied Behavior Analysis, 14,* 345–350.	Number: 3 Sex: male Age range: 1 yr 8 mo–3 yr 8 mo Disability/diagnosis: Autism/developmentally disabled IQ Range: 50–80	Setting: Participant 1: UCLA clinic room Participants 2 & 3: special education classroom Arrangement: individual	Constant and varied reinforcement presentation	Correct responding and on-task behavior
Polaha, J., Allen, K., & Studley, B. (2004). Self-monitoring as an intervention to decrease swimmers' stroke counts. *Behavior Modification, 28,* 261–275.	Number: 11 Sex: 5 male, 6 female Age range: 23 yr to 61 yr and 3 college swimmers Disability/diagnosis: Typical development	Setting: regular fitness or college swim practices Arrangement: group	Self-monitoring	Decrease swimmers' stroke counts
Reyhount, G., & Carter, M. (2007). Social story efficacy with a child with autism spectrum disorder and moderate intellectual disability. *Journal of Autism and Developmental Disabilities, 22,* 173–182.	Number: 1 Sex: male Age Range: 8 yr 9 mo Disability: Autism	Setting: small room adjoining the participant's classroom Arrangement: individual	Social story	Percentage of intervals tapping
Roantree, C. F., & Kennedy, C. H. (2006). A paradoxical effect of presession attention on stereotypy: Antecedent attention as an establishing, not an abolishing, operation. *Journal of Applied Behavior Analysis, 39,* 381–384.	Number: 1 Sex: male Age Range: 10 yrs old Disability/diagnosis: severe mental retardation	Setting: 4 m × 4 m room with chairs and tables Arrangement: individual	Pre-session attention provided 20 minutes of attention to participant prior to functional analysis	Frequency of stereotypical response which included "full-body flex that involved quickly raising his hands above his head while simultaneously extending his legs" (p. 382)

generality of their findings to the extent to which their participants differ (age, disability, gender, ethnicity, etc.) or identify "exceptions to the rule." The importance of this latter point cannot be overstated, for it is through the identification of exceptions that our understanding of human behavior is advanced. You should not be discouraged by a single failure to replicate with a participant in your study, rather you should approach this as an opportunity to identify a solution to a shortcoming of the original intervention for some individuals with whom the intervention may be attempted. When a failure to replicate occurs, identify changes that can be made to the original intervention based on your review and understanding of the literature. You may choose to add to, or in some way modify, the original intervention (e.g., A-B-BC-B-BC) or change to a new intervention completely (e.g., A-B-C-B-C). In single subject research designs, because participants serve as their own controls, you may change your research design during the course of a study in certain ways and still evaluate a functional relation between independent and dependent variables. A simple A-B-A-B design, for example, may be changed to an A-B-BC-B-BC or A-B-C-B-C "multitreatment design." Multitreatment designs are discussed in detail in Chapter 12, "Comparative Intervention Designs."

We also recommend that nontarget behaviors be monitored concurrently when using the A-B-A-B design. This could include monitoring behaviors that are functionally or topographically similar to the target behavior, in which case you are assessing response generalization, but it is also advised that you monitor behaviors that are not functionally or topographically similar to the target behavior. For example, it may be that an intervention designed to decrease the frequency of aggressive behaviors may result in a concurrent increase in attention to task and an improvement in quiz scores. This would be an important positive side effect of the intervention that should be noted. Side effects can be either negative (e.g., when head banging, the target behavior, is decreased in frequency, there is a concomitant increase in the frequency of face slapping) or positive (e.g., when sitting at one's desk, the target behavior, is increased in frequency, there is a concomitant increase in the number of assignments completed). Whichever the case, the concurrent monitoring of nontarget behaviors has practical implications for educators and clinicians interested in identifying both appropriate and inappropriate instances of response generalization. Therefore, whether side effects are positive or negative, we recommend that you continue monitoring these behaviors over the course of the study when resources permit.

Considerations

Guidelines
When using the A-B-A-B design you should:

1. Behaviorally define target behavior(s).
2. Identify, behaviorally define, and concurrently monitor nontarget behaviors of the same response class as well as behaviors that may change as a function of a change in the target behavior.
3. Collect continuous baseline data (A_1) over a minimum of 3 consecutive days.
4. Introduce the intervention (B_1) only after a stable contratherapeutic or zero-celeration trend has been established in the initial baseline condition (A_1).
5. Collect continuous data during intervention (B) over a minimum of 3 days.
6. Withdraw (or reverse) the intervention and return to the baseline condition (A_2) only after acceptable stability in both trend and level has been established in the first intervention condition (B_1).

7. Reintroduce intervention (B_2) procedures after a stable contratherapeutic or zero-celeration trend has been established in the second baseline (A_2).

8. Attempt to replicate the experimental effect with similar participants.

Advantages

The A-B-A-B design provides a most convincing demonstration of causality available to applied researchers. It controls for many of the deficiencies associated with the A-B-A design by (a) ending in an intervention condition and (b) providing two opportunities to replicate the positive effects of intervention (B_1 to A_1; B_2 to A_2). By ending in intervention many of the practical and ethical concerns of teachers and clinicians are dispelled; further, two demonstrations of experimental effect greatly enhance the internal validity of findings. As mentioned, the A-B-A-B design can be extended to a multitreatment design (e.g., A-B-A-B-C-B-C) thereby permitting you the flexibility of comparing other interventions with the initial intervention. This is a particularly useful option when the first intervention to be introduced (B) results in positive changes in the target behavior that approximate but do not meet the therapeutic or educational outcome objective (e.g., Falcomata, Roane, Hovanetz, & Kettering, 2004). In such cases a new intervention may be introduced alone (C) or in combination with the first intervention (BC).

Limitations

The primary limitations of the A-B-A-B design relate to practical and ethical concerns rather than experimental considerations. For many practitioners responsible for programming durable behavior changes, even a brief withdrawal of an effective intervention may be deemed unethical. This is particularly true when target behaviors are dangerous to the client or student (e.g., eye gouging) or others (e.g., fighting). Such concerns are valid and cannot be discounted. However, you may view condition A_2 (withdrawing the intervention) as an empirical check or "probe" to see what effect an abrupt withdrawal will have on the target behavior. If the target behavior returns to unacceptable levels, that indicates that you will have to plan an additional phase after B_2 is reintroduced, one that systematically brings the individual's behavior under self-control (self-management strategy) or under the control of natural environmental events and contingencies. In the latter case you may have to systematically thin the reinforcement schedule (e.g., CRF to FR_2 to VR_3) or teach others to carry out the intervention in the natural environment. Rusch and Kazdin (1981) outlined three strategies (i.e., sequential-withdrawal, partial-withdrawal, and partial-sequential-withdrawal) that may facilitate behavior mainten-ance if the total withdrawal of the intervention in the second baseline condition (A_2) results in a contratherapeutic trend.

Due to ethical concerns, some applied researchers find it difficult not to continue with an effective intervention during the second baseline condition time period. If staff and/or parents are not agreeable to withdrawing an effective intervention for even a brief period, the behavior trend probably will not reverse during the second baseline condition, thus jeopardizing a demonstration of experimental control. For this reason it is critical that procedural-reliability data be collected during A_2, as during all conditions, to ensure planned condition procedures are followed. Staff and parents also should be made aware of the purpose of withdrawing the intervention, i.e., a test of behavior maintenance under nonintervention conditions.

A third limitation of the A-B-A-B design is that it is *not* appropriate for evaluating interven-tions with behaviors that are not likely to be reversed (e.g., writing one's name, completing an assembly task, solving addition problems, learning a mnemonic to self-monitor behavior, etc.). The A-B-A-B design can be used in these and similar situations if the reason for failure on such tasks is one of motivation rather than skill acquisition. Otherwise, a multiple baseline or multiple probe design is more appropriate for evaluating experimental control. The A-B-A-B design also may be used to evaluate the effectiveness of assistive technology and the use of adaptive equipment, including communication devices (Mechling & Gast, 1997), visual activity schedules (Bryan & Gast, 2000; Spriggs, Gast, & Ayres, 2007), and alternative seating equipment (Schilling & Schwartz, 2004).

Applied Example: A-B-A-B

Patel, M. R., Piazza, C. C., Layer, S. A., Coleman, R., & Swartzwelder, D. M. (2005). A systematic evaluation of food textures to decrease packing and increase oral intake in children with pediatric feeding disorders. *Journal of Applied Behavior Analysis, 38*, 89–100.

Patel, Piazza, Layer, Coleman, and Swartzwelder (2005) studied the effects of food texture (puree, wet ground, chopped) on children's food packing. Three males (Dylan, Caden, and Jasper), aged 3 years to 4 years, participated in the study. Each child was diagnosed with a pediatric feeding disorder by an occupational therapist who determined participants had low oral tone, an inability to lateralize food, and immature chewing patterns. As a result of these diagnoses the children were admitted to a day-treatment program for feeding disorders where sessions were conducted in a therapy room with a one-way mirror, a high chair, utensils, and toys.

> Five session blocks were conducted each day (i.e., session blocks were conducted five times per day) with approximately three to four 5-min sessions (15–20 min of total eating time) per session block (for a total of 15–20 sessions per day for Dylan and Caden.
> (p. 93)

Fewer (2–3) but longer (20–30 min) eating-block sessions were conducted with Jasper.

Two dependent variables were measured, percentage of trials with food packing and total grams consumed. Data were collected on laptop computers using event recording to record occurrences of packing. Percentage of packing was computed by dividing number of occurrences by total number of acceptances multiplied by 100. Prior to meal consumption and following meals, participants' food was weighed. The difference in the two weights was used to calculate total grams consumed. Interobserver agreement was calculated as 13%, 23%, and 30% of the sessions for Dylan, Caden, and Jasper, respectively. Mean reliability of food acceptance for Dylan was 93% (range = 74% to 100%), 92% (range = 76% to 100%) for Caden, and 96% (range = 95% to 100%) for Jasper.

Though individual procedures differed slightly, one fruit, one vegetable, one starch, and one protein was identified for each participant. Food presentation order was determined randomly prior to each session and followed throughout the session. If children did not accept a bite, or swallow a bite, an escape extinction procedure was followed. Food textures varied across participants. Dylan received puree and wet ground, Caden received puree, wet ground, and baby food, and Jasper received puree and chopped.

Procedures for Dylan included the therapist presenting a bite approximately every 30 s. If the bite was accepted within 5 s, brief praise was provided. The spoon was not removed until Dylan accepted the food bite and, if the food was expelled, it was re-presented. Incidents of packing were assessed every 30 s. If packing occurred, the therapist used a bristled massaging toothbrush to place the food on his tongue to encourage swallowing. This was paired with the verbal prompt, "Dylan, you need to swallow your bite" (p. 93). This correction procedure was repeated every 30 s until packed food was swallowed. Dylan had continuous access to toys throughout the session. If an inappropriate behavior occurred, it was blocked or ignored. The next bite was presented immediately after swallowing. Intervention procedures for Caden were identical to Dylan's except (a) bites were presented every 15 s, rather than every 30 s from initial acceptance; (b) a brush was not used to redistribute packed food; (c) verbal praise and interaction were provided, however, no toys were used; and (d) expelled bites were re-presented until they were swallowed (p. 93). Procedures for Jasper were different in that food was placed in a bowl every 30 s for initial acceptance. Jasper was allowed to feed himself and, if he fed himself within the 30 s, verbal praise was delivered. If the self-feeding latency exceeded 30 s, the therapist physically guided his hand to the spoon and then to his mouth. Once the spoon reached Jasper's lips, it remained there until the bite was accepted. If bites were expelled, the food was scooped up and place in his bowl. Jasper was given another 30 s to feed himself before the physical guidance was initiated. Similar to other participants, Jasper was verbally prompted if he did not swallow within 30 s of accepting a bite. Toys were provided contingent upon his swallowing. When Jasper engaged in inappropriate behavior, the therapist held his hands down for 20 s.

The relation between food texture on the percentage of trials with packing and total number of grams consumed each session was evaluated within the context of an A-B-A-B withdrawal design (referred to by the authors as a reversal design). Figure 10.5 presents Dylan's data both for percentage of trials with packing (top graph) and number of grams consumed (bottom graph) across experimental conditions. In regards to percentage of trials with packing during the baseline condition, in which Dylan was presented pureed foods, packing was low in A_1 (mean = 6%, range = 0% to 35%). Upon introduction of "wet ground" textures (B_1) there was an immediate and abrupt change in percentage of trials with packing (i.e., absolute level change from 0% to 100%). During B_1 data were highly variable (range = 50% to 100%). There was a 100% non-overlapping data (PND) between conditions A_1 and B_1. With the return to the pureed food condition (A_2), there was an immediate decrease in packing, with no occurrences of packing over the seven sessions of the pureed food-texture condition, and 100% PND between B_1 and A_2. With the return to the "wet ground" food-texture condition (B_2), packing returned to the previously high contratherapeutic level that stabilized at the ceiling (mean = 100%). There was 100% PND between conditions A_2 and B_2. Follow-up data were highly variable across the four observations at 3-month intervals after study completion.

Data were also collected on total number of grams consumed during the puree (A) condition and the "wet ground" (B) condition, as shown in Figure 10.5 (bottom graph). During the initial baseline (A_1) there was a variable decelerating trend in a contratherapeutic direction (median and mean = 58 g). Upon introduction of the "wet ground" condition (B_1) there was an immediate decrease in total number of grams consumed per session (absolute level change 65 g to 35 g). These data reflect a contratherapeutic level under the "wet ground" condition with a mean = 20 g (range = 10 to 35 g). Upon return to the puree condition (A_2) there was an immediate and abrupt change in number of grams consumed (absolute level change from 20 g to 75 g). These therapeutic levels replicated levels of the initial puree condition (A_1). The return to the "wet ground" condition (B_2) resulted in similar low levels of consumption as seen in B_1. There was 100% PND across all adjacent conditions. Overall, the mean number of grams consumed under the puree condition was 60.5 g (range = 40 to 65 g) compared to 18.5 g (range = 10 to 35 g) under the "wet ground" condition.

As displayed in Figure 10.5, these data provide a convincing evaluation and demonstration of a functional relation between food texture and the percentage of trials with packing and the

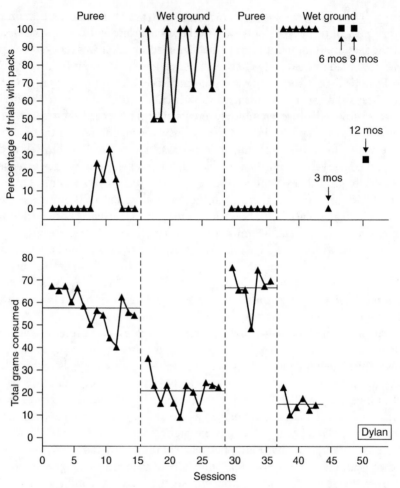

Figure 10.5 Percentage of trials with packing (top panel) and total grams consumed (bottom panel) for Dylan (source: Patel et al., 2005. Copyright by Society for the Experimental Analysis of Behavior, Inc. Reproduced by permission).

number of grams consumed for Dylan. Direct intra-subject replication was achieved within the context of the A-B-A-B design and threats to internal validity were evaluated and controlled. Though not presented here, similar findings were found with the other two study participants, Caden and Jasper, thereby increasing the generality of the findings to the extent to which the three participants were different, i.e., direct inter-subject replication. It is only through systematic replication attempts that we will know the extent to which these findings will generalize.

Applied Example: A-B-A-B with Concurrent Monitoring

Carnine, D. W. (1976). Effects of two teacher-presentation rates on off-task behavior, answering correctly, and participation. *Journal of Applied Behavior Analysis, 9*, 199–206.

The purpose of the Carnine (1976) study was to evaluate the effects of fast and slow presentation rates on off-task, correct answering, and participation behaviors of two "low-achieving" first-grade students. The two participants, one boy and one girl, along with two other children, constituted the lowest-performing first-grade reading group in their school. The children were instructed in reading, using the Level I DISTAR program, 30 min each day. Instruction took place in a small group in the rear of the classroom while other students worked independently at their seats or received small-group instruction in other areas of the room. During the first 33 sessions reading instruction was provided by the classroom teacher and during the last five sessions by a student teacher.

During each instructional session, data were collected on each target participant's off-task, correct answering, and participation behaviors by two data collectors. "Off-task" was defined as any occurrence of a child (a) leaving his or her seat; (b) "blurting out"; (c) talking to other children in the group; or (d) ignoring the teacher. Each of these types of off-task behaviors was coded and recorded by observers. Children were judged to be participating if they responded within 1 s of the teacher's cue. Observers also rated children's responses as correct or incorrect regardless of their participation rating, i.e., a late correct response was scored as answering correctly. Data were collected on one participant at a time. Every 10 trials observers redirected their attention and collected data on all three dependent measures of the other participant. This alternation of recording between participants every 10 trials continued until each child was rated on a total of 30 trials. Different tasks were presented on each trial.

In addition to collecting data on children's behavior, observers recorded task presentation rate. This was done by starting stopwatches with each new block of 10 trials and momentarily stopping stopwatches when children were questioned individually, or if there were interruptions. After each block of 10 trials observers recorded the duration of time it took to complete the block of 10 trials and reset their stopwatches. The presentation rate was calculated by dividing total instructional time for a session by number of tasks presented during that session.

Reliability checks were conducted during 87% of the sessions. Interobserver agreement on each dependent measure was calculated using the point-by-point method, which yielded a mean percentage agreement for all measures above 90% (mean range = 90.2% to 92.9%). Observer checks on presentation rates (i.e., procedural-reliability checks) revealed a consistent difference across all "slow-rate" and "fast-rate" experimental conditions.

The independent variable under investigation was task presentation rate. Two controlled experimental conditions, slow-rate presentation (A) and fast-rate presentation (B), were alternated to assess their effects on the three dependent variables. During the slow-rate presentation condition the teacher silently counted to five after each child's response and then presented the next task. In contrast, during the fast-rate presentation condition the teacher immediately presented the next task after each response. The teacher presented the lesson exactly as it was written in the DISTAR program. The teacher delivered general verbal praise (e.g., "That was really fine") at a constant rate across conditions. This was accomplished by using a preprogrammed tone from an audio-cassette recorder, equipped with an earplug, which served as a cue for the teacher to praise. General praise was delivered on a fixed interval, 90-second schedule (FI 90 s) at the first opportunity after the tone sounded contingent upon a correct response or attending by both participants. This constant schedule across conditions prevented a confounding of verbal praise and presentation rate over the course of the study.

The effect of slow-rate presentation (A) and fast-rate presentation (B) on both participants' off-task, correct answering, and participation behaviors was evaluated within the context of an A-B-A-B-A'-B' design. The certified classroom teacher instructed the reading group during the first four phases of the study (A_1-B_1-A_2-B_2), while the student teacher conducted the group during the last two phases (A'_3-B'_3) of the investigation. The inclusion of the student teacher permitted a brief assessment of stimulus generalization across teachers.

Figures 10.6 and 10.7 graph mean percentage occurrence of the three dependent variables as

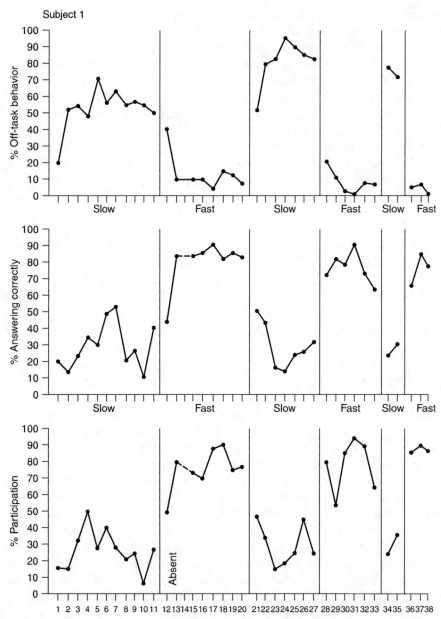

Figure 10.6 Percent occurrence of off-task, answering correctly, and participation for Subject 1 during the slow- and fast-rate presentation phases. The dotted lines indicate when Subject 1 was absent. The student-teacher taught during the final phases (Sessions 34 through 38) (source: Carnine, 1976. Copyright by Society for the Experimental Analysis of Behavior, Inc. Reproduced by permission).

recorded by two data collectors for "Subject 1" and "Subject 2," respectively. It should be noted that off-task data drove the design, i.e., decisions to move to another condition (A to B, B to A) were based on these data. It also should be noted that condition labels were omitted above "% off-task behavior" but are identified above the other two behaviors monitored. For Subject 1, during A_1 (slow-rate condition) both level and trend were stable using an "80% of the data

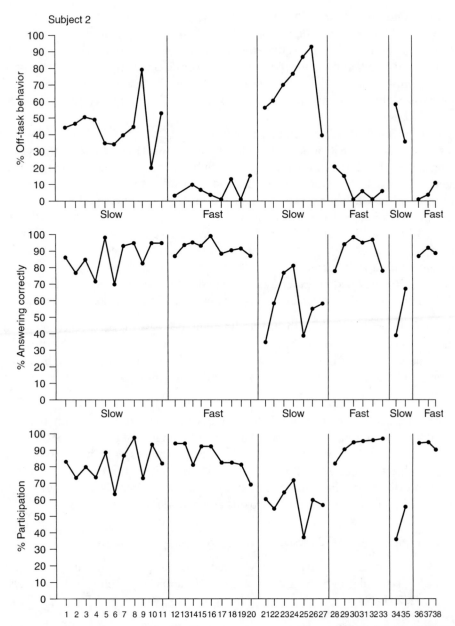

Figure 10.7 Percent occurrence of off-task, answering correctly, and participation for Subject 2 during the slow- and fast-rate presentation phases. The student-teacher taught during the final phases (Sessions 34 through 38) (source: Carnine, 1976. Copyright by Society for the Experimental Analysis of Behavior, Inc. Reproduced by permission).

points falling within a 20% range" as the definition for stability. Upon introduction of B_1 (fast-rate condition) there was an immediate, though modest, absolute change in level. Subsequent days in the fast-rate condition resulted in a stable, zero-celeration trend near the floor. This change in level was replicated across subsequent condition comparisons. The PND was 100% between all adjacent condition comparisons with the exception of B_1 compared to A_1, which was 87.5%. A comparison of the percentages for off-task behavior during the slow-rate presentation condition ($A_1 = 52.6\%$; $A_2 = 81.3\%$; $A_3 = 75.3\%$) and the fast-rate presentation condition ($B_1 = 13.9\%$; $B_2 = 8.7\%$; $B_3 = 4.5\%$) show clear therapeutic differences under the fast-rate presentation condition. Positive effects were also shown under the fast-rate condition with secondary dependent measures, percentage answering correctly and percentage participation, when compared to the slow-rate condition. PND was 100% between all adjacent condition comparisons for both measures with the exception of B_1 compared to A_1 for answering correctly, which was 87.5%.

As shown in Figure 10.7, off-task behavior for Subject 2 in the initial slow-rate condition (A_1) was comparable to that of Subject 1. On the other two dependent variables, percentage answering correctly and percentage participation, Subject 2 was considerably higher; therefore introduction of the fast-rate condition (B_1) had a positive therapeutic effect only on the percentage of off-task behavior. The reinstatement of the slow-rate condition (A_2), however, adversely affected all three dependent measures. The subsequent reinstatement of the fast-rate condition (B_2) resulted in a reversal in trend and level. This pattern of responding on all three dependent measures (A_2-B_2) was replicated with the student teacher (A_3-B_3). These findings replicate those found with Subject 1.

Carnine (1976) provided an experimental analysis of the importance of task presentation rate on children's off-task, correct answering, and participation behaviors. He concluded,

> the present study indicated that the faster rate might decrease the occurrence of students' off-task behavior and increase the occurrence of answering correctly and participation. The technique of more rapidly asking questions or giving instruction can be used by teachers in addition to techniques involving contingent consequences.
>
> (p. 203)

The direct intra-subject replication of effect across the two conditions with two different teachers adds to the internal validity and reliability of findings. The generality of these findings was demonstrated by replicating different responding patterns with two participants, i.e., direct inter-subject replication. Although generality is limited due to the similarity of the two children, external validity can be further enhanced by a systematic replication by other investigators with different types of participants and behaviors.

Applied Example: A-BC-B-A-B Design

Spriggs, A. D., Gast, D. L, & Ayres, K. M. (2007). Using picture activity schedule books to increase on-schedule and on-task behaviors. *Education and Training in Developmental Disabilities, 42*, 209–223.

Spriggs, Gast, and Ayres (2007) studied the effects of a picture activity schedule (PAS) book on the on-schedule and on-task behaviors of four female students, ages 12 years 7 months to 13 years 8 months, with moderate intellectual disabilities. All four participants had difficulty independently transitioning between activities and staying on-task. The study was conducted in the students' self-contained special education classroom during a 45-min independent work period each afternoon. During this period students were to independently transition every 10 min between four randomly scheduled activities when signaled by the teacher saying, "It's time to change." Generalized use of the PAS book was assessed in another self-contained special education classroom at a different time of the day.

Two dependent variables, percentage of on-schedule behaviors emitted during each transition and percentage of time on-task, were measured. The behavioral definitions used by

Bryan and Gast (2000, p. 556) were used. On-task data were collected using a variable time-sample recording procedure in which an independent observer recorded the occurrence or nonoccurrence of a student being on-task at the end of intervals that ranged from 1 to 5 minutes. On-schedule behavior was task analyzed into five steps (remove next activity picture card, move to appropriate center, begin work within 10 s, put materials away when finished, put completed activity card into the "finished" pocket (p. 213)) and the observer recorded either an occurrence or nonoccurrence of each behavior during a transition. Event recording was used to monitor adult prompting, which was not to occur, as a means of evaluating the procedural fidelity of the PAS "Book Only" condition. Interobserver-reliability data were collected in 24.3% of the sessions, while procedural-reliability data were collected in 21.6% of all sessions and at least once during each condition for each participant. The mean percentage agreement for on-schedule and on-task behaviors for all participants and across all conditions was 99% and 98%, respectively. Procedural reliability was 99.8%.

Baseline (A) sessions were conducted to assess each student's on-schedule and on-task behaviors without access to the PAS book. During the "No Book" condition the teacher announced it was time for centers followed by telling students which activities they were to transition to, and in what order, during the 45-min independent work period. The activities and the sequence of activities varied across days to facilitate generalization and to prevent students from memorizing a specific sequence of activities. After four days of the "No Book" baseline condition (A_1), instruction on how to use the PAS book was introduced (BC). During this condition graduated guidance was used in the first session and system of least prompts was used in all subsequent sessions to teach participants how to transition between centers using the PAS book. Instruction continued until a participant reached the criteria of 90% on-schedule and 90% on-task without prompts over three consecutive days. Following PAS book instruction, a "Book Only" condition (B_1) was introduced in which the teacher followed procedures used in the baseline condition (A_1) except for the availability of the PAS book. The teacher and teacher aide were available to answer questions related to assignments but they were not permitted to prompt students to refer to their PAS books.

Figures 10.8 through 10.11 present the percentage of on-schedule and on-task behaviors for all participants across all conditions evaluated within the context of an A-BC-B-A-B experimental design. It should be noted that Generalization Pretest and Posttest data are graphed for each student on each graph. Mary, Cindy, Holly, and Jennifer all showed low percentage of time on-task during the first baseline "No Book" condition (A_1, range = 0% to 31%). Upon introduction of PAS book instruction (BC), an immediate therapeutic change in level and trend of on-task behavior was observed for all participants. There were no overlapping data points between A_1 and BC conditions for any participant, i.e., PND = 100%. Following the PAS book instructional criteria being met, students were presented with the first "Book Only" condition (B_1). This condition resulted in all participants maintaining high percentages of on-task and on-schedule behaviors. After a stable therapeutic level and trend was established for each student the PAS book was withdrawn and the "No Book" condition (A_2) reinstated. For all participants there was an immediate and abrupt drop in level and trend for on-task behavior with 100% PND between A_2 and B_1. The mean percentage of time on-task comparing B_1 to A_1 for Mary was 97.24% to 4%; Cindy, 98.5% to 20%; Holly, 98.5% to 0%; and Jennifer, 95.4% to 0%. Students' low on-task behavior in A_2 replicated their low on-task behavior in A_1. After four days in the "No Book" condition (A_2) and data stability for three of the four students, the "Book Only" condition (B_2) was reintroduced. This resulted in an immediate and abrupt return to therapeutic levels that were evidenced in the first "Book Only" (B_1) condition. There was 100% PND between B_2 and A_2 conditions. Direct intra-subject and inter-subject

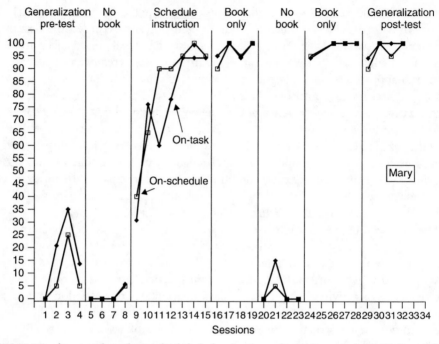

Figure 10.8 Mary's on-task and on schedule behavior (source: Spriggs et al., 2007. Reproduced by permission from the Council for Exceptional Children).

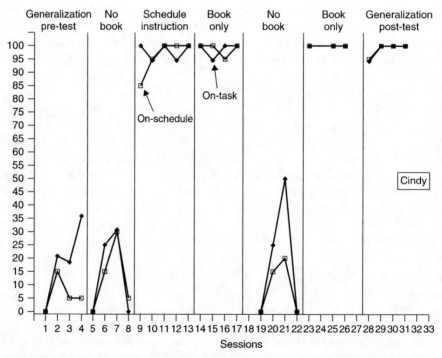

Figure 10.9 Cindy's on-task and on-schedule behavior (source: Spriggs et al., 2007. Reproduced by permission from the Council for Exceptional Children).

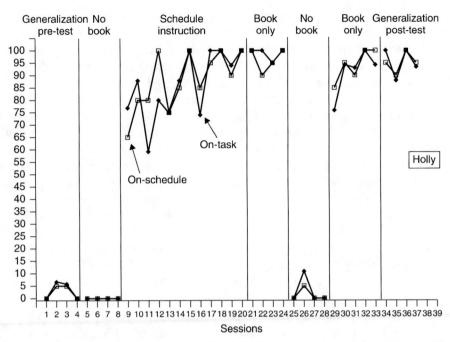

Figure 10.10 Holly's on-task and on-schedule behavior (source: Spriggs et al., 2007. Reproduced by permission from the Council for Exceptional Children).

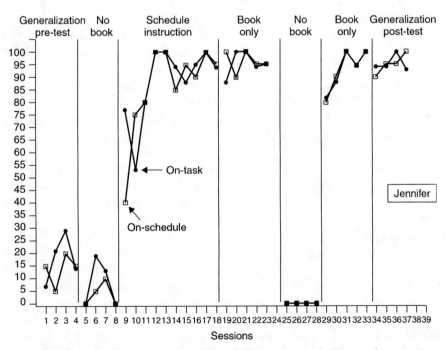

Figure 10.11 Jennifer's on-task and on-schedule behavior (source: Spriggs et al., 2007. Reproduced by permission from the Council for Exceptional Children).

replications were achieved regarding the positive effect the PAS book condition had on all students' on-task behavior.

A visual analysis of the percentage of on-schedule behaviors emitted by students yielded similar findings as those found for on-task behavior. Specifically, Mary, Cindy, Holly, and Jennifer showed a low percentage of on-schedule behaviors during the initial (A_1) "No Book" baseline condition (range = 0% to 30%). Upon introduction of PAS book instruction, an immediate positive change in level and trend for on-schedule behaviors was observed for all participants. After the 90% independent on-schedule criteria were reached in the BC condition, the "Book Only" condition (B_1) was introduced. During this condition percentage of on-schedule behaviors for all participants remained high, indicating that students were able to transition between scheduled activities with minimal, if any, adult prompting. Upon return to the "No Book" condition (A_2) all participants showed an immediate, contratherapeutic drop in level and trend for on-schedule behavior. In comparing on-schedule performance between the "Book Only" (B_1) and "No Book" (A_2) conditions, Mary showed a mean percentage drop from 96.25% to 1.25%; Cindy, 98.75% to 8.75%; Holly, 96.25% to 1.25%; and Jennifer, 90% to 0%. There was 100% PND between B_1 and A_2. On-schedule performance levels in A_2 replicate those in A_1 for all students. Reinstatement of the "Book Only" condition (B_2) resulted in an immediate return to therapeutic levels of on-schedule behaviors achieved in B_1, with 100% PND between the two conditions (B_2 to A_2). Direct intra-subject and inter-subject replications were achieved regarding the positive effect the PAS book condition had on all students' on-schedule behaviors.

A comparison of Generalization Pretest to Posttest data show that all participants generalized their on-task and on-schedule independent behavior gains across settings and activities. Specifically, a positive mean percentage change in on-task behavior was observed for each of the participants from Pretest to Posttest: Mary, 17% (range = 0% to 30%) to 96.25% (range = 90% to 100%); Cindy, 18.25% (range = 0% to 37%) to 99% (range = 95% to 100%); Holly, 3.25% (range = 0% to 7%) to 94.5% (range = 86% to 100%); and Jennifer, 18.25% (range = 6% to 29%) to 95.5% (range = 93% to 100%). The mean percentage of time on-schedule from the Generalization Pretest to Posttest replicated the effect observed with on-task behavior: Mary, 8.75% (range = 0% to 25%) to 96% (range = 90% to 100%); Cindy, 6.25% (range = 0% to 15%) to 99% (range = 95% to 100%); Holly, 2.5% (range = 0% to 5%) to 95.75% (range = 91% to 100%); and Jennifer, 13.75% (range = 5% to 20%) to 94.75% (range = 89% to 100%).

Social validity data collected using a 1–5 point Likert Scale, in which 1 represented "strongly disagree" and 5 represented "strongly agree," yielded unanimous ratings of "strongly agree" (mean = 5) from special education and general education teachers, teacher aides, a speech/language therapist, and an occupational therapist on questions related to: (a) students becoming more independent with picture schedules; (b) picture schedules being a useful management tool; and (c) students "seemed" to accomplish more during center time when using the picture schedule. Unfortunately, social-validity data were not gathered on participants' opinions.

The positive effect the PAS book intervention had on percentage of on-task and on-schedule behaviors of four students with moderate intellectual disabilities was demonstrated through the use of an A-BC-B-A-B withdrawal design. A functional relation was demonstrated when high levels of on-task and on-schedule behaviors were observed in the PAS "Book Only" condition and not in the "No Book" condition. These findings replicated those of Bryan and Gast (2000) and MacDuff, Krantz, and McClannahan (1993), and extended the effectiveness of picture activity schedules to a different population, in different settings, and with different activities (systematic replication).

Concluding Comments

The A-B-A-B design represents the clearest and most convincing research paradigm for evaluating and demonstrating a functional relation between independent and dependent variables when a target behavior is reversible. There is no clearer way to show differences between adjacent conditions than through the systematic presentation and withdrawal of an independent variable. Historically the A-B-A-B withdrawal design has been one of the most frequently used single subject research designs in applied behavior analysis research. It improves upon the A-B and A-B-A designs by providing two opportunities to demonstrate causality with the same participant, thereby strengthening the internal validity of the findings. When a study includes multiple participants, targeting similar behaviors, and employing the same independent variable, it is possible to extend external validity to the extent to which participants, behaviors, settings, materials, etc. differ. For this reason we recommend that you include three or more participants in your study, regardless of the experimental design, in accordance with recommendations by Horner et al. (2005) and others (e.g., Cooper, Heron, & Heward, 2007; Barlow & Hersen, 1984; Tawney & Gast, 1984), and methodically identify even subtle differences between experimental conditions. We also recommend that nontarget behaviors be monitored concurrently as a check on response generalization. When possible, periodic probe measures should be scheduled in other settings, with other individuals, at other times of day, with different materials, etc. to assess stimulus generalization. In light of the flexibility of the A-B-A-B design and clear evaluation of experimental control, it deserves serious consideration by teachers, clinicians, and others engaged in applied behavioral research. Table 10.2 summarizes several studies that used an A-B-A-B design to evaluate experimental control.

Variations of the A-B-A-B Design

All single subject research designs, particularly the A-B-A-B design, are versatile paradigms for evaluating and demonstrating intervention effectiveness. Unlike group research designs, which are static, single subject research designs are dynamic, i.e., rapidly changing. For example, if you design a study using the A-B-A-B design and discover that the effect intervention B has on the target behavior is negligible (i.e., A = B), it is *not* necessary for you to return to baseline condition (A) because conditions A and B are *functionally equivalent*; rather you have the flexibility to introduce a new intervention (C) or to combine a new condition with B (BC). If intervention C, in turn, has a measurable positive effect on the target behavior you can proceed by returning to Condition B. In this example you initially chose the A-B-A-B design to evaluate your intervention (B); however, because it had no effect on the dependent variable, you changed the design to an A-B-C-B-C design (or A-B-BC-B-BC design). Because of such flexibility, there are numerous studies in the applied research literature that differ from the basic A-B-A-B design and yet demonstrate experimental control. In this section we overview some of the more common variations and extensions of the A-B-A-B design. Specifically, the following designs are described and illustrated: (1) B-A-B; (2) A-B-A'-B reversal design; and (3) A-B-A-B-C-B multitreatment design. Additional design variations and expansions, in which a research question focuses on comparing one intervention with another intervention (e.g., A-B-C-B-C, A-B-BC-B-BC), are discussed more extensively in Chapter 12.

B-A-B Design

The B-A-B design is a research paradigm you may find yourself using when a new student or client has been referred who exhibits self-injurious or physically aggressive behaviors. For ethical

Table 10.2 A-B-A-B Design Study Summaries

Reference	Participants	Setting/arrangement	Independent variable	Dependent variable
Ahearn, W. H., Clark, K. M., MacDonald, P. F., & Chung, B. I. (2007). Assessing and treating vocal stereotypy in children with autism. *Journal of Applied Behavior Analysis, 40*, 263–275.	Number: 4 Sex: 2 male, 2 female Age Range: 3 yr to 11 yr Disability/diagnosis: autism spectrum disorder	Setting: therapy room (1.5 m by 3 m) with video camera, microphone, table and two chairs Arrangement: individual	Response interruption and response redirection (RIRD)	Percentage of vocal stereotypy Frequency of appropriate vocalizations
Bruzek, J. L., & Thompson, R. H. (2007). Antecedent effects of observing peer play. *Journal of Applied Analysis, 40*, 327–331.	Number: 4 Sex: 2 female, 2 male Age Range: 2 yrs 2 mo to 3 yrs 8 mo Disability/diagnosis: typically developing	Setting: room equipped with an adjoining observation area Arrangement: dyads	High preference, medium preference and low preference reinforcement	Percentage of time (in-zone) Responses per minute
Bryan, L., & Gast, D. L. (2000). Teaching on-task and on-schedule behaviors to high-functioning children with autism via picture activity schedules. *Journal of Autism and Developmental Disorders, 30*, 553–567.	Number: 4 Sex: 3 male; 1 female Age range: 7 yr 4 mo–8 yr 11 mo Disability/diagnosis: autism	Setting: resource classroom (15 ft by 25 ft) Arrangement: individual	Picture activity schedule book	Percentage of task completed on-schedule Percentage of task completed off-task Percentage of intervals on task with scheduled materials Percentage of on-task with nonscheduled materials Percentage of intervals off-task
Cotnoir-Bichelman, N. M., Thompson, R. H., McKerchar, P. M., & Haremza, J. L. (2006). Training student teachers to reposition infants frequently. *Journal of Applied Behavioral Analysis, 39*, 489–494.	Number: 6 Sex: female Age range: student teachers Disability/diagnosis: typical development	Setting: university-run infant classroom. Arrangement: group	Reposition infants according to a chart plus supervisor feedback. Baseline was chart without supervisor feedback	Mean percentage of correct position changes
Dettmer, S., Simpson, R. L., Myles, B. S., & Ganz, J. B. (2000). The use of visual supports to facilitate transitions of students with autism. *Focus on Autism and Other Developmental Disabilities, 15*, 163–169.	Number: 2 Sex: male Age range: 5–7 yrs Disability/diagnosis: autism	Setting: home environment; community environment Arrangement: individual	Visual supports including fixed and portable schedules	Latency of initiation of directive

Citation	Participants	Setting	Intervention	Dependent measures
Field, C., Nash, H. M., Handwerk, M. L., & Friman, P. C. (2004). A modification of the token economy for nonresponsive youth in family-style residential care. *Behavior Modification, 28,* 438–457.	Number: 3 Sex: 2 male, 1 female Age range: 11 yr to 12 yr Disability/diagnosis: ADHD, conduct disorder, dysthymia, post-traumatic stress disorder, oppositional defiant disorder, reactive attachment disorder IQ range: 90 to 104	Setting; youth's home and school Arrangement: group	Multiple exchange token economy system	Mean frequency of intense behavior episodes Mean percent of privileges earned
Gresham, F. M., Van, M. B., & Cook, C. R. (2006). Social skills training for teaching replacement behaviors: Remediating acquisition deficits in at-risk students. *Behavioral Disorders, 31,* 363–377.	Number: 4 Sex: 2 male, 2 female Age range: 6 to 8 yrs Disability/diagnosis: None. Typical children with difficulties making friends, controlling anger, impulsivity, and inattention. At risk for development of emotional behavior disorders	Setting: pull-out setting as described in SSIG curriculum. Arrangement: group	60 hours (3 hours per week over 20 weeks) of social skills training (SST) and classroom-based interventions Differential reinforcement of other behavior (DRO) delivered in classroom	Duration (percentage of time) for total disruptive behavior (TDB), time alone (TA) and negative social interaction (NSI)
Gulotta, C. S., Piazza, C. C., Patel, M. R., & Layer, S. A. (2005). Using food redistribution to reduce packing in children with severe food refusal. *Journal of Applied Behavior Analysis, 38,* 39–50.	Number: 4 Sex: 2 female, 2 male Age range: 2 yr to 5 yr Disability/diagnosis: Failure to Thrive (FTT), gastroesophageal reflux (GER), post respiratory failure, left vocal cord paralysis, status post Nissen fundoplication, developmental delays, septal optic dysplasia, optic nerve hypoplasia, seizure disorder	Setting: day treatment facility Arrangement: individual	Food redistribution with a bristled massaging toothbrush	Percentage of food packs Mean latency to mouth cleans
Hagopian, L. P., Kuhn, S. A., Long, E. S., & Rush, K. S. (2005). Schedule thinning following communication training: Using competing stimuli to enhance tolerance to decrements in reinforcer density. *Journal of Applied Behavior Analysis, 38,* 177–193.	Number: 3 Sex: male Age range: 7 yr to 13 yr Disability/diagnosis: PDD, ADHD, mild intellectual disability, autism, moderate intellectual disability	Setting: treatment rooms 3 m by 3 m equipped with one way mirrors. Arrangement: individual	FCT with extinction verses FCT with extinction and access to competing stimuli	Responses per minute of problem behavior Responses per minute (communication)

(Continued)

Table 10.2 Continued

Reference	Participants	Setting/arrangement	Independent variable	Dependent variable
Kern, L., Starosta, K., & Adelaman, B. E. (2006). Reducing pica by teaching children to exchange inedible items for edibles. *Behavior Modification, 30,* 135–158.	Number: 2 Sex: males Age range: 8 yr to 18 yr Disability/diagnosis: severe intellectual disability, autism	Setting: Participant 1: hospital room (4.5 m by 6.0 m). Participant 2: across all settings in school (van, store, classroom) Arrangement: individual	Exchanging inedible for preferred edible item	Frequency of pica attempts and exchanges per hour
Kuhn, S. A., Lerman, D. C., Vorndran, C. M., & Addison L. (2006). Analysis of factors that affect responding in a two-response chain in children with developmental disabilities. *Journal of Applied Behavior Analysis, 39,* 263–280.	Number: 5 Sex: 4 male, 1 female Age range: 3 yrs to 11 yrs Disability/diagnosis: autism, developmental delay, down syndrome, obsessive-compulsive disorder, seizure disorder, mental retardation (level unspecified), disruptive behavior disorder, ADHD	Setting: school library, cafeteria and small room, empty classroom, bedroom on the inpatient unit, multipurpose room on impatient unit. Arrangement: individual	Use of extinction, satiation and unchaining in behavior chaining	Frequency of responding
Posavac, H. D., Sheridan, S. M., & Posavac, S. S. (1999). A cueing procedure to control impulsivity in children with attention deficit hyperactivity disorder. *Behavior Modification, 23,* 234–253.	Number: 4 Sex: male Age range: 9 yr Disability/diagnosis: ADHD, depression, bipolar mood disorder, learning disability	Setting: 8-week outpatient treatment program. Arrangement: group	Cueing procedure involving visual reminder, goal evaluation, positive reinforcement and constructive feedback implemented in context of social skills program	Frequency of hand raising and talk-outs

reasons, due to the potential danger to the student, client, or others, you may not have the opportunity to collect baseline data under a non-intervention, "business as usual" condition. It is important to remember, however, that although it may be understandable why baseline data are not collected, it nevertheless weakens the evaluation of experimental control. The absence of pre-intervention behavior measures precludes knowing what the baseline level (mean, range, median, level stability) and trend (accelerating, decelerating, zero celerating, trend stability) were prior to the introduction of the intervention (B_1). Thus, there is no empirical means for (a) comparing the effects of B_1 to the pre-intervention level and trend, and (b) assessing whether the level and trend in A_1, in the B_1-A_1-B_2 design, replicate the level and trend prior to the introduction of B_1. Because of these experimental limitations, few B-A-B designs are found in the recent applied behavioral research literature. For an example of a B-A-B design you may want to review Murphey, Ruprecht, Baggio, and Nunes (1979) and their evaluation of a combination differential reinforcement of other behavior and mild punishment (contingent water squirts) intervention on the high frequency of self-choking behavior (mean = 434 responses per "school" day; range = 345–458) of a young adult with profound intellectual disabilities.

Figure 10.12 displays number of self-chokes emitted by the young man during each condition of the investigation. The data show that the mean frequency for self-chokes during initial treatment (B_1), withdrawal of treatment (A_1), and reinstatement of treatment (B_2) conditions was 22, 265, and 24, respectively. The withdrawal of the treatment package resulted in an immediate and abrupt change in frequency of self-choking in a contratherapeutic direction. This level was reversed immediately upon reintroduction of treatment procedures (B_2).

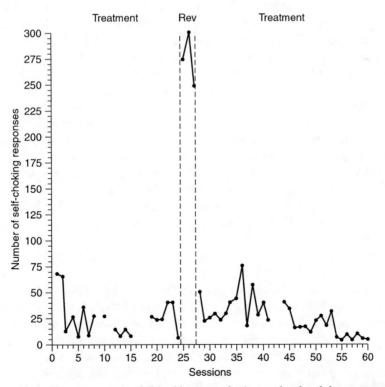

Figure 10.12 Self-choking responses exhibited by Peter during each school day across experimental conditions (source: Murphey et al., 1979. Copyright by Society for the Experimental Analysis of Behavior, Inc. Reproduced by permission).

Although based on current "best practice" you may have concerns with a treatment package that includes a punishment component (contingent verbal reprimands and water squirts), there is no denying the immediate therapeutic effect this intervention had on the self-choking (PND = 100%). Although an initial baseline condition prior to the introduction of the treatment package would have permitted a comparison with the natural frequency of the behavior and strengthened the demonstration of experimental control, the immediate and abrupt level changes between conditions give credence to the effectiveness of the intervention. The investigators' decision to omit an initial baseline condition illustrates the dilemma that sometimes confronts applied researchers who deal with potentially dangerous behaviors in educational and clinical settings.

Although it may be impractical, if not unethical, to collect baseline data over an extended period of time (e.g., three or more data points or until stable) with dangerous behaviors before introducing an intervention, it may be possible to collect baseline data over a shortened observation period to establish a baseline rate. Kennedy and Souza (1995), for example, collected only 6 minutes of baseline data, in one day, in one session for a 19-year-old male with a profound intellectual disability who exhibited a high rate of eye-gouging, before introducing their eye-goggle intervention condition. Although abbreviated, the collection of pre-intervention data strengthened their demonstration of experimental control, clearly showing the effectiveness of the eye-goggle condition in immediately and abruptly decreasing the number of seconds the young man engaged in eye-poking. Figure 10.13 presents Kennedy and Souza's A-B-A-B analysis of the effectiveness of the eye-goggle intervention condition, in which the cumulative seconds of eye-poking are plotted on a cumulative graph.

If you determine it is unethical and/or impractical to collect pre-intervention data, we recommend that you proceed as follows when implementing a B-A-B design: (a) identify a behavior that, if it persists, could result in physical harm to the participant or to others; (b) justify on ethical and/or practical grounds why pre-intervention data cannot be collected; (c) introduce an intervention (B₁), based on a functional behavior analysis (FBA), at the first opportunity and look for an immediate and abrupt level change in behavior in a therapeutic direction; (d) conduct a *brief* withdrawal of the intervention (A₁) after the behavior reaches the established therapeutic criterion level in (B₁); (e) reintroduce the intervention (B₂) after a *brief* reversal in level and/or trend are observed. Assuming you are monitoring the frequency of an inappropriate behavior, experimental control will be demonstrated when the initial introduction of the independent variable results in a low and ideally therapeutic level of the target behavior (B₁), followed by an immediate, though brief, increase in the frequency of the behavior (A₁). Once a change in level or trend is observed (A₁ compared to B₁), reintroduce the intervention (B₂), and ideally, an immediate and abrupt change in level and trend that replicates B₁ will be observed.

As emphasized, when possible it is preferable to collect pre-intervention baseline data, however brief the condition might be, prior to introducing intervention for the first time. Without an initial baseline measure it is impossible to evaluate the effect of the intervention on the natural frequency of the behavior. In contrast to the A-B-A design, however, the B-A-B design has the advantage of ending with intervention and allowing two demonstrations of intervention effectiveness. If practical and ethical considerations permit, a more believable demonstration of causality is possible with the more complete A-B-A-B design.

It is appropriate to point out that within the applied behavior analysis research literature there are studies that report using the B-A-B design with less severe problem behaviors, such as out-of seat (Schilling & Schwartz, 2004), task completion (Robinson, Newby, & Ganzell, 1981; Rowbury, Baer, & Baer, 1976), and on-task behavior (Egel, 1981). In the case of Schilling and

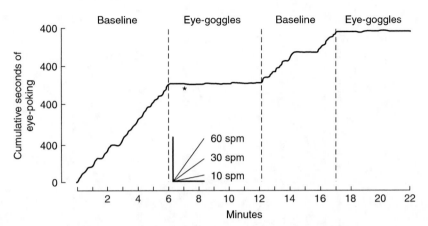

Figure 10.13 Cumulative seconds of eye poking across baseline and goggles conditions. Spm = seconds per minute. The asterisk indicates the occasion when Geof briefly removed the goggles. The goggles were replaced within 5 s by his teacher, who reminded him to continue to wear them (source: Kennedy et al., 1995. Copyright by Society for the Experimental Analysis of Behavior, Inc. Reproduced by permission).

Schwartz (2004), the effectiveness of their independent variable, an alternative seating arrangement, and its effect on the in-seat and engagement behaviors of three of the four preschool children with autism, was assessed within the context of a B-A-B design. Sometimes for practical reasons pre-intervention data may not be collected. Table 10.3 summarizes studies in which at least one B-A-B design was used to evaluate experimental control.

A-B-A′-B Reversal Design

We have chosen to use the notation A-B-A′-B for a class of single subject research designs that are procedurally "true reversals" in that the independent variable is withdrawn from one behavior and applied to a second, possibly incompatible behavior that is being concurrently measured. In this design the independent variable is present in all conditions of the investigation, but its application is applied to two behaviors in a slow alternating pattern. There is disagreement among behavioral researchers as to the appropriateness of referring to an A-B-A-B design as a reversal design when the independent variable (B) only is withdrawn, and not applied to another concurrently monitored behavior in an adjacent condition. As previously discussed, the A-B-A-B design requires that A_1 be procedurally equivalent to A_2, and B_1 be procedurally equivalent to B_2. In other words, there may be no procedural differences between two conditions with the same letter notation.

Withdrawal vs. Reversal Design Distinction ✓✓

Leitenberg (1973), in his discussion of "single-case methodology," we believe convincingly advocates that a distinction be made between the "reversal" design and the "withdrawal" design, a distinction not previously made by Baer et al. (1968). Specifically, Leitenberg (1973) restricts the use of the term *reversal design* to those single subject research designs where the independent variable is truly reversed in the third phase (A_2), *not* simply withdrawn. Operationalized, the reversal design entails concurrently monitoring two *incompatible behaviors* during the first baseline condition (e.g., hands on desk and hands in lap). After a stable baseline

Table 10.3 B-A-B Design Study Summaries

Reference	Participants	Setting/arrangement	Independent variable	Dependent variable
Hernandez, E., Hanley, G. P., Ingvarsson, E. T., & Tiger, J. H. (2007). A preliminary evaluation of the emergence of novel mand forms. *Journal of Applied Behavior Analysis, 40*, 137–156.	Number: 3 Sex: 2 male, 1 female Age range: 1.5 yr to 4 yr Disability/diagnosis: nonspecific developmental delays and typical development	Setting: preference assessment and generalization analysis conducted in room (2.3 m by 2.7 m). Tact assessment and training were conducted in a classroom (12 m by 7 m) Arrangement: individual	Differential reinforcement of undesired, single-word, or framed words	Independent target responses per minute during mand from analysis
Marholin, D., Touchette, P. E., & Stewart, R. M. (1979). Withdrawal or chronic chlorpromazine medication: An experimental analysis. *Journal of Applied Behavior Analysis, 12*, 159–171.	Number: 5 Sex: male Age range: 27 yr to 53 yr Disability/diagnosis: severe intellectual disability	Setting: residential care facility treatment room (5 m by 7 m) Arrangement: individual	Withdrawal of medication (implementation of placebo)	Percentage of ontask rate and accuracy of performance in workshop
Pace, G. M., & Toyer, E. A. (2000). The effects of a vitamin supplement on the pica of a child with severe mental retardation. *Journal of Applied Behavior Analysis, 33*, 619–622.	Number: 1 Sex: female Age range: 9 yr 5 mo Disability/diagnosis: severe mental retardation	Setting: vitamin was given by parents in home environment. Session conducted in treatment room (2.7 m by 2.9 m) Arrangement: individual	Vitamin supplement	Latency to engage in pica

level and trend are established with both behaviors, the independent variable is applied to one of the behaviors (hands on desk) during B_1. If the intervention strategy has a positive effect on this behavior, then it is applied to the concurrently monitored incompatible behavior (hands in lap) in the third phase (commonly referred to as A_2). It is at this juncture that the reversal design is distinguished from the withdrawal design. Not only is the intervention withdrawn from the target behavior in the reversal design, it is applied to an incompatible behavior during the third or "A'_2" condition. If there is a decrease in the one behavior (hands on desk) and a concomitant increase in the incompatible behavior (hands in lap), then a functional relation, between independent and two dependent variables, is demonstrated. When the independent variable is reintroduced to the first behavior (hands on desk), experimental control is further strengthened by reversing data trends of the two behaviors in B_2. The key distinction between reversal and withdrawal designs is that the reversal design (a) withdraws or removes the intervention from one behavior and (b) simultaneously applies it to an incompatible behavior. The withdrawal design, on the other hand, simply removes the intervention during the third phase of the design (A_2). An easy way to distinguish the two designs may be to associate differential reinforcement of an incompatible behavior (DRI), in which you are monitoring two behaviors concurrently, with the reversal design, and extinction (e.g., systematic ignoring) of a single attention-getting behavior with the withdrawal design. We believe that a true reversal design, which we designate as an A-B-A'-B design, is a more "powerful" evaluation and demonstration of experimental control because of the four opportunities to measure the impact the independent variable has on two incompatible behaviors.

In our review of the recent applied behavioral research literature, although not exhaustive, we found no examples of a "true" reversal design. The best example of a "true" reversal design, to the best of our knowledge, continues to be a study conducted by Allen, Hart, Buell, Harris, and Wolf (1964), in which the "isolate" behavior of a nursery-school child was modified through the manipulation of contingent adult attention. Figure 10.14 presents a graphic display of their A-B-A'-B reversal design using the graphic protocol of the day. Figure 10.14 shows the monitoring of two incompatible behaviors: "percent interaction with adults" (top graph) and "percent of interaction with children" (bottom graph). In the first baseline condition (A_1) data show that adult attention was naturally being delivered contingent upon the child's isolate behavior, i.e., adults approached the child when he was alone. Based on what certainly was a result of an FBA, these researchers designed an intervention that provided adult attention *only* when the child was interacting with peers (B_1). This redirection of adult attention resulted in an immediate and abrupt increase in the percentage of peer interactions (PND = 100%), and concomitant decrease in percentage of interaction with adults (PND = 100%), when compared to baseline data. These effects were replicated in subsequent reversals of adult attention (A'_2 and B_2). In the third phase of the study, adults were instructed only to interact with the child when alone, a directive that was *not* part of the A_1 condition, thus the A'_2 designation. This resulted in a reversal of who the child interacted with during the free play period. When the contingency was once again reversed in B_2 the percentage of interactions with peers immediately increased and continued to increase in a therapeutic accelerating trend. It is likely that the Allen et al. demonstration of experimental control in which the third phase of the single subject research design study was labeled "Reversal" influenced subsequent use of the term "reversal" for all A-B-A-B designs, regardless of procedural differences, i.e., withdrawal only vs. withdrawal plus reversal of "independent variable" (e.g., contingent adult attention in the Allen et al. study).

The distinction between the reversal design (A-B-A'-B) and the withdrawal design (A-B-A-B) is small, but nonetheless we believe warranted given the procedural differences relative to the

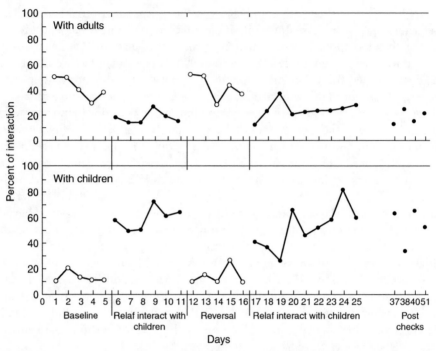

Figure 10.14 Percentages of time spent in social interaction during approximately 2 hours of each morning session (source: Allen et al., 1964. Copyright by Society for Research in Child Development. Reproduced by permission).

third (A_2) condition and the concurrent monitoring of two incompatible behaviors. It is therefore recommended that the A-B-A-B design notation be restricted to those time-series designs in which A_2 procedures are identical to A_1 procedures and when the independent variable is withdrawn. It is our recommendation that an A-B-A'-B design be referred to as a "reversal design" only when (a) the first and third phases of the study are *not* procedurally identical (e.g., a directive is needed to replicate A_1 procedures), and (b) the independent variable is present in all conditions of the design and applied to two different behaviors in an alternating fashion across conditions. We believe that a true reversal design should be assigned the design notation of A-B-A'-B. This having been said, you will discover that currently most behavioral researchers continue to use the term "reversal design" for all A-B-A-B designs. Though this is the case, you should be aware that there are procedural differences between A-B-A'-B reversal and A-B-A-B withdrawal designs.

Multitreatment Designs

Multitreatment designs refer to a class of single subject designs in which two or more planned interventions are compared with one another, or to a baseline condition, to determine which has a greater impact on the dependent variable. In many cases the multitreatment design represents an extension of the A-B-A-B design in which an intervention Condition C is either added to the design sequence (e.g., A-B-A-B-C-B-C) or combined with Condition B (e.g., A-B-A-B-BC-B-BC). In both instances the introduction of C reflects a change in research interest from comparing Condition B to Condition A, to comparing Condition C to Condition B (A-B-A-B-C-B-C) or Condition BC to Condition B (A-B-A-B-BC-B-BC). The difference between these two comparative designs rests with what you wish to say relative to intervention B and intervention C. The A-B-A-B-C-B-C design permits an evaluation of B to C and C to B when both are presented in isolation. The A-B-A-B-BC-B-BC design, on the other hand, permits a comparison of B to BC and BC to B. In this latter design no conclusions can be drawn relative to the effectiveness of C to B when presented in isolation. For example, if Condition A represents noncontingent token reinforcement, Condition B contingent token reinforcement, and Condition C response cost, the latter half of the A-B-A-**B-C-B-C** design provides a comparison of contingent token reinforcement (B) with noncontingent reinforcement and response cost (C). The A-B-A-**B-BC-B-BC** design, however, compares the contingent token-reinforcement condition (B) with the contingent token-reinforcement condition paired with the response-cost condition (BC). The questions are different and thus necessitate different designs.

An in-depth discussion of multitreatment designs and other single subject research designs used to compare two or more interventions are discussed in Chapter 12. Suffice it to say here that variations and extensions of the A-B-A-B design are available if you wish to investigate the relative effectiveness and/or efficiency of two or more interventions.

Summary

In this chapter we have discussed various designs and presented a list of recommendations when you are contemplating using an "A," "B," A-B, A-B-A, A-B-A-B, B-A-B, or A-B-A'-B design. The following basic guidelines are equally important:

1. Introduce a new experimental condition (i.e., baseline or intervention) only after an acceptable data trend has been established in the immediately preceding adjacent condition.
2. Ideally change only one variable at a time when introducing a new experimental condition, and at minimum identify the procedural differences between conditions.
3. Restrict your visual analysis to comparing adjacent conditions.
4. Concurrently monitor nontarget behaviors that may change as a function of applying the intervention to the target behavior (i.e., response generalization).
5. Concurrently monitor target behaviors under "nontraining" stimulus conditions (i.e., stimulus generalization).
6. Attempt to replicate the study with similar participants to enhance the generality of the findings (i.e., external validity).
7. Collect reliability data on both dependent and independent variables.
8. Assess the social validity of the intervention objective(s), procedures, and outcomes.

The A-B-A-B design represents one of the most frequently used single subject designs in behavioral research. This chapter has described and exemplified the basic A-B-A-B design as well as its more common variations. In spite of some educators' and clinician's reluctance to employ an A-B-A-B design because of the brief withdrawal (or reversal) requirement, it continues to be a most convincing and straightforward evaluation paradigm for evaluating experimental control. Its primary advantage, when compared to abbreviated forms of the design (A-B, A-B-A, B-A-B), is that it provides two replications of intervention effectiveness with the same research participant and the same behavior under similar stimulus conditions. This also is an advantage of the A-B-A-B design over the more popular multiple baseline and multiple probe designs.

In the chapters that follow, several alternative experimental designs are discussed. Though each differs from the A-B-A-B design, all are based on baseline logic and represent a rearrangement or elaboration of the more basic A-B design.

References

Allen, K. E., Hart, B., Buell, J. S., Harris, F. R., & Wolf, M. M. (1964). Effects of social reinforcement on isolate behavior of a nursery school child. *Child Development, 35,* 511–518.

Azrin, N. H., & Wesolowski, M. D. (1974). Theft reversal: An overcorrection procedure for eliminating stealing by retarded persons. *Journal of Applied Behavior Analysis, 7,* 577–581.

Baer, D. M., Wolf, M. M., & Risley, T. R. (1968). Some current dimensions of applied behavior analysis. *Journal of Applied Behavior Analysis, 1,* 91–97.

Barlow, D. H., & Hayes, S. C. (1979). Alternating treatments design: One strategy for comparing the effects of two treatments in a single subject. *Archives of General Psychiatry, 29,* 199–210.

Barlow, D. H., & Hersen, M. (1984). *Single case experimental designs: Strategies for studying behavior change* (2nd ed.). New York: Pergamon Press.

Birnbrauer, J. S., Peterson, C. R., & Solnick, J. V. (1974). Design and interpretation of studies of single subjects. *American Journal of mental Deficiency, 79,* 191–203.

Bryan, L. C., & Gast, D. L. (2000). Teaching on-task and on-schedule behaviors to high functioning children with autism via picture schedules. *The Journal of Autism and Developmental Disabilities, 30,* 553–567.

Campbell, D. T., & Stanley, J. C. (1966). *Experimental and quasi-experimental designs for research.* Chicago, IL: Rand McNally.

Carnine, D. W. (1976). Effects of two teacher-presentation rates on off-task behavior, answering correctly, and participation. *Journal of Applied Behavior Analysis, 9,* 199–206.

Christle, C. A., & Schuster, J. W. (2003). The effects of using response cards on student participation, academic achievement, and on-task behavior during whole-class math instruction. *Journal of Behavioral Education, 12,* 147–165.

Cooper, J. O., Heron, T. E., & Heward, W. L. (2007). *Applied Behavior Analysis* (2nd ed.). Upper Saddle River, NJ: Pearson: Merrill Prentice Hall.

Dunlap, G., Clarke, S., & Reyes, L. (1998). An analysis of trends in JABA authorship. *Journal of Applied Behavior Analysis, 31,* 497–500.

Egel, A. L. (1981). Reinforcer variation: Implications for motivating developmentally disabled children. *Journal of Applied Behavior Analysis, 14,* 345–350.

Falcomata, T. S., Roane, H. S., Hovanetz, A. N., & Kettering, T. L. (2004). An evaluation of response cost in the treatment of inappropriate vocalizations maintained by automatic reinforcement. *Journal of Applied Behavior Analysis, 37,* 83–87.

Fraenkel, J. R., & Wallen, N. E. (2006). *How to design and evaluate research in education.* New York: McGraw-Hill Co.

Freeman, K. A. (2006). Treating bedtime resistance with the bedtime pass: A systematic replication and component analysis with 3-year-olds. *Journal of Applied Behavior Analysis, 39,* 423–428.

Glass, G. V., Willson, V. L., & Gottman, L. J. (1975). *Design and analysis of time-series experiments.* Boulder, CO: Colorado Associated University Press.

Harvey, M. T., May, M. E., & Kennedy, C. H. (2004). Nonconcurrent multiple baseline designs and the evaluation of educational systems. *Journal of Behavioral Education, 13,* 267–276

Hersen, A. H., & Barlow, D. H. (1976). *Single case experimental designs: Strategies for studying behavior change.* New York, NY: Pergamon Press.

Horner, R., Carr, E., Halle, J., McGee, G., Odom, S., & Wolery, M. (2005). The use of single-subject research to identify evidence-based practice in special education. *Exceptional Children, 71,* 165–179.

Irwin, D. M., & Bushnell, M. (1980). *Observational strategies for child study.* Columbus, OH: Charles E. Merrill.

Kennedy, C., & Souza, G. (1995). Functional analysis and treatment of eye poking. *Journal of Applied Behavior Analysis, 28,* 27–37.

Kratochwill, T. R. (Ed.). (1978). *Single subject research—Strategies for evaluating change.* New York: Academic Press.

Lazarus, A. A., & Davison, G. C. (1971). Clinical innovation in research and practice. In A. E. Bergin & S. L. Garfield (Eds.), *Handbook of psychotherapy and behavior change: An empirical analysis* (pp. 196–213). New York: Wiley.

Leary, M. (1995). *Introduction to behavioral research methods.* Pacific Grove, CA: Brooks/Cole Publishing Co.

Leitenberg, H. (1973). The use of single-case methodology in psychotherapy research. *Journal of Abnormal Psychology, 82,* 87–101.

Lincoln, Y. S., & Guba, E. G. (1985). *Naturalistic inquiry.* Newberry Park, CA: Sage Publications, Inc.

MacDuff, G. S., Krantz, P. J., & McClannahan, L. E. (1993). Teaching children with autism to use photographic activity schedules: Maintenance and generalization of complex response chains. *Journal of Applied Behavior Analysis, 26,* 89–97.

Mechling, L. C., & Gast, D. L. (1997). Combination audio/visual self-prompting system for teaching chained tasks to students with intellectual disabilities. *Education and Training in Mental Retardation and Developmental Disabilities, 32,* 138–153.

Murphey, R. J., Ruprecht, M. J., Baggio, P., & Nunes, D. L. (1979). The use of mild punishment in combination with reinforcement of alternate behaviors to reduce the self-injurious behavior of a profoundly retarded individual. *AAESPH Review, 4,* 187–195.

Patel, M. R., Piazza, C. C., Layer, S. A., Coleman, R., & Swartzwelder, D. M. (2005). A systematic evaluation of food textures to decrease packing and increase oral intake in children with pediatric feeding disorders. *Journal of Applied Behavior Analysis, 38,* 89–100.

Robinson, P. W., Newby, T. J., & Ganzell, S. L. (1981). A token system for a class of underachieving hyperactive children. *Journal of Applied Behavior Analysis, 14,* 307–315.

Rowbury, T. G., Baer, A. M., & Baer, D. M. (1976). Interactions between teacher guidance and contingent access to play in developing preacademic skills of deviant preschool children. *Journal of Applied Behavior Analysis, 9,* 85–104.

Rusch, F. R., & Kazdin, A. E. (1981). Toward methodology of withdrawal designs for the assessment of response maintenance. *Journal of Applied Behavior Analysis, 14,* 131–140.

Schilling, D. L., & Schwartz, I. S. (2004). Alternative seating for young children with autism spectrum disorder: Effects on classroom behavior. *Journal of Autism and Developmental Disorders, 34,* 423–432.

Sidman, M. (1960). *Tactics of scientific research—Evaluating experimental data in psychology.* New York: Basic Books.

Spriggs, A. D., Gast, D. L, & Ayres, K. M. (2007). Using picture activity schedule books to increase on-schedule and on-task behaviors. *Education and Training in Developmental Disabilities, 42,* 209–223.

Tawney, J. W., & Gast, D. L. (1984). *Single subject research in special education.* Columbus, OH: Charles E. Merrill.

Tincani, M., Crozier, S., & Alazetta, L. (2006). The picture exchange communication system: Effects on manding and speech development for school-aged children with autism. *Education and Training in Developmental Disabilities, 41,* 177–184.

Watson, P. J., & Workman, E. A. (1981). The non-concurrent multiple baseline across individuals design: An extension of the traditional multiple baseline design. *Journal of Behavior Therapy and Experimental Psychiatry, 12,* 257–259.

Weisberg, P., & Waldrop, P. B. (1971). Fixed-interval work habits of congress. *Journal of Applied Behavior Analysis, 5,* 93–97.

11

Multiple Baseline and Multiple Probe Designs

David L. Gast and Jennifer Ledford

Clinicians and educators have been subjected to increasing pressure from consumers, professional organizations, legislatures, and courts to account for their clinical and teaching practices. They have been asked to provide objective, data-based responses to such social-educational questions as: "Are educational and therapy objectives appropriate?"; "Is each child progressing through the curriculum at an optimum rate?"; "When should intervention programs be maintained, modified, or replaced?"; and "Can a student's progress be attributed to identifiable instructional strategies?" Within the framework of applied behavior analysis, there is a class of single subject research designs well-suited for evaluating and demonstrating accountability in clinical and educational settings, namely, multiple baseline and multiple probe designs. Both these designs are flexible (i.e., the learner's behavior controls the pace and choice of programming procedures); are rigorous in their evaluation of threats to internal validity; and are practical for teachers and clinicians who want their research efforts to be wholly compatible with their instructional or therapy activities. For these reasons, and because the public has mandated individualized education and habilitation plans, the demand for and appreciation of single subject experimental designs continues to escalate.

This chapter describes multiple baseline and multiple probe designs and their use by applied researchers investigating the effectiveness of a wide range of interventions within educational and clinical settings. How baseline logic applies to this class of designs, and how threats to internal validity are evaluated, are discussed. We then present general considerations and guidelines for their use, discussing advantages and limitations of both designs. Multiple baseline and multiple probe designs have been used extensively by applied researchers because of their compatibility with educational and clinical practice, and therefore, warrant your serious consideration.

Baseline Logic and Multiple Baseline and Multiple Probe Designs

Baer, Wolf, and Risley (1968) introduced multiple baseline designs to behavioral researchers in their seminal article describing applied behavior analysis. It was 10 years later that Horner and Baer (1978) described a variation of the multiple baseline design that they termed "multiple probe technique." Both designs are based on the same baseline logic for evaluating threats to internal validity and demonstrating experimental control. Procedurally, multiple baseline and multiple probe designs differ in one way, the frequency with which *pre-intervention* data are collected. Where multiple baseline designs require a plan for the continuous measurement of all target behaviors, conditions, or study participants prior to the introduction of the independent variable, the plan for multiple probe designs is to collect data intermittently prior to the introduction of the intervention. As will be discussed, this difference, though small, influences both the experimental rigor and practicality of the two designs. Both designs are, however, well-suited to the practical requirements of applied research in that they (a) lend themselves to program efficacy measures; (b) have no withdrawal of intervention require-ments; and (c) are easy to conceptualize and implement, permitting practicing teachers and clinicians to conduct research in their school or clinical environment.

There are three principal variations or types of multiple baseline and multiple probe designs:

1. Across several different *behaviors* of a single individual or group;
2. Across several different stimulus *conditions* (settings, adults, arrangements, formats, etc.) in which the same behavior of a single individual or group is studied;
3. Across several *participants* (i.e., individuals or group of individuals) displaying the same behavior under the same stimulus conditions.

Because of the similarities of multiple baseline and multiple probe designs, we discuss them together before discussing specific guidelines, advantages, and limitations associated with each. We have chosen to describe general characteristics and considerations of both designs, and their variations (i.e., across behaviors, conditions, participants), using the term "tier." The specific variation of multiple baseline or multiple probe design may be substituted for "tier" in our discussion. For ease of understanding, we use the term baseline, rather than probe, to refer to the pre-intervention condition. In distinguishing these two designs it is important for you to understand that it is only the planned frequency with which data are collected prior to intro-duction of the independent variable that differentiates the two designs. The inclusion of "planned" in this distinction is to account for those infrequent occasions with a multiple baseline design when a participant may be absent due to health or other reasons.

Internal Validity

To demonstrate experimental control with multiple baseline and multiple probe designs, you first collect pre-intervention data simultaneously across three or more tiers (i.e., across behaviors, conditions, or participants). Ideally, when baseline data in all tiers show acceptable stability in level and trend direction, the independent variable is introduced to the first tier. However, if stability is achieved in only one tier you may introduce the independent variable to that tier while maintaining baseline conditions in other tiers. Upon introduction of the independent variable to the first tier there should be an immediate, and ideally abrupt, change in the dependent variable in a therapeutic direction in the first tier, while data in other tiers remain stable and unchanged. When criterion-level performance is attained in the first tier and stability is achieved in the second tier, the independent variable is introduced to the second tier, while maintaining baseline procedures in the third tier. Again the same immediate behavior change should be observed, while uninterrupted baseline data series remain unchanged. This process is repeated in the third tier, and so on, until the independent variable has been introduced to each tier. An immediate change in level, regardless of the magnitude of the change, as well as a change in a therapeutic trend direction, should be observed upon introduc-tion of the independent variable for each tier, not before. If the change in behavior is delayed, the demonstration of experimental control is less clear. Simply stated, to evaluate experimental control, remember that "where intervention is applied, change occurs; where it is not, change does not occur" (Horner & Baer, 1978, p. 189). Figures 11.1a and 11.1b provide graphic prototypes of a multiple baseline design and a multiple probe design, respectively, in which data are collected concurrently across three tiers and a change in the dependent variable occurs immediately upon introduction of the independent variable, not before. Multiple baseline and multiple probe designs can be conceptualized as a series of "stacked" A-B designs in which

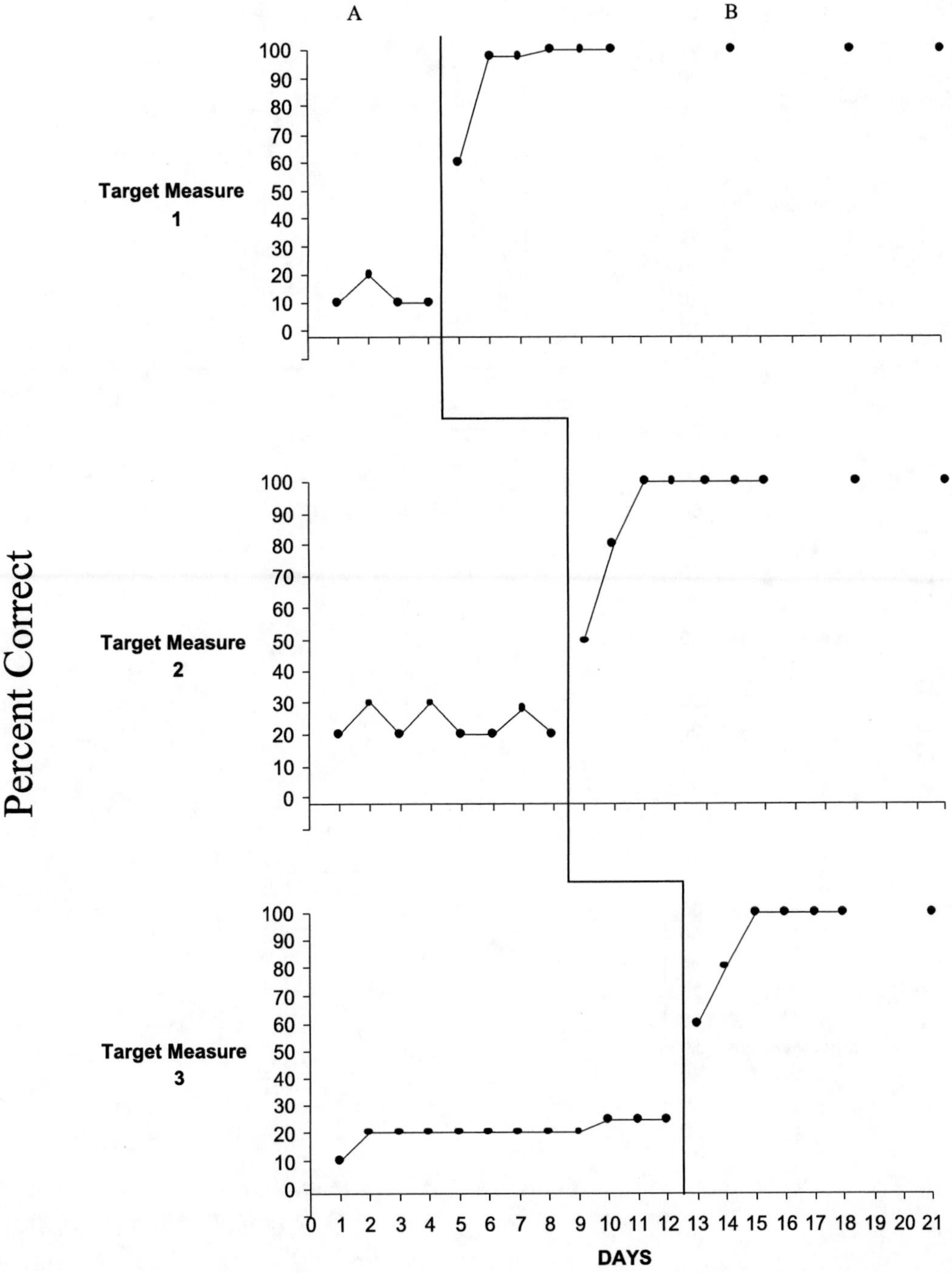

Figure 11.1a Hypothetical data within a multiple baseline design.

the length of the baseline or probe condition (A) is systematically lengthened across tiers of the design prior to introduction of the intervention condition (B).

Specifically, threats to internal validity due to history, maturation, and testing are evaluated by staggering the introduction of the independent variable across tiers. Other threats to internal validity also need to be evaluated, particularly instrumentation (i.e., interobserver

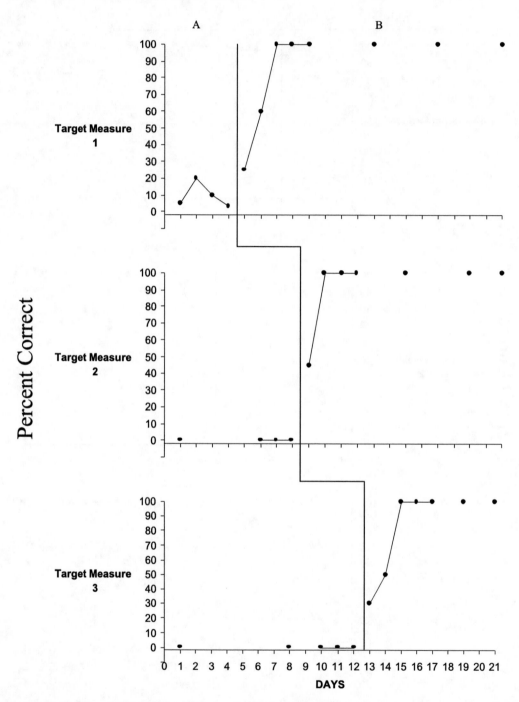

Figure 11.1b Hypothetical data within a multiple probe design.

agreement) and procedural fidelity. Without high-reliability percentages you cannot have confidence in findings regardless of the graphic representation of data.

Considerations

To demonstrate experimental control using multiple baseline and multiple probe designs you must make two predictions prior to initiating your research. First, you must identify behaviors (conditions or participants) that are *functionally independent*, i.e., introduction of the independent variable will not bring about a change in other tiers of the design. Second, behaviors (conditions or participants) should be *functionally similar*, i.e., when the independent variable is introduced to a tier the effect of the independent variable will be replicated across tiers. Should either of these predictions be incorrect, experimental control is lost or, at least, confounded. In the first case, should *behavioral covariation* occur within tiers not yet exposed to the independent variable, you are left with an ambiguous demonstration of effect, "in which it is evident that change has occurred but not that it was due to the intervention" (Birnbrauer, Peterson, & Solnick, 1974, p. 198). Two questions are left unanswered: (1) Was the intervention effective in the first tier, with effects generalizing to the unexposed tiers?; or (2) Was the intervention ineffective, with covarying effects due instead to history, maturation, or testing confounding? In the second case, should one or several of the tiers remain unchanged when the independent variable is directly applied, you again are left with an unconvincing demonstration of experimental control, with the intervention appearing to work in one or a few instances, but not in others, i.e., *inconsistent intervention effects*. Figures 11.2a and 11.2b illustrate these threats to experimental control: (a) behavioral covariance across unexposed tiers and (b) inconsistent effects of the independent variable. Strategies to improve predictions and, thus, to minimize these risks are addressed as each design is described later in the chapter.

General Guidelines

When using multiple baseline and multiple probe designs you should adhere to the following guidelines:

1. Identify three or more tiers (behaviors, conditions, or participants) that are functionally independent (to avoid covariation) but functionally similar (to avoid inconsistent effects).
2. Prior to the start of the study pinpoint a criterion level for staggering the introduction of the independent variable to the next tier in the design.
3. Concurrently and repeatedly monitor all tiers from the start of the study until the independent variable is introduced.
   a. multiple baseline designs—planned continuous measurement;
   b. multiple probe designs—planned intermittent measurement.
4. Introduce the independent variable to one tier when acceptable level stability and a zero celerating or contratherapeutic trend direction are observed.
5. Collect data continuously during the intervention (B) condition.
6. Introduce the independent variable to subsequent tiers only when data are stable, as described in Step 4, and the predetermined criterion level for staggering the introduction of the independent variable has been met.
7. Collect reliability data on the dependent and independent variables in each condition.

Prior to initiating a study, identify a behavior criterion level that you will use to decide when to introduce the independent variable to the next tier. This criterion level will also be used to compare the magnitude of behavior change between adjacent experimental conditions, for example, A-B. Ideally, introduce the intervention only when *all* baseline data series show acceptable stability in level and trend but, if variability is observed in a data series, choose a different data series to introduce the independent variable even if this requires reordering your previously decided upon schedule. A believable demonstration of a functional relation

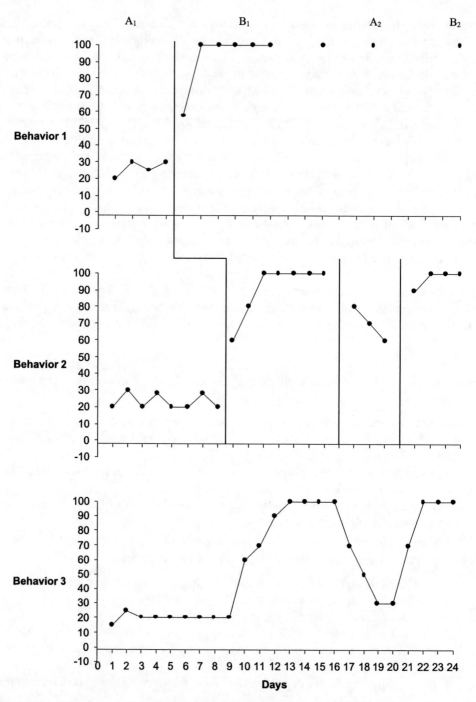

Figure 11.2a Hypothetical data for a multiple baseline design across behaviors demonstrating behavioral covariation of Behavior 3, after the intervention is sequentially applied to Behaviors 1 and 2, followed by withdrawal and reintroduction of B (source: Mayfield & Vollmer, 2007. Copyright by Society for the Experimental Analysis of Behavior, Inc. Reproduced by permission).

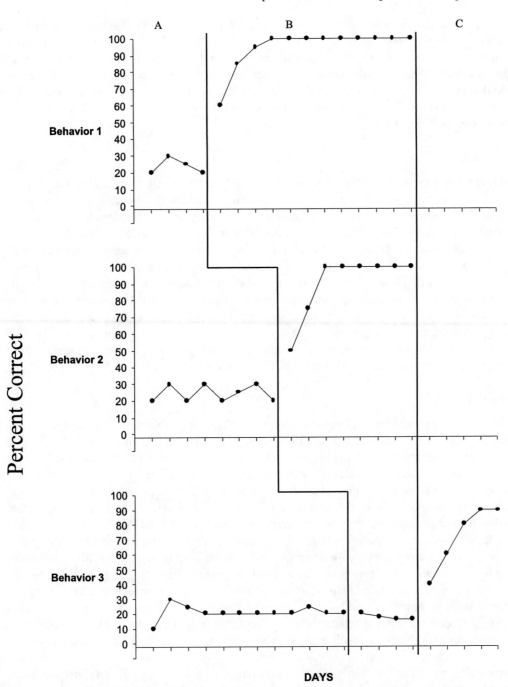

Figure 11.2b Hypothetical data for a multiple baseline design across behaviors demonstrating a failure of intervention effects for Behavior 3, requiring the addition of a new intervention Condition C for that series.

between intervention and behavior change occurs when the effect is replicated across A-B series (Baer et al., 1968). Determination of the appropriate number of replications required for believability is complicated by such factors as trend and level stability of the data series and the rate and magnitude of change upon each sequential introduction of the intervention (Kratochwill, 1978). However, provided there are reliable replications of effect, three or four tiers should be satisfactory (Barlow & Hersen, 1984; Kazdin & Kopel, 1975; Tawney & Gast, 1984; Wolf & Risley, 1971).

Advantages

Multiple baseline and multiple probe designs are better suited to many of the practical demands of applied settings than are A-B-A-B designs. Perhaps the most significant advantage is that it is not necessary to withdraw an effective intervention to demonstrate experimental control. This feature is advantageous because: (a) many behaviors are functionally irreversible, including most academic skills; (b) A-B-A-B withdrawal and reversal designs may be ethically inappropriate, especially regarding behaviors that are injurious to participants or others, or for behaviors that demonstrate therapeutic gains that might not be reinstated easily after withdrawing a condition; and, (c) many parents, teachers, and clinicians find any withdrawal of an effective intervention objectionable. Additionally, multiple baseline and multiple probe designs require the concurrent measurement (i.e., data collection during the same time period) of several target behaviors, conditions, or individuals, thus providing a closer approximation to the goals of most teachers and therapists in the natural environment.

Limitations

Multiple baseline and multiple probe designs also can be problematic. As previously mentioned, multiple baseline and multiple probe designs require the identification and concurrent measurement of several (usually three or four) tiers. This requirement can be limiting because it is sometimes difficult to identify the required number of tiers and because concurrent monitoring of several tiers may prove time consuming, expensive, or otherwise impractical (Horner & Baer, 1978; Scott & Goetz, 1980). Extended baseline or probe conditions, particularly with the multiple baseline design across participants, may result in aversive experiences for learners due to boredom and fatigue, depending how you structure the pre-intervention condition. For example, a baseline or probe condition without reinforcement for some participants may result in an unrepresentative level of performance, thus invalidating findings. Prolonged baseline conditions also may be considered ethically questionable when an effective intervention is postponed with behaviors that require immediate attention (e.g., physical aggression directed toward self or others). The same ethical argument can be made when delaying the introduction of an intervention to participants in the lower tiers of the design.

In the sections that follow we discuss each multiple baseline and multiple probe design separately, describing the similarities and differences of this class of design. First we discuss multiple baseline and multiple probe designs across behaviors, then across conditions, and finally across participants. Though these designs are based on the same baseline logic, each has different advantages and disadvantages that you should consider prior to designing your study or evaluating the study of another researcher.

Multiple Baseline and Multiple Probe Designs Across Behaviors

Internal Validity

When using a multiple baseline or multiple probe design across behaviors, identify a minimum of three similar yet functionally independent behaviors emitted by one individual. Each target behavior is measured concurrently and continuously (multiple baseline) or intermittently (multiple probe) under the same environmental conditions until a stable pre-intervention trend and level are established. Once pre-intervention levels and trends are acceptable, introduce the independent variable to one behavior, while monitoring other behaviors under the pre-intervention condition. It is particularly important that the data path of the behavior you plan to introduce the intervention to shows a stable level and a zero-celerating or a contratherapeutic trend immediately prior to introduction of the intervention. Upon introduction of the independent variable you should see an immediate change in the behavior, not before. After criterion-level responding is attained with the first behavior, the intervention is applied to the second behavior. Following criterion-level responding with the second behavior, the intervention is applied to the third, and so on. This systematic and sequential application of the independent variable across behaviors continues until all target behaviors have been exposed to the same intervention. Target behaviors can range from academic behaviors (e.g., number of words read correctly per minute) to social behaviors (e.g., number of object-throwing episodes per 30-min observation period). The multiple baseline design across behaviors can effectively evaluate an intervention intended to either accelerate the frequency of a nonreversible (e.g., academic, "functional life skill") behavior or decelerate the frequency of a reversible (e.g., aberrant) behavior. The multiple probe design across behaviors, however, to date has been restricted to studying nonreversible behaviors. Table 11.1 and Table 11.2 summarize several applied research studies in which a multiple baseline or multiple probe design across behaviors, respectively, were used to evaluate experimental control.

General Guidelines

When using a multiple baseline or multiple probe design across behaviors:

1. Target a minimum of three behaviors that are functionally independent, yet similar, for each participant.
2. Identify a performance criterion-level for introducing the intervention to the next behavior prior to initiating the study.
3. Introduce the intervention when the data path of at least one behavior (ideally all behaviors) shows acceptable stability in level and trend while maintaining other behaviors in the pre-intervention condition.
4. Introduce the intervention to a new behavior only after criterion-level responding is demonstrated with the preceding behavior.

As previously stated, you must make two predictions prior to initiating a study. First, you must be convinced that target behaviors are functionally independent of one another (i.e., behaviors are not members of the same response class), so that baseline data will remain stable until the intervention is introduced to each. Second, based on your review of the literature, you must be confident that target behaviors are sufficiently similar for each to respond, in turn, to the same intervention. There are many academic behaviors that are reasonably certain to be independent of one another, in that they are unlikely to be acquired without direct instruction

Table 11.1 Studies That Exemplify a Multiple Baseline Across Behaviors Design

Reference	Participants	Setting/arrangement	Independent variable	Dependent variable
Higgins, J. W., Williams, R. L. & McLaughlin, T. F. (2001). The effects of a token economy employing instructional consequences for a third-grade student with learning disabilities: A data-based case study. *Education & Treatment of Children, 24,* 99–106.	Number: 1 Sex: male Age range: elementary Disability diagnosis: LD	Setting: general education classroom. Arrangement: Large group	Token reinforcement	Inapropriate behaviors (out of seat, talking out, poor posture)
Johnson, J. W., Mc Donnell, J., Hohwarth, V. N., & Hinder, K. (2004). The efficacy of embedded instruction for students with developmental disabilities enrolled in general education classes. *Journal of Positive Behavior Interventions, 6,* 214–227.	Number: 3 Sex: 1 male, 2 females Age range: 7–9 years Disabilities/diagnosis: moderate MR (2), autism (1) IQ range: 53–59 (none available for student with autism)	Setting: regular education classroom Arrangement: individual (embedded during transitions, breaks)	Embedded instruction used to teach different targets based on individual students educational needs	Percentage correct and rate of acquisition of targeted information behaviors: (S1) Information from general curriculum, (S2) Sight words related to general curriculum, (S3) One word requests
McDonnell, J., Johnson, J. W., Polychronis, S. & Risen, T. (2002). Effects of embedded instruction on students with moderate disabilities enrolled in general education classes. *Education and Training in Mental Retardation and Developmental Disabilities, 37,* 363–377.	Number: 4 Sex: male Age range: 13–15 years Disability/diagnosis: moderate to severe MR IQ range: 46–57	Setting: regular education classroom Arrangement: individual (embedded during transitions, breaks)	Embedded instruction used to teach sight words or word definitions related to general education curriculum	Percent of correct responses and trials to criterion
Marckel, J. M., Neef, N. A., & Ferreri, S.J. (2006). A preliminary analysis of teaching improvisation with the picture exchange communication system to children with autism. *Journal of Applied Behavior Analysis, 39,* 109–115.	Number: 2 Sex: male Age range: 4–5 years Disability/diagnosis: autism	Setting: clinical Arrangement: individual	Individual instruction using prompt fading for 3 classes or stimuli (functions, colors, and shapes) using descriptors of item when item symbol was unavailable	Number of independent requests with improvisation (e.g. asks for crayon using circle symbol)

| Westerland, D., Granucci, E. A., Gamache, P., & Clark, H. B. (2006). Effects of mentor(s) on work-related performance of adolescents with behavioral and/or learning disabilities. *Journal of Positive Behavior Interventions, 8*, 244–251. | Number: 4
Sex: female
Age range: 16–18
Disability/diagnosis: emotional and/or learning disabilities | Setting: vocational training site
Arrangement: individual | Mentor(s) training | Percentage of steps related to hair styling routine that were completed correctly |
| Williams, G., Perez-Gonzalez L. A., & Vogt, K. (2003). The role of specific consequences in the maintenance of three types of questions. *Journal of Applied Behavior Analysis, 36*, 285–296. | Number: 3
Sex: M
Age-range: 2–9
Disability/diagnosis: autism | Setting: self-contained behavioral program (2), home (1)
Arrangement: small group | Most to Least prompting | Number of questions asked |

Table 11.2 Studies That Exemplify a Multiple Probe Across Behaviors Design

Reference	Participants	Setting/arrangement	Independent variable	Dependent variable
Alberto, P. A., Fredrik, L. Hughes, M. McIntosh, L., & Cihak, D. (2007). Components of visual literacy: Teaching logos. *Focus on Autism and Other Developmental Disabilities, 22* 234–243.	Number: 6 Sex: 3 males, 3 females Age range: 9–14 years Disability diagnosis: moderate to severe MR IQ Range: 38–52	Setting: self contained classroom Arrangement: individual	Individual CTD instruction for identifying logos of community locations and naming items that could be purchase at the named location	Percentage correct for naming logos and items to be purchased
Daugherty, S. Orkham Brown, S., & Hemmeter, M. L. (2001). The effects of embedded skill instruction on the acquisition of target and non-target skills in preschoolers with developmental delays. *Topics in Early Childhood Special Education, 21,* 213–221.	Number: 3 Sex: 1 male, 2 females Age range: 4–5 years Disability: diagnosis: speech and language delays	Setting: inclusive preschool classroom Arrangement: individual (embedded in large group activity)	Individual CTD instruction for counting embedded in ongoing classroom activities	Percentage of correct responses during probe and training sessions
Hughes, T. A., & Fredrick, L. D. (2006). Teaching vocabulary with students with learning disabilities using peer tutoring and constant time delay. *Journal of Behavioral Education, 15,* 1–23.	Number: 3 Sex: 2 males, 1 female Age range: 11–12 years Disability diagnosis: LD	Setting: general education classroom Arrangement Industrial (instruction provided by peer)	CTD instruction provided by peers (dyads: 1 student with LD + 1 student without a disability) for word definitions	Percentage of correct responses during probe and training sessions
Mechling L., Gast, D. L., & Krupa, D. (2007). Impact of SMART Board technology: An investigation of sight word reading and observational learning. *Journal of Autism and Developmental Disorders, 37,* 18–27.	Number: 3 Sex: 2 males, 1 female Age range: 19–20 Disability diagnosis: moderate MR IQ range: 52–54	Setting: transition program for students with disabilities Arrangement: small group	CTD instruction using SMART Board for sight words and non-identity matching	Percentage of correct responses during probe and training sessions
Mechling, L., & Otega-Hundon, F. (2007). Computer-based video instruction to teach young adults with moderate intellectual disabilities to perform multiple-step, job tasks in a generalized setting. *Education and Training in Developmental Disabilities, 42,* 24–37.	Number: 3 Sex: 2 males, 1 female Age range: 20–21 Disability diagnosis: moderate MR IQ range: 40–54	Setting: small office space (instruction), Job site locations throughout the building (generalisation) Arrangement: individual	Computer based video instruction for job tasks	Percentage of correct responses during probe and training sessions

Werts, M. G., Caldwell, N. K. & Wolery, M. (2003). Instructive feedback: Effects of a presentation variable. *The Journal of Special Education, 37,* 124–133.	Number: 4 Sex: male Age: 11 Disability diagnosis: LD (3), Mild MR (1)	Setting: self-contained classroom Arrangement: small group	CTD instruction for sight words (incidental information: images of state outlines)	Percentage of correct responses during probe and training sessions
Wolery, M., Anthony, L., Caldwell, N. K. Snyder, E. D., & Morgarte, J. D. (2002). Embedding and distributing constant time delay in circle time and transitions. *Topics in Early Childhood Education, 22,* 14–25.	Number: 3 Sex: male Age range: 5–7 Disability diagnosis: speech delay (1). Behavior problems (1). ADHD (1)	Setting circle time at integrated summer camp Arrangement: individual (embedded in large group activity)	CTD instruction for sight words (2 participants) and multiplication facts (1 participant)	Percentage of correct responses during probe and training sessions

(e.g., sets of spelling words or sets of arithmetic problems across various math operations). With social behaviors, however, the prediction of independence becomes more problematic. For example, beyond certain thresholds, some behaviors may occasion others, as when a person is taught an appropriate greeting behavior (e.g., saying hello to a familiar adult) that, in turn, may increase the frequency of making eye contact with the individual and responding to a question asked by the adult. In such a case a multiple baseline or probe design across three target social behaviors during a social exchange may result in response generalization, thus precluding a demonstration of experimental control due to behavioral covariation across the three target behaviors. When there is concern about behavioral covariation, consider identifying more than the minimum number of three behaviors, or combining research designs, for example, multiple baseline design across behaviors with a multiple probe design across participants (Cronin & Cuvo, 1979; combination designs are discussed in Chapter 13). Similarly, the deceleration of some behaviors may result in an acceleration of other inappropriate behaviors (e.g., "symptom substitution"), if the net result, otherwise, would be a lower overall frequency of reinforcement (Bandura, 1969). For example, a strategy intended to sequentially suppress spitting, hitting, and object throwing might become progressively less effective for each subsequent behavior, unless the intervention provides alternative avenues for the learner to recruit reinforcement (i.e., differential reinforcement for appropriate behaviors). It is important to remember that with behaviors that are topographically similar, as is the case with some self-injurious behaviors (e.g., slapping face, punching head, poking eye), introduction of an effective intervention to one behavior may result in response generalization, and although clinically ideal, preclude a demonstration of experimental control. If, however, behaviors are reversible you may attempt to salvage experimental control by briefly withdrawing the intervention, as in an A-B-A-B design, and monitoring the effect the withdrawal on the other behaviors. Figure 11.2a exemplifies this strategy. Finally, if you select behaviors that are so topographically or operationally different (e.g., spelling words, adding numbers, reciting a poem) you risk not demonstrating experimental control due to the differences between stimuli or responses associated with each task. Again, if inconsistent intervention effects are of concern a priori, add more behaviors to the design. It is recommended that you stay within the same stimulus or response category (e.g., spelling words across four different sets, emitting three topographically different greeting responses) to evaluate the effectiveness of the independent variable.

Advantages

Multiple baseline and multiple probe designs across behaviors offer several advantages. First, both designs permit an evaluation and demonstration of intra-subject direct replication, thus increasing the internal validity of findings. Second, a return to baseline condition is not required to evaluate experimental control. Third, because withdrawal or reversal of the intervention condition is not required, both designs obviate many of the practical and ethical problems associated with A-B-A-B designs. Fourth, these designs provide a practical means for evaluating programs designed to teach academic and functional skills that are nonreversible once acquired (e.g., spelling, math fact recitation, task assembly) and social behaviors that are difficult to establish and would be inappropriate to reverse (e.g., greeting responses, question asking, walking appropriately). Fifth, because educators and clinicians are interested in behavior maintenance, multiple baseline and multiple probe designs across behaviors provide a paradigm for repeatedly monitoring progress over time.

Challenges and Limitations

Multiple baseline and multiple probe designs across behaviors require adherence to specific guidelines that may present problems for you under some circumstances. First, for each participant a minimum of three behaviors (or sets of behaviors, e.g., reading sight words, naming state capitals, etc.) must be identified, each independent of one another and yet, each responsive to the same independent variable. Second, all behaviors must be monitored repeatedly and concurrently, which may prove time consuming, distracting, cumbersome, or otherwise impractical. This is more likely to be true for multiple baseline designs. Third, a prolonged baseline condition without reinforcement may induce extinction effects in which participants' attempts to respond cease all together. Fourth, an extended pre-intervention condition may raise questions by significant others about the ethics of postponing intervention on behaviors that may require immediate attention.

Applied Example: Multiple Baseline Design Across Behaviors

Mayfield, K H., & Vollmer, T. R. (2007). Teaching math skills to at-risk students using home-based peer tutoring. *Journal of Applied Behavior Analysis, 40,* 223–237.

Mayfield and Vollmer (2007) studied the effects of peer tutoring on math achievement for four females with a history of abuse or neglect (at-risk). Each participant was placed in a dyad with a second participant who resided in the same home. Within each dyad, each participant served as both a tutor and tutee (e.g., Participant 1 tutored Participant 2, and Participant 2 tutored Participant 1). Participants ranged in age from 9 to 16 years. All tutoring took place at participants' current residences (relative's home or group home). The research question was: Will at-risk students with a history of maltreatment improve their accuracy on math skills through home-based peer tutoring?

The dependent variable was the percentage correct on written math tests. Data were collected using an event-recording procedure by scoring each answer on tests as correct or incorrect. Reliability data were collected during 32% of sessions conducted during the intervention condition using the point-by-point method. Mean interobserver agreement was 99% (range: 90–100%).

There were three experimental conditions: baseline, intervention, and maintenance. During baseline condition, each participant completed written math tests on her target skills. Participants earned one penny for each correct answer, but was not given feedback on how she did on any test item.

The intervention condition consisted of two components: tutor training and peer tutoring. During tutor training, the experimenter spent 3 min explaining the target math skill to the peer tutor. During this time the experimenter modeled solutions and provided corrective feedback and praise. Tutor training was repeated for each skill until the tutor completed three consecutive tests with 100% accuracy. After each training session, peer tutoring was implemented. During peer tutoring, the tutor was given 3 min to teach the tutee what she had been taught by the experimenter (with the exception of the long division skill sessions, which were 10 min due to the complexity of the skill and time needed to work a single problem). Both the tutor and tutee received a penny for each problem correctly solved by the tutee. Mastery criterion for the tutee was 100% accuracy on three consecutive tests for each of three targeted skills. Reaching mastery for the tutor and tutee were independent events (i.e., if the tutor reached mastery, she stopped receiving tutor training, but continued implementing peer tutoring). The intervention was modified for three participants by increasing reinforcer magnitude, while adult tutoring, prerequisite skill practice, and an error-correction procedure were implemented for one participant.

During the maintenance condition, participants were given tests for all skills targeted during intervention (skills learned as a tutor and as a tutee). Reinforcement procedures remained the same as in baseline and intervention conditions. The time interval between intervention and maintenance ranged from 3 to 5 months.

Figure 11.3 displays percentage of correct responses on written tests during baseline, intervention, and maintenance conditions evaluated within the context of a multiple baseline design across behaviors (math skills). Prior to the intervention condition, the tutor and tutee maintained low percentages of correct responses (0–10%) with the exception of the skill of solving proportions. For this skill, the tutee had highly variable data that ranged from 0% to 60% correct. Following intervention, both the tutee and tutor reached mastery on the first skill (adding signed numbers). For the other three skills, performance improved following intervention, but both the tutor and tutee failed to meet criterion prior to the end of the peer-tutoring condition. Subsequently, the magnitude of the reinforcer was increased which resulted in criterion-level performances. Similar results were obtained with the three tutor–tutee pairs, although additional changes to the intervention were required for at least one skill set for each participant. After reaching criterion all tutees maintained high percentages of correct responding after 3–5 months with no further instruction.

The current investigation demonstrates that peer tutoring can be effective for teaching math skills to at-risk students, and that mastered skills can be maintained over several months. However, some skills for all students required minor changes to the original intervention. It is important to note that no formal instruction was given to tutors on how they were to teach a tutee. Because there was no prescribed teaching protocol, no procedural-reliability checks were feasible. These researchers concluded that "peer tutoring may be effective at producing initial skill improvements in circumstances when expert help is unavailable . . . but may need to be followed by other academic interventions" (p. 235).

Multiple Baseline Design Across Behaviors: Practical Considerations

Multiple baseline designs have the research benefit of continuous measurement prior to and during intervention, thereby allowing day-to-day data analyses and decisions. This is particularly important when dealing with dangerously aggressive behavior toward self (SIB) or others. Another occasion when we recommend the use of a multiple baseline design rather than a multiple probe design across behaviors is when target behaviors are being observed and measured under *free-operant conditions* (White, 1971), i.e., behaviors are naturally occurring and not dependent on scheduled presentations of a discriminative stimulus as with teacher-paced instruction. Under free-operant conditions, such as monitoring a child's verbal behavior ("positive verbal initiations," "negative verbal initiations," "positive verbal responses," "negative verbal responses") during snack time or during recess in the playground, all target behaviors could be monitored concurrently using a behavior coding system. There would be no practical reason not to collect continuous data on each behavior since they could all occur during the same observation period. From an experimental perspective the more data collected the better, thus when there are *no* major practical inconveniences we recommend that you choose a multiple baseline design over a multiple probe design.

There are practical limitations when using a multiple baseline design across behaviors as previously listed. Some of these limitations can be avoided, particularly during studies

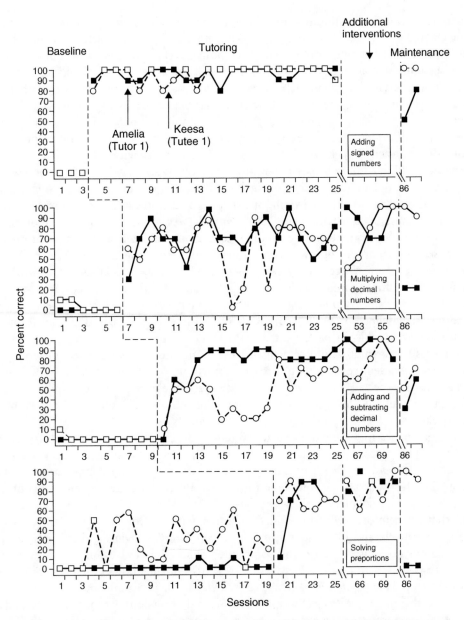

Figure 1. Pair 1's accuracy on the math skills across baseline, tutoring, additional interventions, and maintenance. The five sessions prior to the tutee achieving the mastery criterion are displayed in the additional interventions phase. The filled squares represent the tutor's performance, and the open circles represent the tutee's performance.

Figure 11.3 Graphic display of multiple baseline design across behaviors (source: Mayfield & Vollmer, 2007. Copyright by Society for the Experimental Analysis of Behavior, Inc. Reproduced by permission).

that have an academic or functional skills focus by using a multiple probe design across behaviors. Practical limitations include, first, identifying three or more behaviors (or sets of behaviors) that are similar, yet functionally independent. This requires that you be familiar with the research literature as to stimuli and responses that have resulted in stimulus or response generalization without direct instruction. For example, when teaching object naming and two or more stimuli share a large number of common features (e.g., desk chair, folding chair, dining room chair) *stimulus generalization* is likely, i.e., teaching the name of one results in the child labeling the others "chair" without direct instruction. It would be preferable to choose stimuli that are more different but represent the same class of stimuli (e.g., furniture is the stimulus class, and chairs, tables, beds, couches are the categories within the class). Similarly, if you are teaching response-chain skills that share several common task-analysis step topographies (e.g., packing a grocery bag, packing a suitcase, organizing a dresser drawer) *response generalization* is likely, i.e., teaching one skill results in an increase in other skills without direct instruction. In both cases these stimuli or behaviors should *not* be used in separate tiers within a multiple baseline or multiple probe design. A second limitation with the multiple baseline design across behaviors is that data collection can be *time consuming*, and if you have to collect data while delivering instruction or therapy, it is likely to prove cumbersome. Under these circumstances familiarity with data-collection options is important. For example, observations can be video or audio recorded and analyzed later using your preferred direct observational recording procedure; time-sample recording may be used rather than event recording or interval recording; permanent products may be available, all of which may make use of a multiple baseline design more practical. Third, prolonged baseline conditions can result in *testing threats to internal validity*, either a facilitative or inhibitive effect is possible depending on baseline (or probe) condition procedures. Repeated testing may result in a *facilitative effect* in which a participant's performance improves over time due to response consequences (differential reinforcement of correct and incorrect responses), observation of others, or independent research (e.g., looking something up on the Internet) now knowing what response is expected. An *inhibitive effect* may occur due to response consequences (lack of reinforcement), fatigue (long sessions in number of minutes or number of trials), or task difficulty (lack of understanding of response requirements).

Several strategies may be employed to overcome these potential outcomes of prolonged baseline or probe sessions. First, you can positively reinforce desired behaviors during pre-intervention sessions. You may choose to (a) *contingently reinforce target behaviors* when performed correctly, assuming you are not interested in studying the influence of contingent reinforcement alone (Wolery, Cybriwsky, Gast, & Boyle-Gast, 1991); (b) *intersperse known stimuli* that you reinforce when responded to correctly (Gast, Doyle, Wolery, Ault, & Baklarz, 1991); (c) positively and intermittently *reinforce non-target behaviors* emitted between trials during discrete sessions (VR-3) or on some interval schedule (VI 3 min) or between steps during a response-chain task (Wall & Gast, 1999); (d) inform study participants prior to the start of a session that a *reinforcer menu will be presented immediately after the session* from which they will be able to choose one activity or item. Second, if sessions are long, as indicated by a decrease in response attempts over trial presentations and time, or an increase in aberrant behavior, *shorten the session*. This can be done by dividing sessions into two shorter daily data-collection periods, or by scheduling a "break" midway through the session. Finally, the ethical issue of prolonging the introduction of an intervention to some behaviors can be problematic. Presumably, your project is an experimental investigation and the independent variable is not considered "best practice" with your participants, or with your target behaviors. That is, you are attempting a systematic replication by assessing the generality of the intervention for which there are limited data. In such cases it is prudent to start with one behavior. When using a multiple baseline design across behaviors we advise developing a list of behaviors in the order in which significant others, particularly parents or guardians, would like to see the intervention introduced. We also suggest, if practical, introducing the intervention to the next behavior after a set number of days (e.g., 5) rather than waiting for the preceding tier to reach criterion. This would not typically be recommended but when ethical issues arise you may have limited choices. We normally would recommend waiting until the preceding behavior reaches criterion before introducing the independent variable to the next behavior.

If there are practical concerns regarding the use of a multiple baseline design across behaviors we recommend that you consider a multiple probe design across behaviors. In many settings and situations when you are studying nonreversible behaviors it may be more "user friendly" and equally effective in evaluating experimental control as the multiple baseline design. There are, however, characteristics of multiple probe designs that warrant your attention since pre-intervention data are collected less frequently.

Multiple Probe Design (Days)

Probe Terminology

Multiple probe designs, as a class of single subject research designs, have become increasingly popular with applied researchers because they do not require continuous measurement of all behaviors, conditions or participants *prior* to the introduction of the independent variable, as is the case with multiple baseline designs. Rather, data are collected intermittently during what is referred to as a *probe trial* (i.e., a trial that is operationally identical to a pre-intervention baseline trial) to connote the design type (e.g., multiple probe design rather than a multiple baseline design). A probe trial may occur once daily or several probe trials may be clustered and presented over a short period of time (e.g., 5 min–60 min) in what is referred to as a *probe session*. Several probe sessions may in turn be conducted over 3 or more consecutive days using pre-intervention procedures during what is referred to as a *probe condition*. Remember, as when using the term "baseline," it is recommended that the term "probe" be used as an adjective, not a noun, since it can connote many things related to the design (e.g., probe data, probe trial, probe session, probe day, probe condition, etc.).

Multiple Probe Design Variations

There are two primary variations of the multiple probe design: (a) one that collects probe data periodically across days, and over a minimum of 3 days immediately prior to introduction of the independent variable, which we refer to as a *multiple probe design (days)*, and (b) one that collects probe data across three or more consecutive days or sessions, which we refer to as a *multiple probe design (conditions)*. Figure 11.1b shows a graphic display of the multiple probe design (days) variation and Figure 11.4 presents a prototype of the multiple probe design (conditions) variation. Both variations of the multiple probe design require data to be collected on *all* tiers at the start of the study, ideally all on the first day, but certainly by the third day, regardless of the design type (i.e., across behaviors, conditions, participants). The guidelines for multiple probe designs are identical to those for multiple baseline designs except for the frequency with which pre-intervention data are collected.

The multiple probe design (days variation) was first described by Horner and Baer (1978), which they termed the "*multiple probe technique.*" Horner and Baer, and others (Cooper, 1981; Murphey & Bryan, 1980; Tawney & Gast, 1984), have recommended that intermittent probe data be collected as an alternative to "unnecessary" continuous baseline measures. In educational situations, for example, for students to acquire many skills direct systematic instruction and positive reinforcement will be required. Seldom will a student acquire a new skill through repeated practice alone. For example, it is highly unlikely that a student being taught

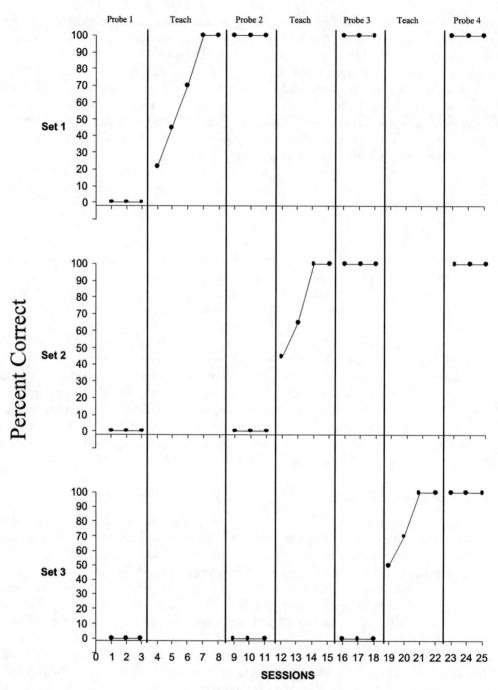

Figure 11.4 Hypothetical data using a multiple probe design (with probe conditions).

to manually sign the labels for a set of functional, though novel objects would acquire other target manual signs without some level of direct instruction. Similarly, it is improbable that a student who cannot add will be able to multiply, or that a student who has not mastered the operation of subtraction will be able to divide. With each of these students a prolonged and continuous baseline would be unnecessary. To quote Horner and Baer, "There is no need to document at the level of well-measured data that behavior does not occur when it cannot" (1978, p. 180). In each of these cases a multiple probe design can provide a demonstration of pre-intervention data stability and experimental control, and thus serve as a practical alternative to a multiple baseline design.

General Guidelines for the Multiple Probe Design (Days)

Guidelines that differentiate the multiple probe design (days) from the multiple baseline design and the multiple probe design (conditions) are presented:

1. Target a minimum of three tiers (behaviors, conditions or participants) that are functionally independent, yet similar.
2. Identify a performance criterion-level for introducing the intervention to the next tier prior to initiating the study.
3. Collect at least one day (or session) of probe data on each tier at the start of the study, ideally on the first day, but certainly within 3 days.
4. With the first tier collect a minimum of 3 consecutive days (or sessions) of probe data, or until stable, immediately prior to introducing the independent variable.
5. During intervention collect data continuously, monitoring performance to criterion.
6. During intervention periodically collect data on other tiers at least once every 5 days.
7. When the first tier reaches criterion, collect at least 1 day or session of probe data on all other tiers.
8. With the second tier collect a minimum of 3 consecutive days (or sessions) of probe data, or until stable, immediately prior to introducing the independent variable.
9. Repeat Steps 1–8 through a minimum of three tiers.

There is no hard-and-fast rule as to how frequently data should be collected after reaching criterion. Generally speaking, it is recommended to periodically collect data using probe procedures to assess whether performance is being maintained. The frequency with which data are collected after criterion has no bearing on whether a design is a multiple baseline or multiple probe design. With both designs you may choose to monitor performance continuously or intermittently, i.e., the type of design, multiple baseline or multiple probe, is based solely on the frequency of data collection *prior* to introducing the intervention.

Applied Example: Multiple Probe Design (Days) Across Behaviors
Flores, M. M., & Ganz, J. B. (2007). Effectiveness of direct instruction for teaching statement inference, use of facts, and analogies to students with developmental disabilities and reading delays. *Focus on Autism and Other Developmental Disabilities, 22,* 244–251.

The effectiveness of Direct Instruction (DI) in teaching three reading-comprehension skills to children with developmental disabilities was studied by Flores and Ganz (2007). The study took place at a private school, in a self-contained classroom for students with developmental disabilities, including intellectual disabilities (ID), autism, and ADHD. Participants in the study were fifth- and sixth-grade students (age range: 10–14). Two students were diagnosed with autism (IQ scores: 95, 87), one student was diagnosed with mild ID (IQ score: 57), and one student was diagnosed with ADHD (IQ score: 75). The two students with autism had average or low average decoding skills (SS: 98, 86), but significantly below-average comprehension skills (SS: 53, 67). The student with mild ID had decoding and comprehension skills that were significantly below average (SS decoding: 61; SS comprehension: 28), and the student with

ADHD had decoding and comprehension skills in the low average range (SS decoding: 89; SS comprehension: 84). The primary research question was: Will a DI program be effective in teaching students with developmental disabilities the following reading-comprehension skills: statement inference, use of facts, and analogies?

The dependent variable was the percentage of correct responses during probe, instruction, and maintenance conditions. Data were collected using an event-recording procedure in which children's responses were scored as correct if they emitted an appropriate oral response to a teacher-delivered question, or incorrect if a child inappropriately responded to a teacher question. Procedural-reliability data were collected once per week (20% of sessions) using a checklist of teacher behaviors from the DI program. The point-by-point method was used to calculate interobserver agreement, which ranged from 96 to 100% (mean = 98%). Procedural reliability was 100%.

The independent variable was the DI program that was used to teach three unrelated reading-comprehension skills (statement inference, using facts, analogies) within the context of a multiple probe design (days) across behaviors. During statement-inference sessions, students were taught to respond to questions related to a statement that was read by the teacher. "An example of a statement is, 'The noisy car drove past the school.' An example of a recall question is, 'What kind of car drove past the school?' " (p. 247). In DI sessions that focused on using facts, the instructor read two facts followed by a series of scenarios. Students were asked to name those facts that explained why the event happened. In analogy-instructional sessions, students were asked to complete simple analogies like, "A rake is to leaves as a shovel is to what?". During instructional sessions, the instructor followed DI program scripts. Sessions occurred for approximately 20 min per day and were conducted by one of two researchers who were not the classroom teachers. Scripts included modeling the skill, "leading" as students demonstrated the skill, and asking students to perform the behavior independently. The instructor followed the DI procedures of choral responding, individual responding, and error correction. Intermittent probe sessions were conducted in a 1:1 arrangement while DI sessions were conducted daily in a small group. Maintenance sessions were conducted 1 month after the final instructional session.

Figures 11.5 and 11.6 present the percentage of correct responses for two students across all sessions evaluated within the context of a multiple probe design (days) across behaviors. Prior to DI instruction all students had low percentages of correct responding on each comprehension skill. Visual analysis shows that levels of independent correct responding changed from a stable zero-celerating or decelerating trend during probe condition (which they label "Baseline") for each skill, to a stable accelerating therapeutic trend immediately upon introduction of the DI condition. Percentage of non-overlapping data (PND) was 100% between probe and DI conditions. This effect was replicated across the three comprehension skills for each of the four students, with each student reaching 100% performance. All students maintained criterion-level performance on the three reading-comprehension skills during their maintenance session 1 month later.

In summary, students with developmental disabilities learned three components of reading comprehension (statement inference, using facts, analogies) through Direct Instruction. The acquisition of comprehension skills was demonstrated within the context of a multiple probe design (days variation) across behaviors. Results demonstrated that DI was an effective teaching method for students with developmental disabilities to increase several skills related to reading comprehension. Further studies are needed to determine the efficacy of DI in relation to other reading interventions. Although intermittent probe sessions were conducted to measure specific target skills, further research is needed to determine whether specific skills acquired

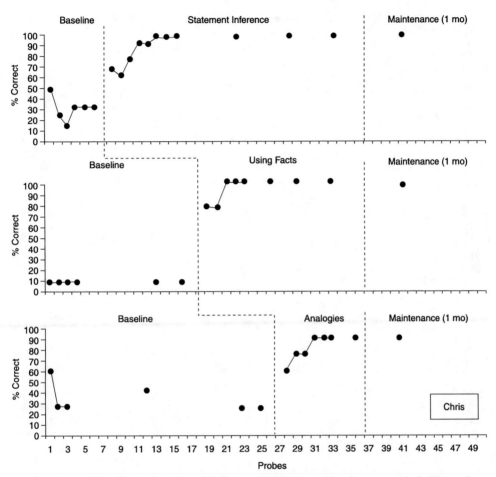

Figures 11.5 Graphic display of multiple probe design (days) across behaviors (source: Flores & Ganz, 2007. Copyright © 2007 Sage Publications. Reproduced by permisssion of Sage Publications).

during DI resulted in gains in other aspects of reading comprehension, such as "passage comprehension across content areas" (p. 251).

Multiple Probe Design (Conditions)

The multiple probe design (conditions) differs from the multiple probe design (days) in when pre-intervention data are collected. In the multiple probe design (conditions variation) a series of *consecutive probe sessions* (or observational days) are introduced at scheduled times over the course of the study. This particular multiple probe design variation is particularly well-suited for teacher- or therapist-paced instruction when a number of stimuli or behaviors are grouped together and taught across three or more tiers. As shown in Figure 11.4, an initial probe condition, labeled Probe 1, assesses all behaviors during the same sessions at the start of the study. During Probe 1 all stimuli/behaviors being tested are randomly intermixed and presented to a participant in a single probe session, after which the participant's responses are separated, according to the tier to which they were assigned, and the percentage correct for each tier for that session is graphed. A minimum of three consecutive sessions, over a

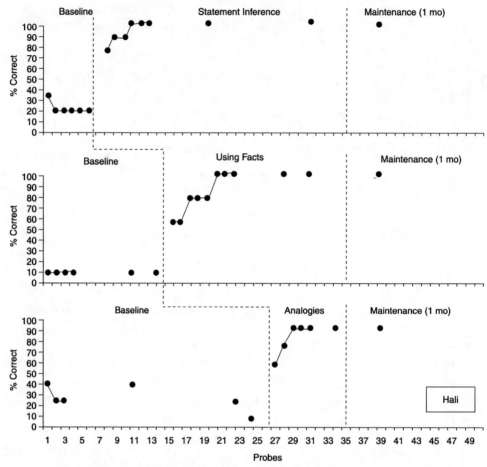

Figures 11.6 Graphic display of multiple probe design (days) across behaviors (source: Flores & Ganz, 2007. Copyright © 2007 Sage Publications. Reproduced by permission of Sage Publications).

minimum of two days, should be conducted, or until data are stable, before introducing the independent variable to the first tier. Once criterion is reached with the first tier, a second probe condition, procedurally identical to Probe 1, is conducted, labeled Probe 2. This alternating sequence of probe condition and intervention condition, staggered across tiers, continues until all tiers have been introduced to the independent variable. Typically there is a final probe condition after all tiers have reached criterion. On some occasions researchers have chosen to thin the schedule of reinforcement during the final probe to facilitate response maintenance.

General Guidelines for the Multiple Probe Design (Conditions)

General guidelines that differentiate the multiple probe design (condition variation) from the multiple baseline design and multiple probe design (day variation) are presented:

1. Target a minimum of three tiers (behaviors, conditions or participants) that are functionally independent, yet similar.
2. Identify a performance criterion-level for introducing the intervention to the next tier prior to initiating the study.

3. Collect probe data across three or more consecutive sessions, over at least 2 days, or until data are stable, on all tiers (i.e., behaviors, conditions, or participants) at the start of the study.
4. Introduce the independent variable to the first tier only. Collect data continuously during intervention until criterion is reached. (It is not necessary to collect data on the other tiers, although you may choose to do so intermittently.)
5. When the first tier reaches criterion, collect probe data across three or more consecutive sessions, over at least 2 days, or until data are stable, on all tiers.
6. Introduce the independent variable to the second tier only. (It is not necessary to collect data on other tiers, although you may choose to do so intermittently.)
7. Repeat Steps 1–6 until all tiers have been introduced to the independent variable.
8. Schedule a final probe condition after all tiers have been introduced to the independent variable to assess maintenance. Thin reinforcement schedule to facilitate maintenance.

This variation of the multiple probe design is practical for use in educational and clinical settings when there is not sufficient time each day to assess students on all target behaviors, e.g., reading 40 Dolch words that have been divided into four sets of 10 words. It has been used frequently when sets of behaviors (e.g., sight word reading, multiplication table recitation, object selection) or multi-step skills (e.g., meal preparation, long division computation, grocery shopping) have been the focus of investigation. Table 11.2 summarizes a number of studies that have used the multiple probe design (conditions) across behaviors (or sets of behaviors).

Applied Example: Multiple Probe Design (Conditions) Across Behaviors

Ledford, J. R., Gast, D. L., Luscre, D., & Ayres, K. M. (2008). Observational and incidental learning by children with autism during small group instruction. *Journal of Autism and Developmental Disorders, 38*, 86–103.

Ledford, Gast, Luscre, and Ayres (2008) studied the acquisition of incidental and observational information presented to six children with autism served in a self-contained elementary public school classroom. Instruction on words commonly found on products and community signs (e.g., *poison, caution*) was delivered using a 3 s constant time-delay (CTD) procedure in a small-group (dyad) instructional arrangement. Six males diagnosed with autism and speech/language impairments, ranging in age from 5 years 9 months to 8 years 4 months, participated in the study. Students were placed into dyads based on entry skills and previous reading instruction. Four specific research questions were asked: During small-group instruction,

> Will children with autism: (a) learn incidental information visually presented (signs) at the same time as the verbal praise statement?; (b) learn another student's target information (sight words)?; (c) learn another student's incidental information (signs)?; and (d) identify targeted and non-targeted instructional stimuli in the natural environment?
>
> (p. 87)

The dependent variables were percentage of words and phrases read correctly (target and non-target words/phrases), percentage of visual stimuli associated with sight words/phrases named correctly (incidental information and observation of incidental information), and percentage of target and non-target words/phrases read correctly. Data were collected using an event-recording procedure across all conditions. During probe, CTD, and generalization conditions a child's response was scored as an *unprompted correct* if the child read (correctly pronounced) the word/phrase or picture sign within 3 s after the task request (e.g., "What word?" or "What is this?"). An *unprompted incorrect* was recorded if the student said anything other than the correct response within 3 s after the question. If the student said nothing during the 3 s response interval, *no response* was recorded. During CTD instruction the teacher-researcher also recorded whether a student emitted a *prompted correct*, a correct response within 3 s after delivery of the prompt, or a *prompted incorrect*, an incorrect response after the teacher's model. Self-corrected responses were scored as incorrect. Echolalic responses, if followed by a correct response, were scored as correct (e.g., "What word?—Caution"). Reliability data were collected, at minimum, during 23% (range: 23% to 50%) of all sessions across all conditions. Using the point-by-point method, interobserver agreement (IOA) ranged from 92 to 100% (mean: 99.4%) and procedural-reliability agreement ranged from 90 to 100% (mean: 99.7%).

The study employed four experimental conditions (Generalization Probe, Word Probe, Picture Probe, CTD). The Generalization Probe condition was implemented as a pretest and posttest that assessed a student's ability to read target and non-target product or community signs/pictures in novel settings. The other three conditions were introduced within the context of a multiple probe design (condition variation) across behaviors (word sets). Word Probe and Picture Probe conditions were scheduled immediately prior to the introduction of the CTD procedure on a word set and immediately following a student reaching criteria on a word set. The purpose of the Word Probe condition was to assess students' acquisition of their target words and their partner's words to which they were exposed, but not directly taught. Acquisition of non-target words was possible only through observational learning. The purpose of the Picture Word Probe condition was to assess a student's acquisition of incidental information (pictures or signs without the word/phrase printed on them) that were presented in the teacher's praise statement following correct responses on their target words/phrases and their partner's target words. Acquisition of the partner's pictures/signs was only possible through observational learning.

All probe condition sessions were conducted in a 1:1 arrangement, while instructional sessions were conducted in a small-group arrangement (two students and one teacher). Sessions were conducted daily whenever both participants in a dyad were present. Generalization Probe pretest and posttest sessions were conducted in novel settings throughout the school building. A summary description of each of the experimental condition is presented in Table 11.3.

The Generalization Probe condition assessed participants' ability to expressively identify signs containing their target sight words (e.g., a yellow diamond with the word "Caution"), and the target word signs assigned to their dyad partner, under novel conditions. While walking through the school with the student, the teacher would stop 3 feet from a sign, point to the sign while saying "Look," and upon directing his eye gaze to the sign, ask the student, "What is this?" Correct responses were followed with social praise, while incorrect or no responses were ignored.

During Word Probe condition sessions, students were assessed on acquisition of their target words and the target words of their partner. On each trial the teacher started with a general attentional cue ("Look") and a specific attentional cue ("Tell me the letters") before asking, "What word?" During Picture Probe condition sessions, students were assessed on their acquisition of their incidental information (a picture of the sign associated with each target word) and the incidental information of their partner. On each trial the teacher followed the same general attentional response protocol before asking, "What is this?" During all probe conditions descriptive verbal praise was delivered on the average of every third trial for appropriate social and attending behaviors (VR-3), as well as after each correct response (CRF).

During the CTD instructional condition, six sight words were taught to each student (two

Table 11.3 Description of Conditions

Generalization	Word probe	Picture probe	CTD
Point & "Look" (General Attentional Cue)	"Look" (General Attentional Cue)	"Look" (General Attentional Cue)	"Look" (General Attentional Cue)
	"Tell me the letters" (Specific Attentional Cue)		"Tell me the letters" (Specific Attentional Cue)
"What is this?"	"What word?"	"What is this?"	"What word?"
Unprompted Correct: Verbal Praise	Unprompted Correct: Verbal praise, token	Unprompted Correct: Verbal praise, token	Unprompted Correct: Verbal praise, presentation of incidental information ("Right! Caution" & present picture)
Unprompted Incorrect: Walk away from the sign	Unprompted Incorrect: Remove written word	Unprompted Incorrect: Remove picture	Unprompted Incorrect: Remove written word ("Wait if you don't know")
No Response: Walk away from the sign	No Response: Remove written word	No Response: Remove picture	No response: Model prompt
			("*Target word)" (Model prompt)*
			Prompted Correct: Verbal praise, presentation of incidental information ("Right! Caution" & present picture of caution sign)
			Prompted Incorrect: Ignore. Remove written word
			No response: Wait 3 s. Ignore & remove word

Source: Ledford et al. (2008), Table 3. With kind permission from Springer Science+Business Media.

per word set). The same general and specific cues/responses required in the Word Probe condition were used in CTD condition. During the initial session for each word set, a 0-s delay was used. During this session, the correct response was modeled immediately following the question, "What word?" During subsequent sessions, a 3-s delay was used in which the student had 3 s to initiate and complete a response before the teacher delivered the controlling prompt. Correct responses emitted before or after the verbal model were reinforced with social praise and a token. When a correct response was emitted, descriptive verbal praise was presented by the teacher ("Right!, Caution!") and incidental information in the form of a related picture/ sign was presented. Incorrect responses before the model prompt resulted in a reminder to wait, while incorrect responses after the teacher's prompt and no responses were ignored. Reinforcement was thinned from a CRF schedule to a VR-3 schedule after one day at 90% unprompted correct responses. It was necessary for students to be correct before the prompt on the first presentation of their two target words in order to meet the criteria.

Figures 11.7 and 11.8 display the percentage of prompted (closed square) and unprompted correct (open triangle) responses for two students across all conditions evaluated within the context of a multiple probe design. Prior to instruction, all students identified 0% of target words. Visual analysis shows that levels of unprompted correct responses changed from a stable trend at 0% to a therapeutic trend that increased to criterion level for all students when each word set was taught during CTD conditions. Percentage correct for words not yet introduced to CTD instruction remained stable at 0%. Mean number of sessions to criterion was seven (range: 4–12) and the mean percentage error across students and word pairs was 3.6% (range:

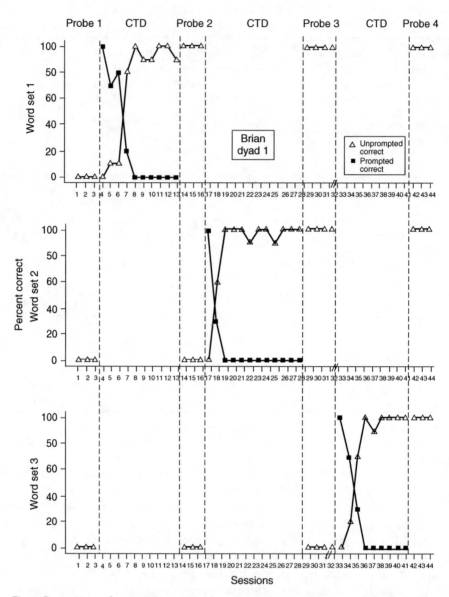

Fig. 1 Percentages of prompted correct and unprompted correct responses during instruction and probe conditions for Brian

Figure 11.7 Graphic display of multiple probe design (condition) across behaviors (source: Ledford et al., 2008. With kind permission from Springer Science+Business Media).

0% to 10%). Each student maintained between 50 and 100% correct responding during post-instruction probes, and five of six participants maintained 100% correct responding for all target words during the final probe.

Table 11.4 presents acquisition percentages for target observational target information (OTI), incidental target information (ITI), and incidental observational information (IOI). Data to the left of the stair step line represent information to which the child had not been exposed, while data to the right of the line represent information that the child had been introduced to through observation or instructional feedback.

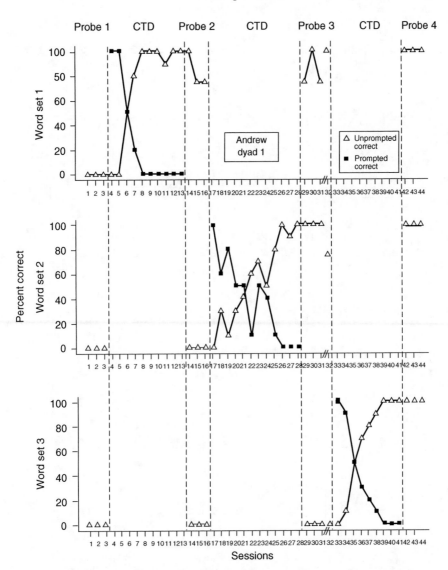

Fig. 2 Percentages of prompted correct and unprompted correct responses during instruction and probe conditions for Andrew

Figure 11.8 Graphic display of multiple probe design (condition) across behaviors (source: Ledford et al., 2008. With kind permission from Springer Science+Business Media).

In addition to target information, all participants acquired some or all observational information (words directly taught to their partner). All students also acquired some or all of the incidental target information (ITI) related to their target words (e.g., when presented with the picture of a yellow diamond, the student identified this as "caution" in the absence of the word). Generalization probe data revealed that students were unable to identify signs in natural contexts prior to instruction. After instruction for all word sets, all students were able to generalize information to natural contexts. Social validity was assessed by reviewing students' individual education plans (IEPs), and requesting parent feedback on study objectives, procedures, and outcomes. Parents returned positive feedback for all measures.

Table 11.4 Display of Probe Data Using Pre- and Post-Intervention Lines

Table 5 Acquisition of OTI, ITI & IOI

Dyad 1: Brian

Word Set		Probe 1	2	3	4
1	OTI	0	100	100	100
	ITI	0	100	100	100
	IOI	0	100	100	100
2	OTI	0	0	100	100
	ITI	0	0	100	100
	IOI	0	0	100	100
3	OTI	0	0	0	100
	ITI	0	0	0	100
	IOI	0	0	0	100

Dyad 2: Keith

Word Set		Probe 1	2	3	4
1	OTI	0	100	100	100
	ITI	0	100	100	100
	IOI	0	100	100	100
2	OTI	0	0	100	100
	ITI	0	0	100	100
	IOI	0	0	100	100
3	OTI	0	0	0	100
	ITI	0	0	0	100
	IOI	0	0	0	100

David 3: Michael

Word Set		Probe 1	2	3	4
1	OTI	0	83	94	100
	ITI	0	100	100	100
	IOI	0	75	100	100
2	OTI	0	0	100	100
	ITI	0	0	100	100
	IOI	0	0	100	100
3	OTI	0	0	0	100
	ITI	0	0	0	100
	IOI	0	0	0	100

Dyad 1: Andrew

Word Set		Probe 1	2	3	4
1	OTI	0	50	81	100
	ITI	0	0	75	100
	IOI	0	25	50	100
2	OTI	0	0	100	50
	ITI	0	0	100	75
	IOI	0	0	100	50
3	OTI	0	0	0	100
	ITI	0	0	0	100
	IOI	0	0	0	100

Dyad 2: David

Word Set		Probe 1	2	3	4
1	OTI	0	100	100	100
	ITI	0	100	100	100
	IOI	0	100	83	50
2	OTI	0	0	100	100
	ITI	0	0	100	50
	IOI	0	0	100	100
3	OTI	0	0	0	100
	ITI	0	0	0	100
	IOI	0	0	0	100

Dyad 3: Ian

Word Set		Probe 1	2	3	4
1	OTI	0	67	56	100
	ITI	0	50	100	100
	IOI	0	0	50	100
2	OTI	0	0	75	100
	ITI	0	0	100	100
	IOI	0	0	100	100
3	OTI	0	0	0	0
	ITI	0	0	0	100
	IOI	0	0	0	0

Source: Ledford et al. (2008), Table 3. With kind permission from Springer Science+Business Media.

During CTD instruction in a small-group arrangement, students with autism learned: (a) target words directly taught; (b) non-target words that were taught to their instructional partner; and (c) incidental information presented in praise statements to both the student and his partner. Results show that a small-group instructional arrangement can be an effective arrangement for students with autism and that these students are likely to acquire information taught to other students through observation alone. In addition, this study demonstrates that presenting incidental information in descriptive praise statements is an effective and unobtrusive way to increase information learned by students with autism.

Multiple Probe Designs: Benefits and Limitations

Multiple probe designs have the practical benefit of not requiring extended periods of time in an assessment condition, particularly when it is highly unlikely, if not impossible, for a participant to respond correctly prior to introduction of the independent variable. In such situations intermittent, rather than continuous, assessments will suffice in documenting behavior stability. If, however, there is variability in either level or trend across the probe data series, you should extend your measurement of the dependent variable under probe conditions and begin collecting data more frequently, for example, every 2 days rather than every 5 days. If you do not extend the probe condition until a stable level and/or trend are established, you risk confounding your results due to potentially uncontrolled history, maturation, practice, and/or adaptation variables. Undetected response generalization is another potential limitation of multiple probe designs. Suppose that after a student participant received direct instruction on the first behavior in the multiple probe design, practice alone improved her correct responding on other behaviors targeted for intervention. In such cases intermittent probes may delay, or altogether prohibit, discovery of response generalization, whereas continuous baseline measures would have alerted you to response covariation from the outset. You must ensure that target behaviors (conditions or participants) are functionally independent, and schedule the optimum number of probe sessions (or days) before introducing the independent variable.

An undetected change in responding within or across tiers due to intermittent data collection is the primary limitation of multiple probe designs. When practical, and always when studying dangerous behavior (aggression, self-injury, etc.), we recommend continuous measurement.

Concluding Comments

Multiple baseline and multiple probe designs across behaviors can be used to evaluate experimental control with a wide range of interventions, in a variety of educational and clinical settings, and across many types of learners exhibiting a multiplicity of behaviors. When compared to other multiple baseline and multiple probe designs, these designs permit direct intra-subject replication, thereby increasing confidence in the findings. Tables 11.1 and 11.2 summarize several studies from the applied research literature that employed a multiple baseline or multiple probe design across behaviors, respectively. These designs are often the single subject research designs of choice for applied researchers when compared to A-B-A-B designs because the withdrawal of an effective intervention is not required to demonstrate experimental control.

Multiple Baseline and Multiple Probe Designs Across Conditions

When using a multiple baseline or multiple probe design across conditions to evaluate experimental control, you sequentially introduce the independent variable to the same behavior across several different stimulus conditions. *Stimulus conditions* can encompass the dimensions of time, instructional arrangement (individual, small group, independent), activity, setting, control agent (therapist, teacher, parent), or composition of peer group. In contrast to the multiple baseline and multiple probe designs across behaviors, these designs require you to target a single behavior and a minimum of three different conditions (e.g., settings) in which you want the behavior to occur (or not occur, depending on the objective of the intervention). The target behavior is monitored continuously (multiple baseline design) or intermittently (multiple probe design) and concurrently under each of three or more conditions until data stability is established. You then introduce the independent variable to the target behavior in one condition, while continuing to measure the same behavior in other conditions using pre-intervention procedures. When the behavior stabilizes at the predetermined criterion level in the first condition, the intervention is then introduced to the same behavior in the second condition. The systematic and sequential introduction of the independent variable across stimulus conditions continues until the criterion level is achieved under all target conditions. For example, target conditions can range from monitoring percentage of time on-task across math, spelling, and social studies periods (across activities) to the frequency of "disruptive behaviors" across a classroom, lunchroom, and playground (across settings), to the number of minutes tardy across morning, lunch, and afternoon recesses (across time).

Internal Validity

The demonstration of experimental control with multiple baseline and multiple probe designs across conditions requires you to first collect "acceptable" pre-intervention data across each stimulus condition and then introduce the intervention in one condition, while maintaining baseline or probe conditions in the other conditions. After criterion-level performance is attained in the first condition, the intervention is applied to the second. Following criterion attainment in the second condition, the intervention is applied to the third, and so on. As with all multiple baseline and multiple probe designs experimental control is achieved when an acceptable pre-intervention data trend is maintained until the intervention is introduced to the behavior in the new condition and, upon introduction of the independent variable, an immediate change in behavior is observed. This effect is replicated across three or more conditions.

The guidelines and threats to internal validity for these two designs are similar to those described for multiple baseline and multiple probe designs across behaviors. The two primary threats to internal validity are behavioral covariation and inconsistent effects. You must make two a priori predictions: (a) that the target behavior will function independently across stimulus conditions, so that pre-intervention data will remain stable and unchanged until the intervention is directly applied; and (b) that the stimulus conditions will be sufficiently similar to permit the replication of effect each time the intervention is applied. There are few guidelines to help you in predicting whether a behavior will be independent across conditions. One recommendation is to avoid using stimulus conditions that are "highly" similar. The greater the similarity between conditions, the greater the likelihood that a participant's behavior will generalize across conditions. To avoid stimulus generalization conduct an analysis of stimulus and response similarities across the three conditions by counting the number of shared stimulus characteristics and response variations. Knowledge of a participant's history under similar stimulus conditions also will be helpful in predicting unwanted stimulus generalization before the start of your study. For example, a student who has a reinforcement history for improving study habits (attention to task, answer questions, active participation in discussions) during reading lessons may exhibit generalized improvements during spelling and math lessons. Such generalization is more likely today than when Stokes and Baer (1977) wrote their seminal article on generalization programming because most teachers and therapists understand the importance of using multiple exemplars during the teaching of new skills. It may be because of the increased use of general case programming procedures (Chadsey-Rusch, Drasgow, Reinoehl, Halle, & Collet-Klingenberg, 1993) that fewer studies using multiple baseline and multiple probe designs across conditions appear in the applied research literature.

Selecting three conditions that are independent, yet similar, is at best an educated guess based on your familiarity with the generalization research literature, a participant's history with the behavior and target conditions, and the number of shared stimulus characteristics across conditions. If there is a concern that the independent variable will have an inconsistent effect across tiers, regardless of the type of multiple baseline or multiple probe design, it is recommended that additional tiers be identified and added. As will be discussed in Chapter 13, it is also possible to combine designs to increase the likelihood of demonstrating experimental control, for example, multiple baseline design across conditions with a multiple probe design across participants. Table 11.5 summarizes several studies in which a multiple baseline design across conditions was used to evaluate experimental control. No multiple probe designs across conditions were found in our review of the literature.

Considerations

Multiple baseline designs across conditions require adherence to specific constraints that may be problematic under some circumstances. First, a minimum of three environmental conditions must be identified, each occasioning the same target behavior, yet each independent enough to permit the replication. Second, if the multiple baseline design across conditions, in which conditions are individuals (e.g., teacher, paraprofessional, and speech pathologist) and school settings (e.g., classroom, individual work station, therapy room), it may be difficult for individuals not to use an effective intervention in their setting until you direct them to do so. A premature introduction of the independent variable will threaten experimental control and, therefore, it is imperative that all involved in the study understand the purpose of staggering the introduction of the intervention. Collection of procedural-reliability data is critical in these situations. Third, the target behavior must be monitored repeatedly and concurrently in each condition, a task that may prove time-consuming, distracting, or otherwise burdensome to you as you try to deliver services and collect data for your research project. And fourth, prolonged pre-intervention measures under conditions in which the intervention has not yet been introduced may raise questions about the ethics of postponing interventions in settings where the behavior requires immediate attention.

Applied Example: Multiple Baseline Design Across Conditions

Miller, C., Collins, B. C., & Hemmeter, M. L. (2002). Using a naturalistic time delay procedure to teach nonverbal adolescents with moderate-to-severe mental disabilities to initiate manual signs. *Journal of Developmental and Physical Disabilities, 14,* 247–261.

Miller, Collins, and Hemmeter (2002) studied the effects of a naturalistic time-delay procedure to teach initiation of manual signs to three nonverbal students with moderate to severe disabilities in a special-education program at a public high school. Two males and one female participated in the study (age range: 19–21 years). All students had significant deficits in academic skills and communication. None of the students were able to initiate appropriate

Table 11.5 Studies That Exemplify a Multiple Baseline Across Conditions Design

Reference	Participants	Setting/arrangement	Independent variable	Dependent variable
Bock, M. A. (2007). The impact of social-behavioral learning strategy training on the social interaction skills of four students with Asperger syndrome. *Focus on Autism and Other Developmental Disabilities, 22,* 88–95.	Number: 4 Sex: male Age range: 9–10 Disability/diagnosis: Asperger syndrome IQ Range: 98–110	Setting: self-contained classroom Arrangement: unknown	A social learning strategy (SODA) that used a story to exemplify cognitive strategies to be used in social situations	Percentage of time spent in cooperative social and learning activities
Hetzioni, O. E., & Tannous, J. (2004). Effects of a computer-based intervention program on the communicative functions of children with autism. *Journal of Autism and Developmental Disorders, 34,* 95–113.	Number: 5 Sex: 3 males, 2 females Age range: 7–12 Disability/diagnosis: autism	Setting: self-contained classroom Arrangement: individual	An interactive computer instruction program with three targets (play, meals, hygiene)	Number of instances of immediate & delayed echolalia, relevant and irrelevant speech, and communication initiations per session across settings
Mancina, C., Tankersley, M., Kamps, D., Kravits, T., & Parrett, J. (2000). Brief report: Reduction of inappropriate vocalizations for a child with autism using a self-management treatment program *Journal of Autism and Developmental Disorders, 30,* 599–606.	Number: 1 Sex: Female Age: 12 Disability/diagnosis: autism & moderate MR	Setting: self-contained classroom Arrangement: individual	Instruction for performing steps of self-management for innapropriate verbalizations	Percentage of intervals which contained inappropriate vocalizations

communication with others and frequently used nonconventional or unintelligible communication attempts to request preferred items or activities. The research question was: Will a naturalistic time-delay procedure be effective in increasing the frequency of manual sign communication initiations by three students with moderate to severe disabilities?

The dependent variable was the number of unprompted correct initiations to request target items in the natural environment. Data were collected using an event-recording procedure. During all sessions a participant's response was scored as an unprompted correct if the participant correctly formed the manual sign within 4 s after an attentional response (i.e., eye contact with the investigator), or a prompted correct if a participant formed the manual sign within 4 s after delivery of a mand or model. An incorrect response was recorded if a student did not respond or incorrectly formed the manual sign within 4 s after an attentional response, mand, or model. Reliability data were collected once per condition per student. Using the point-by-point method, the mean interobserver agreement (IOA) during baseline and maintenance conditions was 100% and during intervention condition IOA ranged from 92 to 100%. Mean procedural reliability was 100% during baseline condition and ranged from 86 to 100% during intervention.

The study employed three experimental conditions: baseline, intervention, and maintenance. The three conditions were introduced within the context of a multiple baseline design across conditions, replicated across participants. All sessions were conducted in a 1:1 arrangement. Sessions were conducted daily at one of three times (morning, noon, afternoon) based on the natural context of the word being taught.

The baseline condition assessed participants' ability to initiate manual signs in natural contexts. During these sessions the investigator manipulated the environment so that a student needed to communicate in order to gain access to a preferred item or activity (e.g., investigator failed to initiate a walk that was scheduled). The investigator first made eye contact with a participant and waited 4 s for a response. Correct responses resulted in verbal praise and incorrect and no responses were ignored. Upon completion of 10 trials, regardless of response correctness, a student was given access to the preferred item or activity.

During intervention sessions, researchers reported using a "naturalistic time delay" procedure. Investigators followed the same procedures as in the baseline condition, but included a general attentional cue ("Look") in addition to making eye contact. If a participant correctly initiated a response, verbal praise was given. If a correct manual sign was not initiated within 4 s, the investigator provided a verbal mand (e.g., "What do you want?") and waited 4 additional seconds for a response. If a correct manual sign was not initiated within 4 s of the mand, the investigator modeled the correct manual sign and waited 4 s for a response. Upon completion of 10 trials, access was given to the item or activity regardless of response correctness. Criterion was set at five initiations above baseline level before introducing the intervention to the next condition (and behavior). Maintenance data were collected during the second, third, and fourth weeks after a participant reached criterion using time-delay conditions.

Figure 11.9 shows the effectiveness of the naturalistic time-delay procedure on number of unprompted correct responses for one of their three participants, Mary, as evaluated within the context of a multiple baseline design across conditions (lunch, afternoon, morning periods) and behaviors. Prior to instruction, Mary initiated no manual signs in any of the three conditions. A visual analysis of the data shows a zero-celeration trend during baseline condition across all tiers. Upon introduction of the independent variable there was an immediate increase in number of initiations that was replicated across conditions and behaviors. This effect was replicated across participants. All participants reached the five initiations criterion, with only one student reaching 100% (10/10 correct initiations) across the three conditions.

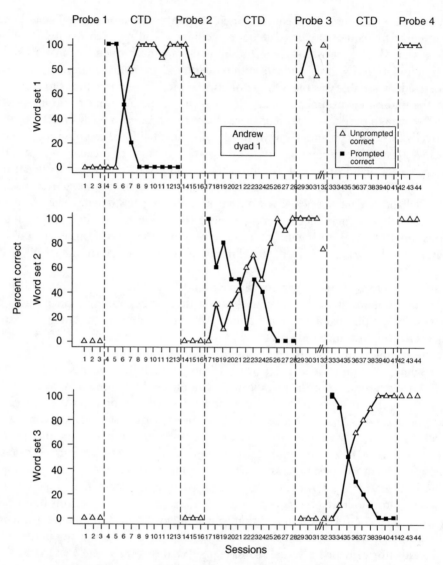

Fig. 2 Percentages of prompted correct and unprompted correct responses during instruction and probe conditions for Andrew

Figure 11.9 Graphic display of multiple baseline design across conditions (source: Miller et al., 2002. With kind permission from Springer Science+Business Media).

During the maintenance condition each student maintained a higher level of manual sign initiation than during baseline condition across all three tiers. Response initiations ranged from 33 to 82%.

Two points should be noted regarding the Miller et al. (2002) study. First, unlike many multiple baseline design across conditions studies, each condition (morning, lunch, afternoon) in the study was paired with a different manual sign. This need not be the case, and is typically not the case. The effectiveness of teaching one manual sign (e.g., "help") could be evaluated across three different activities (e.g., snack, recess, art) within the context of a multiple baseline (or multiple probe) design across conditions. Second, as described by the investigators (p. 54), their intervention more closely resembles a mand-model or system of least prompts procedure (Wolery, Ault, & Doyle, 1992), than a naturalistic time-delay procedure (Halle, Marshall, & Spradlin, 1979), since a hierarchy of prompts (i.e., "general attentional cue," mand, model) was presented if a student failed to respond or responded incorrectly. This investigation demonstrated both intra-subject (across three conditions and behaviors) and inter-subject (across three students) direct replication, providing a convincing demonstration of the effectiveness of their independent variable.

Concluding Comments

The multiple baseline (or multiple probe) design across conditions is appropriate for evaluating the effectiveness of the same intervention across a variety of conditions, including settings, individuals, materials, instructional formats, etc. However, you must proceed with caution since there are few guidelines to help you identify conditions that are functionally independent, yet similar. It is a design that requires your thorough familiarity with the generalization research literature relative to the conditions you have identified to avoid selecting conditions that are so similar that stimulus generalization is likely. If stimulus generalization occurs early (i.e., in one of the first three conditions), experimental control is greatly weakened. You should be aware that few studies appear in the recent applied research literature that employed a multiple baseline design across conditions.

Multiple Baseline and Multiple Probe Designs Across Participants

Multiple baseline and multiple probe designs across participants (frequently referred to as "across subjects") sequentially introduce the independent variable across several individuals (or groups of individuals) who exhibit behaviors that are similar and occur under similar environmental conditions. The ideal, or at least the more conservative research approach, is to identify individuals with similar learning histories and who emit the same target behavior at similar frequencies under similar pre-intervention conditions. For example, if you were interested in assessing the effects of token reinforcement on reading rates across individual students, you may want to initially attempt to identify children of the same age, with similar school backgrounds, and who are currently reading at the same level in the same or a similar classroom. In subsequent investigations, after a series of direct replications, you may choose to evaluate the generality of the intervention by identifying students who vary in one or more ways (e.g., age, skill level) from students used in the initial study. In these replication attempts, the greater the differences across participants the greater the generality of the findings. Initially, however, it is prudent to evaluate the effectiveness of your independent variable on a single target behavior emitted by participants with similar characteristics.

Multiple baseline and multiple probe designs across participants differ from multiple baseline and multiple probe designs across behaviors and across conditions described earlier. In the previously discussed designs the effectiveness of the independent variable is evaluated based on its impact on: (a) the same dependent measure (e.g., frequency, rate, duration) across several similar, yet independent behaviors emitted by the *same participant* (multiple baseline or probe design across behaviors); or (b) one behavior across several similar, yet independent conditions emitted by the *same participant* (multiple baseline or probe across conditions). Intra-subject direct replication is possible with both these designs, whereas with multiple baseline and multiple probe designs across participants, confidence in experimental findings rests solely on inter-subject direct replication. More specifically, independent variable effectiveness is evaluated based on its impact on the same dependent measure, across several functionally similar behaviors, emitted by *several different participants*. In discussing multiple baseline and multiple probe designs across participants, keep in mind that each tier of the design may be either one individual or a group of individuals, such as a classroom of children or particular therapy group. In such cases where three or more groups of individuals are the focus of the study, rather than a series of individuals, we recommend use of the phrase *inter-group direct replication* to describe how experimental control is established. It is important to remember that although we refer to these designs as "single subject," small groups of individuals can also be studied by monitoring group performance (e.g., mean percentage on-task, median test score, etc.) rather than individual performance.

Baseline logic for multiple baseline and multiple probe designs across participants is similar to that used with other multiple baseline and multiple probe designs, in that you identify a minimum of three participants (or groups of participants) who exhibit similar behaviors under similar environmental conditions, but who are independent of one another. Initially you measure the target behavior emitted by each of the participants under pre-intervention conditions until a stable trend and level are established for each. Once an acceptable level and trend are established with one participant, introduce the independent variable to that participant, while continuing to measure the behaviors of other participants under pre-intervention conditions. When the target behavior of the first participant reaches your preset criterion, introduce the independent variable to a second participant whose pre-intervention data are stable, while continuing to monitor the target behavior of other participants under baseline or probe conditions. The systematic and sequential introduction of the independent variable continues until all participants have been introduced to the same intervention. It is worth noting that it is common to monitor each participant's behavior at least intermittently until all participants have reached criterion. Repeated measurement after an individual has reached criterion serves as a maintenance check and helps in determining if the experimental effect is durable over time. It is worth repeating here that the frequency with which data are collected after criterion has been achieved *does not* have a bearing on whether the design is labeled a multiple baseline or multiple probe design.

Internal Validity

Demonstration of experimental control with multiple baseline and multiple probe designs across participants requires that you collect acceptable pre-intervention data across each individual (or group) relative to a common target behavior and then introduce the intervention to one individual (or group), while maintaining baseline or probe conditions with the others. Upon introduction of the independent variable an immediate change should be observed in that participant's behavior, but not in the behavior of others. After criterion performance is reached with the first participant, the intervention is introduced to a second participant whose pre-intervention data are stable. Following the replication of effect with the second participant, the intervention is introduced to the third, and so on. Confidence that the intervention is responsible for observed changes in behavior is gained when there is an immediate change in the dependent variable upon introduction of the independent variable, not before, and that this change is observed by each of the study participants. A delay in effect can weaken a demonstration of experimental control depending on the reason for the delay. For example, an intervention designed to teach participants how to self-monitor their behavior may require several days of teaching before participants are proficient. If you choose to record and graph data during this skill-acquisition period, it would be understandable that the effect may be delayed until after participants reach criterion. Experimental control is also threatened if there is behavioral covariation or inconsistent effects across participants.

Considerations

In keeping with other multiple baseline and multiple probe designs you will need to make two predictions: (a) participants' target behaviors will respond to the same independent variable, and (b) participants are sufficiently independent that a change in one participant's behavior will not influence the behaviors of others. Regarding the first prediction, identifying behaviors that are independent and will respond to the same intervention, it is recommended that you conduct a functional behavior assessment (FBA) to ensure that the intervention addresses the same behavioral function, regardless of behavior topography for each participant in the study. The second prediction may be more difficult to make since many participants in the same study may know one another and may share pertinent information that may influence their behavior. Even if participants do not directly interact with one another about the study, it is possible that participants could learn pertinent information that will influence their behavior through observational learning. For example, introducing a behavioral contingency for some individuals may alter the behavior of other individuals in the same situation, through collateral effects of instructions, modeling, and vicarious reinforcement (Bandura, 1969; Kazdin, 1973; Strain, Shores, & Kerr, 1976). One strategy to minimize such effects is to target individuals in similar but separate settings, or separate periods of the day, in order to insulate students from the intervention until the designated time (Sulzer-Azaroff & Mayer, 1977). For example, a resource teacher investigating a new instructional tactic in reading might schedule each identified child (or group of children) to receive instruction when other participants are occupied elsewhere, or even out of the room.

A decision you will need to make with these designs is when to introduce the independent variable to the next participant. Prior to the start of the study you will want to establish *criteria for staggering the introduction of the intervention*. There are two strategies for doing this: (a) introduce the independent variable to the next participant after a set number of days or sessions (e.g., every 5 days or sessions the intervention is introduced to a new participant); or (b) introduce the independent variable to the next participant when the preceding participant reaches the pre-established criterion (e.g., when Participant 1 doubles the number of baseline initiations, introduce intervention to Participant 2). The advantage of the *set number of days or sessions criterion* is that you can predict how long each participant will need to be in the pre-intervention condition with relative accuracy, barring unstable baseline or probe data. The limitation, however, is that your decision may adversely affect the evaluation of certain threats to internal validity (i.e., history, maturation, testing) by restricting the number of days or sessions you are willing to allow these threats to reveal themselves. For example, if staggering the introduction of the intervention every 3 days across four participants, then a maximum of only 12 days are allowed for threats to internal validity to appear, a relatively short period of time. It would be a better test of threats to internal validity if the intervention were staggered every 5 or 7 days, allowing more days to show themselves. With more tiers in the design, however, you may get by with fewer days. The advantage of *waiting until the preceding participant reaches criterion* is experimental rather than practical. That is, by allowing each participant's performance during the intervention condition to determine when the next participant is introduced to the intervention, you avoid having to make an arbitrary decision as to how long you are willing to wait for threats to internal validity to be revealed. It is a more stringent criterion for evaluating threats to internal validity, provided there is a reasonable stagger and all four participants require more than 3 or 4 days to reach criterion. The disadvantage of this strategy is practical, and potentially ethical; if participants assigned to earlier tiers are exceedingly slow to reach criterion, it will result in prolonged baseline or probe conditions for those assigned to later tiers. In such cases your professional judgment will come into play in deciding how long is too long, and whether threats to internal validity have been adequately assessed.

Multiple baseline and multiple probe designs across participants are well-suited for educational and clinical research when three or more individuals (or groups of individuals) in your charge exhibit similar behavior excesses or deficits that require attention. Assuming that behaviors emitted by prospective participants are not dangerous to self or others, it would be prudent and justifiable to introduce your intervention to one participant at a time before investing your time, and your participants' time, in an intervention that is unproven. Identifying instructional programs and intervention strategies that are effective with several different individuals, or groups of individuals, extends the generality of findings to the extent that participants differ, which is a goal of educational and clinical research.

Applied Example: Multiple Baseline Design Across Participants

Durand, M. (2002). Treating sleep terrors in children with autism. *Journal of Positive Behavior Interventions, 4*, 66–72.

Durand (2002) studied the effects of scheduled awakenings on sleep terrors for children with autism who had been referred to a private sleep study program by their physicians. Three children (two males, one female; age range: 3–7 years), diagnosed with autism, and their parents participated in the study. Parents were instructed on scheduled waking procedures as well as data-collection procedures (daily sleep logs). The research question was: Will a parent-implemented scheduled waking procedure reduce the frequency of night terrors for children with autism?

The dependent variables for this study were the mean number of nights with sleep-terror episodes per week and the mean number of hours of sleep per night. Data were collected using an event-recording procedure. During all conditions, parents collected the following information: time the child was put to bed, amount of time it took the child to fall asleep, the time each sleep terror began, the duration of each sleep terror, the time the child awakened in the morning, and the duration of each nap taken. Reliability data were collected by phone twice per week for all conditions of the study. Information was obtained by the researcher from parents about the previous night's events and was compared with written parent logs to determine agreement using the point-by-point method. In addition, procedural reliability was assessed by asking questions about parent behavior during the previous night's events. Interobserver agreement was 100% for all conditions of the study.

Three conditions were employed during the study: baseline, intervention, and follow-up, all of which occurred in the natural context of each child's home. During baseline condition, parents were instructed in data-collection procedures and then collected data about their child's sleep behaviors each night. Baseline measurement lasted for 3, 6, or 9 weeks for participants, consistent with a multiple baseline across participants design.

During the intervention condition parents were taught the procedure and rationale for a scheduled waking procedure during a single session. Following instructional sessions, parents began waking their child approximately 30 min prior to the typical onset time of the sleep terrors. Parents followed the waking procedure by lightly touching the child and then allowing him to go back to sleep at the scheduled time each night. This procedure was followed each night until there were 7 consecutive nights with no occurrences of sleep terrors. At this time, parents skipped 1 night of scheduled waking the following week. If there were no occurrences of sleep terrors, parents skipped an additional night of scheduled waking each subsequent week. If a sleep terror occurred, parents reverted to nightly scheduled awakenings until there were 7 consecutive nights with no sleep-terror occurrences and then began the fading procedure again.

During the follow-up condition, which occurred 12 months after baseline condition, parents were again asked to collect data on the number of sleep-terror episodes that occurred each night for a 2-week period. Interobserver agreement checks occurred twice weekly via phone calls.

Figure 11.10 displays the number of nights per week that each child experienced sleep terrors during baseline, intervention, and follow-up conditions evaluated within the context of a multiple baseline across participants design. Prior to the intervention, each child experienced sleep terrors at least 1 night per week (range: 1–7). Visual analysis shows that the number of nights per week with sleep-terror occurrences maintained at high, stable levels for two participants, and at variable but high levels for the third participant. During baseline condition,

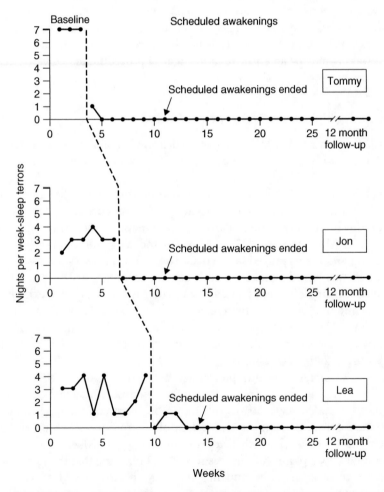

Figure 1. The number of nights per week each child experienced a sleep terror episode across both base-line and intervention.

Figure 11.10 Graphic display of multiple baseline design across participants (source: Durand, 2002. Copyright © 2002 Sage Publications. Reproduced by permission of Sage Publications).

there were no weeks, with no sleep-terror episodes for any of the children. For all participants, number of nights with sleep terrors decreased and maintained at zero or near-zero levels throughout the intervention. For Participant 1, number of nights with sleep terrors decreased from 7 per week during baseline condition to a mean of 0.4 per week during intervention. For Participant 2, number of nights with sleep terrors per week decreased from a mean of 3 during baseline condition to 0 nights during intervention. Participant 3 experienced a mean of 2.5 nights per week with sleep-terror occurrences during baseline condition that decreased to a mean of 0.11 nights with sleep terrors per week during the intervention condition. No occurrences of sleep terrors were reported during the 12-month follow-up condition. Mean sleep time per night increased for two participants and maintained for the third participant.

Social-validity data were collected from parent surveys completed during baseline, intervention, and follow-up conditions. All parents responded positively to statements regarding study procedures and outcomes. In addition, all parents responded "agree" or "strongly agree" to the statement, "My child's sleep terrors are currently a serious problem" (p. 69) during baseline condition, and responded "strongly disagree" to the same statement during follow-up.

Scheduled waking decreased the number of nights per week interrupted with sleep terrors for three children with autism. The efficacy of scheduled waking on decreasing sleep terrors was evaluated within the context of a multiple baseline across participants design. Results show that scheduled waking may be an effective, non-medical procedure to decrease sleep terrors in children with autism.

Applied Example: Multiple Probe Design Across Participants

DiPipi-Hoy, C., & Jitendra, A. (2004). A parent-delivered intervention to teach purchasing skills to young adults with disabilities. *The Journal of Special Education, 38,* 144–157.

DiPipi-Hoy and Jitendra (2004) investigated the effects of teaching parents of young adults with disabilities to implement a constant time-delay (CTD) procedure to teach their children purchasing skills in community settings. Participants in the study were three mother–daughter dyads. Mothers ranged in age from 45 to 48 years and all mothers were living with their daughter. Student participants ranged in age from 16 to 20 years. Two students were diagnosed with "moderate mental retardation" (Full-scale IQ: 49, 55). The third student (Full-scale IQ: 78) demonstrated learning difficulties and, like the other two participants, exhibited difficulty functioning in community settings. The research questions were: (a) Will parents successfully acquire and apply CTD to teach purchasing skills to their child?; (b) To what extent will students acquire the purchasing skill when taught by the parent?; (c) Will parents and students maintain skills during follow-up sessions? (p. 146).

The dependent variables were: (a) percentage of correctly completed parent behaviors during probe, intervention, and maintenance conditions, and (b) percentage of unprompted correct responses by student participants during probe, intervention, and maintenance conditions. Data were collected using an event-recording procedure. For parent behaviors a competency checklist was used which listed the instructional sequence for the purchasing procedure. For each step, a plus or minus was recorded, indicating that the step was performed correctly (+) or incorrectly (−). For student behaviors, an *unprompted correct* was recorded if the daughter completed a step prior to a parent-delivered prompt. An *unprompted incorrect* was recorded if the daughter responded incorrectly prior to the parent prompt. If a daughter did not respond after the parent prompt, *no response* was recorded. During CTD instruction, the observer also recorded whether the daughter emitted a *prompted correct*, a correct response within 2 s after prompt delivery, or a *prompted incorrect*, an incorrect response after the parent's prompt. Self-corrected responses prior to the prompt were recorded as unprompted correct. Reliability data were collected, at minimum, during 30% of all sessions across all conditions. Using the point-by-point method, interobserver agreement ranged from 94 to 100% (mean = 96%) and procedural-reliability agreement ranged from 97 to 100% (mean = 98%).

The study employed three experimental conditions (Probe, Parent Training + CTD Instruction, and Maintenance). The three conditions were introduced within the context of a multiple probe design across participants (mother–child dyads), with the Parent Training + CTD condition applied in a staggered manner across three dyads.

Parent-training sessions were conducted in a 1:1 arrangement in the parent's home by the investigator. Training consisted of reviewing, modeling, and role-playing the CTD procedure. Student training also was conducted in a 1:1 arrangement but with each mother providing instruction to her daughter in a community setting. Probe and CTD sessions occurred an average of twice per week, depending on the occurrence of naturally occurring scheduled shopping trips of each dyad.

During probe sessions, mothers were instructed to complete a purchasing task as usual with their daughter. No other instructions were given. Data were collected on the mothers' behavior using the competency checklist. Data were also collected on the daughters' responses using a multiple-opportunity probe procedure, i.e., students were provided an opportunity to correctly complete each step of the purchasing routine, regardless of the response to previous steps. During the intervention condition CTD instruction was provided to each mother in her home. After this training was complete each mother began CTD training for the purchasing routine in the community setting. At the end of each session, the trainer met the parent to provide corrective feedback regarding her behavior during the session.

Prior to intervention, no parent correctly performed any behavior on the competency checklist. Following the introduction of the Parent Training + CTD Instruction, performance immediately increased and maintained throughout intervention and maintenance conditions. All parents reached 100% correct within 4 weeks and maintained 100% responding.

Figures 11.11 and 11.12 display the percentage of steps completed correctly performed by mothers and percentage of unprompted correct responses by students across all conditions, evaluated within the context of a multiple probe design across participants, respectively. An immediate and abrupt change in each mother's behavior was observed upon introduction of training, not before. All daughters had stable but low levels of correct responding (range: 4–32%) during the probe condition. Visual analysis shows that levels of unprompted correct responses changed from a stable, zero-celerating trend to an accelerating therapeutic trend that reached criterion within 6 to 10 days (mean: 8 days). Each student maintained high levels of independent performance during maintenance (range: 80–100%).

Social-validity data were collected on daughter and mother responses to Likert-scale items. All dyads rated most items "strongly agree"; no negative scores were recorded. This study demonstrated that mothers of adolescent daughters with developmental disabilities could successfully learn to use a CTD instructional program to teach their daughters purchasing skills during community outings. These results reinforce the practice of teaching parents how to implement systematic instructional programs. As demonstrated in this study, use of systematic teaching procedures can result in beneficial learning for both parent and child and skills learned can be maintained.

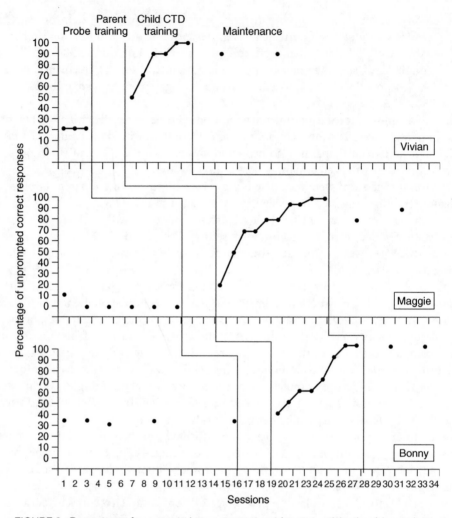

FIGURE 2. Percentage of unprompted correct responses (correct anticipations) by students during probe, intervention, and maintenance conditions. *Note*. CTD = constant time delay.

Figure 11.11 Graphic display of multiple probe design across participants (source: DiPipi-Hoy & Jitendra, 2004. Copyright © 2004 Sage Publications. Reproduced by permission of Sage Publications).

Concluding Comments

Multiple baseline and multiple probe designs across participants are not the panacea that you might think based on the frequency with which they are used by applied researchers. From a research design perspective their primary limitation is that they *do not* assess intra-subject replication, i.e., the independent variable is introduced to each participant only once, thus restricting the demonstration of effectiveness only once with each participant. In spite of this limitation, these designs continue to be popular among researchers. There are other considerations and limitations that may prove problematic, including identifying a minimum of three similar, yet independent individuals; concurrently and repeatedly measuring target behaviors of three or more participants; and delaying the introduction of the intervention for prolonged periods of time to those participants assigned to lower tiers of the design, which may have ethical repercussions.

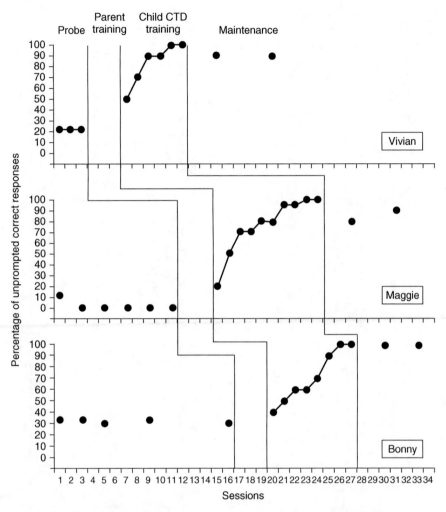

FIGURE 2. Percentage of unprompted correct responses (correct anticipations) by students during probe, intervention, and maintenance conditions. *Note.* CTD = constant time delay.

Figure 11.12 Graphic display of multiple probe design across participants (source: DiPipi-Hoy & Jitendra, 2004. Copyright © 2004 Sage Publications. Reproduced by permission of Sage Publications).

In spite of these limitations they can be used to validate interventions across many types of individuals exhibiting a multiplicity of behaviors in a variety of educational and clinical settings. As will be discusses in Chapter 13, multiple baseline and multiple probe designs across participants can be superimposed over other multiple baseline or multiple probe designs (behaviors or conditions) to enhance the internal and external validity of an intervention, thereby providing a powerful demonstration of experimental control. This pairing of a multiple baseline or multiple probe design across participants with other multiple baseline or multiple probe designs is particularly advisable when the independence of the behaviors or conditions is in doubt. Tables 11.6 and 11.7 summarize studies from the applied research literature that have used multiple baseline or multiple probe designs across participants.

Table 11.6 Studies That Exemplify a Multiple Baseline Across Participants Design

Reference	Participants	Setting/arrangement	Independent variable	Dependent variable
Gureasko-Moore. S., DuPaul, G. J., & White, G. P. (2006). The effects of self-management on the organizational skills of adolescents with ADHD. *Behavior Modification, 30*, 159–183.	Number: 3 Sex: male Age: 12 Disability/diagnosis: ADHD	Setting self-contained (instruction) & general education (target skill performance) Arrangement: individual	Instruction in self-monitoring skills and daily monitoring and self-evaluation for self-monitoring	Percentage of demonstrated classroom preparation skills
Harris, K. R., Friedlinder, B. D. Saddler, B. Frizzelle R. & Graham, S. (2005) Self-monitoring of attention versus self-monitoring of academic performance: Effects among students with ADHD in the general education classroom. *The Journal of Special Education, 39*, 145–156.	Number: 6 Sex: 1 female. 4 males Age range: none given (3rd 5th grade) Disability/diagnosis: ADHD	Setting: general education classroom Arrangement: individual	Self-monitoring of attention or performance	Percentage of intervals on task or number of correct spelling words
Ingersoll B., Lewis. E. & Kruman, E. (in press). Teaching the imitation and spontaneous use of descriptive gestures in young children with autism using a naturalistic behavioral intervention *Journal of Autism and Developmental Disorders.*	Number: 5 Sex: male Age Range: 3–4 years Disability/diagnosis: autism	Setting: Clinical Arrangement: individual	Imitation instruction (contingent instruction, linguistic mapping following the child's lead. physical prompting and contingent reinforcement)	Percentage of intervals in which the participant exhibited in imitative behavior
Jerome, J., Frantino, E. P., & Sturmey P. (2007). The effects of errorless learning and backward chaining on the acquisition of internet skills in adults with developmental disabilities. *Journal of Applied Behavior Analysis, 40*, 185–189.	Number: 3 Sex: male Age range: 24–32 Disability diagnosis: MiH MR (all). Autism (2)	Setting: self-contained classroom Arrangement: individual	Backward chaining and most to least prompting	Number of steps completed to gain access to preferred internet sites

Table 11.7 Studies That Exemplify a Multiple Probe Across Participants Design

Reference	Participants	Setting/arrangement	Independent variable	Dependent variable
Meching, L. C., & Crocin, B. (2006). Computer-based video instruction to teach the use of augmentative and alternative communication devices for ordering at fast-food restaurants. *The Journal of Special Education, 39*, 234–245.	Number: 3 Sex: 2 males, 1 female Age range: 17–21 years Disability/diagnosis: moderate or severe MR IQ range: 36–50	Setting: self-contained classroom and living skills practice site Arrangement: individual	Video modeling of purchasing procedure using an AAC device with a CTD prompting procedure	Percentage of corresponding during probe and instructional sessions
Miller, M. C., Cooke, N. L., Test, D. W., & White, R. (2003). Effects of friendship circles on the social interactions of elementary age students with mild disabilities. *Journal of Behavioral Education, 12*, 167–184.	Number: 3 Sex: male Age: 11 Disability/diagnosis: EBD (1), mild developmental disability (1), hearing impairment (1)	Setting: self-contained classroom Arrangement: inclusion small group	Weekly meetings of "friendship circles" in which a teacher facilitated friendship discussions and role play and cooperative games	Percentage of social interactions during lunch (appropriate, inappropriate, and no interaction)
Olive, M. L., de la Cruz, B., Davis, T. N., Chan, J. M., Lang, R. B. O'Reilly, M. F., Dickson, S. M. (in press). The effects of enhanced milieu teaching and a voice output communication on the requesting of three children with autism. *Journal of Autism and Developmental Disorders.*	Number: 3 Sex: male Age range: 4–5 Disability/diagnosis: ASD	Setting: self-contained classroom Arrangement: individual	Enhanced milieu teaching for communication with AAC devices using time a delay and most-to-least prompting	Number of independent communication attempts
Sigafoos, J, O'Reilly, M., Carnell, H. Upadhyaya, M. Edrisinha C. Lancioni, G. E., et al. (2005). Computer-presented video prompting for teaching microwave oven use to three adults with developmental disabilities. *Journal of Behavioral Education, 14*, 189–201.	Number: 3 Sex: male Age range: 16–18 Disability/diagnosis: moderate MR (3), autism (1) IQ range: 43–50	Setting: self-contained living skills areas Arrangement: individual	Video modeling of popcorn-making procedure	Percentage of steps of a popcorn-making task performed independently
Taylor, P., Collins, B. C., Schuster, J. W., & Klemert, H. (2002). Teaching laundry skills to high school students with disabilities: Generalisation of targeted skills and nontargeted information. *Education and Training in Mental Retardation and Developmental Disabilities, 37*, 172–183.	Number: 4 Sex: male Age range: 16–20 years Disability/diagnosis: moderate MR	Setting: self-contained living skills areas Arrangement: individual	SLP instruction for steps of laundry procedure	Percentage of steps completed independently
Test, D. W., & Ellis, M. F. (2005). The effects of LAP fractions on addition and subtraction of fractions with students with mild disabilities. *Education and Treatment of Children, 28*, 11–24.	Number: 6 Sex: male Age range: middle school Disability/diagnosis: mild disabilities	Setting: self-contained Arrangement: small groups	Mnemonic strategy (LAP Fractions)	Percent correct on addition and subtraction problems

Monitoring the Performance of a Group

Multiple baseline and multiple probe designs may be used to evaluate the behavior of groups of individuals (e.g., classroom, athletic team, choral group). The treatment of group data, however, can be problematic since variability across individuals may be masked when the group is treated as a single organism by averaging individual data points. To resolve this problem, you may maintain several graphs: one summarizing the average group performance and others documenting the individual performance of group members (an approach used by Kirby, Holborn, & Bushby, 1981); or you may plot the individual data paths for each participating group member on one graph, as did Kelly (1980). When research decisions are based on group performance, we recommend maintaining a separate graph showing the average performance of the group, supplemented with either a table, that summarizes individual performance, or individual graphs. Figure 11.13 shows how the individual data of three participants being taught within a small-group arrangement may be graphed. The experimental design is a multiple baseline design across behaviors in which each participant's data are graphed on each tier. Kelly (1980) referred to this design as a "simultaneous replication design" because the effects of the intervention are shown for each participant, on each tier, showing inter-subject replication. Plotting multiple participants' data on one grid and maintaining multiple graphs are most appropriate for smaller groups since too many data paths could be time-consuming to maintain, depending on your access to technology, and would clutter a visual display. We recommend that no more than three data paths be plotted on a single grid. The point we wish to make is that single subject research designs can and have been used to evaluate the effectiveness of interventions designed to change the behavior of groups. There are no better examples than studies evaluating the "Good Behavior Game" (e.g., Barrish, Saunders, & Wolf, 1969) and other interdependent group-oriented contingency intervention strategies (e.g., Babyak, Luze, & Kamps, 2000).

Summary

This chapter has overviewed the three types of multiple baseline and multiple probe designs: across behaviors, across conditions, and across participants. Each of these designs has the distinct advantage of not having to return to pre-intervention conditions to evaluate experimental control, a characteristic and requirement of the A-B-A-B (withdrawal and reversal) design. Multiple probe designs, in contrast to multiple baseline designs, are advantageous when continuous baseline measures are unnecessary, impractical, or reactive. To demonstrate experimental control with multiple baseline and multiple probe designs, you will need to systematically introduce the independent variable into each pre-intervention data series or tier in a time-lagged manner. If, upon introduction of the independent variable, there is (a) an immediate change in level or trend of the dependent variable, while there is (b) no change in level or trend in those data series not exposed to the independent variable, and (c) this effect is replicated across three or more tiers, experimental control has been demonstrated. Intra-subject direct replication increases confidence that the independent variable was responsible for observed changes, as demonstrated in multiple baseline and multiple probe designs across behaviors or conditions. Intra-subject direct replication is not evaluated with multiple baseline and multiple probe designs across participants. Inter-subject direct replication increases the generality of the findings if the effects of the independent variable are repeated across three or more participants in a study. Within a single investigation, the extent to which participants differ will determine the degree to which generality has been extended. As with all single

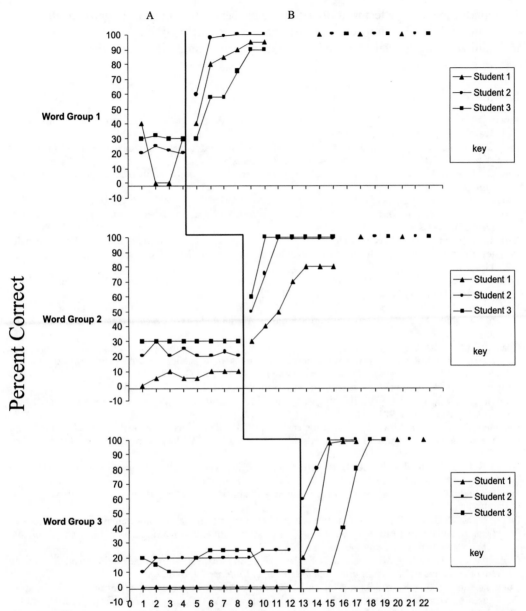

Figure 11.13 Hypothetical data illustrating individual data paths for each of nine students (three per baseline) (source: Reprinted from Kelly, 1980 with permission from Elsevier).

subject research design studies, regardless of the particular experimental design, confidence in research findings increase when other researchers, in other settings, with different participants, studying similar or different behaviors, using the same independent variable replicate the effectiveness of the independent variable, i.e., systematic replication.

Multiple baseline and multiple probe designs are well-suited for educational and clinical research, particularly when it is not possible or desirable to reverse the effects of an intervention, as with academic, aggressive, and self-injurious behaviors. Though these designs provide an eloquent experimental evaluation and demonstration of intervention effectiveness, they do not replicate the cause–effect relation with the same behavior, condition, or participant. Several variations and combinations of these designs are discussed and exemplified in Chapter 13, including the controversial "delayed" or "nonconcurrent" multiple baseline design.

References

Alberto, P. A., Fredrick, L., Hughes, M., McIntosh, L., & Cihak, D. (2007). Components of visual literacy: Teaching logos. *Focus on Autism and Other Developmental Disabilities, 22,* 234–243.

Babyak, A. E., Luze, G. J., & Kamps, D. M. (2000). The good student game: Behavior management for diverse classrooms. *Interventions in School and Clinic, 35,* 216–223.

Baer, D. M., Wolf, M. M., & Risley, T. R. (1968). Some current dimensions of applied behavior analysis. *Journal of Applied Behavior Analysis, 1,* 91–97.

Bandura, A. (1969). *Principles of behavior modification.* New York: Holt, Rinehart, & Winston.

Barlow, D. H., & Hersen, M. (1984). *Single case experimental designs: Strategies for studying behavior change* (2nd ed). New York: Allyn & Bacon.

Barrish, H. H., Saunders, M., & Wolf, M. M. (1969) Good behavior game: Effects of individual contingencies for group consequences on disruptive behavior in a classroom. *Journal of Applied Behavior Analysis, 2,* 119–124.

Birnbrauer, J. S., Peterson, C. R., & Solnick, J. V. (1974). Design and interpretation of studies of single subjects. *American Journal of Mental Deficiency, 79,* 191–203.

Bock, M. A. (2007). The impact of social-behavioral learning strategy training on the social interaction skills of four students with Asperger syndrome. *Focus on Autism and Other Developmental Disabilities, 22,* 88–95.

Chadsey-Rusch, J., Drasgow, E., Reinoehl, B., Halle, J., & Collet-Klingenberg, L. (1993). Using general case instruction to teach spontaneous and generalized requests for assistance to learners with severe disabilities. *Journal of the Association for Persons with Severe Handicaps, 18,* 177–187.

Cooper, J. O. (1981). *Measuring behavior* (2nd ed). Columbus, OH: Charles E. Merrill.

Cronin, K. A., & Cuvo, A. J. (1979). Teaching mending skills to mentally retarded adolescents. *Journal of Applied Behavior Analysis, 12,* 401–406.

Daugherty, S., Grisham-Brown, S., & Hemmeter, M. L. (2001). The effects of embedded skill instruction on the acquisition of target and non-target skills in preschoolers with developmental delays. *Topics in Early Childhood Special Education, 21,* 213–221.

DiPipi-Hoy, C., & Jitendra, A. (2004). A parent-delivered intervention to teach purchasing skills to young adults with disabilities. *The Journal of Special Education, 38,* 144–157.

Durand, M. (2002). Treating sleep terrors in children with autism. *Journal of Positive Behavior Interventions, 4,* 66–72.

Flores, M. M., & Ganz, J. B. (2007). Effectiveness of direct instruction for teaching statement inference, use of facts, and analogies to students with developmental disabilities and reading delays. *Focus on Autism and Other Developmental Disabilities, 22,* 244–251.

Gast, D., Doyle, P., Wolery, M., Ault, M., & Baklarz, N. (1991). Acquisition of incidental information during small group instruction. *Education and Treatment of Children, 14,* 1–18.

Gureasko-Moore, S., DuPaul, G. J., & White, G. P. (2006). The effects of self-management in general education classrooms on the organizational skills of adolescents with ADHD. *Behavior Modification, 30,* 159–183.

Halle, J. W., Marshall, A. M., & Spradlin, J. E. (1979). Time delay: A technique to increase language use and generalization in retarded children. *Journal of Applied Behavior Analysis, 12,* 431–439.

Harris, K. R., Friedlander, B. D., Saddler, B., Frizzelle, R., & Graham, S. (2005). Self-monitoring of attention versus self-monitoring of academic performance: Effects among students with ADHD in the general education classroom. *The Journal of Special Education, 39,* 145–156.

Hetzroni, O. E., & Tannous, J. (2004). Effects of a computer-based intervention program on the communicative functions of children with autism. *Journal of Autism and Developmental Disorders, 34,* 95–113.

Higgins, J. W., Williams, R. L., & McLaughlin, T. F. (2001). The effects of a token economy employing instructional consequences for a third-grade student with learning disabilities: A data-based case study. *Education & Treatment of Children, 24,* 99–106.

Horner, R. D., & Baer, D. M. (1978). Multiple probe technique: A variation of the multiple baseline. *Journal of Applied Behavior Analysis, 11,* 189–196.

Hughes, T. A., & Fredrick, L. D. (2006). Teaching vocabulary with students with learning disabilities using classwide peer tutoring and constant time delay. *Journal of Behavioral Education, 15,* 1–23.

Ingersoll, B., Lewis, E., & Kroman, E. (in press). Teaching the imitation and spontaneous use of descriptive gestures in young children with autism using a naturalistic behavioral intervention. *Journal of Autism and Developmental Disorders*.

Jerome, J., Frantino, E. P., & Sturmey, P. (2007). The effects of errorless learning and backward chaining on the acquisition of internet skills in adults with developmental disabilities. *Journal of Applied Behavior Analysis, 40*, 185–189.

Johnson, J. W., McDonnell, J., Holzwarth, V. N., & Hunter, K. (2004). The efficacy of embedded instruction for students with developmental disabilities enrolled in general education classes. *Journal of Positive Behavior Interventions, 6*, 214–227.

Kazdin, A. E. (1973). Methodological and assessment considerations in evaluating reinforcement programs in applied settings. *Journal of Applied Behavior Analysis, 6*, 517–531.

Kazdin, A. E., & Kopel, S. A. (1975). On resolving ambiguities of the multiple-baseline design: Problems and recommendations. *Behavior Therapy, 6*, 601–608.

Kelly, J. A. (1980). The simultaneous replication design. *Journal of Behavior Therapy and Experimental Psychiatry, 11*, 203–207.

Kirby, K. C., Holborn, S. W., & Bushby, H. T. (1981). Word game bingo: A behavioral treatment package for improving textual responding to sight words. *Journal of Applied Behavior Analysis, 14*, 317–326.

Kratochwill, T. R. (Ed.). (1978). *Single subject research—Strategies for evaluating change.* New York: Academic Press.

Kratochwill, T. R., & Levin, J. R. (1992). *Single-case research design and analysis: New directions for psychology and education.* Hillsdale, NJ: Lawrence Erlbaum Associates, Inc.

Ledford, J. R., Gast, D. L., Luscre, D., & Ayres, K. M. (2008). Observational and incidental learning by children with autism during small group instruction. *Journal of Autism and Developmental Disorders, 38*, 86–104.

Mancina, C., Tankersley, M., Kamps, D., Kravits, T., & Parrett, J. (2000). Brief report: Reduction of inappropriate vocalizations for a child with autism using a self-management treatment program. *Journal of Autism and Developmental Disorders, 30*, 599–606.

Marckel, J. M., Neef, N. A., & Ferreri, S. J. (2006). A preliminary analysis of teaching improvisation with the picture exchange communication system to children with autism. *Journal of Applied Behavior Analysis, 39*, 109–115.

Mayfield, K. H., & Vollmer, T. R. (2007). Teaching math skills to at-risk students using home-based peer tutoring. *Journal of Applied Behavior Analysis, 40*, 223–237.

McDonnell, J., Johnson, J. W., Polychronis, S., & Risen, T. (2002). Effects of embedded instruction on students with moderate disabilities enrolled in general education classes. *Education and Training in Mental Retardation and Developmental Disabilities, 37*, 363–377.

Mechling, L. C., & Cronin, B. (2006). Computer-based video instruction to teach the use of augmentative and alternative communication devices for ordering at fast-food restaurants. *The Journal of Special Education, 39*, 234–245.

Mechling, L., Gast, D. L., & Krupa, D. (2007). Impact of SMART Board technology: An investigation of sight word reading and observational learning. *Journal of Autism and Developmental Disorders, 37*, 18–27.

Mechling, L., & Ortega-Hurndon, F. (2007). Computer-based video instruction to teach young adults with moderate intellectual disabilities to perform multiple-step, job tasks in a generalized setting. *Education and Training in Developmental Disabilities, 42*, 24–37.

Miller, C., Collins, B. C., & Hemmeter, M. L. (2002). Using a naturalistic time delay procedure to teach nonverbal adolescents with moderate-to-severe mental disabilities to initiate manual signs. *Journal of Developmental and Physical Disabilities, 14*, 247–261.

Miller, M. C., Cooke, N. L., Test, D. W., & White, R. (2003). Effects of friendship circles on the social interactions of elementary age students with mild disabilities. *Journal of Behavioral Education, 12*, 167–184.

Murphey, R. J., & Bryan, A. J. (1980). Multiple-baseline and multiple-probe designs: Practical alternatives for special education assessment and evaluation. *The Journal of Special Education, 4*, 325–335.

Olive, M. L., de la Cruz, B., Davis, T. N., Chan, J. M., Lang, R. B., O'Reilly, M. F., & Dickson, S. M. (in press). The effects of enhanced milieu teaching and a voice output communication aid on the requesting of three children with autism. *Journal of Autism & Developmental Disorders*.

Scott, L., & Goetz, E. (1980). Issues in the collection of in-class data by teachers. *Education and Treatment of Children, 3*, 65–71.

Sigafoos, J., O'Reilly, M., Cannell, H., Upadhyaya, M., Edrisinha, C., Lancioni, G. E., et al. (2005). Computer-presented video prompting for teaching microwave oven use to three adults with developmental disabilities. *Journal of Behavioral Education, 14*, 189–201.

Stokes, T., & Baer, D. M. (1977). An implicit technology of generalizations. *Journal of Applied Behavior Analysis, 10*, 349–367.

Strain, P. S., Shores, R. E., & Kerr, M. M. (1976). An experimental analysis of "spillover" effects on the social interaction of behaviorally handicapped preschool children. *Journal of Applied Behavior Analysis, 9*, 31–40.

Sulzer-Azaroff, B., & Mayer, G. R. (1977). *Applying behavior analysis procedures with children and youth.* New York: Holt, Reinhart, & Winston.

Tawney, J. W., & Gast, D. L. (1984). *Single subject research in special education.* New York: Merrill.

Taylor, P., Collins, B. C., Schuster, J. W., & Kleinert, H. (2002). Teaching laundry skills to high school students with disabilities: Generalization of targeted skills and nontargeted information. *Education and Training in Mental Retardation and Developmental Disabilities, 37*, 172–183.

Test, D. W., & Ellis, M. F. (2005). The effects of LAP fractions on addition and subtraction of fractions with students with mild disabilities. *Education & Treatment of Children, 28*, 11–24.

Wall, M., & Gast, D. (1999). Acquisition of incidental information during instruction for a response chain skill. *Research in Developmental Disabilities, 20*, 31–50.

Werts, M. G., Caldwell, N. K., & Wolery, M. (2003). Instructive feedback: Effects of a presentation variable. *The Journal of Special Education, 37*, 124–133.

Westerlund, D., Granucci, E. A., Gamache, P., & Clark, H. B. (2006). Effects of peer mentors on work-related performance of adolescents with behavioral and/or learning disabilities. *Journal of Positive Behavior Interventions, 8*, 244–251.

White, O. (1971). *A glossary of behavioral terminology.* Champaign, IL: Research Press.

Williams, G., Perez-Gonzalez, L. A., & Vogt, K. (2003). The role of specific consequences in the maintenance of three types of questions. *Journal of Applied Behavior Analysis, 36*, 285–296.

Wolery, M., Anthony, L., Caldwell, N. K., Snyder, E. D., & Morgante, J. D. (2002). Embedding and distributing constant time delay in circle time and transitions. *Topics in Early Childhood Education, 22*, 14–25.

Wolery, M., Cybriwsky, C., Gast, D., & Boyle-Gast, K. (1991). Use of constant time delay and attentional responses with adolescents. *Exceptional Children, 57*, 462–474.

Wolery, M., Ault, M. J., & Doyle, P. M. (1992). *Teaching students with moderate to severe disabilities: Use of response prompting strategies.* New York: Longman.

Wolf, M. M., & Risley, T. R. (1971). Reinforcement: Applied research. In R. Glaser (Ed.), *The nature of reinforcement* (pp. 310–325). New York: Academic Press.

12

Comparative Intervention Designs

Mark Wolery, David L. Gast, and Diana Hammond

Members of helping professions often ask, "Does this practice work?" The demonstration designs (withdrawal, reversal, multiple baseline, multiple probe, and changing criterion designs) are ideal for answering this question. Sometimes they ask: (a) Does this practice work better than another practice?; (b) Will this treatment package work as well if a given component (part, element) was eliminated?; (c) Will it work better if a component is added?; (d) Will a practice work as well if used more or less frequently?; or (e) Will a practice work better in one context or another? For such questions, "comparative designs" are needed, and these are discussed in this chapter. Four types of comparisons are described in the first section, followed by a discussion of three issues faced in comparative single subject research. Finally, comparative designs are described. The experimental designs in this chapter address the comparative, component analysis, and parametric research questions discussed in Chapter 4.

Types of Comparative Studies

James Johnston, a noted behavioral scholar, said comparative studies are "the bane of the applied literature. They often lead to (1) inappropriate inferences, (2) with poor generality, (3) based on improper evidence, (4) gathered in the support of the wrong questions, thus (5) wasting the field's limited experimental resources" (1988, p. 2). He argued comparative studies were not done to understand principles of behavior in nature, but to see which intervention "wins." He criticized such research for having unfair and meaningless comparisons of procedures. His criticisms are more applicable to some studies than others, but you should heed them when doing comparative studies. Comparative studies often focus on one of the following endeavors.

Comparison of Competing Interventions

When faced with the same problems or issues, different investigators study different interventions. One may focus on intervention "B" and study it several times through systematic replications, and another may do the same with intervention "C." As a result, two or more effective interventions may be identified for teaching or treating the same participants and behaviors. The question is, "Which of those effective interventions will result in more efficient learning or more rapid deceleration of the challenging behavior?" The goal of such studies is to determine which intervention is superior and should be recommended to practitioners for use. As Johnston (1988) indicated, this is a direct attempt to see which intervention "wins."

In such cases, developers of each intervention ideally join together, plan, and conduct the comparison study. When they do not, the researcher must consider their perspectives when planning the study to ensure a fair test of each intervention. The interventions must be used as the respective developers have described, should use dependent measures the developers find appropriate, and should involve participants and settings similar to those in the original research. If you consider these issues, then the developers are more likely to view the comparison as fair. You may need to contact the developers to get precise information about the procedures to ensure a fair comparison. Use of multiple dependent variables is recommended. For example, when comparing two instructional strategies, the efficiency measures may include the number of trials or sessions to criterion, number of minutes of instruction to criterion, number and percentage of errors to criterion, percentage correct on maintenance (follow-up) sessions, and degree of generalization. You also should have sensitive and appropriate measures of procedural fidelity to document the interventions were used as planned (Billingsley, White, & Munson, 1980; Fiske, 2008; Vollmer, Sloman, & Pipkin, 2008). As in most research areas, one study does not settle which of two effective procedures is superior; multiple studies are needed.

Comparison of an Innovation to an Established Intervention

Sometimes an intervention has a solid research foundation, is recommended widely, and used frequently. You may develop and study an innovation and want to compare it to the established intervention. The goal would be to determine whether the innovation or established intervention results in better outcomes. Two requirements are important in planning such studies. First, the established intervention must be used as its developers recommend and must be applied to behaviors, participants, and contexts similar to those in the original research. Second, the innovation should be sufficiently well studied so an effective and refined form of it can be used. This is accomplished through a series of demonstration studies. You do not want to compare an innovation to an established practice prematurely, because an otherwise useful intervention may be discarded because it was not sufficiently studied before the comparison was attempted. Careful measurement of how the compared procedures are used should occur (Billingsley et al., 1980), and having multiple dependent measures is recommended as in conducting replication studies.

Comparisons to Refine Interventions

Some comparative studies are not of two different interventions but evaluate variations of the same intervention to develop and refine it. The variations may include parametric questions, such as whether using more or less of a procedure results in differential behavior changes. For example, would using 5 or 10 trials per behavior per session result in differential rates of learning; or would having every-day vs. every-other-day sessions result in more rapid learning. Other variations may focus on component analyses; for example, does adding or deleting a given component (part, element) of an intervention package result in differential responding. Studies also can focus on procedural-fidelity issues; specifically does using a procedure with high or low fidelity on some dimension result in different behavioral patterns. The goal of these studies is to identify the most powerful and efficient form of the intervention. When planning such studies, you should compare a form of the intervention that was effective in previous (demonstration) studies to a variation of that form. These studies help refine conclusions about when, in what situations, and for whom an intervention is recommended.

Comparison to Understand Interactions

Sometimes research focuses on whether an intervention or two or more interventions is more or less effective given a couple contextual variables. Contextual variables can be categorized on at least four dimensions: (a) physical space and materials; (b) social structure; (c) temporal structure; and (d) instructional characteristics. Variables of these dimensions are shown in Table 12.1. Below are examples of each type of contextual variation. You may compare individual and group contingencies on the frequency of students' comments when they are seated in rows vs. groups at tables (structuring of physical space as a contextual variable). You may evaluate the use of preferred vs. non-preferred materials on children's social interactions when one or three peers are present (social structure as a contextual variable). You may compare interspersing easy and difficult tasks vs. difficult tasks only on students' engagement during academic time when the previous activity was active or passive (temporal structure as a contextual variable). You may study whether self-monitoring with self-reinforcement vs. teacher-reinforcement differentially influences the accuracy of tasks completed during seat work when children or teacher choose the order for doing assignments (instructional structure as a contextual variable). The goal of such studies is to discern whether one intervention or another produces differential patterns of responding under one or another contextual variables. Ideally, interventions will be effective across contextual variables (Hains & Baer, 1989), but knowing whether an intervention's effectiveness is influenced by contextual variables is important qualifying information. Such information allows more accurate recommendations about the situations under which interventions are likely to produce desirable effects and may hold implications about behavior–environment interactions. The requirements for such studies are (a) interventions should have solid research support; (b) some evidence, logic, or experience should suggest the contextual variable may influence performance; and (c) the interventions

Table 12.1 Examples of Dimensions of Contextual Variables Relating to Comparison Designs

---

Physical dimensions—place, furnishings, and materials (inanimate entities)
- How the space is organized
- Size of space, furnishings, and materials
- Rules of access to space, furnishings, and materials
- Usual use of space, furnishings, and materials
- Regular and irregular variations in the space, furnishings, and materials
- Participants' learning history with similar or the specific space, furnishings, and materials

Social dimensions—others (adults, peers) in the study's context (animate entities)
- Demographic characteristics of those individuals
- Number of individuals in context by type
- The social organization in the context
- Usual patterns of interaction between individuals in the context
- Participants' history of interaction with the individuals in the context

Temporal dimensions—the schedule and organization of events/activities in the context
- Order of events (i.e., activities, routines) in the day
- Predictability of the order of events
- Variations within and across events
- Novelty and familiarity of those events and their order
- Length of events
- Nature of expectations within events
- Practices related to transitions between events
- Participants' control of the order of events

Instructional dimensions—Methods used to transmit knowledge in context
- Usual organization of instructional interactions
- Variation of the instructional interactions
- Person initiation the instructional exchanges (participants, peers, adults)
- Practices used to ensure motivation
- Practices used to ensure attention to instructional stimuli
- Practices used to ensure social and deportment behavior in the context

---

and contextual variables must be under the researcher's control. This last requirement often is difficult.

Special Issues with Comparative Studies

Nothing about comparative studies makes them immune from threats to internal validity faced by demonstration studies (e.g., history, maturation, instrumentation, lack of procedural integrity, attrition; see Chapter 5). However, three issues deserve special note: multitreatment interference, nonreversibility of effects, and separation of treatments (Holcombe, Wolery, & Gast, 1994).

Multitreatment Interference

Multitreatment interference is the influence one experimental condition has on performance under another experimental condition. Historically, two types were recognized: carryover effects, and sequence effects (sequential confounding) (Barlow & Hayes, 1979). Carryover effects are the influence of one experimental condition on performance under another condition due to the nature (characteristics) of the initial condition. Sequence effects are the influence of one condition on another due to the ordering of experimental conditions. A third type of multitreatment interference is alternation effects—the effects on performance due to rapidly changing (alternating) conditions (Hains & Baer, 1989). Carryover effects occur in the context of the sequence of experimental conditions. Specifically, an experimental condition (e.g., Condition B) can only influence subsequent performance in Condition C if the participant experienced Condition B first. Participants must experience a sequence of at least two experimental conditions before multitreatment interference (carryover, sequence, or alternation effects) is possible; logically, a condition (e.g., Condition B) cannot influence performance under another condition (e.g., Condition C) unless the participants first experienced the original condition (Condition B). Thus, Hains and Baer (1989) asserted, "there is little reason to maintain a distinction in terminology between sequence, carry-over, and alternation effects. All that is of issue are sequence effects, sometimes in faster paced sequences, sometimes is slower paced sequences" (p. 60). This assertion is valid, because differences between sequence and carryover effects are subtle and in many cases impossible to disentangle.

Multitreatment interference can have therapeutic (facilitative) or countertherapeutic (inhibitive) effects (Barlow & Hayes, 1979; Holcombe et al., 1994). In the top two panels of Figure 12.1, the effects of Conditions B and C are shown when each is used alone following a baseline condition. Condition B results in an increasing trend and Condition C produces no change. As shown in the third panel, when Condition C follows Condition B, Condition C results in an increasing trend in the behavior—a facilitative effect (due to multitreatment interference) occurs when Condition B precedes Condition C. In the bottom panel, the opposite occurs; when Condition C follows B, Condition C results in deceleration—multitreatment interference has an inhibitive effect. It is possible for combined effects to occur. One condition could enhance performance in another condition, which in turn would inhibit performance when the original condition is reintroduced. When one condition follows another, potential exists for the first condition to influence performance in subsequent conditions (Birnbrauer, 1981); this possibility exists for baseline and intervention conditions as well as two intervention conditions. Methods to detect and control multitreatment interference are discussed in later sections for each comparative design. Multitreatment interference confounds direct comparisons between interventions (Holcombe et al., 1994), but in some cases multitreatment interference may be desirable (Hains & Baer, 1989). For example, an intervention may only work, or work better, when a given contextual variable is present. Knowing this relation (i.e., interaction) will result in more precise conclusions about when and under what situations a functional relation between the intervention and behavior is likely to exist.

Nonreversibility of Effects

In some comparative studies one intervention is used for several observations and later a second intervention is used for several observations. When this occurs, the problem of non-reversibility of effects may arise. If the behavior is not readily reversible (does not revert to baseline levels), then the first intervention may cause the behavior to occur at the ceiling or floor levels of the measurement system. In Figure 12.2, the top graph shows a behavior quickly going to the ceiling when Intervention B is used, and the middle graph shows a behavior quickly moving to the floor when Intervention B is used. In both displays, Intervention C has no room to show an improvement; thus, the comparison is not possible. In some single subject studies the interventions being compared are applied in alternating sessions. In the bottom graph of Figure 12.2, Intervention B quickly drives the behavior to the floor. At issue is whether enough replications exist to argue Intervention B is superior to Intervention C. In all of these cases, these patterns are known as the nonreversibility of effects (Holcombe et al., 1994). This is applicable to both reversible and nonreversible behavior, but is most pronounced in

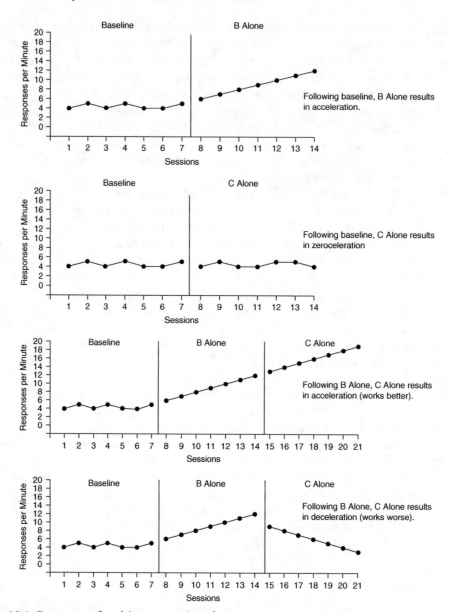

Figure 12.1 Prototype of multitreatment interference.

nonreversible behaviors. The treatment outcome for the participant is desirable, but you have no opportunity to test the relative merits of the interventions being compared.

Separation of Treatments Issue

Most comparative studies are conducted to evaluate the superiority of one intervention over other(s) and to recommend which intervention to use. You want to say, this intervention is superior and can be used to move a behavior from baseline levels to criterion or nonclinical levels. You want to attribute the ultimate results to one and only one intervention. However, *when two or more interventions are applied to the same behavior, the ultimate levels of the*

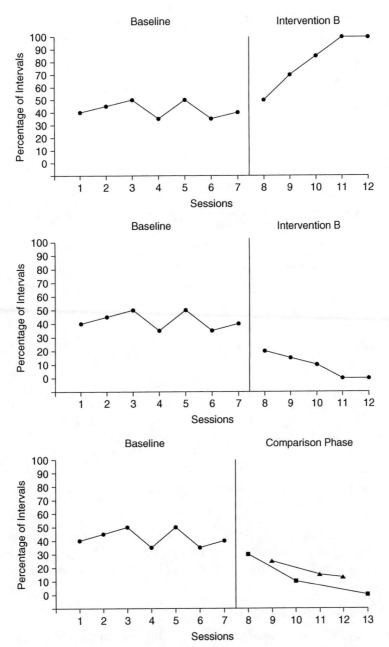

Figure 12.2 Examples of non-reversibility of behaviors precluding a comparison or producing too few replications to draw strong conclusions.

behavior cannot be attributed to only one intervention. This situation is illustrated in Figure 12.3. In the top graph, the behavior got to 100% correct (sessions 12 and 13), but this level of responding cannot be attributed to either intervention alone. Perhaps each intervention individually would establish that level of responding, but that conclusion goes beyond the data. In the bottom graph, the behavior decelerated quickly, and Intervention B appears to be superior to Intervention C, but Intervention B may not have had the same effect if it were not alternated

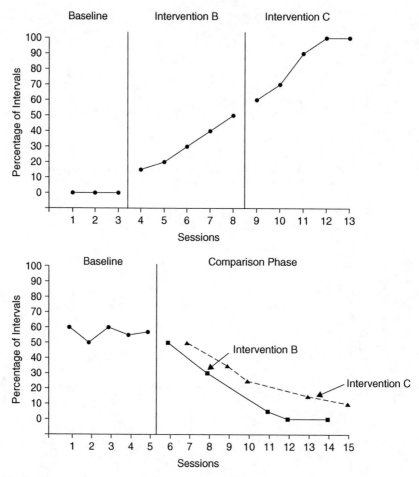

Figure 12.3 Prototype of separation of treatments problem.

with Intervention C. It may have resulted in more rapid deceleration, or perhaps no deceleration at all. This inability to attribute the ultimate behavior change to one and only one intervention is known as the separation of treatment issue (Holcombe et al., 1994).

Comparative Single Subject Designs

Four comparative designs and related variations are discussed in the following sections to use in comparison studies. This section contains a description of the designs, the manner in which they deal with threats to internal validity, guidelines for using them, and their advantages and limitations.

When conducting comparative studies, you must select a design to answer the research question(s), but often more than one design could be used. Some of the issues to consider when deciding which comparative single subject design to use are: (a) whether behaviors being studied are reversible; (b) amount of time available for doing the study; (c) how many participants are accessible; and (d) whether a particular aspect of the research causes one design to be favored. In Table 12.2 the comparative designs are listed by whether they are relatively fast (require little time) and by the type of behavior being studied, reversible or

Table 12.2 Summary of Comparative Designs Categorized by Speed of Comparison and Type of Behavior Studied[a]

	Speed of the comparison	
Type of behavior studied	Fast comparison	Slow comparison
Readily reversible behavior	Alternating treatments design (ATD) Multi-element design (M-ED)	Multi-treatment design (MTD)
Non-reversible behavior	Adapted alternating treatments design (AATD)	Parallel treatments design (PTD)

Note:
a This table was developed by John W. Schuster of the University of Kentucky and was used with his permission.

nonreversible. Comparative single subject designs use at least one of the following rules to order experimental conditions: (a) introduction of the independent variable for a few observations, withdrawal of the independent variable for a few observations, and reinstatement of the independent variable for a few observations; (b) staggered (time-lagged) introduction of the independent variable across tiers; and (c) rapid, iterative implementation of the independent variables across observations (Horner et al., 2005). Some comparative designs use more than one rule. These rules can be combined in a variety of ways to study interactions between two or more interventions or an intervention and multiple contextual variables.

Multitreatment Designs

Description
Multitreatment designs are perhaps the oldest comparative single subject experimental designs (Birnbrauer, Peterson, & Solnick, 1974). These designs use the introduction, withdrawal, and reintroduction of the independent variables rule to order conditions. Multitreatment designs are similar to withdrawal designs (Chapter 10) with an important distinction: A minimum of "two" rather than "one" variable is manipulated when experimental conditions change. One intervention (B) is used for multiple observations, and when it is withdrawn the second intervention (C) is introduced and used instead of returning to baseline condition. Subsequently, the second intervention is withdrawn and the first is reintroduced and used, and finally, the first is again withdrawn and the second is used (e.g., A-B-C-B-C). Each condition remains in effect for multiple observations, as is done with the withdrawal design. The decision to make a change in the experimental conditions is based on stability of the data.

Multitreatment designs, as with withdrawal designs, require only one dependent variable, but more are allowed and are recommended. When multiple behaviors are measured, you should use one behavior to make decisions about when to change experimental conditions. This behavior should be identified before the study begins. Additional behaviors can be viewed as secondary or generalization measures. For example, if a study compares two interventions for a problem behavior, you might also measure adaptive behavior such as on-task or task-completion behaviors. The multitreatment design can be used to study both acceleration and deceleration behaviors. Multitreatment designs should be used only with *reversible behaviors* and may require a large number of observations.

Notation of experimental conditions for multitreatment designs follows the rules described in Chapter 9. "A" refers to baseline conditions. Each intervention is assigned a separate letter using the alphabetical order starting with "B" and reflecting the order in which interventions are applied in the study. Hyphens are placed between letters to indicate when changes in experimental conditions occurred. More than one letter (e.g., BC) without a hyphen indicates the procedures of B and C were used simultaneously. Thus, an A-B-C-B-C design indicates a baseline condition (A) was followed by intervention B, then by intervention C, then by reinstatement of intervention B, and finally by reinstatement of intervention C. Another common multitreatment design is A-BC-B-BC-B; this indicates a baseline condition (A) was followed by an intervention with two components B and C (BC without a hyphen). The BC intervention was followed by the removal of component C but maintenance of component B (B), then the combined components B and C (BC) were used, and finally component B (B) was used alone again. Parametric variations of an independent variable are signified with the use of a prime ('). For example, A-B-B'-B-B' indicates a baseline condition (A) was used, which was followed by use of intervention B (B), followed by a parametric (less or more) variation of the same independent variable B (B'), which was followed by the reinstatement of independent variable B (B), which in turn was followed by reinstatement of the parametric variation (B'). If two parametric variations are used, the design could be depicted as such: A-B-B'-B-B'-B''-B'-B''.

Multitreatment designs can be used with or without a baseline condition. When possible and logically reasonable, baseline conditions should be used. Having a baseline condition allows you to show how each intervention changes performance patterns from a pre-intervention condition. This information is needed to make generalizations about the effects of interventions to no-treatment conditions (Birnbrauer, 1981). Some comparisons, however, do not have a logical baseline condition. For example, a teacher may want to compare two ways of arranging the physical space of the classroom; may want to compare child- or teacher-choice of some instructional variable (e.g., order of completing assignments); or may want to compare individual and group contingencies. In such studies, a baseline condition may not be relevant.

The primary, but not exclusive, use of multitreatment designs is to construct (build) and deconstruct (take apart) treatment packages. It can be used when an initial treatment package is not effective—taking advantage of the dynamic nature of single subject designs. For example, if you began with a baseline and then implemented an intervention, but the intervention did not change the frequency of the behavior, you could add a component to the intervention and evaluate the effects of the modified intervention. The design might be A-B-BC-B-BC. On the other hand, you may begin with a treatment package and systematically remove components to evaluate the relative contribution of each component to the behavior change. In such cases, the design might be: A-BCD-BC-BCD-BC-B-BC-B.

The effects of single subject designs are shown through multiple replications in the study (Edgar & Billingsley, 1974), and multitreatment designs are no exception. An A-B-C multi-treatment design does not have sufficient replications to control for maturation and history and precludes conclusions that a functional relation exists, but correlations may be noted as with an A-B design. At minimum, a demonstration and replication are needed (i.e., A-B-C-B); in practice, a demonstration and two replications are expected: A-B-C-B-C or B-C-B-C. This applies to each experimental manipulation in the study. For example, an A-B-C-B-C-D design has three changes for B and C (B to C, C to B, and B to C) but only one for A to B and C to D. Sufficient replications exist to draw functional conclusions about B and C but not about A and B or C and D. In addition, four to six participants are recommended to ensure adequate inter-subject replications.

When comparing two or more interventions in a multitreatment design the order of using them should be counterbalanced across participants. This is done for two reasons: (a) to help detect sequence effects, and (b) to have each intervention be adjacent to the baseline condition multiple times. In terms of sequence effects, if all participants had the same order of experimental conditions (e.g., A-B-C-B-C) you could not claim intervention C would be effective without following intervention B. A stronger arrangement is to have three participants follow the A-B-C-B-C sequence and three other participants follow the A-C-B-C-B sequence. If this is done, and C is clearly superior to B across all intra- and inter-subject replications, then you could conclude C is superior regardless of its sequence with B. It also allows you to describe the effects of both B and C compared to the baseline condition, which assists in making generalizations and recommendations.

Internal Validity Issues

When using multitreatment designs, experimental control requires you meet several criteria. First, you must attempt to detect plausible threats to internal validity (e.g., instrumentation, lack of treatment fidelity, maturation, history), and if detected take appropriate steps to control those threats. Second, you should introduce or remove only one intervention, component, or parametric variation at a time. An A-BCD-BC-BCD-BC sequence is appropriate, because only the D component is removed when moving to the BC condition, and only the D component is added when reinstating the BCD condition. An A-BCD-B-BCD-B would not be appropriate, because both C and D are simultaneously removed. Third, you must have sufficient number of experimental manipulations (demonstration and replications) to build a believable case that an experimental manipulation was related to resulting shifts, or lack thereof, in data patterns. Thus, an A-B-C-D design would not have replications and should not be used, but an A-B-BC-B-BC has sufficient replications. Fourth, the data must shift in a consistent manner each time experimental manipulations are made. For example, in an A-B-BC-B-BC design, the BC condition must consistently show data patterns distinctly different from B conditions; all B conditions must show similar data patterns and all BC conditions must show similar data patterns. Ideally shifts will be consistent and large each time conditions change, with consistency (not magnitude) of change being most critical. As with other single subject designs you can only analyze data shifts across adjacent conditions. In an A-B-BC-B-BC-BCD-BC-BCD design the only legitimate comparisons of are B and BC, and BC and BCD. You cannot conclude BCD is more or less effective than B, because they are not adjacent. All interventions in a multitreatment design study are used to treat the same behavior; thus, the *separation of treatments* issue applies. You may be able to conclude one intervention is superior to another (depending upon the data patterns) but you cannot attribute the ultimate levels of behavior change to a single intervention.

Also, because interventions are applied to the same behavior, *multitreatment interference* is likely in the form of slow-paced sequence effects. When multitreatment interference is suspected, extending the length of a condition will help control for this effect. This is illustrated in Figure 12.4; Intervention B resulted in an increase in level and an accelerating trend. When Intervention C was used, the first few data points had values similar to those in B. By extending the C condition, the data subsequently dropped, indicating multitreatment interference may have been operating when Intervention C initially was used.

Multitreatment designs tend to be quite long. If each condition only had three data points, the simplest multitreatment design would require at least 15 observations. The more usual case is that two or three times that number of observations is needed. The length of the design means many *threats to internal validity* can occur. *Observer drift and bias* are more likely with each additional observation and condition. Interobserver agreement assessments (IOA) should occur regularly (20–30% of the sessions) and should be collected on each participant in each condition. Similarly, because procedures change from one condition to the next, direct assessment of *procedural fidelity* should occur in each condition for each participant, usually in

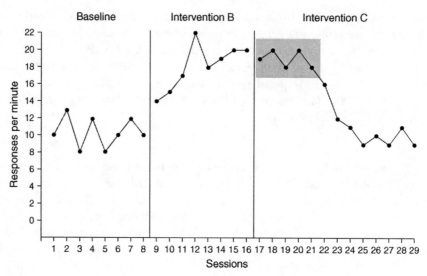

Figure 12.4 Prototype of slow sequence effects.

20–30% of sessions. More frequent assessment of procedural fidelity is needed when doing component analyses, because implementers will be expected to use and not use different components across conditions, increasing the likelihood of procedural errors. The length of the design also increases the probability that *maturation* and *history* threats will occur. *Attrition* (loss of participants) also is possible given design length. You must be alert to the possibility of these effects when planning and conducting such studies. In this design (a) separation of treatments issue applies—all interventions are applied to the same behavior; (b) nonreversibility of effects is possible, thus, the design only should be used with readily reversible behaviors; and (c) multitreatment interference in the form of slow-paced sequence effects is likely—extend conditions when it is suspected and counterbalance the order of experimental conditions across participants to detect sequential confounding.

External Validity Issues
Systematic replication requires careful description of experimental procedures and parameters and detailed description of factors controlling participants' pre-experimental and baseline functioning (Birnbrauer, 1981). Generalizations are made to baseline conditions and to individuals in situations similar to the baseline conditions whose behavior is controlled by factors similar to those of study participants. For this reason having a baseline condition in multitreatment designs is desirable. When a baseline condition is not logical, then knowing factors controlling participants' pre-experimental behavior is critical information in making sound generalizations from multitreatment design studies. Another problematic issue in making generalizations from these designs deals with sequence issues. For example, in an A-B-BC-B-BC design, generalizations about the effects of BC can only be made to the B condition and not to the A condition. You can stipulate that given participants whose behavior is similar to the patterns in the A condition and controlled by the same factors, then BC is likely to influence their behavior if they initially experience the B condition alone.

In comparative studies, including those with multitreatment designs, you want to make recommendations (generalizations) about the relative merits of one intervention or component over another. You may discover, for example, intervention C is superior in some important way to intervention B, but all findings are conditional and limited. Conditional means the finding is dependent upon the situation in which it was studied and identified. In different situations, the finding may not be replicated. Thus, you must identify the "key" study variables to define for whom and under what situations the finding is likely to replicate. Likely candidates are factors controlling participants' pre-experimental behavior, their entry-level skills, active variables in the setting where the study occurred, and components and parameters of the procedures used.

Guidelines

Multitreatment designs are useful for answering many research questions, including comparisons of two different interventions, analyses of components of treatment packages, and parametric analyses. Guidelines for using a basic A-B-C-B-C multitreatment design are listed below. You should:

1. Identify and define a reversible target behavior; and select and use a sensitive, reliable, valid, and feasible data-collection system.
2. Identify and define nontarget behaviors of the same response class as target behaviors or other nontarget behaviors which may co-vary (positively or negatively) with changes in the target behavior; select and use a sensitive, reliable, valid, and feasible data-collection system.
3. Use and specify the inclusion criteria to select participants, ideally this includes some quantification of their performance on variables used in the selection process.
4. Collect continuous baseline data (A) on target behaviors for a minimum of 3 consecutive days or until data are stable.
5. Collect, calculate, and analyze interobserver-agreement (IOA) data and procedural-fidelity (PF) data for each participant during all experimental conditions (e.g., A, B, C).
6. Introduce Intervention B only after a stable contratherapeutic or zero-celeration trend has been established in the initial baseline (A) condition.
7. Collect continuous data during Intervention B on target behaviors for a minimum of 3 consecutive days or until data are stable, and continue to monitor nontarget behaviors on a regular schedule.
8. After a stable data pattern occurs under Intervention B, withdraw Intervention B and introduce Intervention C.
9. Collect continuous data during Intervention C on the target behaviors for a minimum of 3 consecutive days or until the data are stable, and continue to monitor nontarget behaviors on a regular schedule.
10. After a stable data pattern occurs under Intervention C, withdraw Intervention C and reintroduce Intervention B.
11. Repeat steps 7–10.
12. Replicate with similar participants, and counterbalance the order of implementing interventions if sufficient participants are available. For some participants use A-B-C-B-C and for others use A-C-B-C-B.

Advantages

Multitreatment designs are flexible, making them useful for a variety of important comparisons with reversible behaviors. They can be used to compare different interventions (e.g., A-B-C-B-C); in component analyses to build interventions (A-B-BC-B-BC-BCD-BC-BCD) or to take treatment packages apart (A-BCD-BC-BCD-BC-B-BC-B); and in studying parametric variations of an independent variable (A-B-B'-B-B'-B''-B'-B''). Multitreatment designs are useful with a variety of different types of interventions, such as environmental arrangements (room arrangements, manipulations of materials), consequence-based interventions (contingencies), and antecedent-based interventions (e.g., self-monitoring, rule statements). The designs can be used when the goal is to accelerate target behaviors or to decelerate behaviors. Besides its flexibility, these designs only require measurement of one reversible behavior. Data-analysis procedures are similar to those used with withdrawal designs.

Limitations

Despite the advantages, these designs have limitations. Multitreatment designs should only be used with reversible behaviors. It is not useful for evaluating strategies to promote acquisition of new behaviors. Sequence effects are likely, and it does not solve the separation of treatments issue. The design also requires a long time to complete, producing an increased risk of important threats to internal validity, including instrumentation (observer drift and bias), lack of procedural fidelity, maturation, history, and attrition.

Variations

The design has a many variations, all following the above guidelines and using the introduction, withdrawal, and reintroduction rule to order experimental conditions. Another variation is to add the time-lagged rule to order experimental conditions. When used across participants, the baseline condition can be time-lagged to add evidence that the first independent variable changed performance from the baseline data patterns. This variation is recommended when the multitreatment design is used across participants. Table 12.3 summarizes studies using a multitreatment design to evaluate behavior change.

Applied Example: A-B-BC-A-BC-B-BC Design

Falcomata, T. S., Roane, H. S., Hovanetz, A. N., Kettering, T. L., & Keeney, K. M. (2004). An evaluation of response cost in the treatment of inappropriate vocalizations maintained by automatic reinforcement. *Journal of Applied Behavior Analysis, 37,* 83–87.

Falcomata, Roane, Hovanetz, Kettering, and Keeney (2004) evaluated the effects of noncontingent reinforcement (NCR) and NCR plus Response Cost in treating inappropriate vocalizations maintained by automatic reinforcement. Derek, an 18-year-old male diagnosed with autism participated. Sessions were 10 min and conducted in small rooms approximately 4 by 5 meters. Data were collected on (a) the duration of inappropriate vocalizations (reported as percentage of session time) using total-duration recording and (b) choice behavior (Derek being inside one of two rooms) by trained observers.

Prior to intervention, a functional analysis was conducted to identify the reinforcer maintaining inappropriate vocalizations. Results indicated the behavior was maintained by "automatic reinforcement," as shown by the high percentage of session time Derek engaged in the target behavior during the "Alone" condition (see Figure 12.5, top panel). During the treatment study the Alone condition served as baseline condition (A), except that Derek was placed in a room with a therapist and Walkman. The Walkman had been identified as a preferred item and would be used in the NCR (B) and NCR plus Response Cost (BC) intervention conditions. During baseline condition, the Walkman was present but Derek was denied access to it. Its use during baseline condition was to control for its presence alone being responsible

Table 12.3 Summary of Several Studies That Used a Multitreatment Design (MT) to Evaluate Experimental Control

Reference	Participants	Setting/arrangement	Independent variable	Dependent variable
Ahearn, W. H., Kerwin, M. E., Eicher, P. S., & Lukens, C. T. (2001). An ABAC comparison of two intensive interventions for food refusal. *Behavior Modification, 25*, 385–405.	Number: 2 Sex: male Age range: 4 yr Disability/diagnosis: PDD-NOS, autoimmune enteropaty, chronic anemia, anal condyloma, failure to thrive, and gastroesophal geal	Setting: hospital room and therapy room (3.1 m by 3.7 m) Arrangement: individual	Non-removal of spoon and physical guidance	Percentage of trials with the occurrence of acceptance, disruption, negative vocalizations
Buckley, S. D., & Newchok, D. K. (2005). An evaluation of simultaneous presentation and differential reinforcement with response cost to reduce packing. *Journal of Applied Behavior Analysis, 38*, 405–409.	Number: 1 Sex: female Age range: 9 yr Disability/diagnosis: autism	Setting: Private schools' assessment room (3 m by 2.3 m) Arrangement: individual	Simultaneous presentation Differential reinforcement paired with response cost	Number of intervals of food retention in the mouth (packing)
Call, N. A., & Falcomata, T. S. (2005). A preliminary analysis of adaptive responding under open and closed economies. *Journal of Applied Behavior Analysis, 38*, 335–348.	Number: 2 Sex: male Age range: 14 yr–18 yr Disability/diagnosis: autism/mild mental retardation/Smith-Magenis Syndrome	Setting: 9 m by 9 m classroom located in school facility and 4 m by 4 m padded therapy room Arrangement: individual	Open economy reinforcement verses closed economy reinforcement	Frequency of responding
Embrey, D. G., Yates, L., & Mott, D. H. (1990). Effects of neuro-developmental treatment and orthoses on knee flexion during gait: A single-subject design. *Physical Therapy, 70*, 626–637	Number: 1 Sex: female Age range: 2yr 8 mo Disability/diagnosis: diplegia, limb hypotonia with hyperextensible joints, decreased should co-contraction	Setting: Children's Therapy Unit of Good Samaritan Hospital Arrangement: individual	Orthoses	Reduce excessive knee flexion during gait
Freeman, K. A., & Dexter-Mazza, E. T. (2004). Using self-monitoring with an adolescent with disruptive classroom behavior. *Behavior Modification, 28*, 402–419.	Number: 1 Sex: male Age range: 13 yr Disability/diagnosis: ADHD, conduct disorder, adjustment disorder, mathematics disorder	Setting: residential facility for youth with conduct problems Arrangement: individual	Self-monitoring Self-monitoring plus matching (paraprofessional recorded behavior at same time)	Percent combined of off-task and disruptive behavior
Fisher, W. W., Thompson, R. H., Hagopian, L. P., Bowman, L. G., & Krug, A. (2000). Facilitating tolerance of delayed reinforcement during functional communication training. *Behavior Modification, 24*, 3–29.	Experiment 1 Number: 1 Sex: male Age range: 3yr Disability/diagnosis: cerebral palsy and severe to profound intellectual disability	Setting: padded treatment room Arrangement: individual	Functional Communication Training (FCT) FCT plus extinction (EXT)	Responses of destructive behavior and communication per minute (rate)

(Continued)

Table 12.3 Continued

Reference	Participants	Setting/arrangement	Independent variable	Dependent variable
Hanley, G. P., Piazza, C. C., Fisher, W. W., & Maglieri, K. A. (2005). On the effectiveness of and preference for punishment and extinction components of function-based interventions. *Journal of Applied Behavior Analysis, 38*, 51–65.	Number: 2 Sex: 1 male; 1 female Age range: 5 yr–8 yr Disability/diagnosis: moderate intellectual disabilities, autism, seizure disorder, ADD, oppositional defiant disorder	Setting: treatment rooms (3 m × 3 m) Arrangement: individual	FCT plus punishment for one participant FCT vs. NCR for another participant	Aggressive responses per minute and problem behaviors per minute
McCord, B. E., Grosser, J. W., Iwata, B. A., & Powers, L. A. (2005). An analysis of response-blocking parameters in the prevention of pica. *Journal of Applied Behavior Analysis, 38*, 391–394.	Number: 3 Sex: male Age range: 40 yr–48 yr Disability/diagnosis: profound mental retardation	Setting: 3.1 m by 3.4 m assessment room in state residential center Arrangement: individual	Response blocking	Frequency of pica successes and attempts
Roane, H. S., Call, N. A., & Falcomata, T. S. (2005). A preliminary analysis of adaptive responding under open and closed economies. *Journal of Applied Behavior Analysis, 38*, 335–348.	Number: 2 Sex: male Age range: 14 yr–18 yr Disability/diagnosis: autism/mild mental retardation/Smith-Magenis Syndrome	Setting: Participant 1: 9 m by 9 m classroom in treatment/school facility Participant 2: 4 m by 4 m padded room Arrangement: individual	Open and closed economies	Frequency of responses (envelope sorting, math worksheets that contained 25 single-digit addition problems)
Saunders, R. R., McEntee, J. E., & Saunders, M. D. (2005). Interaction of reinforcement schedule, a behavioral prosthesis, and work-related behavior in adults with mental retardation. *Journal of Applied Behavior Analysis, 38*, 163–176.	Number: 3 Sex: male Age range: adults Disability/diagnosis: severe/profound intellectual disability	Setting: simulated sheltered workshop workstation Arrangement: individual	Variable-interval (VI) and fixed-ration (FR) schedules of reinforcement	Percentage of sessions on task
Smith, S. L., & Ward, P. (2006). Behavioral interventions to improve performance in collegiate football. *Journal of Applied Behavior Analysis, 39*, 385–391.	Number: 3 Sex: male Age range: college age Disability/diagnosis: typical	Setting: college football field Arrangement: group	Public posting of performance plus error correction verses public posting of performance plus error correction and goal setting	Percent correct of block, routes and releases during practice sessions and games
Tarbox, R. S., Tarbox, J., Ghezzi, P. M., & Wallace, M. D. (2007). The effects of blocking mouthing of leisure items on their effectiveness as reinforcers. *Journal of Applied Behavior Analysis, 40*, 761–765.	Number: 2 Sex: male Age range: 4 yr–5 yr Disability/diagnosis: Autism	Setting: room (2.5 m by 2.5 m) Arrangement: individual	Blocking stereotypic mouthing of leisure reinforcers.	Percentage of intervals with object mouth and toy contact

Citation	Participants	Setting	Independent variable	Dependent variable
Tiger, J. H., & Hanley, G. P. (2005). An example of discovery research involving the transfer of stimulus control. *Journal of Applied Behavior Analysis, 38*, 499–509.	Number: 2 Sex: 1 male; 1 female Age range: 5 yr Disability/diagnosis: 1 typical development 1 non-specified developmental delays	Setting: 5 m by 5 m room designed to emulate classroom Arrangement: group (2:1)	Multiple schedules involving extinction and reinforcement	The number of social approach responses
Wilder, D. A., Zonneveld, K., Harris, C., Marcus, A., & Reagan, R. (2007). Further analysis of antecedent interventions on preschoolers' compliance. *Journal of Applied Behavior Analysis, 40*, 535–539.	Number: 3 Sex: male Age range: 30–42 mo Disability/diagnosis: 2 typical; 1 diagnosed with Fragile X	Session: small room at children's hospital and home Arrangement: individual	Noncontingent reinforcement condition compared to warning condition	Percentage of compliance
Zanolli, K., Daggett, J., Ortiz, K., & Mullins, J. (1999). Using rapidly alternating multiple schedules to assess and treat aberrant behavior in natural settings. *Behavior Modification, 23*, 358–378.	Number: 4 Sex: 3 male, 1 female Age range: 29 mo–11 yr Disability/diagnosis: seriously emotionally disturbed, typical development autistic	Settings: 1 participant: university-based day care, 2 participants: school setting, 1 participant home Arrangement: individual	Rapidly alternating multiple schedules (RAMS) (consequent component and no consequent component) Differential reinforcement of alternative behavior (DRA)	Rate of disruptive and aggressive behaviors

for behavior changes in other conditions. In NCR, Derek had continuous access to the Walkman, and no consequences were imposed for occurrences of inappropriate vocalizations. NCR plus Response Cost was identical to the NCR condition except the Walkman was removed for 5 s contingent upon each occurrence of the target behavior. After the intervention study, a choice analysis verified that Derek preferred the Walkman rather than engaging in inappropriate vocalizations.

IOA data were calculated using the "gross method" (smaller duration divided by larger duration multiplied by 100) during 39% of the functional-analysis sessions, 67% of treatment sessions, and 100% of choice-analysis sessions. IOA during functional analysis ranged from 80 to 100% (mean = 93.5%); baseline and intervention conditions ranged from 53.3 to 100% (mean = 94.5%); and choice-making sessions ranged from 96.9 to 100% (mean = 98.5%).

Figure 12.5 presents Derek's data for the functional analysis (top panel), using an alternating treatments design (ATD, M-ED variation), treatment comparison study (middle panel), using a multitreatment design, and choice analysis (bottom panel). In the middle panel, an A_1-B_1-BC_1-A_2-BC_2-B_2-BC_3 multitreatment design was used. Results indicate high levels of inappropriate vocalizations during baseline conditions (A_1 and A_2) with lower percentages of time engaged in inappropriate vocalizations during both treatment conditions. In the initial baseline condition (A_1), Derek's mean percentage of time engaged in the target behavior was 99.1% and was stable in level and trend across the three sessions of the condition. Upon introduction of NCR (B_1) there was an immediate decrease in level, however, this abrupt change in level was followed by a variable increasing trend in a contratherapeutic direction. Introduction of NCR plus Response Cost (BC_1) resulted in an immediate and abrupt change in level to near zero (mean = 1.2%). Upon reintroduction of baseline condition (A_2) there was an immediate and abrupt change in level with a mean of 98.9% of session time engaged in inappropriate vocalizations. Reintroduction of NCR plus Response Cost (BC_2) replicated levels shown in BC_1 (mean = 0.3%). Researchers subsequently withdrew the response-cost component and returned to NCR alone (B_2), which replicated higher levels of inappropriate vocalizations shown in B_1 (mean = 60.9%). Once high levels of responding were established in B_2 a return to the more effective treatment (BC) was reinstated. Once again, an immediate decrease in level (mean = 1.6%) with a stable and therapeutic pattern occurred. The BC_1-A_2-BC_2 comparison showed the superiority of NCR plus Response Cost over the Alone condition, while the BC_2-B_2-BC_3 showed its superiority over the NCR condition without the response-cost component. In both cases, a functional relation was demonstrated, however, because only one participant was studied, a need exists to replicate the findings before generalizing to other individuals and other inappropriate behaviors. Only a correlation relation can be deduced regarding NCR being superior to the baseline Alone condition (B_1 to A_1) since there was no return to the Alone condition immediately following B_1.

Alternating Treatments Design (ATD) and Multi-element Design (M-ED)

Description
The alternating treatments design (ATD; Barlow & Hayes, 1979) and the multi-element design (M-ED; Ulman & Sulzer-Azaroff, 1975) are similar procedurally, but many variations of the designs exist as described below. The ATD is often used to evaluate two or three interventions; thus, it is used to compare interventions. The M-ED can be used to compare interventions, but more often it is used to assess factors that may be maintaining challenging behavior. As a result

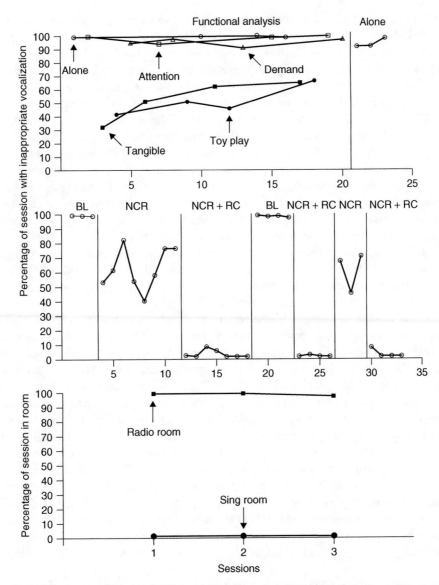

Figure 1. Average percentage of engagement in inappropriate vocalizations during the functional analysis (top panel) and treatment analysis (middle panel) and choice responding during the choice analysis (bottom panel). BL = baseline.

Figure 12.5 Average percentage of engagement in inappropriate vocalization during the functional analysis (top panel) and treatment analysis (middle panel) and choice responding during the choice analysis (bottom panel). BL = baseline (source: Falcomata et al., 2004. Figure 1. Copyright by Society for the Experimental Analysis of Behavior, Inc. Reproduced by permission).

four or five conditions are used (compared) and none may be considered an intervention. Nonetheless, the ATD also can be used to assess the effects of different conditions rather than comparing interventions, and the M-ED can be used to compare interventions. Thus, in this chapter, these designs are treated as the same basic design, and are referred to as the ATD. Barlow and Hersen (1984, pp. 254–256) discuss the array of terminology related to the design variations.

The ATD uses rapid and repeated manipulation of two or more conditions (independent variables and ideally a baseline condition) across observations as the rule for ordering experimental conditions (Horner et al., 2005). In other words, the compared conditions are alternated across sessions or days. This rapid alternation often is done randomly with a stipulation that no more than two consecutive observations are of the same condition. An ATD study does not require an extended time making it useful to practitioners and researchers.

The ATD requires measurement of one *reversible behavior*. More than one behavior is allowed, and can be conceptualized as side-effect or corollary behaviors. Usually, however, one behavior is viewed as the behavior of interest and is used to make decisions. The design is useful only for reversible behaviors, because the behavior must be free to increase or decrease depending on the intervention being used. The ATD can be used with acceleration and deceleration behaviors. Acceleration behaviors are those you want to increase, such as engagement, appropriate peer interactions, quiz performance, and fluency on academic tasks. Deceleration targets include challenging behaviors such as disruptive, aggressive, stereotypic, and self-injurious behaviors. The duration of observations with the ATD is often short (e.g., 5 to 20 min), although observation duration can be of any length. The base rate of the behavior should be considered in selecting the duration of the observation. The session duration should be long enough to capture several occurrences of the target behavior.

The ATD is flexible, making it useful for many purposes. A major purpose is to assess factors maintaining challenging behaviors (M-ED variation). The intent of such assessments is to identify interventions or characteristics of interventions to treat those behaviors. Often this is done in the context of a broader functional analysis of behaviors (Dunlap et al., 2006) and may use an analogue functional analysis (Iwata, Dorsey, Slifer, Bauman, & Richman, 1994). Such assessments often include four or five conditions designed to identify the motivating operation maintaining the problem behavior; these might be: the participant being alone, contingent attention, contingent receipt of a tangible item, escape from demands, and play (Neef & Peterson, 2007). Other conditions, of course, can be included and individualized to the participant, behavior, and suspected maintaining variables. The conditions (independent variables) are not viewed as interventions; rather, the question is, "Which of the independent variables can be used to devise an intervention?" In general, interventions based on assessments using the M-ED variation of the ATD often result in more effective interventions than when interventions are devised without such assessment (Herzinger & Campbell, 2007). The top panel in Figure 12.5 of the Falcomata et al. study exemplifies the M-ED variation of the ATD.

Another purpose of the ATD is to compare two or more interventions. Interventions could be environmental arrangements such as various seating arrangements during a storybook activity, placement of high- and low-preference items in different classroom areas, or using or not using buddies during classroom transitions. The interventions could be modifications of materials, such as the format (columns or rows) of math problems children are asked to solve, two different adaptive devices for magnifying print for students with low vision, or use of picture or video recipes for independent cooking tasks. They also can be antecedent interventions such as child or teacher choice of the order of completing assignments, types of instructions given to clean up a work area, or various types of attending cues on participant engagement. Interventions also can be consequences for the behavior being studied such as different adult responses to problem behaviors or different consequences for rule infractions. When comparing interventions the ATD can be used to compare two variations of the same intervention, including different parametric variations or the presence or absence of a given intervention component. A parametric comparison of a self-monitoring intervention might involve comparing self-recording every 5 min, every 15 min, or once per hour. The simplest ATD design, which is appropriate for answering comparative questions, is depicted in Figure 12.6 in which Logan et al. (1998) evaluated the effects of small-group composition (typical developing peers compared to peers with disabilities) on the frequency of "happiness behaviors" (smiling, eyes open) of five primary-age children with profound multiple disabilities. Data were collected using a 10-s partial-interval recording procedure, alternated with a 5-s recording period, during small-group activities (gross motor game, music, art) in which time of day, teacher behavior, activities, materials, and number of peers in the group were controlled. The independent variables, group of typical peers vs. a group of peers with disabilities, were

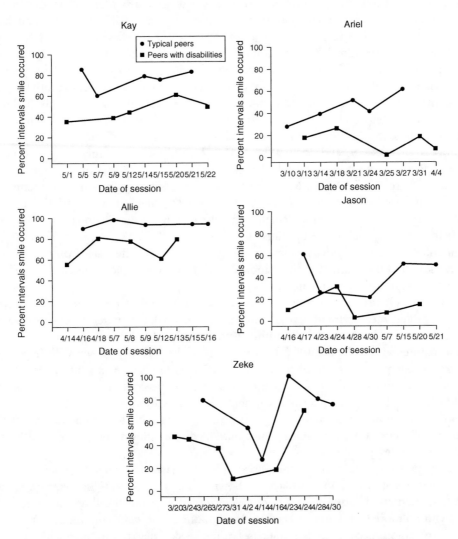

Figure 1. Comparison of peer groups. Percentage intervals that happiness behavior occurred. Circles represent sessions with typical peers. Squares represent sessions with peers with disabilities.

Figure 12.6 Comparison of peer groups. Percentage intervals that "happiness" behavior occurred. Circles represent sessions with typical peers. Squares represent sessions with peers with disabilities (source: Logan et al., 1998. Figure 1. Copyright by The Association for Persons with Severe Handicaps. Reproduced by permission).

randomly scheduled across days with no more than 2 consecutive days of the same group composition. As shown in Figure 12.6, smiles/open eyes were recorded in a higher percentage of intervals for all five children when the group comprised typical peers rather than peers with special needs. There was 100% non-overlapping data points (PND) for four of five children and 80% for the other child, giving credence to students' ability to discriminate between conditions. This simple variation of the ATD is well-suited for studying similar comparative research questions.

Because of the rapid alternation of conditions across observations, a special requirement of the ATD is that a participant must discriminate which condition is in effect in any given session (i.e., stimulus discrimination). This requirement is less of an issue with interventions based on antecedent practices, environmental arrangements, or material modifications. It is, however, a major concern when the intervention is a consequence for a behavior—the behavior must occur before an intervention is used. A strategy for dealing with this is to tell participants which intervention is being used. However, with participants whose language is limited, simply telling them which intervention is in effect will not allow them to make the discrimination. With such participants researchers have used different colored lights, vests, or format boards, had different people implement each of the interventions, or used different rooms or room arrangements to facilitate the discrimination as to which intervention is in effect.

Barlow and Hayes (1979) described the ATD as having four experimental phases: Phase 1 (baseline), Phase 2 (comparison of independent variables), Phase 3 (use of superior treatment alone), and Phase 4 (follow-up). Note: the term, "phase," as used here, refers to conditions being used in the experiment; sometimes, "phase" is used to refer to a small variation in a given condition (e.g., a change in reinforcement schedule during an instructional program), however, in this case, "phase" is used because the second "condition" has two or more separate experimental conditions (independent variables) being rapidly alternated. Unfortunately, an extensive search of the applied literature indicated almost no examples of researchers using the third phase—superior condition alone.

In the ATD, Phase 1, or baseline condition is optional, but recommended. If planned, it involves repeated measurement across consecutive sessions/days under baseline procedures. This condition should remain in effect until data are stable, but unlike other designs stability is not a requirement. In Figure 12.7, five variations of the ATD are shown with hypothetical data: (a) all four phases described by Barlow and Hayes (1979); (b) a study with a baseline and comparison phase without the superior treatment alone condition; (c) a study with the comparison phase and the superior treatment alone condition; (d) a study with only the comparison phase and two interventions; and (e) a study with four interventions without a baseline or superior treatment alone condition. The display shown in panel "e" is often called a multi-element design (M-ED).

After the baseline condition, the comparison phase (Phase 2) is applied by rapidly alternating interventions across sessions or days, as shown in Figure 12.7 (a, right column). As noted previously, alternation should be randomly determined to avoid the threat of cyclical variability, with no more than two consecutive observations of the same condition. In many ATD studies, two sessions occur each day, one observation session per condition, in which the order is counterbalanced across days, as shown in Figure 12.7 (a, left column). An equal number of observations should be scheduled for each condition during the comparison phase with a minimum of five observations per condition. A common and recommended variation of the ATD during the comparison phase is to include baseline condition observations in the alternation. The purpose of alternating baseline condition observations is to detect multitreatment interference. If the behavior during baseline condition sessions remains stable and similar to

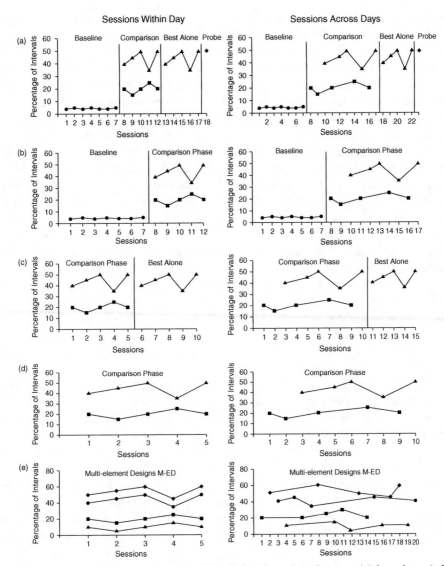

Figure 12.7 Prototype of ATD variations within (left column) and across (right column) days.

data patterns in the initial baseline condition, then multitreatment interference is less likely. If the behavior in these baseline observations deviates from initial baseline patterns (level, trend, variability), then multitreatment interference is likely.

During the comparison phase, data patterns of each experimental condition are compared to one another. A conclusion that one intervention is more "effective" than other(s) is made when the data pattern for that intervention shows a more therapeutic level or trend than data patterns of other conditions. This differentiation can often be accomplished with as few as five observations with each condition. As with other single subject designs, evidence of an effect is based on replications of findings. With the ATD, replications occur within the comparison phase. With each change of conditions in alternating sessions or days, another replication occurs. More alternations are generally better, but when a clear difference exists, more alternations may add relatively little evidence.

Calculation of percentage of non-overlapping data (PND) between conditions being compared is how replication of differences is quantified. Calculating PND with an ATD is different from other single subject designs in that you are looking for consistent differences between data-point values of the conditions alternated during the comparison phase, rather than comparing the data path of each condition against pre-comparison phase (baseline alone) or post-comparison phase (superior condition alone) data. You may choose to do this but the PND operation conducted within the comparison phase is most critical. In calculating PND within the ATD you compare each condition being alternated against each other, for example, you compare the first data-point value of B to the first data-point value of C, then the second data-point value of B to the second data-point value of C, and so on until all data-point values are compared, first to first, second to second, third to third, and so forth. This is done with each condition you are alternating during the comparison phase, for example, B to A, C to A, C to B (see Figure 12.8). Variability in the data paths of each condition is less important; rather, the focus is on whether one condition is consistently superior to the other condition being compared, e.g., over 15 comparison sessions Condition B is superior to Condition C on 5 of the 5 sessions, yielding a PND of 100%. PND is the most critical statistic to report when comparing conditions with the ATD. On occasion, trend may be important when the data paths of compared conditions separate over the course of the comparison phase. In such cases the first part of the comparison phase may show considerable overlap between conditions, but toward the end of the phase, one condition will be consistently higher or lower than the other. This can be analyzed by calculating PND for the first and second halves of the comparison phase, or first and final third of the phase.

When the ATD is used to compare interventions, inter-subject replications are recommended. At minimum three and ideally five or more participants should be included. When the ATD M-ED variation is used to assess the influence of various factors to devise an intervention for a participant, then inter-subject replications are not necessary because the factors maintaining a given problem behavior for one participant may be different for another participant with the same challenging behavior (Neef & Peterson, 2007).

The third phase, superior intervention alone, is used when one of the compared interventions produces a more therapeutic data pattern than the other(s). The intervention producing the more therapeutic data pattern is used without alternating it with other interventions or the baseline condition. This condition is a control for the possibility of a specific type of multi-

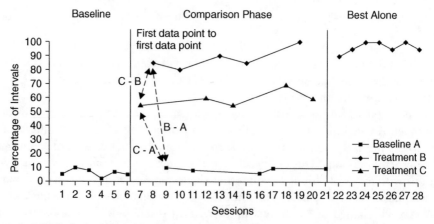

Figure 12.8 Calculating PND with ATD, comparing first data point of each condition to one another, second data point of each condition to one another, etc.

treatment interference called alternation effects (rapid sequence effects; Hains & Baer, 1989). Interventions may function differently when they are used alone in contrast to when they are rapidly alternated with other conditions. In treatment programs an intervention is usually used alone; thus, this superior treatment alone condition attempts to replicate that arrangement. Further, assuming the data pattern does not change in the superior treatment alone condition, this is additional evidence the differences were not due to multitreatment interference.

These three phases (baseline, comparison, superior treatment alone) often are completed in a relatively short time period, especially when multiple sessions occur each day. Some studies with the ATD can be done in 10–20 days. The final phase, follow-up, is seldom included in ATD studies. It can, however, provide an evaluation of how an intervention continues to function when it is used over time; thus, its importance should not be minimized.

To summarize, several variations of the ATD exist. First, a baseline condition does not need to be included, but it is recommended to evaluate multitreatment interference. Second, the ATD can be used to compare a large number of interventions or conditions, including as few as two and as many as five or six. With each additional intervention or condition, the design complexity, the likelihood of multitreatment interference, the study length, and potential difficulties in visually analyzing the data increase. With the comparison of two or three conditions, the design is relatively straightforward. Third, you can choose to alternate baseline sessions with the interventions during comparison phase, which is recommended. Fourth, you can choose to include the superior treatment alone condition, which is recommended. It is not required, although it provides useful information.

Internal Validity Issues
Standard threats to internal validity apply to ATD studies, but the relatively short time frame and rapid alternation of independent variables guards against many threats. Maturation and history threats are assumed to be minimal because ATD studies are conducted over a short time period. Further, and perhaps more convincing, rapid alternation should mean maturation and extra-experimental events would influence performance under all conditions equally. Instrumentation threats, of course, can occur any time data are collected. Lack of procedural integrity is possible with the ATD. Procedural drift is less likely to occur, because interventions are used for relatively short periods of time. However, procedural errors are likely because the rapid alternation of interventions in the comparison phase increase the chances of humans making errors in implementation. Procedural-fidelity data should be collected in each condition and phase of the study as well as for each participant. Keeping all factors other than the independent variables the same is critical in ATD studies. Thus the procedural-fidelity assessment should focus on the components of independent variables and on variables that should not change across conditions. Attrition is possible but less likely than with longer designs (e.g., multitreatment designs).

Multitreatment interference is likely in the comparison phase of the ATD in the form of rapid alternation effects (Hains & Baer, 1989). The superior treatment alone condition is designed to deal with this threat to internal validity (Barlow & Hayes, 1979). If there are changes in level, trend, or variability between the intervention and initial baseline alone conditions and baseline condition data in the comparison phase, multitreatment interference is probable. This detection leaves open the possibility that one of the interventions is influencing performance in sessions of other interventions as well as the baseline sessions. A strategy for dealing with this problem is to increase the amount of time between sessions (McGonigle, Rojahn, Dixon, & Strain, 1987). For example, if multiple sessions are conducted each day and multitreatment interference is detected, conducting only one session per day is advised. A minimum of 1 hour between conditions should be scheduled when multiple conditions are used on the same day.

The ATD does not solve the separation of treatments issue. All interventions are applied to the same behavior being studied. Thus, the ultimate therapeutic levels of the behavior cannot be attributed only to the more (most) effective intervention. *Reversibility of the behavior is critical* in ATD studies. The behavior must be one that is influenced by the immediate change in conditions. If this is not the case, a totally benign intervention will seem to produce an intervention effect because the effective intervention would move the behavior to new levels with each application. If the behavior did not readily reverse, then the benign intervention's data would be at the same level as the previous session with the effective intervention.

External Validity Issues
For the ATD, external validity is in part dependent upon the purpose of the study. If the purpose is to compare two or more interventions or two or more variations of a single intervention, then external validity is similar to other single subject designs. ATD studies carry an important qualifier when making recommendations. Specifically, conclusions must note that the performance under the intervention producing the more (most) therapeutic changes was found in the context of the intervention being alternated with another (other) intervention(s). Using the superior treatment alone condition must include the qualifier that it was done with a history of the alternation with another (other) intervention(s).

If the purpose of the ATD study is to assess factors controlling behavior to devise an individualized intervention (M-ED variation) and if another design is used to evaluate the devised intervention (multiple baseline, or withdrawal design), then the ATD portion of the study provides critical information in making generalizations from the study. Specifically, it describes important information about the types of individuals for whom the devised intervention is likely to be successful. The M-ED portion of study may indicate that contingent attention maintained the problematic behavior. An intervention could be devised and in a subsequent portion of the study be found effective. We would conclude the intervention is more likely to be effective with non-study individuals whose behavior also was maintained by attention rather than some other factor (e.g., escape from tasks). Ideally, all studies would have precise information on key factors influencing participants' relevant behavior, because this fits with the logic of external validity with single subject experimental designs.

Guidelines
When using the ATD, you should:

1. Identify the purpose of the study; is it to compare two or more interventions or two or more variations of the same intervention, or is it to identify factors influencing the participant's behavior to devise an intervention?
2. Use and specify the inclusion criteria to select participants, ideally this includes some quantification of their performance on the variables used in the selection process.
3. When comparing interventions, determine whether a baseline condition is possible; if logical, use a baseline condition.
4. Collect IOA and procedural fidelity data in 20–33% of all conditions.
5. Determine how independent variables to be compared will be applied. Will they be alternated within or across sessions/days? Will their use be determined randomly or intentionally counterbalanced? How many consecutive sessions/days of the same condition will you allow (two are recommended)?

6. Include the baseline or control condition during the comparison phase.
7. Implement the comparison phase by rapidly alternating conditions, and continue until a clear pattern exists in the data with a minimum of five sessions per condition and an equal number of sessions for each condition.
8. When comparing interventions, use the superior independent variable alone for several sessions. When conducting an assessment to identify factors maintaining a behavior, devise an intervention from the assessment and evaluate it.
9. Conduct follow-up assessments if possible.

Advantages

The ATD has three major advantages. First, it provides a rapid method for evaluating two or more interventions or two or more variations of an intervention. The benefits of this rapidity are (a) less investigator time is spent conducting the study; (b) fewer resources are used; and (c) less participant time is devoted to study activities. Second, the ATD is an efficient method for assessing factors maintaining participants' problem behavior and is useful for selecting success-ful interventions. This assessment information is also a solid foundation for making generaliza-tions to other non-study individuals. A third positive feature of the ATD is its flexibility. It can be used with a wide range of interventions and in several different variations.

Limitations

A limitation of the ATD is it is restricted to reversible behaviors. Another limitation is that multitreatment interference can emerge from rapidly alternating interventions across sessions/days. Starting with a baseline alone condition, inserting baseline sessions in the comparison phase, and using a superior treatment alone condition can provide information on multi-treatment interference. Finally, the design provides little information about the effects of an intervention from repeated and continuous use, but this is not the purpose of the design although it is relevant when making practice recommendations. Table 12.4 summarizes selected studies using an ATD to evaluate behavior change.

Variations

As noted above, the ATD has a number of variations, including the number of experimental phases and the number of interventions used. Another variation, referred to as the simultaneous-treatment design involves the participant choosing from two or more interventions to be used (Browning, 1967). Although rarely used (Barlow & Hersen, 1984), a recent example has emerged that is procedurally similar to the simultaneous-treatment design. Heal and Hanley (2007) compared four types of activities preschoolers would choose and measured their choices, the number of tasks completed, and the percentage of intervals of undesirable behavior. The four activities were (a) play; (b) highly preferred materials with praise for correct responses; (c) less-preferred teaching materials and praise and preferred consumable delivered for correct responses; and (d) less-preferred materials with praise as a consequence for correct responses. The children tended to make consistent choices among the activities, and restricting access to the most frequently chosen resulted in consistent selection of another. The number of tasks completed tended to be similar across activity types, but for some children, less problem-atic behavior occurred when they chose the first two types of activities. This study seems to be a model for identifying elements of treatments that could be used.

Table 12.4 Summary of Several Studies That Used an Alternating Treatments Design (ATD) or Multi-Element Design (M-ED) to Evaluate Experimental Control

Reference	Participants	Setting/arrangement	Independent variable	Dependent variable
Erbas, D. (2005). Responses to communication breakdowns by nonverbal children with developmental disabilities. *Education and Training in Developmental Disabilities, 40,* 145–157.	Number: 3 Sex: 2 male, 1 female Age range: 3 yr–4 yr Disability/diagnosis: developmental disabilities	Setting: self-contained classroom at university, during snack Arrangement: individual	Gestural request condition Wrong response condition Ignore condition	Percentage of repair breakdowns (behaviors)
Gast, D. L., Jacobs, H. A., Logan, K. R., Murray, A. S., Holloway, A., & Long, L. (2000). Presession assessment of preferences for students with profound multiple disabilities. *Education and Training in Developmental Disabilities, 35,* 393–405.	Number: 4 Sex: 3 male, 1 female Age range: 6 yr 2 mo–9 yr 1 mo Disability/diagnosis: cerebral palsy, profound intellectual disabilities	Setting: multiple settings Arrangement: individual	Neutral compared to preferred conditions	Total duration of target behavior
Harris, S. R., & Riffle, K. (1986). Effects of inhibitive ankle-foot orthoses on standing balance in a child with cerebral palsy. *Physical Therapy, 66,* 663–667.	Number: 1 Sex: male Age range: 4 yr 6 mo Disability/diagnosis: moderate spastic quadriplegia; cerebral palsy	Setting: not specified Arrangement: individual	Orthoses	Duration of independent standing with and without orthoses
Kodak, T., Northup, J., & Kelley, M. E. (2007). An evaluation of the types of attention that maintain problem behavior. *Journal of Applied Behavior Analysis, 40,* 167–171.	Number: 2 Sex: 1 male; 1 female Age range: 5 yr–9 yr Disability/diagnosis: ADHD, PDD-NOS	Setting: private room in participant's home or therapy room Arrangement: individual	Attention, Demand, Toy Play and Alone conditions	Rate of problem behavior per minute
Logan, K. R., Jacobs, H. A., Gast, D. L., Murray, A., Daimo, K., & Skala, C. (1998). The impact of typical peers on the perceived happiness of students with profound multiple disabilities. *Journal of the Association for Persons with Severe Handicaps, 23,* 309–318.	Number: 5 Sex: 2 male, 3 female Age range: 5 yr 5 mo–10 yr 4 mo Disability/diagnosis: cerebral palsy, developmental delay, hearing impairment, visual impairment, profound intellectual disabilities	Setting: self-contained classroom Arrangement: small group	Typical peers compared with peers with disabilities	Percentage of target behavior (smiling, eyes open) occurred
Mechling, L. C. (2006). Comparison of the effects of three-approaches on the frequency of stimulus activations, via a single switch by students with profound intellectual disabilities. *Journal of Special Education, 40,* 94–102.	Number: 3 Sex: male Age range: 5 yr 6 mo–18 yr 10 mo Disability/diagnosis: cerebral palsy	Setting: multiple settings Arrangement: individual	Adapted toys and devices Cause-and-effect commercial software Instructor-created video programs	Number of stimulus activations
Neef, N. A., Cihon, T., Kettering, T., Guld, A., Axe, J. B., Itoi, M., & DeBar, R. (2007). A comparison of study session formats on attendance and quiz performance in a college course. *Journal of Behavioral Education, 16,* 235–249.	Number: 44 Sex: male and female Age range: college students in special education, psychology and physical education Disability/diagnosis: not applicable	Setting: college classroom Arrangement: group	Game study format Q & A study format No study session Baseline	Mean percentage of correct quiz responses Mean percentage of students who attended study sessions

Citation	Participants	Setting/Arrangement	Conditions	Dependent measures
Paramore, N. W., & Higbee, T. S. (2005). An evaluation of a brief multi-stimulus preference assessment with adolescents with emotional-behavioral disorders in an educational setting. *Journal of Applied Behavioral Analysis, 38,* 399–403.	Number: 3 Sex: male Age range: 9 yr–11 yr Disability/diagnosis: classified as emotional-behavioral disorders	Setting: special education teacher's private office Arrangement: individual	Low, medium, and high preferred items	Percentage of intervals on task
Peyton, R. T., Lindauer, S. E., & Richman, D. M. (2005). The effects of directive and nondirective prompts on noncompliant vocal behavior exhibited by a child with autism. *Journal of Applied Behavior Analysis, 38,* 251–255.	Number: 1 Sex: female Age range: 10 yr Disability/diagnosis: autism and developmental delays	Setting: home Arrangement: individual	Four conditions: no task removal Task removal Directive prompts Nondirective prompts	Rate of noncompliant vocal behavior per minute
Reinhartsen, D. R., Garfinkle, A. N., & Wolery, M. (2002). Engagement with toys in two-year-old children with autism: Teacher selection and child choice. *Journal of the Association for Persons with Severe Handicaps, 27,* 175–187.	Number: 3 Sex: male Age range: 2 yrs Disability/diagnosis: autism and developmental delays	Setting: toddler classroom Arrangement: individual	Two conditions: Teacher selected toy from pool Child chose toy from choice of two from a pool of toys	Percentage of intervals of engagement with toy, and percentage of intervals of problematic behavior
Spooner, F. (1984). Comparisons on backward chaining and total task presentation in training severely handicapped persons. *Education and Training in Developmental Disabilities, 19,* 15–22.	Number: 8 Sex: 5 females, 3 males Age range: 18 yrs to 58 yrs Disability/diagnosis: severe and profound intellectual disabilities	Setting: school therapy room Arrangement: individual	Backward changing verses total task presentation	Percentage of vocational task completed
Tarnowski, K. J., & Drabman, R. S. (1986). Increasing the communicator usage skills of a cerebral palsied adolescent. *Journal of Pediatric Psychology, 11,* 573–581.	Number: 1 Sex: female Age range: 13 yrs Disability/diagnosis: spastic quadriplegia secondary to cerebral palsy	Setting: inpatient care facility Arrangement: individual	Prosthetic assistance device	Task completion time Number of errors Client Subjective ratings or performance difficulty
Tincani, M. (2004). Comparing the picture exchange communication system and sign language training for children with autism. *Focus on Autism and Other Developmental Disabilities, 19,* 152–163.	Number: 2 Sex: 1 male; 1 female Age Range: 5 yr–10 yr Disability/diagnosis: autism	Setting: school classroom Arrangement: individual	PECS Sign language training	Percentage of independent mands
VanDerHeyden, A. M., Snyder, P., Smith, A., Sevin, B., & Longwell, J. (2005). Effects of complete learning trials on child engagement. *Topics in Early Childhood Special Education, 25,* 81–94.	Number: 3 Sex: male Age range: 2 yr 6 mo Disability/diagnosis: two participants diagnosed with moderate intellectual disabilities, one typical developing peer	Setting: each participant's classroom during one activity center-choice period of the day. Arrangement: individual	Elaborate and ensure task completion compared to elaborate and praise only New toy plus no consequence	Percentage intervals differentiated engagement Percentage intervals contact engagement

Adapted Alternating Treatments Design (AATD)

Description

The adapted alternating treatments design (AATD), which was based on the ATD, was developed to compare instructional practices with *nonreversible behaviors* (Sindelar, Rosenberg, & Wilson, 1985). The AATD is useful when comparing interventions for teaching functional, developmental, or academic behaviors. A wide range of strategies can be studied, but the purpose must be to facilitate acquisition of new behaviors. The AATD is not useful for evaluating strategies for promoting the deceleration of challenging behaviors, and it often is not useful for evaluating interventions for influencing the rate of previously acquired behaviors (e.g., to increase fluency). When comparing two different instructional strategies with the AATD, interventions should have been studied sufficiently with demonstration designs to document they are effective, defined as resulting in learning. The interventions also should be refined through a series of studies to identify their most "powerful" form.

A major use of the AATD is to compare the efficiency of instructional strategies. The definition of efficiency has two dimensions. First, to be efficient, a strategy must reliably produce learning (be effective). Second, to be efficient, a strategy must be superior to another strategy on an important dimension. Common dimensions of superiority include (a) the rapidity of learning; (b) the extent of maintenance and generalization; (c) the breadth of learning (e.g., learning two things rather than one); (d) acquiring untrained relations; and (e) influencing future learning (Wolery, Ault, & Doyle, 1992). The most common dimension of efficiency is the rapidity of learning. It often is measured by comparing number of minutes of instruction, number of sessions or trials, number and percentage of errors, and number of trials or sessions to criterion.

The AATD also can be used to refine an intervention, including component analyses. For example, a number of studies documented the effectiveness of a procedure called instructive feedback (Werts, Wolery, Holcombe, & Gast, 1995). It involved presenting extra nontarget information in praise statements during direct instruction but not asking students to respond to that information. When this was done, students learned a great deal of the extra information. In initial studies, the extra nontarget information always had been related to target behaviors. Werts, Wolery, Holcombe, and Frederick (1993) used the AATD to compare two conditions: one in which instructive feedback information was related to target behaviors and one in which it was unrelated. The AATD also can be used to study parametric variations of an intervention. For example, Holcombe, Wolery, and Snyder (1994) used the AATD to compare two high and low levels of procedural fidelity for an instructional strategy.

With the AATD, *instructional strategies (independent variables) are each applied to different behavior sets or behavior chains.* This makes the AATD different from the ATD in which all interventions are applied to the same behavior. A behavior set is a collection of discrete responses (single behaviors of relatively short duration); for example, a list of five words to be read, 10 mathematic problems, or a list of 10 facts to be learned. Response chains are a series of behaviors that when sequenced together to form a complex skill, such as completing a long division problem, putting on a garment, setting a table, making a purchase at a store, or cooking a meal. Target behaviors in AATD studies must meet five criteria. First, behaviors must be nonreversible—the behaviors will continue to be performed after instruction has stopped. Second, behaviors should not be in the participants' repertoire. Third, behaviors must be independent, meaning one behavior set/chain can be acquired without influencing performance on other behavior sets/chains. Fourth, behaviors also must be functionally equivalent, meaning behaviors are likely to be influenced by the same environmental variables (e.g., the instructional strategies being studied). Finally, *behaviors sets/chains must be of equal difficulty*.

This last criterion, behaviors of equal difficulty, is tremendously challenging but extremely important. Behavior sets/chains must be of equal difficulty because the instructional strategies are applied to separate behavior sets or response chains. If the behavior set taught with one strategy were easier than the behavior set taught with the other intervention, then the test of the two interventions would be unfair. Before the study, you must select behaviors to be studied and ensure they are of equal difficulty. Determining whether behavior sets/chains are of equal difficulty is done for each participant individually.

Several methods exist for ensuring behavior sets/chains are of equal difficulty (Romer, Billingsley, & White, 1988). A convincing method is an *experimental evaluation* of the difficulty of behavior sets/chains. This can be accomplished by teaching behaviors to non-participant individuals who are similar to participants who will be recruited for the actual study. The sets/chains would all be taught using the same intervention using the following assumption: If the behavior sets/chains are of equal difficulty, then the same procedure should require the same amount of instruction to establish criterion-level responding. This is a time-consuming and expensive approach, but it is a stringent test of whether the behavior sets/chains are of equal difficulty. Another method is to select behaviors from pools of responses for which *norms* exist. For example, reading, spelling, and other academic behaviors are often listed by grade level and often by divisions within the grade. This method is weak, because a good deal of variability in difficulty can exist even within the same grade level and the same segment of a grade level. A third method is to conduct a *logical analysis* of the difficulty of the responses and discriminations required to perform correctly. This method is perhaps the most commonly used; and if used, you should report the dimensions on which behaviors were logically analyzed. For example, if the target behavior was reading sight words, the logical analysis would focus on (a) number of syllables in each word; (b) configuration of the words; (c) initial consonants; (d) part of speech for each word; (e) any redundant letters across words; (f) the participant's knowledge of the referent of the word; and (g) participant's ability to say each word. Yet another method is to ask *experts to rate* the difficulty of potential target behaviors. When using this method, consult with multiple experts independently and exclude the behaviors on which they disagree.

Another method is to evaluate participants' performance on *related behaviors*. For example, a study may compare two procedures in teaching preschoolers to name pictures (i.e., an expressive-language task). In this case, you should select only pictures the children cannot initially name. You also should assess their ability to point to the correct picture when presented with an array of four pictures and you say, "Point to [name of a picture]" (i.e., a receptive-language task). If children accurately and consistently point to some pictures but not others, then those to which they can point are not of equal difficulty to those to which they cannot accurately point. You should select only those pictures on which the child was correct at chance levels, or only those pictures for which the child was correct at 100% on the receptive-language task. However, having pictures the child could point to when named in one set and those the child could not point to correctly would result in unequal difficulty of sets. The above methods are not mutually exclusive. Combinations of the methods should be used in the same study. Ensuring equal difficulty of behavior sets/chains is fundamental to conducting a fair comparison with the AATD. As a result, plan extra time at the beginning of the study to document carefully that the behavior sets/chains are of equal difficulty. Simply showing that a participant cannot perform behaviors is not sufficient to document that the behaviors are of equal difficulty. When multiple participants are taught the same behavior sets/chains, another option is available: Behaviors can be assigned randomly or counterbalanced across compared strategies. This practice is highly recommended if the same behaviors are taught to two or more participants.

Three behavior sets/chains are recommended in studies comparing two strategies. One for each instructional strategy and one called a control set/chain. If three instructional strategies were being compared, then four behavior sets/chains are recommended. The control set is used to detect whether history or maturation influenced participants' performance. Without the control set, you have no way to detect the presence of these threats to internal validity.

In most cases, the AATD has three sequentially implemented conditions. The first is an initial probe (baseline) condition in which all behavior sets/chains are assessed in multiple sessions. This condition is similar to the multiple probe design (conditions variation; see Chapter 11). With this design a minimum of three observations are needed for each behavior set/chain, but more may be necessary to ensure data are stable. Initial probe condition sessions should be about as long and contain a similar number of trials as later instructional sessions. Ideally, behaviors of the different sets would be assessed in the same probe sessions during the initial probe condition. In probe sessions, correct responses should be reinforced. Although this may seem counterintuitive, the rationale is as follows. First, AATD studies are not about reinforcement effectiveness; their purpose is to compare the efficiency of instructional strategies. By using reinforcement in probe sessions, the purpose of the comparison is preserved. Second, reinforcing behaviors during probe sessions ensures learners will respond and show their optimal performance rather than an artificially deflated performance level. This can be ensured by interspersing some known behaviors and delivering reinforcers for those behaviors.

The second experimental phase is a comparison phase in which the instructional strategies are applied to their respective assigned behavior sets/chains in alternating sessions. *Unlike the ATD, instructional strategies are applied to separate behavior sets/chains.* These sessions may be alternated across days and conducted at the same time each day. Sessions also may occur within the same day; however, the order of sessions should be counterbalanced to detect the effects of time of day. When sessions occur in the same day, at least 1 hour should occur between them to minimize multitreatment interference. If you are concerned about possible multitreatment interference, the time between the sessions can be lengthened (e.g., 3 hours). All aspects other than the instructional strategies should be identical across sessions with different interventions. Examples of such variables are the instructor, reinforcers, type of materials (unless the independent variable is about type of materials), session length, and setting in which the sessions occur. Any variables that are different across sessions may separately or in combination with the instructional strategies be responsible for differences in the data.

The instructional comparison phase usually continues until behaviors meet a predetermined criterion level for each intervention. A common criterion is: three consecutive sessions of 100% correct unprompted responding with continuous reinforcement (CRF) followed by three consecutive sessions of 100% correct unprompted responding when an average of every third response is reinforced (VR3). If one strategy produces criterion-level responding before the other, then periodic review trials/sessions can be conducted for the behavior set/chain which is at criterion. When one strategy produces criterion-level responding before the other, you must decide how long you will continue to use the less-effective strategy if it does not also reach criterion. An acceptable guideline is 1.5 or 2 times the number of sessions it took the effective strategy to reach criterion. Of course an arbitrary cut off would be ignored if the less-effective strategy was on its way to producing criterion-level responding.

The final study phase is a probe condition in which all behavior sets/chains are assessed, including the control set/chain. The procedures of this condition should be identical to those of the initial probe condition.

Internal Validity Issues
The usual threats to internal validity (maturation, history, lack of procedural integrity, instrumentation, attrition) may occur with the AATD design. The detection of maturation and history is accomplished by measuring the control behavior set/chain during the initial and final probe conditions. If therapeutic performance changes occur from the initial to final probe conditions, then maturation or history may be present and account for changes in the behavior sets/chains to which the instructional strategies were applied. Collecting intermittent data on the control behavior set/chain during the comparison phase increases your opportunities to detect maturation or history effects. Since no intervention is applied to the control behavior set/chain, intermittent data collection can be done during probe sessions separate from the instructional sessions. If the control set/chain is not included in the design, maturation and history threats cannot be detected. When this occurs, it is usually because several previous studies using multiple baseline or multiple probe designs have shown the effectiveness of the interventions and absence of maturation and history threats. Instrumentation, of course, is assessed through regular collection of IOA data, which should be done for each participant and behavior set/chain during each condition. Similarly, lack of procedural integrity is detected by regularly collecting procedural fidelity data on each participant and behavior set/chain in each condition. Attrition can be problematic, but each participant in the AATD design stands alone. Showing a functional relation does not depend upon inter-subject replications, but inter-subject replications are important. No firm number of participants is needed in AATD studies, but because these studies focus on instructional efficiency, four or more is recommended.

Multitreatment interference is possible in AATD studies. The effects of multitreatment interference can be minimized by increasing the time between sessions of the different instructional strategies in the comparison phase. Alternating sessions by day is often adequate to minimize multitreatment interference, but it takes longer to complete the study than having multiple sessions each day. However, when conducting the study with several participants at the same time it may be more feasible. Multitreatment interference may be detected by intermittent measurement of the control behavior set/chain during the comparison phase. The AATD solves the separation of treatments issue, because each strategy is applied to separate behavior sets/chains. The AATD is not compromised by the reversibility issue; nonreversible behaviors are selected and the independent variables are applied to separate, but equally difficult behaviors sets/chains. Those behaviors can move from low levels in the initial probe condition to criterion levels in the comparison phase without negatively influencing findings. Unlike demonstration designs (multiple baseline, multiple probe, A-B-A-B) and multitreatment and ATD comparative designs, the AATD presents an additional threat to internal validity: lack of equal difficulty of behavior sets/chains. If the interventions are applied to behavior sets/chains that are *not* of equal difficulty, the comparison is seriously confounded.

External Validity Issues
With the AATD you usually want to make two types of conclusions or generalizations. The first deals with the effectiveness of the instructional strategies—did they result in criterion-level responding? The second deals with the relative efficiency of the compared strategies—did one result in more rapid learning or greater generalization than another? The use of the initial probe condition documenting low levels of correct performance followed by the use of the

instructional strategies during the comparison phase allows an evaluation of the first type of conclusion. However, you should describe the criteria used for selecting participants (e.g., their prerequisite skills). The second type of conclusion is based on data from the comparison phase, usually the efficiency data. You should analyze the data by measure and by participant, and then sum it across participants. When making judgments about the superiority of one strategy over others, several questions arise. Are differences in data for the compared strategies consistent across measures (e.g., minutes to criterion, and trials to criterion)? Are differences consistent across participants? Are differences large enough to be meaningful? Consistency of differences across measures and participants is necessary to conclude one strategy is more efficient than another. You should report all relevant data related to the research questions. Note: the findings apply to participants who meet the selection criteria and are taught behaviors similar to those in the study.

Guidelines
When using the AATD, you should:

1. Identify nonreversible behavior sets/chains participants need to acquire that are independent and functionally equivalent. Identify one behavior set/chain for each instructional strategy and one control set/chain.
2. Use and specify the inclusion criteria to select participants; ideally this includes some quantification of their performance on variables used in the selection process.
3. For each participant, ensure the behavior sets/chains are equally difficult.
4. Establish a learning criterion and a criterion for stopping the comparison if one of the compared instructional strategies is not effective.
5. Conduct an initial probe condition by collecting data on all behavior sets/chains for a minimum of three sessions or until data are stable for each behavior set/chain.
6. Collect IOA and PF data for each participant in 20–33% of the sessions of each study phase and for each strategy.
7. Implement the comparison phase by applying each strategy to its respective behavior set/chain in alternating sessions. If multiple sessions are conducted each day, use counterbalancing to detect effects of time of day.
8. When the compared instructional strategies result in criterion-level responding, initiate the final probe condition.
9. Collect data in the final probe condition for all behavior sets/chains for a minimum of three sessions or until the data are stable for each behavior set/chain.
10. Replicate across three or more additional participants.
11. Conduct follow-up or maintenance checks when appropriate and possible.
12. Summarize and analyze the efficiency data.

Advantages
The primary advantage of the AATD over the multitreatment design and the ATD is that it allows you to compare instructional strategies with nonreversible behaviors, including evaluations of effectiveness and efficiency. Further, unlike the multitreatment design and ATD, it solves the separation of treatments issue and it is not confounded by the reversibility problem. Studies using an AATD can be completed in a relatively short time period. Given an adequate amount of replications across participants, the AATD can provide useful information about the efficiency of one instructional strategy over another.

Limitations

A major limitation of the AATD is the requirement that behavior sets/chains must be of equal difficulty. Failure to establish equal difficulty will result in an unfair evaluation of the compared strategies and in spurious conclusions. Another weakness is the design's inability to detect maturation and history effects until it is too late (i.e., in the final probe condition). This weakness can be abated by collecting intermittent data on the control set/chain during the comparison phase. This practice also potentially allows detections of multitreatment interference. A third limitation is there typically is only one evaluation of the relative efficiency between the compared strategies. If time permits you could use a parallel-treatments design (PTD), discussed in the next section. However, a more practical approach may be to repeat the comparison with two new behavior sets/chains of equal difficulty with another AATD. If the superiority of one intervention over another is consistent with the first comparison, there is greater confidence in the differences between conditions because of the intra-subject replication.

Variations

Two variations are worth noting. In the standard AATD, data are collected on the control set/ chain during the initial and final probe conditions. A variation to detect multitreatment interference, maturation, and history effects is to collect data intermittently on the control set/chain during the comparison phase. This requires more measurement, but is worth the effort. A second variation is to apply the superior (more efficient) strategy to the control set after the final probe condition. This constitutes an intra-subject replication for the more (most) efficient strategy, and it allows you to show how the intervention works when it is not being alternated with another instructional strategy (as during the comparison phase). Table 12.5 summarizes selected studies using an AATD to evaluate the relative effectiveness and efficiency of instructional strategies.

Applied Example: AATD

Cihak, D., Alberto, P. A., Taber-Doughty, T., & Gama, R. I. (2006). A comparison of static picture prompting and video prompting simulation strategies using group instructional procedures. *Focus on Autism and Other Developmental Disabilities, 21,* 89–99.

Cihak, Alberto, Taber-Doughty, and Gama (2006) compared using video and picture prompts in teaching responses chains to six male participants, aged 11 to 12 years, who functioned in the moderate range of intellectual disability (IQ = 38 to 51). Two response chains, withdrawing $20 from the automated teller machine (ATM) and purchasing two items with a debit card, were counterbalanced across prompting procedures. An AATD was used to compare the effectiveness and efficiency of the prompts. Group instruction occurred in each participant's special education class and data were collected in community-based instruction (CBI). The six participants were divided into two groups. Group 1 attended a middle school in the Southeast and Group 2 attended a middle school in the Midwest. The inclusion criteria were: (a) age range 11 to 15 years; (b) cognitive abilities in the moderate intellectual disability range; (c) attended middle school; (d) no sensory deficits; (e) no prior training on target tasks; (f) participation in CBI; (g) parental permission; and (h) participants' verbal consent. Picture prompts were used to teach Group 1 to purchase two items and Group 2 to withdraw $20 from the ATM. Video prompts were used to teach Group 1 how to withdraw $20 and Group 2 how to purchase two items. The chains were deemed equivalent based on each task analysis requiring

Table 12.5 Summary of Several Studies That Used an Adapted Alternating Treatments Design (AATD) to Evaluate Experimental Control

Reference	Participants	Setting/arrangement	Independent variable	Dependent variable
Baumgart, D., & Van Walleghem, J. (1987). Teaching sight words: A comparison between computer-assisted and teacher-taught methods. *Education and Training in Mental Retardation, 22,* 56–65.	Number: 3 Sex: 1 male, 2 female Age range: 18 yr to 45 yr Disabilities/diagnosis: moderate intellectual disabilities	Setting: university summer program office (5 m × 3 m) Arrangement: individual	Computer assisted instruction compared with teacher instruction	Percent of words at criterion
Chavez-Brown, M., Scott, J., & Ross, D. E. (2005). Antecedent selection: Comparing simplified and typical verbal antecedents for children with autism. *Journal of Behavioral Education, 14,* 153–165.	Number: 4 Sex: 3 male; 1 female Age range: 2 yr 4 mo–3 yrs 3 mo Disabilities/diagnosis: autism	Setting: participant's homes Arrangement: individual	Typical verbal antecedents compared to simplified verbal antecedents	Percentage of correct picture selection responses
Hitchcock, C. H., & Noonan, M. J. (2000). Computer-assisted instruction of early academic skills. *Topics in Early Childhood Special Education, 20,* 145–158.	Number: 5 Sex: 3 male; 2 female Age range: 3 yrs 2 mo– 4 yrs 7 mo Disabilities/diagnosis: early childhood learning impairment	Setting: self-contained classroom with 8 students, 3 full-time adults Arrangement: individual	Direct instruction, teacher-assisted instruction and computer-assisted instruction	Percentage of correct matches on the selected skill
Kircaali-Iftar, G., Birkan, B., & Uysal, A. (1998). Comparing the effects of structural and natural language use during direct instruction with children with mental retardation. *Education and Training in Mental Retardation and Developmental Disabilities, 33,* 375–385.	Number: 8 Sex: 7 male, 1 female Age range: 6 yr–11 yr Disabilities/diagnosis: moderate mental retardation	Setting: preschool program in Turkey Arrangement: individual	Structural compared to natural language	Number of correctly identified shapes or colors
Laarhoven, T. V., & Laarhoven-Myers, T. V. (2006). Comparison of three video-based instructional procedures for teaching daily living skills to persons with developmental disabilities. *Education and Training in Developmental Disabilities, 41,* 365–381.	Number: 3 Sex: 2 male, 1 female Age range: 17 yr to 19 yr Disabilities/diagnosis: autism, Down Syndrome, moderate intellectual disabilities	Setting: participant's home (dining room or kitchen) or home school classroom Arrangement: individual	Video rehearsal Video rehearsal plus photos during task engagement	Percentage score for levels of assistance Percentage of independent correct responses Number of prompts to use instructional materials Number of sessions to reach criterion Percentage score for levels of assistance on measures of generalization Percentage of independent correct responses on measures of generalization

Citation	Participants	Setting	Intervention	Dependent measures
Nies, K. A., & Belfiore, P. J. (2006). Enhancing spelling performance in students with learning disabilities. *Journal of Behavioral Education, 15*, 163–170.	Number: 2 Sex: 1 female; 1 male Age range: 8 yr Disability/diagnosis: learning disability	Setting: special education classroom Arrangement: individual	Cover, Copy, Compare Copy only	Number of words spelled correctly
Polychronis, S. C., McDonnell, J., Johnson, J. W., Riesen, T., & Jameson, M. (2004). A comparison of two trial distribution schedules in embedded instruction. *Focus on Autism and Other Developmental Disabilities, 19*, 140–151.	Number: 4 Sex: male Age range: 5 yr–11 yr Disability/diagnosis: multiple disabilities, Down Syndrome, moderate intellectual disabilities, autism	Setting: inclusive classroom Arrangement: individual	30 minute compared to 120 distribution schedules	Percentage correct responses during testing probes, naturalistic probes and the total number of trials to criterion
Poncy, B. C., Skinner, C. H., & Jaspers, K. E. (2007). Evaluating and comparing interventions designed to enhance math fact accuracy and fluency: Cover, copy and compare versus taped problems. *Journal of Behavior Education, 16*, 27–37.	Number: 1 Sex: female Age range: 10 yr Disability/diagnosis: moderate intellectual disabilities	Setting: participant's classroom Arrangement: individual	Cover, Copy, Compare Taped Problems Control	Percentage of correct problems Rate of digits correct per minute
Preis, J. (2006). The effect of picture communication symbols on the verbal comprehension of commands by young children with autism. *Focus on Autism and Other Developmental Disabilities, 21*, 194–210.	Number: 5 Sex: 2 males, 3 females Age range: 5 yr–7 yr Disability/diagnosis: autism	Setting: university speech-language pathology center Arrangement: varied	Picture communication symbol (PCS) compared to no picture communication symbol	Number of commands
Schlosser, R. W., & Blischak, D. M. (2004). Effects of speech and print feedback on spelling by children with autism. *Journal of Speech Language and Hearing Research, 47*, 848–862.	Number: 4 Sex: male Age range: 9 yr–12 yr Disability/diagnosis: autism	Setting: quiet corner of participant's classroom Arrangement: individual	Interventions compared: Print Speech Speech-Print	Percentage of correct words
Schlosser, R. W., Blischak, D. M., Belfiore, P. J., Bartley, C., & Barnett, N. (1998). Effects of synthetic speech output and orthographic feedback on spelling in a student with autism: A preliminary study. *Journal of Autism and Developmental Disorders, 28*, 309–318.	Number: 1 Sex: male Age range: 10 yr Disability/diagnosis: autism	Setting: school library or quiet corner in the classroom Arrangement: individual	Visual Auditory Auditory-Visual	Percentage of words spelled correctly Percentage of correct letter sequences Number of sessions to criterion

(Continued)

Table 12.5 Continued

Reference	Participants	Setting/arrangement	Independent variable	Dependent variable
Singleton, D. K., Schuster, J. W., Morse, T. E., & Collins, B. C. (1999). A comparison of antecedent prompt and test and simultaneous prompting procedures in teaching grocery words to adolescents with mental retardation. *Education and Training in Developmental Disabilities, 34, 182–199.*	Number: 4 Sex: 3 male, 1 female Age Range: 15 yr 3 mo–19 yr 9 mo Disabilities/diagnosis: moderate intellectual disabilities	Setting: self-contained classroom Arrangement: individual	Simultaneous prompting compared to antecedent prompt and test. Included a control set of words	Percentage correct across sets of words
Venn, M. L., Wolery, M., & Greco, M. (1996). Effects of every-day and every-other-day instruction. *Focus on Autism and Other Developmental Disabilities, 11, 15–28.*	Number: 6 Sex: 3 male, 3 female Age range: 3 yr 7 mo to 5 yr 6 mo Disabilities/diagnosis: 4 typically developing, 1 autism, 1 pervasive developmental disorder	Setting: preschool classroom Arrangement: 2 small groups—1 child with disabilities and 2 typically developing peers in each group	Every day instruction with constant time delay, and every-otherday instruction with constant time delay	Percentage of correct responses Number of sessions, trials, minutes of instruction Number and percentage of errors Observational learning
Viel-Ruma, K., Houchins, D., & Fredrick, L. (2007). Error self-correction and spelling: Improving the spelling accuracy of secondary students with disabilities in written expression. *Journal of Behavioral Education, 16, 291–301.*	Number: 3 Sex: male Age range: 16 yr to 18 yr Disabilities/diagnosis: learning disabilities	Setting: special education resource classroom Arrangement: group	Traditional repeated practice Error self-correction	Percentage of correctly spelled words
Holcombe, A., Wolery, M., & Snyder, E. (1994). Effects of two levels of procedural fidelity with constant time delay on children's learning. *Journal of Behavioral Education, 4, 49–73.*	Number: 6 Sex: 3 male, 3 female Age range: 3 yr 5 mo to 4 yr 4 mo Disability: moderate intellectual impairments	Setting: preschool special education classroom Arrangement: two small groups of 3 students each	Constant time delay delivered at high fidelity, and constant time delay with programmed procedural errors on delivery of the controlling prompt	Percentage of correct responses Number of sessions, number and percentage of errors, number and percentage of no responses

12 steps with similar motor responses and equally difficult based on initial baseline group performance (Group 1, 11.2% and Group 2, 11.5% on debit card purchase task; Group 1, 13.3% and Group 2 22.2% on $20 ATM withdrawal task). Data were collected during three phases: (a) initial probe sessions; (b) comparison phase; and (c) one follow-up probe session.

Initial probe-session data were collected during CBI. In each of five sessions, the participant was assessed on both chains. A task direction was delivered and participants had 15 s to initiate the chain. If the participant did not initiate the behavior within 15 s, he was asked if he was finished. If the participant responded "yes" or did not respond within 1 min., probe sessions were discontinued (single-opportunity probe method).

Two group instructional sessions occurred each day, one session per prompting strategy, and order within the day was randomized. For the picture prompts, pictures of each task-analysis step were taken with a digital camera and copied onto a transparency. During instruction the transparencies were displayed on a screen in front of the group for 4 s. For the video-prompts strategy, tapes were made using a Sony 72x camera and iMovie 4.01. A 4-s video clip of each task-analysis step was shown during the video prompting instruction. CBI data collection on target behaviors was scheduled 90 min following instruction. One trial on each chain was conducted during each CBI session, with 15 min between trials. A system of least prompts strategy was used; the hierarchy was: (a) verbal prompt; (b) gesture prompt; and (c) gesture plus verbal prompt. Data were collected using event recording on the number of steps completed independently and the prompt level needed to complete each step. Mastery was set at 100% independent responding for three consecutive sessions. Two weeks after each group met criterion, a follow-up probe session was conducted.

Interobserver and procedural-reliability data were collected simultaneously during 25% of sessions across both conditions. The point-by-point method was used to calculate IOA, and it ranged from 95 to 100% (mean = 98%). Procedural-fidelity data were calculated by dividing the number of observed teacher behaviors by the number of planned teacher behaviors and multiplying by 100. Procedural fidelity ranged from 96 to 100% (mean = 99%).

Results for Group 1 are presented in Figure 12.9. All participants had low stable performance in the initial probe condition for both chains. The picture prompts resulted in an abrupt change in level and a gradual stable accelerating trend to criterion. Similar patterns were observed during baseline and video-prompting conditions for Group 1. These findings were replicated with Group 2. Both prompting strategies resulted in children learning the chains.

Efficiency data for Groups 1 and 2 are shown in Table 12.6. Little difference existed in the number of sessions to criterion for the two prompting strategies, although Edgar had twice as many sessions in the video-prompting instruction. In terms of number of errors to criterion, the four boys had similar numbers across both chains, but Carlos and Drew had more in the video-prompt condition than in the picture-prompt condition.

Parallel-Treatments Design (PTD)

Description

The parallel-treatments design (PTD) was devised to compare instructional practices with *nonreversible behaviors* (Gast & Wolery, 1988). It can be conceptualized as two concurrently operating multiple probe designs—one instructional strategy is evaluated with one multiple probe design, and the second is evaluated with another multiple probe design. The PTD is useful when comparing interventions for teaching functional, developmental, and academic behaviors. As with the AATD, a wide range of strategies can be studied, but the purpose should be to evaluate procedures for teaching new behaviors. The PTD is not useful for evaluating

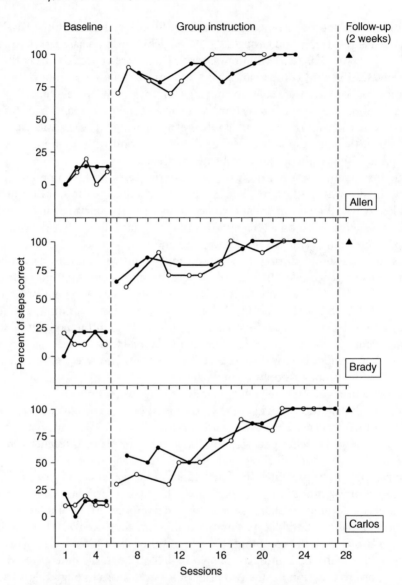

FIGURE 1. The percentage correct for Group 1 students, taught using static picture prompts to purchase two items, and taught using video prompts to withdraw $20. • = picture prompt; o = video prompt; ▲ = follow-up probe.

Figure 12.9 The percentage correct for Group 1 students, taught using static picture prompts to purchase two items, and taught using video prompts to withdraw $20 (source: Cihak et al., 2006. Figure 1. Copyright by PRO-ED, Inc. Reproduced by permission).

interventions to decrease the frequency of problematic behaviors or to promote fluency. The strategies compared with the PTD should be effective with a history of solid development research. The PTD is ideally suited for comparing the efficiency of interventions.

As with the AATD the instructional strategies being compared with the PTD are applied to separate behavior sets/chains. Target behaviors must meet the same criteria as with the AATD. Also, as with the multiple probe design, a strong a priori assumption should exist that the behaviors will not change until instruction occurs. Procedures for determining whether

Table 12.6 Students' Mean Performance, Number of Errors, and Number of Sessions to Criterion Using Static Picture Prompts and Video Prompts Across Baseline and Intervention Phases

Student	Video prompting Baseline (%)	Instruction (%)	Errors	Sessions	Picture prompting Baseline (%)	Instruction (%)	Errors	Sessions
Group 1 (mean)	13.3	79.4	21.3	10	11.2	84.5	18.3	10
Allen	10.5	86.3	11	8	7.5	90.9	11	10
Brady	12.6	84.5	12	11	12.0	86.7	12	9
Carlos	16.8	67.3	41	11	14.0	75.9[a]	32	11
Group 2 (mean)	11.5	78.9	30.7	11	22.2	77.9	25	6.7
Drew	7.2	63.4	66	16	19.8	70.9[a]	52	15
Edgar	5.6	88.6	13	10	25.2	81.0	12	5
Frank	21.6	84.7	13	7	21.6	81.8	11	5
Overall (mean)	12.4	77.0	26.0	10.5	16.7	81.2	21.7	9.2

Note:
a Wilcoxon signed-ranks matched-pairs W test, $p < .05$.
Source: Cihak et al. (2006), Table 3, p. 96. Copyright by PRO-ED, Inc. Reproduced by permission.

behaviors are of equal difficulty are identical to those discussed for the AATD. When the same behaviors are taught to more than one participant in a study, then you should counterbalance sets/chains across instructional strategies. With the PTD you should identify three or more behavior sets/chains for each instructional strategy being compared. Usually only two instructional strategies are compared, which means six total behavior sets/chains need to be identified. Six behavior sets/chains is a minimum, but eight sets/chains are recommended to increase intra-subject replications. Although all sets/chains should be equally difficult, at a minimum *pairs of behavior sets/chains must be equated* (e.g., sets 1 and 2 are equal but may be more or less difficult than sets 3 and 4). If sets are not equally difficult, the comparison is fatally flawed.

When six sets/chains are used with two independent variables, the PTD has seven sequentially implemented experimental conditions. In Probe 1, all behavior sets/chains are assessed for a minimum of three sessions or until the data are stable. All behaviors are assessed, and ideally the behaviors for the various sets are assessed in an intermixed arrangement (within the same sessions). The learner is faced with many behavior sets that are not in her repertoire, thus she initially encounters a great deal of failure. For example, if each set includes three behaviors, a total of 18 behaviors are needed ($3 \times 6 = 18$). If each behavior is assessed on five trials (presented in random order), a total of 90 trials ($5 \times 18 = 90$) must be delivered. The learner has 90 trials on unknown behaviors, such a barrage of trials without reinforcement is not recommended. You should intersperse known behaviors, similar to the target behaviors, in probe sessions; when the learner responds correctly, deliver reinforcement. Also, participants can be reinforced during inter-trial intervals for attending and participating appropriately in the session. This reinforcement can be delivered on the average of every third trial (VR3) in which the child behaved appropriately.

After all behavior sets/chains have been assessed in Probe 1, the first instructional comparison is initiated. In this phase, each strategy being compared is applied to separate but equally difficult behavior sets/chains; Instructional Procedure X is applied to set 1, and Instructional Procedure Y is applied to set 2. Instructional strategies are alternated across sessions as with the AATD. If the two procedures are used in the same day, you should counterbalance the order of the daily sessions to detect effects due to time of day. A minimum 1 hour should occur between sessions. All factors other than the instructional strategies should be identical across sessions. The strategies are used until the participant achieves the predetermined learning criterion for each behavior set/chain. If one behavior set/chain reaches criterion before the other, review trials can be administered with the set/chain that is at criterion. When both reach criterion, Probe 2 is conducted.

Probe 2 uses identical procedures to Probe 1. This condition is an immediate maintenance check for sets 1 and 2, and is additional "baseline" assessment for the remaining sets/chains. The probe condition is in effect for three sessions or until data are stable. After Probe 2, the second instructional comparison is implemented. In this condition, instructional procedure X is applied to set 3, and instructional procedure Y is applied to set 4. This sequence is continued across all pairs of sets/chains. An example of PTD with probe-condition data are shown in Figure 12.10. These data are from a study comparing two prompting procedures (constant and progressive time delay) in teaching students with moderate intellectual disabilities to read community-sign words (Ault, Gast, & Wolery, 1988). As shown in Figure 12.10, an initial probe condition occurred indicating the participant could not read any of the targeted words. Probe 1A occurred before and Probe 1B after winter holidays; because certain breaks (winter holidays, spring break) are natural occurrences in schools, maintaining the

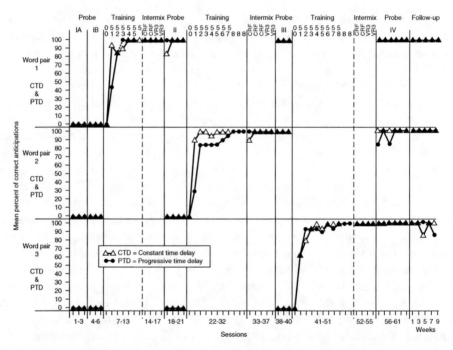

FIGURE 1. Frequency of correct responses for Erin during the baseline, peer modeling, and maintenance phases.

Figure 12.10 Percentage of correct responses by Elliot across word pairs taught with progressive time delay and constant time delay. Open triangles = constant time delay, and closed circles = progressive time delay data. The numbers above the data points in the training conditions indicated delay intervals during each session. The top row of numbers indicated constant delay intervals, and the bottom row of numbers indicated progressive time delay intervals (source: Ault et al. 1988. Figure 3. Copyright by American Association on Mental Retardation, Reproduced by permission).

same condition across breaks is recommended. Instruction on two behavior sets, one with progressive and one with constant time delay, was applied after Probe 1. During the instructional comparison phase, no assessments occurred on the untaught behavior sets. After criterion-level performance on the two instructed sets, Probe 2 was conducted and measured performance on all behavior sets. This was followed by the second instructional comparison phase. This sequence was repeated until all six behavior sets had been taught. The study also included follow-up sessions 1, 3, 5, 7, and 9 weeks after completion of Probe condition 4.

Generalization of acquired behaviors across settings, other assessors, and materials or stimulus conditions also can be assessed with the PTD. Usually, these are conducted during the probe conditions. As such, it allows you to assess the relative effects of the two instructional strategies on generalization of the instructed behaviors. In addition, you can assess the relative maintenance of any generalization that occurs.

The PTD uses two rules to order the experimental conditions: (a) rapid iterative implementation of the instructional procedures (independent variables) across sessions, and (b) time-lagged application of the instructional procedures across pairs of sets/chains. The rapid iterative implementation of procedures across sessions allows for a comparison of two procedures, particularly on efficiency measures. The time-lagged application of procedures across sets/chains provides evidence supporting a functional relation as with a multiple probe design. The repeated probes allows for a realistic assessment of maintenance.

Internal Validity Issues

Threats to internal validity (maturation, history, instrumentation, lack of procedural integrity, attrition) are assessed with the PTD. Maturation and history are assessed during each introduction of the probe condition. Before instructional strategies are applied to the sets/chains, behaviors should remain unchanged if history and maturation are not occurring. If change occurs, then more frequent assessment should be done and additional behavior sets/chains should be identified. Instrumentation, of course, is detected by collecting frequent IOA data for each participant in each probe condition on each behavior set/chain and in each instructional comparison phase. Similarly, procedural-fidelity data should be collected for each participant in each probe condition for each behavior set/chain and in each instructional comparison phase. Procedural-fidelity data are particularly important when comparing instructional strategies, because they document the levels at which the procedures were used correctly. Incorrect use may account for differences found in the data. The PTD can be used with one or two participants, but usual practice is to include three or four. To avoid a problem with attrition, begin PTD studies with four participants.

Multitreatment interference is possible with the PTD. As with the AATD, multitreatment interference can be minimized by increasing the amount of time between sessions during instructional comparison phases. Although alternating sessions by day is possible, the length of PTD studies usually calls for having multiple sessions per day, usually one with each strategy being compared. When this is done, have a morning and afternoon session. Collect intermittent data on behavior sets/chains that have not yet been taught to detect multitreatment interference. The PTD solves the separation of treatments issue, because each strategy is applied to separate sets/chains. The PTD is not compromised by the reversibility issue; nonreversible behaviors are selected and independent variables are applied to separate (but equally difficult) sets/chains. As with the AATD, the PTD presents a special threat to internal validity. If the behavior sets/chains are not of equal difficulty, the comparison is flawed. Thus, ensuring equal difficulty of behavior sets/chains is an extremely important issue.

External Validity Issues

The PTD can be used to answer questions about the effectiveness, relative efficiency, and relative maintenance of compared instructional strategies. Studying efficiency is the primary reason for using the PTD. If questions exist about the effectiveness of one of the strategies, use a multiple baseline or multiple probe design. The PTD is superior to the AATD, because it evaluates history and maturation threats by staggering interventions across several behavior sets/chains thus permitting more intra-subject replications. These added replications increase confidence that one strategy is more efficient than the other. Further, the PTD allows you to study the efficiency of instructional strategies as they are applied across several sets/chains over time, compared to once as in the AATD. For efficiency to be relevant to practitioners, a strategy should repeatedly (across behaviors and over time) be superior to other strategies. The repeated probe conditions in the PTD allow you to evaluate maintenance with the instructional strategies being compared.

As with the AATD, studies of instructional efficiency with the PTD should monitor multiple efficiency measures. You should report these data for each behavior set/chain, for each measure, and for each participant, and then sum them across participants for each measure. To conclude that one instructional strategy is more efficient than another, the data should consistently (across tiers within each participant) be superior for one procedure than another; furthermore, one would expect this consistency to extend to each efficiency measure. When this is the case, you must determine whether the differences are sufficiently large to recommend use of one strategy over the other. No firm rules can be proposed for how much difference must exist before the label of "more efficient" can be applied. However, in analyzing the data it is useful to put it in the context of actual use. Questions should be asked, such as: How many sessions would be saved in a month (4 months, 1 year) if one procedure were used over another? How many minutes of instruction would be saved in a month (4 months, 1 year)? How many more behaviors would be learned in a month (4 months, 1 year)?

Given one strategy is consistently superior to another on efficiency measures (based on intra- and inter-subject replications) and an educationally (clinically) relevant difference exists, then making generalizations to non-study individuals is based on three issues. First, you must use and clearly describe participants' prerequisite behaviors (inclusion criteria). We do not expect the same findings with individuals who did not have the same prerequisite behaviors. Second, the type of behaviors and the amount of instruction provided must be described. We only expect similar findings when similar behaviors are taught with a similar amount of instruction. Third, levels of correct implementation of the instructional strategies should be reported. We only expect similar findings when the procedures are used at the same level of fidelity.

Guidelines

When using the PTD, you should:

1. Use and specify the inclusion criteria to select participants; ideally this includes some quantification of their performance on the variables used in the selection process.
2. Select at least three or four participants; more is usually better, but may be impractical.
3. Identify a minimum of six behavior sets/chains for each participant. Behavior sets/chains should be those (a) participants have not acquired but need to learn; (b) independent; (c) functionally equivalent; (d) nonreversible; and (e) unlikely to change without instruction.

4. For each participant, ensure behavior sets/chains are equally difficult.
5. Establish a learning criterion for instructional strategies.
6. Conduct Probe 1 condition by collecting data for a minimum of three sessions/ days, or until data are stable for each behavior set/chain. All behavior sets/chains are assessed, ideally in an intermixed arrangement.
7. Collect IOA data and procedural-fidelity data for each participant during 20–33% of Probe 1 and all subsequent study phases and conditions.
8. Implement first instructional comparison phase by applying one instructional strategy to behavior set 1, and the other instructional strategy to behavior set 2 in alternating sessions. If multiple sessions are conducted per day, use counter-balancing to allow detection of time-of-day effects. Schedule at least 1 hour between sessions.
9. When the compared instructional strategies result in criterion-level responding, initiate Probe 2 using Probe 1 procedures.
10. Implement the second instructional comparison phase by applying one instructional strategy to behavior set 3 and the other strategy to behavior set 4 in alternating sessions.
11. When the compared instructional strategies result in criterion-level responding, initiate Probe 3.
12. Implement the third instructional comparison phase by applying one instructional strategy to behavior set 5 and the other strategy to behavior set 6 in alternating sessions.
13. When the compared instructional strategies result in criterion-level responding, initiate Probe 4.
14. Summarize the efficiency data and report the results.

Advantages
The primary advantage of the PTD is studying effectiveness *and* efficiency under conditions similar to how instructional strategies are used—teaching multiple behavior sets/chains over time. Intra-subject replications produce considerable evidence for making judgments about the relative efficiency of strategies. If consistency exists across intra- and inter-subject replications, then strong evidence can be provided to argue one strategy should be used over the other. If consistency does not exist (both strategies produce similar efficiency data), then decisions about which strategy to use should be based on other factors. Another advantage is the repeated probe conditions of previously taught sets/chains allow study of the relative maintenance of the strategies. Two strategies may be effective and equally efficient, but one may result in greater maintenance. Adding a generalization measure can provide a comprehensive evaluation of two strategies.

Limitations
Three major limitations exist with the PTD. First, identifying six equally difficult behavior sets/ chains is challenging. Although procedures exist for determining whether sets/chains are equally difficult (Romer et al., 1988), it is often time consuming to find a sufficient number of behaviors. However, this extra effort and time is beneficial because of the large number of intra-subject replications the design provides. Second, a great deal of time is spent conducting probe sessions. Interspersing known behaviors which allow participants to respond correctly and have those behaviors reinforced and delivering reinforcement for attention in the inter-trial intervals are recommended. Third, the design requires a great deal of time to

complete; thus, the PTD should only be used when adequate time and availability of partici-pants exist. For example, the AATD traditionally has three conditions (initial probe, instructional comparison, and final probe), and these are similar to Probe 1, the first instructional comparison, and Probe 2 of the PTD design. The PTD provides more intra-subject replications than the AATD when studying effectiveness, efficiency, and maintenance; but if time does not allow, the AATD design should be used.

Variations

Few variations of the PTD exist. One is to collect probe data intermittently on untreated behavior sets/chains during instructional comparison phases. This provides added evidence that maturation and history are controlled and allows for detection of multitreatment inter-ference, but it adds to an already large amount of testing during probe condition. Another variation is to add generalization measures to probe conditions. Finally, you could use the superior instructional strategy alone at the end of the study to show how it works when it is not alternated with the less-efficient strategy. Table 12.7 summarizes studies that report using a PTD to compare instructional strategies.

Applied Example: PTD (Probe Days)

Jones, C. D., & Schwartz, I. S. (2004). Siblings, peers, and adults: Differential effects of models for children with autism. *Topics in Early Childhood Special Education*, 24, 187–198.

Jones and Schwartz (2004) compared three types of models (peers, siblings, and adults) on the acquisition of language skills by three preschoolers with autism. The models were a sibling of the child with autism who attended the same school, a peer without disabilities from the child's class, and an adult (teacher or assistant) from the child's class. Two participants (children with autism, Erin and Jerry) were taught three sets of three types of language skills (actions, professions, and opposites); and one participant (Jennifer) was taught three sets of two types of skills (actions and professions). Each set contained three behaviors (e.g., three different actions). For each participant, one set of each type of language skills had a different model (peer, sibling, adult). Sessions occurred at a table outside each participant's classroom in the hallway.

A PTD was used involving intermittent single probe days after three consecutive days of stable baseline performance, rather than probe conditions. The order of experimental condi-tions was: (a) pre-baseline in which stimuli were identified and selected; (b) baseline; (c) the instructional comparison phase involving the three model types (peer, sibling, and adult) was time-lagged across the three language skills; and (d) maintenance probes. In baseline, the investigator conducted individual sessions to assess all behavior sets before the modeling intervention was used. For each the participant was shown a picture and asked a specific task question (for actions, "What is this person doing?"; for professions, "Who is this person?"; and for opposites, "If this is [e.g., *open*], then this is _____.") The models (peers, siblings, and adults) were taught to answer the questions correctly in sessions not attended by the child with autism.

During the instructional comparison, 15-min sessions had three 5-min segments. In each segment a different set of the same type of language behaviors (e.g., actions) were taught, and in each segment a different model was present. In each segment, three trials were delivered on each of the three behaviors of the set. First, the investigator would show the model a picture, deliver the task direction, and provide a response interval. After the model responded correctly,

Table 12.7 Summary of Several Studies That Used a Parallel Treatments Design (PTD) to Evaluate Experimental Control

Reference	Participants	Setting/arrangement	Independent variable	Dependent variable
Ault, M., J., Wolery, M., Gast, D. L., Doyle, P. M., & Eizenstat, V. (1988). Comparison of response prompting procedures in teaching numeral identification to autistic subjects. *Journal of Autism and Developmental Disorders, 18,* 627–636.	Number: 2 Sex: male Age range: 8 yr 3 mo –8 yr 5 mo Disability/diagnosis: moderate intellectual disabilities, "autistic continuum," pervasive developmental disorder	Setting: self-contained classroom Arrangement: individual	Constant time delay and system of least prompts	Mean percentage of correct responses (numerals)
Bennett, D. L., Gast, D. L., Wolery, M., & Schuster, J. (1986). Time delay and system of least prompts: A comparison in teaching manual sign production. *Education and Training of the Mentally Retarded, 21,* 117–129.	Number: 3 Sex: 1 male, 2 female Age range: 14 yr to 17 yr Disability/diagnosis: severe ID, moderate ID	Setting: 10 m × 12 m unoccupied classroom Arrangement: individual	Progressive time delay compared with constant time delay	Percentage of correct responses correct responses
Collins, B. C., Hall, M., Branson, T. A., & Holder, M. (1999). Acquisition of related and unrelated factual information delivered by a teacher within an inclusive setting. *Journal of Behavioral Education, 9,* 223–237.	Number: 2 Sex: 1 male, 1 female Age range: 21 yr Disability/diagnosis: moderate intellectual disabilities	Setting: rural secondary school in each participant's homeroom class Arrangement: individual	Nontargeted related factual and unrelated factual information	Percent correct responses
Doyle, P. M., Wolery, M., Gast, D. L., & Ault, M. J. (1990). Comparison of constant time delay and the system of least prompts in teaching preschoolers with developmental delays. *Research in Developmental Disabilities, 11,* 1–22.	Number: 3 Sex: 2 male, 1 female Age range: 4 yr 1 mo –6 yr 5 mo Disability/diagnosis: Down Syndrome, developmental delay	Setting: multiple: preschool classroom for 4 and 5 year old and kindergarten room. Arrangement: individual	Constant time delay System of least prompts	Percent correct responses
Knight, M. G., Ross, D. E., Taylor, R. L., & Ramasamy, R. (2003). Constant time delay and interspersal of known items to teach sight words to students with mental retardation and learning disabilities. *Education and Training in Developmental Disabilities, 38,* 179–191.	Number: 4 Sex: 1 male, 3 female Age range: 8 yr old Disability/diagnosis: significant learning disabilities, mild intellectual disabilities	Setting: small room within the self-contained special education. Arrangement: individual	Constant time delay and interspersal of known items	Percentage of target words read correctly Mean number of instructional minutes through criterion Percentage of errors through criterion
Murzynski, N. T., & Bourrett, J. C. (2007). Combining video modeling and least-to-most prompting for establishing response chains. *Behavioral Interventions, 22,* 147–152.	Number: 2 Sex: male Age range: 8 yr–9 yr Disability/diagnosis: autism	Setting: participant's residential homes Arrangement: individual	Video modeling plus least-to-most prompting compare to least-to-most alone	Number of steps completed independently

(Continued)

Table 12.7 Continued

Reference	Participants	Setting/arrangement	Independent variable	Dependent variable
Pufpaff, L. A., Blischak, D. M., & Lloyd, L. L. (2000). Effects of modified orthography on the identification of printed words. *American Journal on Mental Retardation, 105,* 14–24.	Number: 4 Sex: 3 male, 1 female Age range: 20 yr–38 yr Disability/diagnosis: moderate/severe intellectual disabilities, cerebral palsy, Down Syndrome	Setting: center isolated hallway or center's cafeteria Arrangement: individual	Traditional orthography compared to modified orthography	Percentage of correct responses
Rohena, E. I., Jitendra, A. K., & Browder, D. M. (2002). Comparison of the effects of Spanish and English constant time delay instruction on sight word reading by hispanic learners with mental retardation. *Journal of Special Education, 36,* 169–184.	Number: 4 Sex: 2 male, 2 female Age range: 12 yr–15 yr Disability/diagnosis: moderate intellectual disabilities.	Setting: life-skills classroom Arrangement: individual	4-second constant time delay or 4-second Spanish constant time delay.	Percentage correct of English words read in Spanish constant time delay, English time day and no-treatment.
Schuster, J. W., Griffen, A. K., & Wolery, M. (1992). Comparison of simultaneous prompting and constant time delay procedures in teaching sight words to elementary students with moderate mental retardation. *Journal of Behavioral Education, 2,* 305–325.	Number: 4 Sex: 2 male, 2 female Age range: 10 yr to 11 yr Disability/diagnosis: moderate ID	Setting: participants classroom at table located in front of room Arrangement: individual	Constant time delay compared with simultaneous prompting	Percentage of correct responses
West, E. A., & Billingsley, F. (2005). Improving the system of least prompts: A comparison of procedural variations. *Education and Training in Developmental Disabilities, 40,* 131–144.	Number: 4 Sex: 3 male, 1 female Age range: 5 yr 10 mo–6 yr 2 mo Disability/diagnosis: autism	Setting: children's early childhood inclusive classroom Arrangement: individual	Traditional least to most procedure (TLM) compared to revised least to most procedure (RLM)	Independent correct responses
Wolery, M., Ault, M. J., Gast, D. L., Doyle, P. M., & Griffen, A. K. (1990). Comparison of constant time delay and the system of least prompts in teaching chained tasks. *Education and Training in Developmental Disabilities, 25,* 243–257.	Number: 4 Sex: 2 male, 2 female Age range: 10 yr 8 mo–14 yr 7 mo Disability/diagnosis: moderate intellectual disabilities, Down Syndrome, microcephaly, articulation disorder	Setting: student's classroom Arrangement: individual	Constant time delay compared to system of least prompts	Mean percentage of independent responses

the investigator would show the preschooler with autism the picture, deliver the task direction, and provide a response interval. Correct responses were praised and errors and no responses were ignored. When nine trials were completed, the investigator took the model and participant back to the classroom and got another model; the investigator, new model, and participant completed another 5-min segment with another set of behaviors. When this segment was completed, the process was repeated with the third model. The daily order of models was the same for each type of language skill, but was randomly determined for each language skill. Criterion was 66% correct (6/9 daily trials) with each model type. IOA data were collected on 21% of the sessions with at least one check per condition for each child. Mean IOA was 97% (range = 95–100%). Maintenance data were collected intermittently on each language skill after criterion-level performance had been demonstrated in the instructional (modeling) comparison phase. The procedures of maintenance sessions were identical to the initial probe condition.

In Figure 12.11, Erin's performance is shown for each model type across the three types of language skills. In the initial baseline sessions, Erin did not answer correctly to any of the trials. When the modeling intervention comparison phase was implemented for actions, her number of correct responses immediately increased from zero in probe to three correct responses on peer-modeled set, seven on adult-modeled set, and eight on sibling-modeled set. Correct responding reached 100% on sibling and adult sets and 66% on the peer set. After criterion-level responding on action behaviors, probe data were collected on behavior sets for professions and opposites. Both remained at zero correct responses. The model-comparison condition was implemented for the profession behavior sets. Performance replicated that of the action behaviors sets; Erin's number of correct responses increased on behaviors modeled by her peer, sibling, and adult. When criterion-level responding occurred, probe sessions were conducted on the behavior sets for opposites; performance remained at zero. The instructional comparison was implemented on the opposites behavior sets. Erin's correct performance immediately increased on these sets as well. Correct responding reached 100% on peer and adult sets and 66% on sibling set. Maintenance probes were conducted on the behavior sets of each language skill after the respective comparison conditions. Erin's performance maintained at criterion levels or above across all sets for all language skills, regardless of the type of model used. Similar findings were reported with the other participants. The researchers concluded all three models were effective in increasing the number of correct responses, and child models were as effective as adult models.

Summary

In this chapter four experimental designs (MTD, ATD, AATD, and PTD) were discussed; in Table 12.8, the four designs are compared on various dimensions. All of the designs can be used to compare interventions, although the AATD and PTD are restricted to instructional strategies. Component and parametric analyses are possible with all designs. The ATD can be used for comparing different levels of procedural fidelity with reversible behaviors, and the AATD is well-suited for comparing different levels of procedural fidelity in nonreversible behaviors. The MTD and ATD require reversible behaviors, and the AATD and PTD require nonreversible behaviors. With the MTD and ATD, only one behavior is required and it can be an acceleration or deceleration target. With the AATD, three behavior sets/chains are required, and with the PTD at least six behavior sets/chains are required. Generalization of the interventions can be evaluated in all designs, but often is difficult with the ATD. Only the PTD has built-in assessments of maintenance, although follow-up assessments can be done with all four

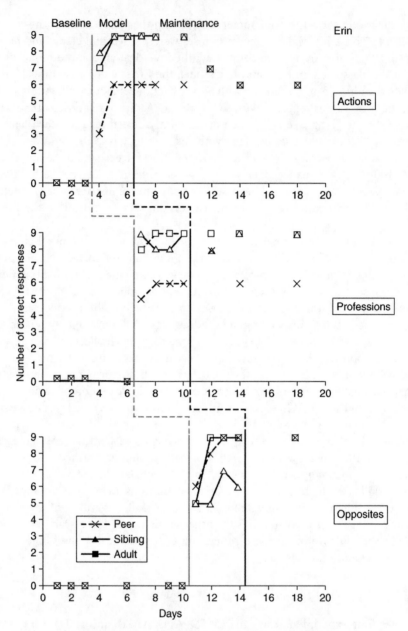

FIGURE 1. Frequency of correct responses for Erin during the baseline, peer modeling, and maintenance phases.

Figure 12.11 Frequency of correct responses for Erin during the baseline, peer modeling, and maintenance phases (source: Jones & Schwartz, 2004. Figure 1. Copyright by PRO-ED Inc. Reproduced by permission).

designs. With the MTD and ATD only one participant is required, but more should be used to secure inter-subject replications. The AATD and PTD should have at least three participants. Multitreatment interference is likely with all of these designs, and methods for detecting and controlling it when detected is specific to each design. The AATD and PTD solve the separation of treatments issue, and these two designs are not bothered by the reversibility issue.

Table 12.8 Illustration of the Similarities and Differences of the Multitreatment Design, Alternating Treatments Design, Adapted Alternating Treatments Design, and Parallel Treatments Design

Dimension	Multitreatment design	Alternating treatments design	Adapted alternating treatments design	Parallel treatments design
Types of comparison questions for which design is useful	Compare IVs Component analyses Parametric analyses	Compare IVs Assess factors maintaining behavior Component analyses Parametric analyses	Compare instructional strategies Efficiency questions Parametric analyses Procedural fidelity of instructional strategies	Compare instructional strategies Parametric analyses Efficiency questions Maintenance questions
Reversible or Nonreversible behavior?	Reversible	Reversible	Nonreversible	Nonreversible
Minimum number of behaviors required	1	1	3 behavior sets/chains	6 behavior sets/chains
Types of behavior (acceleration or deceleration)	Acceleration or deceleration behaviors	Acceleration or deceleration behaviors	Acceleration only	Acceleration only
Generalization measures feasible?	Yes	Yes, but difficult	Yes	Yes
Maintenance of effects part of the design?	No	No	No	Yes
Minimum number of participants	1	1	3	2
Multitreatment interference likely?	Yes	Yes	Yes	Yes
How is multitreatment interference detected?	Change in conditions does not result in change in data pattern	Collect baseline data during comparison phase	Collect probe data on control set during comparison phase	Collect probe data on untreated behaviors during comparison phases
If multitreatment interference detected, what is solution?	Extend condition	Increase time between sessions	Increase time between sessions	Increase time between sessions
Is reversibility issue solved?	No	No	Yes	Yes
Is separation of treatments issue solved?	No	No	Yes	Yes
Special considerations	None	Participant must discriminate when each condition is in effect	Behaviors must be of equal difficulty	Behaviors must be of equal difficulty

With the ATD and consequent-based interventions, participants must discriminate which condition is in effect. With the AATD and the PTD, behavior sets/chains must be of equal difficulty.

References

Ault, M. J., Gast, D. L., & Wolery, M. (1988). Comparison of progressive and constant time delay procedures in teaching community-sign word reading. *American Journal on Mental Retardation, 93,* 44–56.

Barlow, D. H., & Hayes, S. C. (1979). Alternating treatments design: One strategy for comparing the effects of two treatments in a single subject. *Journal of Applied Behavior Analysis, 12,* 199–210.

Barlow, D. H., & Hersen, M. (1984). *Single case experimental designs: Strategies for studying behavior change* (2nd ed.). Boston, MA: Allyn & Bacon.

Billingsley, F. F., White, O. R., & Munson, A. R. (1980). Procedural reliability: A rationale and an example. *Behavioral Assessment, 2,* 229–241.

Birnbrauer, J. S. (1981). External validity and experimental investigation of individual behavior. *Analysis and Intervention in Developmental Disabilities, 1,* 117–132.

Birnbrauer, J. S., Peterson, C. R., & Solnick, J. V. (1974). Design and interpretation of studies of single subjects. *American Journal of Mental Deficiency, 79,* 191–203.

Browning, R. M. (1967). A same-subject design for simultaneous comparison of three reinforcement contingencies. *Behaviour Research and Therapy, 5,* 237–243.

Cihak, D., Alberto, P. A., Taber-Doughty, T., & Gama, R. I. (2006). A comparison of static picture prompting and video prompting simulation strategies using group instructional procedures. *Focus on Autism and Other Developmental Disabilities, 21,* 89–99.

Dunlap, G., Strain, P. S., Fox, L., Carta, J. J., Conroy, M., Smith, B. J., et al. (2006). Prevention and intervention with young children's challenging behavior: Perspective regarding current knowledge. *Behavioral Disorders, 32,* 29–45.

Edgar, E. B., & Billingsley, F. F. (1974). Believability when N = 1. *The Psychological Record, 24,* 147–160.

Falcomata, T. S., Roane, H. S., Hovanetz, A. N., Kettering, T. L., & Keeney, K. M. (2004). An evaluation of response cost in the treatment of inappropriate vocalizations maintained by automatic reinforcement. *Journal of Applied Behavior Analysis, 37,* 83–87.

Fiske, K. E. (2008). Treatment integrity of school-based behavior analytic interventions: A review of research. *Behavior Analysis and Practice, 1, 2,* 19–25.

Gast, D. L., & Wolery, M. (1988). Parallel treatments design: A nested single subject design for comparing instructional procedures. *Education and Treatment of Children, 11,* 270–285.

Hains, A. H., & Baer, D. M. (1989). Interaction effects in multi-element designs: Inevitable, desirable, and ignorable. *Journal of Applied Behavior Analysis, 22,* 57–69.

Heal, N. A., & Hanley, G. P. (2007). Evaluating preschool children's preferences for motivational systems during instruction. *Journal of Applied Behavior Analysis, 40,* 249–261.

Herzinger, C. V., & Campbell, J. M. (2007). Comparing functional assessment methodologies: A quantitative synthesis. *Journal of Autism and Developmental Disorders, 37,* 1430–1445.

Holcombe, A., Wolery, M., & Gast, D. L. (1994). Comparative single subject research: Description of designs and discussion of problems. *Topics in Early Childhood Special Education, 14,* 119–145.

Holcombe, A., Wolery, M., & Snyder, E. (1994). Effects of two levels of procedural fidelity with constant time delay on children's learning. *Journal of Behavioral Education, 4,* 49–73.

Horner, R. H., Carr, E. G., Halle, J., McGee, G., Odom, S. L., & Wolery, M. (2005). The use of single-subject research to identify evidence-based practices in special education. *Exceptional Children, 71,* 165–179.

Iwata, B. A., Dorsey, M. F., Slifer, K. J., Bauman, K. E., & Richman, G. S. (1994). Toward a functional analysis of self-injury. *Journal of Applied Behavior Analysis, 27,* 197–209 (Reprinted from *Analysis and Intervention in Developmental Disabilities, 2,* 3–20).

Johnston, J. M. (1988). Strategic and tactical limits of comparison studies. *The Behavior Analyst, 11,* 1–9.

Jones, C. D., & Schwartz, I. S. (2004). Siblings, peers, and adults: Differential effects of models for children with autism. *Topics in Early Childhood Special Education, 24,* 187–198.

Logan, K. R., Jacobs, H. A., Gast, D., L., Murray, A. S., Daino, K., & Skala, C. (1998). The impact of typical peers on the perceived happiness of students with profound multiple disabilities. *Journal of the Association for Persons with Severe Handicaps, 23,* 309–318.

McGonigle, J. J., Rojahn, J., Dixon, J., & Strain, P. S. (1987). Multiple treatment interference in the alternating treatments design as a function of the intercomponent interval length. *Journal of Applied Behavior Analysis, 20,* 171–178.

Neef, N. A., & Peterson, S. M. (2007). Functional behavior assessment. In J. O. Cooper, T. E Heron, & W. L. Heward (Eds.), *Applied behavior analysis* (2nd ed., pp. 500–524). Upper Saddle River, NJ: Pearson.

Romer, L. T., Billingsley, F. F., & White, O. R. (1988). The behavior equivalence problem in within-subject treatment comparisons. *Research in Developmental Disabilities, 9,* 305–315.

Sindelar, P. T., Rosenberg, M. S., & Wilson, R. J. (1985). An adapted alternating treatments design for instructional research. *Education and Treatment of Children, 8,* 67–76.

Ulman, J. D., & Sulzer-Azaroff, B. (1975). Multi-element baseline design in educational research. In E. Ramp & G. Semb (Eds.), *Behavior analysis: Areas of research and application* (pp. 377–391). Englewood Cliffs, NJ: Prentice-Hall.

Vollmer, T., Sloman, K., & Pipkin, C. (2008). Practical implications of data reliability and treatment integrity monitoring. *Behavior Analysis in Practice, 1*, 2, 4–11.

Werts, M. G., Wolery, M., Holcombe, A., & Frederick, C. (1993). Effects of instructive feedback related and unrelated to the target behaviors. *Exceptionality, 4*, 81–95.

Werts, M. G., Wolery, M., Holcombe, A., & Gast, D. L. (1995). Instructive feedback: Review of parameters and effects. *Journal of Behavioral Education, 5*, 55–75.

Wolery, M., Ault, M. J., & Doyle, P. M. (1992). *Teaching students with moderate and severe disabilities: Use of response prompting strategies.* White Plains, NY: Longman.

13

Variations of Multiple Baseline Designs and Combination Designs

David L. Gast and Jennifer Ledford

In Chapter 11 we described multiple baseline and multiple probe designs and their three principal variations: multiple baseline/probe designs across behaviors, conditions, and participants. In this chapter we elaborate on two variations of the multiple baseline design: changing criterion design (Hartmann & Hall, 1976), and the "delayed" (Watson & Workman, 1981) or "nonconcurrent" (Harvey, May, & Kennedy, 2004) multiple baseline design. In addition, we provide examples of how researchers have combined single subject research designs to strengthen their evaluation of experimental control and to resolve some of the ambiguities that may arise during the course of an experiment. The changing criterion design and nonconcurrent multiple baseline design require your attention and caution before using. As will be discussed, though these two designs have some practical advantages, they have serious internal-validity limitations and may be best used in combination with an A-B-A-B design, multiple baseline design, or multiple probe design.

Changing Criterion Design

Sidman (1960) described a research design that Hall (1971) named the changing criterion design. This design may be appropriate for teachers, clinicians, and other applied researchers who wish to evaluate instructional or therapy programs that require gradual, stepwise changes in behavior. Hartmann and Hall (1976) describe the changing criterion design as follows:

> The design requires initial baseline observations on a single target behavior. This baseline phase is followed by implementation of a treatment program in each of a series of treatment phases. Each treatment phase is associated with a stepwise change in criterion rate for the target behavior. Thus, each phase of the design provides a baseline for the following phase. When the rate of the target behavior changes with each stepwise change in the criterion, therapeutic change is replicated and experimental control is demonstrated.
>
> (p. 527)

Though the changing criterion design has not been widely cited in the applied research literature, Hartman and Hall (1976) have suggested it may be useful to monitor a wide range of programs (e.g., systematically increasing correct homework completion, decreasing number of cigarettes smoked per day, etc.). Any intervention program that employs differential reinforcement of other behavior (DRO), differential reinforcement of high-rate behavior (DRH), or differential reinforcement of low-rate behavior (DRL) may find the changing criterion design appropriate for monitoring program effectiveness.

Internal Validity

To demonstrate experimental control using the changing criterion design you must show that each time the criterion level is changed (increased or decreased), there is concomitant change in the dependent variable. This change should be immediate and should follow a stable level and trend in the data at the preceding criterion level. It is imperative to demonstrate stability before changing the criterion level, for each phase serves as a baseline measure for the subsequent phase. McDougall, Hawkins, Brady, and Jenkins (2006), in their discussion of changing criterion variations, emphasized the importance that with each change in criterion the data of each subsequent phase fall within a set range, rather than simply anywhere above the designated criterion. Replication of effect is demonstrated if each stepwise change in criterion level results in a behavior change to the new criterion level. Figure 13.1 illustrates, with hypothetical data, the use of a changing criterion design to evaluate the effectiveness of an intervention designed to decrease number of talk-outs.

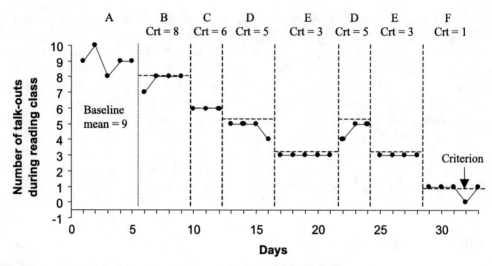

Figure 13.1 Prototype changing criterion design (talk-outs, decrease).

Guidelines and Considerations

Hartman and Hall (1976) recommended that applied researchers attend to the following design requirements (refer to Figure 13.1):

1. Introduce the intervention (i.e., the first criterion change) only after the initial baseline data show acceptable stability in level and trend.
2. Change the criterion level only after stable criterion-level responding has been attained in the preceding phase.
3. Plan, at minimum, four changes in criterion level (i.e., replications).
4. Pinpoint criterion levels, or a strategy for determining criterion levels, prior to initiating the study.
5. Vary the size of criterion changes (e.g., decrease the number of talk-outs by 1–3 talk-outs across phases)
6. Vary the length of time that a participant must maintain responding at a criterion level (e.g., 4 days, 3 days, 5 days).
7. Revert to a former criterion level at some point in the stepwise progression that will permit an "A-B-A" design analysis.

The strength of the changing criterion design is in its demonstration of a close correspondence between criterion-level change and behavior change, i.e., data fall within a pre-established range at each criterion level. It is possible, however, that the correlation between the two could be explained by naturally occurring, uncontrolled historical, maturational, or measurement factors. These guidelines are intended to dispel such a possibility.

The most essential prerequisite to a demonstration of experimental control is the stepwise replication of stable, criterion-level responding (guidelines 1–3); however, there are additional strategies to increase believability (guidelines 4–7). To minimize the risks of bias, you should pinpoint criterion levels, or a strategy for determining criterion changes before initiating a study. These predictions are, however, subject to change, depending on the variability of the data (e.g., the greater data variability, the larger the required criterion change in order to demonstrate visible differences across phases). As additional assurances of experimental control, you are advised to vary the length of each phase, vary the magnitude of each criterion change, and revert to a former criterion level at some point in the progression to ensure changes in the dependent variable are not naturally occurring. If data consistently follow each of these criterion changes, there is a high probability that the intervention is responsible for changes in the target behavior.

Advantages

The changing criterion design is appropriate to evaluate programs designed to shape behaviors that are in a person's repertoire but do not occur at an acceptable rate. The changing criterion design has been employed to monitor desensitization (Koegel, Openden, & Koegel, 2004; Ricciardi, Luiselli, & Camre, 2006), prompt fading (Luiselli, 2000; Flood & Wilder, 2004), fluency building (Nes, 2005), exercise (DeLuca & Holborn, 1992), and self-monitoring (Ganz & Sigafoos, 2005) programs. It also can be used to evaluate behavior deceleration programs (e.g., smoking reduction, talk-outs, out-of-seat, abusive language). Unlike multiple baseline and multiple probe designs across behaviors, the changing criterion design has the advantage of requiring only one target behavior. In contrast to the A-B-A-B design, no withdrawal condition is required, though one return to a preceding criterion level is recommended, which can strengthen the demonstration of experimental control. Most importantly, at least from an educator's or therapist's perspective, the changing criterion design, through its small-step increments in criterion level, permits a student or client to change behavior without being "overwhelmed" by an initial, seemingly impossible criterion demand.

Limitations

There are, perhaps, two reasons that the changing criterion design has been used infrequently: first, it is limited to a relatively small range of target behaviors and instructional procedures and, second, a demonstration of experimental control depends upon the "subjective" prediction of criterion levels, which may or may not conform to the data. The changing criterion design is not an appropriate paradigm to validate "acquisition stage" instructional procedures (e.g., constant time delay, system of least prompts, graduated guidance, etc.) because any procedural alterations (stimulus shaping and fading, response prompting and fading, or response chaining) across design phases would alter the independent variable and, thus, confound the demonstration of experimental control. Consequently, *the changing criterion design is limited to programs that manipulate consequences for the purpose of increasing or decreasing the frequency of behaviors already established in an individual's repertoire.*

A second problem associated with the changing criterion design pertains to setting and changing criterion levels. Whenever you are required to specify a criterion level of acceptable performance, there is always some degree of subjectivity or "professional guesswork" involved. The investigator who uses the changing criterion design has the tedious responsibility of making criterion changes that are large enough to be "detectable" though small enough to be "achievable," but not so small that the behavior will far exceed the criterion level. In other words, a demonstration of experimental control depends upon an "a priori" prediction or strategy for setting a progression of criterion levels, as well as acceptable response ranges at each criterion level, predictions that may or may not prove appropriate. One strategy that takes some of the guesswork out of deciding individual criterion levels is to decide upon a percentage to change the criterion in each subsequent phase (e.g., 10–20% based on your stability criterion; see Chapter 9). For example, if during the baseline condition the mean frequency of daily talk-outs for a class of 12 students was 27, you could use a "criterion size change rule" of 12% of the preceding phase to determine the acceptable number of talk-outs for the next phase. The first criterion level would be three fewer talk-outs by the group ($27 \times 0.12 = 3.36$ rounded to the lower whole number), that is, 24 talk-outs for the group to access the reinforcer; the second criterion level would be 12% lower than the preceding criterion level ($24 \times 0.12 = 2.88$ rounded up to the nearest whole number), or three fewer talk-outs by the group, 21; the third criterion level would be 12% lower than the preceding criterion level ($21 \times 0.12 = 2.52$ rounded down to the nearest whole number) or two fewer talk-outs by the group, 19. The decision to round up or down, in this example, was based on <0.6 to round down; >0.6 to round up. Such a rule will help systematize the process of changing criterion levels across design phases.

Applied Example: Changing Criterion Design—Increase Behavior

Johnston, R. J., & McLaughlin, T. F. (1982). The effects of free time on assignment completion and accuracy in arithmetic: A case study. *Education and Treatment of Children, 5*, 33–40.

Johnston and McLaughlin (1982) employed a changing criterion design to assess the effect of contingently dispensed free time on improved arithmetic assignment completion. The child, a 7-year-old girl enrolled in a self-contained second-grade classroom, presented an average daily math worksheet completion of 35%, a level far below her expected ability, given that she consistently scored above her grade level on achievement tests and, in fact, averaged 100% correct on daily worksheet problems she attempted. The present study was conducted during her daily 35-minute arithmetic lesson.

Daily assignments ranged from 6 to 43 items, including computational and "thought" problems. The two dependent variables were percentage of problems completed per daily assignment and percentage correct per assignment. To provide interobserver-reliability checks a parent-aide regraded at least one daily assignment during each phase of the study. For both dependent measures, point-by-point (i.e., problem-by-problem) reliability checks yielded 100% agreement.

During an initial 10-day baseline condition the second-grade teacher presented the child with her daily math assignment, worked one of the problems as a model, and asked the student to complete as many problems as possible within the 35-min session. At the end of this baseline period, an average daily baseline completion rate was computed at 35%. A changing criterion procedure was then introduced in which investigators "successfully changed the criterion for reinforcement, usually in graduated steps, from baseline level until the desired terminal behavior was achieved" (p. 35). Most new criterion levels required a 5% increment in percentage completion above the preceding level (i.e., Phase 1 = 35%, Phase 2 = 40%, Phase 3 = 45%, . . . Phase 16 = 100%) for 3 consecutive days. Throughout the intervention condition the teacher continued to present the child with the daily assignment and worked one example as a model; however, in addition she informed the child of the minimum number of problems that had to be completed accurately in order for criterion to be met and reminded her that, upon meeting the criterion, she was eligible to enjoy free time for the remainder of the 35-min time period. If she did not meet criterion within the allowable 35 min, she was required to remain at her desk until criterion was attained.

Johnston and McLaughlin employed a changing criterion design, shown in Figure 13.2, which included 16 criterion changes during the intervention condition. During Sessions 38–40 a brief reversal in criterion level was instituted to strengthen the demonstration of experimental control. The investigation concluded with a three-session follow-up baseline condition extended over 25 days, which permitted a pretest–posttest analysis of the data. Results showed

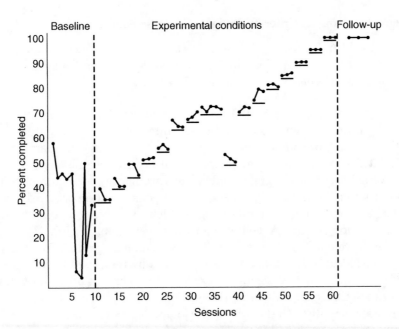

Figure 1. The percent of problems completed for each assignment during each of the experimental conditions. The solid horizontal lines indicate the reinforcement criterion set for each session.

Figure 13.2 The percent of problems completed for each assignment during each of the experimental conditions. The solid horizontal lines indicate the reinforcement criterion set for each session (source: Johnston & McLaughlin, 1982. Reproduced with permission from West Virginia University Press).

that the child "met or exceeded the criterion each time that it was changed" (p. 36). Whereas her mean baseline completion was 35%, by the final intervention phase she averaged 100% assignment completion. Furthermore, her accuracy remained stable throughout the study (≥95%), even though greater numbers of more difficult problems were being assigned.

Johnston and McLaughlin (1982) provided a simple and convincing strategy to shape a child's percentage of task completion by requiring small increments in performance to ensure continued successful responding. Interestingly, after the 60th session the investigators withdrew the free-time contingency (i.e., reinstated baseline condition) and found that 100% task completion and accuracy were maintained when measured by three follow-up probes conducted 5, 15, and 25 days after terminating the intervention condition. This shows that the use of extrinsic reinforcement can be a temporary procedure useful to initiate new patterns of responding without necessarily "addicting" the student to its continued availability. Furthermore, the researchers reported that the free-time contingency required very little teacher time or expense. As a final note, you might suspect that the choice of 5% level increments may have been smaller than actually required since the child abruptly reached and often exceeded each new criterion level. Perhaps the outcome objective could have been attained more rapidly had the step-wise requirements been greater. However, this is problematic with all changing criterion designs, i.e., the challenge of identifying criterion levels that will permit the demonstration of experimental control without impeding optimal learning rates.

Applied Example: Changing Criterion Design—Decrease Behavior

Koegel, R. L., Openden, D., & Koegel, L. K. (2004). A systematic desensitization paradigm to treat hypersensitivity to auditory stimuli in children with autism in family contexts. *Research and Practice for Persons with Severe Disabilities, 29,* 122–134.

Koegel, Openden, and Koegel (2004) used a changing criterion design to assess the effectiveness of a systematic desensitization procedure to treat three children with autism who showed hypersensitivity to auditory stimuli (age range: 2 years 6 months to 3 years 7 months). All children exhibited hypersensitivity to environmental noises, and the target stimuli for the intervention varied based on the child's individual sensitivities (Lori: flushing toilets; Jamie: musical toys; Jeff: vacuum cleaners and blenders). Lori's intervention occurred in an inclusive preschool, Jamie's occurred in a clinical setting, and Jeff's intervention occurred in his home. The changing criterion design was replicated for two target stimuli for Jeff.

Criterion levels were different for each child based on target stimuli. For example, several steps for Lori included: toilet flushed while Lori walks by the closed bathroom door; toilet flushed while Lori walks by the "slightly cracked" open bathroom door; toilet flushed while Lori walks by the quarter-open bathroom door. The final step was: toilet flushed repeatedly while Lori is inside the bathroom stall with door closed. Dependent measures were the number of steps completed per week and the mean level of anxiety per session (comfortable, mild anxiety, high anxiety, or intolerable). Criterion for moving to the next step was two to four consecutive 3-min intervals scored as "comfortable." Sessions were terminated if rated "intolerable." Interobserver agreement was calculated using the point-by-point method by dividing the number of agreements by the number of agreements plus disagreements multiplied by 100. Mean interobserver agreement was 96.8%.

Prior to intervention, all participants failed to reach criterion levels with "intolerable" scores. During intervention, all participants reached the final step with each step being rated as "comfortable." Visual analyses of graphic data show that each child was rated as comfortable as the criterion changed for each level. The amount of time needed to reach criterion for each level varied greatly across participants, with some children achieving criterion for several steps in a single day and others requiring several weeks to achieve criterion for a single step. The amount of time needed to complete all steps ranged from 4 days to 25 weeks.

Results of the study, presented in Figure 13.3, show that a systematic desensitization program can effectively treat hypersensitivity to auditory stimuli, and such programs can be evaluated within the context of a changing criterion design. These findings also lend support that hypersensitivity may be related to phobic behavior rather than pain. Parents reported the findings to be socially significant because of the positive impact the intervention had on children's abilities to participate in everyday settings. Similar treatment programs that address challenging behaviors may be evaluated with a similar changing criterion design.

Concluding Comments

The changing criterion design is one of several experimental paradigms available to educators and clinicians to evaluate the effectiveness of intervention programs. Table 13.1 summarizes several studies that have used the changing criterion design in clinical and educational settings. Though it has not been cited frequently in the applied research literature, it does offer a practical way to monitor performance when stepwise criterion changes are both desirable and practical. It can be used to monitor programs designed to increase or decrease the rate of responding. Those who decide to employ the changing criterion design must closely follow

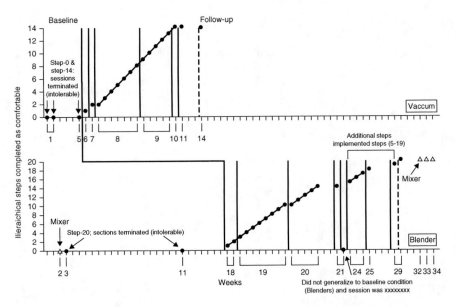

Figure 2. Number of steps in the systematic desensitization hierarchy completed as comfortable per session and per week for the vacuum, blender, and hand-mixer for Child 3 (Jeff) presented in a multiple baseline across stimuli design.

Figure 13.3 Number of steps in the systematic desensitization hierarchy completed as comfortable per session and per week for the vacuum, blender, and hand-mixer for Child 3 (Jeff) presented in a multiple baseline across stimuli design (source: Koegel et al., 2004).

guidelines previously discussed. You are cautioned to use the changing criterion design only if the target response is in the individual's repertoire and the objective of the intervention is to increase or decrease the frequency of responding. Under these conditions you will find the changing criterion design appropriate and useful in evaluating program effectiveness.

Nonconcurrent (or Delayed) Multiple Baseline Design

In an effort to reduce the length of baseline conditions, increase flexibility to include new behaviors, conditions, or participants as they become available, and address research questions related to organization (schools, hospitals, clinics, etc.) behavior rather than the behavior of individuals, some researchers have proposed the use of a "delayed multiple baseline design" (Watson & Workman, 1981), or "nonconcurrent multiple baseline design" (Harvey et al., 2004; Christ, 2007). In recent descriptions the design has been advocated for use to evaluate "practices used by state education agencies, local education agencies, and schools," suggesting that

> some important topics in educational research do not lend themselves to traditional single-case designs. In fact, substantive policy decisions about educational practices often occur at the school system and/or school building level, not at the student or classroom level, although their effects can also be realized at these latter levels, as well.
>
> (Harvey et al., pp. 267–268)

One could hardly argue against the importance of such system-wide research questions, however, the question that must be raised is whether the nonconcurrent multiple baseline design, or any single subject research design, is appropriate for answering large organization policy research questions. If we believe that single subject research designs can be used with such

Table 13.1 Studies That Used Changing Criterion Designs

Reference	Participants	Setting/arrangement	Independent variable	Dependent variable
DeLuca, R. V., & Holborn, S. W. (1992). Effects of a variable-ratio reinforcement schedule with changing criteria on exercise in obese & nonobese boys. *Journal of Applied Behavior Analysis, 25,* 671–679.	Number: 6 Sex: male Age range: 11 years Disability/diagnosis: obesity (3)	Setting: public school clinic Arrangement: individual	Tangible reinforcement based on reaching criterion levels of responding	Revolutions per minute, duration of session
Easterbrooks, S. R., & Stoner, M. (2006). Using a visual tool to increase adjectives in the written language of students who are deaf or hard of hearing. *Communication Disorders Quarterly, 27,* 95–109.	Number: 3 Sex: 2 males, 1 female Age range: 17–18 years Disability/diagnosis: severe to profound hearing loss	Setting: self-contained classroom Arrangement: individual	Printed visual aid for writing	Number of adjectives included in a written product
Flood, W. A., & Wilder, D. A. (2004). The use of differential reinforcement and fading to increase time away from a caregiver in a child with separation anxiety disorder. *Education and Treatment of Children, 27,* 1–8.	Number: 1 Sex: male Age: 11 years Disability/diagnosis: ADD and anxiety disorder	Setting: clinical Arrangement: individual	DRO procedure (student was reinforced for absence of emotional behavior)	Latency to emotional behavior after departure of mother
Ganz, J. B., & Sigafoos, J. (2005). Self-monitoring: Are young adults with MR and autism able to utilize cognitive strategies independently? *Education and Training in Developmental Disabilities, 40,* 24–33.	Number: 2 Sex: male Age range: 19–20 years Disability/diagnosis: autism (1), ID (2) IQ range: 20–26	Setting: self-contained classroom Arrangement: individual	Self-monitoring training (visual system to track successes and reinforcement for an identified number of tokens)	P1: Number of independent tasks completed, P2: Number of independent requests for help
Luiselli, J. K. (2000). Cueing, demand fading, and positive reinforcement to establish self-feeding and oral consumption in a child with food refusal. *Behavior Modification, 24,* 348–358.	Number: 1 Sex: male Age: 4 Disability/diagnosis: lung disease and gastronomy tube dependence	Setting: home Arrangement: individual (instruction provided by parents)	Positive reinforcement in the form of tangibles for self-feeding	Number of self-fed bites per session
Nes, S. L. (2005). Using paired reading to enhance the fluency skills of less-skilled readers. *Reading Improvement,* 179–192.	Number: 4 Sex: 3 males, 1 female Age range: 9–12 years Disability/diagnosis: low-performance in reading	Setting: school library Arrangement: individual	Oral reading by a more skilled reading prior to reading of the passage by the target participant	Number of words read per minute
Ricciardi, J. N., Luiselli, J. K., & Camare, M. (2006). Shaping approach responses as intervention for specific phobia in a child with autism. *Journal of Applied Behavior Analysis, 39,* 445–448.	Number: 1 Sex: male Age: 8 years Disability/diagnosis: autism and specific phobia	Setting: inpatient clinical setting Arrangement: individual	Differential reinforcement of approach responses	Distance from avoided stimuli
Warnes, E., & Allen, K. D. (2005). Biofeedback treatment of paradoxical respiratory distress in an adolescent girl. *Journal of Applied Behavior Analysis, 38,* 529–532.	Number: 1 Sex: female Age: 16 years Disability/diagnosis: paradoxical vocal fold motion	Setting: outpatient clinic Arrangement: individual	Biofeedback instruction	Electromyographic measures, anecdotal pain and adaptive functioning reports

questions, then we must use research designs that adequately evaluate and control threats to internal validity. In a recent search of Google of "nonconcurrent multiple baseline designs" (April 29, 2008) we were surprised to find no citations or references to their use with large organizations, such as schools or clinics, and were equally surprised to discover the number of citations and references for their use with individuals.

As proposed in the literature (e.g., Carr, 2005; Harvey et al., 2004; Watson & Workman, 1981) the nonconcurrent or delayed multiple baseline design obviates the need for concurrent data collection across baseline data series, i.e., tiers. Assume you are interested in studying the effects of a school-wide positive behavior support strategy to reduce principal office referrals. You have identified three middle schools in three different school districts that have agreed to participate in your investigation. Consistent with nonconcurrent multiple baseline design guidelines, in year one you collect baseline data at one of the three schools; no baseline data are collected at the other two schools in the first year. Data are collected repeatedly (e.g., weekly) on the number of discipline office referrals, and when baseline data are stable the intervention is introduced school-wide. Data continue to be collected repeatedly across weeks until the end of the school year. In the second year of the research project, you collect baseline data at the second school for a longer period of time than at the first school (e.g., 6 weeks rather than 3 weeks), or until baseline data are stable, after which you implement the same intervention as you did at the first school, monitoring office referrals until the end of the school year. Like in the first year of the project, no baseline data are collected at the third school, and you may or may not chose to collect maintenance data at the first school. This sequence of conditions is replicated at the third school, the third year with the important exception that the baseline condition must exceed the length of the baseline condition at the second school (e.g., 9 weeks rather than 6 weeks), or until data are stable. In other words, the nonconcurrent multiple baseline design requires that the same independent variable be implemented across tiers, that the same dependent variable be repeatedly measured, and that each subsequent tier's baseline condition be longer than preceding tiers. The assumption by those who advocate its use is that by requiring longer baseline conditions across tiers (e.g., 3 weeks, 6 weeks, 9 weeks) maturational threats to internal validity are adequately evaluated, i.e., the mere passage of time will not influence the dependent variable. This assumption is predicated on the position that organizations, clinics, individuals, etc. do not change over time, or if they do change, they change in a predictable way. Without baseline or probe data to substantiate these assumptions it would be unwise to rule out maturation as a threat to internal validity. Figure 13.4 is a prototype of a nonconcurrent multiple baseline design.

Advocates of this design recognize that "A primary limitation of the nonconcurrent multiple baseline design is the inability to identify history effects that may be coincidental with the application of a prescribed intervention, or occur at another time during the analysis" (Harvey et al., 2004, p. 274) History threats, as well as maturation threats, are major concerns to applied researchers who use multiple baseline and multiple probe designs. *Confidence that maturation and history threats are under control is based on observing (a) an immediate change in the dependent variable upon introduction of the independent variable, and (b) baseline (or probe) condition levels remaining stable while other tiers are being exposed to the intervention.* Without the latter you cannot conclude, with confidence, that the intervention alone is responsible for observed behavior changes since baseline (or probe) data are not concurrently collected on all tiers from the start of the investigation. Only through repeated measurement across all tiers from the start of a study can you be confident that maturation and history threats are not influencing observed outcomes.

The advantage of the nonconcurrent multiple baseline design is strictly logistical, not

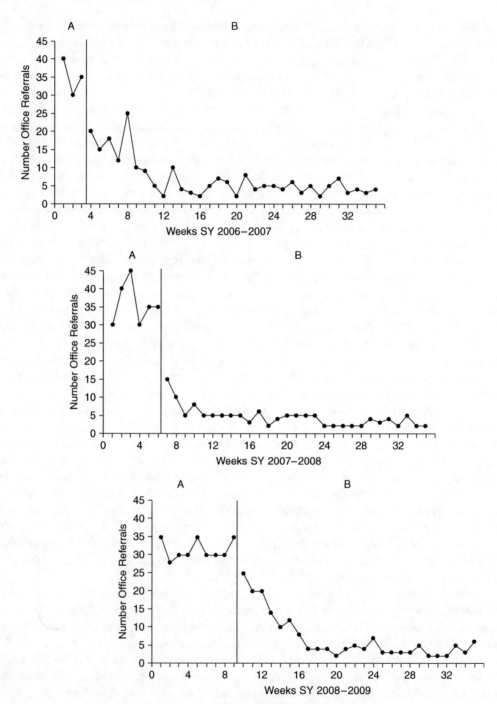

Figure 13.4 Prototype nonconcurrent multiple baseline design across schools; appropriate.

experimental. The design allows researchers to add participants who exhibit rare behaviors as they become available by implementing a series of A-B designs. In a similar vein, researchers interested in studying organization policies and their effect on behavior may not have the resources to collect frequent and repeated measures across three or more schools, hospitals, or clinics. The decision to use a nonconcurrent multiple baseline design is based on practical rather than research considerations. In studying rare cases when only one case is referred every 6 months or once a year, you should consider all other single subject research design options before settling on an A-B design, regardless of your intent to lengthen the baseline condition over previous clients. To quote Carr (2005, p. 220), "The nonconcurrent MB design is essentially a series of A-B replications in which the length of each baseline phase differs," and, "Although the nonconcurrent MB design is useful when designs that are more rigorous are unavailable, especially for scientist-practitioners (Hayes, 1985), the inference one can make regarding the independent variable is weakened (Harris & Jenkins, 1985)." In the case of studying organization policies, it is unclear why periodic probe data could not be collected intermittently, though infrequently, to dispel concerns regarding maturation and history threats to internal validity. Multiple probe designs are well-suited for such research questions since pre-intervention data are collected intermittently.

A word of caution is in order to you as a consumer of research. Figure 13.4 shows the most appropriate and least misleading way to graphically present data generated within the context of a nonconcurrent multiple baseline design. Data on each tier show when baseline data collection was initiated over the course of the 21 weeks of the study, clearly showing that data were not collected concurrently across tiers. Figure 13.5 shows an alternative graph format plotting the same data as shown in Figure 13.4, however, the first week of data collection on each tier is aligned with the first week noted along the abscissa giving the visual appearance that baseline data were collected concurrently across all tiers. Though dates may be added along the abscissa of each tier, it is highly likely that readers will, at first glance, identify the design as a "true" multiple baseline design, rather than a nonconcurrent multiple baseline design, and incorrectly visually analyze findings without attention to possible maturation and history threats that were not evaluated. We believe, as do others (Carr, 2005), that a graphic representation of this type is deceptive and should be avoided, and thus we recommend a graphic format similar to that in Figure 13.4.

Although the nonconcurrent multiple baseline design may have more flexibility than traditional multiple baseline and multiple probe designs, it does not, and cannot, provide as convincing a demonstration of experimental control because it fails to concurrently evaluate dependent variable levels in the initial sessions, days, weeks, or months of the investigation. The visual analysis of such data is limited to a simple A-B design, with all its shortcomings, followed by a series of A-B replications across data series. In spite of its limitations, it continues to be used to evaluate clinical programs that address a wide range of behaviors of individuals, including bladder control (Duker, Averink, & Melein, 2001), sleep disturbance and sleepwalking (France & Hudson, 1990; Frank, Spirito, Stark, & Owens-Stively, 1997), instruction compliance (Everett, Olmi, Edwards, & Tingstrom, 2005) and expressive communication (Hanser & Erickson, 2007; Tincani, Crozier, & Alazetta, 2006; Lancioni, O'Reilly, Oliva, & Coppa, 2001). In reviewing these and other nonconcurrent multiple baseline design studies, it is important to attend to their compliance with the "baselines of different lengths" guideline and use of a graphic display format that accurately shows their attempts to evaluate threats to internal validity. Some researchers who have recognized the limitations of the nonconcurrent multiple baseline design and have combined it with other single subject designs, such as the A-B-A-B design (e.g., Freeman, 2006; Tiger, Hanley, & Hernandez, 2006) or multiple baseline design (Schindler & Horner, 2005), while others have

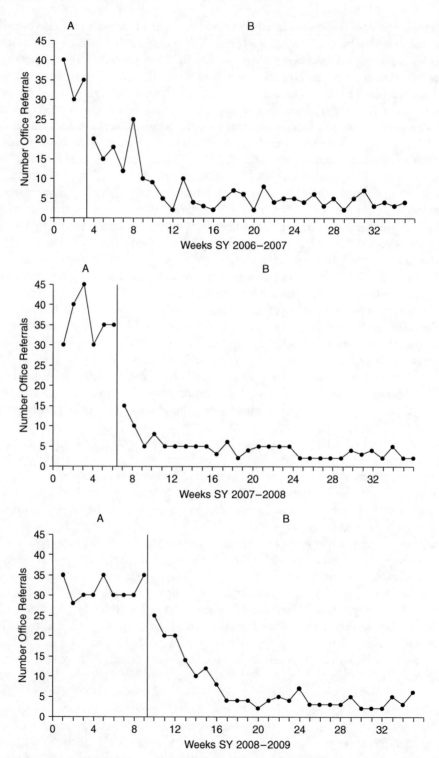

Figure 13.5 Prototype nonconcurrent multiple baseline design across schools; inappropriate.

developed variations of the design, e.g., longer baseline conditions on earlier tiers and systematically shorter baseline conditions on later tiers (Barry & Singer, 2001). It is a design that should be considered only as a last resort when more stringent single subject designs cannot be used.

Combination Designs

In this section we present a case for combining single subject research designs when the research question(s) or circumstances call for it. Single subject research designs are combined when (a) planning a study, or (b) attempting to salvage experimental control during a study in progress. More specifically, applied researchers are combining designs to:

1. Answer more than one research question in one investigation, for example, a functional assessment of a behavior (e.g., ATD–MED variation) followed by an analysis of proposed intervention effectiveness (e.g., A-B-A-B).
2. Address the inherent limitations of a research design (e.g., multiple baseline design across participants) and strengthen the demonstration of experimental control by adding another design (e.g., multiple probe design across behaviors).
3. Respond to covariation if behaviors, participants, or conditions were not independent, as believed prior to the start of a multiple baseline or multiple probe design study, by changing to an A-B-A-B design with concurrent monitoring across untreated behaviors, participants or conditions.

Table 13.2 identifies and briefly summarizes several studies that have combined single subject research designs for one or more of these reasons. A common practice by researchers interested in the functional analysis of challenging behavior has been to combine an alternating treatments design (ATD–MED variation) with an A-B-A design (Roundtree & Kennedy, 2006; Baker, Hanley, & Mathews, 2006) or A-B-A-B withdrawal design (Hanley, Piazza, Fisher, & Maglieri, 2005; Dwyer-Moore & Dixon, 2007). Researchers who recognize the limitations of the nonconcurrent multiple baseline design have strengthened their evaluation of experimental control by combining it with an A-B-A-B withdrawal or "reversal" design (Freeman, 2006; Tiger et al., 2006), multiple baseline design (Schindler & Horner, 2005), or changing criterion design (Najdowski, Wallace, Doney, & Ghezzi, 2003). Others, who recognize the importance of intra-subject replication and its not being addressed in multiple baseline (or probe) designs across participants, have combined them with multiple probe designs across behaviors (Trent, Kaiser, & Wolery, 2005), across conditions (Charlop-Christy, Lee, & Freeman, 2000), A-B-A-B withdrawal designs (Koegel, Werner, Vismara, & Koegel, 2005), and changing criterion designs (Levin & Carr, 2001). Multiple baseline across participants have also been combined with A-B-A-B designs (Charlop-Christy & Haymes, 1998), alternating treatments designs (ATD; Lloyd, Bateman, Landrum, & Hallahan, 1989), and adapted alternating treatments designs (AATD; Cuvo & Klatt, 1992; Worsdell et al., 2005; Canella-Malone et al., 2006.) These studies, and those presented in Table 13.2, illustrate the range of combination designs that have been used by applied researchers, but this sample is by no means exhaustive. The important thing when designing your study is to select a research design, or combination of designs, that evaluate threats to internal validity and answers the research question(s) posed. As Baer, Wolf, and Risley (1987) stated,

a good design is one that answers the question convincingly, and as such needs to be constructed in response to the question and then tested through argument in that context (sometimes called "thinking through") rather than imitated from a book. . . . Perhaps

Table **13.2** Studies That Combined Single Subject Research Designs

Design	Reference	Participants	Setting/arrangement	Independent variable	Dependent variable
MP across conditions + ABAB	Alberto, P. L., Heflin, J., & Andrews, D. (2002). Use of the timeout ribbon procedure during community-based instruction. *Behavior Modification, 26,* 297–311.	Number: 2 Sex: male Age range: 10–11 years Disability/diagnosis: ID IQ range: 46–50	Setting: community work sites and school gym Arrangement: individual	Timeout ribbon procedure with token reinforcement for exhibiting appropriate behaviors	Percentage of innapropriate behaviors that interfered with successful community participation
MP across participants + MP across conditions	Charlop-Christy, M., Le, L., & Freeman, K. A. (2000). A comparison of video modeling with in vivo modeling for teaching children with autism. *Journal of Autism and Developmental Disorders, 30,* 537–552.	Number: 5 Sex: 4 males, 1 female Age range: 7–11 years Disability/diagnosis: autism	Setting: private therapy center Arrangement: individual	In-vivo or video modeling for social, adaptive, or cognitive skills	Number of correct responses
MP across conditions + ABAB	Hughes, M. A., Alberto, P. A., & Fredrick, L. L. (2006). Self-operated auditory prompting systems as a function-based intervention in public community settings. *Journal of Positive Behavior Interventions, 8,* 230–243.	Number: 4 Sex: 2 males, 2 females Age range: 16–18 years Disability/diagnosis: moderate ID IQ range: 40–55	Setting: community work sites Arrangement: individual	Self-operated auditory prompting systems with prompts that provided reinforcement for attention or escape-maintained behavior	Escape- and attention-maintained target behaviors (different for each child)
MB across participants + ABAB	Koegel, R. L., Werner, G. A., Vismara, L. A., Koegel, L. K. (2005). The effectiveness of contextually supported play date interactions between children with autism and typically developing peers. *Research & Practice for Persons with Severe Disabilities, 30,* 93–102.	Number: 2 Sex: 1 male, 1 female Age range: 8–9 Disability/diagnosis: autism	Setting: community/home play sites Arrangement: integrated small group	Contextual support provided by providing set-up and structure that encouraged participation by both the child with autism and typically developing peer	Reciprocal interaction between child with autism and typically developing peer; child affect
MB across participants and CC	Levin, L., & Carr, E. G. (2001). Food selectivity and problem behavior in children with developmental disabilities: Analysis and intervention. *Behavior Modification, 25,* 443–470.	Number: 3 Sex: 2 males, 1 female Age range: 5–7 Disability/diagnosis: autism (3), moderate to severe ID (3)	Setting: self-contained classroom Arrangement: individual	Positive reinforcement for consumption in the form of preferred edibles and witholding access to preferred foods prior to meals	Number of bites of non-preferred foods consumed during each session

the more important point is that convincing designs should be more important than "proper" designs.

(pp. 319, 320)

Guidelines and Considerations for Combining Designs

The decision to combine two single subject research designs should be made after recognition of the experimental analysis limitations of using one design alone and the advantages of combining two designs. We recommend that you approach your decision to combine designs as follows:

1. Write your rationale for combining designs. This will necessitate identifying the limitations of each individual design you may be considering to answer your research question(s).
2. Select the two simplest research designs that will (a) answer your research question(s); (b) control for threats to internal validity; and (c) be practical given the demands of your setting.
3. Identify the primary design for your study, the one that will "drive" the decision-making process. This will typically be the one that you wanted to use in the first place, but in recognition of its limitations, you decide to add a second design to address those limitations. For example, in recognition of the failure of a multiple baseline (or probe) design across participants to evaluate intra-subject replication, you decide to combine a multiple probe design across participants ($N = 3$) and a multiple probe design across behaviors ($N = 2$). When Participant 1 reaches criterion on the first behavior, you will introduce the independent variable to the second behavior for Participant 1, while concurrently introducing the independent variable to the first behavior for Participant 2. When Participant 2 reaches criterion on the first behavior, you will introduce the independent variable to the second behavior for Participant 2, while concurrently introducing the independent variable to the first behavior for Participant 3. In this example the primary design is the multiple probe design across participants, with the multiple probe design across two behaviors addressing the primary limitation of the multiple probe design across participants, i.e., direct intra-subject replication. Figure 13.6 graphically depicts this combination design.
4. Consider the logistics when choosing designs to combine. If you can combine a multiple probe design across participants with a multiple probe design across behaviors there are practical advantages for doing so. Yes, you could combine multiple baseline designs that would generate continuous rather than intermittent measures prior to introduction of the independent variable, but it is likely to be impractical, particularly if the research is to be conducted in a classroom or clinic setting. Though the frequency of measures will be less, the combined multiple probe designs will still permit an evaluation of history and maturation threats, and testing threats to a lesser degree, and will be more practical to implement in an applied research setting.
5. Follow the design recommendations and guidelines for each of the two designs you have chosen to combine.

When designing your study, whether it is with a single design or combination of designs, your first priority is to choose a design that will answer your research question(s). This should be done using the simplest research design and data-collection procedures that will evaluate potential threats to internal validity. When combining designs the same principle of parsimony applies. You should "be your worst critic"; anticipate criticisms and adjust your measurement

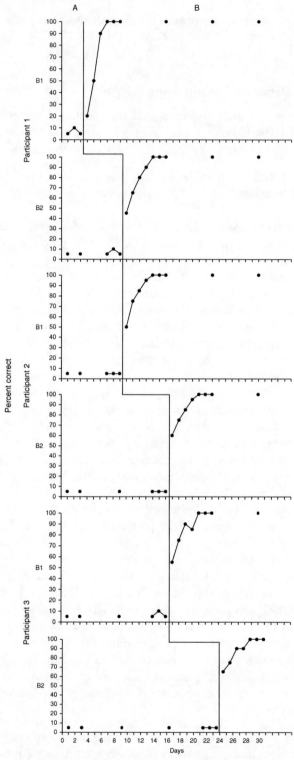

Figure 13.6 Prototype multiple probe design across participants and multiple probe design across behaviors.

and research-design decisions based on the shortcomings you identify. Keep your research design and measurement procedures simple, but not so simple as to fail to adequately address threats to internal validity that would undermine your findings.

Applied Example: Multiple Baseline Design Across Behaviors and Participants

Trent, J. A., Kaiser, A. P., & Wolery, M. (2005). The use of responsive interaction strategies by siblings. *Topics in Early Childhood Special Education, 25,* 107–118.

Trent, Kaiser, and Wolery (2005) studied the effectiveness of teaching siblings of children with Down syndrome positive-interaction strategies to facilitate interactions between the typically developing child and the sibling with Down syndrome. Participants were two sibling dyads, each with an older, typically developing sister and a younger sister with Down syndrome. Sibling dyads were 7 and 5 years, and 9 and 7 years old. Instruction on nonverbal mirroring and verbal responding were taught to typically developing siblings in each child's home. The primary purpose of the study was to evaluate "procedures for teaching two responsive interaction strategies (mirroring and verbal responding) to two older, typically developing children in the context of play sessions with their younger siblings with Down syndrome" (p. 108). The second purpose was to evaluate the effectiveness of a "child-implemented responsive interaction intervention on the communicative behavior of the siblings with Down syndrome" (p. 108).

The dependent variables were the number of 10-s intervals in which target siblings used a responsive intervention strategy; the target siblings' percentage of responsiveness to the verbal turns of their siblings; the number of 10-s intervals in which siblings with Down syndrome took verbal turns; and the number of investigator prompts per session. Data were collected on percentage of responsiveness to verbal turns and the number of investigator prompts using an event-recording procedure. Data were collected on the number of intervals in which target siblings used a responsive intervention strategy and number of intervals in which siblings with Down syndrome took a verbal turn using a 10-s partial-interval recording procedure. Mirroring and responding by the typical siblings were coded as occurring or not occurring during each 10-s interval, and verbal turns by the children with Down syndrome were recorded as occurring or not occurring during the same 10-s intervals. In addition, these turns were coded as verbal turns (any vocalization) and topic-related verbal turns (intelligible to the observer). Reliability data were collected during 25% of all sessions across all conditions. Using the point-by-point (interval-by-interval) method, interobserver agreement (IOA) ranged from 83 to 100% and procedural-reliability agreement ranged from 89 to 100%.

There were three experimental conditions (baseline, intervention, and follow-up) in the study. The intervention condition was evaluated within the context of a multiple baseline design across behaviors and participants. Sessions were conducted in the family home twice each week, each lasting 30–60 min. During baseline sessions, the observer asked siblings to play together for 10 min with no other family members in the room. Use of responsive intervention strategies by the typical sibling and verbal turns by the sibling with Down syndrome were recorded using the 10-s partial-interval recording system. Each intervention session was divided into three segments. The first segment consisted of teaching or reviewing interactive response strategies to the typically developing sibling. The second segment consisted of a 10-min play session with both siblings. During the third segment, both siblings and the observer watched the videotape of the play session while the observer provided positive and corrective feedback. Follow-up sessions, which were conducted identical to baseline sessions, were conducted one month after completion of the intervention condition.

Figure 13.7 displays the number of 10-s intervals in which typically developing siblings used a responsive interactive strategy during baseline, intervention, and follow-up conditions evaluated within the context of a multiple baseline across behaviors and participants design. Prior to instruction, there were few intervals during which they used responsive interaction strategies when interacting with their sister with Down syndrome. A visual analysis of the data shows

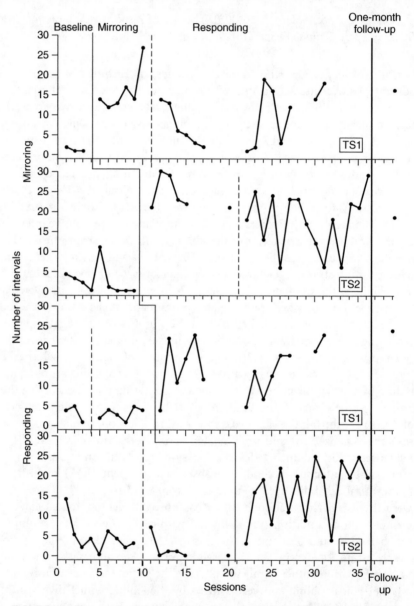

FIGURE 1. The number of 10-s intervals in which target siblings used either mirroring or verbal responding during baseline, mirroring training, responding training, and follow-up sessions. Gaps in the data indicate missed training sessions.

Figure 13.7 The number of 10-s intervals in which target siblings used either mirroring or verbal responding during baseline, mirroring training, responding training, and follow-up sessions. Gaps in the data indicate missed training sessions (source: Trent et al., 2005. Copyright © 2005 by Sage Publications. Reproduced by permission of Sage publications).

that the use of responsive interactive strategies changed from a stable, low level, and zero or decelerating trend in baseline conditions, to a variable accelerating trend in a therapeutic direction upon introduction of training. These data were replicated across siblings. During the one-month follow-up session, siblings maintained use of responsive interaction strategies above baseline levels.

Figure 13.8 presents the percentage of intervals in which the typically developing siblings responded to the verbal turns of their sibling with Down syndrome. During the baseline condition and mirroring training, levels of responding remained low. Upon introduction of responding training, there was an immediate change in level and a variable accelerating therapeutic trend. Gains observed in the responding training condition were maintained during the follow-up session for both children.

Data on behaviors of the siblings with Down syndrome were more variable than those of the typically developing siblings. Number of verbal turns remained variable across all conditions of the study. Although typical siblings took more verbal turns than their sibling with Down syndrome throughout the intervention, the ratio of turns taken by the typically developing sibling and the sibling with Down syndrome was more balanced at the end of intervention condition compared to baseline condition.

The effectiveness of teaching typically developing siblings responsive interaction strategies to increase responsiveness to sisters with Down syndrome was demonstrated within the context of a multiple baseline across behaviors and participants design. Effects on the communicative behavior of participants with Down syndrome were more variable, although there were some

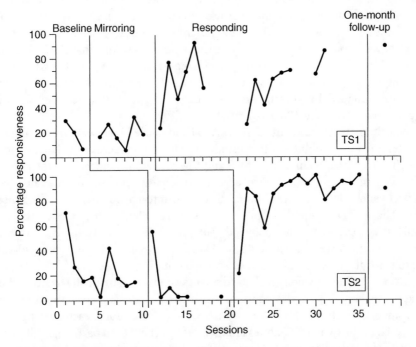

FIGURE 2. Target siblings' percentage of responsiveness to the verbal turns taken by their siblings with Down syndrome.

Figure 13.8 Target siblings' percentage of responsiveness to the verbal turns taken by their siblings with Down Syndrome (source: Trent et al., 2005. Copyright © 2005 by Sage Publications. Reproduced by permission of Sage Publications).

modest gains. Follow-up data suggest that siblings were able to continue using these strategies in the absence of continued instruction.

Applied Example: Multiple Probe Design Across Participants and Adapted Alternating Treatments Design (AATD)

Cannella-Malone, H., Sigafoos, J., O'Reilly, M., de la Cruz, B., Edrisinha, C., & Lancioni, G. E. (2006). Comparing video prompting to video modeling for teaching daily living skills to six adults with developmental disabilities. *Education and Training in Developmental Disabilities*, *41*, 344–356.

Cannella-Malone et al. (2006) compared video prompting (VP) and video modeling (VM) for teaching two chained tasks to six adults with disabilities. The participants ranged in age from 27 to 41 years and were all diagnosed with mild to moderate intellectual disabilities (IQ range: 36–69) and an autism spectrum disorder. Each participant was judged to have substantial deficits in domestic living skills. All participants lived in a group home and attended the same vocational day program. The study was conducted in the dining room and kitchen areas of the vocational center. The purpose of the study was to compare the effectiveness of VM and VP for teaching two domestic tasks (unpacking groceries and setting the table).

Three experimental phases were employed during the study: (a) probe phase; (b) comparison phase: VP vs. VM; (c) "Best Alone" phase. The dependent variable was the percentage of task-analysis steps performed correctly by each participant. An event recording system was used to record the correct or incorrect completion of each step in the task analysis. During the comparison phase the VP procedure was used to teach one task and the VM procedure was used to teach the second task. Procedure assignment was counterbalanced across participants and tasks. Data were collected twice-weekly during training sessions that lasted approximately 10 min each. Reliability data were collected during at least 55% of all sessions across all conditions. Interobserver agreement was calculated using the point-by-point method in which agreements were divided by agreements plus disagreements multiplied by 100. Reliability percentages ranged from 90 to 100% (M = 99%).

An adapted alternating treatments design (AATD; identified by researchers as an alternating treatments design) was combined with a multiple probe design across participants to evaluate the relative effectiveness and efficiency of VP and VM procedures in teaching the two response-chain tasks. The multiple probe design across participants permitted an evaluation of VP and VM effectiveness by controlling several threats to internal validity, including history and maturation. The AATD comparison phase assessed the relative efficiency of the two video instructional strategies, as measured by percentage of steps correct for each chained task. Following the comparative phase, the "Best Alone" phase used the superior video training procedure to teach the task that had not yet reached criterion.

During probe condition sessions each participant was taken individually to either the kitchen (unpacking grocery bag task) or dining room (setting table task) and given the appropriate task directive. A single opportunity probe procedure was used to evaluate each participant's ability to complete each of the two task analyses independently. That is, if a participant did not initiate the first step of the task within 30 s, complete any step initiated within 30 s, or complete any step within 30 s after completion of the preceding step, the probe session was stopped. An edible reinforcer was delivered noncontingent on performance following each probe session. This reinforcement strategy was used at the end of VP and VM sessions as well in subsequent phases. The purpose of probe sessions was to determine if participants were able to complete either task, in their entirety, independently and to determine whether tasks were of equal difficulty, a requirement of the AATD.

During the VP vs. VM condition, each participant was taken individually to the kitchen or dining room, as in the probe condition. The trainer gave a direction to "watch this" before showing the appropriate video. Following the video, the trainer gave the direction to complete the task (or task step). During both the VP and VM sessions, a one-sentence voice-over direction was given for each step of the task analysis.

During the VP sessions, 10 separate video clips depicting each step of a task analysis were shown to a participant. Participants were expected to perform each step of the chained task after the corresponding step was shown via video. Participants were not expected to complete the entire chained task at once. Only steps completed correctly within 30 s after viewing were scored as correct. During the VP condition the video clip was filmed from a participant's perspective.

During VM condition a single video clip depicting all 10 steps of the task analysis was shown to a participant prior to the participant having the opportunity to perform the entire task. The participant was given 30 s to initiate the step and 2 min to complete all steps, with no contingencies for duration or latency of any other single step in the chained task. Participants were allowed to complete steps out of sequence, but were required to perform the task in its entirety after watching the video clip. This video clip in the VM condition was filmed from a spectator's perspective.

During final "Best Alone" phase, both tasks were taught using the VP procedure. During this condition, an error-correction procedure was implemented for one participant who consistently made mistakes in utensil placement.

As is shown in Figure 13.9, all students had low and stable levels of correct responding ranging between 0% and 30% during the probe condition. For two participants (Gina and Steve), immediate and abrupt changes in level and trend were noted with the VP condition, while no or small changes in level and trend were noted with the VM condition. For the third participant (John), an immediate change in level and trend was observed with both conditions, although the absolute level change was greater with the VP condition.

> This phase continued until either one task had been taught to criterion (i.e., 100% correct over 2 of 3 successive sessions) or until visual analysis of the graphed data showed a clear and consistent separation in data paths of the two conditions over the last nine sessions.
>
> (p. 349)

During the "Best Alone" phase, each of three participants whose data are depicted in Figure 13.9 reached or maintained criterion levels of responding on both tasks using the VP procedure. Similar results were found for the remaining three participants, although one participant failed to reach criterion using either procedure.

A combination multiple probe design across participants and adapted alternating treatments design was used to evaluate the relative effectiveness of two video presentation instructional procedures counterbalanced across participants and tasks. The VP procedure resulted in more efficient acquisition of skills across participants and both tasks. More studies are needed, however, considering the research base showing that VM has been effective with participants with disabilities, though it was "generally ineffective" (p. 353) in this study. Several factors may contribute to the success of VP in comparison to VM, including the lower attention and retention demands of VP. In the VM condition, participants were required to watch a video that was more than 1 min in length (M = 1 min, 37 s; 2 min, 42 s), while the video clips in the VP condition were an average of only 12 s for one task and 19 s for the other task. In

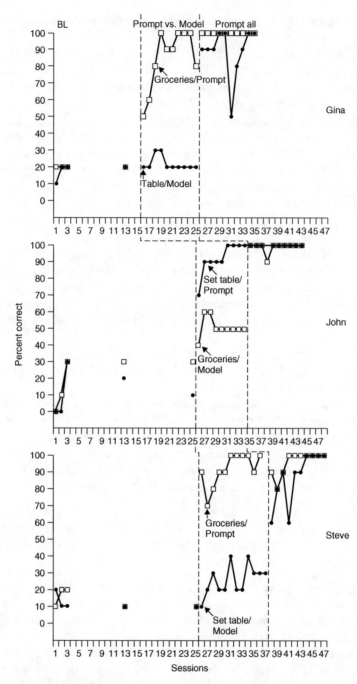

Figure 1b. Percentage of steps completed correctly across sessions and tasks for Gina, John, and Steve.

Figure 13.9 Percentage of steps completed correctly across sessions and tasks for Gina, John, and Steve (source: Canella-Malone et al., 2006. Reproduced by permission from the Council for Exceptional Children, Division on Developmental Disabilities).

addition, the perspective from which the film was viewed may have had an impact on task acquisition. In the VP condition, the film was viewed from the participant's perspective (i.e., participant watched a video of a hand/arm picking up fruit from a bag and putting it in a bowl, similar to what they would see if they were completing the task themselves). In the VM condition, the film was viewed from a spectator's perspective (i.e., participant watched a video of someone else completing the task). Future studies are needed to replicate findings and determine the factors that are important in contributing to the superiority of one video training procedure over the other.

Applied Example: Multiple Baseline Design Across Settings and Nonconcurrent Multiple Baseline Design Across Participants

Schindler, H. R., & Horner, R. H. (2005). Generalized reduction of problem behavior of young children with autism: Building trans-situational interventions. *American Journal on Mental Retardation, 110,* 36–47.

Schindler and Horner (2005) assessed the interaction effects of implementing functional communication training (FCT) in a school context and a lower effort intervention in secondary settings on reduction in problem behaviors and increases in the use of functional communication skills in all four settings. Participants enrolled in an early-intervention program were selected based on a formal diagnosis of an autism spectrum disorder (ASD), nomination from a teacher as a student with significant behavioral problems, and observable levels of problem behaviors in multiple school and home environments. Participants were 4 to 5 years of age and were all diagnosed with autism. One participant was also diagnosed with Charge Syndrome.

Three preschool settings and one home setting routine were identified for each student. Preschool settings included: (a) one-on-one training; (b) snack; and (c) "explore time," which was a routine where students transitioned between play and sensory-based activities. The transitions in explore time were teacher-directed. At home, two students worked with their parents on activities similar to those used in one-on-one training at school, and one student transitioned between home activities similar to those used in explore time.

A functional behavior assessment (FBA) was conducted via teacher and parent interview. Neal's problem behaviors were most likely to occur when he was engaged in a less-preferred activity when more-preferred activities were available, and they were thought to be maintained by access to preferred activities. The antecedent stimuli for Ellie's problem behaviors were tasks on which she was unsuccessful, and her behaviors were thought to be maintained by adult assistance. Antecedent stimuli for Kit's problem behaviors were teacher-directed transitions. His problem behaviors were thought to be maintained by avoidance of transitions. Each child was assigned FCT behaviors to be taught based on the FBA: (a) Neal: pointing to a preferred activity or card depicting the preferred activity; (b) Ellie: saying "help" or pointing to a "help card"; (c) Kit: using a transition book by receiving visual information given by the teacher indicating a transition.

The dependent variables were: (a) percentage of intervals during which target problem behaviors occurred, and (b) percentage of intervals during which students used FCT skills. FCT skills "were identified as socially appropriate responses that were (a) perceived as equal or more efficient than problem behaviors and (b) produced the same maintaining function as the problem behaviors" (p. 40). Data were collected using a 10-s partial-interval recording system. Each interval was recorded as including a problem behavior, if a problem behavior occurred at any time during the 10-s interval, or a functional communication, if a functional communication behavior was used at any time during the 10-s interval.

Interobserver-agreement data were collected during 64% of all sessions, "distributed nearly equally across all students, settings, and phases" (p. 41). The mean IOA was at least 94% for problem behavior, and at least 95% for functional communication behaviors for each student. Procedural-fidelity procedures were in place during 90% of class observations and 100% of home sessions, which included the supervision of each session by the primary researcher who provided prompts, as needed, to complete procedures appropriately. Authors reported that this procedure "resulted in correct implementation of phase procedures in all monitored sessions" (p. 41).

An "adapted" multiple baseline design across settings was used to evaluate the effectiveness of functional communication training to reduce problem behaviors in one context, and to produce generalized reduction of problem behaviors when combined with a second, lower-effort intervention in other settings. Data from the primary setting were also analyzed using a nonconcurrent multiple baseline design across participants, although data from this comparison were not visually displayed. The study employed three conditions: (a) baseline; (b) low effort; and (c) FCT. In the primary setting, baseline data were collected, followed by FCT. In the other three settings, the low-effort condition was employed during the same time as the baseline condition for the primary settings. Then, baseline conditions were employed, followed by the second low-effort condition. Figure 13.10 shows the order of conditions during the study.

During baseline condition, teachers or parents were instructed to retain features of the setting that were observed during the initial observation. This included giving nonpreferred task demands for Neal, providing activities that could not be performed successfully for Ellie, and giving transition directions from one activity to another for Kit. Results of the FBA were used to develop interventions for the low-effort condition. However, these interventions involved minimal effort or set-up. Prompting and rewarding of functional communication was used for each child, to include making sure that visual aids were available and using the prompt to "ask the right way." Consequences for problem behavior (e.g., helping Ellie with a difficult task) were maintained. FCT occurred during one-on-one training and involved multiple opportunities to use functional communication behaviors that had been previously taught following the baseline condition. During FCT, use of functional communication behaviors resulted in teacher praise plus access to the maintaining reinforcer. Problem behavior resulted in redirection and did not result in access to the maintaining reinforcer.

In order to assess the interaction effects of implementing a high-effort intervention in one setting and a low-effort intervention in multiple secondary settings, it was necessary to demonstrate that the low-effort procedures were not effective alone, and that the implementation of the high-effort procedures in one setting was insufficient to achieve a reduction in problem behavior in secondary settings. Analysis of Figure 13.10 shows that both the ineffectiveness of first low-effort condition prior to FCT and the lack of generalization during baseline condition to the three secondary settings demonstrate the interaction effects of the two intervention components resulting in generalized reduction in problem behaviors during the second low-effort condition.

Analysis of Figure 13.10 also shows that problem behavior was maintained at high and variable levels for Neal (M = 41%). Following the implementation of FCT, the level and trend of the data changed such that Neal was emitting low, stable levels of problem behavior (M = 14%). In addition, Neal's use of functional communication increased from 0% in the baseline condition to a mean of 3.1% during FCT condition. In the secondary settings, Neal's problem behavior was also high but variable (M = 53.3%). During baseline, no reliable changes in level or trend occurred (M = 53.9%) when compared to the low-effort condition, and functional communication remained at 0%, suggesting that the behaviors learned during FCT

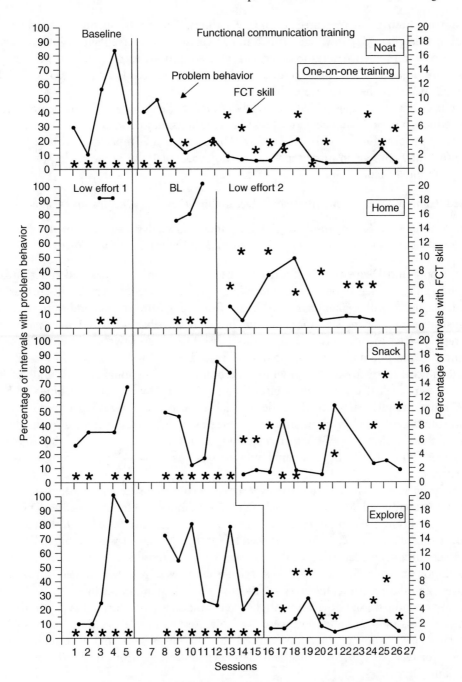

Figure 2. Percentage of observation intervals with problem behavior and functional communication training skill (FCT) performance by Neal across experimental phases.

Figure 13.10 Percentage of observation intervals with problem behavior and functional communication training skill (FCT) performance by Neal across experimental phases (source: Schindler & Horner, 2005. Reproduced by permission from the American Association on Intellectual Development Disabilities).

were not generalizing to the three secondary settings. The reintroduction of the low-effort condition following FCT, however, resulted in a decrease in the percentage of intervals during which behavior problems were observed (M = 9.2%) and an increase in the percentage of intervals during which functional communication skills were used (M = 5.6%). These findings were replicated with the other two children.

Results of this study suggest that, while low-effort interventions alone may be unsuccessful in the reduction of problem behaviors, these interventions may be successful if combined with high-effort interventions in only one setting. These results are important because providing high-effort interventions in more than one setting, particularly in home settings, may not be feasible in some situations.

Applied Example: Alternating Treatments Design and A-B-A-B Withdrawal Design

Dwyer-Moore, K. J., & Dixon, M. R. (2007). Functional analysis and treatment of problem behavior of elderly adults in long-term care. *Journal of Applied Behavior Analysis, 40*, 679–683.

Dwyer-Moore and Dixon (2007) studied the use of functional analysis and function-based treatments in three elderly participants in a long-term care facility. Participants in the study were all diagnosed with dementia, ranged in age from 70 to 90 years old, and were referred by administrative and nursing staff for exhibiting problematic behaviors. Two female participants were referred due to disruptive vocalizations (obscenities, repetitive statements, "irrelevant utterances"), and one male participant was referred due to wandering from the facility that made it difficult to ensure his safety within the home. The functional analysis and results of treatment were evaluated within the context of an ATD (MED variation) combined within an A-B-A-B withdrawal design. The dependent variable was number of responses per minute for the target undesirable behavior. Interobserver agreement (IOA) was calculated by dividing the smaller frequency count by the larger frequency count and multiplying by 100. Agreement ranged from 90 to 100% for functional-analysis sessions (M = 94%) and from 92 to 100% for treatment sessions (M = 97%).

During the functional analysis, four experimental conditions (attention, demand, control, alone) were conducted for 10 min each with 5-min breaks between sessions. During the attention condition, the experimenter sat across the room and interacted with the participant only by giving 5–10 s of social attention when the problem behavior was exhibited. During the demand condition, an occurrence of the problem behavior resulted in removal of the demand (gross motor or academic tasks) for 30 s. Leisure items were readily available in the control condition, and the experimenter provided 5–10 s of social attention during each 30-s interval. In the alone condition, the experimenter observed "unobtrusively" through a gap in the door; no leisure items or social attention were available. Results of the functional-analysis (ATD, MED variation) portion of the study showed that the target behaviors were maintained by attention for two participants (Alice and Carmen), and escape from demands for the third participant (Derek).

Intervention sessions were conducted individually in the family room of the facility. Sessions were 10 min in length. For Alice, a DRA procedure was used that consisted of 3–5 s of social attention contingent upon an appropriate vocalization. Inappropriate vocalizations were ignored. Derek's intervention consisted of noncontingent access to attention (NCA) on a FT-30 s schedule and access to his most preferred leisure items, as chosen during a "multiple-stimulus without replacement (MSWO) preference assessment" (p. 681). No consequences were provided during wandering. If he wandered out of the room he was redirected back to the family room once he was observed engaged in appropriate behavior. Carmen's intervention entailed FCT with extinction during demand situations. Demands were presented continuously and the experimenter prompted her to hand a break card to her. Presentation of the break card, prompted or unprompted, resulted in a 30-s break from the activity. Inappropriate vocalizations resulted in continued demands, with a prompt to use the card after 5 s with no vocalizations.

Figure 13.11 shows the results from the functional analysis and treatment for each participant. For Alice, the ATD showed that inappropriate vocalizations were maintained by attention. Treatment, using DRA for appropriate vocalizations, resulted in a 40% decrease in inappropriate vocalizations, and a 400% increase in appropriate vocalizations. The effectiveness of the intervention was demonstrated within the context of the A-B-A-B withdrawal design. Derek's wandering behavior also was maintained by attention and his treatment package of noncontingent attention and access to preferred leisure activities resulted in an 85% decrease in his wandering behavior. The functional analysis showed that Carmen's disruptive vocalizations were maintained by escape from demands. Functional communication training and extinction resulted in an 82% decrease in inappropriate vocalizations from the baseline condition to the intervention condition.

Although problem behavior is common in long-term care facilities, and although elderly adults living in these facilities represent a growing part of the population, few research studies have examined treatments for these behaviors. This study supports the appropriateness of using functional analysis to determine the cause of problem behavior in older adults with dementia. In addition, by combining the ATD design with a withdrawal design, the effectiveness of each function-based intervention allowed clear demonstration of experimental control.

Resolving "Ambiguities" of Multiple Baseline and Multiple Probe Designs

Internal Validity Issues

An essential requirement for any experiment or investigation is internal validity. As previously discussed, internal validity is attained when a researcher demonstrates that (a) an intervention has an effect on the dependent variable and (b) the effect is replicated within the study. Regardless of the single subject design used to evaluate a functional relation between independent and dependent variables, a number of threats to internal validity are possible. For applied researchers who use multiple baseline and multiple probe designs, the following threats to internal validity must be controlled: history, maturation, testing, instrumentation, data variability, and reactive intervention (Campbell & Stanley, 1968; Glass, Willson, & Gottman, 1975; Kratochwill, 1978). In addition to these potentially confounding variables an investigator must also attend to procedural contrast, i.e., the number and magnitude of differences between the procedures employed in two adjacent conditions (Cuvo, 1979). Chapter 11 discussed several suggestions for controlling threats to internal validity. Here, we describe other strategies to guard against confounding due to history, testing, and procedural contrast.

History

Historical confounding refers to extraneous events that occur concurrently with the introduction of the independent variable and that influence the dependent variable (see Chapter 5). Multiple baseline and multiple probe designs control for historical confounding by demonstrating immediate and, ideally, abrupt changes in the dependent variable across three or more data series over time. However, behavioral covariation (i.e., response generalization) across untreated data series threatens a demonstration of experimental control.

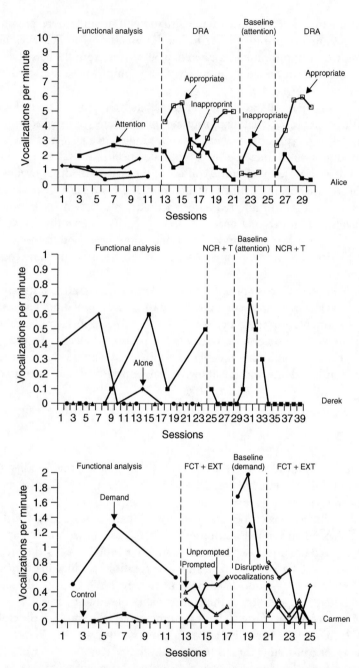

Figure 1. The number of problem behaviors per minute during the analogue functional analyses and interventions for Alice (vocalizations, top), Derek (wandering, middle), and Carmen (vocalizations, bottom). Alternative appropriate behaviors in the intervention phases are designated by open squares (Alice) and open diamonds and triangles (Carmen).

Figure 13.11 The number of problem behaviors per minute during the analogue functional analyses and interventions for Alice (vocalizations, top), Derek (wandering, middle), and Carmen (vocalizations, bottom). Alternative appropriate behaviors in the intervention phases are designated by open squares (Alice) and open diamonds and triangles (Carmen) (source: Dwyer-Moore & Dixon, 2007. Reproduced by permission from *Journal of Applied Behavior Analysis*).

Behavioral covariation may be prevented from interfering with a demonstration of experimental control if you: (a) carefully target behaviors (conditions or participants) that are as functionally independent as possible; (b) identify, a priori, four or more behaviors (conditions or participants) rather than the minimum recommendation of three; or (c) combine a multiple baseline (or probe) design across behaviors with a multiple baseline (or probe) design across participants. Figure 13.12 graphically displays a study by Cronin and Cuvo (1979) in which they combined a multiple probe design across three behaviors (sewing of buttons, hems, and seams) with a multiple probe design across five participants. Given the topographic similarities of the three behaviors, the multiple probe design across participants was a safeguard for salvaging experimental control if the investigators had "guessed" incorrectly about the independence of three behaviors and had behavioral covariation occurred. The multiple probe design across behaviors was a way they strengthened their demonstration of experimental control by evaluating intra-subject replication, a limitation of the multiple probe (and baseline) designs across participants. The data in Figure 13.12 show how only upon introduction across the three behaviors and across the participants was there a positive change in behavior. The discussion of other reasons for combining single subject research designs is addressed in the next section.

As discussed in Chapter 11 and graphically presented in Figure 11.2a, in the event that behavioral covariation emerges during the course of an investigation, and the behavior is "reversible," a "brief" reintroduction of baseline conditions with the last data series introduced to the intervention may salvage a demonstration of experimental control (Kazdin & Kopel, 1975; Russo & Koegel, 1977). With this "return to baseline condition strategy" you should closely monitor the effect the withdrawal (or reversal) of the intervention has on all data series. If other data series also show a reversal in trend and/or level, there is evidence of a generalized intervention effect, i.e., response generalization. This effect is further verified by the subsequent reintroduction of the independent variable and reversal in trend.

Though the change from a multiple baseline (or probe) design to an A-B-A-B design, with one or more participants, may be the only way to salvage experimental control, there are, however, circumstances that may preclude you from doing so. First, it is unlikely that some behaviors, once learned, will return to earlier baseline levels when the independent variable is withdrawn (e.g., academic skills). Second, practical constraints, such as parent or staff resistance, may prohibit the withdrawal of an effective intervention. Third, ethical constraints, as with a child who exhibits self-injurious or dangerously aggressive behaviors, may prevent a reintroduction of baseline conditions for even a brief period. If behavioral covariation does occur and (a) you have not combined your multiple baseline or multiple probe design with another design in advance, and (b) one or more of the three circumstances arise, thereby precluding an A-B-A-B analysis, the outcome is clear—a failure to demonstrate experimental control with the participant. If this situation were to occur with all participants, you would be left with a series of A-B analyses and correlational rather functional conclusions. Our recommendations is, if you suspect covariation is possible and lack confidence in the independence of behaviors, conditions, or participants, it would be prudent to combine designs in the event that your suspicions are realized.

Testing and Procedural Contrast

Multiple baseline and multiple probe designs are particularly susceptible to confounding due to the contrast between baseline condition and intervention condition procedures. Confounding due to prolonged testing, using untrained items, may generate two distinctly

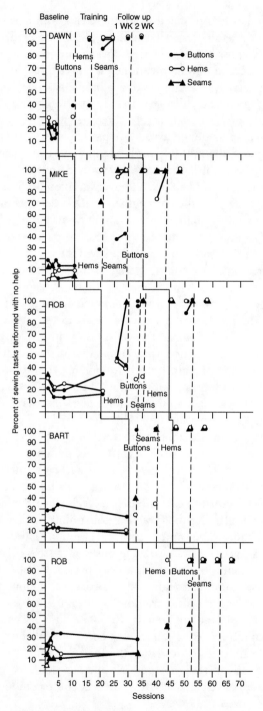

FIGURE 11-5 **Performance on Sewing Skills Test in various phases of the experiment for five mentally retarded adolescents.**

Figure 13.12 Performance on Sewing Skills Test in various phases of the experiment for five mentally retarded adolescents (source: Cronin & Cuvo, 1979. Reproduced by permission from *Journal of Applied Behavior Analysis*).

different patterns of responding. As discussed in Chapter 11, prolonged baseline conditions can (a) suppress responding, resulting in a data path that resembles an extinction curve (e.g., nonreinforced baseline condition); or (b) facilitate responding, generating a data trend that resembles learning (e.g., reinforced baseline condition). The type of baseline data trend will depend upon such variables as the frequency of observation periods, response requirements (e.g., task difficulty), and the procedures employed in the baseline condition (e.g., reinforcement schedule). These potential side effects have been advanced as rationales for using a multiple probe design, rather than the multiple baseline design; however, it is unfair to suggest that multiple baseline designs necessarily evoke reactive responding from participants. As preventive measures, Cuvo (1979) suggested: (a) to minimize the length of baseline sessions by including fewer items and/or fewer trials while still validly sampling learner performance; (b) to maintain as dense a reinforcement schedule during baseline as during intervention by reinforcing appropriate "test-taking behaviors" (e.g., attending to task or by interspersing previously learned "competency items" for which correct responding can be reinforced); and (c) to delete unnecessary components of an intervention package. By following these guidelines the risks of confounding due to prolonged baseline conditions can be minimized, whether you choose a multiple baseline or multiple probe design.

Premature Introduction of the Independent Variable

In Chapter 11 we recommended that the independent variable not be introduced until the preceding behavior (participant or condition) reaches a pre-established criteria. By doing so there is no arbitrary investigator-imposed time frame for threats to validity (e.g., history, maturation, testing) to show an effect. By following this guideline you can avoid criticism that you did not allow sufficient time for threats to be revealed. There are, however, situations in which you may be justified in setting a schedule for introducing an intervention to the next participant due to your ethical concerns of a prolonged baseline condition on a participant. For example, you may decide to introduce your independent variable to each of four participants every five days in your multiple baseline design across participants study, thereby allowing a maximum of 20 days for internal validity threats to be revealed. This may or may not satisfy reviewers. Be aware that although your decision may have an ethical or practical basis, depending on the "number of day stagger" (e.g., 2 days vs. 4 days vs. 6 days), you may or may not convince your audience that threats to validity were adequately assessed. We strongly recommend that you do not strictly adhere to an intervention-introduction schedule if your visual analysis of baseline data (trend direction or level stability) contra-indicate its introduction. If you decide to employ such a schedule you may choose to combine single subject research designs, for example, multiple probe across behaviors and a multiple baseline across participants. Once again we advise that you be conservative in your research decisions, assuming the role of critical reviewer, a role you should also assume in the research decisions of others.

Summary

In this chapter we reviewed and exemplified two variations of the multiple baseline design, the changing criterion design and the nonconcurrent multiple baseline design, both of which have been used by applied researchers, but which have inherent limitations in their evaluation of threats to internal validity. For this reason we do not recommend that they be the design of first choice when designs that more thoroughly evaluate experimental control are available. Guidelines were presented for each of these designs, with the recommendation that they be combined with other single subject research designs to address their limitations. Increasingly, applied researchers are combining single subject research designs as a means of answering more than one research question in their investigations (e.g., ATD to assess the function of a behavior and an A-B-A-B to evaluate intervention effectiveness), and addressing the limitations of some designs, such as no intra-subject replication (e.g., multiple probe across participants combined with a multiple probe across behaviors). Because of the dynamic nature of single subject research designs, researchers have been able to add, or change, their experimental design mid-course for one or more study participants in an effort to salvage experimental control in response to behavior covariation. In our discussion of combining single subject research designs we have advocated that the simplest combination of designs be employed, provided that the research question can be answered and threats to internal validity controlled. Prior to design selection we recommend that you assume the role of critic, systematically identifying all potential threats to internal validity and criticisms from reviewers that may arise. By doing so you will be better prepared to justify your design choice and explain its strengths and weaknesses in evaluating experimental control.

References

Ahearn, W. H. (2003). Using simultaneous presentation to increase vegetable consumption in a mildly selective child with autism. *Journal of Applied Behavior Analysis, 36,* 361–365.

Alberto, P. L., Heflin, J., & Andrews, D. (2002). Use of the timeout ribbon procedure during community-based instruction. *Behavior Modification, 26,* 297–311.

Baer, D. M., Wolf, M. M., & Risley, T. R. (1987). Some still-current dimensions of applied behavior analysis. *Journal of Applied Behavior Analysis, 20,* 313–327.

Baker, J. C., Hanley, G. P., & Mathews, R. M. (2006). Staff-administered functional analysis and treatment of aggression by an elder with dementia. *Journal of Applied Behavior Analysis, 39,* 469–474.

Barry, L. M., & Singer, G. H. S. (2001). A family in crisis: Replacing the aggressive behavior of a child with autism toward an infant sibling. *Journal of Positive Behavior Interventions, 3,* 28–38.

Campbell, D. T., & Stanley, J. C. (1968). *Experimental and quasi-experimental designs for research.* Chicago: Rand McNally, 1966.

Canella-Malone, H., Sigafoos, J., O'Reilly, M., de la Cruz, B., Edrisinha, C., & Lancioni, G. E. (2006). Comparing video prompting to video modeling for teaching daily living skills to six adults with developmental disabilities. *Education and Training in Developmental Disabilities, 41,* 344–356.

Carr, J. E. (2005). Recommendations for reporting multiple-baseline designs across participants. *Behavioral Interventions, 20,* 219–224.

Charlop-Christy, M. H., & Haymes, L. K. (1998). Using objects of obsession as token reinforcers for children with autism. *Journal of Autism and Developmental Disorders, 28,* 189–198.

Charlop-Christy, M. H., Le, L., & Freeman, K. A. (2000). A comparison of video modeling with in vivo modeling for teaching children with autism. *Journal of Autism and Developmental Disorders, 30,* 537–552.

Christ, T. J. (2007). Experimental control and threats to internal validity of concurrent and nonconcurrent multiple baseline designs. *Psychology in the Schools, 44,* 451–459.

Cronin, K. A., and Cuvo, A. J. (1979). Teaching mending skills to mentally retarded adolescents. *Journal of Applied Behavior Analysis, 12,* 401–406.

Cuvo, A. J. (1979). Multiple-baseline design in instructional research: Pitfalls of measurement and procedural advantages. *American Journal of Mental Deficiency, 84,* 219–228.

Cuvo, A. J., & Klatt, K. P. (1992). Effects of community-based, videotape, and flash card instruction of community-referenced sight words on students with mental retardation. *Journal of Applied Behavior Analysis, 25,* 499–512.

DeLuca, R. V., & Holborn, S. W. (1992). Effects of variable-ratio reinforcement schedule with changing criterion on exercise in obese and non-obese boys. *Journal of Applied Behavior Analysis, 25,* 671–679.

Duker, P. C., Averink, M., & Melein, L. (2001). Response restriction as a method to establish diurnal bladder control. *American Journal on Mental Retardation, 106,* 209–215.

Dwyer-Moore, K. J., & Dixon, M. R. (2007). Functional analysis and treatment of problem behavior of elderly adults in long-term care. *Journal of Applied Behavior Analysis, 40,* 679–683.

Easterbrooks, S. R., & Stoner, M. (2006). Using a visual tool to increase adjectives in the written language of students who are deaf or hard of hearing. *Communication Disorders Quarterly, 27,* 95–109.

Everett, G. E., Olmi, D. J., Edwards, R. P., & Tingstrom, D. H. (2005). The contributions of eye contact and contingent praise to effective instruction delivery in compliance training. *Education & Treatment of Children, 28,* 48–62.

Flood, W. A., & Wilder, D. A. (2004). The use of differential reinforcement and fading to increase time away from a caregiver in a child with separation anxiety disorder. *Education and Treatment of Children, 27,* 1–8.

France, K. G., & Hudson, S. M. (1990). Behavior management of infant sleep disturbance. *Journal of Applied Behavior Analysis, 23,* 91–98.

Frank, N. C., Spirito, A., Stark, L., & Owens-Stively, J. (1997). The use of scheduled awakenings to eliminate childhood sleepwalking. *Journal of Pediatric Psychology, 22,* 345–353.

Freeman, K. A. (2006). Treating bedtime resistance with the bedtime pass: A systematic replication and component analysis with 3-year olds. *Journal of Applied Behavior Analysis, 39,* 423–428.

Ganz, J. B., & Sigafoos, J. (2005). Self-monitoring: Are young adults with MR and autism able to utilize cognitive strategies independently? *Education and Training in Developmental Disabilities, 40,* 24–33.

Glass, G. V., Willson, V. L., & Gottman, J. M. (1975). *Design and analysis of time-series experiments.* Boulder, CO: Colorado Associated University Press, 1975.

Hall, R. V. (1971). *Managing behavior: Behavior modification, the measurement of behavior.* Lawrence, Kan: H & H Enterprises.

Hanley, G. P., Piazza, C. C., Fisher, W. W., & Maglieri, K. A. (2005). On the effectiveness of and preference for punishment and extinction components of function-based interventions. *Journal of Applied Behavior Analysis, 38,* 51–65.

Hanser, G. A., & Erickson, K. A. (2007). Integrated word identification and communication instruction for students with complex communication needs: Preliminary results. *Focus on Autism and Other Developmental Disabilities, 22,* 268–278.

Harris, F. N., & Jenson, W. R. (1985). Comparisons of multiple-baseline across persons designs and AB designs with replication: Issues and confusions. *Behavioral Assessment, 7,* 121–129.

Hartmann, D. P., & Hall, R. V. (1976). The changing criterion design. *Journal of Applied Behavior Analysis, 9,* 527–532.

Harvey, M. T., May, M. E., & Kennedy, C. H. (2004). Nonconcurrent multiple baseline designs and the evaluation of educational systems. *Journal of Behavioral Education, 13,* 267–276.

Hayes, S. C. (1985). Natural multiple baselines across persons: A reply to Harris and Jenson. *Behavioral Assessment, 7,* 129–132.

Hughes, M. A., Alberto, P. A., & Fredrick, L. L. (2006). Self-operated auditory prompting systems as a function-based intervention in public community settings. *Journal of Positive Behavior Interventions, 8,* 230–243.

Johnston, R. J., & McLaughlin, T. F. (1982) The effects of free time on assignment completion and accuracy in arithmetic: A case study. *Education and Treatment of Children, 5,* 35–40.

Kazdin, A. E., & Kopel, S. A. (1975). On resolving ambiguities of the multiple-baseline design: Problems and recommendations. *Behavior Therapy, 6,* 601–608.

Koegel, R. L., Openden, D., & Koegel, L. K. (2004). A systematic desensitization paradigm to treat hypersensitivity to auditory stimuli in children with autism in family contexts. *Research & Practice for Persons with Severe Disabilities, 29,* 122–134.

Koegel, R. L., Werner, G. A., Vismara, L. A., & Koegel, L. K. (2005). The effectiveness of contextually supported play date interactions between children with autism and typically developing peers. *Research & Practice for Persons with Severe Disabilities, 30,* 93–102.

Kratochwill, T. R. (Ed.). (1978). *Single subject research—Strategies for evaluating change.* New York: Academic Press.

Lancioni, G. E., O'Reilly, M. F., Oliva, D., & Coppa, M. M. (2001). A microswitch for vocalization responses to foster environmental control in children with multiple disabilities. *Journal of Intellectual Disability Research, 45,* 271–275.

Levin, L., & Carr, E. G. (2001). Food selectivity and problem behavior in children with developmental disabilities: Analysis and intervention. *Behavior Modification, 25,* 443–470.

Lloyd, J. W., Bateman, D. F., Landrum, T. J., & Hallahan, D. P. (1989). *Journal of Applied Behavior Analysis, 22,* 315–323.

Luiselli, J. K. (2000). Cueing, demand fading, and positive reinforcement to establish self-feeding and oral consumption in a child with food refusal. *Behavior Modification, 24,* 348–358.

McDougall, D., Hawkins, J., Brady, M., & Jenkins, A., (2006). Recent innovations in the changing criterion design: Implications for research and practice in special education. *Journal of Special Education, 40,* 2–15.

Najdowski, A. C., Wallace, M. D., Doney, J. K., & Ghezzi, P. M. (2003). Parental assessment and treatment of food selectivity in natural settings. *Journal of Applied Behavior Analysis, 36,* 383–386.

Nes, S. L. (2005). Using paired reading to enhance the fluency skills of less-skilled readers. *Reading Improvement, 40,* 179–192.

Ricciardi, J. N., Luiselli, J. K., & Camre, M. (2006). Shaping approach responses as intervention for specific phobia in a child with autism. *Journal of Applied Behavior Analysis, 39*, 445–448.

Roantree, C. F., & Kennedy, C. H. (2006). A paradoxical effect of presession attention on stereotypy: Antecedent attention as an establishing, not an abolishing, operation. *Journal of Applied Behavior Analysis, 39*, 381–384.

Russo D. C., & Koegel, R. L. (1977). A method for integrating an autistic child into a normal public-school classroom. *Journal of Applied Behavior Analysis, 10*, 579–590.

Schindler, H. R., & Horner, R. H. (2005). Generalized reduction of problem behavior of young children with autism: Building trans-situational interventions. *American Journal on Mental Retardation, 110*, 36–47.

Sidman, M. (1960). *Tactics of scientific research—Evaluating experimental data in psychology.* New York: Basic Books.

Tiger, J. H., Hanley, G. P., & Hernandez, E. (2006). An evaluation of the value of choice with preschool children. *Journal of Applied Behavior Analysis, 39*, 1–16.

Tincani, M., Crozier, S., & Alazetta, L. (2006). The picture exchange communication system: Effects on manding and speech development for school-aged children with autism. *Education and Training in Developmental Disabilities, 41*, 177–184.

Trent, J. A., Kaiser, A. P., & Wolery, M. (2005). The use of responsive interaction strategies by siblings. *Topics in Early Childhood Special Education, 25*, 107–118.

Warnes, E., & Allen, K. D. (2005). Biofeedback treatment of paradoxical vocal fold motion and respiratory distress in an adolescent girl. *Journal of Applied Behavior Analysis, 38*, 529–532.

Watson, P. J., & Workman E. A. (1981). The non-concurrent multiple baseline across individuals design: An extension of the traditional multiple baseline design. *Journal of Behavior Therapy and Experimental Psychiatry, 12*, 257–259.

Worsdell, A. S., Iwata, B. A., Dozier, C. L., Johnson, A. D., Neibert, P. L., & Thomason, J. L. (2005). Analysis of response repetition as an error-correction strategy during sight-word reading. *Journal of Applied Behavior Analysis, 38*, 511–527.

Statistics and Single Subject Research Methodology

Jonathan M. Campbell and Caitlin V. Herzinger

Our overall objective for this chapter is to describe and illustrate several statistical methods for analyzing single subject research design data. As such, we begin the chapter by introducing the long-standing debate between visual and statistical analysis of single subject data. We outline limitations of visual analysis as documented in the research literature, which has, in part, served as justification for using statistical techniques to evaluate single subject data. We then move on to introduce a few methods of statistical analysis that have been proposed and used with single subject design data, illustrating their calculation with a few hypothetical data sets. We also identify several statistical programs that have been created to assist with the statistical analysis of these data. Due to the large number of proposed statistical analytic strategies for use with single subject research data, our discussion is selective and brief. Our aim is to provide readers with a reasonable introduction to several statistical methods that include illustrative calculations which are supplemented by references and resources for further inquiry and use.

Due to the increasing interest in aggregation and reporting of single subject research data in the form of quantitative synthesis, we also introduce meta-analytic techniques that have been proposed for synthesizing data from single subject investigations. We illustrate the calculation of several effect-size measures that have been proposed and report findings from several recently published meta-analyses. In our discussion of meta-analysis, we describe the rationale for meta-analysis of both group-based synthesis and single subject synthesis. The chapter concludes with a discussion of the complementary use of visual and statistical analysis and the potential impact of single subject meta-analyses.

Prior to introducing methods of statistical analysis, we believe it is important to disclose our opinions and biases about the use of such procedures within the field. First and foremost, our chapter should not be interpreted as reflecting the opinions of the other authors who have contributed to the text. Second, we believe that no statistical procedure exists to date that effectively solves or handles all types of single-case data. Third, we believe that statistical procedures, particularly those involving quantitative synthesis of individual outcomes, will be used with increasing frequency in the literature; therefore, investigators using single subject methodology should be familiar with some of the basic statistical procedures. Fourth, we expect inquiry in this area to increase in the near future, which will include the development and evaluation of additional statistical procedures for use with single subject data sets. Finally, we do not consider ourselves to be strong advocates of statistical analysis of single-case data, but rather invested consumers of statistical procedures. As such, we attempt to provide a reasonable introduction to statistical procedures with a particular eye toward identifying unresolved problems with them.

Visual Analysis and Statistical Analysis

After implementation of a well-designed intervention that features a sound experimental design, the educator or behavioral interventionist turns toward evaluating the effectiveness of the intervention. A cautionary note is in order prior to our discussion of visual and statistical analysis: an inappropriately designed study does not allow the individual to justifiably ask the question of whether intervention worked. In the presence of an appropriately designed intervention that features methodological controls and reliable measurement, the experimenter can pose the question, "Did my intervention work?" In response to this question, the "inter-ocular traumatic test" (Edwards, Lindman, & Savage, 1963, p. 217) might be invoked to describe the threshold for concluding that an intervention is effective. That is, graphical representation of data should be of sufficient magnitude that the effect of treatment should "hit [you] between the eyes" (Edwards et al., 1963, p. 217). Of course, treatment effects of this kind are uncommon within the behavioral sciences, which has led to the creation of rules and guidelines regarding how to evaluate if a treatment is effective or not. In Chapter 9, Gast and Spriggs outlined various procedures used to guide the visual analysis of data in order to render a decision about the presence of a treatment effect. The purpose of our chapter is to introduce methods of statistical analysis that attempt to answer questions of whether treatment was effective or not (a dichotomous decision) but also provide an estimate of the strength of an effective treatment (a description along a continuum).

The Argument for Visual Analysis

As described earlier in the text, the majority of single subject research data-based decisions are reached through visual analysis of data plotted in graph form. In Chapter 9, Gast and Spriggs illustrated visual-analysis techniques, such as documenting the degree of trend observed within the baseline and intervention conditions by the use of trend lines and calculating several percentages that will be relevant to our discussion of statistical analysis of data in this chapter, such as the mean level change percentage, median level change percentages, and percentage of non-overlapping data (PND).

The roots of visual-analysis techniques are grounded firmly in the behavior-analysis literature, with frequent reference to Skinner (1963) as an ardent supporter of the visual analysis of data. When arguing for the superiority of direct behavioral observation over measuring "inner states," Skinner also contrasted statistical and visual-analysis methods associated with the superiority:

> The simpler [direct observation] procedure is possible because rate of responding and changes in rate can be directly observed . . . The effect is similar to increasing the resolving power of a microscope: A new subject matter is suddenly open to direct inspection. Statistical methods are unnecessary. When a variable is changed and the effect on performance observed, it is for most purposes idle to prove statistically that a change has indeed occurred.

> (p. 508)

Within the published literature, supporters of visual analysis often cite: (a) the conservative nature of decision-making based on this method; (b) the benefits of access to the "primary" data which is not hindered or clouded by statistical summation; and (c) its dynamic nature (e.g., Parsonson & Baer, 1986).

Visual Analysis Results in Conservative Judgments about Intervention Effects
When compared to statistical analysis, some authors propose that the use of visual analysis provides a more conservative threshold in decision making. For example, Parsonson and Baer (1986) concluded that research findings seemed "to imply that time-series analysis [a statistical technique] is usually less conservative than visual analysis" (p. 159). From an inferential decision-making perspective, a conservative decision threshold results in reduced probability of Type I error, which is to conclude that an effect exists when it does not (Figure 14.1). The argument for conservative judgment associated with visual analysis is that conservatism serves to "filter" weak treatment effects so that only robust treatment effects are applied to clinical problems (Parsonson & Baer). The conservative emphasis built into visual analysis corresponds with a differential tolerability for errors of inference: Type II errors are more acceptable than Type I errors. That is, overlooking small effects, on occasion (i.e., Type II error), is preferable to incorrectly concluding that effects are present when they are not (i.e., Type I error). Invoking the "inter-ocular traumatic test" of significance once again, a conservative decision-making approach means the effects should be readily apparent prior to deciding that a treatment is effective.

| | | **"Reality"** | |
		Treatment is Effective (Yes)	Treatment is Not Effective (No)
Visual/Statistical Analysis Decision	Treatment is Effective (Yes)	True positive	False positive (Type I error)
	Treatment is Not Effective (No)	False negative (Type II error)	True negative

Figure 14.1 Outcomes for statistical/visual analysis decisions and "reality."

Visual Analysis Allows for Direct and Verifiable Analysis of Data

Parsonson and Baer (1986) also argued that visual analysis of graphed data allows for a detailed inspection of observations that are verifiable across judges. By providing access to the primary data set, investigators allow for independent verifiability of their conclusions that is not encumbered by statistical analyses. According to Parsonson and Baer, direct access to data prevents statistical manipulation whereby "nearly significant results are made significant either by finding a statistical test that after all will give significant results from the current data, or by increasing the amount of that data until a statistically significant result emerges" (p. 160). The intimate access to primary data is also thought to allow for discovery of unexpected findings, which may generate new hypotheses to be tested empirically, such as altering an intervention protocol. In contrast to statistical aggregation, such as presenting averages, visual presentation and analysis allows the reader to "look into the fine grain of the data, and perhaps start down a new line of research" (p. 165). Continuing to use the analogy proposed by Skinner (1963), visual analysts argue that access to raw data significantly increases the analytic "resolution" available to the reader.

Visual Analysis Allows for Continuous Evaluation of Treatment

Through the use of ongoing data collection, graphic presentation, and visual analysis, interventions may be tailored to individual clients. Visual analysis allows for response-guided decision making, such as collection of baseline data until behavior reaches a stable level and/or trend prior to implementing intervention. Also, response-guided decision making is required for a growing number of manualized treatment protocols, such as parent–child interaction therapy. Similarly, visual analysis of data allows for modifications in the treatment protocol based on changes in client responding, in essence providing a built-in feedback mechanism to inform treatment. When used in this manner, visual analysis provides for a dynamic evaluation process that is individualized.

Limitations of Visual Analysis

Despite the advantages of visual analysis identified within the literature, multiple authors have criticized the use of visual analysis as the sole decision-making method for determining if an intervention is effective. Criticisms are leveled in the areas of questionable reliability and accuracy for the judgments based upon visual analysis.

Unreliability Across Raters

When subjected to tests of inter-judge agreement, visual analysis has been shown to be unreliable. For example, Ottenbacher (1993) conducted a quantitative review of 14 studies representing 789 participants and found that overall agreement was unsatisfactorily low ($M = 0.58$; $Mdn = 0.58$; $SD = 0.12$; $Range = 0.39$–0.84). Ottenbacher also found that agreement did not differ when training was included (0.62) or excluded (0.57) prior to judging graphed data. Similarly, the presence (0.64) vs. absence (0.59) of trend lines did not improve inter-rater agreement. Normand and Bailey (2006) recently documented 72% average accuracy between (a) five Board Certified Behavior Analysts' decisions about treatment effectiveness and (b) pre-established criteria for treatment effectiveness. The authors also reconfirmed the finding that the presence (67%) vs. absence (78%) of trend lines resulted in no improvement in accuracy. In sum, research findings question the *reliability* of judgments based on visual analysis.

Visual Analysis is Prone to Type I Errors

Despite the argument that visual analysis yields conservative judgments about the effectiveness of treatment, raters are prone to making Type I errors in the range of 0.24 to 0.25 (e.g., Matyas & Greenwood, 1990; Ferron & Jones, 2006). That is, visual analysis has been shown to incorrectly conclude that ineffective treatments are effective up to 25% of the time. Although Type I errors characterize general findings in the literature, Bobrovitz and Ottenbacher (1998) found good general agreement (86%) between statistical analysis and visual analysis and low Type I errors (4.8%). Type I errors in visual analysis have also been shown to be related to autocorrelated data. Matyas and Greenwood, for example, documented Type I error rates as high as 84% in the presence of autocorrelated data and random variability. Overall, research findings question the *accuracy* (i.e., criterion validity) of conclusions reached using visual analysis.

No Universal Decision Rules

The poor reliability and accuracy findings for visual analysis have been attributed, in part, to the lack of consensus regarding decision rules to guide visual analysis. The consistent call for visual analysts to look for "large and convincing" experimental effects is not accompanied by a specific definition of what is meant by large, which results in the possibility that visual analysts rely on "visual common sense" (Bengali & Ottenbacher, 1998, p. 651).

In response to these criticisms, recent work in the area of visual analysis has been initiated by Hagopian et al. (1997) and Fisher, Kelley, and Lomas (2003) to create explicit decision rules. Hagopian et al. produced a set of structured criteria to identify behavioral function from data typically collected during multi-element functional analysis, i.e., alternating treatments design. The authors trained interns in their use and found that inter-rater reliability improved from a pre-training mean of 0.46 to a post-training mean of 0.81. As such, Hagopian et al. demonstrated that explicit decision rules could be used to improve *reliability* of visual analysis.

Fisher et al. (2003) created two sets of decision rules (one more conservative than another) to evaluate treatment effects in A-B panels based on two baseline trend lines extended to the intervention condition. According to the decision rules, an intervention was deemed effective when intervention-condition observations exceeded both baseline predictions in numbers that exceeded chance. One baseline trend line was based on the split-middle method described in Chapter 9, the second trend line was the baseline mean value extended into the intervention condition. Fisher et al. demonstrated the utility of the explicit criteria in training five participants; thereby demonstrating that explicit decision rules can be used to improve the *accuracy* of visual analysis. Even so, others have questioned the value of creating formal, standardized procedures for visual analysis, citing the potential loss of freedom to evaluate data and reach individual conclusions that may contradict the decision rules (e.g., Parsonson & Baer, 1986).

Why Consider Statistical Analysis of Single Subject Data?

In response to the problems identified above with visual analysis, varied statistical-analysis procedures have been proposed. Authors, such as Huitema (1986b) who have advocated for the use of statistical analysis, frequently point to the following advantages:

> (a) statistical methods allow the identification of small but potentially important effects that might be ignored in a visual analysis, (b) statistical methods can evaluate intervention effects when there this is instability and/or trend during the baseline phase, and (c) statistical methods are more objective than visual methods.

(p. 228)

Statistical Analysis May also Increase Confidence in Visual Analysis
In addition to Huitema's (1986b) reasons, supporters of statistical analysis of single subject research data have argued the point that visual judgments may be strengthened in the presence of statistical corroboration. In cases where visual analysis and statistical analysis agree, the conclusions reached are more convincing and allow us to state our conclusions about intervention effectiveness (or ineffectiveness) with greater confidence.

Statistical Analysis May also Quantify Strength of Outcome
Visual analysis is frequently used to determine whether treatment is effective or not (a dichotomous outcome) yet does not yield an estimate of strength of the effect (a judgment placed on a continuum). Statistical analysis allows for improved quantification of treatment effects via summary statistics that reflect magnitude of treatment effect. The ability to quantify intervention effects is important, as several fields now frequently require researchers to report effect sizes in research reports, regardless of the final statistical test result reported.

A Note about Increased "Objectivity" in Statistical Analysis
In contrast to Parsonson and Baer's (1986) skepticism about statistical test results, proponents of statistical analysis often assert that statistical procedures are less subjective when compared to visual analysis. At face value, this seems reasonable; statistical formula and statistical software programs are dispassionate about the results being calculated. Of course, the investigator is typically not so disinterested in the findings, which can result in the misuse of statistical procedures.

In addition to the standard arguments we reviewed, Huitema (1986b) offered additional justifications for the use of statistical analysis over 20 years ago that continue to be relevant today. Huitema cogently argued that the inclusion of statistical analysis in single-case research may allow for greater influence of behavior analysis. A clear example of this lies in the U.S. Department of Education's What Works Clearinghouse that emphasizes randomized trials and quantitative analysis of data to guide educational policy decisions.

Proposed Statistical Procedures for Use with Single Subject Research Data

For the purposes of demonstrating some of the statistical techniques used with single subject research data, we continue to use Gast and Spriggs's data set. Recall in the example, the purpose of the investigation was to determine if contingent adult attention (independent variable) had an effect on a child's engagement with peers (dependent variable). The raw data are presented in Table 14.1 and the data are presented in graphic form in Figure 14.2; note that the data are presented as a simple A-B design. To illustrate some of the statistical procedures, we modified the data set presented in Chapter 9 either through adding observation points or combining the data with other hypothetical data sets.

Table 14.1 Hypothetical Data Set to Illustrate Statistical Procedures for A-B Designs

	Baseline						Intervention												
Day	1	2	3	4	5	6	7	8	9	10	11	12	13	14	15	16	17	18	19
Data	22	42	11	20	8	26	40	81	63	70	80	57	96	90	78	28	86	79	94

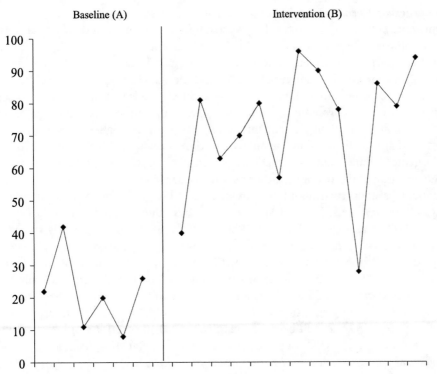

Figure 14.2 Hypothetical data showing simple A-B contrast for effects of adult attention in increasing peer interaction.

Two Important Points to Consider for Statistical Analysis of Single Subject Research Data
Prior to introducing specific statistical analytic procedures for use with single subject data, we introduce two important points that transcend our introduction of statistics. The first involves the difference between evaluating for treatment level effects, slope effects, or combined level and slope effects; the second involves the role of autocorrelation.

Evaluating for the Presence of Level Change, Slope Change, or Both
As described in Chapter 9, treatment effects may present in the form of level changes, slope changes, or combined level and slope changes. The distinctions are important to keep in mind, because treatment may affect any or all of these outcomes. To review, level changes between baseline and treatment conditions indicate that an absolute difference of behavior has occurred, usually characterized by mean or median differences. For example, the child in our example may show an average increase in peer interaction contingent upon adult attention. Slope changes indicate that the rate of behavior has changed in some way, either increasing or decreasing as a result of treatment. In our example, this might be characterized by an increasing rate of engaging in peer interaction due to adult attention. Finally, level and slope changes may be involved in an interaction, such as the overall amount of peer interaction showing an improvement, but also that the improvement may increase in a systematic manner over the course of the intervention. Throughout our introduction and discussion of statistical-analysis techniques, we identify what type of treatment outcome is being evaluated for each method.

Problems of Serial Dependency and Autocorrelation

The term *serial dependency* refers to the predictability of a value in a data sequence through either *prior values* or the *passage of time* (Matyas & Greenwood, 1996). Autocorrelation refers to the extent to which an observed value is related to a previously observed value, such as an adjacent observation within a single subject research design. The typical method for detecting the degree of autocorrelation within a data set is to calculate a lag-1 autocorrelation coefficient (r_1). Fairly similar to a correlation coefficient, r_1 provides a numerical indicator of relations between data points and their subsequent data points; with the higher the value the stronger the relations. Lag-1 indicates that the autocorrelation is calculated from adjacent points, i.e., one set "lagging" behind the other. In addition to strength of relations, r_1 provides information about the direction of the relations, either positive or negative.

We should be concerned about the presence of autocorrelation because it impacts the accuracy of visual *and* statistical analysis when it reaches values as small as 0.10 to 0.25 (Busk & Marascuilo, 1988; Sharpley & Alavosius, 1988). In the presence of sufficiently strong *positive* autocorrelation, error variances for parametric tests will be artificially decreased, thereby inflating values of resulting test statistics (e.g., t or F). This means that we may incorrectly conclude that there is an effect when there is not because our p-value of 0.05 would actually be a 0.10 without the autocorrelation. If autocorrelation is sufficiently *negative*, standard errors will be increased and the resulting statistic too conservative (Crosbie, 1987). This means that we may incorrectly fail to reject the null because our p-value is 0.10 when it would actually be 0.05 without the autocorrelation. Throughout our discussion of statistical techniques, we identify the impact that autocorrelation may have on each procedure.

How Much Autocorrelation Exists in Single Subject Research Data?

In his review of 441 lag-1 autocorrelation coefficients, Huitema (1985) found a mean of −0.01 and argued that single subject data were not autocorrelated. Huitema's findings were challenged subsequently by several authors (e.g., Busk & Marascuilo, 1988; Sharpley & Alavosius, 1988) who reported that autocorrelated data are frequently observed in single-case data, which creates problems for the majority of statistical tests that assume that observations are independent. For example, Busk and Marascuilo reported that roughly 40% of baseline and 60% of intervention autocorrelation coefficients reported in Huitema's review met or exceed values that would significantly increase Type I errors for many statistical tests. Sharpley and Alavosius similarly argued that even a small degree of autocorrelation will result in overestimated test values for traditional statistical procedures.

Subsequent studies have confirmed the presence of significant autocorrelation in single subject research literature. For example, Robey, Schultz, Crawford, and Sinner (1999) calculated the degree of autocorrelation for A-B designs from the aphasia treatment literature and documented a significant degree of lag-1 autocorrelation for baseline conditions ($M = -0.11$, $SD = 0.33$), intervention conditions ($M = 0.27$, $SD = 0.24$), and for the total number of observations ($M = 0.63$, $SD = 0.18$). Similarly, Bengali and Ottenbacher (1998) reported significant lag-1 autocorrelation for both baseline ($M = 0.23$, $SD = 0.21$) and treatment ($M = 0.30$, $SD = 0.23$) conditions for published single subject research studies within the rehabilitation literature. The degree of lag-1 and lag-2 (data separated by two observations) autocorrelation in the sample data set was calculated using SPSS Version 15.0 and is presented in Table 14.2. The degree of autocorrelation in our data appears to be comparable to that reported in the literature.

Table 14.2 Degree of Autocorrelation in the Sample Data Set

Example of lag design for baseline

Baseline observation	Data	Day 1 Lag	Day 2 Lag
1	22	–	–
2	42	22	–
3	11	42	22
4	50	11	42
5	8	50	11
6	26	8	50

Resulting autocorrelation coefficients

Condition	Lag 1	Lag 2
Baseline	−0.312	0.135
	$(n = 5)$	$(n = 4)$
Intervention	−0.186	−0.082
	$(n = 12)$	$(n = 11)$
Total	0.538*	0.473**
	$(n = 18)$	$(n = 17)$

Note:
* $= p < 0.05$; ** $= p < 0.01$.

Procedures for Statistical Analysis

t *Tests and Analysis of Variance (ANOVA)*

Some authors have proposed the use of parametric statistical procedures for the statistical analysis of single-case data, such as the use of ANOVA or *t* tests. These tests were proposed in order to detect *level* changes across baseline and intervention conditions, for example, the traditional *t* test involves comparing mean differences between groups of interest which is divided by error variance. Given the degree of autocorrelation observed within single-subject data, these tests are generally considered to be inappropriate. The reason for this involves the violation of the assumption that individual observations are statistically independent from one another. Although ANOVA and *t* tests are robust when violations of homogeneity of variance and normality are encountered, violation of the non-independence of observations results in increased chances of either Type I or Type II errors. That is, when observations are non-independent, the statistical test becomes too liberal or conservative in determining if treatment is effective or not. Our hypothetical data set produces a t (17) = 5.58, $p < 0.001$ and $F(1, 17) = 31.18$, $p < 0.001$. Recall that t equals the square root of F, so findings are identical in a two-group analysis such as this.

Binomial Sign Test

The binomial sign test has been proposed for single subject data analysis to detect changes in *level* between baseline and intervention conditions. The approach involves calculation of a baseline trend line which is extended into the adjacent intervention condition. Several trend line options have been proposed, such as the use of the split-middle technique, the celeration trend line, and a trend line based on ordinary least squares regression. Regardless of the calculation method, the baseline trend line is extended into the treatment condition and the proportions of points falling above and below the trend line are calculated. This statistical approach assumes that treatment observations have an equal probability of falling above or below the baseline prediction line. Therefore the expected probability for each "successful" treatment observation is 0.50 (i.e., 50%) which reflects a unique binomial test known as the binomial sign test. As the number of observation deviates from the expected 0.50 value, we are more likely to reject the null hypothesis. For our sample data set, we calculated a baseline trend line using ordinary least squares regression, which resulted in the following prediction equation:

$$Y = 28.80 - 2.09 \times day$$

The regression equation establishes the y-intercept at 28.80 and predicts an average decrease in 2.09 number of minutes of peer interaction per observation period. Two points to make here. The first is that the regression line is reflecting what appears to be a negative trend in the data. The second is that the regression line will result in impossible prediction values, that is, negative minutes of peer interaction, by day 14 of the intervention. At day 14, predicted minutes of peer interaction is $28.80 - (2.09 \times 14) = -0.46$ minutes. This situation arises due to the negative slope in baseline and illustrates some problems with regression approaches in general. Regression prediction equations may yield impossible values that need to be accounted for in other procedures, such as some of the effect size calculations introduced later in the chapter.

We extended the line into the adjacent treatment condition which resulted in 13 observations above the line and zero observations below the line. The associated one-tailed probability of finding that all 13 observations fell above the trend line is $p = 0.0001$. For a binomial sign test value to reach significance at the 0.05 level, 10 of 13 observations would need to fall above the predicted value. An easy-to-use binomial sign test program may be accessed via: www.graphpad.com/quickcalcs/binomial1.cfm. We could also calculate a Z value using Fisher's Exact Test, which is recommended with small numbers of observations. The (tedious) computational form follows:

$$Z = p1 - p2 / [P(1 - P) / n1 + P(1 - P) / n2]^{1/2},$$

where $p1$ is 0.50 due to the baseline trend line evenly dividing the baseline phase and the observed proportion of values exceeding the baseline in the intervention phase. The P value is based upon the following formula: $P = n1p1 + n2p2 / n1 + n2$ or 0.55 in our example. The Z statistic and corresponding p-value is:

$$Z = 0.50 - 1.00 / [(0.55)(0.45) / 6 + (0.55)(0.45) / 13]^{1/2}$$

$$Z = -0.50 / 0.245 = -2.04, p < 0.021$$

Fortunately, Fisher's Exact Test is calculated using statistical software programs, such as the chi-square procedure in SPSS. Note that the formula produces a negative value in our example due to the $p1 - p2$ ordering; however, the importance is the absolute magnitude of the difference. In our case, we adjust the Z-value to reflect our hypothesis that we are expecting our treatment to increase the dependent variable.

As with other statistical techniques, the binomial sign test based on baseline prediction lines appears to be unduly influenced by the presence of significant autocorrelation. In a simulation study, Crosbie (1987) found that the binomial test does not control Type I error when data are autocorrelated. Similar to problems with other statistical tests, autocorrelation affects the binomial sign test, leading to an overly liberal statistical result. Crosbie also suggested that problems with Type I error were compounded when a split-middle line was used with the binomial sign test procedure.

C Statistic

Tryon (1982) proposed application of the C statistic to evaluate the presence of significant changes in *slope* across baseline and treatment conditions. When applied to single-case data, Tryon argued that the C statistic provides a measure of slope within a phase, and that the C statistic works best when there is no significant slope found in the baseline condition. In the presence of non-significant baseline slope (i.e., the C statistic produces a non-significant finding) a significant change in slope may be tested by calculating the C statistic with combined baseline and treatment data, converting this to a standard normal distribution score (i.e., Z score). The change from a non-significant baseline C to a significant baseline plus treatment C indicates the presence of significant slope change and treatment effect. Baseline data in our example resulted in a C statistic of -0.09, a non-significant trend, $Z = 0.17$, ns. In our case, we would need to append treatment scores to the baseline scores and calculate another C statistic (see Figure 14.3). This calculation resulted in a C statistic $= 0.63$ and a significant finding, $Z = 2.88$, $p < 0.01$. According to Tryon, our result indicates that there was a significant change in slope from baseline to treatment, suggesting that treatment increased peer interaction.

The C statistic has been used infrequently in statistical analysis of single subject data. This is likely to be the case, in part, due to Crosbie's (1989) findings that the C statistic is strongly correlated with lag-1 autocorrelation in simulated data ($r = 0.98$). Indeed, Crosbie argued that any relationship between the C statistic and slope was due to autocorrelation entirely. In addition, Crosbie found that C does not control for Type I error and results in too-liberal judgments of treatment effects on slope in the presence of autocorrelated data. Overall, Crosbie argued strongly against the use of C for statistical analysis of single-subject data.

Interrupted Time-Series Analyses (ITSA)

The autocorrelation solution offered by ITSA approaches is to remove autocorrelation prior to testing for changes in level and slope. Time-series methods accomplish this by transforming data to statistically correct for autocorrelation prior to conducting statistical tests. As you might expect, time-series analyses involve sophisticated statistical analysis and considerable statistical expertise. In addition, the methods typically require large numbers of data points per condition (often 50 or more) in order to adequately account for autocorrelation and determine if level and slope changes exist within a data set. Due to the technical sophistication involved in these approaches, our purpose here is simply to familiarize readers with the logic of the methods and make them aware of their availability.

Crosbie's (1993) ITSACORR program was developed to more accurately account for autocorrelation in single subject research data than earlier ITSA statistical programs. The advantages offered by ITSACORR include smaller number of required observations (10–20 observations per condition) necessary to model the degree of autocorrelation, which is probably why ITSACORR has been widely employed. ITSACORR provides an overall statistical test of changes between level and slope (F test) across baseline and treatment phases. Follow-up t test values are also produced that indicate whether level changes and slope changes are statistically significant. Level change is based on the difference between the y-intercept values

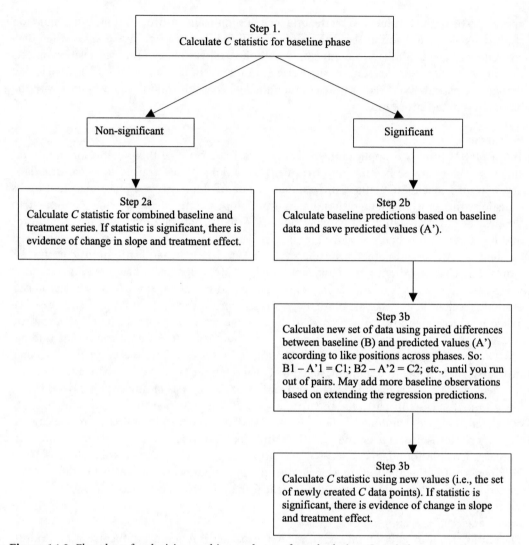

Figure 14.3 Flowchart for decision making and steps for calculating C statistic.

for baseline and treatment phases, which results in the t test. Based on published meta-analyses, ITSACORR typically yields changes in level vs. slope. For example, Stage and Quiroz (1997) analyzed 183 single-case designs using ITSACORR and found almost no significant changes in slopes. Maughan, Christiansen, Jenson, Olympia, and Clark (2005) also found that ITSACORR detected more level ($n = 9$) vs. slope differences ($n = 2$).

Randomization Tests

The methodological and statistical controls that are used via random assignment in group-based research designs have been proposed for use with single-case designs (e.g., Onghena & Edgington, 2005; Scruggs, Mastropieri, & Regan, 2006). From a statistical perspective, randomization tests attempt to address the problem of autocorrelation by not relying on probability values generated from parametric tests, such as t and F distributions. Rather, statistical probabilities are determined using the observed data. Randomization tests can be used with "phase" designs (i.e., sequences of repeated measures divided according to treatment conditions, such as A-B or A-B-A-B designs) or alternating treatments designs as well as sequential or simultaneous replications (Onghena & Edgington, 2005). The logic of the randomization design and subsequent statistical analysis draws from the between-group design literature. Within the between-group literature, the random assignment of individuals to conditions (e.g., treatment vs. control) allows for statistical control over threats to internal validity that may confound results of the investigation, such as maturation or participant characteristics that may influence treatment outcomes.

Onghena and Edgington (2005) illustrate the use of randomization and statistical tests for two designs, baseline-treatment condition designs (called "phase" designs by the authors) and alternating treatment designs. The reader will recall that these designs were introduced and described earlier in the text. Across all randomization designs, however, five general steps are involved in their use (Sierra, Solanas, & Quera, 2005):

1. Some aspect of the design must be randomized (e.g., onset of intervention).
2. A relevant test statistic must be calculated from the data (e.g., A-B difference at point of intervention).
3. The same statistic is calculated from all other like conditional units (e.g., A-B differences for all other possible points of intervention initiation).
4. Calculated values are sorted in ascending or descending order.
5. Statistical significance of the test statistic is obtained from the resulting distribution obtained in step 4.

We identify each step within the phase design example that follows.

Condition ("Phase") Design Example (e.g., A-B Design)
For the phase design, the randomization of the point of onset of intervention may be determined randomly from within a sequence of baseline-intervention observations. The randomization test yields a probability (p) value which indicates the probability that the observed value would have been selected by chance from the other values calculated from the data. Thus, the probability of obtaining a mean difference (by chance alone) that is larger than or equal to the observed mean difference is determined by keeping the ordering of observations constant (e.g., A always precedes B), calculating all possible mean differences from the potential phase shifts, sorting the values, and determining where the observed difference falls within the sort. The p value is equal to the number of values greater than or equal to the test value (plus 1) divided by the possible number of values.

To illustrate the application of the randomization test for phase data, we analyze the data presented in Chapter 9 of the text. Recall that the data were presented in a simple A-B design and consisted of six baseline observations and 13 intervention observations. In Table 14.1, A condition data are presented in the first six columns, while B condition data are bolded and presented in columns 7–19. Let us assume that the clinician implementing the intervention required a minimum of five observations for each condition, which corresponds to a reasonable expectation of baseline observations reported in the published literature (e.g., Huitema, 1986a). The requirement that five observations appear in each condition will reduce the number of possible values calculated from 18 (i.e., all possible A-B values with only one observation within each condition) to 10 (i.e., intervention can begin somewhere between Day 6 and Day 15, inclusive).

Based on the logic of the randomization design, let us assume that the intervention was randomly selected and assigned to begin on Day 7 from the set of 10 possible points (Step 1). Recall that the purpose of our study is to evaluate if contingent adult attention increases the number of minutes a child engages with peers; therefore, the null hypothesis being evaluated with the randomization test is that there is no difference between A and B. The value tested within our example is the observed difference between M_A (21.50) and M_B (72.46), which is calculated as $M_B - M_A$ due to our directional hypothesis that the intervention (i.e., contingent adult attention) will increase the dependent variable (i.e., minutes of engagement with peers). The difference ($M_B - M_A$) equals 50.96 (Step 2).

The randomization test yields a probability value based on the comparison between the observed value and all other possible values calculated in the data set if the condition change were located elsewhere ($n = 10$ in our example). The randomization test assumes equal probability that the treatment could have occurred at any other allowable point in the design. The probability will be determined, in part, based on the parameters of the design. For example, if the minimum number of observations within a condition was set at six, then the number of condition shifts that could be randomized in the example would be reduced to eight and the resulting probability test reduced in power. Table 14.3 illustrates all possible mean difference for this design (Step 3).

Next, we sorted the observed values for the 10 possible treatment initiation points (i.e., Day 6 to Day 15) from greatest to least (Step 4). As shown in Table 14.4, the data point where intervention began was the second largest value from the group of 10. The probability value (p) associated with the A-B randomization test is calculated by totaling the number of values that meet or exceed the test value from the array of scores (including the test value) and dividing by the total number of calculated values. In the present example, the probability of achieving a mean difference of 50.96 or greater at the phase shift was observed to be 2/10 or 0.20, which is interpreted as the likelihood that a value of this magnitude would be expected by chance (Step 5). The finding from the randomization test indicates that we fail to reject the null hypothesis that the intervention produced an effect. Two points to keep in mind as we illustrate the use of the randomization test: (a) obviously, we did not select the intervention onset randomly, and (b) we did not include a sufficient number of observations to allow for adequate statistical power to detect a statistically unlikely (or significant) finding. That is, even if our test value (50.96) were the largest observed from all possible values, the probability of achieving

Table 14.3 Observed Mean Differences for All Possible Condition Assignments for a Randomized A-B Design with 19 Observations and a Minimum of Five Observations per Condition

Treatment begins	Design notation	M_A	M_B	M_B-M_A
Day 6	A_1-A_5/B_6-B_{19}	20.60	69.14	48.54
Day 7	A_1-A_6/B_7-B_{19}	21.50	72.46	50.96
Day 8	A_1-A_7/B_8-B_{19}	24.14	75.17	51.03
Day 9	A_1-A_8/B_9-B_{19}	31.25	74.64	43.39
Day 10	$A_1-A_9/B_{10}-B_{19}$	34.78	75.80	41.02
Day 11	$A_1-A_{10}/B_{11}-B_{19}$	38.30	76.44	38.14
Day 12	$A_1-A_{11}/B_{12}-B_{19}$	42.09	76.00	33.91
Day 13	$A_1-A_{12}/B_{13}-B_{19}$	43.33	78.71	35.38
Day 14	$A_1-A_{13}/B_{14}-B_{19}$	47.38	75.83	28.45
Day 15	$A_1-A_{14}/B_{15}-B_{19}$	50.43	73.00	22.57

Note:

Design notation shows number of consecutive phase points used to calculate mean values for A and B conditions (e.g., A_1-A_6) denotes that the first six A observations were used to calculate the mean value for the A phase. Shaded box contains the test value.

this value by chance from the array would only be 1/10 or 0.10, which is an unacceptably large Type I error value.

To further illustrate the application of the randomization test for phase designs, we opted to require a minimum of five observations per condition and added 10 additional intervention observations the median value of 79 for the intervention condition for convenience (see Table 14.5). The increase in number of observations to 29 allowed us to calculate 20 possible condition shift values that included at least five observations per phase. By increasing the number of calculations to 20, we increase the power to detect a treatment effect. In illustrating the randomization test for this example, we use a presentation format similar to that adopted by Scruggs et al. (2006) where bolded values indicate the implementation of intervention in Condition B. To abbreviate our presentation of the example, we only show calculations for the first three means and the final three means (out of 20 possible). Note also again that we are testing a directional hypothesis that intervention will increase the dependent variable as noted by our mean score calculation of $M_B - M_A$; this has implications for the calculation of positive vs. negative values, but also specifies the critical region of our statistical test at $\alpha = 0.05$ as opposed to a two-tailed test where the critical region is divided between the distribution, i.e., $\alpha = 0.025$.

After we computed all possible permutations ($N = 20$; Table 14.6), we ranked the values and calculated the p value associated with the observed value (53.80) in the design (see Table 14.7). In this example, we found no other values that equaled or exceeded the observed value (range from 52.77 to 17.92); therefore, the p value equaled 1/20 or 0.05. Recall that in this example, we are assuming that the intervention starting point was selected at random; therefore, the

Table 14.4 Mean Differences Sorted According to Decreasing Values

Treatment begins	Design notation	M_A	M_B	$M_B - M_A$
Day 8	A_1-A_7/B_8-B_{19}	24.14	75.17	51.03
Day 7	A_1-A_6/B_7-B_{19}	21.50	72.46	50.96
Day 6	A_1-A_5/B_6-B_{19}	20.60	69.14	48.54
Day 9	A_1-A_8/B_9-B_{19}	31.25	74.64	43.39
Day 10	$A_1-A_9/B_{10}-B_{19}$	34.78	75.80	41.02
Day 11	$A_1-A_{10}/B_{11}-B_{19}$	38.30	76.44	38.14
Day 13	$A_1-A_{12}/B_{13}-B_{19}$	43.33	78.71	35.38
Day 12	$A_1-A_{11}/B_{12}-B_{19}$	42.09	76.00	33.91
Day 14	$A_1-A_{13}/B_{14}-B_{19}$	47.38	75.83	28.45
Day 15	$A_1-A_{14}/B_{15}-B_{19}$	50.43	73.00	22.57

Note:
Design notation shows number of consecutive points used to calculate mean values for A and B conditions. For example, A_1-A_6 denotes that the first six A observations were used to calculate the mean value for the A phase. The shaded row contains the test value.

Table 14.5 Modified Hypothetical Data Set to Illustrate Randomization Test for A–B Design

Day	1	2	3	4	5	6	7	8	9	10	11	12	13	14	15	16	17	18	19
Data	22	42	11	20	8	26	**40**	**81**	**63**	**70**	**80**	**57**	**96**	**90**	**78**	**28**	**86**	**79**	**94**

Day	20	21	22	23	24	25	26	27	28	29
Data	**79**	**79**	**79**	**79**	**79**	**79**	**79**	**79**	**79**	**79**

Table 14.6 Observed Mean Differences for a Sample of Possible Condition Assignments for a Randomized Condition (or "Phase") Design with 29 Observations and Minimum of Five Observations per Condition

Treatment begins	Design notation	M_A	M_B	M_B-M_A
Day 6	A_1-A_5/B_6-B_{29}	20.60	73.25	52.65
Day 7	A_1-A_6/B_7-B_{29}	21.50	75.30	53.80
Day 8	A_1-A_7/B_8-B_{29}	24.14	76.91	52.77
	...	...	...	...
Day 23	$A_1-A_{22}/B_{23}-B_{29}$	54.28	79.00	19.55
Day 24	$A_1-A_{23}/B_{24}-B_{29}$	60.30	79.00	18.70
Day 25	$A_1-A_{24}/B_{25}-B_{29}$	61.08	79.00	17.92

Note:
Design notation shows number of consecutive points used to calculate mean values for A and B conditions. For example, A_1-A_6 denotes that the first six A observations were used to calculate the mean value for the A condition. The shaded row contains the test value.

Table 14.7 Mean Differences Sorted According to Increasing Values

Treatment begins	Design notation	M_A	M_B	M_B-M_A
Day 7	A_1-A_6/B_7-B_{29}	21.50	75.30	53.80
Day 8	A_1-A_7/B_8-B_{29}	24.14	76.91	52.77
Day 6	A_1-A_5/B_6-B_{29}	20.60	73.25	52.65
...	...	...	...	...
Day 23	$A_1-A_{22}/B_{23}-B_{29}$	54.28	79.00	19.55
Day 24	$A_1-A_{23}/B_{24}-B_{29}$	60.30	79.00	18.70
Day 25	$A_1-A_{24}/B_{25}-B_{29}$	61.08	79.00	17.92

Note:
Design notation shows number of consecutive points used to calculate mean values for A and B conditions. The shaded row contains the test value.

probability of obtaining this value at chance is 0.05. As such, we reject the null hypothesis that contingent adult attention did not effect peer engagement.

Todman and Dugard (2001) developed a set of useful statistical software programs to run randomization tests such as this based on a large number of random calculation runs (1,000–2,000 depending on program) for data provided. In our examples, we ran three separate randomization tests using the Todman and Dugard SPSS program for A-B randomization designs (see Tables 14.8a and b).

Table 14.8a AB Randomization Test Results Obtained for Sample Data ($n = 19$) Using Todman and Dugard's SPSS Computer Program

Program output	Run 1	Run 2	Run 3	Mean: runs 1 to 3
Test value	50.96	50.96	50.96	50.96
No. of calculated values ≥ 50.96 from possible total of 2,000	426	364	388	392.6
One-tailed probability	0.213	0.182	0.194	0.196

Table 14.8b AB Randomization Test Results Obtained for Sample Data ($n = 29$) Using Todman and Dugard's SPSS Computer Program

Program output	Run 1	Run 2	Run 3	Mean: runs 1 to 3
Test value	53.80	53.80	53.80	53.80
No. of calculated values ≥ 53.80 from possible total of 2,000	89	94	81	88
One-tailed probability	0.045	0.047	0.041	0.044

Note that the generated probabilities fell roughly in line with what we calculated from our randomization tests. For example, the A-B randomization test result for the 19 observation examples indicated that the test value (or greater) would be found approximately 20% of the time, the software program identified values (from a total of 2,000) that equaled or exceeded our test value between 18.2 and 21.3% of the time. Similarly, the statistical software found a value equal to or greater than our test value 4.1%–4.7% of the time for the A-B randomization test using 29 observations.

Simultaneous Replication with A-B Randomization Designs

As seen in the example above, we added observations to the design in order to reach an acceptable decision rule of 0.05, which demonstrates the power limitations of employing the randomized phase design with a single participant. Marascuilo and Busk (1988) described statistical procedures to combine A-B designs for data that are replicated simultaneously (e.g., multiple baseline across participants), a design feature that significantly increases statistical power. To continue to build upon the original data set reported in Chapter 9, let us assume that two children participated in the intervention (Table 14.9a). Day 7 was randomly selected as the treatment starting point for Participant 1 and Day 11 was randomly selected for Participant 2. Therefore, we have collected similar data across two participants, each with a total of 19 observations and minimum of five observations within each phase. Based on the requirement that at least five observations appear within each phase, intervention must begin on Day 6, 7, 8, 9, 10, 11, 12, 13, 14, or 15, which allows for 10 mean values to be calculated for each participant. As before, mean differences are calculated for each participant (Table 14.9b).

In order to evaluate the effectiveness of the intervention, the results from both participants

Table 14.9a Hypothetical Data Set to Illustrate Randomization Test Procedures for use with Simultaneous Replication with A–B Designs

Day	1	2	3	4	5	6	7	8	9	10	11	12	13	14	15	16	17	18	19
									Participant 1										
Condition	A	A	A	A	A	A	B	B	B	B	B	B	B	B	B	B	B	B	B
Value	22	42	11	20	8	26	40	81	63	70	80	57	96	90	78	28	86	79	94
									Participant 2										
Condition	A	A	A	A	A	A	A	A	A	A	B	B	B	B	B	B	B	B	B
Value	22	42	11	20	8	26	25	20	18	28	80	57	96	90	78	28	86	79	94

Table 14.9b Mean Differences for Two Participants

Intervention	Participant 1			Participant 2		
	M_A	M_B	M_B-M_A	M_A	M_B	M_B-M_A
6	20.60	69.14	48.54	20.60	57.50	36.90
7	21.50	72.46	50.96	21.50	59.92	38.45
8	24.14	75.17	51.03	22.00	62.83	40.83
9	31.25	74.64	43.39	21.75	66.73	44.98
10	34.78	75.80	41.02	21.33	71.60	50.27
11	38.30	76.44	38.14	22.00	76.44	54.44
12	42.09	76.00	33.91	27.27	76.00	48.73
13	43.33	78.71	35.38	29.75	78.71	48.96
14	47.38	75.83	28.45	34.85	75.84	40.99
15	50.43	73.00	22.57	38.79	34.00	34.21

Note:
The shaded rows contain the test value of interest.

Table 14.10 Summed Values Presented in Ascending Rank from Participants 1 and 2 That Yield a Randomization Distribution

		Participant 1 (M_B-M_A)									
		51	51*	49	43	41	38	35	34	28	23
Participant 2 (M_B-M_A)	54*	105	**105**	103	97	95	92	89	88	82	77
	50	101	101	99	93	91	88	85	84	78	73
	49	100	100	98	92	90	87	84	83	77	72
	49	100	100	98	92	90	87	84	83	77	72
	45	96	96	94	88	86	83	80	79	73	68
	41	92	92	90	84	82	79	76	75	69	64
	41	92	92	90	84	82	79	76	75	69	64
	39	89	89	87	81	79	76	73	72	66	61
	37	88	88	88	80	78	75	72	71	65	60
	34	85	85	83	77	75	72	69	68	62	57

Note:
* = Observed (test) value for each participant. Darkly shaded values within distribution indicate critical region for rejecting null hypothesis that there is no effect of intervention; observed (test) value is bolded within the distribution. Values presented are absolute values and rounded to the nearest integer for ease of presentation.

are summed to create a larger range of possible values. Given the parameters of the design, each participant yields 10 outcomes which are paired and summed to produce 100 possible outcomes for the replication (i.e., 10 outcomes for Participant 1 × 10 outcomes for Participant 2; Table 14.10). Therefore, each sum has a probability of $p = (p1) \times (p2) = 1/100 = 0.01$. Marascuilo and Busk (1988) provide the calculation formula for the number of observations that define the critical test region (C) as [the number of observations × probability decision point] or $100 \times (0.05) = 5$ in our example. The five largest values in the combined distribution of 100 scores are: 105.47, 105.40, 102.98, 101.30, and 101.23. The observed (test) value of 105.40 falls within the set of five largest values; therefore, we reject the null hypothesis that treatment had no effect.

For the interested reader, Regan, Mastropieri, and Scruggs (2005) provide a published example using simultaneous replication across five participants using randomization designs and statistical tests. The authors utilized the Todman and Dugard (2001) software in their statistical analysis and illustrate the application of the randomization approach within an educational setting.

Randomization Tests for Use with Alternating Treatments Designs (ATD)
Recall in our introduction of randomization designs and tests that randomization procedures also exist for ATD (Onghena & Edgington, 2005). In cases of ATD, the use of randomization to conditions and associated statistical testing involves the random selection of a treatment *sequence* from a list of possible treatment sequences. For example, if a researcher were interested in contrasting the effects of two treatments, A and B, with three observations per condition, the total number of treatment sequences is 20 as follows:

AAABBB	BBBAAA
AABABB	BBABAA
AABBAB	BBAABA
AABBBA	BBAAAB
ABABBA	BABAAB
ABBABA	BAABAB
ABBBAA	BAAABB
ABAABB	BABBAA
ABBAAB	BAABBA
ABABAB	BABABA

In this example, the steps for the randomization test might be:

1. Randomize treatment sequence (i.e., randomly select from one of the 20 options listed above).
2. Calculate a mean difference (test statistic) between A-B for the selected sequence.
3. Calculate mean differences for the remaining A-B sequences.
4. Sort all mean differences in order from highest to lowest.
5. Calculate probability for the randomly selected treatment sequence depending on its position within the sorted distribution. Note that with 20 possible sequences, the observed test statistic may reach statistical significance only if it appears first in the distribution (i.e., $1/20 = 0.05$).

Ranking Procedures for Use with Randomization Designs
Busk and Marascuilo (1992) and Edgington (1982) illustrated analytic procedures that use ranked data within the context of randomization designs to determine if an intervention is effective. The five-step process remains consistent, however, regardless of the specific statistical procedure used. An example of a ranking test used with randomization is the binomial sign test introduced earlier, where the outcome of interest involves a known probability of 0.50. Busk and Marascuilo provide other examples of ranking statistical procedures for use with simultaneous A-B replications and simultaneous A-B-A-B replications.

From methodological and statistical perspectives, randomization designs and associated tests demonstrate significant benefits. Randomization designs allow for valid inference due to the randomization of treatment onset, as in the case of phase designs, or treatment sequence, as in the case of ATD. As Scruggs et al. (2006) note, educational research policy is favorable toward designs that include randomization procedures. Although not immune to autocorrelation, randomization designs appear to handle the problem of autocorrelation better than other statistical tests, particularly when mean values are analyzed (Ferron, Foster-Johnson, & Kromrey, 2003). There are some authors that have identified autocorrelation as a problem for randomization tests (Sierra et al., 2005); however, Type I errors appear to be better controlled than for other statistics, such as the binomial test and C statistic. The most significant statistical limitation of randomization tests involves low statistical power, particularly when used with one participant, as illustrated in the chapter.

In addition to low power, there are clinical limitations associated with randomization tests. In contrast to response-guided designs, the randomization design must be planned at the outset of intervention and, as such, does not allow modifications once the design has been implemented. Due to the lack of clinical flexibility, randomization designs and associated statistical tests are not frequently used within single subject research designs. Their omission is justifiable on grounds that randomization is not always suitable when addressing significant behavior problems. For example, if a child is exhibiting severe self-injurious behavior, random selection of a starting point for an intervention would not be acceptable. Randomization tests are designed to measure change of *level* only.

General Statements about Statistical Analysis of Data

As evidenced by our presentation of statistical analysis of data, there is no consensus for the "correct" method to analyze data; therefore, considerable judgment is involved, not unlike the judgment necessary in visual analysis. In light of findings that results from single-case statistical analyses do not correlate very well (Parker et al., 2005), the role of judgment in selecting a statistical analytic procedure cannot be overemphasized. Indeed, in the Parker et al. investigation, correlations between statistical tests and effect sizes ranged from 0.09 to 0.82, comparable to the variable agreements for visual analysis. Nourbakhsh and Ottenbacher (1994) argued that there was a clear need for the field to establish decision-making rules for determining when certain statistical techniques should and should not be used. The need identified by the researchers is identical to the need for well-accepted decision rules to guide visual analysis.

Universal statistical decision rules do not exist; however, we argue that, at a minimum, single-case statistical analysts provide information regarding the degree of autocorrelation observed in the data set, particularly for baseline data. This is due to the profound influence that autocorrelation plays across virtually all of the statistical procedures described in this chapter. If significant autocorrelation is observed in the data, which seems likely, the data analyst may opt to omit the analysis altogether, account for the autocorrelation via sophisticated time-series procedures, or conduct the analysis with appropriate caveats about the potential role of autocorrelation. As multiple authors have suggested, when appropriate, statistical analysis should be used as an adjunct to visual analysis and vice versa. The two processes need not be in competition, but rather, may complement one another as suggested by Huitema (1986b) and others.

In our opinion, several possibilities exist regarding the relationship between visual and statistical analysis when rendering a decision about the presence of a functional relation between intervention and outcome. First, the two types of analysis could be viewed as *mutually exclusive* and conclusions about the presence of a functional relation proceed without considering input from the other analysis (an *isolated* decision-making model). The majority of single subject designs feature isolated decision making, most typically involving the use of visual analysis. Second, decisions about the presence of a functional relation could include supporting evidence from *either* visual analysis *or* statistical analysis (an *independent* decision-making model). If such a model were utilized in a design, the strategy should be explicitly identified and employed a priori. Such a model seems to feature an inherent bias toward Type I error inflation by allowing two opportunities for concluding a functional relation exists and is not recommended. Finally, conclusions about the presence of functional relation could require supporting evidence from *both* visual analysis *and* statistical analysis (a *mutual* decision-making model). Of the three options identified, the mutual model constitutes the most conservative threshold.

A mutual decision-making model involving complementary visual and statistical analysis could take several forms. The visual-analysis tradition involves a dichotomous decision-making process as does the statistical-analysis tradition. Therefore, one possible relationship would involve an attempt to disconfirm the binary conclusion that a functional relation exists or not. Another possibility involves quantification of the functional relation. That is, the dichotomous decision-making tradition of visual analysis would be supplemented with a quantitative summary of the strength of the treatment effect, or an effect size.

Meta-Analysis and Evidenced-Based Practice

Early suggestions (e.g., Gorman-Smith & Matson, 1985; Scruggs, Mastropieri, & Casto, 1987) that single subject research outcomes may be quantified and synthesized using varied procedures, such as Cohen's *d* statistic and the PND statistic, have been followed by a growing interest by practitioners and methodologists alike. Part of the emergent interest in statistical analysis and aggregation of single subject research data has developed from the increasing emphasis on evidence-based practice across professions, such as medicine, psychology, education, and special education. To establish the degree of interest, we conducted a cursory Social Sciences Citation Index search of the published literature using the terms "single subject" and "meta-analysis" (producing 44 hits) which identified meta-analyses in the areas of: purchasing skill instruction with individuals with developmental disabilities (Xin, Grasso, DiPipi-Hoy, & Jitendra, 2005), writing instruction with adolescents (Graham & Perin, 2007), and social skills interventions for individuals with autism (Bellini, Peters, Benner, & Hopf, 2007). From a methodological perspective, a large number of papers has also been recently published addressing the limitations of effect sizes for single subject research designs, resulting in a growing number of possible effect sizes and analytic procedures. Part of the growing interest in single subject meta-analysis is because methodologists have argued that single subject research should be included in evidence-based decision-making (Shadish & Rindskopf, 2007).

The growing number of published single-case meta-analyses should not be taken as universal endorsement of this method of literature review and synthesis (cf., Salzberg, Strain, & Baer, 1987; Strain, Kohler, & Gresham, 1998). Opponents to the application of meta-analytic techniques to single-subject data acknowledge that a core principle of applied behavior analysis is individualized assessment and intervention. Philosophical differences between two experimental paradigms within psychology lie at the core of the dissatisfaction with single-case meta-analysis. Group-based approaches focus on aggregated differences between two groups (nomothetic approach), single-case research designs focus on the intensive study of the individual (idiographic approach) and, opponents to single-subject meta-analysis argue, belie statistical summary.

Due to the likelihood of many procedural variations in single subject research studies, aggregating of data *within* a single-subject design has been identified as troublesome (Salzberg et al., 1987). Aggregation of data *across* single-subject outcomes is also criticized due to the prevailing emphasis on broad categories of treatment approaches, such as reinforcement-based or punishment-based, and individual characteristics, such as degree of impairment of participants. When this occurs, the comparability of treatments is compromised, such as treatment equivalence on the critical domains of duration, timing, and therapist competence (Salzberg et al.). Comparability of individuals is similarly compromised resulting in significant loss of information.

As you may have guessed from our introduction of statistical analysis, single subject meta-analysis methodology is in the early stages of development, although statistical improvements with newer analytic techniques continue to be developed. In contrast to the well-established and validated methods of meta-analysis for between-group designs, single-case meta-analysis is in its infancy. The philosophical issues notwithstanding, the core methodological problem for single subject meta-analysis is closely related to the statistical issues we identified earlier, i.e., how does one summarize treatment effects from single subject research designs and present this information in the form of an effect size? Statistical test results, such as t, F, and Z, may be transformed into effect-size values, such as d; however, the limitations of parametric tests are well-documented. Stated another way, if we had consensus regarding the appropriate statistical-analysis procedure, we would have the effect size.

Meta-Analysis: What Is It and What Is Its Purpose?

For many researchers, practitioners, and rule-makers (i.e., governing bodies), it is often the cumulative findings of a body of literature rather than the specific results of individual studies that guide research, practice, and legislation. Literature reviews, narrative summaries, descriptive analyses, and integrative reviews are all methods of examining sets of primary studies in order to derive general summary statements about a body of research. It is the integrative research review that attempts to synthesize knowledge from related fields of research in order to make generalizations (Cooper & Hedges, 1994; Jackson, 1980). In 1976, Glass coined the term *meta-analysis* to refer to the "statistical analysis of a large collection of analyses" (Glass, 1976, p. 3). Also known as a quantitative research synthesis, a meta-analysis is the process of compiling the results of multiple research studies and combining the findings into one summative product. With meta-analyses, quantitative comparisons are made across primary studies through the use of statistical analyses (Glass, 1976; Mostert, 1996; Cooper & Hedges, 1994). Initially developed for group research (Glass, McGraw, & Smith, 1981), meta-analyses have become standard tools for integrating related studies (both published and unpublished) using single subject research designs to make generalizations. This is done by transforming the findings of the primary studies to some common metric, coding characteristics of the studies, and using statistical procedures to determine overall effects, moderating and mediating effects, and relations between characteristics of the studies and findings (Jackson, 1980).

Several examples of meta-analyses exist within the social and behavioral sciences and cover many different topics of interest. Meta-analyses are often defined by the diagnoses of the population studied (e.g., intellectual disability, autism, learning disabilities, emotional and behavioral disorders, ADHD); type of treatment or assessment involved (e.g., behavioral approach, psychopharmacological treatment, assessment of intelligence); specific behaviors targeted for reduction or increase (e.g., social skills, maladaptive behaviors) or a combination of factors.

Guidelines for Conducting a Meta-Analysis

Despite the pervasive use of meta-analysis in the behavioral sciences, the methods for conducting such a study are not as clearly defined as the strategies used to address primary study methodology. However, many researchers have made efforts to define the procedural parameters necessary to conduct a meta-analysis (Jackson, 1980; Mostert, 1996). We identify and discuss six important general steps to follow when conducting a single subject meta-analysis.

Step 1: Select a Compelling Question or Hypothesis

Defining the research question and formulating the hypothesis to be tested is the first step in the method of meta-analysis. According to Jackson (1980), there are four major sources that must be consulted when developing questions or formulating hypotheses for a review: available theory, primary studies, existing reviews, and one's own insight. Theory will no doubt guide potential questions regarding relationships within the research topic but also aids in creating a basic structure for a set of related research questions. Primary and secondary articles that may be included in the meta-analysis should be reviewed prior to formulating the hypothesis as the consistencies and inconsistencies reported may guide additional research questions and the general direction and goal of the meta-analysis. Carefully constructed research questions will also aid in the development of specific inclusion categories (Bangert-Drowns, 1986).

Step 2: Search the Literature and Sample Research to be Reviewed

As with primary research, beginning the literature review for a meta-analysis is an exhausting enterprise. Searching the existing literature for relevant studies is an arduous but necessary task. Clearly reporting the search methods used to collect the primary studies is important as it helps to clarify the scope of the meta-analysis. The use of online search engines (e.g., ERIC, PsycINFO, and Medline) and the descriptors used during the search should be reported. The specifics of any manual, hand-searches, or ancestral searches of existing articles should also be reported.

Establishing criteria for inclusion (and exclusion) is of the greatest importance. These criteria typically include: type of study presented (e.g., single subject research design); research topic (e.g., treatment of maladaptive behavior); characteristics of the participants (e.g., adults with autism); publication status (e.g., published in peer-review journal); and date of data collection or publication. Subsequently, identifying exclusion criteria and giving specific examples of the utilization of the criteria is recommended as it will focus the study more rigorously (Mostert, 2003). There is controversy regarding the inclusion/exclusion of non-published and methodologically flawed studies in a meta-analysis (Jackson, 1980). The general view is that studies should not be excluded based on perceived quality as this determination is based on subjectivity (Hunter & Schmidt, 1990; Cooper, 1984). The possibility of reporting bias exists and is a limitation of any synthesis of literature.

Step 3: Code Variables from Primary Studies and Document Reliability of Coding Decisions

Once the relevant literature has been gathered, the important data within the articles must be coded and recorded. Decisions must be made regarding the classes of variables selected for coding and the level of detail to include in such codes. For example, if one is interested in the treatment of maladaptive behaviors, the topography of target behavior (e.g., aggression, self-injurious behavior) may be an important variable for later analyses. It may also be relevant to code subtypes of each behavior (e.g., hitting and kicking, or head banging and self-bites). Nevertheless, the information garnered from the primary studies will be used to make comparisons across studies and the data collected must be coded in an objective manner. Objective coding is accomplished through the use of operationalized codes. Clearly defining, and subsequently reporting, the variables obtained from the primary articles is necessary as the coding of independent variables (a) helps to define the parameters of the independent variables (Halvorsen, 1994) and (b) allows for replication by other researchers (Cooper & Hedges, 1994). Using Herzinger and Campbell's (2007) coding scheme as an example, the variables were coded in each of the following categories: participant characteristics; assessment or pre-intervention data; target-behavior characteristics; and intervention data. For the interested reader, an example of a comprehensive coding protocol for single subject designs is accessible at: www.sp-ebi.org/projects.html. The coding protocol was developed by the Task Force on Evidence-Based Interventions in School Psychology of Division 16 of the American Psychological Association and has been used in several published meta-analyses.

Establishing the reliability of coding decisions is an integral part of validating the methodology of meta-analysis. Independent coding of the variables presented in the primary articles should be conducted in order to verify the validity of coding definitions. Inter-rater or inter-observer reliability is used to assess the degree to which two or more independent raters agree and is most often calculated through the percentage agreement method (no. of agreements / no. of agreements + no. of disagreements × 100). There is some disagreement regarding acceptable levels of reliability in the literature, but generally, reliability above 90% is desirable and reliability below 80% indicates significant problems with measurement (Wolery, Ault, & Doyle, 1992).

Step 4: Calculate Individual Study Outcomes: Multiple Effect Size Calculations
At the heart of the meta-analysis is the calculation of an effect size that represents the efficacy or effectiveness of the intervention under study. The procedures for effect-size calculations are well-established for group-based designs; however, as seen in our discussion of statistical analysis, little consensus exists regarding the appropriate calculation of effect sizes for single-case designs. Due to the disagreement regarding the most appropriate effect size, we recommend calculating multiple effect sizes appropriate to the research question. For example, in our meta-analyses in the area of problem-behavior reduction, we utilized three effect sizes. In this section, we introduce commonly reported effect sizes from the single subject research literature. To illustrate the calculation of various effect sizes, we introduce a second set of data (Figure 14.4). In this example, assume that a differential reinforcement of other behavior (DRO) intervention has been implemented to reduce the frequency of face-slapping behavior for a boy with autism. Number of face slaps is plotted in the ordinate and days plotted along the abscissa.

Mean Baseline Difference (MBD)
The MBD is designed to provide an index of the change of *level* of behavior across baseline-treatment conditions. We used the MBD to quantify outcomes of interventions to reduce problem behavior; in this context we referred to the MBD as the Mean Baseline Reduction (MBLR) statistic to indicate our interest in problem-behavior reduction (Herzinger & Campbell, 2007). Another name for this metric is the percentage reduction measure (Marquis et al., 2000). The MBD or MBLR is easily calculated by subtracting the mean of treatment observations from the mean of baseline observations then dividing by the mean of baseline observations and multiplying by 100 (Campbell, 2003). In our example:

$$MBLR = M_A - M_B / M_A \times 100 = 5.6 - 2.0 / 5.6 \times 100 = 64.29$$

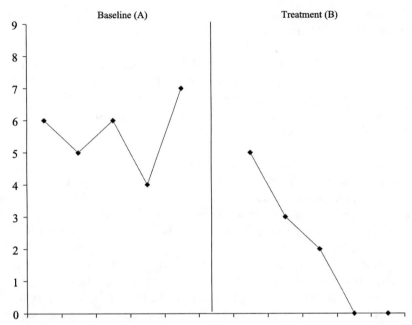

Figure 14.4 Hypothetical data showing simple A-B contrast for effects of treatment in reducing face slapping for a child with developmental disability.

Variations exist for calculating the MBD, such as using the last three baseline and treatment data points within a phase as opposed to using the entire data set (e.g., Marquis et al., 2000). Of course, if the interest is in behavioral improvement, the difference would be calculated as $M_B - M_A / M_A \times 100$, with positive values indicating greater improvement.

Percent of Non-Overlapping Data (PND; Scruggs et al., 1987)
The PND is aligned with the tradition of visual analysis to note degree of non-overlap between data points across conditions. The PND statistic is calculated as the percentage of treatment data points that do not overlap with baseline data points. The PND can range from 0 to 100; a PND greater than 90% reflects a highly effective treatment, a PND of 70–90% is considered a fair treatment outcome, and a PND of less than 50% indicates unreliable/ineffective intervention (Scruggs et al.). Didden, Duker, and Korzilius (1997) proposed a modification for PND calculation to handle the problem of baseline data points that may fall at the abscissa. Didden et al.'s (1997) modification is to identify the number of baseline data points that fall at the abscissa and exclude the same number of data points from the treatment phase prior to calculating the PND. In the present example, our DRO intervention produces a PND score of 80 because four of the five intervention data points (i.e., observed face slaps on Days 7, 8, 9, and 10) fall below the lowest baseline data point (i.e., four observed face slaps on Day 4).

For A-B-A-B designs, Scruggs et al. (1987) proposed calculating a total PND score from both baseline-intervention (i.e., A-B) condition shifts by summing numerator and denominators across both shifts, dividing summed numerators by summed denominators and multiplying by 100. Suppose we opted to conduct a condition withdrawal with our DRO intervention and collected three additional baseline observations (A_2) and three additional intervention observations (B_2). Let us also suppose that there was no overlap between conditions A_2 and B_2, this would result in a PND = 4/5 (A_1 / B_1) + 3/3 (A_2 / B_2) = 7/8 ($A_1 + A_2 / B_1 + B_2$) = 87.5%.

The PND offers the following advantages. First, it is easy to calculate. Second, it is closely aligned with the visual-analysis tradition as evidenced by its inclusion in Chapter 9 of the present text describing methods of visual analysis. It also holds intuitive appeal. Perhaps due to its simple calculation and intuitive appeal, the PND has been used frequently in single-case meta-analyses (see Table 14.11). On the negative side of the ledger, however, the PND is skewed by the presence of outliers in the baseline condition, which is why Didden et al. (1997) proposed their modification. This is illustrated easily in our example; if one baseline point reached zero, the PND value would equal zero.

Percent of Zero Data (PZD; Scotti, Evans, Meyer, & Walker, 1991)

The PZD statistic is calculated by computing the percentage of data points that reached zero after locating the first intervention data point that reached zero. This first zero point is included (Scotti, Evans, Meyer, & Walker, 1991). The PZD score is considered a more stringent indicator of treatment outcome as the PZD score requires target behaviors to reach and stay at zero levels throughout treatment to be considered effective. Campbell (2004) noted that the PZD score represents a "degree of behavior suppression versus degree of behavior reduction" (p. 235). The independence between the PND and PZD scores has been established in meta-analyses with correlations between the two ranging from 0.00 to 0.29 (Campbell; Scotti et al., 1991) The PZD score will only be relevant to those studies that are targeting the reduction or suppression of undesirable behavior. The PZD can range from 0 to 100; according to Scotti et al., a PZD

Table 14.11 Sample Percentage of Non-overlapping Data (PND) Effect Sizes from Published Meta-Analyses Reviewing Treatments to Reduce Problem Behaviors

Author	Topic	No. of articles	M	SD	Range
Campbell (2003)	Problem behavior reduction for autism	117	84.40	23.80	0–100
Herzinger & Campbell (2007)	Functional analysis (FA) versus behavioral assessment (BA)	58	FA: 81.00 BA: 89.02	FA: 31.23 BA: 89.02	FA: 0–100 BA: 10.33–100
Didden et al. (1997)	Problem behavior reduction for mental retardation	482	73.41	33.42	0–100
Didden et al. (2006)	Problem behavior reduction for mild mental retardation	80	75	30	0–100
Scotti et al. (1991)	Problem behavior reduction for developmental disabled	318	NR	NR	NR
Gresham et al. (2004)	Effects of functional behavioral assessment (FBA). Not all targets problem behaviors	150	51.41–67.11 (depending on FBA)	26.00–37.74 (depending on FBA)	NR
Shogren et al. (2004)	Effects of choice on problem behaviors	13	65.7	41.0	0–100
Wehmeyer (1995)	Reduction of stereotyped behaviors	33	81.0	32.0	NR

greater than 80% reflects a highly effective treatment, a PZD of 80–55% reflects fair treatment outcome, a PZD of 18–54% reflects questionable outcome, and a PZD <18% indicates an ineffective treatment. In the present example, our DRO intervention produces a PZD score of 100 because the final two intervention data points indicated zero frequency of face slapping (i.e., [2/2 × 100 = 100]). If another observation were taken on Day 11 and face slapping were observed, the PZD score would fall to 66.67 (i.e., [2/3 × 100 = 66.67]).

The PZD has been calculated in several meta-analyses that have reviewed varied interventions to reduce problem behaviors exhibited by individuals with developmental disabilities (see Table 14.12). Campbell (2003) and Herzinger and Campbell (2007) both found that PZD was sensitive to detecting moderators of treatment. The PZD features a similar profile when compared to the PND. It is easy to calculate and makes intuitive sense; however, it can be unduly influenced by outliers. For example, a treatment may yield a PZD score of 100% by virtue of achieving a final treatment observation of zero.

Percent of Data Exceeding the Median of Baseline (PEM; Ma, 2006)

The PEM is calculated by dividing the number of treatment data points that exceed the median of the baseline phase over the total number of treatment data points. The PEM statistic can be used to make comparisons across consecutive phases within an assessment or an overall mean effect size. Ma proposed the PEM in order to reduce the impact of data outliers on the calculation of an effect size. In the present example, the baseline data produces a median of 6 and our DRO intervention produces a PEM score of 100 because all of our intervention data points (range 0–5) fall below the median of the baseline phase.

Ma (2006) compared original authors' judgments regarding treatment effects to both the PEM and PND statistics. Spearman correlations were used to decide which statistic shared greater relationship with the authors' judgments. Ma (2006) found that the PEM had higher correlation with the original researchers' judgments than the PND. The PEM has also been

Table 14.12 Sample of Percentage of Zero Data (PZD) Effect Sizes from Published Meta-Analyses Reviewing Treatments to Reduce Problem Behaviors

Author	Topic	No. of articles	M	SD	Range
Campbell (2003)	Problem behavior reduction for autism	117	42.86	35.69	0–100
Herzinger & Campbell (2007)	Effects of functional analysis (FA) versus behavioral assessment (BA)	58	FA: 62.55 BA: 35.61	FA: 31.87 BA: 42.86	FA: 0–100 BA: 0–100
Didden et al. (2006)	Problem behavior reduction for mild mental retardation	80	35	32	0–100
Shogren et al. (2004)	Effects of choice on problem behaviors	13	42.3	42.4	0–100
Wehmeyer (1995)	Reduction of stereotyped behaviors	33	36.0	38.0	NR
Scotti et al. (1991)	Problem behavior reduction for developmental disabled	318	NR	NR	NR

independently evaluated by Parker and Hagan-Burke (2007) who compared PEM with several other effect-size indicators and found modest support for its use.

A few points are required with respect to the summary methods presented in this section. Although the methods presented here are intuitively appealing as effect sizes, these statistics are not effect sizes as defined in the traditional sense, such as *r* or *d*, which are introduced in the next section. As such, the methods described in this section do not yield outcomes that could be combined with group designs.

Non-Regression Parametric Approach

Standardized mean difference (SMD; Busk & Serlin, 1992)
Gingerich (1984) introduced the SMD as a possible method for effect-size calculation of single subject data, which involves calculating the difference between the mean of the treatment condition and the mean of the baseline condition and dividing by the standard deviation of the baseline condition.

$$M_B - M_A / SD_A$$

The SMD is typically calculated using all data points within the comparison conditions of interest; however, modified forms exist, such as using all baseline data points and last five treatment data points (Gorman-Smith & Matson, 1985), and using the final three baseline data points and final three treatment data points (*SMD3*; Marquis et al., 2000). Also, the meta-analyst must decide which conditions will be contrasted in the investigation. For example, will first baseline and final treatment condition means be used to calculate SMD, or perhaps all baseline and treatment phases combined (e.g., for A-B-A-B designs) in the calculation of SMD?

Several variations exist for the SMD approach depending on statistical assumptions hypothesized to be met in the data, such as the equality of variances between conditions (Busk & Serlin, 1992). Busk and Serlin's Approach One: No Assumptions is a procedure that does not hold any assumptions about the nature of the data, and its calculation is illustrated with our hypothetical data. As seen in Table 14.13, the DRO intervention resulted in an effect

Table 14.13 Hypothetical Data Set for Intervention to Reduce Face Slapping for a Child with Developmental Disability. Effect Size Calculation Illustrated Using Busk and Serlin's (1992) Approach One

Day	Condition	Value	Means	SDs	Effect size calculation
1	Baseline (A)	6			
2	A	5			
3	A	6			
4	A	4			
5	A	7	$M_A = 5.6$	$SD_A = 1.14$	
6	Treatment (B)	5			
7	B	3			
8	B	2			
9	B	0			
10	B	0	$M_B = 2.0$	$SD_B = 2.12$	$ES = [2.0–5.6] / 1.14 = -3.16$

size of −3.16, which is extremely large when evaluated by group-based effect-size standards. Due to the purpose of the intervention, our effect size is assigned a negative value (i.e., −3.16) in order to indicate that our intervention was found to reduce the behavior being measured.

Approach One is what is typically reported in the published literature, and authors using the SMD in their meta-analyses have reported very large values (Table 14.14). For example, Robey et al.'s (1999) review of the aphasia-treatment literature yielded 12 SMD effect sizes that ranged from 2.01 to 23.93. The large values reported in the literature are likely due to violating the assumptions inherent in calculating the SMD, namely, data represent independent observations. As described earlier in the chapter, when observations are serially dependent, results from statistical analyses tend to produce biased results. In the case of the SMD, the procedure appears to produce effect sizes that are inflated due to serial dependency present in each phase.

One important point to note is that there are different methods to produce a statistical equivalent to the SMD, such as transforming t values, F values, Z values, and regression statistics to SMD scores using mathematical formulae. One such transformation from R^2 to SMD is illustrated below via regression.

Regression-Based Approaches
For baseline-treatment contrasts, we have seen that the data represent a unique type of design called an *interrupted time-series* whereby pre- and posttest data are presented in reference to the implementation (and possible withdrawal) of an intervention. Due to the serial nature of the data collection, as we have found, statisticians have proposed a variety of statistical tests that attempt to incorporate and account for trends and autocorrelation often observed in single subject research data.

Regression-Based Standardized Mean Difference (d_{REG})
Several regression-based mean difference score procedures have been proposed in the literature (e.g., Allison & Gorman, 1993; Faith, Allison, & Gorman, 1996; White, Rusch, Kazdin, & Hartmann, 1989). Allison and Gorman (1993) and Faith et al. (1996) proposed a linear regression technique that removes trend from repeated observations by calculating predicted values based on baseline data only. In order to calculate an effect size based on this method, the following steps are followed:

Step 1. Calculate regression equation of dependent variable on day or observation number.

Table 14.14 Sample Standardized Mean Difference (SMD; *d*) Effect Sizes from Published Meta-Analyses

Author	Topic	No. of articles	M	SD	Range
Robey et al. (1999)	Aphasia treatments	12	6.29	6.14	2.01–23.93
Gorman-Smith & Matson (1985)	Treatment for self injury and stereotypy	41	4.29	6.27	0.84–13.73
Gresham et al. (2004)	Effects of functional behavioral assessment (FBA)	150	0.70–6.77 (depending on FBA)	1.37–18.69 (depending on FBA)	NR

Note:
For Robey et al. (1999) *M* and *SD* calculated from data presented in Table 2.

Step 2. Calculate residuals for baseline data, this can be accomplished in SPSS software by saving nonstandardized residuals.

Step 3. Apply the regression equation calculated in (1) to predict dependent variable values for the intervention condition.

Step 4. Predicted intervention condition values are subtracted from observed data and saved as "detrended" data. The residual values calculated for the baseline condition are combined with the residual values calculated for the intervention condition.

Step 5. Zero-order correlations are calculated between (a) treatment condition and "detrended" data, and (b) treatment condition by time interaction and "detrended" data. If the zero-order correlations share the same sign, the "detrended" data is regressed on treatment and treatment by time interaction via the following linear model:

$$Y = b_0 + b_1X + b_3X(t) + e,$$

with the b_2t term (i.e., effect of passage of time) removed from the model. If the zero-order correlations do not share the same sign, treatment effects are calculated for treatment condition alone, i.e., the $b_3X(t)$ term was removed from the model.

Step 6. The resulting adjusted R^2 value from the regression equation calculated in (5) is converted to d via a standard formula:

$$d = [4R^2 / (1 - R^2)]^{1/2}$$

and assigned the same sign as the zero-order correlations obtained in (5). Therefore, a negative sign indicates a lower value in the dependent variable across conditions, while a positive sign indicates a higher value in the dependent variable across conditions.

Using the DRO intervention data as an example, we obtain an effect size as follows:

Step 1. Regression equation using baseline data only:

$$Y = 5.30 + .10 \times day$$

Steps 2–4. Residual values were calculated (Table 14.15).

Step 5. The zero-order correlation between condition and detrended data was −0.79; for condition × day interaction and detrended data the correlation was −0.89; therefore, both terms were included in the regression equation, which resulted in an adjusted R^2 of 0.882.

Table 14.15 Calculation of Residuals used in Regression-Based Method for Single Subject Effect Size

Day	Condition	Observed value	Predicted value	Residual value	Day	Condition	Observed value	Predicted value	Residual value
1	A	6	5.4	0.6	6	B	5	5.9	−0.9
2	A	5	5.5	−0.5	7	B	3	6.0	−3.0
3	A	6	5.6	0.4	8	B	2	6.1	−4.1
4	A	4	5.7	−1.7	9	B	0	6.2	−6.2
5	A	7	5.8	1.2	10	B	0	6.3	−6.3

Step 6. The adjusted R^2 of 0.882 resulted in an effect size, $d = -5.47$, which indicates a strong effect of the DRO intervention in reducing face slaps. Note that the resulting effect size using this approach is larger than the SMD approach above (i.e., −3.16), this is due to the inclusion of the treatment by time interaction term (i.e., $b_3X(t)$) in the regression equation.

Allison, Faith, and Franklin (1995) used this method to summarize the efficacy of antecedent exercise in reducing disruptive behavior. Campbell (2004) also used the approach to summarize treatment outcomes for individuals with autism, but found the effect size estimates to be unreasonably large and not sensitive in detecting moderators of treatment outcomes.

With normally distributed observations in between-group designs, an effect size can be transformed to represent the proportion of control-group scores that are less than the average score in the experimental group (Hedges & Olkin, 1985). For example, an effect size of $d = -0.5$ indicates that the score of the average individual in the experimental condition is less than 69% of individuals in the control group. With single subject effect sizes, d represents the proportion of treatment data points that are less (or greater, depending on direction) than the average data point in the baseline condition (Scruggs & Mastropieri, 1998). Therefore, an effect size of $d = -0.5$ indicates that 69% percent of treatment data points fall below the average baseline data point.

Marquis et al. (2000) also calculated a regression-based SMD by taking the difference between two predicted values at the end of treatment: (a) one value based upon a best-fitting regression equation created from baseline data ($\hat{y}_{base}$) and (b) another value based upon a best-fitting regression equation created from treatment data ($\hat{y}_{treat}$). The difference between the two predicted values ($\hat{y}_{base} - \hat{y}_{treat}$) was divided by the standard deviation of the residual scores calculated from the baseline regression equation.

Hierarchical Linear Modeling (HLM)
Recently, hierarchical linear modeling (HLM) approaches have been proposed for combining and analyzing data from single subject research designs (e.g., Van den Noortgate & Onghena, 2003). We introduce HLM within the regression-based discussion due to the nature of the analytic technique. HLM analyzes single subject data in a hierarchical format whereby one level involves analysis of the individual via a regression equation to estimate baseline and treatment intercepts and slopes. The baseline and treatment slopes and intercepts from the first-level analysis constitute the dependent variables included in a second-level analysis. If significant differences are documented between baseline and treatment intercepts (level) and slopes (rates of behavior change), additional statistical testing is conducted to determine if variables of interest (e.g., sex of participant; age; diagnosis) influence treatment outcomes (Rindskopf, 2008). Similar to the time-series analyses, HLM requires advanced statistical expertise and access to appropriate statistical software. For the purposes of our chapter, we merely introduce this analytic strategy as readers may encounter its use with more frequency in the published literature in the future.

Concluding Comments About Effect Sizes
Similar to statistical-analysis methods, single subject effect sizes do not correlate well with each other (Campbell, 2004; Parker & Hagan-Burke, 2007; Parker, Hagan-Burke, & Vannest, 2007), which is not the case for group-based effect sizes (Ray & Shadish, 1996). Due to the differences between various effect sizes, there is no consensus regarding which effect size to use within single-case meta-analysis. As such, the current state of knowledge prohibits recommendation

of a single subject effect size for the purposes of quantitative synthesis. In the next decade, we anticipate ongoing development and refinement of single subject effect sizes which will yield new alternatives. One may emerge as a clear choice from the fray; however, at this point, our recommendation is to calculate a small number of effect sizes that approximate different types of effects, such as level and slope, and report these in the analysis. Although not our preference, another defensible alternative is to call for a moratorium on single-case effect-size calculations until greater consensus is reached regarding the most appropriate method.

Step 5: Interpret and Report Results
For group-based meta-analyses, effect sizes are weighted per study according to the number of participants who contributed to the calculation of the effect size. Weighting is based on the reasoning that effect sizes calculated from larger samples are more stable and that this should be reflected in the statistical aggregation of outcomes. Once effect sizes are calculated, an overall mean effect is reported to describe the general effects of intervention for the population of interest. For parametric effect sizes, such as SMD and d_{REG}, confidence intervals are reported and the overall mean tested via Z test. In the presence of a significant overall effect of treatment, follow-up analyses are also conducted to discover if the general effects of the intervention are moderated by certain variables of interest, such as sex, age, or therapist type. In the presence of strong a priori justification, group contrasts might be examined in the absence of a significant overall effect of treatment. For the majority of single-case meta-analyses, follow-up analyses are typically conducted using non-parametric statistics (e.g., Mann-Whitney U tests) due to the findings that the distributions for the effect sizes are non-normal or that variances across groups are sufficiently different (see Herzinger & Campbell, 2007, for an example). The use of non-parametric statistics for tests of moderators is due to the utilization of percentage-based effect sizes, such as the MBLR, PND, and PZD.

Step 6: Offer Summative Statements and Identify Limits of the Meta-Analysis
Once the statistical analyses are completed, the meta-analyst reviews the substantive findings of the investigation by emphasizing the main treatment findings and their moderation across different variables included in the investigation. Due to the aggregation of data across multiple individual studies, findings from meta-analyses can be of particular value in guiding practice, informing legislation, and identifying areas within large domains of the literature that are in need of additional clarification. Once this is completed, the meta-analyst typically offers some critique of the methods utilized, such as limits of literature included or population sampled. Of course, identifying limitations typically justifies direction for future research, either through primary study or additional quantitative review.

Adoption of QUOROM Guidelines for Single-Case Meta-Analysis

We advocate the adoption of methodological guidelines produced by the Quality of Reporting of Meta-analyses (QUOROM; Moher et al., 1999), which were developed for meta-analysis of randomized group-based studies. The QUOROM standards were produced to improve the methodological rigor of meta-analytic reviews (e.g., appropriate calculation of effect sizes; establishing inter-rater agreement for coding decisions) and assist meta-analysts in explicitly stating methods used in reviews (e.g., literature search procedures, study selection criteria). QUOROM guidelines serve as quality-control guidelines for conducting and evaluating meta-analyses. A modified excerpt from the QUOROM guidelines is presented that is pertinent to documenting the flow of manuscripts throughout different inclusion and exclusion decision points that arise during the meta-analysis (see Figure 14.5). Although developed for use with group-based studies, the flowchart is applicable for single subject meta-analyses. Use of the QUOROM flow diagram for study selection procedures requires specification of the number of articles identified, screened, reviewed, excluded, and included in the meta-analysis. Other procedural guidelines are delineated in the QUOROM document that we encourage readers to review.

Summary

The call for empirically based medicine, psychological treatments, and educational practice will continue for the foreseeable future. Single subject research designs offer important data in the quest to identify "what works" across disparate professional domains. In our opinion, the meaningful contributions of single subject research outcomes will be ignored if statistical analysis is excluded as part of the evaluation. Huitema (1986b) argued effectively for the inclusion of statistical analysis with this very point by suggesting that researchers "employ statistical as well as visual methods when [they] are attempting to communicate with a nonbehavioral audience that is likely to be influenced by the presentation of statistical tests" (p. 229). Who might be members of the nonbehavioral audience? Huitema identifies members as most administrators, program evaluators, and granting agencies; to omit statistical methods of analysis is to omit *the* most familiar type of empirical evidence for many. "Besides that, statistics make people feel good" (Huitema, 1986b, p. 229).

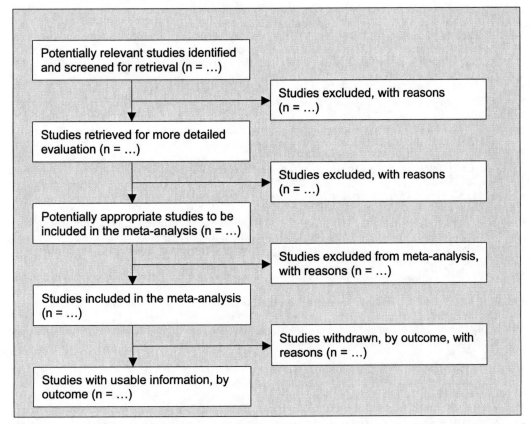

Figure 14.5 A modified QUOROM statement flow diagram showing progress through the stages of literature search, study selection, and study inclusion for meta-analyses.

Supplementing visual analysis with statistical analysis, which we support, will require collaboration between single subject applied researchers and data analysts. This will require willingness of visual analysts to collaborate with statistical analysts, and vice versa. One immediate outcome from this type of partnership would involve further field testing and refinement of the structured decision criteria developed to date. Overall, neither visual nor statistical analytic procedures have sufficiently solved the problem of how best to analyze single-case data, perhaps through collaboration significant improvements can be achieved in this area.

References

Allison, D. B., Faith, M. S., & Franklin, R. D. (1995). Antecedent exercise in the treatment of disruptive behavior: A meta-analytic review. *Clinical Psychology: Science and Practice, 2,* 279–303.

Allison, D. B., & Gorman, B. S. (1993). Calculating effect sizes for meta-analysis: The case of the single case. *Behaviour Research and Therapy, 31,* 621–631.

Bangert-Drowns, R. L. (1986). Review of developments in meta-analytic method. *Psychological Bulletin, 99,* 388–399.

Bellini, S., Peters, J. K., Benner, L., & Hopf, A. (2007). A meta-analysis of school-based social skills interventions for children with autism spectrum disorders. *Remedial and Special Education, 28,* 153–162.

Bengali, M. K., & Ottenbacher, K. J. (1998). The effect of autocorrelation on the results of visually analyzing data from single subject designs. *The American Journal of Occupational Therapy, 52,* 650–655.

Bobrovitz, C. D., & Ottenbacher, K. J. (1998). Comparison of visual inspection and statistical analysis of single subject data in rehabilitation research. *American Journal of Physical Medicine and Rehabilitation, 77,* 94–102.

Busk, P. L., & Marascuilo, L. A. (1988). Autocorrelation in single subject research: A counterargument to the myth of no autocorrelation. *Behavioral Assessment, 10,* 229–242.

Busk, P. L., & Marascuilo, L. A. (1992). Statistical analysis in single-case research: Issues, procedures and recommendations, with applications to multiple behaviors. In T. R. Kratochwill & J. R. Levin (Eds.), *Single-case research designs and analysis: New directions for psychology and education* (pp. 159–185). Hillsdale, NJ: Lawrence Erlbaum.

Busk, P. L., & Serlin, R. C. (1992). Meta-analysis for single-case research. In T. R. Kratochwill & J. R. Levin (Eds.), *Single-case research designs and analysis: New directions for psychology and education* (pp. 187–212). Hillsdale, NJ: Lawrence Erlbaum.

Campbell, J. M. (2003). Efficacy of behavioral intervention for reducing problematic behaviors in persons with autism: A quantitative synthesis of single subject research. *Research in Developmental Disabilities, 24,* 120–138.

Campbell, J. M. (2004). Statistical comparison of four effect sizes for single-subject designs. *Behavior Modification, 28,* 234–246.

Cooper, H. M. (1984). *The integrative research review: a systematic approach.* Beverly Hills, CA: Sage Publications.

Cooper, H., & Hedges, L. V. (1994). Research synthesis as a scientific enterprise. In H. Cooper & L. V. Hedges (Eds.), *Handbook of research synthesis* (pp. 1–13). New York: Russell Sage Foundation.

Crosbie, J. (1987). The inability of the binomial test to control Type I error with single-subject data. *Behavioral Assessment, 9,* 141–150.

Crosbie, J. (1989). The inappropriateness of the C statistic for assessing stability or treatment effects with single subject data. *Behavioral Assessment, 11,* 315–325.

Crosbie, J. (1993). Interrupted time-series analysis with brief single subject data. *Journal of Consulting and Clinical Psychology, 61,* 966–974.

Didden, R., Duker, P. C., & Korzilius, H. (1997). Meta-analytic study on treatment effectiveness for problem behaviors with individuals who have mental retardation. *American Journal on Mental Retardation, 101,* 387–399.

Didden, R., Korzilius, H., van Oorsouw, W., & Sturmey, P. (2006). Behavioral treatment of challenging behaviors in individuals with mild mental retardation: Meta-analysis of single subject research. *American Journal on Mental Retardation, 111,* 290–298.

Edgington, E. S. (1982). Nonparametric tests for single subject multiple schedule experiments. *Behavioral Assessment, 4,* 83–91.

Edwards, W., Lindman, H., & Savage, L. J. (1963). Bayesian statistical inference for psychological research. *Psychological Review, 70,* 193–242.

Faith, M. S., Allison, D. B., & Gorman, B. S. (1996). Meta-analysis of single-case research. In R. D. Franklin, Allison, D. B., & Gorman, B. S. (Eds.), *Design and analysis of single-case research* (pp. 245–277). Mahwah, NJ: Lawrence Erlbaum Associates.

Fisher, W. W., Kelley, M. E., & Lomas, J. E. (2003). Visual aids and structured criteria for improving visual inspection and interpretation of single-case designs. *Journal of Applied Behavior Analysis, 36,* 387–406.

Ferron, J., Foster-Johnson, L., & Kromrey, J. D. (2003). The functioning of single-case randomization tests with and without random assignment. *The Journal of Experimental Education, 71,* 267–288.

Ferron, J., & Jones, P. K. (2006). Tests for the visual analysis of response-guided multiple-baseline data. *The Journal of Experimental Education, 75,* 66–81.

Gingerich, W. J. (1984). Methodological observations on applied behavioral science. *The Journal of Applied Behavioral Science, 20,* 71–79.

Glass, G. V. (1976). Primary, secondary, and meta-analysis of research. *Educational Researcher, 5,* 3–8.

Glass, G. V., McGraw, B., & Smith, M. L. (1981). *Meta-analysis in social research.* Beverly Hills, CA: Sage.

Gorman-Smith, D., & Matson, J. L. (1985). A review of treatment research for self-injurious and stereotyped responding. *Journal of Mental Deficiency Research, 29,* 295–308.

Graham, S., & Perin, D. (2007). What we know, what we still need to know: Teaching adolescents to write. *Scientific Studies of Reading, 11,* 313–335.

Gresham, F. M., McIntyre, L. L., Olson-Tinker, H., Dolstra, L., McLaughlin, V., & Van, M. (2004). Relevance of functional behavioral assessment research for school-based interventions and positive behavioral support. *Research in Developmental Disabilities, 24,* 19–37.

Hagopian, L. P., Fisher, W. W., Thompson, R. H., Owen-DeSchryver, J., Iwata, B. A., & Wacker, D. P. (1997). Toward the development of structured criteria for interpretation of functional analysis data. *Journal of Applied Behavior Analysis, 30,* 313–326.

Halvorsen, K. T. (1994). The reporting format. In H. Cooper & L. V. Hedges (Eds.), *Handbook of research synthesis* (pp. 425–437). New York: Sage.

Hedges, L. V., & Olkin, I. (1985). *Statistical methods for meta-analysis.* Orlando, FL: Academic Press.

Herzinger, C. V., & Campbell, J. M. (2007). Comparing functional assessment methodologies: A quantitative synthesis. *Journal of Autism and Developmental Disorders, 37,* 1430–1445.

Huitema, B. E. (1985). Autocorrelation in applied behavior analysis: A myth. *Behavioral Assessment, 7,* 107–118.

Huitema, B. E. (1986a). Autocorrelation in behavioral research: Wherefore art thou? In A. S. Bellack & M. Hersen (Series Ed.) & A. Poling & R. W. Fuqua (Vol. Eds.), *Applied clinical psychology: Research methods in applied behavior analysis: Issues and advances* (pp. 187–208). New York: Plenum.

Huitema, B. E. (1986b). Statistical analysis and single subject designs: Some misunderstandings. In A. S. Bellack & M. Hersen (Series Ed.) & A. Poling & R. W. Fuqua (Vol. Eds.), *Applied clinical psychology: Research methods in applied behavior analysis: Issues and advances* (pp. 209–232). New York: Plenum.

Hunter, J. E., & Schmidt, F. L. (1990). *Methods of meta-analysis: correcting error and bias in research findings.* Newbury Park, CA: Sage.

Jackson, G. B. (1980). Methods for integrative reviews. *Review of Educational Research, 50,* 438–460.

Ma, H. (2006). An alternative method for quantitative synthesis of single subject researches: Percentage of data points exceeding the median. *Behavior Modification, 30,* 598–617.

Marascuilo, L. A., & Busk, P. L. (1988). Combining statistics for multiple-baseline AB and replicated ABAB designs across subjects. *Behavioral Assessment, 10,* 1–28.

Marquis, J. G., Horner, R. H., Carr, E. G., Turnbull, A. P., Thompson, M., Behrens, G. A., et al. (2000). A meta-analysis of positive behavior support. In R. Gersten, E. P. Schiller, & S. Vaugh (Eds.), *Contemporary special education research: Syntheses of the knowledge base on critical instructional issues* (pp. 137–178). Mahwah, NJ: Lawrence Erlbaum Associates.

Matyas, T. A., & Greenwood, K. M. (1990). Visual analysis of single-case time series: Effects of variability, serial dependence, and magnitude of intervention effects. *Journal of Applied Behavior Analysis, 23,* 341–351.

Matyas, T. A., & Greenwood, K. M. (1996). Serial dependency in single-case time series. In R. D. Franklin, Allison, D. B., & Gorman, B. S. (Eds.), *Design and analysis of single-case research* (pp. 215–243). Mahwah, NJ: Lawrence Erlbaum Associates.

Maughan, D. R., Christiansen, E., Jenson, W. R., Olympia, D., & Clark, E. (2005). Behavioral parent training as a treatment for externalizing disorders and disruptive behavior disorders: A meta-analysis. *School Psychology Review, 34,* 267–286.

Moher, D., Cook, D. J., Eastwood, S., Olkin, I., Rennie, D., Stroup, D. F., et al. (1999). Improving the quality of reports of meta-analyses of randomised controlled trials: The QUORUM statement. *Lancet, 354,* 1896–1900.

Mostert, M. P. (1996). Reporting meta-analyses in learning disabilities. *Learning Disabilities Research and Practice, 11*, 2–14.

Mostert, M. P. (2003). Meta-analyses in mental retardation. *Education and Training in Developmental Disabilities, 38*, 229–249.

Normand, M. P., & Bailey, J. S. (2006). The effects of celeration lines on visual data analysis. *Behavior Modification, 30*, 395–314.

Nourbakhsh, M. R., & Ottenbacher, K. J. (1994). The statistical analysis of single subject data: A comparative examination. *Physical Therapy, 74*, 768–776.

Onghena, P., & Edgington, E. S. (2005). Customization of pain treatments: Single-case design and analysis. *The Clinical Journal of Pain, 21*, 56–68.

Ottenbacher, K. J. (1993). Interrater agreement of visual analysis in single subject decisions: Quantitative review and analysis. *American Journal on Mental Retardation, 98*, 135–142.

Parker, R. I., Brossart, D. F., Vannest, K. J., Long, J. R., De-Alba, R. G. Baugh, F. G., et al. (2005). Effect sizes in single case research: How large is large? *School Psychology Review, 34*, 116–132.

Parker, R. I., & Hagan-Burke, S. (2007). Median-based overlap analysis for single case data: A second study. *Behavior Modification, 31*, 919–936.

Parker, R. I., Hagan-Burke, S., & Vannest, K. (2007). Percentage of all non-overlapping data (PAND): An alternative to PND. *The Journal of Special Education, 40*, 194–204.

Parsonson, B. S., & Baer, D. M. (1986). The graphic analysis of data. In A. S. Bellack & M. Hersen (Series Ed.) & A. Poling & R. W. Fuqua (Vol. Eds.), *Applied clinical psychology: Research methods in applied behavior analysis: Issues and advances* (pp. 157–186). New York: Plenum.

Ray, J. W., & Shadish, W. R. (1996). How interchangeable are different estimators of effect size? *Journal of Consulting and Clinical Psychology, 64*, 1316–1325.

Regan, K. S., Mastropieri, M. A., & Scruggs, T. E. (2005). Promoting expressive writing among students with emotional and behavioral disturbance via dialogue journals. *Behavioral Disorders, 31*, 33–50.

Rindskopf, D. (2008, April). *Using multilevel models to analyze data from small-N designs: Introduction and overview.* Presented at the Institute of Education Sciences Research Training Institute: Single-Case Design. Washington, DC.

Robey, R. R., Schultz, M. C., Crawford, A. B., & Sinner, C. A. (1999). Single subject clinical-outcome research: Designs, data, effect sizes, and analyses. *Aphasiology, 13*, 445–473.

Salzberg, C. L, Strain, P. S., & Baer, D. M. (1987). Meta-analysis for single subject research: When does it clarify, when does it obscure? *Remedial and Special Education, 8*, 43–48.

Scotti, J. R., Evans, I. M., Meyer, L. H., & Walker, P. (1991). A meta-analysis of intervention research with problem behavior: Treatment validity and standards of practice. *American Journal on Mental Retardation, 96*, 233–256.

Scruggs, T. E., & Mastropieri, M. A. (1998). Summarizing single subject research: Issues and applications. *Behavior Modification, 22*, 221–242.

Scruggs, T. E., Mastropieri, M. A., & Casto, G. (1987). The quantitative synthesis of single subject research: Methodology and validation. *Remedial and Special Education, 8*, 24–33.

Scruggs, T. E., Mastropieri, M. A., & Regan, K. S. (2006). Statistical analysis for single subject research designs. In T. E. Scruggs & M. A. Mastropieri (Series Ed.) & T. E. Scruggs & M. A. Mastropieri (Vol. Eds.), *Advances in learning and behavioral disabilities: Vol. 19: Applications of research methodology* (pp. 33–53). New York: Elsevier.

Shadish, W. R., & Rindskopf, D. M. (2007). Methods for evidence-based practice: Quantitative synthesis of single subject designs. *New Directions for Evaluation, 113*, 95–109.

Sharpley, C. F., & Alavosius, M. P. (1988). Autocorrelation in behavioral data: An alternative perspective. *Behavioral Assessment, 10*, 243–251.

Shogren, K. A., Fagella-Luby, M. N., Bae, S. J., & Wehmeyer, M. L. (2004). The effect of choice-making as a intervention for problem behavior: A meta-analysis. *Journal of Positive Behavior Interventions, 6*, 228–237.

Sierra, V., Solanas, A., & Quera, V. (2005). Randomization tests for systematic single-case designs are not always appropriate. *The Journal of Experimental Education, 73*, 140–160.

Skinner, B. F. (1963). Operant behavior. *American Psychologist, 18*, 503–515.

Stage, S. A., & Quiroz, D. R. (1997). A meta-analysis of interventions to decrease disruptive classroom behavior in public education settings. *School Psychology Review, 26*, 333–368.

Strain, P. S., Kohler, F. W., & Gresham, F. (1998). Problems in the logic and interpretation with quantitative syntheses of single-case research: Mathur and colleagues (1998) as a case in point. *Behavioral Disorders, 24*, 74–85.

Todman, J. B., & Dugard, P. (2001). *Single-case and small-n experimental designs: A practical guide to randomization tests.* Mahwah, NJ: Lawrence Erlbaum Associates, Inc.

Tryon, W. W. (1982). A simplified time-series analysis for evaluating treatment interventions. *Journal of Applied Behavior Analysis, 15,* 423–429.

Van den Noortgate, W., & Onghena, P. (2003). Combining single-case experimental data using hierarchical linear models. *School Psychology Quarterly, 18,* 325–346.

Wehmeyer, M. L. (1995). Intra-individual factors influencing efficacy of interventions for stereotyped behaviors: A meta-analysis. *Journal of Intellectual Disability Research, 39,* 205–214.

White, D. M., Rusch, F. R., Kazdin, A. E., & Hartmann, D. P. (1989). Applications of meta analysis in individual-subject research. *Behavioral Assessment, 11,* 281–296.

Wolery, M., Ault, M., & Doyle, P. M. (1992). *Teaching students with moderate to severe disabilities: Use of response prompting strategies.* White Plains, NY: Longman.

Xin, Y. P., Grasso, E., DiPipi-Hoy, C. M., & Jitendra, A. (2005). The effects of purchasing skill instruction for individuals with developmental disabilities: A meta-analysis. *Exceptional Children, 71,* 379–400.

Contributors

Kevin Ayres, Ph.D., is Assistant Professor of Special Education at The University of Georgia. His research interests include video modeling, instructional technology, and behavioral methods of instruction for individuals with autism and other developmental disabilities.

Jonathan M. Campbell, Ph.D., is Associate Professor in the Department of Educational Psychology and Instructional Technology at The University of Georgia. His research interests include facilitating inclusion for students with autism spectrum disorders through peer education, the analysis and summary of single-subject research data, and differential diagnosis within the autism spectrum.

Diana Hammond is a Ph.D. student in Special Education at The University of Georgia. Her research interests include using technology in individual and small group arrangements, the instruction of functional skills, and observational and incidental learning by children with autism spectrum disorders and moderate to severe intellectual disabilities.

Caitlin V. Herzinger, Ph.D., BCBA-D is a program coordinator at the Marcus Autism Center in Atlanta, Georgia. Her current research interests include comparisons of functional assessment methodologies across diagnostic populations, understanding the relations between verbal operants, and assessing the efficiency of current teaching modalities.

Kathleen Lynne Lane, Ph.D., is Associate Professor of Special Education at Peabody College at Vanderbilt University. Her research interests focus on designing, implementing, and evaluating multi-level, school-based interventions to prevent the development of learning and behavior problems for students at-risk for EBD and remediate the deleterious effects of existing problems exhibited by students with EBD.

Jennifer Ledford is a Ph.D. student in Special Education at Peabody College at Vanderbilt University. Her research interests include observational and incidental learning and response to intervention for young students with autism spectrum disorders.

Linda Mechling, Ph.D., is Associate Professor of Special Education at the University of North Carolina Wilmington. Her research interests include multi-media instruction, assistive technology, teaching of functional skills, and community-based instruction.

Amy D. Spriggs is a Ph.D. student in Special Education at The University of Georgia. Her research interests include using technology as a means of instructional delivery, incidental and observational learning in small group arrangements for children in settings with autism spectrum disorders and moderate to severe intellectual disabilities.

Mark Wolery, Ph.D., is Professor of Special Education at Peabody College of Vanderbilt University. His research interests focus on evaluating the effectiveness and efficiency of instructional practices in inclusive preschool classrooms.

Author Index

Subject Index

A

A design, 235–239

A-B design, 218, 235, 239–242, 249, 278–279, 393; combination designs, 411; randomization tests, 428–435; statistical analysis, 422–423

A-B-A design, 242–248, 249, 395

A-B-A-B design, 14, 201, 218–219, 242, 248–263, 273, 284; advantages, 251; applied examples, 252–262, 408–409, 410; baseline logic, 235; combination designs, 395, 396, 408–409, 410, 411; cumulative graphs, 175, 177; cyclical variability, 107; guidelines, 250–251; interobserver agreement, 161; limitations, 251–252; randomization tests, 428–429; replication, 111, 113, 115; stability envelope, 203–204; validity, 248–250; variations, 263–273; visual analysis summary table, 221

A-B-A'-B design, 269, 271–272

A-B-A-B-BC-B-BC design, 272–273

A-B-A-B-C-B-C- design, 272–273

ABC notation, 200, 223

A-BC-B-A-B design, 258–262

abscissa, 168, 169, 178, 181–182, 185, 186, 393

abstracts, 64, 73

accountability, 1, 277

accumulating evidence approach, 74

accuracy, 98, 99, 100, 157, 421

action research, 11

adaptation, 107

adapted alternating treatments design (AATD), 337, 358–367, 369, 374, 377–379; advantages, 362; applied examples, 363–367, 402–405; combination designs, 395, 402–405; external validity, 361–362; guidelines, 362; internal validity, 361; limitations, 363; variations, 363

affirmation, 113

alternating treatments design (ATD), 216, 337, 346–357, 377–379; advantages, 355; combination designs, 395, 408–409, 410; decision rules, 421; external validity, 354; guidelines, 354–355; internal validity, 15, 353–354; limitations, 355; randomization tests, 429, 435; variations, 355

alternation effects, 332–333, 352–353

American Journal on Mental Retardation (AJMR), 236, 237

American Psychological Association (APA): coding protocol, 440; *Ethical Principles*, 33–35, 55; journal submission guidelines, 86, 111; *Publication Manual*, 51, 58, 190

analysis of variance (ANOVA), 425

anonymity, 38, 50–51

applied behavior analysis (ABA), 1–2, 3, 13, 23–24, 102; benefits to participants, 122–123, 247; measurement and evaluation, 91–92; professional ethics, 16

assent, 51–54

Assessment of Practices in Early Elementary Classrooms, 76

Association of Behavior Analysis International (ABAI), 3, 29, 35

attrition, 27, 106, 151; A-B-A design, 244; adapted alternating treatments design, 361; alternating treatments design, 353; group research approach, 9; multitreatment design, 340, 342; parallel-treatments design, 371

auditing, 12

auditory hypersensitivity, 388, 389

authorship, 55, 81–84

autism: Direct Instruction, 297–299; functional communication training, 405–408; modeling of language skills, 374–377, 378; research, 3–4; sleep terrors, 316–318; small group instruction, 301–307; systematic desensitization, 388, 389

autocorrelation, 424–425, 427, 436

automated-quantitative recording, 137–139, 153

B

B design, 235, 236–239

B-A-B design, 263–269, 270

bar graphs, 169, 172, 173, 174, 175; combination graphs, 178, 179–180; Microsoft Excel, 195–197

baseline, 14, 15, 411; A design, 236; A-B design, 239–240, 242, 422, 423; A-B-A design, 242–243; A-B-A-B design, 248, 250, 263; ABC notation, 200; adapted alternating treatments design, 360; alternating treatments design, 350–351, 353, 355; autocorrelation, 425; B-A-B design, 267, 268; between-condition analysis, 216–217; changing criterion design, 383, 386–387; combination designs, 399–401, 406; condition length, 202; content validity, 103; decision rules, 421; hierarchical linear modeling, 447; inter-subject replication, 125; line graphs, 168, 170; literature reviews, 66; mean baseline difference, 440–441; multitreatment design, 337–338, 339, 342, 346;